# BALKAN TRAGEDY

SUSAN L. WOODWARD

# BALKAN TRAGEDY

## CHAOS AND DISSOLUTION
## AFTER THE COLD WAR

THE BROOKINGS INSTITUTION
WASHINGTON, D.C.

*Library of Congress Cataloging-in-Publication data*

Woodward, Susan L.
    Balkan tragedy : chaos and dissolution after the Cold War / Susan
L. Woodward.
        p.    cm.
    Includes bibliographical references and index.
    ISBN 0-8157-9514-9 : alk. paper — ISBN 0-8157-9513-0 (pbk.: alk. paper)
    1. Yugoslav War, 1991–    —Causes.   2. Nationalism—Yugoslavia.
    I. Brookings Institution.   II. Title.
DR1313.W66   1995
949.702′4—dc20                                                       94-12742
                                                                          CIP


Digital printing

Typeset in Bembo

Composition by Harlowe Typography, Inc.
Cottage City, Maryland

Maps by Parrot Graphics
Stillwater, Minnesota

# Foreword

Few issues of foreign policy and world order in our time have evoked as much division, emotion, and disillusionment as the war in Bosnia-Herzegovina. Although major powers considered the conflict of little strategic consequence, their inability to prevent the violence, reverse its course, or resolve the crisis was widely judged a failure of Western leadership and corroded the credibility of regional and international institutions. These international institutions, and many domestic institutions in Europe, had been created after World War II precisely to prevent the repetition of such developments in Europe. Even the successes that were claimed for international intervention, of containment and humanitarian relief, were under constant threat of reversal with a new round of fighting that could escalate and spread.

In this book, Susan L. Woodward, senior fellow in the Brookings Foreign Policy Studies program, argues that the failure arose from a lack of understanding of the causes of the conflict, and the application of cold war thinking and instruments that were not appropriate to the case. Although many books have attempted to bring the plight of Bosnia and the fall of Yugoslavia to the attention of the outside world, this is one of the few that attempts to analyze the causes of these events and that weaves into the story of decline and war the influence of the international environment and outside actors.

The significance of the Yugoslav case cannot be overestimated as an early warning of other such conflicts currently brewing. The collapse of political orders under international pressures, economic austerity, and policies of economic reform and liberalization during the 1980s has led in many parts of the world to a massive upheaval. The stabilizing social, economic, and political mechanisms that countries used over the past fifty years are often proving inadequate to new circumstances. Dealing with each instance as a separate case disguises the common elements and the need for a collective response.

This book grows out of the decades of gracious hospitality, scholarly exchange, and open encounters with strangers for which the former Yugoslavia was at one time justly famous. Two visits by the author were particularly helpful in sensing the change, in July 1991 to Belgrade and Zagreb, and in early February 1992 to Belgrade and Sarajevo. The author would like to give particular thanks to friends and colleagues who shared their efforts to come to terms with events after the mid-1980s and in 1990–93—especially Silva Mežnarić, Vasil Tupurkovski, Vladimir Gligorov, Milorad Pupovac, Vesna Pešić, Vesna Pusić, Radmila Nakarada, Zdravko Grebo, Kemal Kurspahić, Miša Tomičić, and Tomislav Jakić. She feels unusually fortunate to have benefited from the knowledge of Obrad Kesić, Julie Mostov, Herbert S. Okun, Dennison Rusinow, Paul Shoup, Misha Glenny, and Arthur Keys; and from the advice and support of three colleagues at Brookings—the late Ed Hewett, Catherine Kelleher, and William Quandt—and from Claire Fudrain, Gail Kligman, Martha Lampland, Sarah Lampland, Celia Morris, David Binder, Mario Blejer, and C. Vann Woodward. Special thanks go to John Steinbruner, who suggested the study, supported its travails, and carefully read drafts of the manuscript.

Although the manuscript was fully drafted before the author took up the offer of Yasushi Akashi, special representative of the UN Secretary General for former Yugoslavia, to create an analysis and assessment unit for the UN Protection Forces at its headquarters in Zagreb, Croatia, its revision benefited immeasurably from that experience over seven and one-half months. She wishes to express here her deep gratitude to those who taught her so much in that difficult operation, particularly Yasushi Akashi, John Almstrom, Yelena Guskova, Andreas Corti, Nicholas Morris, Lt. General Bertrand de la Presle, Kai Eide, Maj. General John Archer MacInnis, Shashi Tharoor, Aracelly Santana, Slava Guerrasev, Charles McLeod, Lt. Col. Jan-Dirk van Merveldt, Lt. Col. Kent Koebke, Major Brad Smith, Lt. Col. Marc Rebhun, Laura Vaccari, and Michael Williams.

At Brookings, research assistance was provided by Daniel Turner and Ian Campbell, assisted by interns Irene Schmid and Ellen Ginzbursky. The wide range of tasks performed with skill by the author's staff assistant, Stacey Seaman, who also typed the final manuscript, deserves special notice. Nancy Campbell and Deborah Styles edited the manuscript, and Andrew Solomon, with Diane Chido, Michael Levin, and Alexander Ratz, verified its factual content. Norman Turpin arranged for the maps, Susan Woollen prepared the manuscript for typesetting and made arrangements for the cover, Ellen Garschick proofread the manuscript, and Julia Petrakis prepared the index.

Brookings gratefully acknowledges the financial support provided for this book by The Carnegie Corporation of New York and The John D. and Catherine T. MacArthur Foundation.

The views expressed in this study are those of the author alone and should not be ascribed to any of the persons or organizations mentioned above, or to the trustees, officers, or other staff members of the Brookings Institution.

Bruce K. MacLaury
*President*

*March 1995*
*Washington, D.C.*

# Contents

## Tables

## Figures

*To the rebuilding of the Mostar Bridge
and what it represented, and to the
people who will have to do it.*

*Yugoslavia in 1990–91*

*Croatia, Showing UN Protected Areas, and Bosnia-Herzegovina*

*"Europe, Now"*

Slogan of the Eleventh Congress, League of
Communists of Slovenia, December 1989

*"Why should I be a minority in your
state when you can be a minority in
mine?"*

Vladimir Gligorov

*"The disease of this country is fear."*

General Philippe Morillon

# Chapter 1

# *Introduction*

O n the eve of the 1989 revolutions in eastern and central
Europe, Yugoslavia was better poised than any other socialist country to make a successful transition to a market economy and
to the West. It had, after all, been moving toward full global integration
since its Communist party leadership broke with Stalin in 1948. As early
as 1955, Yugoslavia's borders were open to the movement of its citizens,
foreigners, and trade. Since 1949 it had regularly negotiated loans from
the International Monetary Fund (IMF) and implemented marketizing and
decentralizing economic reforms to satisfy IMF conditions and—between
1958 and 1965—the conditions of membership in the General Agreement
on Tariffs and Trade (GATT). The consequence was a socialist country
with extensive economic liberalization and political decentralization, earning association agreements with the European Community (EC) and the
European Free Trade Association (EFTA) long before the nations of central
Europe made their requests. Even after a decade of economic hardship and
political uncertainty in 1979–89, the relative prosperity, freedom to travel
and work abroad, and landscape of multicultural pluralism and contrasts
that Yugoslavs enjoyed were the envy of eastern Europeans.

Two years later the country had ceased to exist, and devastating local
wars were being waged to create new states. Between the fall of the Berlin
Wall in November 1989 and the start of the war in Bosnia-Herzegovina in
March 1992, the path of disintegration moved at astonishing speed: from
a shock-therapy program of economic reform enthusiastically welcomed
by Western creditors and advisers to the disbanding of the country's Communist party, the beginnings of democratization with multiparty elections
in the six republics that had composed the federal state, and declarations
of independence by two republics—Slovenia and Croatia. Six months later
the war in Croatia had created the largest refugee crisis in Europe since
World War II. Yet the more than 200,000 refugees, approximately 20,000
dead, and more than 350,000 displaced persons from the Croatian war
soon looked mild in comparison with the war in neighboring Bosnia-
Herzegovina. In the first two years alone, the death toll in Bosnia was
greater than 70,000. More than 2 million people of a population of 4.3
million became refugees or were displaced to other parts of the republic,

1

expelled from their homes—probably never to return—by fear, war, or nationalist extremists aiming to rid their town or village of people whose ethnicity was different. Among its repercussions was the largest global dispersement of children since World War II.

The collapse of Yugoslavia into nationalist regimes led not only to horrendous fratricidal cruelty and incomprehensible destruction but also to a crisis of Western security regimes. Coming at the height of euphoria over the end of the cold war, the conflict faced Western governments and the international community with a set of tasks that was the opposite of their expectations. Plans to spend the "peace dividend" on domestic economic recovery and strained welfare systems in the West were not compatible with calls for military intervention or peacekeeping missions. Wanting to move gradually in transforming cold war security alliances, such as the North Atlantic Treaty Organization (NATO), the Conference on Security and Cooperation in Europe (CSCE), and even the United Nations, Western leaders were reluctant to act in Yugoslavia. But their initial assessment that the conflict was of little strategic significance or national interest could not be sustained in light of its consequences: the possibility that the wars could lead to regional conflagration; the threat to European identity itself; the growing outrage at the failure to prevent war in Europe in the late twentieth century and to protect civilians against rape, torture, forced detention, and the threat of genocide in clear violation of conventions written after World War II to ensure its atrocities would not recur.

By 1994 this conflict of little significance had emerged as the most challenging threat to existing norms and institutions that Western leaders faced. Step by step, they began to alter those institutions with little thought to what the result might be. Germany sent pilots to participate in a NATO-enforced no-fly zone over Bosnia (on April 9, 1993). This decision required a revolutionary ruling by the constitutional court, allowing the use of German military power outside NATO frontiers for the first time since the Nazi defeat.[1] NATO used air strikes against the army of Bosnian Serbs, its first combat action since its founding.[2] The West European Union (WEU) joined with NATO in enforcing a naval blockade in the Adriatic Sea, and deployed its first police contingent when the European Union took on the administration of Mostar in Herzegovina. The United Nations sent troops to Europe for the first time ever, a peacekeeping operation that quickly became the largest, most complex, and most expensive in UN history. Russia became recognized as an equal partner in major-power decisionmaking on European security through efforts to negotiate a peace in Bosnia, including a five-power Contact Group set up in April 1994. And major disagreements among Western powers within the UN, NATO, and CSCE, particularly between the United States and its European allies, threatened to disrupt irreparably those security organizations because their leaders and journalists began to define their actions in Bosnia as an issue of credibility. The optimism in 1989–90 that marketization and democratization in the East would effortlessly replace military and ideological confrontation between East and West with a Europe "whole and free" had been dashed almost as quickly as it had arisen. In its place rose a sobering view of a future overcome by ethnic conflict, state fragmentation, and tribal wars.

## The Purpose of This Book

The link between the Yugoslav crisis and the crisis that developed among major powers over the war in Bosnia is the underlying theme of this book. Conventional wisdom, which emerged rapidly after war broke out in 1991, is that the war resulted from peculiarly Balkan hatreds or Serbian aggression. In fact, however, the Yugoslav conflict is inseparable from international change and interdependence, and it is not confined to the Balkans but is part of a more widespread phenomenon of political disintegration. The conflict grew and infected Western alliances because those making policy and shaping public opinion toward Yugoslavia misunderstood the nature and origins of the conflict from the beginning. Central to this misunderstanding was their underestimation of the interrelation that exists between the internal affairs of most countries and the international environment. Ignoring that interdependence in dealing with the Yugoslav crisis led to many paradoxes and had counterintuitive results. One was that the external effects of the conflict on Western powers could have been reduced substantially if there had been a greater appreciation for the influence that actions by foreign governments and international organizations were having on Yugoslav politics throughout its path of dissolution. Nor is the Yugoslav conflict unique. Because of their country's international position in the cold war, the Yugoslavs were simply early in demonstrating a broader syndrome facing the world at the end of the cold war. Finally, the Yugoslav crisis was not one but many conflicts. It evolved over time, having a different character at subsequent stages and requiring different actions to prevent its continuation, particularly the descent into territorial war and ethnic violence—which was never inevitable.

The purpose of this book is to explain what happened to Yugoslavia and what can be learned from the response of outsiders to its crisis. This book is being published at a particularly difficult time in the evolution of the conflict. Emotions about the violence and atrocities in the Bosnian war are most raw. The most compelling emotion is to take sides in the war in Bosnia-Herzegovina, and all who propose instead to analyze the conflict are accused of assigning moral equivalence between victims and aggressors—or worse, of justifying the actions being explained. The conflict is moving at an accelerating pace, and its significance for outsiders has taken numerous turns. Moreover, the story is far from over. This book is being published before much information on many details of the events and the politics behind decisions recorded here is available. The first phase of self-justifying memoirs and exposés has begun, but these works have only added to the many disagreements over what actually happened and who played what role.[3]

Nonetheless, the issues at stake are already clear. As more and more countries and regions within countries threaten to follow the Yugoslav path, these issues are too vital to world order to await closure in the Yugoslav case before analyzing its causes and calling for more appropriate policy and institutions. In fact, this significance makes the origins and evolution of the Yugoslav conflict more important, in contrast to those who entered the story later and were inclined to consider its early stages irrelevant ancient history or those who had little time for such perspective in their race to stop the violence. Among the most difficult and painful lessons of the conflict, moreover, in terms of both its moral challenge and policy formulation, is that taking sides made matters worse for the most vulnerable in former Yugoslavia, inhibiting policy that could have protected them.

The story recorded and analyzed in this book begins a decade before the fall of the Berlin Wall, when the economic austerity and reforms required by a foreign debt crisis triggered a slide toward political disintegration. It stops in March 1994, three years after Yugoslavia's collapse. There was no settled outcome at that point. The Bosnian war and its forced population movements were actually intensifying, and there was scant assurance that further disintegration would not bring war eventually to other parts of the former country, especially the autonomous province of Kosovo in Serbia and the former republic of Macedonia. There was, however, a psychological divide during February–March 1994. An auspicious conjunction of events—a major power confrontation at a NATO summit, the arrival of a civilian head for UN forces on the ground and a new military commander in Bosnia-Herzegovina, and a tragic massacre by mortar fire in a market in central Sarajevo—jolted the momentum away from war toward peace and substantially raised hopes that political settlements would soon follow. Encouraged by their view that a NATO ultimatum to bomb Bosnian Serb positions had created that momentum and propelled by their own impatience since the fall of 1993 with the length of the war and the cost of the UN operation, the major powers resolved to work in concert to end the Bosnian war before the next winter.

The result was a shift in tactics. The changes addressed the three primary criticisms of international intervention until then: that there had been insufficient willingness to threaten the use of military force to support negotiators in pressing parties for a political settlement; that disunity among the major powers had allowed warring parties to play one off against the other; and that the sole remaining global power, the United States, had not been sufficiently engaged in the problem. Without altering their strategy toward the conflict (part of which was that their national interests still did not support direct use of military force to end the war), the major powers and international negotiators sought new leverage over the warring parties: the threat of NATO air power to obtain cease-fires and political settlements; a consensus that unity among the major powers (defined as Britain, France, Germany, Russia, and the United States) was a precondition of all their objectives in their engagement in the conflict; and the willingness of the United States to become a permanent player in the diplomatic search for a settlement.

The grand hopes of March had a more modest result. A string of localized, piecemeal cease-fire agreements, to be monitored by UN peace-keeping forces, appeared to lay the conditions on the ground for peace. A fragile cease-fire signed on March 29 in the former federal republic of Croatia covered an armed stalemate between its government and rebel Serb forces, which held one-fourth of Croatian territory and refused to be incorporated into the new state. Another hopeful but fragile cease-fire in mid-February appeared finally to end a twenty-two month siege of the Bosnian capital, Sarajevo, by the Bosnian Serb army, enabling the city's trapped inhabitants to take small steps toward freedom of movement and economic revival. A third cease-fire, signed in Washington on March 1, promulgated a binational federation as an alternative to the ferocious fighting in one-third of Bosnian territory between two of the three warring parties in the republic, the Bosnian Croats and Bosnian Muslims (Bosniacs).

The next step was a cease-fire to stop the fighting between the Muslim-led Bosnian government forces and the third party, the Bosnian Serbs. With an end to open hostilities, the task of finding a political settlement could resume, thereby preventing the cease-fires from turning into long-term stalemates—a complex Cyprusization of the Yugoslav conflict, with UN forces on the ground for an interminable future. With the active role of the United States, aided by Russia and the heads of the UN operation, in achieving these cease-fires, the parallel tracks of international mediation—cease-fires to stop the fighting as soon as possible and political settlements to end the conflict—might begin to converge and, in their mutual reinforcement, end the wars.

## Foreign Policy Quagmire

From the beginning of the Yugoslavs' resort to force to solve their conflicts, the leaders of the major powers who had initiated and backed international negotiations insisted that it was up to the warring parties to find a solution. This was their war, of little intrinsic interest to the Europeans or to the United States. The worry associated historically with Balkan conflict, that World War I had its prelude in the Balkan Wars of 1912–13 and ignited at Sarajevo, was explicitly dismissed with the observation that the great power interests and competition for spheres of interest which fueled this proverbial "tinder box" were lacking.[4] Western security was protected by the NATO alliance, by the norms and conflict-resolving institutions of the CSCE, and by agreement among the powers to act in concert to contain the war in Bosnia-Herzegovina and to assist the warring parties to implement whatever political settlement they reached.

In fact, these assumptions could not have been further from the truth. To proceed to the final two steps—to obtain a cease-fire between the two parties still at war in Bosnia and to complement the string of cease-fires with a political settlement—the major powers had to confront the fact that they did not agree on the parameters of a permissible outcome or the means to achieve it. They could agree that maintaining a united front was more important than any particular outcome in the Balkans, but this was not the same as leadership or agreement on a specific outcome and was not sufficient to override their competing interests and commitments and the contradictory signals they had been sending to the warring parties for the preceding three years.

The result was once again to slow the momentum toward a resolution, to threaten the existing cease-fires, and to endanger the UN personnel sent to contain the conflict with humanitarian assistance and constraints on the conduct of warring parties. The parallel tracks of negotiations did not become complementary but worked at cross-purposes. The use of NATO air power for both tracks and the role of the United States put such strains on the agreement of the major powers to remain united that the NATO alliance looked seriously threatened by the end of 1994, and the UN forces came very close to withdrawing from Bosnia altogether.

At the most transparent level, the issues of disagreement included the cause of the fighting; what was necessary to bring the conflict to an end and the method of obtaining peace; and the goal of intervention. At a less visible level, however, was a far more disquieting problem: the fact that these disagreements revealed the lack of leadership and conception of the security regime that should replace the cold war division (including the survival and purpose of NATO) in Europe. This included the role of the United States as the sole remaining global power, the relations of the United States with its European allies in a new Europe, and the place that Russia would assume in that new world order. Already in January 1993, soon after assuming the presidency, William Clinton called the conflict "the most frustrating and complex foreign policy issue in the world today."[5]

But this was not sufficient to override the one area of clear agreement among the major powers that the two issues were separate: the Yugoslav conflict was not of sufficient strategic or national interest to contribute the political and military resources necessary to solve it and end the war.

The disagreements over the cause and nature of the conflict could be seen to fall into one of two views, both focused on the war in Bosnia-Herzegovina. One view held that the war was an act of aggression by Serbs against the legitimate government of a sovereign member of the United Nations. According to this view, this was part of a pattern of aggression that had begun earlier in Slovenia and Croatia, when one nation within multinational Yugoslavia—the Serbs under the leadership of the president of the former federal republic of Serbia, Slobodan Milošević—sought, in alliance with the federal army of Yugoslavia, to create a Greater Serbia. Achieving this goal required annexing territory in the neighboring republics of Croatia and of Bosnia and Herzegovina where Serbs lived; securing control by expelling or killing all inhabitants who were not Serbs, most egregiously Slavic Muslims in Bosnia; and then completing a process begun in the 1980s of retracting autonomy from two provinces within Serbia by expelling the minority populations of ethnic Albanians, Hungarians, Croats, and others.

This view came to be identified most consistently with the U.S. government and portions of its political and intellectual elite, although it originated with leaders in Austria, Slovenia, Croatia, and, somewhat later, Germany, when the issue at stake was sovereignty in Slovenia and Croatia. It had become the basis, however, for the identification of a more general pattern in the post–cold war period of what American officials called rogue or renegade states, headed by "new Hitlers" such as Saddam Hussein in Iraq and Slobodan Milošević, who defied all norms of civilized behavior and had to be punished to protect those norms and to protect innocent people. A package of indirect measures, designed to turn such leaders into international pariahs and to reduce their military advantage, was used to stop such behavior and to discourage others from emulating it. These measures included political exclusion from international bodies, diplomatic isolation, economic isolation through trade sanctions, an arms embargo, a no-fly zone, and the threat of air power against attempts to attack civilians with heavy weapons.

A second view, more common in Europe and Canada, though not without its adherents in the United States, was that the Yugoslav and Bosnian conflicts constituted a civil war based on the revival of ethnic conflict after the fall of communism. The argument was that communist regimes had kept their populations in a deep freeze for forty years, repressing ethnic identities and freedoms. Freedom throughout the region had restored to countries their national histories of the precommunist era, which had been interrupted and which included, as in Yugoslavia, enduring and venomous animosities between ethnic groups that had exploded into new cycles of revenge when the repression lifted.[6]

According to this view, the conflict that erupted between the Croatian government and one segment of the republic's Serbian minority after nationalists won in the presidential and parliamentary elections of April 1990 was thus a revival of an ancient Croat-Serb conflict. In the republic of Bosnia-Herzegovina, Europeans saw a three-sided war, which they had tried to prevent in February 1992 before recognizing it as a sovereign state by negotiating an ethnic partition of the republic into three cantons. They were not averse to the use of sanctions to change Serbian behavior and to declarations of Helsinki norms on the sanctity of internationally recognized borders as applied to the republics, but they saw no solution without a political settlement among the three parties over their territorial disputes. Because this view was largely held by countries that had sent soldiers to the UN protection forces in Croatia and in Bosnia-Herzegovina, it was not in conflict with—and usually was complementary to—the idea that an early cessation of hostilities monitored by outsiders facilitated the work of external mediators.

In contrast, the first view, that the wars were caused by Serbian aggression, saw a cease-fire as consolidating, and therefore rewarding, the military gains of aggressors. A cease-fire, therefore, was only welcome if it was accompanied by a political agreement that reversed those gains and obtained Serb acceptance of the internationally recognized borders of the republics. The difficulty was that this view was represented among negotiators by countries that did not have soldiers at risk on the ground and that would not send troops to reverse the aggression.

The disagreements over explanations of the conflict and diplomatic strategies were compounded by differences in goals. Proponents of the first view were primarily concerned with protecting principles of international order and stability. This objective had led the U.S. government in early 1991, in fact, to follow a conservative path, opposing the breakup of Yugoslavia and the independence of Slovenia and Croatia. In early 1992 that perspective shifted under the same Bush administration to a defense of the Helsinki norms underlying European security after 1975 of inviolable borders (transferred to the borders of the federal republics) and of human rights. The Bosnian war was particularly conducive to such a policy, based on a liberal perspective of individual rights and political arrangements guaranteeing those rights.[7] This policy could justify support for the sovereignty and borders of multinational Bosnia-Herzegovina against Serbian aggression as simultaneously protecting the international commitment to human rights and the dual foundations of European and global peace and stability. But such a view was increasingly difficult to distinguish from support for the republic's Muslim population, whose very survival appeared at risk when war broke out. In early 1993 the new U.S. administration reversed the two principles, demanding a just territorial settlement for the Muslims of Bosnia and a more forceful attitude against Serbian aggression, even if that necessitated a continuation of the war, on the grounds that individual Muslims were victims of gross violations of international humanitarian law.[8] Although the policy of the new administration retained its insistence on the norm of inviolable borders and therefore the territorial integrity of a sovereign Bosnia-Herzegovina, it was increasingly difficult to differentiate support for a particular ethnonational group (the Muslims) from the assumption of ethnic conflict that underlay the second interpretation of civil war.

The ethnic conflict perspective had also dictated a conservative policy against dissolution. Countries such as Britain and France espoused this position because they foresaw a threat to stability from a snowballing of autonomist struggles, which they recognized from their own experience. But by mid-1993 Europeans also adjusted their policy to what some called a realistic (others, a cynical) approach. This was a reaction to their experience as members of UN forces in Bosnia and impatience with a war that had escalated beyond all expectations and with the repeated failures of international negotiators to achieve a political agreement. The major powers with soldiers on the ground argued that the territorial gains of ethnic armies were largely irreversible and that ethnic partition (preferably within a Bosnia-Herzegovina because they had also recognized its sovereignty and territorial integrity) was inevitable.[9] Their view of stability and the threat to European security led them to be less concerned about the general principles of international order, applied in this instance to what the United States and Germany were calling a just solution for the Muslims in Bosnia and the need to punish Serbian aggression; they were more concerned about the growing risk that war would escalate and spread. Because they were closer to the scene, they had all along defined the threat in more immediate, concrete terms: the flow of refugees into their own fragile political environments and the threat of additional waves; the possible spillover of war beyond Bosnia-Herzegovina; the destabilization of economics in neighboring states as a result of the sanctions on Serbia and Montenegro; and the disruption of transcontinental commerce and the process of integration. The goal for them was to contain the conflict and to negotiate a compromise political settlement acceptable to all three warring parties in Bosnia-Herzegovina so as to end the war.

As approaches on which to base the search for a political agreement, peace, and long-term stability, these two interpretations of the cause of conflict in former Yugoslavia and on an acceptable political outcome in relation to the resources necessary to achieve it were incompatible. The incompatibility was papered over, for a remarkably long time, by the use of a UN peacekeeping and humanitarian operation. The UN mandate to monitor and negotiate cease-fires, based on the consent of parties on the ground, appeared to succeed in containing the conflict and suited both the interpretation and goals of those who supported the theory that the conflict was a civil war. The UN mandate to provide humanitarian assistance to alleviate the suffering of civilian victims, including safe areas for six cities with a Muslim majority in range of Bosnian Serb artillery, and to impose rules on the conduct of war by its monitoring and reporting activities suited the interpretation and goals of those who considered the war a result of Serb aggression.

The five permanent members of the UN Security Council had originally resisted intervention in the Yugoslav conflict on other than humanitarian grounds. Such a mandate to protect civilian lives and aid the displaced and refugees, particularly in the conditions of war, depended on the consent of those who controlled the terrain—in effect, operational neutrality among the parties and the perspective that this was a civil war. But the UN General Assembly had also admitted to membership in May 1992 three of the six former Yugoslav republics—Slovenia, Croatia, and Bosnia-Herzegovina. The legitimate governments of each of these new states represented one nation in contests that pitted two or three nations against each other, so their recognized sovereignty gave support to the proponents of the view that Serbian fighting in Croatia and Bosnia-Herzegovina constituted aggression across internationally recognized borders against legitimate states. The United States, joined more and more by Islamic states concerned for the fate of Bosnian Muslims, considered the principle of neutrality on the ground a pretense to appease aggressors, to facilitate genocidal policies and truculent violation of humanitarian law, and to stand in the way of policies that would bring a just solution by continuing to treat the Bosnian Serbs as an equal party to conflict. The proponents of the other view countered that intervention was not intended to take sides in a civil war and must remain neutral, helping civilian victims regardless of their ethnic background and facilitating the necessary precondition of peace, a political settlement among warring parties, rather than encouraging more slaughter.

Instead of providing a common denominator among them, the UN operation exacerbated these differences. Frequent amendments to the mandate (see appendix) aimed to quell dissatisfaction with actual results and the failure to achieve peace and disagreements among major powers played out around the table of the Security Council. But this only increased the contradictions in the UN mandate, leading to ever greater difficulties of implementation and need for more troops. Moreover, unlike all UN operations in the past, this conflict was occurring on the European continent.

The longer the war in Bosnia and its televised atrocities continued and the further from a political settlement the warring parties in both Bosnia-Herzegovina and Croatia appeared, the more it eroded the one basis of agreement among the major powers: that the conflict held little consequence for their mutual relations and the institutions of European security and the NATO alliance. Their inability to act collectively and effectively toward the Bosnian challenge threatened what mattered. Pressures on the United States to show the necessary leadership led it to pressure for the use of NATO air power to improve the protection of humanitarian aid and to punish the Serbs. The resulting danger that war would escalate and also put at risk the lives of UN soldiers, the consent from all warring parties on which humanitarian aid depended, and the policy of containment led the troop-contributing countries to retain control within the UN command over the use of NATO air power with a "dual key" system on the decision to bomb requiring that requests originate with the UN forces.

The resulting vicious circle increasingly translated their disagreements over the Bosnian crisis into a crisis of confidence in their regional and international security institutions. The United Nations became trapped between its commitment to protect the universal norm of sovereignty for all states and its obligation to protect universal human rights, such as the right of asylum and the conventions on war, and the norms of humanitarian law and global peace that were being defied. The U.S. administration, angered by the refusal of the UN peacekeeping operation to adopt the U.S. position and go to war against Serbs, led the campaign against the United Nations at the same time that it, as sole superpower, needed the UN more than other countries—to legitimize its actions in protecting global security, take over policing actions that it had begun in the meantime in countries such as Haiti, Somalia, and Rwanda, and to enforce international law and the universal norms of a world order it had created after World War II and still led.[10] Exasperation at the ineffectiveness of NATO in ending the conflict, although not the task it defined for itself, raised doubts about its purpose and intensified calls for it to demonstrate its credibility by a greater show of force against the Serbs. U.S. frustration at the limitations placed by UN commanders on the use of air power grew into a conflict between the United States and its European allies over policy in Bosnia and the risk that Europeans saw in U.S. policy. NATO discomfort over its assigned role in a Chapter 8 action (by which a regional organization assists a UN mission) revived unilateralists in the U.S. Congress who attacked multilateralism and the idea that NATO would be subordinated to the UN and the United States to its allies in NATO.[11] These quarrels inevitably reverberated to capitals where early disagreements between departments of defense and foreign affairs over the use of force to end the Yugoslav crisis at a time of military downsizing, on the one hand, and the lack of direction on political goals in the case, on the other, were growing into deep divisions.

Moreover, in its attempt to avoid committing troops, the United States had also sought assistance from Russia to move the diplomatic process forward. Russian negotiators were to entice Serbs to the bargaining table and to concede territorial gains to the Muslim-led Bosnian government by giving assurances of protection for Serb interests, but without abandoning the U.S.-led policy of reversing and punishing Serbian aggression by diplomatic isolation, economic sanctions, and threat of NATO bombs. But Russia was caught in a political dynamic similar to that which had caused the conflict in Yugoslavia. Its leaders were therefore more aware of the war's actual causes. They were also facing an assertive parliament and opposition from Russian nationalists who had made Western policy toward the Yugoslav conflict into a litmus test. The leadership thus chose to cooperate for its own national interest in this period of transition in winning recognition as a major power in economic and diplomatic forums in the post–cold war world, such as the Group of Seven (G-7) and the new European security architecture, but it also opposed this policy. Moreover, Russian cooperation was explained in the West, in the same terms they applied to the former Yugoslavs, as a result of historical, nationalist, and religious sympathies between Russians and Serbs or of Russian imperialist designs in the Balkans. The United States found itself unprepared for increasing conflict with Russia over Bosnia policy. The key benefit of the end of the cold war, improved U.S.-Russian relations and Russian cooperation in the Security Council, was also at risk.

Acting very much like the warring parties on Yugoslav soil, the major powers were unwilling to concede to each other's view of the conflict, in large part because of the long-term political implications for both the Balkans and major power relations. Why were major European powers, with substantial troops on the ground in their own backyard, unable to achieve a political settlement of ethnic conflicts over territory without the military power and political leadership of the United States? What did it mean for the United States to be the sole superpower if it was unwilling to put troops on the ground in Bosnia in defense of a policy that insisted on rolling back military aggression and leveling the military playing field with the use of air power? Was Russia a part of Europe? Without answers to these questions, the UN protection forces and international negotiators in former Yugoslavia resorted increasingly to building a "piecemeal peace" on the basis of cease-fires.[12] Stopgap measures to avoid worse alternatives resulted in multiple stalemates of negotiated zones of separation between warring parties and in hope that, in the absence of agreement on how to solve the conflict, they might in the end build peace from the ground up.

## Escaping the Diplomatic Deadlock

The only solution to the Yugoslav problem is to address directly the real origins and fundamental issues of the conflict: the collapse of states, the problematic meaning of national self-determination in relation to human rights and borders, and the process of incorporating (or excluding) former socialist states into the West. The two interpretations that were driving Western policies were ideological, based on a conceptual apparatus still moored in the cold war. The first identified aggression as that which the West had mobilized decades of resources to prevent from the East: a deliberate, planned, military, cross-border denial of independence to a sovereign state. The fact that former Communist party leaders had been reelected in Serbia (true also in Macedonia and Slovenia, but disregarded) made it easy to apply wholesale anticommunist attitudes to this new aggression, to see this as the last stand of communism in Europe, and to ignore the fundamental disputes about the locus of sovereignty and of new borders that had been created by the breakup of the state. The second view was more attuned to the fact that a system was collapsing, but its focus on the internal characteristics of these societies reflected a different kind of misunderstanding—a Western, stylized view of communist regimes as centralistic, repressive dictatorships. The fact that the collapse had more to do with the transition of a particular constitutional order, its social and economic rights, and a society much transformed over forty years to another type of political order and its procedural and civil rights was beyond common knowledge about these regimes.

In fact, the conflict was simultaneously a matter of domestic transformation and of the transformation of the European and international order. Domestic conflicts became defined in terms of sovereignty and independence, whereas the actions of regional and international institutions were undermining state sovereignty and at the same time so based on unquestioning protection of the principle of sovereignty that they could not address the issue of sovereignty itself. The international prerogative to intervene to protect fundamental human rights appeared to lack both the instruments and the conception of how and when to intervene in circumstances when the process of transforming citizenship rights becomes a matter of national rights, group survival, and incompatible territorial claims. Major powers saw no strategic interest in acting to prevent territorial war, only to find the wars challenging all the premises of their security regimes.

To the extent that the Yugoslav crisis is recognized correctly as an early case of a larger phenomenon that must be addressed, it has been defined as ethnic conflict. Although the major powers attempting to resolve that crisis had fundamental disagreements, they in fact began from the same premise that the conflict was caused by personal hatreds and animosities that they labeled ethnic. The black-and-white portrayal of ethnic conflict that characterized discussion of the Yugoslav case is, in fact, an understandable and potent way to generate sympathy and mobilize loyalties and support for action, particularly when there are clearly innocent victims of armed aggression and when the weaponry of late twentieth-century warfare is so destructive and in abundant supply. This tendency is reinforced by the effects of global interdependence on the formulation of domestic foreign policy. Political and intellectual migration has made ethnic lobbies of émigrés potent single-interest groups in major capitals. The global mass media can truly internationalize the tactics of local contests through vivid televised images of human cruelty and through the use of apparently familiar religious, racial, and cultural symbols. The resulting empathy and personal identification are more influential the less governments see a strategic interest to define early action because foreign policy is then more vulnerable to the domestic electoral calculations of governing parties and the political pressures of legislative assemblies.

The definition of the Yugoslav crisis as ethnic conflict was a major source of the quicksand into which intervention fell. Although they were accused of excusing the crimes of nationalist demagogues, those who held the view that this was ethnic conflict and civil war ran into difficulty because they accepted the argument of nationalists, giving credence to the war propaganda of politicians and generals who sought national states and accepted the necessity of war to that end. Those who insisted that this was not civil war but external aggression were drawn increasingly toward the same conclusion—an ethnically defined solution in Bosnia-Herzegovina and in Croatia, because they defined that aggression and its victims ethnically—Serbs against Bosnian Muslims or Croats. But by giving in to an ethnic account of the conflict and defending only one nation in a multinational context, proponents of the aggression theory abandoned the *non*-ethnic understanding and constitutional mechanisms necessary to protect that group (and all citizens in general) against discrimination, expulsion, and death on the basis of their ethnicity/nationality.[13]

That these wars are a form of aggression is indisputable. But the focus on aggression diverts attention from its immediate cause—the breakup of a country and the contest over the location of new frontiers—and from the role that the United States and European powers together played in that process in 1990–92. And while the distinction between external and internal aggression and between aggressive and defensive military action may be the only perch for international actors who seek to hold to international norms those responsible for the atrocities, detention camps, and forced migrations, it is of very little use in influencing behavior when the driving political dynamic is nationalism. In order to combine moral principles with effective policy, the interactive character of competing nationalisms cannot be ignored, and the escalatory spiral of defensive perception and aggressive behavior must be counteracted to stop the violence.

The counterintuitive character of such a dynamic can be seen particularly in the outcome of the argument that such aggression in the Yugoslav case was the plan of one man, Slobodan Milošević. This argument ignores the conditions that make such leaders possible and popular and therefore also ignores the policies necessary to end their rule. It also led people to ascribe so much power to the man that foreign governments came to rely on him to end the wars and therefore could not risk his fall from power even while they accused him of crimes against humanity. Why did Yugoslav society take the turn it did at the end of the 1980s? Why did the economic and political reform of a socialist country bring nationalists to the fore in most of its regions? Why is the dynamic in the former Yugoslavia so similar to that seen elsewhere in the former Soviet Union and in parts of Africa?

## The Argument in Brief

The real origin of the Yugoslav conflict is the disintegration of governmental authority and the breakdown of a political and civil order. This process occurred over a prolonged period. The conflict is not a result of historical animosities and it is not a return to the precommunist past; it is the result of the politics of transforming a socialist society to a market economy and democracy. A critical element of this failure was economic decline, caused largely by a program intended to resolve a foreign debt crisis. More than a decade of austerity and declining living standards corroded the social fabric and the rights and securities that individuals and families had come to rely on. Normal political conflicts over economic resources between central and regional governments and over the economic and political reforms of the debt-repayment package became constitutional conflicts and then a crisis of the state itself among politicians who were unwilling to compromise. Such a contest over fundamentally different views of the role of government and its economic powers would be fought between competing political parties in parliamentary and democratic regimes. But in this transitional, one-party, but highly decentralized federation, the contestants were government leaders fighting to retain or enhance their political jurisdictions and public property rights over economic resources within their territories. The more they quarreled, the more they contributed to the incapacity and declining authority of the central government to regulate and to resolve those conflicts over economic rights and political powers of subordinate governments.

This story would be incomplete and might easily have had a quite different outcome, however, if the internal events had not been accompanied by a disintegration of the international order in which the country found its place. As is characteristic of small states, the domestic order of socialist Yugoslavia was strongly influenced by its place in the international order: its geopolitical location, its patterns of trade and foreign alliances, and the requirements of participation in the international economy and its various organizations. The viability of the Yugoslav regime, in fact, depended on its foreign position and a policy of national independence and nonalignment tied to the organization of the cold war world. By the 1960s that viability had also come to depend on access to foreign credits and capital markets on the basis of Yugoslavia's strategic position in the Balkans and its independent foreign policy. The process that brought the cold war to an end challenged and undermined that strategic significance, the role of the Yugoslav army, and the country's alternative markets in the East and in the third world without providing any new bases for security and domestic political and economic viability.

In the collapse of Yugoslavia the link between these two processes, the domestic and the international, is the state. The global campaign of major powers and financiers during the 1980s to promote economic liberalization had as a premise the idea that states had taken on too much control in managing their economies during the stagflationary conditions of the world economy during the 1970s. Economic revival required liberalization, privatization, and cuts in public expenditures for welfare, public employment, and social services. At the same time anticommunists within communist-ruled countries and in the West were declaring the problem of socialism to be the power of their states—so-called totalitarian control and overweening bureaucracies. The West's euphoria over the collapse of communist states and its insistence on market reform, privatization, and slashed budgets as conditions for economic aid and trade paid little regard to the alternative hypotheses—that the crisis of these countries grew from governments that were too weak; that to achieve the prescribed reforms required an extremely effective administrative capacity; that foreign creditors will lend only to governments that guarantee repayment; and that foreign investors demand favorable governmental regulations and political stability.

The more unstable an international order, the more governments must resume responsibility for external defense and for negotiating foreign trade and the conditions for it on which all modern economies depend. Radical reorientation to market demand of exports and production cannot occur without new investment for structural adjustments, and successful open-market economies require a centralized capacity for macroeconomic policy. Entrepreneurship and civil freedoms depend on a context of civil order, predictability, and individual security.

Economic reforms such as those demanded of Yugoslavia by foreign creditors and Western governments ask for political suicide: they require governments to reduce their own powers. They also do so at the same time that the demands on governments, particularly the necessity to protect civil order and to provide stability in the midst of rapid change, are ever greater. Without a stable civil and legal order, the social conditions that are created can be explosive: large-scale unemployment among young people and unskilled urban dwellers; demobilized soldiers and security police looking for private employment; thriving conditions for black market activities and crime; and flourishing local and global traffic in small arms and ammunition. A sense of community under these circumstances is highly prized, but not because of the historical persistence and power of ethnic identities and cultural attachments, as the ethnic conflict school insists, but because the bases of existing communities have collapsed and governments are radically narrowing what they will or can provide in terms of previously guaranteed rights to subsistence, land, public employment, and even citizenship.[14]

## The Road to Tragedy

This is the broader story told in this book, which begins by describing the complex system of constitutional rights and international relations that made Yugoslavia stable after 1945. The country's breakdown over a decade of economic reform and constitutional crisis is detailed in chapters 3, 4, and 5. The speed of the process of disintegration, particularly when it entered a nationalist dynamic, is a major lesson of the Yugoslav crisis. That speed increasingly deprived alternative forces of the time needed to do the political work that would reverse disintegration: to create new political alliances, to bargain compromises, to develop alternatives to the previous order, to create procedures for resolving systemic conflicts peacefully, to build new governmental capacity, and to await adjustment and membership in Western organizations for which they were redesigning their domestic order.

Less than six months after the first democratic elections were held in the former Yugoslav republics, the country was at war. In July 1991, three weeks after war had broken out between an independence-seeking Croatia and units of the Yugoslav army defending the country's territorial integrity and, in some localities, Serbs who opposed Croatia's secession, top-level political advisers in Zagreb and Belgrade insisted that a political solution would still be found.[15] While barricades were being erected in the city of Mostar in Bosnia-Herzegovina and the main transport link between Bosnia and Croatia—the bridge at Bosanski Šamac—was being blown up on February 5, 1992, the Bosnian government was still preparing a referendum on independence, and all of Sarajevo was convinced it would be spared war. Two months later the more than two-year-long siege of Sarajevo by Bosnian Serb artillery fire began. In the summer of 1993, three weeks before the central Bosnian town of Vitez was nearly leveled by bombs and fire and its Muslim citizens massacred by Bosnian Croats, a high-level delegation visiting from a Western defense ministry insisted that Vitez was calm and safe from war.[16]

Unprepared for the rapidity of the political changes, inexperienced in creating new governments, and preoccupied with revolution against the previous regime and their own ambitions, the politicians who emerged in this rapidly changing scene were neither predisposed nor well prepared to develop the guarantees and procedures for human rights and free debate and to accept the compromises and temporary defeats necessary to stable, pluralistic democracies. A top adviser to Russian president Boris Yeltsin characterized the general problem in August 1992: "The most important thing to know about the Russian democrats and Yeltsin is that power came to us unexpectedly."[17] Under these circumstances, the positive assistance, or absence of negative influence, from major powers and international organizations takes on critical importance.

Already deep Western involvement in Yugoslavia shifted belatedly to explicit intervention to try to save the country or to mediate its dissolution (chronicled in chapter 6) only when nationalist and autonomist goals had taken over. Understanding little about the concept of national self-determination and the consequence of pursuing national states in a multinational setting (as laid out in chapters 7 and 8), external actors did little to counteract the escalating momentum of confrontation and violence and did much to make matters worse.

Ethnic differences, even substantial differences, do not set a society inexorably on a path toward war. Few states are free of the potential for animosity along ethnic, religious, racial, or communal lines. All countries have histories, even unresolved quarrels and unexpunged traumas, but they do not inevitably become the cause of war. In societies like the United States, ethnic differences are valued for enhancing the quality of life through variety and creative tension, even if ethnic conflicts also arise. Tensions along ethnic, racial, or historical fault lines can lead to civil violence, but to explain the Yugoslav crisis as a result of ethnic hatred is to turn the story upside down and begin at its end.

One does not need to understand the Yugoslav conflict to feel the agony and the sadness of the deliberate destruction of precious cultural and religious monuments more than four centuries old—mosques, churches, bridges, libraries, medieval towns; the generation of children left homeless, orphaned, and exposed to the traumas of hatred and the rape, dismemberment, or murder of their parents; the thousands of women sexually assaulted; and the deep psychological toll on soldiers and their supporters who are simultaneously perpetrators and victims. One does need to understand the conflict to have prevented its violent course and to bring it to a resolution. The title *Balkan Tragedy* is chosen to incorporate two other tragic aspects of the story: the roles played by the main actors and by the onlookers.

The Yugoslav crisis and disintegration into war is a story of many small steps taken in separate scenes and locales, and of the power of words that gather momentum in a particular direction. The politicians who play the major roles must be held responsible for their part in writing the story; at the same time they are also trapped in the roles they have written and must eventually take the action to its tragic conclusion unless someone intervenes to rewrite the script. Despite substantial warning of the consequences, Western governments did not intervene to alter the roles and perceptions that were feeding the escalating cycle of disintegration and violence; instead, they contributed substantially to the drama. Even with foreknowledge that there would be carnage if they did not act to prevent it or change their own behavior, actors within Yugoslavia and in the West stuck to their assigned parts.

As for the onlookers, their role has prolonged the tragedy. The death of the Yugoslav state in 1991 and the violent convulsions that followed did evoke moral outrage and anguish for its victims in public opinion and an outpouring of private sympathy and myriad nongovernmental initiatives to help refugees, children, women, and whole communities come to terms with their trauma. But many onlookers believed that the fate of the Yugoslavs was not undeserved—was there not, after all, a long history of ethnic animosity? Onlookers were not convinced of any threat to their own security or that the same fate could strike down others. Officials struggled to define the conflict so as to keep at a distance, seeing little incentive to confront the Yugoslav misfortunes directly—to recognize the tragedy and attempt to reverse it.

The war in Bosnia and Herzegovina did eventually evoke pity for Muslim victims and for the people of Sarajevo, leading to the largest UN operation ever to deliver humanitarian relief and protect relief workers. But this operation was part of a policy (analyzed in chapter 9) that aimed to do everything possible to avoid military involvement in support of a particular political objective. Instead, outsiders insisted that the Yugoslavs were not like them, that such atrocities always characterized the troublesome region and its penchant for war and balkanization, that more than anything else the violence demonstrated the difference between *them* and *us*. Continuing to view the conflict as irrelevant to their national interests and collective security, Western leaders defined it as anachronistic, an unpleasant reminder of old ethnic and religious conflicts that modern Europe had left behind, rather than as part of their own national competition to redefine Europe and respond to the end of the cold war. Even the morally outraged used a language of distinctions in their label of barbarism: the "otherness" of nations capable of such evil. This act of dismissal—itself profoundly nationalist in its core sentiment of prejudicial exclusion of whole peoples defined by their origin as different, even subhuman, and thus of little consequence—justified inaction. It was thus for most surviving Yugoslavs the greater tragedy of the wars.[18]

# Chapter 2

# The Bases of Prewar Stability

L ooking back in time from a land so ravaged by war and
brutality among former neighbors and compatriots that
talk of living together again commonly evokes derision, one finds it difficult to imagine that the dissolution of Yugoslavia into national states and
civil war was not inevitable. The most frequently heard explanation suggests just that. It was an *artificial* country, the refrain goes, which never
deserved to last its seventy-three years.

This characterization comes not only from nationalists who favored
the country's breakup but also from some political scientists and historians
who argue that ethnically homogeneous states are more stable and durable
than multiethnic or multinational states.[1] Two explanations are commonly
offered for Yugoslavia's defiance of this principle in 1945–90. One version
was that the country had held together only because of the charismatic
leadership of President Josip Broz Tito, whose death in May 1980 presaged
its collapse. A second version was that communist dictatorship could force
peoples with intense historical animosities and profoundly different political cultures to live together. The end of the communist regime unleashed
these hatreds and permitted the smaller nations of the former Yugoslavia
to choose independence, which they had sought in the precommunist era.

Neither version, however, can explain why there should have been
war, if the country's disintegration into its national parts was inevitable,
or why this collapse occurred when it did. The claims of historical ethnic
animosities and a return to the precommunist past are ways of dismissing
from consideration what collapsed and why. They are a way of saying there
is nothing to understand. But this denial has serious consequences. Either
the conclusion is that all multiethnic societies (much of the globe) must
disintegrate (and there is nothing that outsiders can do to prevent this or
its violence unless the international community actively facilitates ethnic
apartheid); or the conclusion is that Yugoslavia was unique, and no lessons
can be learned from its tragedy.

In fact, Yugoslavia was held together not by Tito's charisma, political
dictatorship, or repression of national sentiments, but by a complex bal-

ancing act in the international arena and a mixed economy and political system that provided governmental protections of social and economic equality and of shared sovereignty among its many nations. Both elements established a modus vivendi with the principles of international order that were chosen by the major powers after the two great wars of the twentieth century. The Versailles system of national self-determination was used to legitimize the breakup of empires after World War I but did not fit the multinational environment of the Balkans. The bipolar division between free world and communist aimed to contain the power of Germany and of the Soviet Union after World War II, but did not satisfy either the independent-minded Yugoslav Communist party or the contest between East and West over the Balkans and access to the Mediterranean. Although the Titoist system, as it came to be called, depended in the same way as other political systems on ruling myths that fell short in practice, the structure of the system was quite different from that of Western countries and from Western stereotypes about eastern countries. Its distortion by works written after the fall of Yugoslavia belongs to the same process of creating myths to legitimize revolution against it.[2]

Summing up the events around them in 1991 and early 1992, many Yugoslavs were inclined simply to speak of "a collapse of the system."[3] But because it was a complex system, its collapse was not simple. Pressures from social and generational change during the 1970s and 1980s were intense. The political system was characterized by nearly constant reform, including work during the 1980s on the fifth constitution. But critical to its breakdown was change from the outside, in the foreign economic and strategic environment on which the country's stability had come to depend. Contrary to the myth that has formed since Yugoslavia's demise, the cracks in the system were not the fault lines between civilizations that came together in the Balkans, but those that defined the country's domestic order and international position during the socialist period.[4] The country's institutions of civil order and common purpose were the object of erosion and attack, and division occurred according to the system of national defense, the concurrent rights and jurisdictions of the political and economic system, and social strata.[5] The disintegration of Yugoslavia cannot be understood, nor can lessons be learned for more timely intervention in similar cases, without an understanding of what broke down.

## International Security

There were two Yugoslavias, 1918–41 and 1945–91, and both were shaped by the postwar settlements of the European powers. The creation of Yugoslavia in 1918 after World War I was the outcome of nationalist struggles against the empires of Austria, Hungary, and Turkey during the nineteenth century. The great powers at Versailles determined the composition of the new country. They used the new principle of the right to national self-determination to justify the dissolution of the Habsburg and Ottoman empires which had ruled the region for half a millennium, but they created a country that was in fact multinational. South Slav politicians claiming to represent three nations—Serbs, Croats, and Slovenes—maneuvered a political compromise that joined the independent states of Serbia and Montenegro with provinces of the dissolved empires.[6] Croats—who in the mid-nineteenth century originated the Yugoslav idea of one south Slav people—and Slovenes, both from Austria-Hungary, thus escaped absorption by Italy and Austria. The great powers gained a state they hoped would not only create regional stability in place of many small states and border conflicts but also create a buffer between Austria and Serbia, the two states that had ignited the world war. Representatives from Serbia were not so favorably disposed to the idea of a Yugoslav state. Serbia had fought as an independent state on the side of the Allies, losing nearly half its adult male population to complete its nineteenth-century nation-building process. Paralleling unification in German and Italian lands, that process had aimed to incorporate all Serbs into one state, including, above all, those living in the territory that makes up today's Bosnia-Herzegovina. However, that had been given to Austria as a protectorate by the Treaty of Berlin in 1878 and it was annexed by Austria in 1908. As compensation, Serbia's political system—the Serbian royal house, its governing class, and its army—became the core of the new state and its unitary constitution: the Kingdom of the Serbs, Croats, and Slovenes (called Yugoslavia after 1929).[7]

Political instability plagued this interwar kingdom. Quarrels over the choice of a unitary constitution instead of a federation became deep-seated discontent over the lack of autonomy for particular nations (especially Croats).[8] But equally important was the extraordinarily difficult task, under the economic conditions of the 1920s and 1930s, of integrating into one state the territories, bureaucracies, legal and transportation systems, and peoples of very different historical experiences. Nonetheless, the result was a country with an unusual richness of cultures: Habsburg, Venetian, and Ottoman legacies; Roman Catholic, Greek Orthodox, Muslim, Jewish, and Protestant religions; Slavic dominance mixed with non-Slav indigenous and immigrant traditions.

By the mid-1920s world demand for agricultural exports—the kingdom's primary source of trade revenues—had collapsed. The liberal democratic constitution written at Versailles gave way to dictatorship in the face of worldwide economic depression and continuing constitutional quarrels at home when British and French financial credits were withdrawn on the eve of the Great Depression. The return to democracy in 1935 became dangerously tied to German economic penetration and to an economic recovery based on German rearmament and expansion after 1936.[9] Yugoslavia was militantly anti-Bolshevik, but its fascist leanings, in contrast to those of its neighbors, were limited to the introduction of corporatist institutions in the economy and state. In April 1941 an air force coup staged to protest a pact the Yugoslav prince regent had secretly signed with Hitler brought immediate retaliation. Belgrade was bombed and the Axis powers invaded, splintering the country among occupying armies from Germany, Italy, Hungary, and Bulgaria. Croatian fascists in exile in Italy returned to accept the German offer of an independent state of Croatia (*Nezavisna Država Hrvatske*, or NDH), including Croatian annexation of the territories of Bosnia and Herzegovina. The Yugoslav government went into exile in London, and the Serbian royal army broke down into guerrilla bands. The Communist party organized a partisan army of national liberation, combining elite mobile units and regionally autonomous commands. It eventually linked the separate provincial committees of liberated areas into a provisional government of national unity comprising antifascist groups.

Nationalist anti-imperialism of the nineteenth century had therefore been revived as a shared bond among Yugoslav peoples, although it had now taken the form of antifascism under Communist party leadership. As a result of World War II the new governing party was imbued with the region's geopolitical sensibility: the persistent threat of conquest from outsiders and war over territory and between competing political systems. Moreover, despite its later reputation for fierce independence, the communist leadership under Tito also had to operate within the constraints of another compromise envisioned by the major powers for stability and influence in the region after the war: the infamous percentages agreement between Churchill and Stalin of October 1944, which divided influence in Yugoslavia, 50-50, between the West and the East. The British would retain their sphere of interest in the Balkans (a position that the United States took over with the Truman Doctrine of February 1947), but Tito's forces would be permitted local governance. Stalin was more concerned at the time with maintaining the wartime alliance than with socialist internationalism. Furthermore, this was no threat to the security of the Soviet Union because it had no common border with Yugoslavia.

The resulting tensions in the Balkans from 1945 to 1949 had a significant role in the origins of the cold war. Among these tensions were Yugoslavia's grievance with the Allies for awarding Trieste and a surrounding area to Italy;[10] conflicts between Tito and Stalin over defense policy, development strategy, and independence in the Balkans (including military domination of Albania, defense coordination with Romania, and a bilateral treaty with Bulgaria in place of Stalin's proposed political union); and quarrels with Britain and the United States over their attempt to undermine Tito's regime by economic sabotage and over Yugoslav support for the guerrillas in the Greek civil war.

To the surprise of those in the West who had propagandized Tito as the most fanatical Stalinist in Eastern Europe, a quarrel between Stalin and Tito, made public on June 28, 1948, led to Yugoslavia's exclusion from the newly forming eastern bloc. In contrast to East Europeans, whose nationalism focused on the symbol of Yalta, where allied powers agreed to a Soviet sphere of influence in Eastern Europe, the Yugoslavs created a nationalist symbol out of their anti-Soviet stand of 1948, and a second civil war in less than ten years ensued.[11] In the political purge that followed, the majority of the Yugoslav population sided with Tito over Stalin. Nonetheless, tens of thousands chose loyalty to international communism, fell victim to local vendettas, or, in confusion over the choice between the two leaders, were sent to jail, to prison camp, or to their death.[12] During World War II 1 million to 2 million people died in a population of less than 15 million. Within five years, another 51,000 were arrested or disappeared, and many members of the political elite were excluded from further participation in public life. Making virtue out of necessity a decade before Romania and China, the Yugoslav leadership chose the anomalous position that the United States called national communism. The country would be simultaneously socialist and independent of Moscow.

The regime survived thanks to U.S. military aid; U.S.-orchestrated economic assistance from the International Monetary Fund, World Bank, U.S. Export-Import Bank, and foreign banks; and the restoration of trade relations with the West after August 1949.[13] In exchange, socialist Yugoslavia played a critical role for U.S. global leadership during the cold war: as a propaganda tool in its anticommunist and anti-Soviet campaign and as an integral element of NATO's policy in the eastern Mediterranean. Jealously guarding its neutrality, Yugoslavia became an important element in the West's policy of containment of the Soviet Union. It prevented the Soviets from gaining a toehold in the Mediterranean and protected routes to Italy and Greece by providing a strong military deterrence to potential Soviet aggression in the Balkans.

Yugoslavia's foreign economic relations were less satisfying. The United States refused to reconsider Yugoslavia's request for inclusion in the Marshall Plan and therefore early membership in Europe, and the USSR blocked its participation in the Council for Mutual Economic Assistance (CMEA). The country found a modus vivendi in associate or observer status in both alliances after 1955, with the Organization for Economic Cooperation and Development (OECD), the CMEA, and the Warsaw Treaty Organization (WTO). Between 1958 and 1965 the Yugoslavs reformed their economy to meet the conditions for full membership in the General Agreement on Tariffs and Trade (GATT). Beginning in 1971 they negotiated association agreements with the European Community and after 1979 with the European Free Trade Association (EFTA). But Tito directed much of his energies to the third world by helping to found the Nonaligned Movement (NAM) and the Group of 77 as alternatives to the superpower blocs.[14]

The United States frequently demonstrated its discomfort with the NAM and with Yugoslav independence by stopping economic assistance to Yugoslavia. As an alternative to superpower confrontation, however, this coalition of developing countries was a moderating force against class war at the international level. Yugoslav leaders became leading advocates of peaceful coexistence between ideological camps and of the redistribution of wealth from rich countries to poor in the form of economic assistance (the program of the new international economic order—NIEO) as a substitute for worldwide communist revolution or direct North-South confrontation. The country played an active role in the United Nations, participating in peacekeeping efforts and in the United Nations Conference on Trade and Development (UNCTAD) and sending Yugoslav technical advisers and aid to developing countries.

The domestic economic and political system of socialist Yugoslavia was structured around the needs of this policy of neutrality and independence. The system of national defense depended on a certain level of self-reliance: state protection of strategic industries; location in the mountainous, defensible interior of the country of the most critical defense plants, airfields, and strategic stockpiles; and governmental regulation of agriculture to ensure self-sufficiency in food. To reduce vulnerability to East-West relations and possible attack from either side, the leadership spread its military purchases among NATO, the WTO, and domestic producers (who supplied at least one-third) and distributed the stages of armaments production among factories in different regions.[15]

This balancing act extended to the organization of the armed forces and strategic doctrine as well. At the federal level a standing army, air force, and navy (the Yugoslav People's Army, YPA) were deployed with technologically advanced weaponry capable of mounting direct resistance against a conventional invasion. This force could not resist a dedicated assault from either alliance, but it could extract an appreciable immediate price for any such aggression and provide a barrier for the second force. An all-people's civilian militia (the territorial defense forces, TDF), designed to present a systematically organized, prolonged, guerrilla resistance to any invader, was under the control of republics and localities. These guerrilla units followed the doctrine of people's war and were inspired by the impressive record of partisan resistance against the invading Germans, Italians, Bulgarians, Hungarians, and Austrians during World War II. They would, if necessary, retreat ever farther into the interior of the country (especially to Bosnia-Herzegovina), where armaments factories, airstrips, and underground stockpiles of food, fuel, and weapons would supply them. But their primary virtue was their familiarity with local terrain and commitment to defense of their own homes. No high school or university graduate could receive a diploma without passing the obligatory four-year course in premilitary training. There was universal conscription of males, with active duty lasting eighteen months to two years (depending on the conscript's level of education). After 1974 all adult citizens were required to spend time each year in the active reserves.[16] Civil defense and TDF units were organized at every workplace in the public sector, and local authorities were obliged to maintain stockpiles of weapons and supplies.

Although operational control of the armed forces belonged to the general staff of the YPA and the ministry of defense in Belgrade, the emphasis in defense doctrine and policy priority between the YPA and the TDF shifted periodically depending on assessments of external developments and the most likely security threat. The system of military command and control was substantially decentralized, but the balance between federal (YPA) and republican (TDF) authority was not always clear. Moreover, the internal security and intelligence apparatus of the ministry of the interior included a separate armed militia. The third-largest regular land force in Europe in 1948, the YPA was a moderately sized force of 220,000 in 1980, when budget cuts had already begun to force reductions; it was projected to shrink to 150,000 by 1992.[17]

Yugoslavia's foreign economic relations also operated in three distinct markets: the West, from which it borrowed capital (suppliers' credits, commercial loans, and public grants and loans) and imported advanced technology and spare parts; and the third world (especially oil-rich Iraq and Libya) and the second world of the USSR and the CMEA, in both of which state-negotiated bilateral contracts predominated to secure access to fuel and other strategic resources in exchange for armaments, construction projects, and manufactured goods.

Yugoslav openness to economic relations with all three divisions of the cold-war world gave it flexibility in a world where economic aid and access to capital and goods markets was politically governed and largely unpredictable.[18] Many producers could buy time for adjusting to shifts in demand for their exports by shifting sales among markets, although foreign loans and commercial credits played a significant role as well. But increasing participation in Western markets also required being technologically competitive at the same time that barriers remained high against Yugoslav exports, particularly those of higher value added, and often in arbitrary fashion. The result was a growing dependence of Yugoslav producers (for both domestic and export markets) on imported technology, spare parts, and trade credit from the West and a persistent trade imbalance. In addition, the short-run solution of loans to finance trade depended on remaining strategically significant to the West.

Liberals argued that the solution to this deficit with convertible-currency countries was full incorporation in global markets through currency convertibility. Developmentalists, however, saw nonconvertibility as necessary to retain control over economic development policy, including the policy of strategic self-reliance on which their special relationship with the West was based. Domestic views on economic policy swung between these two camps, depending on the availability of credit and export revenues in the West. But periodic attempts at liberalizing economic reforms (usually required by an IMF loan and conditionality program to restore credibility in capital markets) as a long-term solution always ran up against the actual limits of Western demand for Yugoslav goods and political restraints on Western trade, leaving the debate unresolved. By the eve of the world debt crisis in 1981, the Yugoslav foreign debt was $19.3 billion.[19]

The Western stereotype of socialist countries is one of autarchy and command economies based on central planning. Once a socialist country opens up to Western foreign trade and aid, however, as Yugoslavia did after 1949 (and particularly after 1954) and as countries in Eastern Europe (especially Hungary and Poland) did somewhat later, it must reform its domestic political and economic system accordingly. The result is a hybrid system that combines market and socialist elements emphasizing increasing autonomy for firms and territorial decentralization. In place of planned quotas, economic regulation is conducted through the financial instruments of monetary, credit, and fiscal policy (according to the closed accounting system of monetary planning), and producers are expected to respond to consumer demand (both domestic and foreign). Sectoral planning and its functional bureaucracies are subordinated to territorial economic coordination, regional planning, and parliamentary approval of budgets, economic plans, and taxation. Foreign borrowing reinforces this government role in managing money because public loans (such as those from the IMF and World Bank) are made only to governments, and commercial banks require governments to guarantee repayment. Periodic foreign exchange crises and resort to IMF credits bring repeated rounds of economic reform aimed at improving financial discipline and incentives for efficiency through more governmental decentralization and enterprise autonomy.

The combination of territorial organization of economic decision-making, strategically based industrial policy, and preference for long-term stability and economies of scale through production specialization gave a distinct geopolitical character to the reform socialist economy. The economies of different localities and regions tended to become identified with certain specializations, including foreign trade. These specializations often reinforced inherited patterns. For example, of the six republics composing the Yugoslav federation, Slovenia and Croatia were far more integrated into European networks because of the Habsburg legacy, geographic proximity, and industrial policy favoring export production (including tourism). Producers and traders from the republics of Macedonia and Bosnia-Herzegovina inclined toward the Middle East and the Greek port of Thessaloniki. The republic of Serbia had relatively more business in Eastern-bloc clearing markets because of its substantial metal industry and heavy manufacturing and the importance of Danube River commerce. Exploitation of primary commodities tended to occur in the poorer regions of the south, such as Mediterranean crops in Macedonia, and mining for coal, iron ore, bauxite, copper, lead, zinc, antimony, and mercury in Bosnia and the autonomous province of Kosovo (in Serbia). The exception was grain production, which was concentrated largely in the northern plains of Slavonia (a region in Croatia) and neighboring Vojvodina (an autonomous province in Serbia). These biases were relative, and the decentralization of regional development policy to the republics after 1958 had led to substantial duplication of capital and consumer goods industries.[20] But the economic differences among republics, given their shared dependence for production and employment on imports and their preference for Western technology to improve international competitiveness and productivity, made federal policy on foreign trade and foreign exchange particularly contentious.

The collapse of the international postwar order in which states were divided into ideological camps was particularly disturbing to Yugoslavia because it straddled those divisions. Its domestic order accommodated its mixed personality—both West and East, communist-ruled and internationally open, second and third world. Its citizens could simultaneously hold separate ideological and regional identities and share in the prestige of Yugoslavia's international role. The survival of the Yugoslav regime had been tied to its national independence and organization of defense, which grew out of the critical role it played in European security and the Western anti-Soviet campaign, and its resulting ability to play off of the rivalry between the superpowers.

## Internal Sovereignty: The Constitutional Order

The second source of stability and survival of socialist Yugoslavia was its constitutional order. Through a complex web of public property rights, federalism, and individual, group, and national rights to social and economic equality, the ruling Communist party attempted to resolve two crises of the first Yugoslavia: the Wilsonian dilemma of how to guarantee the right to national self-determination in a multinational state, and the economic crises of an agrarian economy exposed to world depression.[21]

The second Yugoslavia began with the formation during World War II of a provisional government called AVNOJ (the Anti-Fascist Liberation Council of Yugoslavia), which declared its intention in November 1943 to replace the monarchy with a republic and to create a federation based on the territorial organization of the partisan, antifascist resistance. These principles formed the basis of the postwar constitution, which was ratified in 1946 but was substantially revised in 1953 after the country's international position stabilized.[22] Although many have argued that the constitution was a close copy of Stalin's 1936 constitution, it in fact reflected Lenin's approach to the national question in the 1920s and the commitment made by the Communist party of Yugoslavia in 1928 to replace the kingdom's unitary state with a federal order. It is generally accepted that this commitment to recognize the separate existence of Yugoslav nations and their sovereign rights in a federal system was critical to the communist victory after 1943.

The right of nations to self-determination, however, was only one aspect of the fundamental principle on which the communist leadership built this postwar system—a broad concept of popular self-governance or sovereignty. It shaped the leaders' perception of the world, that all nations were free and equal and that national independence had both military and economic aspects: freedom from dependence on military overlords or on foreign capital and its exploitation. The concept also was a defining constitutional principle for the country: "The Socialist Federative Republic of Yugoslavia is a federal State of voluntarily united and equal peoples and a socialist democratic community based on the power of the working people and on self-government."[23]

The Slavic word *narod* makes no distinction between "people" and "nation." The peoples of Yugoslavia had rights as founding nations of the member states of the federation (the republics) and also as individual members of those nations (ethnic peoples) to express their nationality and culture freely, without discrimination. At the same time, all people employed in the socially owned sector of the economy had rights of self-management (*samoupravljanje*) to participate in the management of their firm or social service and to be politically represented as such through elected delegates from their workplace in legislative assemblies.

The principle of sovereignty, in other words, was simultaneously political and economic, incorporating a long tradition of local self-government in the Balkans, the principle of national self-determination that created the first Yugoslavia, and democratic and socialist ideas of popular sovereignty. But, as the primary foreign interpreter of these relations noted in 1968, "Sovereignty is a rather inflexible legal concept which does not easily lend itself to new interpretations. . . . The idea of sovereignty as a single, supreme power simply did not fit into a State envisaged as a network of self-governing communities."[24] For Yugoslavs faced with national assertiveness in the late 1980s, the concept of sovereignty needed revision to reflect their reality of a layering of partial sovereignties and shared rights to self-governance and popular checks on power.

The primary constitutional problem lay with the dual concept of a nation—ethnic peoples and peoples of territories. The founding (constituent) peoples of Yugoslavia were Croats, Macedonians, Montenegrins, Serbs, and Slovenes, and, after the 1963 constitution, Muslims (in the sense of a political community, not a religion).[25] The six republics of the federation recognized nations as historical-territorial communities. Individual members of the six constituent nations (not fully coincident with the territorial boundaries of the republics) had rights as members of those nations as ethnic peoples (defined by a common religion, language, and political consciousness).

In addition, there were many citizens who identified ethnically with a people who had a national homeland elsewhere, called nationalities.[26] These individuals, such as Jews, Czechs, Romanians, Russians, Bulgarians, Turks, and Italians, and also individuals whose nation had no homeland, such as the seminomadic Romany and Vlachs, had guaranteed cultural rights to preserve their sense of community and its inheritance. Albanians and Hungarians, the largest of these groups, were also given local self-government in two autonomous regions in the republic of Serbia where they predominated (Kosovo and Vojvodina, respectively).

Because the organization of the economy emphasized territorial over functional organization and became more and more decentralized with successive marketizing reforms, the primary practice of sovereignty came over time to be associated with the republics. These six federal units had administrative and budgetary autonomy over their economies, education, and culture, but it remained a matter of intense dispute whether republican sovereignty included the right of secession from the federation.[27] Borders between the republics were drawn according to the territorial-historical concept of the nation, which based national claims to territory on a long history of common life. Since only Serbia and Montenegro had been internationally recognized as states (in 1878), the internal borders were based on a variety of historical treaties and on political negotiations held between 1944 and 1947 (and again in 1953 and 1956) by a number of border commissions and federal committees. Disputes between Croatia and Slovenia over the Istrian peninsula, between Serbia and Macedonia over their common border, between Croatia, Serbia, and Bosnia-Herzegovina over much

TABLE 2-1. *National Composition of Yugoslavia, 1961–91*
Percent (except total)

| National group | 1961 | 1971 | 1981 | 1991 |
|---|---|---|---|---|
| Total | 18,549,291 | 20,522,972 | 22,427,585 | 23,528,230 |
| Serbs | 42.0 | 39.7 | 36.3 | 36.2 |
| Croats | 23.1 | 22.1 | 19.8 | 19.7 |
| Muslims | 5.2 | 8.4 | 8.9 | 10.0 |
| Albanians | 5.0 | 6.4 | 7.7 | 9.3 |
| Slovenes | 8.5 | 8.2 | 7.8 | 7.5 |
| Macedonians | 5.6 | 5.8 | 6.0 | 5.8 |
| Montenegrins | 2.8 | 2.5 | 2.6 | 2.3 |
| Yugoslavs | 1.7 | 1.3 | 5.4 | 3.0 |
| Other | 6.1 | 5.6 | 5.5 | 6.2 |

Sources: Frits Hondius, *The Yugoslav Community of Nations* (The Hague: Mouton, 1969), p. 13; Ruža Petrović, "The National Composition of the Population," *Yugoslav Survey*, no. 3 (1983), p. 22; Petrović, "The National Composition of Yugoslavia's Population, 1991," *Yugoslav Survey*, no. 1 (1992), p. 12.

of the Bosnian border, and above all between Croatia and Serbia over Vojvodina and Srem (Srijem) were as prickly and contested as the international disputes between Slovenia and Italy over Trieste, the Soča valley, Julian March, and parts of Istria; between Slovenia and Austria over Carinthia; and between Macedonia, Bulgaria, and Greece.[28]

The construction of the republics as national homelands was insufficient for constitutional protection of *individuals'* rights to national equality, however, because the ethnic geography of the country did not conform to these historical territories. In ethnonational terms, Yugoslavia was a land of minorities (see table 2-1 and table 2-2). No group had more than a regional majority, and most communities were ethnically mixed. But as a scholar of Serb ethnicity from Croatia poignantly suggested in 1993, "with the exception of minorities such as Hungarians, Romany, Turks, Czechs, Slovaks, Romanians, Italians, and Jews, no one else, and especially not Serbs and Croats, either felt or wanted to feel a minority."[29]

Many people lived in relatively compact ethnonational communities that were not within the republic associated with their nation. Large parts of the country—including cities and most towns—were ethnically mixed. This was particularly the case in exposed plains and movable borderlands between empires, because these areas were settled by political initiative to establish defensive buffers or to repopulate areas decimated by war. The most striking example was the area running through the center of the country, where the buffer between the Habsburg and Ottoman empires—the military border, or *krajina*—had been governed under an entirely separate administration by the Austrian war

TABLE 2-2. *National Composition of Yugoslavia by Republics and Provinces, 1961–91*

Percent

| Republic | 1961 | 1971 | 1981 | 1991 |
|---|---|---|---|---|
| Bosnia-Herzegovina | 100.0 | 100.0 | 100.0 | 100.0 |
| Serbs | 42.8 | 37.3 | 32.2 | 31.4 |
| Muslims | 25.6 | 39.6 | 39.5 | 43.7 |
| Croats | 21.7 | 20.6 | 18.4 | 17.3 |
| Yugoslavs | 8.4 | 1.2 | 7.9 | 5.5 |
| Montenegrins | 0.4 | 0.3 | 0.3 | |
| Albanians | 0.1 | 0.1 | 0.1 | |
| Slovenes | 0.1 | 0.1 | 0.1 | |
| Macedonians | 0.0 | 0.0 | 0.0 | 0.0 |
| Other | 0.9 | 0.8 | 1.5 | 2.1[a] |
| Croatia | 100.0 | 100.0 | 100.0 | 100.0 |
| Croats | 80.2 | 79.4 | 75.1 | 78.1 |
| Serbs | 15.0 | 14.2 | 11.6 | 12.2 |
| Yugoslavs | 0.4 | 1.9 | 8.2 | 2.2 |
| Slovenes | 0.9 | 0.7 | 0.5 | 0.5 |
| Montenegrins | 0.2 | 0.2 | 0.2 | 0.2 |
| Muslims | 0.1 | 0.4 | 0.5 | 0.9 |
| Albanians | 0.0 | 0.1 | 0.1 | 0.3 |
| Macedonians | 0.1 | 0.1 | 0.1 | 0.1 |
| Other | 3.1 | 3.0 | 3.7 | 5.5 |
| Macedonia | 100.0 | 100.0 | 100.0 | 100.0 |
| Macedonians | 71.1 | 69.3 | 67.0 | 64.6 |
| Albanians | 13.0 | 17.0 | 19.7 | 21.0 |
| Serbs | 3.0 | 2.8 | 2.4 | 2.2 |
| Muslims | 0.2 | 0.1 | 2.1 | |
| Yugoslavs | 0.1 | 0.2 | 0.8 | |
| Croats | 0.3 | 0.2 | 0.2 | |
| Montenegrins | 0.2 | 0.2 | 0.2 | |
| Slovenes | 0.1 | 0.1 | 0.1 | |
| Other | 12.0 | 10.1 | 7.5 | 12.2[a] |
| Montenegro | 100.0 | 100.0 | 100.0 | 100.0 |
| Montenegrins | 81.3 | 67.2 | 68.5 | 61.8 |
| Muslims | 6.5 | 13.3 | 13.4 | 14.6 |
| Albanians | 5.5 | 6.7 | 6.5 | 6.6 |
| Serbs | 3.0 | 7.5 | 3.3 | 9.3 |
| Yugoslavs | 0.3 | 2.1 | 5.4 | 4.0 |
| Croats | 2.2 | 1.7 | 1.2 | |
| Slovenes | 0.2 | 0.1 | 0.2 | |
| Macedonians | 0.1 | 0.1 | 0.2 | |
| Other | 0.9 | 1.3 | 1.3 | 3.7[a] |

TABLE 2-2. *National Composition of Yugoslavia by Republics and Provinces,*
*1961–91 (Continued)*

Percent

| Republic | 1961 | 1971 | 1981 | 1991 |
|---|---|---|---|---|
| Serbia | | | | |
| Total Republic | 100.0 | 100.0 | 100.0 | 100.0 |
| Serbs | 74.6 | 71.2 | 66.4 | 65.8 |
| Albanians | 9.2 | 11.7 | 14.0 | 17.2 |
| Yugoslavs | 0.3 | 1.5 | 4.8 | 3.2 |
| Muslims | 1.2 | 1.8 | 2.3 | 2.4 |
| Croats | 2.6 | 2.2 | 1.6 | 1.1 |
| Montenegrins | 1.4 | 1.5 | 1.6 | 1.4 |
| Macedonians | 0.5 | 0.5 | 0.5 | 0.4 |
| Slovenes | 0.3 | 0.2 | 0.1 | 0.1 |
| Other | 9.9 | 9.4 | 8.7 | 8.4 |
| Serbia "proper" | 100.0 | 100.0 | 100.0 | 100.0 |
| Serbs | 92.4 | 89.5 | 85.4 | 87.3 |
| Muslims | 1.7 | 2.4 | 2.7 | |
| Yugoslavs | 0.2 | 1.4 | 4.3 | 2.5 |
| Albanians | 1.1 | 1.2 | 1.3 | |
| Montenegrins | 0.7 | 1.1 | 1.4 | |
| Croats | 0.9 | 0.7 | 0.6 | |
| Macedonians | 0.4 | 1.1 | 0.5 | |
| Slovenes | 0.3 | 0.2 | 0.1 | |
| Other | 2.3 | 2.4 | 3.7 | 10.2[a] |
| Vojvodina | 100.0 | 100.0 | 100.0 | 100.0 |
| Serbs | 54.9 | 55.8 | 54.4 | 57.2 |
| Hungarians | 23.8 | 21.7 | 19.3 | 16.9 |
| Yugoslavs | 0.2 | 2.4 | 8.3 | 8.4 |
| Croats | 7.8 | 7.1 | 5.4 | 4.8 |
| Montenegrins | 1.8 | 1.9 | 2.1 | 2.2 |
| Slovenes | 0.8 | 0.8 | 0.9 | 0.8 |
| Albanians | 0.3 | 0.2 | 0.1 | 0.0 |
| Muslims | 0.1 | 0.2 | 0.2 | 0.0 |
| Other | 10.2 | 9.7 | 9.1 | 9.7 |
| Kosovo | 100.0 | 100.0 | 100.0 | 100.0 |
| Albanians | 67.0 | 73.7 | 77.5 | 90.0[b] |
| Serbs | 23.5 | 18.4 | 13.3 | 10.0 |
| Montenegrins | 3.9 | 2.5 | 1.7 | |
| Muslims | 0.8 | 2.1 | 3.7 | |
| Croats | 0.7 | 0.7 | 0.6 | |
| Yugoslavs | 0.5 | 0.1 | 0.2 | 0.2 |
| Macedonians | 0.1 | 0.1 | 0.1 | |
| Slovenes | 0.0 | 0.0 | 0.0 | |
| Other | 3.5 | 2.4 | 2.9 | |

TABLE 2-2. *National Composition of Yugoslavia by Republics and Provinces,
1961–91 (Continued)*
Percent

| Republic | 1961 | 1971 | 1981 | 1991 |
|---|---|---|---|---|
| Slovenia | 100.0 | 100.0 | 100.0 | 100.0 |
| Slovenes | 95.6 | 94.0 | 90.5 | 87.6 |
| Croats | 2.0 | 2.5 | 3.0 | 2.7 |
| Serbs | 0.8 | 1.2 | 2.2 | 2.4 |
| Muslims | 0.0 | 0.2 | 0.7 | 1.4 |
| Yugoslavs | 0.2 | 0.4 | 1.5 | 0.6 |
| Macedonians | 0.1 | 0.1 | 0.2 | 0.2 |
| Montenegrins | 0.1 | 0.1 | 0.2 | 0.2 |
| Albanians | 0.0 | 0.1 | 0.1 | 0.2 |
| Other | 1.2 | 1.4 | 1.6 | 4.7 |

Sources: Frits Hondius, *The Yugoslav Community of Nations* (Mouton: The Hague, 1969), p.
13; Ruža Petrović, "The National Composition of the Population," *Yugoslav Survey*, no. 3
(1983), pp. 22, 30; Petrović, "The National Composition of Yugoslavia's Population, 1991,"
*Yugoslav Survey*, no. 1 (1992), pp. 4–11.

ªIncludes other listed groups for which values are not given. The results of the 1991 census
were processed individually by each republic, and there was no uniform system of classification.

ᵇThis approximate figure for Kosovo was taken from "Preventing War In Kosovo" (Lund,
Sweden: Transnational Foundation for Peace and Future Research, July 9, 1992), p. 14.

ministry. Migrants from Ottoman territory, particularly Serbs, had
been invited to settle here in exchange for defending the border, serving
in the imperial army, and acceding to strict regulation of their movements and persons. This area was thus populated by ethnically mixed
communities. It also did not conform to the borders of the two different
republics, Croatia and Bosnia-Herzegovina.[30] The exigencies of household survival and distant empires had produced, over centuries, occupational traditions of long-distance seasonal labor migration, traveling
merchants, nomadic or transhumant herding, and flight to escape imperial exactions. After 1945, industrialization had brought massive population shifts from rural to industrial and urban areas, particularly rapid
urbanization in the 1960s and 1970s, and economic migration abroad or
to other republics. The result of all these influences was a residential
landscape far different from that of the historical states giving rise to
nations and large areas that were a patchwork quilt of ethnicity.

Moreover, historians have demonstrated that the very idea of ethnic
or national identity is never fixed, but is contingent on historically specific
definitions of political identity or the particular state in which one is a

subject or a citizen. For example, Macedonian political identity was officially granted for the first time in 1948 even though the political consciousness of Slavic Macedonians preceded the Balkan Wars of 1912–13. The political identity of Muslims as a nation (as opposed to the ruling stratum under Ottoman rule in the Balkans) was not recognized until the 1963 constitution. While many Muslims shifted their chosen identity from Yugoslav to Muslim in the 1971 census, when the option first arose, the very large numbers of people who viewed their nation as Bosnian—as a people of that territory with a common history, not as an ethnic people—did not have that option in the census listing because Bosnian was neither a constituent nation nor nationality. A growing number of people also identified themselves officially as Yugoslavs by nationality in place of an ethnic identity, although there was no republican homeland for Yugoslavs. For many people, such as army officers and idealistic party members, this choice reflected a commitment to the Yugoslav idea or to socialism. For others, it reflected a view of what was more modern and appropriate, as suggested by the growing number of those among the younger generation who claimed Yugoslav nationality in the 1981 census.[31] For still others, it was an alternative to forcing a single choice from their mixed ethnic background. Even when national identity is relatively stable for some time, demographic change, labor mobility, intermarriage, and the rise of competing identities, such as occupation and schooling, change the ethnic landscape of particular plots of land and the very meaning of national identity. More than 3 million in a population of over 22 million in the 1980s were the product of ethnically mixed marriages or were themselves married to someone of different ethnicity.[32]

The concept of constituent nation can be seen as an accommodation to this reality. Individuals retained their national right to self-governance even if they lived outside their home nation's republic. Where such individuals congregated in territorially compact areas, such as the Serbs in parts of the Croatian *krajina* and the Muslims in the *sandžak* in Serbia, it was considered politically and economically pragmatic to avoid partitioning the republics into autonomous regions any more than was necessary. The choice of a national identity was voluntary—citizens had a right *not* to choose—and was registered in the census and official documents such as school and military records, voters' registries, birth and marriage certificates, and employment cards (but not, as in the USSR, in passports). The concept not only conferred language rights and psychological security about the survival of cultural community but also required that all federal activities (from appointments to public office such as army generals or the rotation of the prime minister to the distribution of federal investments and representation at cultural festivals) take directly into account the proportional representation of individuals by constituent nationality—called the national key (*ključ*, or quota system).[33]

Explicit constitutional provisions to accommodate the conflict between the territorial and the personal concept of a nation were critical for areas that for historical reasons were nationally mixed, such as the *krajina* in Croatia, the *sandžak* in Serbia, and above all, the multinational republic of Bosnia-Herzegovina. Bosnia and Herzegovina had a clear historical-territorial identity at least as old as the others, but its population comprised three national communities (simultaneously religious, social, and administrative, according to the nonterritorial Ottoman *millet* system of governance in place before 1878). None of these had a numerical majority. As a result of Croatian and Serbian opposition to recognition of the territorial nation of "Bosnians," only two of its south Slav nations (Croats, Serbs) were recognized as founding nations. The quarrel was settled in the 1960s with recognition of a third ethnic people, Muslims, as a constituent nation of Yugoslavia. In Serbia the mixture of peoples and presence of nationalities was so great in two regions that they were granted partial self-governance as autonomous provinces. In Vojvodina, in the north, Hungarians composed 19.3 percent of the population in the 1981 census.[34] They lived alongside Serbs, Croats, Romanians, Czechs, Slovaks, Ruthenians, Romany, and others. In Kosovo, in the south, Albanians formed 67 percent of the population in 1961 and 85 percent by 1981. They lived alongside Serbs, Montenegrins, and Romany.

Constitutional protections also guaranteed freedom of cultural expression for nationalities—to use their own language in public forums; to have their own newspapers and other media; to form cultural associations and, where they were locally concentrated, to be educated in their own language.

Underlying this complex system of rights was a political commitment to multiethnic coexistence. The constitution prohibited "propagating or practicing national inequality and any incitement of national, racial, or religious hatred and intolerance."[35] While cultural rights of national expression were not only permitted but also funded, any political expression of national*ism* was treated as a threat to the socialist regime and prosecuted. Although these measures were repressive, they were applied evenhandedly to maintain the concept of equality. Authorities often went out of their way to balance a particular prosecution with charges against persons from other ethnic groups in the area—what Varady calls a "civilization-shield against open animosities" and a "protection of ethnic minorities."[36] The role of the Communist party, which was also a federation of national (republican) committees, was to knit this all together. Simultaneously representing the ideal of Yugoslavia and the many nations and social strata within it, the party had the task of creating political harmony through party loyalty, rules of democratic centralism, and the patriotic principle—under the slogan "brotherhood and unity"—of equal nations in one state.

From the perspective of war and ethnonational conflict over territorial rights to self-determination in 1991–94, outsiders tend to see nationality in terms of individual identity alone and to give it overriding importance in the lives of Yugoslavs. Yet in the Yugoslav period, the ideas of ethnicity and national rights were far more tied to governmental assurances of equality among national groups and to economic governance in a progressively decentralizing system of reform communism. Its driving administrative principle was what is now commonly referred to in Europe as subsidiarity: operational and managerial decisions should be made as close to the ground as possible. Republican and local governments had ever more autonomy over their economic affairs, budgets, and taxes, sharing ownership and managerial rights with self-governing enterprises.[37] Independent agencies multiplied to provide social services. The functions, powers, and budget of the federal government declined accordingly.

Federal institutions were based on the cooperative idea of government based on councils (*saveti*) in which representatives from the republics and provinces (in the parliament, executive branch, central bank, collective state presidency, and so forth) were consulted, deliberated, and made decisions on the basis of consensus. The system of parity representation of nations and of consensus aimed to prevent any single national group from gaining political dominance over the state. It was designed by numerically smaller nations (especially Slovenes and Croats) explicitly in reaction to the interwar political dominance of the Serbian state apparatus (1919–41).[38] Therefore, all federal policy depended on cooperation from republican leaders, who could veto any decision.

The country had a mixed economy, in which economic coordination occurred through a hybrid of instruments. Free prices regulated retail markets, but bilateral supply contracts governed most transactions between public enterprises or between processing firms and private farmers.[39] Corporatist negotiations between unions, business chambers, and governments set rules over wages and benefits for firms. An indicative social plan, similar to the French system of planning, gave information about future trends and government preferences on credit policy. The plan was based on wide consultation of firms, localities, republics, producers' associations, and civil servants, and approved by the federal parliament, not on the ministerial hierarchy of central planning. Most economic decisions were a matter of wide consultation, debate, and participation. For a number of institutional reasons including the country's international position, the Achilles' heel of this reform-socialist economy was inflation.[40] The difficulty of maintaining monetary stability led to frequent (and unsuccessful) resort to anti-inflationary macroeconomic stabilization policies, placing an even greater burden on fiscal policy and on special grants and funds to manage the economy. Governments quarrelled endlessly—because of these frequent restrictions on money and credit—over rules for allocating money. Federal economic policy was driven by revenues and their redistribution.[41]

Politics revolved around the tug and pull between states' rights and the powers of the federal government. Some of these conflicts were reduced by functional specialization. The federal government was responsible for their common market (therefore, monetary and trade policy) and for defense and foreign affairs, but it owned no productive assets. Republican governments were responsible for manufacturing, agriculture, transportation and communications, and labor within their territory, and they had autonomy over education and science. Local governments were responsible for consumer markets, welfare, housing, local roads, elementary schools, health care, unemployment, and relations between the public and private sectors of the economy. Most of agriculture, much of trades and services, and the large number of unemployed were private. Nonetheless, because the republics owned major productive assets, a portion of their revenues was taxed to support common (federal) expenditures. Because the constitution required all government budgets to balance, when federal revenues from turnover and sales taxes and customs duties (its jurisdictions) fell short of expectations, republican governments were obliged to make up the difference.

The armed forces were also shared. The YPA was fully under federal jurisdiction and therefore the federal budget, including veterans' pensions, housing credits for serving and retired military officers, military industries contracting to the secretariat of national defense, and the office of trade in special (strategic) goods. The TDF system was under republican authority, but was organized within localities and workplaces, financed accordingly from republican, local, and enterprise revenues. By the early 1960s decentralization and devolution were so extensive that the federal budget was largely a defense budget (on average 67 percent of the total budget, around 4–6 percent of GNP), other expenditures having been handed down.

The elaborate system of rights for individual economic security and national equality (both individual and collective) also infused constant tensions into the federal-republican relationship. Conflicts arose between federally mandated standards such as the minimum wage, welfare rights, cultural rights for minorities, and ethnic quotas in public employment; federal subsidies to poorer communities; federal aid to less developed regions; the federal army; and bailouts of strategic industries on the one hand, and republican assertions of their rights to independent governance—including less government regulation, local self-rule, and homogeneous communities—on the other.

While republican governments were economically independent, they were often also in need of federal funds (including World Bank funds, disaster relief, and various grants and subsidies). The more developed republics (Slovenia, Croatia, and Serbia) with above average per capita income were taxed accordingly to support these funds and the federal budget. The government was far more decentralized, with greater emphasis on states' rights than in the United States, but the two countries shared the same commitment to local self-government and extensive local control over schools, roads, police, unemployment relief, and housing.

In practice the functional division of governmental jurisdictions meant that the balance between republican sovereignty and federal authority shifted according to economic policy priorities. World economic conditions in the 1970s created particularly serious tensions in the federal-republic relationship. The source of new capital was largely foreign loans; but Western demand for Yugoslav products weakened after 1975 (in part because of Western trade barriers), undermining the country's ability to service foreign loans. The demand restrictions of anti-inflationary stabilization policy dominated Yugoslav federal policy during this period of global stagflation. Enterprises also redirected their exports of machinery and processed goods to less demanding Eastern markets, and trade with petroleum-producing countries became particularly important because of rising OPEC oil prices. This meant that far more foreign trade flowed through the federal government through clearing or bilateral contracts. Since East-West relations were also more tense during the 1970s, national defense policy also had priority.

These policies, which followed a period in the 1960s of liberalizing economic reform and Western-oriented trade, caused liberals to think that reform had been abandoned for recentralization. In fact, a new constitution in 1974 (actually, amendments adopted between 1967 and 1971) had decentralized most political power to the republics and localities, in part because of defense doctrine shifting emphasis to the territorial defense forces and further devolution of the police, military, and party. Even the two provinces within Serbia (Vojvodina and Kosovo) gained full autonomy over their parliaments, budgets, and judicial systems after 1974, giving them near-republic status.

Decentralization by the early 1970s had led to so much *de facto* independence that political life was primarily centered in the republics. The republics' authority over culture and education had substantially eroded all-Yugoslav means of communication. Each republican party controlled its own cadre, and republic-level elections and party congresses preceded the federal. To combat fears of majority tyranny, voting rights emphasized minority protections through consensus, parity, and proportional representation of republican-based organizations.

At the same time, however, people in different republics had many bonds. The one-party state meant that political organizations such as the League of Communists and League of Youth convened all-Yugoslav conferences, youth work brigades, and other forums. Vacation travel and second homes brought people from different regions into contact. Periods of marketizing reform encouraged capital and goods to move around the country, and much production was integrated across republics. There was a shared national pride in Yugoslavia's international stature. And although federal authorities had little independent power to enforce their decisions and depended on consensus among republican representatives, they did make federal policy with regard to the army, the party (renamed the League of Communists, LCY, in 1952 to reflect its federal composition and non-directive role), a federal constitutional court, the federal business chamber (representing the interests of public sector firms, especially large manufacturers), and the federal parliament, which set the basic rights and principles upon which republics, provinces, and localities wrote legislation and regulations. The country's complex system of shared sovereignties among levels of government and extensive economic democracy thus produced both centripetal and centrifugal tendencies.

## Individual Security

The third source of stability depended on the provision of individual security that all states provide in the form of political, civil, and social rights.

Despite the extensive autonomy of the republics and provinces, the real center of the Titoist system and its concept of self-determination was the idea that individual workers and citizens, in association, would govern their workplaces and local communities (called communes). This system combining local, social, and worker self-government was the Yugoslav contribution to socialist experience—its response to the effect on peasants, workers, and even the urban middle class of the economic crises of the 1920s and 1930s. It replaced private property and markets for capital and labor with the idea of shared, equal property rights for all employed persons and equal participation in managing that property. The power of bureaucracies and managers would be checked by the constitutional obligation to consult with elected representatives of workers and citizens. In practice, it was a system of checks and balances over the expenditure of monies (such as wages and local revenues) in a regime of decentralized managerial and political power.

The idea of self-management, as the concept was usually translated, was that people with long-term stable employment and residence and rights to participate in budgetary and managerial decisions would develop a sense of property and propriety. This would create higher incentives to work, to raise productivity, and to take local initiative. Alienation and the psychological and social costs of the labor market would disappear. Commitment to coworkers and neighbors would develop the long time horizons on savings and investment associated with employers in capitalism.

Alongside this system of economic democracy was an entire society based, as in other socialist countries, on the concept of guaranteed welfare. The constitution guaranteed the right to equal treatment in the economy (for example, equal pay for equal work); limited sources of private wealth through restrictions on the amount of income-yielding private property and through progressive taxation on individual income and wealth from market profits; and guaranteed subsistence. People were citizens of both Yugoslavia and their republics, but citizens' rights were protected by the federal government.

Federal and local governments shared responsibility for individual welfare. The federal government set standards for wage rates; the guaranteed minimum wage in public sector firms; social benefits such as pensions, health care, and child allowances; and guidelines for the republics on education, taxation, health care, and social security. But realizing these rights was a matter of local coffers. Economic decentralization meant that the standard of living depended greatly on where citizens lived. The particular interests of republics and provinces held sway in the upper chamber of the federal parliament, where delegations voted *en bloc* by republic. Social welfare—scholarships, retraining, income supplements, and travel allowances and social insurance for the unemployed—was provided by local governments, supplemented if necessary by federal grants-in-aid to localities that fell below countrywide income averages and thus might not be able to meet federally mandated standards. The exception was the army, which fell under federal jurisdiction for defense and which received federal funds for veterans' pensions, army officers' housing, and other military-related benefits.

Even more noticeable than local differences in standards of living was the effect of their system of guaranteed subsistence, which divided the population into two worlds: those with employment in the public sector and those left in the private sector until jobs could be created. As in other socialist countries, social benefits in the public sector—health care, child allowances, housing, subsidized transport and hot meals, winter food staples, social insurance for sickness and retirement, and vacation retreats—

were distributed at the workplace rather than through market purchase. The primary source of household living standards was not private wealth but a public sector job. But the policies of economic reform had eroded the tenet of job security found in other socialist countries and created an ever-increasing number of people who could not get a public sector job and were stuck in the private sector or unemployed. Reform policies also transferred an ever-larger portion of goods and services to market provision and the ability of households to buy or bribe. Long waiting lines for housing credits from one's public sector workplace or for services of doctors and dentists, for example, could be avoided by paying on the open market (often astronomical prices). Firms adjusted to declining profits first by delaying wage payments or reassigning less skilled or redundant workers downward, to jobs more in line with their qualifications. The first to be fired were those considered, rightly or wrongly, to have alternative sources of material support (women, young people, and rural residents). Federal standards did not, therefore, lead to economic equality—only to equal treatment within a job category. Take-home pay depended on the profitability of one's employer and the level of one's education and skills.

The government program for unemployment was to prevent concentration in the private sector by placing limits on the sale of land and urban real estate, on the size of private workshops, and on the number of employees whom independent artisans and services could hire. Landownership of a smallholding became an insurance policy for households, and economic reformers told critics of unemployment that people could always go back to the farm. As in the rest of southern Europe, from Portugal to Greece, the family protected unemployed young people and women, thus retaining its critical social functions and the primary role in the survival of its members. The division between the two worlds, public and private sectors of employment, applied to political rights as well as economic privilege. The unemployed did not participate in the system of workers' self-government or have the double representation in parliament through the workplace in addition to residence.

The result of this system was that, as a rule, people remained settled if they had a secure public sector job and housing (most characteristic of those in the upper brackets of education, income, and status). Identities with a locality, territory, and, in many cases, ethnic group, had not weakened as a result of the labor mobility characteristic of most industrial societies. Relocation across republican boundaries in search of jobs was discouraged by the chronic shortage of housing and republican control over education. At the same time, there was a substantial rural exodus to towns and cities in the postwar period. People left villages primarily for secondary or university education, and therefore paths of migration followed mainly ethnocultural lines. Croats would be more likely to go to Zagreb Univer-

sity and Serbs to Belgrade University, for example. Upward mobility out
of a poor region or family was also possible through a political career or
government job, but this created a huge informal network of people who
lived by their connections and political associations. In the urban areas,
teeming with the influx of rural and small town migrants, support networks also tended to develop along lines of hometowns, regions, and
extended kin. When middle-class young people were increasingly affected
by unemployment after 1971, they resented those who appeared to get jobs
through their political work and connections, considering them corrupt.

The tenacity of local bonds did not mean homogeneous environments.
Because there were few economic or social mechanisms to incorporate
newcomers into communities other than the informal networks of kinship
or friends from home areas, migrants often remained second-class citizens.
Areas that were ethnically mixed as a result of government programs to
resettle areas affected by wars or to defend exposed borderlands—especially those in the rich agricultural plains of Slavonia and Vojvodina—
retained a sharp distinction between old settlers and recent ones.[42] The
very poor and the unskilled tended to roam for temporary construction
and odd jobs. Large numbers of migrant workers went abroad temporarily
to western Europe after 1960 (especially to Germany, but also to Sweden,
Belgium, and Austria), sending home their earnings to build spacious
homes filled with modern appliances. In the 1970s migrants from Kosovo
and Bosnia followed the same pattern in Slovenia. Those who moved from
poor rural areas to cities in search of better opportunities often remained
outsiders, however. Members of this group, like economic migrants in
most societies, were often the most ambitious and talented persons within
their home environment. Once in the city, however, they often had to resort
to political activism or informal networks of people from their village or
region of origin to obtain employment (particularly when unemployment
began to soar after 1971). Reminded by this or by older residents of their
rural origins, newcomers could not always avoid a sense of second-class
status, inferiority, and marginality.[43] The rural communities they left behind, moreover, were disproportionately made up of the elderly or people
of poor or no education.

Despite the rhetoric of official obeisance to national equality in many
forms and the preoccupation of foreign media with "ethnic animosities"
in the wars of 1991–94, the primary social divisions and inequalities in
Yugoslav society were not defined by ethnicity but by job status and growing unemployment. In terms of how people saw themselves, ethnicity was
less important than either occupation and the social status it conveyed or
place of residence—urban or rural—and its related culture. Residents of
cosmopolitan cities had different prospects and world views than those of
heartland farming communities or poorer mining and timbering towns in

the interior of the country. Villagers had deep cultural and psychological attachments to the land, and households survived periods of severe inflation and unemployment by relying on their own production of food, on neighbors, or—for urban dwellers—on rural relatives. Status and ethnicity could be mutually reinforcing—particularly in poorer areas of mixed ethnicity, where criteria for rationing scarce jobs drew on traditional loyalties—but the importance of ethnic or national identity was primarily a matter of self-identification and choice. And over all these distinctions hung the public-private divide. Although access to supplementary income in the private sector (moonlighting, bribes and side-payments, private practice) was an important source of wealth and inequality in Yugoslavia, those who did not also have public sector employment were excluded from the full rights of economic citizenship and social welfare. This included most farmers, many artisans and traders in small shops, day laborers, the truly unemployed, and an underworld of criminals. Neither the Communist party nor the system of local and worker self-management provided political avenues to manage these various social divisions.

## Conclusion

Yugoslav society was not held together by Tito's charisma, political dictatorship, or repression of national sentiments but by a complex balancing act at the international level and an extensive system of rights and of overlapping sovereignties. Far from being repressed, national identity and rights were institutionalized—by the federal system, which granted near statehood to the republics, and by the multiple rights of national self-determination for individuals.

Just as the mixture of civilizations in the Balkans did not program its members for confrontation, producing a rich tapestry of religious and cultural diversity when the outside world was not in conflict along religious or imperial lines, so the mixture of constitutional principles and international ties that defined Yugoslavia had produced a relatively prosperous, open, and stable society. It had no small measure of international prestige as a leader of the nonaligned movement and site of numerous world sports competitions, and borrowed capital had helped fuel three decades of rapid economic growth that relative equality and consumer orientation had shared broadly in comparative terms.[44] But during the 1980s, all three elements composing that stability and the security that holds any society together were increasingly threatened: international position; constitutional order defining governmental powers and property rights; and social order and concept of citizenship. A new round of economic reforms to westernize, liberalize, and promote manufactured exports in the changed international conditions of the 1980s required fundamental changes in the country's hybrid system of rights and sovereignties, leading first to increasing austerity and individual insecurity and then to quarrels between the federal and the republican governments over economic assets and constitutional jurisdictions.

Chapter 3

# The Politics of
# Economic Reform and
# Global Integration

Yugoslavia's dissolution began with fundamental changes in the international environment. The attempt, led largely by the International Monetary Fund (IMF), to salvage the international monetary system in the 1970s through massive global lending of recycled petrodollars came to a halt after 1979. Banks retreated. The interest rate on the U.S. dollar skyrocketed, and with it the foreign debt of all countries holding debt in those dollars. The Western recession that started in 1975 intensified into a worldwide economic depression in the 1980s. In 1985 Western Europe entered a new stage of economic integration in the European Community (EC), which set the goal of complete financial unification by 1992, accompanied by a deepening of political institutions.

This apparent hardening of the division of Europe and the economic borders of the West, however, saw an opposite trend in the very same year. Talks on economic cooperation between the EC and the Council for Mutual Economic Assistance (CMEA) resumed after a hiatus caused by the Afghan war and U.S. President Reagan's "evil empire" campaign. Real progress began in the negotiations over strategic arms and conventional force reductions between the two military alliances of East and West, the Warsaw Treaty Organization (WTO) and the North Atlantic Treaty Organization (NATO).

Although this period ended on a positive note—with the possibilities now identified with the end of the cold war—it began with severe hardship. Like so many countries in the second and third worlds, from Poland to Mexico, the Yugoslav government had fueled growth during the 1970s with foreign borrowing. The loans served two purposes. First, they allowed the country to import advanced technology to improve its international competitiveness. Second, they bought time for domestic industry to adjust to both higher prices for oil and other primary commodities and a variety of erratic, nontariff barriers against Yugoslav exports of steel, textiles, tobacco, and beef to European (hard currency) markets. Demand for Yugoslav exports to Western markets, necessary to service debt and finance imports, had shifted dramatically from higher to lower value-added products, with an ever higher proportion of primary commodities in relation to manufactures. Manufacturers dependent on Western imports for production were increasingly less able to purchase the machinery they considered necessary for global competitiveness, and were even threatened with bankruptcy. This change in demand to primary commodities had meant declining revenues overall and a relative shift of purchases and earnings to areas producing primary commodities—areas such as Serbia, Kosovo, the poorer interior in Croatia, Bosnia-Herzegovina, and Macedonia. The country shifted investment priorities of the social plan away from the manufacturing associated with modern economies and toward industries that required far more governmental involvement in capital investment and negotiated trade in the eastern bloc and the Middle East. Not fully aware of the reasons behind these changes, ordinary people who experienced declining economic fortunes began to nurture political explanations and grievances.

The 1970s ended with even more extreme external shocks, however. A second oil price rise occurred in 1978–79. Interest rates for U.S. dollars, in which Yugoslav debt was denominated, jumped into double digits. At the same time the country's borrowing from commercial banks at free-market rates had reached 58 percent of total debt. Commercial bank lending to Eastern Europe nearly stopped altogether after 1978, and that trend was given political impetus in 1979–80 by the Polish crisis and the Soviet invasion of Afghanistan. For Yugoslavia, an economic crisis originating in the foreign sector could no longer be averted by minor adjustments. With seriously depleted foreign reserves, failing exports, and an increasingly intractable foreign debt of about $20 billion, the government had no choice but to focus all its attention on foreign liquidity.

Because governments must guarantee repayment of their country's foreign debt, the sharp reversal in lending from Western commercial banks forced the Yugoslav government—like its counterparts in Poland and Hungary, which found themselves in the same situation in 1979—to turn first to domestic resources to restore its ability to finance crucial imports. By the end of 1979 the government had introduced austerity measures to cut domestic consumption of imported goods and to increase exports. This was insufficient to improve the trade balance, however. Facing a further decline in workers' remittances and a series of natural disasters (such as an earthquake in tourist areas of Dalmatia), the government sought a compensatory loan from the IMF. By 1982, a change in prime minister and cabinet, according to the normal rotation, had unblocked the resistance of the previous government to another return to the IMF, which created a new facility called a three-year standby loan. The IMF conditions were that the government introduce domestic economic reforms to make the country better able to service its debt. It proposed, in effect, an anti-inflationary macroeconomic stabilization policy of radical austerity, trade and price liberalization, and institutional reforms to impose on firms and governments monetary discipline and real price incentives. But the IMF and other international creditors were not alone in this call for liberalization and marketization; economic liberals (mainly economists) within the various republics and the federal government also took up the cry. In their view, economic growth and successful international adjustment would not occur without economic reform favoring export orientation to Western hard currency markets; increased labor productivity, above all with imported Western technology; and improved microeconomic efficiency. Over the preceding thirty years each round of such reforms was aimed, according to the usual slogan, to "integrate [the country] into the world division of labor."

Nonetheless, international conditions were not felicitous. Beginning in 1975 remittances from workers temporarily employed in western Europe (especially Germany) had begun to fall dramatically as recession set in the West. By 1981 these remittances—which had financed half the Yugoslav trade deficit since the early 1960s—provided for only 25 percent of the deficit. Hundreds of thousands of these workers were sent home to Yugoslavia, where unemployment had been rising sharply since 1971. Negotiations to renew Yugoslavia's association agreement with the European Community, begun in 1976, encountered frequent delays until 1980. Even then, trade concessions were fewer than the Yugoslavs had expected. Their hopes for trade talks begun in 1979 with the European Free Trade Association (EFTA) were even longer in coming to fruition. Moreover, in early 1982 IMF negotiations begun in 1979 unexpectedly took a serious turn for the worse when the IMF team, reflecting a change of policy in Washington, stiffened its terms and bargaining position. Unlike the debate that accompanied these conditions in Latin America, however, there was no discussion in Yugoslavia of defaulting on its loans—the dispute was over whether to restructure and refinance the debt. Yugoslav leaders had always given priority in economic policy to maintaining the confidence of foreign creditors because of the import dependency of Yugoslav domestic production (including production for export) and the precarious position of Yugoslav independence outside the trade and military blocs of the two superpowers.

Because of the links between domestic producers and even regions and Yugoslavia's international position, reorientation to Western markets would involve huge restructuring and domestic costs. It was also risky because of the West's trade recession and political restrictions in capital markets. Trade reorientation would also require transforming the entire basis of Yugoslavia's national security, forcing reductions in military expenditures when East-West tensions were on the rise. The proposed economic changes could even threaten the special relationship with third world suppliers—particularly for energy—and with Western financial markets.

Economists claimed the problem was political. Successive Yugoslav governments during the 1970s had failed to adjust to the changing terms of foreign trade because of too much government regulation, political interference in investment decisions, an overvalued exchange rate that protected domestic manufacturers, and especially the political reversal to the market-oriented reforms of the 1960s that economists claimed conservative party forces had engineered after 1971. No effective economic reform, in their view, would occur without accompanying political change. By 1983 the leadership of the League of Communists of Yugoslavia (LCY) had concurred and appointed a party commission to discuss the political system. The commission's preliminary proposals for amendments to the 1974 Constitution entered public debate in 1985. So the entire constitution of the state was open for criticism and revision at the same time as the systematic shocks of drastic austerity and proposals to curtail the economic powers and resources of governments.

Just as with monetary integration in the European Community or trade liberalization in the General Agreement on Tariffs and Trade (GATT), the method for integrating a socialist system into the global economy *appears* to be economic and technical; in fact, it is fraught with political implications. As in the case of negotiations over and confirmation of the Maastricht Treaty in western Europe during 1991–92, the return in Yugoslavia to a program of long-term macroeconomic stabilization and export-oriented economic reform after 1982 unleashed an intense and multilayered political struggle.[1] At a minimum, the political process to negotiate, formulate, fight, legislate, implement, retreat, and revive this program of economic reform and macroeconomic stabilization dominated the entire decade of 1979 to 1989 and spanned the careers of three prime ministers (Milka Planinc, Branko Mikulić, and Ante Marković). The problem also consumed the economic policy of the federal government, had a drastic effect on most citizens' welfare, and led to major political quarrels between the republics and the federal government over the federal budget, taxation, and jurisdiction over foreign trade and investment. Expectations of greater economic integration were not realized. Instead, the result by the end of the decade was a breakdown in all elements of the domestic order, political disintegration, and rising nationalism.

## Austerity

The first stage of this decade-long process was the emergency response to foreign illiquidity and debt. The problem was a shortage of foreign currency, although experts blamed distortions in the economic system. The immediate solution was to seek short-term coverage (through IMF credits), to try to refinance the debt, to cut imports to the bone, and to promote all conceivable commodity exports to hard currency markets in the West.

For the population this meant austerity as the government sought every possible way to cut domestic consumption and squeeze foreign currency and exports out of the economy. Food subsidies were abandoned in 1982. Prices for gasoline and heating fuel, food, and transportation rose by one-third in 1983. All imports not critical to production were prohibited, including all consumer goods. Two currency devaluations and a decision to allow the currency to float cut the value of the dinar by 90 percent between 1979 and 1985. This further squeezed imports but was a source of windfall profits to firms holding foreign currency earnings. To gain greater access to the foreign currency holdings of private households, which would help repay the debt, the government allowed interest rates on foreign currency bank accounts to rise substantially. In addition to these privileges granted overnight to individuals holding dollars and deutschemarks, groceries and shops favored buyers who paid in hard currency. All new investment for social services, infrastructure, and government projects was frozen.

Firms showing losses were obliged to lay off workers instead of carrying them with lower wages. The small firms in the private sector—the government's primary hope for employing those laid-off workers and those affected by the slowdown in new jobs in the public sector—were cut off from access to credit by its prohibitively high cost under a real-interest-rate policy in conditions of rapid price inflation. An underclass of unemployed, unskilled workers emerged, concentrated in urban areas. Wage and income restrictions, price increases, and unemployment among young people and women sent average household incomes plummeting to levels of twenty years before. Savings were rapidly depleted for 80 percent of all households, who found it increasingly difficult to live on their incomes. Official unemployment was at 14 percent by 1984, varying from full employment in Slovenia to 50 percent in Kosovo, 27 percent in Macedonia, and 23 percent in Bosnia and Herzegovina and in large parts of Serbia, including the capital, Belgrade (see figures 3-1 and 3-2).

Inflation rose by 50 percent a year, and by more after 1984, as shown in figure 3-3. Citizens accustomed for more than twenty years to full stores faced shortages and long lines for goods such as meat, coffee, detergent, cooking oil, sugar, gasoline and heating fuel, and electricity, commodities that were affected by import restrictions and the export push. Against its economic judgment, but to prevent the deterioration of social order, the federal cabinet permitted republican governments to issue ration

FIGURE 3-1.  *Yugoslav Rate of Unemployment, 1979–88*

Percent

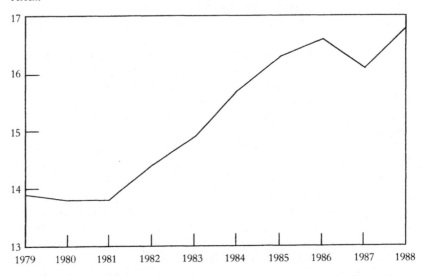

Source: Jože Mencinger, "Privredna Reforma i Nezaposlenost," in *Privredna Kretanja Jugoslavije,* vol. 3 (1989), p. 37.

coupons. As early as 1983 the government acknowledged a deep depression. Gross domestic product fell 1.3 percent in 1983, and average capacity utilization in industry was below 70 percent (see figure 3-4). Table 3-1 shows how drastically economic indicators fell during this period; all economic indicators were negative and worsening after 1982. By the end of 1984 the average income was approximately 70 percent of the official minimum for a family of four, and the population living below the poverty line increased from 17 to 25 percent.[2]

It would be difficult to say which element of this austerity—escalating inflation, falling real incomes, consumer goods shortages, or unemployment (or the threat of unemployment)—contributed most to the sense of insecurity. Individuals had different buffers against its effects. Rural households could continue to grow their own food, whereas poorer urban dwellers with declining wages and without rural kin had few nonmarket sources of food and were also unlikely to have foreign-currency bank accounts. Unemployment disproportionately affected unskilled workers and young people, so households, particularly poorer urban families, had to feed and clothe more mouths with less money. Yugoslav *Gastarbeiter* who had returned from jobs in northern Europe and many urban professionals had Western currency, but they feared the government would freeze those ac-

FIGURE 3-2.  *Unemployment Rates in Yugoslavia by Republic, 1979–90*

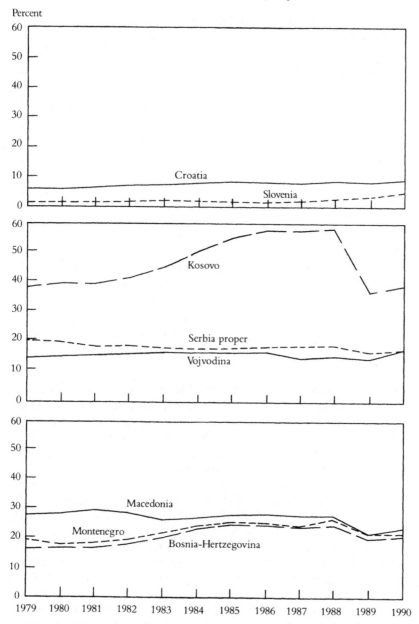

Sources: For 1979–88; Jože Mencinger, "Privredna Reforma i Nezaposlenost," in *Privredna Kretanja Jugoslavije*, vol. 3 (1989), p. 27, table 1. For 1989 and 1990, Statistički Godišnjak Jugoslavije (1990).

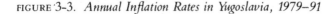

FIGURE 3-3. *Annual Inflation Rates in Yugoslavia, 1979–91*

Percent change over previous year, CPI (1985 = 100)

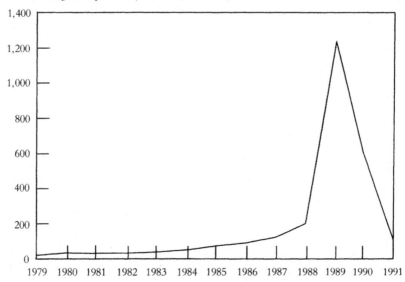

Source: International Monetary Fund, *International Financial Statistics Yearbook: 1992* (Washington: 1992), pp. 748–49; and IMF, *International Financial Statistics* (Washington: November 1992), p. 566.

counts in its desperation over the debt.[3] Shop employees squirreled away goods for friends and relatives before they reached store shelves. The incentives to indulge in absenteeism in order to moonlight on second jobs and to take advantage of the opportunities for black-market transactions, bribery, barter, and theft were obvious (leading to suspicions perhaps greater than facts, but it was the suspicions that mattered politically).

The consequence of greatest long-term political significance was the erosion of the substantial middle class, which had been growing since the late 1950s. This solid social middle consisted of public sector managers, urban professionals, skilled industrial workers, and a portion of private sector shopowners, artisans, and farmers. They were the most likely to benefit from successful liberal reforms, and they could also provide the basis of a moderate political center by cutting across the urban-rural and public-private sector divisions of the economic and political system. Instead, they were being polarized economically and socially by the austere conditions. Sixteen percent were able to sustain or improve their standards; the remaining 84 percent felt their economic fortunes and sense of personal security begin to decline.[4] Even those who could maintain their standard

FIGURE 3-4. *Growth of GDP in Yugoslavia, 1979–91*

Percent change over previous years

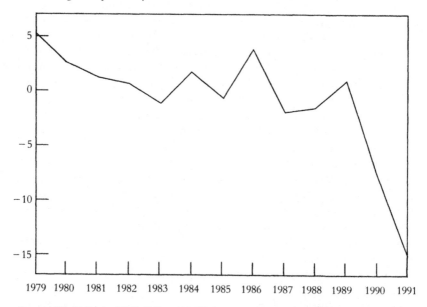

Source: World Bank, *World Tables 1991* (Washington, 1991), pp. 624–25; and *World Tables 1992* (Washington, 1992), p. 653. The 1991 figure is an estimate from the United Nations Economic Commission for Europe, *Economic Survey of Europe in 1991–1992* (Geneva, 1992), table 3.2.2, p. 60.

TABLE 3-1. *Economic Adjustment, Output Indicators, 1979–83*

| Indicator | 1979 | 1980 | 1981 | 1982 | 1983 |
|---|---|---|---|---|---|
| Gross material product (produced) | 7.0 | 2.2 | 1.4 | 0.9 | −1.3 |
| Gross material product (consumed) | 9.7 | 1.3 | −0.8 | −4.8 | −3.6 |
| Personal consumption | 5.2 | 0.7 | −1.0 | −0.1 | −1.7 |
| Social consumption | 7.9 | 2.7 | −4.8 | −1.7 | −5.0 |
| Fixed investment | 6.4 | −1.7 | −9.8 | −6.2 | −13.0 |
| Final domestic demand | 5.8 | −1.8 | −4.4 | −2.2 | −5.5 |

Source: Chris Martin and Laura D'Andrea Tyson, "Can Titoism Survive Tito? Economic Problems and Policy Choices Confronting Tito's Successors," in Pedro Ramet, ed., *Yugoslavia in the 1980s* (Westview Press, 1985), p. 191.

of living feared the future and the prospect of isolation from the global economy. Import restrictions, for example, had stopped all subscriptions to foreign scientific journals; this had a demoralizing impact on professionals, who viewed themselves as part of the West and the world community and had been free to travel abroad since the mid-1950s.

Nonetheless, the unequal distribution of the burden of austerity did not lead to political mobilization on these grounds; the civic and political organizations of the socialist system generally did not work this way. There was some opportunity within the self-management structure in large public sector firms for industrial workers to protest wage cuts to management or local authorities—especially in the mining industry, where countrywide wage restrictions and inflation were compounded by a dramatic drop in demand. Work stoppages and strikes increased 80 percent between 1982 and 1983. By 1987, 1,570 work stoppages involving 365,000 workers were reported officially. By the fall of 1988 massive delegations of workers from Croatia, Vojvodina, and Serbia proper took their protest, for the first time in the postwar period, to the federal parliament in Belgrade. For most of Yugoslav society, however, reaction to austerity was restricted to the personal level and to a growing realm of antipolitics.

People looked for ways to forestall the decline in purchasing power by supplementing their increasingly worthless money with barter, gifts, friendships, political networks and connections, and the reciprocal obligations of kinship and ritual kinship.[5] Instead of encouraging market behavior as intended, the reforms—by forcing people to resort to the older norms of reciprocity and mutuality—reinforced the localization of economic distribution and the social divisions within the labor force prevalent in preceding decades (see chapter 2). They increased the use of personalistic criteria in access to jobs and goods, as well as the barriers to collective political action for change. Pressures to employ relatives, finding scapegoats on the basis of social prejudice, antifeminist backlash, and rightwing nationalist incidents became more common. Resentment against those with political sinecures—or what were assumed to be party-based privileges—was informed by old stereotypes (for example, the belief that Serbs dominated political offices). In those poorer communities where job cuts were most severe and federal government subsidies and employment had been critical to the local economy, the employment requirement of proportionality and parity among national groups made ethnicity more salient rather than less. Suspicion of ethnic bias was as powerful as its reality, and such resentments particularly threatened poorer, ethnically mixed communities. Authorities worried aloud about religious revival, an example of which was the number (6,000–10,000) of pilgrims who traveled each day to Medjugorje in western Herzegovina, where the Virgin Mary had allegedly visited six children daily since June 1981. Elaborate new mosques arose in northern Yugoslav cities such as Zagreb, Croatia, which also saw the establishment of a new Islamic theological faculty.[6]

Unemployment among young people had been consistently increasing since 1972. By 1985, 59.6 percent of the total registered unemployed were under the age of twenty-five (and 38.7 percent of people under age twenty-five were unemployed). Alienation and resentment that education did not bring its promised rewards translated into generational conflict with those who had secure jobs and increasing criticism of the system itself.[7] The fraying social fabric, already evident by 1982, became manifest in crumbling norms of civility and hospitality, leading tourists to complain that the problem of high prices was compounded by rudeness from a once welcoming and relaxed people.

While signs of social dislocation and anomie were growing at the mass level, the restrictive monetary, fiscal, and foreign trade policies also required a fundamental change in political authority over economic assets—specifically, over the social property rights of governments. In contrast to the extreme territorial decentralization of the 1970s, these emergency policies required federal assertion of economic authority over the republics, leaving little room for negotiation. In its scramble to gain access to all available sources of foreign currency and to impose monetary discipline, the federal cabinet issued a series of decrees and penalties. Banks and enterprises were required to give priority to debt repayment over new lending and contracts. Republican governments had to project import needs quarterly or have it done for them. And, perhaps most significant, control over foreign exchange operations and allocation was returned to the National Bank in Belgrade; only five years earlier, as part of decentralization, the assets and debits of the balance of payments of this same bank had been distributed among republican governments, and they had been granted corresponding authority for foreign economic relations.[8]

Terms negotiated with the IMF for a three-year standby loan were railroaded through a tumultuous federal parliament. This incited particular animosity from the Slovene delegation and its republican government when they lost their battle against devaluation and the assignment of authority over debt repayment, and therefore foreign exchange, to the National Bank.[9] At the same time the U.S. embassy in Belgrade and the U.S. State Department organized an extraordinary campaign to help refinance and reschedule the country's debt (although public opinion had not yet agreed that this was the correct course). This project was completed by 1985, when the second stage of the debt crisis program began. The second stage was to legislate economic reforms on the basis of a "long-term program for economic stabilization" created by external creditors and an ad hoc commission of economists and politicians and approved, at least in principle, by the parliament.[10]

## Economic Reform

The emergency nature of this unwanted federal and executive assertion of economic authority gave way to a more determined stage with the adoption of the IMF program and the political commitment to integrate into the "world division of labor." Domestic liberal economists and IMF advisers alike felt that the country had to reorient to production of exports that were competitive in Western markets and had to generate growth by improving efficiency at home in order to escape the trap of persistent trade deficits and debt.

These reforms shifted the balance of economic policy in favor of certain firms, sectors, and areas. Exporters to Western markets had a built-in advantage over those with contractual markets in the East and South; areas with developed transportation and cultural links with the West had the edge over those farther from or cut off from such links; and persons with skills appropriate to marketing and to activities that earned hard currency enjoyed an advantage over those who did not. The reform aimed also to shift export composition to higher value-added manufacturing, in part because of the economic interests of the reformers and in part because terms of trade in world markets shifted dramatically in 1980 against the primary commodities—such as energy and petroleum-based industries (petrochemicals, for instance) and shipbuilding—that had dominated demand in the 1970s. Export subsidies, tax incentives, and foreign exchange and permission to import would go to such producers of manufactured exports rather than to producers for the domestic market and suppliers of raw and intermediate materials. Because the primary earning capacities in foreign trade varied significantly among the republics, Slovenia and large areas of Croatia had a significant advantage, and Serbia somewhat less; demand declined for producers in agriculture, mining and metallurgy, and defense, which tended to concentrate in Bosnia and Herzegovina, Macedonia, and Serbia proper and its two provinces, Kosovo and Vojvodina. This second group of producers also needed to restructure old industries, making them far more vulnerable to immediate unemployment than the northwest.

But more than economic policy and interests were affected in a system where political institutions were based on control over economic assets and their distribution. Liberalization and the transformation to a market economy were intended to restore financial stability and discipline by sending price signals to all economic participants rather than by reorganizing and decentralizing the economy and focusing on production, as in the 1970s. Because this meant fundamental changes in the locus of economic decisionmaking, it required constitutional and political reform.

It had long been the stock-in-trade of economic liberals in Yugoslavia and most foreign economists to blame the country's political system for the economic crisis. In the early 1980s nearly all agreed on the problems. They criticized the stalemate of decisionmaking in the federal government, the myriad mechanisms of negotiated redistribution (of wages, profits, taxes, and transfers), and the role of political forces (the League of Communists, workers' councils in firms, police, army, socialist alliance, and unions) in economic decisions such as managerial appointments, investments, and local patronage. But within the camp of promarket, liberal reformers, there were very different views about what political changes were necessary.

There were two camps at the ideological level. Keynesian liberals argued that mechanisms of market integration and effective macroeconomic management were preconditions to economic recovery, and trickle-down liberals opposed redistribution and the role it gave to federal institutions. These different economic ideologies had direct implications for political reform. The Keynesian liberals were federalists, favoring the market and its institutions; the trickle-down neoliberals were antifederalists concerned about protecting the rights of property owners (that is, profitable firms and the republics in general).[11]

Because the priorities of economic reform were financial stabilization and external equilibrium, the early positions were staked out, however, by those with the most influence and interest in finance and foreign trade—on the one hand, by the IMF and the federal government reformers, and on the other hand, by the Slovene government (with occasional support from Croatia) and primary export producers.

Despite years of pushing decentralization in Yugoslavia, the IMF advisers and economic liberals now attributed the lack of monetary discipline to excessive decentralization of the banking and foreign exchange systems. In their view, the central bank had long ago lost the capacity to discipline its member banks and control the money supply. The dispersed authority over money, credit, and foreign exchange made it impossible to have any effective monetary and exchange rate policy, let alone effective industrial and foreign trade policy.[12] Global integration now required a unified domestic market, which meant reintegration of the segmented economies of the republics, and the free movement of labor, capital, and goods across local and republican borders according to price signals and opportunities for profit. The country needed to break down the complex system of bilateral contracts between suppliers and manufacturers; of payment arrangements through producers' cartels that rationed foreign exchange to prevent production bottlenecks; of corporatist social compacts among firms, governments, and unions to regulate wages and salaries; and of local party and government networks that had developed during the 1969–79 period. Monetary authority should be returned to the National Bank, and the independence of the bank strengthened, so that the government could implement a true macroeconomic policy to manage demand.

Criticism of the government focused on the virtual stalemate in federal decisionmaking due to republican and provincial autonomy, the conflicts between federal and provincial authority, and the procedure for making federal decisions. Federal policy took a long time to negotiate. All interested parties had to be consulted and consensus had to be reached. Although these procedures aimed to protect smaller republics and to prevent majority tyranny, they tended to end in deadlock, which could be broken only by temporary measures that delayed real agreements. Or, as in the case of the IMF package, they produced a paper unity that had little chance of successful implementation. According to an Italian diplomat who attempted to negotiate, during 1985–88, the dispersal among republics and projects of a massive program of economic assistance, "the political situation was in total fragmentation and deadlock. You couldn't get any decision; and if the republics finally did agree, the agreement was so rigid, there was nothing to negotiate."[13] The consensual voting rules gave each party to the negotiation a veto. For those who believed their bargaining position was strong, there was little incentive to negotiate trade-offs and compromises and much potential gain from obstructionist tactics, stubbornness, or the threat of a walkout. Economic improvement, the critics concluded, depended on increasing the competence and effectiveness of the federal government to make and implement tough decisions. A primary target of the critics was the system of consensual decisionmaking, especially among the governors of the central bank.

The strongest resistance to these criticisms and to the proposed reforms came from those who stood to lose economic power and privilege. Wealthier republican and provincial governments felt their control over the flow of labor, capital, and goods in and out of their territories threatened by instruments for internal marketization. Poorer republics and provinces dependent on federal grants felt that marketization might improve their wealth in the long run, but it carried serious risks of loss of political power. Those governments with more substantial foreign exchange holdings and economically powerful territorial banks perceived liberalization as recentralization of monetary authority to the central bank. Many manufacturers, exporters, and powerful republic-level business associations for foreign trade had privileges in price and tariff regulations, received export-promoting subsidies, and particularly benefited from the rights of firms and republics ("the right of those who earn") to retain a certain portion of their foreign exchange earnings for their own importing needs. Such groups foresaw a loss of special privilege and felt threatened by market competition.

These antifederalists believed that the problem did not lie with republican and provincial economic autonomy but with the powers still held by the federal government over economic resources that were rightfully theirs.

In their view, the economic crisis was the result of inappropriate investment choices, waste of funds transferred as aid or subsidies to poorer republican or provincial governments, and politically influenced choices by monetary authorities. The problem was the policies of redistribution of their earnings to maintain federal commitments to guaranteed minimum wages, development credits for less developed areas, and defense expenditures, all of which they saw as lowering resources for new investment and diminishing the incentives of the most productive workers and firms. The remedy lay instead in strengthening the rights of enterprises and republics over their incomes; cutting federal taxes, transfers, and jurisdiction; and giving priority in federal allocations to export producers.

In the early discussion of political reform, members of this camp were staunch defenders of the status quo as represented by the decentralized 1974 Constitution. But when the IMF program and economic reform began to legislate reforms in banking, foreign economic relations, and the monetary system, and when political contests arose over cuts in the federal budget, the rights to foreign exchange earnings, and wage controls, they shifted to a more radical confederalist position. The safeguards of the present constitution were no longer sufficient; their economic independence required further political protections. This meant eliminating the remaining political functions of the central government—the federal courts, police, army, procedural rules, and the fund for development assistance that bound the republics and provinces together—in favor of republican sovereignty.

Foreign observers of the politics of economic reform in socialist (and later postcommunist) countries tend to see the fight as one between reformers and conservatives, between liberals and communists, or between those in favor of change and those opposed to it. If that fight turns into nationalist assertion for independence, it is assumed that the opponents—whether they are called antireform forces, conservatives, or communists—have resorted to mobilizing nationalist hatreds and anti-Western sentiments in their desperate struggle to prevent change. But in the Yugoslav case—because of previous decentralization and participation in Western markets—it was not the central government or the poorer areas that had political and economic privileges to protect, but rather the republican politicians, especially those in the wealthier and more western regions. Those whose views might seem more liberal and Western were, in fact, the most conservative about change, the most antireform, and the most nationalistic. They insisted on exclusive priority to what they defined as the national interests (and therefore national rights) of their republic. At the same time there were many political supporters of the federal government, which was by jurisdiction charged with implementing the IMF program and economic reform. Except for the federal army, however, this group was an unorganized assortment of economic liberals, federalists, and scattered segments of voters of all nationalities in each republic who had no institutional base.

The idea of a battle royal between reformers and conservatives also mistakenly places people in one of two opposite camps. In fact, most politically active forces were in neither camp, but instead had one perspective on the economic changes and another on the political changes that reform implies. Most individual citizens were neither proreform or antireform. Their views were based on their immediate economic circumstances and on the increasingly difficult economic choices imposed by the austerity program. Because they were not being mobilized by politicians who wanted their votes, however, they had no need to choose sides and were more likely to look to their particular employer, locality, republic, or social status—the factors that most influenced the economic fate of their families.

The position of republican governments was most important because their representatives would debate constitutional reform. The two loudest opponents of the institutional aspects of reform were Slovenia and Croatia. Clearly benefiting more from export promotion to Western markets and, as the richer republics, able to withstand austerity better than others, these republics stood to lose privileges within the Yugoslav context. In June 1985 their parliaments accordingly rejected the three laws dealing with reform of foreign economic relations. As the main proponents of consensual decisionmaking and a republican veto (as a protection for smaller nations within Yugoslavia), they were particularly antagonistic toward pressure from foreign creditors to end the stalemate in federal decisionmaking by introducing majority rule. But even those republics and provinces that they criticized for misuse of development credits and that needed federal subsidies—such as Bosnia and Herzegovina, Macedonia, and Kosovo—opposed recentralization when it would cut into their governments' control over local assets. The recipient of the greatest amount of federal funds, the province of Kosovo, had long been nurturing a political movement for gaining the status of a republic, and independence from Serbia.[14]

In Serbia most economists were arguing that the economic problem was structural—having to do with the global recession and the import dependence of export production. They recommended an economywide evaluation of productivity and a federal industrial policy for structural adjustment.[15] Serbia's political leadership at the time was made up of primarily promarket, federalist economic liberals. The issue of constitutional reform that most preoccupied them was not the weakness of federal institutions, however, but the effect of full autonomy (equivalent to republican powers) that had been granted Serbia's two provinces by the 1974 Constitution and the need to reintegrate the Serbian economy and government and restore its own effective economic management.

In addition to these general tendencies, the positions of republican and provincial political leaders on constitutional reform were subject to change because of conflicts within the republics. Most common was conflict between the executive branch (both party and government leadership) and the legislature, in which specific fights over legislation, budgets, and social consequences and the elected legislators' greater localism led republican parliaments to act quite independently.

## The Shifting Prospects of Key Political Actors

To understand the different positions taken by key players in the ensuing fight over reform—the governments of the six republics and two provinces, the army (YPA), the federal government, and external creditors—it is important to note that each faced very different conditions.

The key actors in the unfolding drama over constitutional reform were the three most economically influential republics—Croatia, Serbia, and Slovenia (those which saw themselves as the original founding nations of Yugoslavia)—and the army. The YPA had a voting role in the federal party presidency equivalent to that of the republics (earning it the name of the ninth republic) and was the sole federal institution explicitly affected by economic reform in the same way as the republics. Slovenia was particularly important. It had always been the bellwether of change for the country, and in this case, it benefited most from westernization. It had been the leader in economic policy since 1945, in large part as a result of its flexibility in foreign markets.

Although outsiders wishing to emphasize the historical character of contemporary Yugoslav politics insist on a long-standing Serb-Croat conflict, the far more important relationship in Yugoslavia was between Slovenia and Serbia. Political alliances between Slovenia and Serbia had been essential to stability in the first Yugoslavia, and it was generally believed that Slovenia acted as a brake on autonomist forces in Croatia (which periodically appeared, most recently in 1967–71) in the interests of political stability in the second Yugoslavia.[16] The absence of confrontation between Slovenia and Serbia was far more crucial than the presence of conflict between Serbia and Croatia.[17]

Policymakers in Slovenia were preoccupied in the early 1980s with economic data that showed a decline in the productivity of Slovene firms relative to global trends.[18] To restore their position, they decided to modernize older industries with new technology, and this required massive foreign exchange. The drop in primary commodity prices on the world market after 1979 had enabled Slovene firms to redirect sources of supply from Yugoslav producers to foreign markets, and the policy return to export orientation and its supports was a boon to the Slovene economy. During the 1980s indicators of Slovene integration into the Yugoslav economy fell dramatically.[19] Although Slovenia still faced labor shortages—it was the only republic to have full employment throughout the postwar period, actually importing labor to economic benefit—authorities decided that the number of Bosnian and ethnic Albanian workers in Slovenia (nearly a quarter of the Slovene labor force) had reached the social maximum. The reasons for this were cultural—fearing a loss of Slovene national distinctiveness and cultural identity if any more southerners arrived—and also economic—calculating that the costs of additional housing, social benefits, and other infrastructure would begin to eat into Slovene standards of living. Slovene policymakers preferred to ignore federal wage controls and allow wages to rise in order to entice back highly skilled Slovene workers and professionals who were working abroad, particularly in Austria, for better incomes.[20]

Politically, Slovenia was experiencing the strains familiar to other socialist countries open to the world economy but having full employment (especially Poland and Hungary): a radical youth press, burgeoning civil society, and workers' strikes against the wage and benefit restrictions of the austerity policy. Already unhappy about its contributions to the federal budget (especially for the army and the federal fund for less developed republics), Slovenia favored market reforms in order to *reduce* federal activity further and support export trade to Western markets. Its enterprises were already well ensconced in the Yugoslav market through direct contracts for raw materials, direct investments, and captive consumer markets. It saw little economic or political benefit and much to oppose in the proposals for reintegrating the Yugoslav market.

The contrast with Serbia is striking. There, leaders faced a deteriorating economic scene of serious proportions.[21] Unemployment in Serbia proper was 17 to 18 percent in 1981–85. In Belgrade, it had risen 13.7 percent in the 1970s alone. In Kosovo it was over 50 percent. Planners preparing studies for the 1986–90 development plan discovered that a new wave of rural exodus within Serbia was beginning. Their concern was compounded after 1981 (if not numerically, certainly psychologically) when the growing social movement of ethnic Albanians in Kosovo to obtain separate republic status led many Serbs and Montenegrins to leave the province for Serbia proper. Belgrade was already groaning under the weight of upwardly mobile Serb immigrants from rural areas of other republics—particularly Bosnia-Herzegovina and Montenegro—and the economic austerity program was giving new impetus to this flow. Although Serbia was assessed in the federal system of taxes and transfers as a developed republic, along with Slovenia and Croatia, planners discovered that on all relevant indicators Serbia had fallen below average during the

1970s. This made its relations with its two autonomous provinces particularly sensitive. In contrast to the federal credits available to Kosovo as an underdeveloped region, republican budgetary expenditures for equally poor areas within Serbia proper had become an increasing burden on its capacity for growth.

Serbia was the only republic with autonomous provinces (sometimes also called federal units), and these had been granted autonomy over investment and budgets during the decentralizing phase of 1967–74. As an economic unit it was therefore deprived of resources that had previously been channeled through Belgrade. It also lacked the economic, legislative, and judicial authority necessary (in its leaders' view) to govern effectively. The governments of Vojvodina and Kosovo could veto any policy from Belgrade that applied to the entire territory, while Serbia proper had no equivalent power over decisions within the two provinces. When rioting exploded in Kosovo in 1981 and federal and local authorities imposed a state of emergency, Kosovo and its Albanian population became the central topic, some might even say fixation, of public opinion and the parliament within Serbia proper. At the same time, in the economic reform debate, Vojvodina expressed the most vocal opposition of all the republics and provinces to strengthening federal economic authority and losing its control over local investments. Foreign trade reorientation called for a sharp decline in Serbia's substantial markets in the East, while its primary export markets in the West were largely for those goods most vulnerable to erratic protectionism—textiles and agricultural products.

Politically, the liberal faction of the LCY was in power in Serbia. It favored reintegrating the Yugoslav market where Serbian producers might have a chance to recover; reintegrating Serbia administratively to make industrial policy more effective; and strengthening federal economic authority along lines proposed by the IMF so that it could introduce a program of investments to reverse the recession. Despite worsening tensions over Kosovo, the Serbian political scene was alive with intellectuals' criticism of the system. But in contrast to the political ferment occurring in Slovenia, demands for greater pluralism and constitutional democracy in Serbia were aimed at federal-level reform and against the disintegrative federalism of the 1943 principles established by the war-time partisan government, the Anti-Fascist Council of National Liberation of Yugoslavia (AVNOJ). The Slovenes cherished these principles.[22] These critical non-party intellectuals constituted a small stratum, but one that ranged across the entire political spectrum, from socialists to social democrats, liberals, human rightists, and Serbian nationalists.

Croatia at the time was a composite of Serbia and Slovenia. Economically, it had always been divided between domestic-oriented and export-oriented production. Poorer regions in the interior depended on outside assistance, produced primary commodities (timber, bauxite, aluminum, and the railroads necessary to such traffic), and exported labor.[23] Wealthy cities and the coastline thrived on foreign exchange earnings in tourism, shipbuilding, or light manufacturing and processing, especially oil, although many were cyclically vulnerable.[24] The rich farmlands and agroindustrial complexes in the eastern plains of Slavonia and Baranja operated in both domestic and export markets. Planners in the early 1980s had focused on the stark inequalities in levels of economic and social development among communes and the problem of regional development across Croatia. However, they chose a growth poles approach, favoring the concentration of investment in the cities from which economic growth would then be an engine of growth for outlying areas and more local autonomy in the poorer areas to encourage their local initiative. Economists urged export orientation and sharply criticized 1970s investments in railroads and aluminum in the interior as inappropriate industrialization, creating white elephants that had to be put up for auction.[25] Like the Slovene government, Croatian leaders protested federal tax levels and the waste of monies in the country's south, arguing as trickle-down liberals that they could use their earnings far more productively. They favored marketization insofar as it meant export orientation, but not where it entailed a revived federal authority.

Politically, however, the leadership of the LCY in Croatia was still dominated by the conservatives who had come to power after a purge of nationalist liberal reformers in 1972. They tended to be pro-Yugoslav, from the poorer and ethnically mixed hinterland, and cautious about greater political pluralism for fear of reawakening Croatian nationalist sentiment. Even the intellectual scene was divided on political reform, producing articulate briefs for both federalist and antifederalist camps.[26] In contrast to the political ferment in Slovenia and Serbia, however, there prevailed what locals called a great silence. Political caution and private pursuits were the norm.

The final player of consequence in the emerging debate over constitutional reform, the military, was a voice for the federalist position. The armed forces comprised both the federal army and the territorial defense forces (TDF) of the republics and communes. They had a constitutional obligation to safeguard Yugoslavia's territorial integrity against external attack and to protect the state against internal threats to the constitutional order. Its economic interests lay both in domestic production essential to military self-reliance (stockpiles of food, clothing, and other necessities; domestic armaments and military equipment) and in exports (arms and equipment sales, especially to the South and Middle East) to finance imports.[27]

Cuts in the military budget for the five years preceding the economic crisis had already led, by 1981, to allotments of less than what the secretary of national defense had declared a rock bottom level. Obliged to economize further, the army began to cut personnel. It undertook an internal reorganization effort to improve command and control using fewer resources. To save scarce foreign currency for technological modernization, the YPA pledged to become self-sufficient in armaments by the end of the decade. The general staff was operating, moreover, in what it perceived as an internationally hostile environment—the war in Afghanistan, NATO rearmament, and Reagan's offensive posture—leading military strategists to expect and prepare for a blitzkrieg attack from abroad.

Meanwhile partisan strongholds were being depopulated. The 1981 census revealed that the process of urbanization had progressed even faster than previously recognized; the agricultural population had fallen from 73 percent in 1945 to 19.9 percent, leaving rural areas largely inhabited by older women. Thus the rural basis of the partisan guerrilla strategy of the territorial defense forces appeared to be no longer viable at a time when the YPA's task of defending cities and towns was becoming more vital. Urbanization and worker migration abroad had also made army recruitment more difficult. Falling pay and amenities made military careers increasingly less attractive to those in the richer areas of Slovenia and Croatia. They also created morale problems among the majority of Serbs in the middle ranks of the officer corps, whose chances for promotion into the top ranks were limited by the requirements of national proportionality. Evidence that reservists were poorly trained and that their unit cohesion was declining compounded concerns.

In light of its role to protect the constitutional order, the army leadership became increasingly vocal about mounting threats to the social order and political stability as a result of the economic crisis. Military leaders were convinced that the causes of both economic crisis and political disintegration were a weakened party and federal government. It combined its worries about strategic preparedness and the increasing uncertainty over funding for the military budget in calls for a stronger League of Communists and federal government and for integration of the country's basic infrastructure (railroads, postal and telephone services, and the electricity grid).[28] In the midst of an ongoing process of reorganization, initiated in response to Croatian and Kosovo disturbances of 1967–71 and aimed at improved command and control over the TDF, however, opponents of the armed forces became convinced the army was preparing a coup.[29]

## Fiscal Crisis and Constitutional Reform

By 1985 prospects were not good for either economic or political reform. The current account surplus achieved through austerity in 1983 and 1984 could not be sustained into 1985, as exports fell. The federal cabinet was under pressure from industries, the less developed republics, and one school of economists and politicians favoring more gradual stabilization and economic stimulus to reverse the recession. A confrontation was brewing among republics and with the federal cabinet over financing for the federal budget.

Social disorder strengthened political conservatives, who won the elections to the federal state presidency in May 1984. A Slovene party initiative to run multiple candidates for republic-level elections to the presidency was withdrawn as premature. Political trials and threatened witch-hunts of critical intellectuals intensified as party conservatives attempted to prevent the emergence of political leaders outside the party who might capitalize on growing popular discontent.

This combination of economic liberalism and political conservatism was a global trend at the time, from Hungary and Poland to Britain and the United States to Chile. In Yugoslavia, however, a crisis over the federal budget cuts agreed with the IMF brought a retreat on economic reform. The crisis sharpened political divisions over reform in the fight between antifederalists, who favored the status quo, and federalists, who urged reintegration. The political debate over economic reform would thus be played out at two levels: over the constitutional changes in the federal government required by the economic reform and over the federal budget. Moreover, the two issues could never really be separated, for the economic sovereignty of the republics meant that quarrels over money for federal expenditures or over federal transfers between the republics could always be seen as issues of ownership and jurisdiction. The political question of *rights* to assets might be ignored under conditions of prosperity and economic growth, but not easily under conditions of long-term recession and a federal austerity program.

The federal government still had the authority to negotiate foreign assistance and its conditions and, given the emergency of foreign illiquidity and tough bargaining tactics of external creditors, to impose more or less unilaterally those conditions on domestic players. But the cabinet had to bargain over the distributive consequences of stabilization and economic reform, particularly the federal budget. By 1985 the effect of foreign trade liberalization and the deliberate contraction of domestic consumption on the two main sources of federal revenue (the customs duties and the sales tax) had produced a dramatic drop in revenues.[30] The budget deficit rose, defying the balanced budget principle of monetary stabilization in a reformed socialist economy and of the conditions set for IMF credits. Moreover, for five years or longer, outlays had not met legislated commitments (for example, that pensions be indexed to wage increases and that a certain *percentage* of national income go to defense and the federal fund for development aid). The federal government had two choices: to ignore the reform program, the IMF, and monetary stability by printing money or to ask for higher contributions from the republics.

With the loss to the National Bank of authority over foreign exchange and the elimination of socially managed agencies to fund public services, republic governments were similarly facing the prospects of declining revenues at a time when they needed resources to revive the growth and export-earning capacity of their own economies.[31] Although federal expenditures had represented only 13 to 14 percent of GDP at the high point in the 1970s, the republics balked at the idea of increased contributions.[32] Some were already behind on their payments. Some even refused to pay their share for the army. Such recipients of federal expenditure—particularly the army—soon became lightning rods for broader political conflict. The Croatian parliament voted to oppose federal financing for defense in principle. The Slovene government rejected the alternative proposed by the secretary of national defense, that the department of defense receive a portion of the income tax and manage it autonomously. The federal government finessed the debate on defense in 1985 by responding to demands for greater accountability on budgets, but not to those for their total elimination. The solution involved isolating the components of the budget into three separate budgets: one for defense, one for export incentives and material reserves, and one for all other beneficiaries. But only one year later, in November 1986, the government agreed to break all further links between the federal and republican budgets and to finance the federal budget from federal revenues alone.

The Slovene and Croatian governments, basing their reasoning on trickle-down orthodoxy, opposed expenditures for defense and development credits in the south, justified withholding tax monies from the federal government, and opposed moves to strengthen federal capacities. (Ironically, this economic theory was also favored by the IMF and commercial banks to seek the opposite outcome: reintegration and a strengthened federal government.) They argued that productivity was declining because redistribution sapped the incentive of firms and workers and that growth and exports would revive fastest if firms that were profitable (and the republics in which they were located) made decisions on investment. This was clearly against the interests of the poorer republics and localities in need of federal aid. Yet if these regions played down their opposition, they could be silent beneficiaries of the political half of this platform—the arguments against the return of economic authority to the center.

Far more influential than this trickle-down theory, however, was a second argument made by Slovenia and Croatia. Combining the economic and political goals of the antifederalists, the republics argued that constitutionally they were final owners of productive assets within their territory and that this included the right to dispose of income earned by their firms and workers. The misuse of their taxed earnings by other republics was a form of national exploitation, based on the populist understanding of exploitation through exchange common to nationalists in general and to states created by reform communists. Although in theory not all nations could be exploited, decades of debate over the net effect of resource allocation within the economy (through taxes and transfers, government subsidies, export incentives, price regulations, and so forth) had never been resolved. Macedonia, for example, was particularly outspoken about the system of price regulations and export incentives, which had the effect of awarding to the more developed republics of Slovenia and Croatia greater economic transfers than did the system of federal credits and investment grants to the less developed republics. They were net losers in the system of redistribution. However, the taxation on income and fixed assets was far more politically visible than were prices and industrial subsidies. The severity of the economic decline and the net capital outflow to repay the debt compounded the zero-sum character of budgetary thinking in the socialist economy. Regardless of the facts, hardship encouraged on all sides the notion that each was a victim of unfair economic exchange by others.

In the absence of political democracy and competitive political organization, the contests over federal expenditures and economic reform could not be decided by popular vote or by public opinion. Political stability depended on keeping social disorder at a minimum because there were few established procedures for channeling and defusing mass activism. The methods preferred to outright repression were popular self-restraint out of fear of repression or a quick resolution of localized grievances. At the same time, however, a politician's ability to threaten to mobilize popular support or social discontent was a powerful bargaining chip in inter-republican and federal politics. As the debate over economic reform and federal institutions became ever more public and political in its language, it provided an opportunity for those who helped shape public perceptions through language and symbols to influence politicians and for politicians in turn to influence the public. Thus the climate of public opinion created by intellectuals of various inclinations who were actively engaged in proposing ways out of the economic crisis, by journalists, and by party leaders was critical.

The climate of intellectual opinion and of the mass media was increasingly open, critical, and even permissive by the early 1980s, especially in Slovenia and Serbia. It was also particularly conducive to the language of national exploitation in confronting economic hardship. In Slovenia, more affluent and stable economic conditions had favored ever greater pluralism. In part because it was the easiest way for youth to challenge the party establishment and in part because it was a form of protectionist reaction to threats of economic decline (similar to the anti-immigrant xenophobia in western Europe), nationalist expression became increasingly common in literature, economic policy, and youth manifestations.[33]

Since the mid-1970s, the extensive economic decentralization had narrowed Yugoslav political life, much of communication, and the perspectives of the younger generation to the point where people were inclined to see their jobs and fortunes as tied to their republic rather than to the country as a whole. In Croatia, sullen but silent discontent remained over Tito's purge, in 1971–72, of leaders who, in the view of party leaders and the army, had taken their nationalism too far and should be held responsible for the social turmoil that resulted from the previous marketizing economic reform. In Serbia, resentment still lingered at Tito's compensatory purge of liberal reformers and economic managers who had responded to market opportunities to expand into other republics. By 1977 this resentment had nationalist tones, a manifestation of which was the appearance of a Blue Book that charged persistent discrimination against Serbia in Tito's Yugoslavia.[34] Intellectuals spoke ever more openly of their anger at the purge of Serbia's managerial stratum and liberal party leadership. This openness, in turn, seemed to give permission to broader segments of the intellectual elite and the professional middle class to express Serbian nationalist sentiments, which were perceptible by 1983–84, exacerbated in no small measure by the incipient revolt among ethnic Albanians in the province of Kosovo. By 1983 members of the Serbian Academy of Sciences and Arts (SANU) were meeting to analyze the "political and economic crisis" and to write a platform—in draft by 1986—defining Serbian national identity and interests.

In addition, throughout the country a generational change was taking place in political and intellectual life. People convicted during the 1970s for "inciting nationalist hatred" were at the end of their jail sentences. The death of the last wartime leaders (Edvard Kardelj in 1979, Tito in 1980, and Vladimir Bakarić in early 1983) brought some who had retired prematurely during other political purges cautiously back into public life. By the time of the thirteenth party congress (June 25–28, 1986) 127 of the 165-member central committee were under age 40. A generational turnover in historians, on the one hand, and the memoir production of wartime leaders in retirement, on the other, produced an explosion of new research and public debate about the wartime and immediate postwar history of Yugoslavia. Issues that had been politically taboo—from the real extent of atrocities committed by domestic fascists to revelations about massacres by Partisan forces and reexamination of the purge of Cominformists after 1948—dominated weekly magazines, plays, and novels.[35] Countrywide, the one public entity recognized politically outside the party and its affiliated organizations—religious institutions (above all the three largest denominations: Roman Catholic, Greek [Serbian] Orthodox, and Muslim)—became more active in recruitment and social action. Parallels were found throughout central and eastern Europe at the time, in the rise of autonomous social organizations (such as Solidarity in Poland or Charter 77 in Czechoslovakia), the public reexamination of immediate postwar history (such as the legacy of Yalta in Poland, the expulsion of Germans from Czechoslovakia after World War II, the truth about the events of 1956 in Hungary), and generational conflict.

At least as important, the international environment in which this political debate and social turmoil in Yugoslavia was taking place changed dramatically in 1985–86. As dwindling internal resources required increasingly harsher choices and exacerbated political conflict, events in Europe pushed those conflicts one step further by seeming to offer new options to some and to limit or worsen choices for others. In 1985 the European Community committed to accomplish the next stage of market integration by 1992. The CMEA and the EC resumed talks on freer mutual trade that had broken off in 1979. Gorbachev came to power in Moscow with a program of westernization and a "common European home." The revival of commercial bank lending to Eastern Europe gave profitable exporters in Yugoslavia an alternative to federal restrictions on foreign exchange. Foreign investment began to flow into Slovenia and Croatia, and the two republics became intensely involved in a new tourist and cultural organization of regions along the border of Italy, Austria, and Yugoslavia called Alpe-Adria. Both Italy and Austria initiated policies to develop economic ties to and expand interests in central and Eastern Europe (including formation of the Pentagonale to coordinate interests among Italy, Austria, Hungary, and Yugoslavia).[36] The Vatican initiated a policy of active reengagement in central Europe. At the same time, however, demand in Yugoslavia's traditional Eastern and Middle Eastern markets was declining as a result of the Soviet attempts to find Western partners and the consequences of the Iran-Iraq war.

Although economic opportunities were expanding westward and declining eastward, mutual arms reduction talks between the two blocs did little to assuage the feelings held by the members of the Yugoslav national security establishment of growing danger. Renewed attention by NATO to its southern European theater, where it held its maneuvers in 1985 and 1986, persuaded the Yugoslav army that the environment was more, not less, hostile. Already embroiled in attacks on the army's budget and concerned about internal instability, the minister of national defense, Admiral Branko Mamula, became more outspoken about the YPA's guardian role and about a growing threat to territorial integrity from renewed fascism abroad.[37]

## Nationalist Momentum and the Insidious Decline
of the Old Order

By 1985–86 the preconditions of a revolutionary situation were apparent. One million people were officially registered as unemployed. The increasing rate of unemployment was above 20 percent in all republics except Slovenia and Croatia. Inflation was at 50 percent a year and climbing. The household savings of approximately 80 percent of the population were depleted. Western currencies such as the deutschemark and the U.S. dollar were given preference in domestic exchange. Allocation decisions increasingly became stark questions of survival. Attempts to alleviate the pressures made inflation worse and undermined economic management. This economic polarization led to social polarization. While most people were preoccupied with making ends meet under the austerity program and the dominant mood was that of localism, personalism, scapegoating against minorities (ethnic and women), and antipolitics, independent political activity and new civic groups were also bubbling up.

The outcome of these conditions was a growing political polarization between official alternatives: a federal government pushing ever more radical economic reform and confronting republican governments asserting their sovereignty and "national" interest with equal conviction. This confrontation and the final showdown was not apparent until 1988–90 because the events leading up to it operated on two parallel tracks. On the one hand was a gradual but insidious breakdown of the old order, particularly its system of multinational guarantees and federal contributions to social welfare. On the other hand were the increasingly open resort by republican politicians, from Slovenia to Serbia, to nationalism in their fight over constitutional reform and the political difficulties facing liberals within and across republican lines.

The challenges to the constitutional order began as temporary measures taken in response to the emergency of economic crisis. As early as 1982, Prime Minister Milka Planinc accepted her mandate to move rapidly on stabilization, the IMF program, and economic reform on the condition that she be released from the rule obliging national proportionality (among constituent nations) in making cabinet appointments. The principle that professional criteria and the discretion of the prime minister should outweigh ethnic parity thus received a boost, while the principle of republican parity in the appointment of prime ministers, by rotating alphabetically among the republics, fell victim to bargaining among the republics. In 1986, when the prime minster, by constitutional rotation, should have been a Slovene, Slovenia horsetraded concessions on economic reform in exchange for the appointment of a Bosnian, Branko Mikulić.[38]

The economic reforms brought more permanent political changes. The makeup of the governing board of the contested federal fund for development credits to underdeveloped areas changed in 1982 in response to demands by enterprises that their representatives, and not those chosen by republican and provincial governments, compose the board. If the goal was more profit-oriented investments and efficient use of declining resources—as the enterprises argued—then businessmen, not politicians or planning offices, should make its policy. Republican parity received an additional blow in October 1986, when the IMF began to tie conditions for new credits to political reform. Its first demand for restrengthening the governing capacity of the federal administration (despite growing intransigence on the parts of Slovenia, Vojvodina, Croatia, and occasionally Macedonia and Kosovo) was to change the voting rules in the National Bank from consensus to majority decision.[39]

The fights among republics over the federal budget and federal legislation were moving in the opposite direction, however. While reformers and the IMF insisted on a more effective federal government, the specific victories of the republics were draining what little power the existing federal institutions had. In the fall of 1985, for example, Slovenia concluded a campaign begun the previous March against the authority of the federal constitutional court to rule on the constitutionality of an agreement between republican and provincial assemblies by refusing to accept the court's ruling. The Slovenes insisted that parliament was supreme in their legal system and thus that the republics had supremacy over the executive branch. In March 1987 they refused to implement the wage restrictions of the federal incomes policy. In the first six months of 1986, all republics and provinces except Slovenia and Bosnia and Herzegovina failed to pay their obligatory portion of the federal budget. The continuing quarrels over financing the budget were settled, in November 1986, by an agreement to rely on federal revenues only, without republican contributions, and thus to give republics fiscal sovereignty. This break in the fundamental commitment of the republics to their common fate and the forty-year system of "brotherhood and unity" among the nations that had helped form Yugoslavia had already been made in Slovene political speech. In a subtle shift from "brotherhood and unity" to the slogan "togetherness," the idea of a whole that was larger than its parts seemed to vanish.

At the same time that both federal and republican leaders, in their responses to the economic crisis and bargaining over political elements of the economic reform, were picking apart the fundamental principles of the constitutional order of multinational Yugoslavia, its legitimating principles were eroding at the popular level. Challenges to authority and to the myths of the Tito era—including the late Marshal Tito himself—were ever more freely expressed.[40]

In Slovenia the realm of tolerance exploded as youth used forms of expression (including nationalism and neofascism) designed to shock elders into more rapid change. Newspapers published works censored in other republics, and public accountants (employed by the government) used bank data to fight openly the government decision to revise downward the measure for calculating the minimum wage and social assistance. The young staff of the Slovene youth journal, *Mladina*, began an open campaign against the army. Their demands included the right to conscientious objection (a campaign instigated by Jehovah's Witnesses in the republic's second-largest city, Maribor), the right to be posted in one's home republic, the creation of ethnically homogeneous units, and implementation of the existing but rarely practiced right to use the Slovene language at any time in the military. As early as January 1985, Stane Dolanc (a Slovene member of the federal presidency and a political conservative) noted the drift of public attention, warning that a "free united Slovenia, joined in a central European catholic federation . . . means a destruction of Yugo-slavia."[41]

In Croatia, the Catholic Church reopened a particularly sensitive issue by campaigning to rehabilitate Archbishop Stepinac (who was charged as a traitor after World War II for collaborating with the Germans). Bombings occurred in Yugoslav cities and were blamed on Ustashe.[42] This name, from World War II Croatian fascist paramilitary troops, had become an epithet for contemporary right-wing Croatian nationalists, who were usu-ally assumed to have foreign support. Although Croatia's conservative reign maintained tighter wraps on political debate, there were local revivals of nonparty cultural and religious groups, cases of blatant nationalism and gender intolerance in the press, and even acts of vicarious (largely youthful) violence against non-Croats.

In Serbia, intellectual ferment had begun with historical reflections, such as the novels written in the 1970s by the popular writer Dobrica Ćosić chronicling the Serb losses but glory in World War I; in scholarly studies by Vladimir Dedijer, Kosta Čavoški, Vojislav Koštunica, and others that opened new archives on the pluralist alternatives and political purges of the immediate postwar period; and debate on American constitutional history on the origins of the Bill of Rights and the constitutional review powers of the Supreme Court.[43] In addition to the growing nationalism of urban professionals and intellectuals, by the mid-1980s the Orthodox Church and Serb leaders from Kosovo began to organize rallies in smaller cities and towns in the interior to champion the rights of Serbs in Kosovo. Both demographic growth, which had raised the proportion of ethnic Albanians in Kosovo from 67 percent to 78 percent between the 1961 and 1981 cen-suses, and the movement for a separate republic had increased the fears of Serbs living in the province. Tales spun of forced expulsion and even rape of Serbs and Montenegrins by rebellious Albanians became the basis for emotional appeals to a receptive parliament to prevent what was increasingly called genocide against Serbs.[44] Muslim nationalists became active in the *Sandžak* region, linking up with groups on trial in Bosnia and Herzegovina for propagating pan-Islamic views.[45]

Party conservatives and security apparatuses—particularly at the federal level and in Croatia and Bosnia-Herzegovina—worried out loud about these developments and about a repeat of the social disorder of the 1960s, when marketization and liberalizing economic reforms led to youth rebellion, worker militancy, and assertions of nationalism. But they were in a difficult position. Many opposed the economic reforms, including LCY president Stipe Šuvar, who complained openly as late as October 1988 that, with only 6 million employed out of a population of 23 million, the last thing the country needed was an "efficiency-oriented reform."[46] But the economic reform was policy, and the party was constitutionally separate from the government. The party could appoint the commission on government reform in 1983 to amend the constitution, just as it appointed the commission to write the economic reform program in 1981, but it had to abide by the vote of the parliament and the enabling legislation initiated by the federal executive council (the cabinet).

The party leadership was responsible primarily for guarding the constitutional and social order while the constitution was under revision. Dominated by political conservatives, it followed its institutional inclination to govern as it always had, relying on habit rather than risking innovation. In proposing a new conception for the constitution that could bridge the deep chasm between the federal government and Slovenia and accommodate most of those in between, the party's constitutional commission (named for its chair, Josip Vrhovec from Croatia) attempted to manufacture a consensus. This procedure, known in reform-communist circles as the "harmonization of differences," is an alternative to majority rule, in which there are winners and losers.[47] The Vrhovec Commission yielded a report in 1985 that included a nearly indecipherable and eminently vague compromise.[48] The proposed constitutional amendments conformed with the principles of economic liberals aiming to reduce the power of the party and government. They also acknowledged the IMF requirement that the authority of central monetary institutions be increased and the ability of the federal administration to make effective decisions strengthened. At the same time, however, the report also reasserted the autonomy of the republics and of enterprises that had been established by the 1974 Constitution. The constitutional position of the ruling party remained untouched.

The party's concern for social order thus produced a conservative, habitual response: to try to strengthen the party while preventing the perceived threat to the political system posed by political liberals, critical intellectuals, and civil libertarians. The real danger, in the party's view, lay in the activities of nonparty liberals and social democrats who were fighting for greater rights of expression in general, independent organization, and individually based voting rights. Civil liberties groups campaigned to give "workers and citizens" who had economic grievances an opportunity to organize in self-defense. Party president Šuvar had even drawn up a "White List" of enemies in the fall of 1984 that was so long that self-respecting intellectuals left off the list felt insulted. Those who gathered in private apartments for political discussions in Belgrade were arrested. Leaders of large workers' strikes were harassed. Police activity intensified, often crudely, with the special aim of trying to prevent alliances of intellectuals, workers, or potential leaders *across republican lines*. It was clear from both government actions and words that the example of the Solidarity movement in Poland in 1980–81, with its horizontalist movement among party cadre and alliance between workers and intellectuals, defined the party leaders' greatest fears.

The consequence of this rearguard action, however, was the opposite of what was intended: it made the party increasingly irrelevant to the needs of the day, weakening it further. Instead of viewing the right-wing revivals of unresolved historical issues from previous wars, of religious fervor, of fascist tendencies, and of ethnic conflict as a danger to both the state and the economic reforms, the party leadership made the task of the political right easier by seriously undercutting the efforts of political liberals and moderates who could have built a political center throughout the country, and thus an alternative to the republic-centered nationalists. Instead of counterbalancing the world of segregated intellectual universes and their burgeoning civic activity—the result of republican jurisdiction over education, culture, and the mass media—the party's response reinforced it. Moreover, while economic hardship encouraged scapegoating, self-serving historical revision, and nationalist tensions, the party deprived the country of the one potential antidote: a liberal press and communication across ethnic and national communities to challenge political perceptions, prejudices, and interpretations of events. This failure strengthened the political forces operating within republican arenas by preventing competition and isolated those forces most inclined to fight destructive nationalism. Most important, because the federal government was preoccupied with economic and constitutional reform rather than with building a popular constituency, the party leaders handed the political resource of popular discontent, alienation, and scapegoating over to republican and provincial leaders to mobilize in their bargaining over federal policy.

The first to use this resource of popular discontent and oppositional activity to their political advantage were the antifederalist Slovene party and government. Slovenia was the furthest along the road to political pluralism as a result of its economic situation. With full employment and persistent labor shortages, they were able to respond to workers' strikes—at the time most numerous in Slovenia—by refusing to abide by the wage limits of the IMF stabilization program. Wage concessions helped buy political allegiance, making it possible to keep Slovene workers from emigrating for higher incomes or to entice their return from abroad so that non-Slovene workers could be limited and even sent home. The leadership also could use the excuse of popular pressure, in the event, to deny federal authority over social policy in Slovenia, thus striking another victory for republican sovereignty. The government was skilled at exploiting youth discontent and the young people's campaign against the army for use in the republican leaders' fight against the federal budget and the army's political authority. By agreeing to fund the youth and mainstream press at a time when other republics were responding with censorship and police repression, the Slovene government gained the political loyalty of activist youth and the media—despite specific criticisms—while the party retained ultimate control.

In Serbia, however, the centrist party leadership faced a very different political problem because nonparty political activity and intellectual fervor focused on an internal problem—Kosovo. In contrast to the Slovene anti-federalists, the Serb leaders supported the liberal economic policies and stronger federal government of the reform program. But it faced a nearly impossible political task: to make Serbia's government more capable of liberal policies by reducing the autonomy of Kosovo and Vojvodina, while remaining politically liberal and forestalling mounting pressure from the public and parliament for a tighter rein on Kosovo Albanians. Under the conditions of economic hardship, this was even more difficult. In September 1986 the liberal party press attempted to expose the nationalist-based opposition among intellectuals by printing leaked portions of a draft of the SANU discussion memorandum; however, the attempt backfired. Although it aroused immediate condemnation from outside Serbia, it also gave publicity to the memorandum's nationalist theme of a long history of victimization against the Serb nation. Its portrayal of that history cited discrimination since 1945 at the hands of economically dominant Slovenia and Croatia; the partition of the Serb nation among republics in Yugoslavia, making it the only Yugoslav nation without its own state; claims of genocide against Serbs in Kosovo; the need to restore the "integrity" of the Serb nation, starting with the position of Serbs in Croatia, as the best way to strengthen the federal government, and, implicitly, to "rectify" internal borders.[49]

Moreover, because economic conditions were far less able than in Slovenia, for example, to support a politically liberal approach, political liberals were unlikely to succeed in Serbia without forming a broader base for democratic reform throughout the country as a whole. Intellectuals who tried to establish such links were singled out for attack by the federal party led by the political conservative (though social radical) Šuvar.[50] (It did not go unnoticed that he was a Croat from Croatia.) Liberals in Croatia and Slovenia were not much inclined toward alliances because they were increasingly nationalist and antifederalist about securing republican rights and had a greater interest in developments in central Europe. Alliances with liberals in other parts of Yugoslavia might potentially undercut this "Catholic alliance," as both they and their critics increasingly called it, revealing the ever more open activities of the Church and revelation of religious identities with Europe. But they would have to overcome intellectual prejudices formed in the interwar kingdom that tended to view all pro-federalist, pro-Yugoslav Serbs as unitarist.

In effect, the same problem emerged in Croatia under a conservative party leadership more concerned about the threat from political liberals than that from political nationalists. Government censorship and attempts at repression focused largely on liberal intellectuals and the media. Authorities paid far less attention to the growth of nonparty cultural and religious groups, nationalist and antifeminist excesses in the youth press, isolated gang attacks on minorities, and historical revisionism. Since the party was still governing Croatia under the great silence it adopted after the 1972 purge of its leadership, conflicts between liberal and conservative factions remained behind closed doors. While the Croatian parliament was actively pursuing Croatian interests in the fight over taxation and the federal budget, the party leadership had yet to enter the broader political debate over reform and thus to instigate or reach out to groups in society.

## Conclusion

This period of harsh austerity, budgetary conflicts, economic policy aimed at westernization to reduce trade deficits and foreign debt, and quarrels over constitutional reform of the federal government was dominated by the sense of economic crisis and a political turbulence, the outlines of which were still vague. Critical elements of the political system were under serious challenge. In pursuing their interests in economic policy and reform, republican politicians were willing to abandon fundamental guarantees of national equality, such as republican rotation of the prime ministership and national quotas for cabinet ministers, to defy tax obligations to the federal government and the authority of the constitutional court, and to question openly the ruling myths of the Tito period, the party's means of coming to power, and the Partisan army. Most believed that political change was needed, but for the republican leaders this meant shoring up their political control over economic resources. If doing so threatened the federal guarantees of their common existence—the multiple rules to guarantee national rights to both republics and constituent nations; the redistribution of monies for poorer regions and localities; the complex, shared economic sovereignty between republics and federal government; federal executive power as inhered in institutions such as the constitutional court and central bank; the army—then so be it. If the economic crisis was, at the same time, threatening the minimal securities of social existence for an ever larger portion of the population, and if the youth unemployment, growing urban underclass, and increasing autonomy (or abandonment) of localities and the private sector were reducing the party's ability to control social turmoil, then—in the absence of electoral democracy—these were also largely outside the republican leaders' scope of concern.

In this still inchoate period of political erosion, in fact, most battles were over ad hoc emergency arrangements and specific pieces of legislation. Even the debate over amending the constitution was bogged down in the process of "harmonizing differences" through party and legislative committees and public information campaigns, which were largely ignored, in the newspapers. To the extent that anyone had an agenda for change broader than reaction to specific issues, it was those who could afford economically to exit the system if it collapsed. Although not without losses, they could risk obstructing an agreement to insist on their own position. In contests subject to influence and decision by the republics, Slovenia was the one able to risk no compromise; in setting the program and pace of federal reforms, foreign creditors and advisers, led by the IMF, held the position of strength.

Although these two economic powers, Slovenia and foreign creditors, represented the two extremes in the confrontation over constitutional reform of the state, their actions were leading in the same direction. Politically, they both attacked the stabilizing political mechanisms of the socialist period—the constitutional rules aimed to protect a perception of national equality, the limits on political nationalism in or by republics that could destroy the country's multinational composition, and the symbols and institutions of Yugoslav identity at the federal level. Economically, they both took aim at the redistributive transfers at the federal level and social protections that, however minimally, prevented total exclusion of individuals who would lose under economic liberalism.

The Slovene leadership was already ahead in its use of popular Slovene national sentiment and protest activity to serve the republic's objectives in federal policy and reform. In 1987–88 the party leadership made the links between elite and mass politics ever more explicit and open in its fight with the political aspects of the IMF and federal government program. Serbia's leadership was not far behind in connecting with popular discontent. In the interim period of 1985–86, federal authorities were divided between a government attuned to popular discontent, if not actively using it for public gain, and a party leadership actively trying to moderate its expression for fear that it would lose control of political change.

A forecaster of Yugoslavia's path of political transformation away from socialism would have cited the responsiveness of the federal cabinet and the federal party presidency as containing the seeds of an all-Yugoslav democracy.[51] The choice of Branko Mikulić as prime minister in 1986 reflected in part the opinions of those who disapproved of orthodox stabilization responses to debt. For similar reasons many groups in Latin America also proposed heterodox policies for debt repayment. While attempting to sustain an economic policy within the budget constraints required by foreign debt rescheduling, the Mikulić cabinet sought to buy a measure of social peace with the army, the less developed republics, and domestic industries through a more graduated program of stabilization. The collective party presidency was particularly concerned about carefully maneuvering the shoals of political change so as to prevent both conservative backlash against too rapid change and the equal danger of too little reform. Emphasizing incrementalism, the party leadership experimented with new forms of checks and balances—such as seating members alphabetically instead of by republic so they could no longer caucus by republic in the actual course of meeting and assigning responsibility for nationalist disturbances within a republic to a representative from another republic— as means of counteracting growing nationalism and republican assertiveness without provoking further radicalization.[52]

In the following period, both federal leaderships failed in their efforts to maintain a centrist balance. The republics became more assertive in defining and pursuing what they called national interests. And international conditions changed profoundly.

# Chapter 4

# *Escalation*

On February 11, 1987, the presidency of the League of Communists of Yugoslavia (LCY) opened the next stage of political reform by recommending to the lower house of the federal parliament 130 amendments to the 406 articles of the federal constitution. No sooner had this happened than the foreign economic policy necessitating this reform took another about face. The rising trade deficit in February forced Prime Minister Branko Mikulić to reopen negotiations to finance the deficit with International Monetary Fund (IMF) credits. The IMF's conditions required much more drastic economic reform, thus forcing Mikulić to abandon his effort to revive growth and to build a more inclusive political coalition around reform with a moderate course.[1]

The return to an orthodox, anti-inflationary program in October 1987 raised prices on oil, food, gas, and transport; cut wages; raised interest rates in order to cut domestic lending; introduced a federal value-added tax; devalued the currency twice in two months (24.6 percent in November alone) and allowed it to depreciate rapidly against Western currencies.[2] Nevertheless, the republican assemblies of Slovenia, Croatia, and Serbia called the program insufficient. When it reached the federal parliament in November, the entire Slovene delegation and some Croatian delegates voted against it.

Even more important was the political message accompanying the economic program, which was bound to complicate federal-republican relations. The IMF team told federal representatives that the IMF and the World Bank were ready to support Yugoslavia substantially in a thorough reform of the financial system and the structural changes necessary to a supply response. In return, however, Yugoslavia could not rely on "plastic surgery or Band-Aids" to correct its economic problems, but must undergo "radical surgery and a long period of rehabilitation."[3] Shifting tactics from the political advice accompanying harsh economic conditionality of 1982–85, they were conditioning new credits on constitutional change: a strengthened federal administration and a change in the voting rules of the central bank from consensus to majority. Their assumption was that these changes would restore the government's capacity to establish monetary discipline and to repay debt.

The state presidency seemed to agree, for in May 1987 it published its approval of the LCY's proposed constitutional amendments with the declaration that the system of "polycentric statism" (whereby decentralization had led not to marketization but to the republics' acting like states) had caused the disintegration of the economy and, as a result, the growth of nationalism. In late September 1987, the LCY presidency approved twenty-nine of the proposed economic amendments and announced that parliamentary debate would resume the next April. But the federal government, inferring that a radical therapy had to be accomplished with speed, cut short the parliamentary debate. In November 1987, it proclaimed that the debate on the draft amendments was concluded—to the great outcry of the Slovene government. The process was not complete, however, until the republican assemblies had, as constitutionally obliged, approved the amendments and also amended their constitutions in accordance with the revised federal constitution (which was finally adopted a year later on November 29, 1988, by changing 135 articles—one-third of the 1974 Constitution—with thirty-nine amendments). This meant that the first year of the government's return to a policy of austerity and an even more radical economic program of liberalization would be focused on debating and rewriting the constitutions in the republics.

## The Problem: The Political System

Despite the leaders' commitment to speed, their proposed revisions retained all the ambiguity of the compromises in the original commission draft. The draft accepted both the IMF demands for a stronger federal administration and independent central bank and the republics' demands to retain their sovereignty. At the same time, it continued the constitutional prerogatives and political role of the Communist party in binding the republics together.

There were already three fundamentally different constitutional programs on the table—the confederalist concept proposed by Slovenia; the liberal economic concept of a centralized capacity for macroeconomic policy appropriate to an open, market economy proposed by the IMF and the federal cabinet; and the federalist views held by a motley coalition but associated most with Serbia. Nevertheless, the political leadership's method of resolving the growing confrontation reflected no change in its own conception of the political system. The primary principle of decentralization and a brokering of compromises among representatives of the republics and federation—in effect, deal-making within the territorialized political elite—was retained.

This "harmonization of differences" (in socialist jargon), or "incrementalism" (in Western jargon), might apply well to the pork-barrel politics of normal legislation and distribution of money and credit. Giving something to each on a matter as fundamental and untradeable as the character of the state would satisfy no one. Slovenia won the fight for republican sovereignty with the retention of the principle of consensual decisionmaking in federal political councils and parliamentary sovereignty at the federal level, but it was still unwilling to accept the strengthening of federal economic institutions. A year later (in 1988) Serbia was permitted to strengthen its institutions by reducing the autonomy granted Kosovo and Vojvodina in the 1974 Constitution, but the constitutional commission either ignored or rejected its proposals (and those of all political federalists) to strengthen the federal executive branch by replacing the system of republican and provincial veto over federal decisions with majority rule. And the commission made no attempt to explain how upholding the principle of republican economic sovereignty was compatible with a recentralization of monetary policy and more effective federal economic administration, or vice versa.

A year later the issue was again subordinated to economic reality. It was only clear politically on December 30, 1988, when Prime Minister Mikulić felt forced to resign before his mandate expired, that the gradualists on federal economic policy had lost in their attempt to balance the tension between policies for foreign debt repayment and trade liquidity, on the one hand, and policies to revive economic growth at home, on the other. With the administration of Prime Minister Ante Marković, the federal reform agenda—as well as the program to replace the socialist economic system with a market economy—became even more radical in pace. In 1989 Marković insisted on a federal system based not on parliamentary sovereignty and territorial autonomy but on functional integration. In the meantime, however, political events had taken their own course, further weakening the governing capacity of the federal government and leading to growing polarization among proponents of competing visions of constitutional reform.

The constitutional quarrels contained two separate political problems, both of which were ignored by the economic reformers. Their resolution would decide the fate of the reforms and of the country. First, there was no procedure for reaching agreement on reform of their common state, jurisdiction between federal and republican governments, and the form of government that was appropriate to a market economy. The system of federal decisionmaking by consensus and veto had no procedure for resolving differences between truly incompatible projects. The federal cabinet was an interested party and, at best, a coequal player with the republics and the army in what was basically a bargaining system.

The effect of the economic reform was to deprive the governing party of most of its few remaining resources to compel compliance other than its powers of persuasion and its members' loyalty. Moreover, the remaining powers became the primary political target for change during 1988.[4]

Slovenia's attempts to enhance its sovereignty by denying federal authority in ever more fields was systematically depriving the federal government of the means to enforce any decision. None of the republics had been punished for noncompliance during the 1980s. By 1987–88, the only uncontested federal power left to force a choice and obtain compliance was the government's access to foreign credits and its role as intermediary with foreign capital for the republics. Even the constitutional obligation of the federal army and police to protect the constitutional order, which was exercised occasionally in Kosovo, was under the authority of the federal presidency and therefore the rules of consensus among the republics. Coalitions could form on negative grounds, where politicians agreed on what they opposed, but there were ever fewer coalitions being formed on positive grounds. It was far easier to attack the current system or to abstain from participation than it was to find agreement on what should replace it.

The second political problem contained in the constitutional quarrels was hardly discussed. This was the lack of attention paid in the constitutional debates and amendments to the representation of popular grievances about federal policy. The revolutionary preconditions of social disintegration present after 1985, resulting from the austerity policy and economic decline, screamed out for political change at the level of relations between the political elite and the population. By keeping republican sovereignty, the one-party system, and the federal structure of the Communist party, however, the revised constitution ensured that the republics would continue to be the intermediary between the interests of citizens and federal policy. Horizontal and interest-based associations independent of republican borders were precluded, despite the talk of a market economy and the character of issues confronting citizens from the austerity program. Citizens would continue to have their interests represented, if at all, by the republics where they lived. Even the Slovene pressure for greater political pluralism—such as competitive candidacies for the state-presidency elections in 1984, lauded by many as a democratic initiative frustrated by opposition from other republics—was strictly limited to reforms within the republics. It blocked any initiative at the all-Yugoslav or federal level that might weaken republican sovereignty and the control of republican governments and parties over political representation and competition over federal policy and reform.

Despite the absence of apparent solutions to these two problems or even the ability to confront them head on, the combination of economic reform and economic hardship had created an increasingly fluid political scene. In the course of 1987, there were many signs of civic activity and popular self-organization on economic interests that might provide the pressure from the bottom up for breaking the political logjam between the republics and the federal government and for a new political system. In February, for example, intellectuals in Croatia began to break the fifteen-year political silence within the republic and to talk publicly, including on television, about multiparty elections.[5] Unions sought to become independent representatives of workers' interests and to replace the corporatist system of government-negotiated wage regulations with collective bargaining. Strikes increased throughout the country. They were most numerous in Slovenia, followed by Serbia.[6] The most notable, an impressively organized miners' strike in Labin, Croatia, started in April 1987 and lasted thirty-three days. This strike, according to observers, had not just the usual economic demands of self-management but also the political goal of creating mechanisms for regulating conflict directly between workers and the state.[7]

Elsewhere, enterprising mayors were turning some cities into economic miracles despite the global depression and federal austerity. Local elites and economists in poor areas began to draw up plans for regional development across republican boundaries (such as ties between Knin in Croatia and Banja Luka in Bosnia and Herzegovina, for the impoverished *krajina*, experiencing severe deindustrialization), and to bring professionals of many disciplines together to discuss implementation.[8] Social democratic and liberal democratic intellectuals formed political associations (parties were not yet permitted) that crossed republican boundaries and tried to improve regular communication among colleagues in different republics. Data gathered in 1991 suggest that measures of economic integration across republican borders began to improve around 1987, reversing the process of republicanization of the economy that had received so much commentary and criticism in the preceding decade.[9] New proto-political civic groups such as environmentalists, pacifists, antinuclear protestors, and public debating clubs sprang up, particularly among young people and intellectuals, and they were having an effect on policy, even though such activities were still viewed with suspicion by party conservatives as a danger to be quashed.

At the same time, citizens' responses to the deteriorating economy remained largely antipolitical, manifest in the appearance of cultural nationalism, religious solidarity, and the popularity of surrealism with the younger generation.[10] The reason was the absence of political outlets independent of the party and its affiliated groups and the continuing attempt by LCY conservatives to contain social turmoil by preventing the emergence of alternative leaders who might seek to organize nonparty people.

Attacks on existing federal and countrywide institutions became more open as well. After a year of crisis, at its annual parliament in June 1987, the Yugoslav Writers' Union (the only all-Yugoslav cultural organization) simply dissolved when the Slovene delegation broke tradition and voted against the candidate for president of the Union proposed by the Serbian Writers' Association. Until then the post was filled formalistically, as a matter of republican prerogative in the regularized system of rotation for all federal bodies that institutionalized republican sovereignty. It was particularly ominous, however, that the candidate rejected, Miodrag Bulatović, was a Serb who, in fact, lived and worked in Slovenia. Attacks increased on the Yugoslav People's Army (YPA), the largest recipient of federal funds and the only economic institution that, by federal jurisdiction and the structure of defense production and planning, was all-Yugoslav.[11] In October the Slovene delegation and part of the Croatian delegation walked out of the federal parliament, refusing to contribute any longer to the federal budget.

The hopes that many had for evolutionary change to new political alliances and economic relations across republican lines were particularly damaged in September 1987, when a major corruption scandal in Bosnia was exposed by the federal party newspaper, *Borba*.[12] Agrokomerc was a huge agroindustrial and trade conglomerate, with its headquarters in Velika Kladuša in the northwestern corner of the republic and a board of directors closely tied to current Bosnian party and governmental leaders at the federal level and to much of Bosnia's economy. This conglomerate was found to have issued unsupported promissory notes to at least fifty-seven banks in four republics.[13] The notes, countersigned by the Bank of Bihać, totaled $865 million. Though the republican government had been issuing warnings for three years, beginning in July 1984, banks throughout the country holding the notes had accepted reassurances from political leaders on the assumption that the government would bail them out if necessary. The Agrokomerc directors had resorted to long-time practices to find independent financing when federal grants were cut. However, they were caught in the reformers' campaign against corruption initiated by the party leadership to demonstrate greater accountability. They were arrested, tried, and convicted in a civil court. The scandal reverberated through a vast network of family and political connections, leading to the arrest, dismissal, or resignation of scores of economic managers and party officials in Bosnia-Herzegovina and the core of its federal party leaders. One of the leaders, Hamdija Pozderac, was vice-president of the state presidency.

The scandal left a vacuum in the Bosnian political (and profederal) leadership at the very moment when new political associations were beginning to form within the republic, above all among Muslim intellectuals. It also contributed to the decline in stature of the federal party, striking an additional blow to any political alliance that supported an all-Yugoslav option of economic and political integration. And because the majority of the promissory notes had been bought by the republican bank of Slovenia— the Ljubljana Bank—the scandal also put a brake on one of the most hopeful developments of the decade, namely, the developing economic relations between Slovene and Bosnian firms and the two economies.[14]

The confrontation between Serbian authorities and ethnic Albanians in Kosovo over the Albanians' campaign for republic status and the debate since the mid-1970s within Serbia over the constitutional status of its provinces had begun to heat up by the end of 1986. The issue of Kosovo, more than any other, revealed the growing difficulty facing Yugoslavia of keeping the two spheres of political activity separate: the emergence of ever more explicit, popular, associational and protest activity, on the one hand, and the political struggle over the constitutional relations between federal and republican governments and the weakening of federal institutions, on the other.

The liberal party leaders ruling Serbia, aided by the federal presidency, had attempted to steer a middle course, to prevent Kosovar separatists from gaining popular support in the Albanian community by isolating leaders and repressing open dissent. At the same time it had tried to resist popular pressures from the Serbian public and parliament to take a hard line on Albanians and to protect the Serbian minority feeling pressure to leave the province. This course began to lose ground during 1987. Police harassment and repression of Albanians escalated, as did the number and size of protest delegations mounted by Serbs and Montenegrins from Kosovo to the Serbian parliament in Belgrade.[15] The issue implicated the federal and republican leaderships, both party and state, because the continuing strife was an issue of civil order, and therefore a matter of federal concern and jurisdiction, and an issue of constitutional reform. Kosovo had become the question on which the intellectual and political elite of Serbia had focused its constitutional and political debate. In 1987 and 1988, entire sessions of the LCY central committee were frequently devoted to the problem. The Kosovo party committee was purged in late 1987. On October 25, 1987, the federal state presidency suspended the authority of the provincial police and judiciary, dispatching federal police units in their place.

## Who Does the Organizing?

The political consequence of popular protest depends less on who is protesting and why than on who seeks to organize the discontent.[16] At some point the differences within the political elite over economic and constitutional reform in Yugoslavia and the views and activities of ordinary citizens over the consequences of these reforms would meet. The political groups and personalities that took the step to link elite and mass politics by mobilizing popular support and grievances directly for a particular political platform would be most likely to define the agenda and path of political change.

Two sets of events in 1987, one in Slovenia and the other in Serbia, were critical. In Slovenia, the policy of protecting and enhancing Slovene sovereignty by opposing all federal institutions that seemed to interfere with republican rights and were not founded on parliamentary and republic supremacy linked up with a campaign of radical young people and intellectuals against the YPA. In Serbia, the new president of the party, Slobodan Milošević, took up the appeals for help from Serbs in Kosovo and used the issue to stage an inner-party coup, replacing liberal party and state leaders, who were equivocating on the issue of Kosovo, with his party faction. In both cases, the result was a tactical shift by both party leaderships away from party etiquette and toward a direct link with the rhetoric and demands of nationalist intellectuals and with popular protest. Their goals were simultaneously to enhance their bargaining strength at the federal level over republican rights and constitutional reform and to preempt or coopt real and potential rivals emerging among nationalist, opposition intellectuals within their republics. The political rhetoric of national interest and nationalism increasingly framed public debate and participation. The initiative for political change was coming from the republics.

By the time the amendments to the federal constitution had been adopted, in November 1988, events in Serbia and Slovenia had made the constitution's focus on economic reforms and avoidance of substantial political reform obsolete.[17] Yet another round of proposals for a federal constitution became necessary. Furthermore, because the austerity program, economic reform, and debate over the federal budget were also raising doubts about federal guarantees of individual rights—to welfare and to national equality regardless of residence and republic—the act of linking the elite and mass levels made the issue of constitutional and economic reform one of citizenship and political identity as well.

Already in 1986, the YPA had become the object of particular criticism from Slovene nationalist intellectuals and radical youth, and the Slovene government had supported, against army opposition, young people who campaigned for conscientious objectors' right to alternative civilian service.[18] By 1987 the Slovene government had adopted its call for the army's "socialization" as part of its policy against a stronger federation (and the federal budget). "Socialization" in Yugoslav socialist jargon meant devolution of federal powers to the republics or localities, principles of self-management (financial accountability by autonomous, balanced budgets), and, in the case of the army, priority of republican and local territorial defense forces (TDFs) over the YPA. A similar campaign begun in 1968 to decentralize national security to the republics had succeeded but was partially reversed in the early 1970s when the YPA insisted on clearer lines of command and control among the branches of the armed forces. The rhetoric alone, therefore, made Slovene intent clear.

During 1987 and into 1988, the confrontation grew. Young people demanded that they be allowed to do their military service at home in Slovenia rather than be sent to another republic, as was army policy (with exceptions), and also to use the Slovene language in all military circumstances (a constitutional right practiced more often in the breach). Investigative journalists in the radical youth and nationalist press, such as the journals *Mladina* and *Nova Revija*, pushed harder and harder against the limits of army secrecy, to the point of publishing military secrets.[19] In the view of the army's general staff and the minister of defense, the army's honor, authority as guardian of the constitutional order, and fighting unity were increasingly threatened by Slovene and Croatian opposition to their budget, by Slovene youth demands for local postings, by intellectuals' calls for "nationally homogeneous armies" in each republic, and by the intentional insults of the youth campaign.

Beginning in April 1987, the Serbian party also shifted tactics in the constitutional fight by adopting the increasingly nationalist language of critical intellectuals and issues of popular protest within the republic. The Serbian shift was part of a factional struggle within the Serbian party, which culminated at the eighth party plenum (September 23–24), when Slobodan Milošević made a successful move to oust his former patron and friend Ivan Stambolić as president of Serbia and to engineer a coup against its Belgrade party organization, Serbia's most powerful (and liberal). Milošević accused Stambolić's crowd of being too lenient on Albanians in Kosovo and of failing to protect Serbian territorial integrity and Serbs and Montenegrins from forced expulsion. He was thus continuing a line he began in the spring at a speech on April 24 on the Kosovo battlefield (site of the most famous battle of Serbian history and epic poetry). To an assembled crowd of 10,000 to 15,000 (at which the police used excessive force, for which they were later disciplined), he appealed to "Serbs" with the slogan "No one should be allowed to beat you!"[20]

Like Milan Kučan, the Slovene party leader, Milošević was choosing to preempt or incorporate anticommunist nationalists who were beginning to organize an opposition, but who also had, in this case, made inroads in organizing cultural revivals of an anticommunist flavor among Serbs in other republics. In Serbia these intellectuals were mobilizing around the goal of Serbian unity and national interests. Their rhetoric had strong undertones of historical redress, such as were displayed in the draft of a Serbian Academy of Sciences and Arts (SANU) memorandum leaked in September 1986, in the popular historical novels about World War I published by Dobrica Ćosić in the 1970s, or in the revival of World War II memorabilia and heroes (such as Draža Mihailović) and the themes of church and monarchy by poet and later party leader Vuk Drašković. (Croatian party leaders in the 1980s tended to be cautious, drawing on lessons of an earlier instance when the party leaders who preceded them, attempting to mobilize popular support for their position on economic reform and constitutional issues around national symbols, created and then lost control over a mass social movement.)

Although the two party leaderships, those of Slovene president Kučan and Serb president Milošević, were different in style—the first far more discreet and the second playing directly and personally to the crowd—the issues were also strikingly similar (and, in retrospect, ominous).[21] Both claimed national rights over territory and a duty to protect the nation and its territory: in one case, asserting the right of Slovenia to define the terms of its defense of territory and the individual rights of Slovenes in the army, and in the other, asserting the right of Serbia to territorial integrity and the individual rights of Serbs "not to be beaten [in] their lands." But unlike the Slovene party, which was managing to build and consolidate a national-liberal coalition across Slovene groups, Milošević and his faction were moving to divide the Serbian party and defeat the liberal wing. Between September and December 1987, they used their new-found power in the party executive and Belgrade party organization to purge large parts of the Serbian political class in the government, party, and mass media that they considered too harsh on Serb nationalists. This move far from consolidated the power of Milošević's faction, however, as is often claimed later, but it did succeed in neutralizing liberal forces, with substantial help from the campaign—in the years immediately preceding—by the political conservatives who dominated the federal party (led by Croat Stipe Šuvar) to repress and divide democratic forces, above all in Serbia.[22]

The formation of Milošević's political coalition had a profound consequence. In this transitional period of economic and constitutional reform, with no blueprint for or agreement on political reform, Communist party leaders were only beginning to respond directly to popular grievances, and explicitly political alternatives to mobilize and organize citizens were still forbidden. Milošević nonetheless eventually captured a large part of the political spectrum. Serbia's economic decline had worsened as a result of changes in its foreign markets and of the investment priorities and monetary restrictions of the stabilization program. The stabilization program, in particular, was rapidly reducing, to a segment of the urban and professional classes, the obvious beneficiaries of liberal policies while expanding dramatically the number of those it had lost or would hurt. It promised to increase unemployment; to expose land ownership to the market; and to cut farm subsidies, veterans' pensions, and the size of the police forces and army. These last three categories, of federal and republican expenditures affecting individual incomes, hit Serbia hard because of its large farming population, high unemployment, and substantial participation in the army. Moreover, politics in Serbia had long been defined by local political machines. Budget cuts and political rhetoric against the patronage networks of local power to justify those cuts thus hit squarely at the party's base on both economic and political fronts.

Milošević, however, was at a disadvantage not suffered by the other five republics or by Serbia's two provinces in forging a political coalition around issues of federal economic policy. The federal government was located in Serbia's capital, and the traditional discourse of anticenter nationalists from the first Yugoslavia in the 1920s and 1930s was anti-Serbian. The antifederalist camp had already begun to create a coalition across republics and economic and social strata with rhetoric that was anti-Belgrade, antifederalist, and anti-Serb. A Serb choosing to mobilize opponents of federal policy would have to find other arguments.

In commandeering the historical language of Serb nationalism from the anticommunists, Milošević found a language to overcome the problem of opposing a state that nationalists in other republics propagandized as Serbian. This language was the Serbian national myth of victimization: the defeat of the medieval Serb empire by the Ottomans on the "field of blackbirds" (Kosovo in 1389).[23] Milošević adopted the interwar political slogan, revived by nationalists, that "Serbs win wars, but lose the peace" because Serbia's huge war losses on the side of the Allies in both world wars had not won it a state. He capitalized on the widespread belief in the 1980s that Serbs and Montenegrins were being forced once again to flee their historic cradle. And he helped propagate the analysis of many Serbian intellectuals that Serbia had been maltreated in Tito's Yugoslavia—that the federal state was constructed to divide and weaken Serbia and to prevent the Serb nation from having its own state (in contrast to Slovenes, Croats, Montenegrins, and Macedonians, nations whose locations more closely matched the geographic boundaries of their republics).

By turning this language of victimization against the Titoist system, but not against Yugoslavia itself, and by using the idea of protection, Milošević was able to link nationalist intellectuals, ordinary people hurting from the effects of economic reform, and all those politically expelled or economically derogated to the private sector who had felt like outsiders in the socialist system. He was able to do this and still use the organizational network of the Communist party and the police. This extraordinary political coalition included Serb nationalists of all social strata, both anticommunist and communist; unskilled and semiskilled workers; police; junior army officers of predominantly Serbian nationality; anti-Titoists purged from the party in campaigns that included a hint of anti-Serb bias (especially in 1948–49, 1966, and 1972); country people; and local party bosses.

There were two dangers in this coalition. The first was that Milošević was appealing, indirectly, to groups that were not represented in the prevailing political system and who clearly stood outside the circle of privilege and gain projected by the westernizing, liberalizing reforms. No other established political force had sought to give these groups a voice. And did it also mean that a man who still claimed to be an economic reformer would be captured by those he sought to lead? The second danger grew directly from the constitution criticized by Serb nationalists. Because policies to limit Serb power in 1945–87 had indeed divided the Serb people among political units, any appeal to individual Serbs (rather than to the Serbian republic)—because they lived throughout Yugoslav territory—implied a political threat to the power of republican leaders who did not want competition for constituents and perceived such outside influence as interference with their republican sovereignty. Although not the first to use mass meetings for political ends or the only leader whose national appeal would cross republican borders, Milošević was the only one who could aspire to a democratic victory on national appeals. The Serb people were numerically preponderant within Yugoslavia, although their low birth rate relative to the high birth rate of Slavic Muslims and ethnic Albanians had reduced their proportion substantially since the 1960s. But if other politicians confined their activities to their republican bastions or mobilized support on national grounds *and* if, against all historical experience, Serbs united politically, they might still produce a voting plurality. This, in turn, could lead other nationalist politicians to view Serbs living in their republics, by virtue of their ethnicity, as of questionable loyalty and to escalate the dynamic of nationalist rhetoric and perceived threats.

## The Dynamic of Escalation

Leaders in Slovenia and Serbia were now pursuing the same goal: putting what they defined as the national interests of their republics and nations above those of Yugoslavia. Their view of power was different. If the republics had been political parties instead, they would have had partisan differences on the balance of parliamentary and executive power and on economic policy. But they were not. Rather than compete to control the government, the two leaderships could pursue their goals to enhance their sovereignty in tandem—even collaborating, one might say, in the effects. Slovenia was systematically protecting its political autonomy by challenging the constitutionality of federal powers. The effect of this, combined with fights over the federal budget and the stabilization program, was an ever weaker central government. At the same time, the transfer of power in Serbia from federalist liberals to a leader oriented to Serbian sovereignty dislodged from the federalist camp its longest standing and most reliable support. Opponents of Milošević throughout the country argue that he was a centralist attempting to become a new Tito or to create a Yugoslav dictatorship that Slovenia, and eventually other republics, would have to oppose. On the contrary, however, his populist nationalism was republican and could not even pretend to internationalism. Moreover, an appeal based on Serbian nationalism had built-in limits. But in terms of the political path his critics were taking, Milošević's nationalism removed what might have been an important obstacle to Slovenian independence. The situation had the dangerous potential of escalation by the dynamic called a security dilemma. Without a common authority and accepted procedures to resolve conflict, leaders in independent states can perceive themselves to be acting defensively against an external threat but can be perceived by others as acting aggressively, thereby setting in motion a process of competitive, defensive reactions with no limit.

Opposition intellectuals in both republics had published well-developed nationalist platforms, the SANU draft memorandum in Belgrade, leaked to the press in September 1986, and the Slovene program published in *Nova Revija* in February 1987.[24] The Slovene and Serbian leaders are thus accused of following a plan (particularly Milošević, as regards a "Greater Serbia"). This is unlikely. Responding to specific events politically, they were choosing tactics of consequence, but they were not necessarily thinking out the chain of those consequences or the logic of their daily steps. This is important in understanding the political dynamic, if not the responsibility.

Slovenia viewed its sovereignty as a direct trade-off with federal authority. Milošević's objective, widely shared by the population and political class of Serbia, was to restore the constitutional integrity of the republic by ending the extensive autonomy granted Kosovo and Vojvodina by the 1974 Constitution (in fact, by the eighteenth amendment of 1968). The Serbian government began this process to revise its republican constitution in January 1988; police harassment continued in Kosovo. In October 1988, the LCY central committee—in a deal that omitted or modified all amendments to the federal constitution that Slovenia found objectionable (including that on funding the army)—approved the Serbian parliament's revisions, reducing to provincial status what Serbia claimed was the de facto republican status of the two provinces. The central committee also expelled the two main Kosovo Albanian party leaders, Azem Vllasi and Katcuša

Jašari, from the LCY, although it was apparently restrained by the Slovene leadership from granting other Serbian demands.[25] This was not the end of the story for Albanians, however.

Demonstrations by Serbs and Montenegrins from Kosovo or in sympathy with their cry for a hearing were originally a response to their political mobilization beginning in 1981. Demonstrations by ethnic Albanians in response to the actions of the Serbian government now increased. Mass demonstrations occurred in towns throughout Kosovo during October 17–21, 1988, with people protesting the LCY decision to reduce Kosovo's autonomy. A month later, gatherings of Albanian young people and workers protested the removal of Vllasi and Jašari from the party leadership. In February 1989 miners at Stari Trg protested both in a political strike that lasted many days.

Meanwhile, in Slovenia, in April 1988 the YPA decided to go on the offensive and pick up the gauntlet tossed down repeatedly by Slovene young people, who had structured a political society and constant antiestablishment happening around their journal, *Mladina*.[26] At a meeting of the federal parliamentary committee for national defense on June 16, three journalists (Janez Janša, Ivan Borstner, and David Tasić) were placed under house arrest for revealing army secrets as part of a campaign against arms sales and charges of counterinsurgent activities by the YPA. At their subsequent military trial, little regard was shown for their civil rights, such as the right to be tried in the Slovene language. Their conviction to prison in the late fall instigated large protests in Slovenia that lasted into the spring of 1989. For a Slovene public already antagonistic to federal power, there could scarcely have been a better lightning rod of solidarity or confirmation of their views.

Slovenes had not participated much in the Partisan army during the war, and as a result did not have a strong veterans' organization (which tended to be politically powerful in Yugoslav localities). But many Slovenes (such as the ranking admiral, Stane Brovet) had distinguished themselves in the officer corps. By the early 1980s, the Slovene government saw little need for a standing army or the strategic principles of the YPA for its defense. A largely mountainous republic in the western corner of Yugoslavia, Slovenia had resolved its border disputes with Italy and Austria in 1975. In one of its first contests with the federal government in the 1980s, over its right to define its own tax principles and to ignore the economic reform that removed limits on landholding, the republican government had altered the basis for calculating taxation on farmers so as to encourage those with smallholdings in the Alpine borderlands to remain on their land and keep viable the system of territorial defense.

The army leadership retreated during 1989 to a less combative and more conciliatory position on Slovene demands for local postings, language, nationally homogeneous units, and control over some weapons stockpiles. The damage, however, was done. The battle tarnished the army's legitimacy further and sealed Slovene resolve. In contrast to the situation in the other republics, conflict with the federal army unified Slovene public opinion behind the republic's Communist party and government leadership without destroying the seeds of political pluralism. The Slovene Communist party leadership, its popularity enhanced by its stand against the army and for civil rights, could thus distance itself from the declining authority of the federal party and was spared much of an anticommunist revolt within the republic in 1990.

The federal government was largely preoccupied with drawing up new IMF-conditioned stabilization restrictions as part of the second phase of debt rescheduling with Paris Club banks. Payments the previous summer had had to be postponed, for the first time since rescheduling began in 1983, for lack of cash. After failing to get a proposed three-year moratorium with Western banks and a reduction of debt servicing from 40 percent to 25 percent of foreign exchange earnings so as to prevent total economic collapse, Prime Minister Mikulić sought more IMF help. The October 1987 anti-inflationary demand restrictions were followed by an agreed IMF package—the "May Measures" of 1988. This plan defined three nominal anchors for bringing down inflation: limits on wages, on the money supply, and on public expenditures. The program also opened the economy to full foreign ownership rights and ended the system of workers' participation in firms, including the procedural protections against precipitate and large-scale unemployment.[27] By June all targets had been met except those for public expenditures, but inflation continued to spiral upward. It rose from 190 percent in 1986 to 419 percent in 1987 and 1,232 percent in 1988.[28]

At the same time, from July 1988 to January 1989, Milošević had turned his attention to issues that needed federal decision and began to use popular support for that purpose. Pursuing his tactics of appealing directly to the crowd, which he had used successfully in April–May 1987, Milošević turned the increasing number and size of popular demonstrations against austerity measures to his advantage and organized others to gain voting allies in Vojvodina and Montenegro as he had done in Serbia proper. These "meetings" (as they were called in Serbian) gathered thousands of Serbs in town squares to demand a political hearing. The demonstrations began with small groups of protesters from Kosovo, but expanded to crowds numbering from 10,000 to as many as 1 million. The demonstrators were often paid by their employers to attend, but increasingly came from among the unemployed, who needed a handout or had nothing else to do.

Milošević acknowledged his complicity in this increasing resort to "the street" to generate support by proclaiming an "antibureaucratic revolution"—the code word used throughout the Titoist period for revolution from below against established power and official privilege. By October 1988, when the LCY plenum was approving some reductions in the autonomy of Kosovo and Vojvodina, governments of the two provinces resigned in the face of recurring populist demonstrations and were replaced by governments comprising Milošević allies.[29] In November the two Albanians representing Kosovo province on the federal party presidency were removed from their posts by the provincial party committee. The moderate Montenegrin leadership withstood five months of mass demonstrations (many genuinely spontaneous, including the miners of the Nikšić steel mill) before it also resigned in January 1989.

Milošević's political use of crowds in 1988–89 was perceived by others as an aggression against the rest of Yugoslavia, but it did not in fact reflect his political support among the Serb population or Serbian views on the fate of the country. The majority still favored a liberal, Europeanist, and pro-Yugoslav option.[30] Yet because the number of those in the secure or independent middle stratum who would support economic reforms was falling sharply as a result of the serious economic decline, Serb liberals could not long sustain an opposition alone. To protect their nonnationalist option or restrain rising militancy, they had to form alliances and gain support from liberals in other republics. At a minimum, this meant doing so in Slovenia and Croatia, where economic interests in Western-oriented liberal policies were most substantial. An ever-larger portion of liberals in those republics, however, was antifederalist, increasingly nationalist, and unwilling to work with Serbs.

## Confrontation

This escalating internal dynamic was not independent of international circumstances, which were changing rapidly. The only power the federal government had independent of the republics was its ability to conduct business with international financial institutions and to act as an intermediary in access to foreign loans and capital markets. Slovene pursuit of national independence had gained speed after 1985, with correspondingly greater opportunities for trade, finance, and political association in Western Europe. In the course of 1988, Austrian economic overtures, such as the opening of four bank affiliates in the Slovene capital of Ljubljana, began to suggest real options to Slovenia if it chose to leave the federation. This realization gave Slovenia ever less reason to compromise on its sovereignty claims.

Whether consciously or not, the Slovene leadership became ever more emboldened. The parliament adopted the amended federal constitution on

November 25, 1988, but the Slovene government refused to participate in an all-Yugoslav referendum, insisting that this was a matter of republican parliamentary authority.[31] A mass meeting was called in Ljubljana on February 27, 1989, in support of the Albanian miners on strike at Stari Trg in Kosovo. Slovene Communist party leader Milan Kučan, other government officials, and leaders of various opposition groupings appeared on the podium. Appealing to the crowd, Kučan called the miners' strike a defense of AVNOJ Yugoslavia—the 1943 federal pact that had come to symbolize to Serbian nationalists the fractioning of the Serb nation. This was like waving a red flag. Kučan thus acknowledged that the miners' strike was political, signaled his solidarity with the Slovene protestors on the issue of Kosovar rights, and linked Albanian civil rights with the constitutional principle of territorial sovereignty and the right of secession claimed by Slovenes. As recently as the previous October, Slovenia had won federal concessions on the constitutional amendments in exchange for agreeing to the object of the miners' protest—the reduction of Kosovo's autonomy in the revised Serbian constitution. Now Kučan portrayed Serbia as the enemy of Slovene democracy, as witnessed by its repression of Albanian rights.[32] The act was a more open appeal to Slovene public opinion on the constitutional question than before. In aligning himself and the Slovene cause with Albanian human rights, Kučan was introducing an essential and useful confusion in the ideas of self-determination—an elision between rights of territorial governance and individual rights and political freedoms, between human rights and territorial autonomy. The shift was a critical transition in the meaning of nationalism and the process of disintegration in Yugoslavia and in the way that outsiders would perceive the issues at stake.

Most students of Yugoslav history agree that periods of crisis in both the first and the second Yugoslavias had been diverted by an alliance of self-interest between Slovenes and Serbs. By identifying Slovenia's claims for sovereignty with individual rights and shifting its focus from the federal government to Serbia as the generalized enemy of both, Kučan thus took a momentous step. His challenge to duel, allegorically, on the field of Kosovo was merely a proxy war (as the Slovene foreign minister after 1990, Dimitrij Rupel, later admitted) over the future of Yugoslavia. Mass public protests in Serbia erupted in March 1989, and the republic's parliament rushed adoption on March 28 of the constitutional revisions approved by the federal party the previous October, reducing the provinces' autonomy. In Kosovo, Albanian party leaders were arrested on March 2 on charges that they had organized the February 1989 miners' strike. Massive demonstrations called on the day that the Serbian parliament met to protest the constitutional changes turned violent, with twenty-two demonstrators and two policemen killed, and many injured. The federal state presidency responded by imposing emergency rule over Kosovo. Slovenia's representative voted in favor of this action, committing Slovenia to participation in the contingent of internal security forces sent immediately to the province.

Kučan's decision to go on the offensive against Serbia before Slovene crowds, mixing issues of sovereignty and individual rights, also played right into the hands of Milošević, whose speeches since April 1987 had attempted to equate the rights of individual Serbs with those of the nation and its unity and to identify Milošević himself as the protector of the Serb nation against external foes. Although Milošević's personal popularity was on the rise, Serbian public opinion was spread among competing political programs, and Milošević was being challenged by a number of openly anticommunist nationalists, many of whom were more outspoken against Albanians in Kosovo and in their support of Serbs outside of Serbia.

The confrontation spread to the mass media, where Slovene and Serb intellectuals traded ever more vicious accusations.[33] The constitutional fight among politicians at all levels began increasingly to adopt the language of nationalist intellectuals, as the politicians reached out openly to get public support of their programs and to establish themselves as personal leaders, independent of the party. The language of national exploitation, national integrity, and moral right portrayed these issues in ethical terms, replacing economic ideology and legalistic disquisitions on governments' economic property rights brought on by the severe restrictions of the stabilization program. This shift only escalated conflict further because it transformed conflict within elite circles over economic choices, which could temporarily be evaded with inflation, into nonnegotiable questions of identity. Campaigns to mobilize public support in terms of the morality of a cause could not easily yield to political compromise and instead stiffened resolve and stubbornness. Each leader began to portray his or her program (whether the federal prime minister, republican leaders, or activist intellectuals) as necessary to freedom or to the righting of wrongs, without regard to the consequences for others. Nor was it sufficient simply to claim the higher ground; the purpose was to get others to recognize one's claim—to be heard. The Slovenes and Serbs, in particular, talked most about being misunderstood by their critics and being victims of greater powers.[34]

Once the Slovene leadership identified Serbia as the main obstacle to an autonomous political life, it had accepted the consequences of its fight for sovereignty. In the early 1980s it had campaigned in favor of the weak federal powers and extensive republican rights of the 1974 constitution, on the grounds that it reflected the arrangement of the European Community and Reagan's "new federalism."[35] During 1989 Slovene leaders began to speak openly of confederation, making praiseworthy references to the U.S. articles of confederation. They proposed that Yugoslavia be transformed into a voluntary union of separate states cooperating on issues of mutual interest and with a monetary union sufficient only to facilitate the states' eventual inclusion in the European Community.

This direct attack on the federal government—essentially a declaration that it was irrelevant—came at the very moment when a new federal prime minister was assuming a mandate of radical change in the opposite direction. On December 30, 1988, the Mikulić cabinet had resigned en masse, accepting economic failure. Mikulić's successor, the representative of Croatia, Ante Marković, was handed the mandate of the IMF program, and, with the assistance of Western economic advisers, went immediately to work on the next stage of economic reform.[36] The goal was to remove the remaining limits on foreign ownership, management, and profit repatriation; to begin the process of privatizing public property; and to remove the political barriers to full market integration within Yugoslavia imposed by republican governments to protect their economic sovereignty. Politically, the state would remain federal, but reform of its economy and institutions would be based on functional integration appropriate to a market.

On January 19, 1989, Marković introduced legislation that ended the property rights of the socialist system. Gone were the legal limits on holdings and sales of land; job security; the restrictions on managers' freedom to hire and fire or obligation to consult the workers' council on wages and plans; the local government's solidarity wage fund; and the system of party approval for managerial positions and supervision over nominations for candidates for elected position. Struggling to increase foreign currency reserves for the assault on convertibility planned for the beginning of 1990, Marković ended the National Bank's ability to make automatic advances to exporters operating in state-negotiated trade in Council for Mutual Economic Assistance (CMEA) and third world markets.

Although these economic reforms were intended to revitalize the economy and the federal government, their economic consequences played directly into the shift made by Kučan in February and the civil libertarian language of Slovene nationalists: the argument that individual rights were a matter of republican protection, not Yugoslav. In attempting to create a market economy and a government appropriate to it, particularly under conditions of severe austerity, Marković was eroding the equal protections the socialist system afforded individuals regardless of the republic in which they resided and the functions assigned the federal government to maintain "brotherhood and unity" among the republics and nations. While further budget cuts and marketization threatened all those with public employment and intensified competition for the reduced number of political appointments, Marković's reforms threatened to eliminate completely the right of national equality guaranteed to constituent nations through rules on national and republican proportionality in government employment (the *ključ*), which had been eroding at the very top of the political system during the 1980s. In its continuing pressure for exports to Western markets, the federal government also abandoned its foreign trade role as intermediary between Eastern and Western markets. In this position it had given some protection to producers with fewer direct ties in Western markets, who tended to cluster in the southern republics.

There was even a hint that the reforms encouraged a sentiment growing within a faction of the Serbian leadership at the time in response to Slovene actions: that Serbia could do without Slovenia economically. With the effects of these reforms and the loss of Eastern markets and without Slovene competition for domestic consumers or governmental policy toward western markets, Serbia might even do better. Although Marković, Kučan, and Milošević had incompatible political goals, were they, unwittingly, working toward the same end in their desire to change the existing Yugoslav state?

## The International Context

Political change within Yugoslavia at this juncture was also receiving major impetus from changes in the international environment. The events in Eastern Europe appear to have had a particularly powerful impact on the Croatian Communist party, leading it to enter as an active player in the constitutional conflict. Following the central and east European pattern in the 1980s, the Croatian leadership was internally divided between reform and conservative factions. Despite the actively antifederalist positions of the Croatian parliament and its representatives at the federal level throughout the 1980s (even though the majority were party members), the party leadership in Croatia (like that in Hungary, Poland, and the German Democratic Republic) had been trying to slow social mobilization rather than capture it for a program of national assertion, as was happening in Slovenia and in Serbia. The events of 1988–89 in Eastern Europe made clear that the choice of silence and leaving the initiative to Serbia and Slovenia was no longer politically safe. Encouraged to be more assertive, the reform faction of the party maneuvered a shift, from the leadership's attempt to slow social mobilization by suppressing liberal intellectuals and potential leaders to an approach designed to manage the pace of change by opening a dialogue.

Until 1989, the stalemate in the party leadership between economic reformers and political conservatives was the result of very real concern that there not be a repeat of the nationalism that accompanied the westernizing, marketizing economic reform during 1968–71. For the conservative majority, the resurgence in segments of Croat public opinion of nationalist, anti-Serbian, and anti-army sentiments revived painful memories of the social and political explosions of that time and seemed predictably dangerous to social order. The danger was intensified by the rise of Serbian nationalism, which had not been a factor in the 1960s, and Milošević's appeals to Serbs (rather than strictly to Serbia), because 12.2 percent of the population of Croatia, about 583,680 people (in the 1991 census), identified their nationality as Serb. Although Serbs lived throughout Croatia, about one-third were concentrated in ethnically mixed, poorer regions in the interior. These regions were experiencing far harsher economic consequences of deindustrialization and had local industries that were poorly adapted to exports to western markets. Their economic base comprised railroads, heavy industrial sectors such as aluminum processing and steel, timber, and subsistence farming, all of which had recent memories of economic neglect and political discrimination under similar policies in the 1960s. Nonetheless, the debate over the constitutional revisions within Croatia made another division within the party leadership more salient in 1988–89—that between confederalists in sympathy with Slovenia and committed federalists. The explicitly antifederal positions of the Croatian parliament throughout the 1980s and the tilt within the party leadership toward the reformers as events in the region, particularly in Hungary, seemed to argue forcefully for a preemptive strategy had their effect by early 1989.

The party leaders began by reaching out to independent intellectuals and legal experts to help formulate constitutional initiatives. In February, they permitted a group of independent urban intellectuals from different republics, who allied to counteract the nationalist momentum and fight for democratic reform (the Association for a Yugoslav Democratic Initiative, or UJDI), to register as a political association in Croatia. They chose not to interfere, moreover, with the chain reaction of organizing that followed, with the formation of a Croatian Social-Liberal Alliance, a Green party, and two nationalist parties, the Croatian Democratic Union and the Croatian Democratic party. The police were apparently given no instructions about how to respond to requests for registration. Perplexed by the constitutional free-for-all, encouraged by a constitutional court ruling accepting the freedom of association, and unaided but not inhibited by legislative silence on procedures, they permitted the registration to take place.[37] This automatically opened discussions on the crucial attributes of political citizenship at the same time as the constitutional debate was redefining citizenship itself: who may organize, who may vote, and according to what rules and protections?

At the same time, the Croatian parliament was engaged in revising its constitution. Following an initiative taken already in Slovenia, the parliament rewrote the constitution's preamble, redefining the essence of the republic's sovereignty as residing in the Croatian people. This replaced the concept, embodied in the previous two constitutions, that each republic was a community of the people of the republic, which, in the case of Croatia, read: "the Croatian people in brotherly unity with the Serbs of Croatia."[38] For Serbs, the largest community of the other constituent nations of Yugoslavia who found their historical home or residence within the territory of the republic, this was a demotion in status of major consequence. They were to be granted the cultural and social rights of a minority but not the equal political status and full rights to self-determination that belonged constitutionally to nations in Yugoslavia. Croatia was the state of the Croatian nation, but the implication for rights of citizenship of those who were not Croat but who resided in Croatia, perhaps for many generations, became very uncertain.

Equally momentous, the Croatian government began to talk openly about confederation to replace the federal government, making it clear that it had chosen to side with Slovenia in the constitutional battle. By the summer of 1989 the alliance was made explicit when the two governments announced they would withdraw their internal security forces from the federal police action in Kosovo. The rapid opening to political debate and organizing after February 1989 revealed a broad range of partisan views in the Croatian public, including pro-Yugoslav and nonnationalist groups. At the same time, the shift taking place in Slovenia over national rights—melding issues concerning the republic's constitutional jurisdiction with issues concerning citizenship rights—was also occurring in Croatia. And in Macedonia, the same process was beginning with a parliamentary revision of the republic's constitution to redefine Macedonia as a state of the Macedonian nation. This revision similarly created minorities out of other constituent nations (including 2 percent Serbs) and nationalities (above all, the approximately 25 percent Albanians in its population). The only difference was that in Macedonia, the party leadership had not moved to the extreme confederal position as a consequence of declaring republican sovereignty, but remained pro-Yugoslav.

The Croatian party was not the only one to be influenced by foreign developments among actors of consequence in the ongoing conflict. Opportunities in central Europe after 1985, particularly Austrian economic initiatives, had clearly emboldened the Slovene party and government leadership. The simultaneous economic reforms and shift westward in the Soviet Union after 1985 were creating shock waves economically, strategically, and politically. Soviet President Mikhail Gorbachev apparently made clear in a visit to Belgrade in May 1988 that its Western orientation and budget cuts would mean a reduction of Soviet military or diplomatic aid in support of communist regimes elsewhere. Given Yugoslav neutrality, the result for Yugoslavs was not as momentous as it was in the rest of

Eastern Europe, but it did mean that conservatives in the party and the army could not automatically count on Soviet power in a showdown with an anticommunist movement. Of far more immediate consequence, however, was the momentous effect on American policy.

In April 1989, Warren Zimmermann, a new U.S. ambassador to Yugoslavia, with a new set of instructions, presented his credentials to the federal government. U.S.-Soviet strategic parity, the progress of arms and force reduction talks between the two blocs, and Gorbachev's reforms made Yugoslavia's role in NATO policy superfluous. For forty years Yugoslavia had had a special relationship with the United States, including the implicit guarantee of special access to Western credits to keep Yugoslavia's trade deficit afloat in exchange for Yugoslav neutrality and military capacity to deter Warsaw Pact forces from western Europe. Now, however, Yugoslavia was unnecessary to U.S. vital security. It was being moved from a special category in the U.S. State Department and international organizations, a category in which it stood alone or shared its status with southern Europe, and returned to its pre-1949 category, defined geopolitically, of eastern and southeastern Europe. No longer restrained by the priority on national security, the U.S. ambassador could now turn far greater attention to other issues of concern to his government, such as human rights. For Zimmermann, newly arrived from a post at the Conference on Security and Co-operation in Europe (CSCE), where the United States was pushing "Basket Three" issues (human rights), the repression of Albanian civil rights in Kosovo was an obvious target.

In May 1989 the foreign minister of Hungary, Gyula Horn, began the series of decisions that finally ended the cold war and the Warsaw Pact, by dismantling the barbed wire on the Austrian border. In August, as a result of secret negotiations with West Germany and the Soviet Union, he opened the western border for escaping East Germans. Austria's strategy to expand its sphere of economic influence eastward gained a major boost. On November 9 the Berlin Wall came down.

Yugoslavia's special relationship with Europe seemed to become obsolete overnight. Central Europeans rushed to join West European institutions as full members, and Yugoslavs had to enter this new competition on the same terms as the others, abandoning the habits of special treatment. Moreover, those terms were very different from those of the previous forty years, and they suggested a return to earlier definitions of geopolitics that could be very threatening to Yugoslavia. The revolutions in central Europe were already redefining the East on the basis of cultural criteria. Intellectuals and political dissidents in central Europe had been claiming since the early 1970s (and substantially aided by the Helsinki Accords of 1975) that their countries should be included in Europe because they had been members of "European civilization" for centuries. As early as 1989,

Western governments began to declare that the central European countries were better prepared to make the economic and political transition from socialism to capitalism and from East to West than those in southeastern Europe.

But this historico-cultural criterion, largely of Mitteleuropa, Roman Catholicism, and Habsburg tradition, cut straight through the center of Yugoslavia. It left a great gash undefined where the military border of mixed populations between Habsburg and Ottoman rule had been, and it reinforced the separatist arguments already being made by Slovene and Croat nationalists. These intellectuals began to talk about the existence of "two worlds" in Yugoslavia, and both groups proclaimed their greater preparedness for European membership as central Europeans, talk that had led LCY leader Stane Dolanc to warn in January 1985 would mean the destruction of Yugoslavia. If the new Western policy of "differentiation" continued, and the historico-cultural arguments prevailed so that Yugoslavia was moved from the head of the queue, where it had been since 1955, to an entirely second-class status, then it was clearly in the interest of those parts of Yugoslavia (such as the republics of Slovenia and Croatia) that could claim—on historico-cultural grounds (as the republics had been defined in 1943–45)—to belong to the first tier that they begin a campaign to persuade Europe of their deserved eligibility.

For citizens in the rest of Yugoslavia, who also yearned to be received as the full-fledged members of Europe that they considered themselves, after more than thirty years of partial integration, the only hope lay in keeping the country together and meeting the criteria for membership in European associations as a whole. The economic imperatives also intensified. With the change in U.S. policy and the collapse of the Warsaw Pact, the rationale for a substantial armed forces and for a strategy of self-reliance was unclear. Now the army's growing demands for imports, which had been financed largely through arms exports to the Middle East after 1985, were increasingly threatened by the effects of the Iran-Iraq war on oil, arms purchases, and payments of past due accounts. The collapse of trade with the East and increasing arrears on delivered contracts by Middle Eastern partners were devastating to the economies of Bosnia-Herzegovina, Macedonia, and, somewhat less, Serbia.

## Human Rights or Territorial Rights?

These international developments were more than just background to the escalating internal crisis in Yugoslavia. As direct influences on the perceptions, options, and constraints of individual participants, however, their message was full of conflicting signals. On the one hand, the driving force behind these constitutional reforms and redefinition of citizenship rights was still the economic policies designed to refinance and repay Yugoslavia's foreign debt, reorient trade to Western markets, and improve the country's capacity for international economic adjustment through marketization. This program of reform was still very much under the direction of the IMF and the refinancing and rescheduling package put together under U.S. initiative. But both were based on a special relationship, which made Yugoslav territorial integrity and independence a matter of strategic interest to the West, and that special relationship was rapidly coming to an end.

In addition, the shift of the U.S. embassy in Belgrade to concerns of human rights with a focus on Kosovo occurred only after the issue had become one of territorial autonomy, or even a separate republic, and after Slovene president Kučan had clearly linked human rights and national sovereignty in his reference to AVNOJ principles in February 1989. The rights to territorial self-governance on the basis of national self-determination or to national sovereignty were not at all clear in the case of the ethnic Albanians. Their constitutional classification as a nationality rather than a constituent nation made them ineligible for such rights, and this classification was a cornerstone of the Serbian position. The relation to Albanian human rights of the entire constitutional framework on self-determination would have to be addressed. The United States saw the situation in Kosovo as a problem created by the leadership in Serbia and in a way that perpetuated the confusion between human rights and sovereignty. The U.S. approach thus reinforced not only Kučan's position but also the increasingly open anti-Belgrade and anti-Serb rhetoric of Croatian nationalists and confederalists. A new round of diplomatic protests from the U.S. ambassador, from the State Department, and from some members of Congress, far from having their intended effect, brought powerful international backing to the Slovene arguments and the growing anti-Serbian coalition and at the same time bolstered Milošević's efforts to claim to best represent Serbian national interests, including the policy in Kosovo, and therefore added to his stature and position. By May 1989 the Serbian parliament elected Milošević president of Serbia (he was already leader of the party). The next December, in a popular referendum on the presidency, 86 percent of the population gave him their vote.

Milošević's victory over the Serbian League of Communists is often cited, because of the war and Western policy in 1991–94, as the beginning of the end of Yugoslavia. But this view was not shared by Western banks and governments, or by other departments of the U.S. government. They supported him because he appeared to be an economic liberal (with excellent English), who might have greater authority to implement the reform. Although Western governments were later accused of complicity, or foolishness in the extreme, Milošević was an economic liberal (and political conservative). He was director of a major Belgrade bank in 1978–82 and an economic reformer even as Belgrade party boss in 1984–86. The policy proposals commissioned by the "Milošević Commission" in May 1988 were written by liberal economists and could have been a leaf straight out of the IMF book.[39] It was common at the time (indeed into the 1990s) for Westerners and banks to choose "commitment to economic reform" as their prime criterion for supporting East European and Soviet leaders (as well as many in developing countries) and to ignore the consequences that their idea of economic reform might have on democratic development. The man who replaced János Kádár as leader of Hungary in May 1988, Károly Grósz, was similarly welcomed for the same profile of economic liberalism and political conservatism—what locals at the time called the Pinochet model. Moreover, despite the U.S. position on human rights, on the constitutional front, Serbian criticism of the stalemate created by consensual voting and de facto confederation and criticism of the economic irrationality of republicanized economies harmonized with the advice of the IMF and Western banks, many of the country's best economists, and large numbers of political liberals.

The interaction between the politics of constitutional reform in different republics, pushed along as well by the relation between constitutional changes and public behavior, escalated further in the summer of 1989, when republics were finalizing revisions of their constitutions. Croatia and Macedonia accompanied their declaration as national states with a permissive atmosphere of intolerant speech, extremist attacks, and instances of very real discrimination against and diminution of rights of, respectively, Serbs (in Croatia) and Albanians (in Macedonia).[40] The Croatian government, to cite an example of major consequence for the republic's move toward ever greater national sovereignty, did little to protect its citizens from a vicious outburst of anti-Serb terror in some mixed communities in Dalmatia and in the interior in the summer months of 1989, when Croat zealots smashed storefronts, firebombed homes, and harassed or arrested potential Serb leaders. In many parts of Croatia, Serbs were expelled from jobs because of their nationality, discrimination that was not limited to this early flare-up but increased over the following years. This and the anti-Serb innuendo of much Croatian political rhetoric not only aroused considerable fear, understandably, but also gave further credibility to Milošević's rhetoric, supported by the revisions taking place in the Serbian constitution, which committed Serbia to protect Serbs living elsewhere.[41]

Although Serbs in Croatia were not the only group in the country who were losing from the redefinitions taking place in economic, national, and citizenship rights, they were the next (after Albanians in Kosovo) to create a political movement around the principle of nationality and their loss of civil rights. Unfortunately, the first to organize protests against the Croatian government were Serbs who lived in areas of mixed population in the Croatian interior that were historically contested. Like demonstrations in Montenegro the previous year, these were blamed on Milošević, contributing further to his aura of omnipotence. The Serbs in this region, called the *krajina* because it had formed the military border between the Habsburg and Ottoman empires, not only considered this their historical home but also had a long tradition of bearing arms to defend those homesteads, which they were given in exchange for military service to defend Croatia and the Habsburg empire.[42] These Serbs wanted restoration of the same right to national self-determination that Croats had. When their petitions fell on deaf ears, they began to demand local autonomy.

The revised republican constitutions and rhetoric of national rights and interest therefore opened the question that the complex system of constitutional rights had been created to avoid and that Kučan had confused. Did rights to self-determination belong to peoples as nations or as republics, if a choice had to be made? The decision was made that these rights belonged to republics and their majority nation. Those members of nations that were now demoted from equal rights to the status of minority began, in areas where they lived in more ethnically concentrated communities, to demand regional autonomy.[43] Whether in Serbia, Slovenia, Croatia, or Macedonia, the move toward majority rule on national grounds led not to a movement for civil rights of minorities but to movements for territorial autonomy.[44] Why not write one's own rules rather than fight politically to remove imposed limits or end discrimination? This option was even more attractive in areas of mixed populations along republican borders, which cut across nationally identified groups and were historically contested. As Yugoslav political theorist Vladimir Gligorov observes, "Why should I be a minority in your state when you can be a minority in mine?"[45]

The still overriding politics of economic reform played into this buildup of mutual fears and self-defensive mobilization across the republics as a result of constitutional reforms. By 1989, the economic reforms had reached the stage of marketization and property rights with direct implications for individuals' rights to jobs, land, and welfare. This contributed to the personalization of political rhetoric and threat. Political campaigns for economic reform throughout the socialist period—and this most recent one was no exception—tended to identify obstacles to reform with people in political positions whose jobs were destined for cuts: the police, the army, holders of local political office, and the federal administration. Two conventional arguments justified such cuts. One was that these positions were held by "Partisan veterans"—people who had been rewarded politically for World War II service on the side of the antifascist resistance but who, it was assumed, did not have the requisite professional qualifications.

The other was the assertion of ethnic bias, based on the historical example of the interwar period and local traditions in the areas of the former military border, which equated political positions with Serbian power and Serbs.

Although this language of reform bothered little with reality and was supported by tendentious analysis, there was enough truth to the second accusation by the mid-1970s in some places to satisfy those it served.[46] The decentralization to the republics had gone so far that the prime jobs were no longer in Belgrade, leaving more federal jobs to local residents and especially immigrants, who were disproportionately of Serb nationality. The nearly continuous demand-cutting economic policy of the 1980s had also reduced the pay and privileges of political jobs in relation to market opportunities in the wealthier republics and some urban centers and to the salaries of professional and administrative positions in the public sector, which were indexed to local wage rates in production. The army's complaint that it could not attract Slovenes and Croats to military careers and fill senior officer quotas was a reflection of a larger phenomenon, as were the complaints of junior officers, a majority of whom were Serb for historical and economic reasons and who were restricted in opportunities for promotion by the quotas for national equality, against declining salaries and perquisites. Political connections had greater relative importance in managerial positions as unemployment rose among the educated strata after 1971. Such positions paid well only in relation to salaries in the poorer regions. A special problem existed in Croatia, moreover, because the 1972–73 purge of Croatian nationalists from government posts and the subsequent political alienation of many Croatian citizens had had the effect of increasing substantially the proportion of Serbs in local government jobs in many communities.[47]

Identifying Serbs as persons with antireform views and with political positions in the army, police, appointive office, and veterans' organizations, however, was blatantly unjust to the many proreform Serbs and to the many non-Serbs who held such public positions. It also made it far more difficult to debate the real employment consequences of the economic reforms and to form multiethnic political alliances for and against economic reform. Instead, it nourished the arguments of Serbian nationalists.

Reversing this ready-made anti-Serb catechism into the language of victimization took scarcely any political skill on Milošević's part. There was no better demonstration of Milošević's argument that Serbs outside of Serbia were also in danger than the threatening language prevalent in other republics. Serbs who did feel threatened by the most recent economic reform or who had felt tossed aside, politically purged, or economically excluded from Titoist Yugoslavia were consequently pushed further into the Milošević camp. There the theme was developing of "rectification" (for Serbia and Serbs everywhere) of the wrongs of the Tito era. One example of this approach was the ultranationalist call for redrawing internal borders that anticommunist Serbian nationalists began to popularize in the mid-1980s. Moreover, since many of the emerging Serbian leaders were, in fact, upwardly mobile migrants from peripheral areas (especially those in Bosnia-Herzegovina, Montenegro, and Croatia) who had used political avenues to overcome the disadvantages of their origins, the Serb nationalist argument of victimization reinforced prejudices on both sides. It gave authenticity to the nationalists' claims to represent those who felt marginalized and especially Serbs from outside Serbia proper. To Serbs' enemies, the prominence of these migrants among nationalist leaders contributed to the propaganda of two worlds and the leaders' cultural inferiority that magnified their threat.

The rhetoric of reform also reinforced the insulting effect of the campaign by pacifist or nationalist young people against the army at a time when its entire raison d'être was at stake, and when the Kosovo question and increasing threats to civil order confronted the Yugoslav minister of defense and general staff with an extremely delicate question. Could they interpret their constitutional obligation as it had been in the socialist period: to protect the constitutional order as well as the country's territorial integrity? Slovenia was challenging the definition of the army's duty; the prime minister was cutting the defense budget; and the changes in Soviet and U.S. foreign policy raised doubts about the army's external role and potential allies in protecting Yugoslav national security. In the Croatian *krajina*, some citizens of Serb identity began to secure arms for self-defense, and extremists laid plans to take control of local territorial defense forces and demanded arms from local YPA posts or army protection.

At the end of September 1989, Slovenia's parliament adopted constitutional amendments that initiated a process of dissociation from the Yugoslav federation, declaring the "complete and unalienable right" to "self-determination, including the right of secession" and specifying the conditions under which federal legislation and decisions would be invalid in Slovenia.[48] The federal party presidency responded to Slovenia's initiative in November, circulating a revised draft of the federal constitution to each of the republics for opinion.[49] Slovenia answered with an entirely different proposal, making official for the first time its plan for Yugoslavia to become a confederation of sovereign states.[50] The Bosnian party proposed a compromise formula that was more confederal than the constitution that would result from the current amendments, but that retained some essential powers for the federal government. The federal government, however, remained locked on its commitment to economic reform and the political reforms that were necessary to make the government executive more effective.

Rather than defend against the Slovene challenge to the political system, the Marković cabinet—in the spirit of economic shock therapy—ignored constitutional practice, whereby the federal party initiated major policy, and bypassed the consultation with and consensus from the republics considered obligatory. Instead, it presented its own proposal for functional integration in monetary and fiscal policy—including direct federal taxes and a federal agency for privatization—and sent it directly to the parliament.

## Conclusion

It was the reform-oriented Croatian prime minister Milka Planinc who first made formal exception to the constitutional principle of proportionality and parity to push through the IMF stabilization program of 1982–83. Political decisions still took place within narrow circles and involved substantial horsetrading among members of the same political party, and the liberal Serbian party leadership failed to win a change in federal voting rules from consensus to majority. This led Milošević in 1988–89 to encourage and exploit popular demonstrations where he could by using Serbian nationalism to replace sitting republican leaders with his own people. In contrast to Planinc, Milošević was playing by the rules, but he was attacking the spirit behind them and thus also contributing to the process of dismantling the corporatist voting rules and the system of power-sharing that the IMF and the federal cabinet had begun. His opponents labeled both actions anticonstitutional.

Milošević was responding in 1987–88 to pressures from a radicalizing parliament, and he was joined by the Croatian party leadership in 1989. Parliamentary actions in Croatia to define greater republican sovereignty during the 1980s combined with Slovene insistence on parliamentary sovereignty to deprive the federal government of ever more of its enforcement power and, by continuing to insist on consensus among republics for federal decisions, to prevent any decision with which one or the other disagreed. Although the anticonstitutional charge against Milošević's actions was made for his populist (some said demagogic) majoritarianism, what these critics really had in mind was his defiance of essential assumption of all the constitutions since 1945—the limits on Serbian power that they considered necessary to the security of less numerous Yugoslav nations. But such criticism reinforced the views of Serbian nationalists because the deeply felt injustice of these limits had given rise to much of contemporary Serbian nationalism, including support for Milošević by 1988. When Slovenia voted to pursue "dissociation" and a confederation, Milošević attempted, in December 1989, to organize mass meetings in

Ljubljana as well, to "bring the truth" of Serbian views to the Slovenes and simultaneously to warn Slovenia that there would be trouble if it continued on this path. The Slovene response was to close the border and to prohibit the demonstrations. The more open the expression of Serbian nationalism, the freer Croatian nationalists felt to jettison the restraint they had displayed since 1971–72 in expressing their views.

During 1988–89, the specific contests within republics and between republics and federal authorities began to interact at an escalating pace. Claims for control over economic resources or political authority were necessarily a denial of resources, authority, and rights to others. Protectionist economics and aggressive politics tended to incite defensive responses, and the interaction could escalate rapidly if not restrained. Popular protest excited counterprotests, and the rhetoric of national interest became increasingly nationalist in the sense of defining one group and its goals in opposition to another. The more assertive each republic became in its own political project, the more this impinged on politics in other republics and on the prospects for political and economic activities that crossed republican borders and ignored ethnic identity.

Despite the deterioration of the economy, social order, and political system over the decade 1979–89, there was also still room for major actors to pull back from confrontation, for political groups to emerge with an outcome other than militant nationalism, and for political management to divert the momentum of incompatible national interests and economic reform into a peaceful compromise and genuine political reform.

Some of the groups taking advantage of the moment did propose new political programs and made explicit efforts to reverse the nationalist momentum, giving hope to many that fears of civil war or military coup were exaggerated.[51] For example, at the extraordinary congress of the Montenegrin Communist party, called in April 1989, a program of political reform emerged with the support of new local groups such as the Committee for Human Rights, the Association for the Improvement of Democratic Processes, and the Association of Unemployed.[52] Privatization provided newspapers and journals an opportunity to become independent of the party and the state, leading in some cases to new voices for civil rights and liberties regardless of ethnicity and to the beginnings of investigative and watchdog journalism. Although strikes were mounting almost daily, workers in particularly large factories in Croatia and Serbia chose to take their demands to the federal parliament, reversing the focus of collective bargaining in local and republican enclaves and pushing the federal government into greater political accountability for its reforms.

Nevertheless, the balance of economic and political resources lay heavily on the side of destructive forces—those who preferred to push their own political goals regardless of the consequences for Yugoslavia. Unwilling to compromise in what they still treated as a bargaining game within one system where maximalist tactics by the most powerful were rewarded, politicians and politically active intellectuals were also using nationalist tactics to mobilize support within their republics. Other republics or the federal government were increasingly identified as external enemies to be defeated. At the same time the economic reforms of the federal government had become even more politically destabilizing.[53]

Chapter 5

# Interrupted Democratization: The Path to War

T he profound shift in possibilities within Europe in the fall
of 1989 intensified the conviction of economists and reformers gathered around the federal government of Ante Marković, the
liberal from Croatia, that the effectiveness of the program for global integration depended on speed, and that the demands by the IMF and World
Bank for radical transformation were correct.[1] On December 1 the Marković government announced a "shock therapy" stabilization program for
rapid convertibility of the dinar and an end to hyperinflation, to begin
mid-December. The program was similar to the approach introduced at
the same time in Poland, because Marković used the same advisers.[2]

Also with an eye to external events, but in this case the rapid demise
of communist parties in Eastern Europe, the Croatian party leadership
during the fall of 1989 submitted to pressure from opposition intellectuals
to hold competitive elections, but it would not yield on their demand to
organize political parties. But before elections could be held, the rapid pace
of political organizing and the victory of the reform (and potentially confederalist) faction within the Croatian party (and noted at the party's
congress in November by the addition of the label Party of Democratic
Changes) made this compromise obsolete. In December the Croatian party
leadership agreed to revolutionary concessions: the legalization of political
parties and free, multiparty elections to be held in April 1990. When mass
rallies organized by the opposition (and openly supported by the president
of the Croatian parliament) demanded more radical change along the lines
of Hungary and Poland, the party agreed to hold round-table talks with
opposition groups on a new electoral law.

The other pillar of the political conservatives in the country, the army
leadership (representing the nation of Yugoslavia), also sought to adjust to
the pace of change. While turning more conciliatory on Slovene demands
during 1989, it intensified its call for an extraordinary LCY congress on

the argument it had been pushing for some time, that to counteract the process of disintegration, the federal League of Communists needed to take a stronger lead.[3]

The Marković program had an uphill political climb, however. Even before the federal parliament adopted what was basically a program to remove political barriers to a market economy, these barriers were being reinforced by a political confrontation between Slovenia and Serbia. At the end of November 1989 the Slovene government asserted full constitutional sovereignty over its borders by forbidding the right to assemble, on threat of military force, to an association representing Serbs and Montenegrins from Kosovo who sought to hold a "meeting of truth" in Ljubljana on December 1 of about 40,000 people to inform Slovenes about events in Kosovo.[4] Political forces in Serbia responded tit for tat. The Serbian party's mass organization, the Socialist Alliance of Working People (SAWPY),[5] called immediately for a boycott, which the Serbian parliament secretly approved, of all Slovene goods in Serbia.[6] Slovenia then countered by refusing to pay its assessed share of the federal fund for underdeveloped regions and sent the monies earmarked for Kosovo directly to its provincial government, in defiance of the constitutional change in Serbia.[7] In response, Marković delayed the start of the shock therapy program until January 1, 1990.[8]

By the end of January 1990, the Extraordinary Congress of the League of Communists, which the YPA had been urging since 1986, convened. The army's objective backfired, however, when the congress became an opportunity for the next step in the Slovene goal of transforming the country into a confederation of states—in this case, by transforming the League of Communists into a confederation of "free and independent republican communist parties" and then accepting the end of its constitutional status by adopting multiparty elections.[9] The inchoate conflict over the form of the state was now an open confrontation among republican leaderships. When the Slovene delegation failed to win support for its idea of an "asymmetric federation," it walked out.[10] The Croatian party leader, Ivica Račan, took the position that his delegation should abstain until the Slovenes returned. The congress split in two. One bloc combined Serbia, its two provinces, and Montenegro, and was led by Serbian President Slobodan Milošević, who insisted that the congress continue without the Slovenes and recalculate voting procedures accordingly. The other bloc was formed by the newly assertive Croatian party with the two other republics (Bosnia-Herzegovina and Macedonia) and the army. When the Slovenes did not return, these four voted for adjournment.[11]

This sealed the fate of the party, whose privileged constitutional position rested on such weak soil that it succumbed to the deadlock over the constitution for the common state it had created in 1943–45 and to the willingness of Slovenia to go its own way.[12] To make things worse, within days of the congress called to resuscitate the party, the federal state presidency ordered the army—whose legitimacy had depended on the League of Communists—to establish martial law in Kosovo on the assessment that civil war was imminent. The army's actions against demonstrations in several towns—including one involving 20,000 people in the capital, Priština, demanding free elections and the release of political prisoners, on the first two days of February—left twenty-eight dead and ninety-seven injured and further compromised the neutrality upon which its own authority would have to be rebuilt in the eyes of its opponents. A debate unresolved since the nationalist events in Croatia in 1971 over the role of the army to preserve internal order was, under the threat of system collapse, bound to revive and to escalate the growing political confrontation. Subsequently, on February 4, Slovenia followed through on its pledge of the previous summer to withdraw its unit of the federal police forces, which were already stationed in Kosovo. Croatia did the same.[13] The consequence was to expose both the army and the Albanian population to a federal policy that would by default become defined by a Serbian voting majority and to concede the very power over its provinces that Serbia sought and that Slovene party leader Milan Kučan had opposed rhetorically to gain popular support at home.[14]

To outsiders, Yugoslavia continued to give the appearance of a functioning state, from the visits of foreign bankers, businesses, IMF teams, and diplomats to the daily pilgrimage of children to school. Warnings of civil war or an impending military coup had been made so often that they were losing much of their currency. Even the collapse of the Communist party at the federal level seemed no more momentous than the revolutions taking place throughout eastern Europe. Yet the existing system was ceasing to function. While politicians and parliaments bent on sovereignty or radical change were challenging the legitimacy of the federal government and party, all the less visible bonds that hold any society together were collapsing—the rules of mutual obligation, the checks and balances, the equilibrating mechanisms, the assumption of minimal security of one's person and status. In the contest of wills over economic and political reform, still dominated by the two extremes of the Marković reforms and Slovene dissociation from Yugoslavia, there was no longer any uncontested authority, only competing authorities of circumscribed legitimacy and uncertain legality. The political opening and free-for-all also encouraged others to pursue ambitions of political power and avenge perceived wrongs. The more the system dissolved, the greater was the incentive to seize the moment—such as the millennialism of certain Croatian nationalists who began to speak of the first and possibly last chance, after 1,000 years, to establish their statehood—and there were ever fewer restraints to prevent the situation from escalating out of control. It was in this atmosphere that democratic elections were held.

## Democratization

We tend to think of competitive elections in terms of long-functioning, stable democracies, as a way for citizens to choose their government among competing parties and as a set of rules to guarantee the conditions necessary to that choice among a plurality of options—including the right to dissent and the right of defeated parties to compete again—what political theorist Robert Dahl refers to as being "willing to lose."[15] But when such elections originated in the eighteenth-century doctrine of popular sovereignty, they were an elite project whereby local gentry reached out for the people's support in their struggle against the crown. In the spring of 1990, elections in Slovenia and Croatia became such a vehicle for local republican politicians.

The demand for elections did not originate from popular pressure, but with politicians seeking more political power over their territories and opposition intellectuals seeking more political influence over the course of events.[16] Moreover, one should not confuse either elections or increasing participation in mass demonstrations and civic associations with a democratic system. Democracy means a set of formal rules for ending a conflict over contestants or policies peacefully because those who lose are willing to accept the choice. They go along because the rules and methods for deciding the conflict guarantee them the chance to continue to participate and win at another round, and the costs of the alternative are greater.[17] By 1989–90 the Slovene political and cultural elite was becoming convinced (rightly or wrongly) that Serbian nationalism would create a system in which it would be worse off than it would be alone. Rather than seek to build a coalition within the country for an alternative political system or for a coordinated movement toward confederation, the Slovene leadership took heart in foreign encouragement for Slovenia's position and instead refused to participate in federal institutions, sought to protect Slovenia's internal order against alternatives, and threatened to exit if others did not agree to their position.[18] Slovenia's democratic elections were an instrument of this strategy.

The goal of multiparty elections had gained momentum, ironically, with the project of pro-Yugoslav, reform-communist, and nonparty intellectuals in Croatia to create an alternative within Yugoslavia to the radical projects of Slovene and Serb nationalism. Moreover, Croatian Communist party leaders were still confident of victory in January 1990, when they insisted in the round-table talks that the electoral law enact a majority two-round system instead of the proportional representation sought by opposition parties and adopted by Slovenia. By the time of the elections in April–May 1990, however, the federal party had bloodlessly collapsed, and the federal government's reform project had legislated an end to the entire system of socialist self-management. The resulting electoral competition among political and cultural elites brought into the open political arena all manner of persons who had been or felt excluded from political life—persons jailed for incitement to nationalist hatred, purged from the party for ideological views too liberal or too conservative, resentful toward real or imagined discrimination for not being a party member or a certain nationality, and political or economic émigrés awaiting a chance to return. To the issues and language of the ongoing constitutional struggle, they introduced anticommunism.

Despite Prime Minister Marković's expectations that federal elections would follow republican elections at the end of the year and would demonstrate the popular mandate for change, Slovene initiative defined the political momentum. Slovenia had insisted successfully that republican elections occur first, and it continued to veto any countrywide expression of preferences, from a proposed federal referendum on the constitutional amendments at the end of 1988 to a referendum on the fate of the country scheduled in 1990. The first democratic elections were thus not the opening of choice for Yugoslavs but its closure.[19]

The multiparty elections in Yugoslavia in 1990, rather than being a regular instrument of popular choice and expression of political freedom or the transition to a democratic system, became the critical turning point in the process of political disintegration over a decade of economic crisis and constitutional conflict. Despite the propaganda surrounding the wars of Yugoslav succession that began the next year, however, the voters did not make a clear choice for nationalists and independence. They did push the nationalist momentum further, not because of the voting results themselves, but because of the use politicians made of them.

Although the elections were to choose republican legislatures and executives, those who won fought on a nationalist platform, combining successfully the many different issues at stake into the negative symbol of Belgrade and of Serbs. To the Slovene linkage of its national sovereignty with individual liberty, the campaign in Croatia of right-wing nationalist Franjo Tudjman added "decommunization," linking a vote against the Communist party to a purge of persons in any way associated with the former regime. In one case, the leader of the Slovene League of Communists, and in the second, a former communist general, took their victories as a mandate for independence, even though neither received even 50 percent of their republic's vote.

The republic of Slovenia held elections on April 8 and 22. Croatia followed suit on April 22–23 and May 6–7. The other four republics did not go to the polls until November and December. Just as in central Europe, there was a proliferation of political parties contesting elections—seventeen in Slovenia, thirty-three in Croatia. Given the mandate claimed by the victors, it is particularly notable that voters did not, in fact, give nationalists a majority. The nationalist vote was strongest in Slovenia, but even there the party that had initiated and pushed Slovene sovereignty and that was the largest vote-getter—the Communist party (renamed the Party of Democratic Renewal)—received only 17 percent of the vote. Its leader, Milan Kučan, won the presidential election with 44 percent of the vote in the first round and 58 percent in the second, but the government was formed by an electoral coalition, DEMOS (Democratic-United Opposition of Slovenia), of seven opposition parties. Together they gained 55 percent of the vote on an anticommunist and pro-independence platform, but individually they took from 3.5 percent to 13 percent of the electorate.[20]

In Croatia the radical nationalist, anticommunist, and anti-Serb campaign of Franjo Tudjman and his party, the Croatian Democratic Union (HDZ, the "party of all Croats in the world"), won only 41.5 percent of the vote in the parliamentary election, but was the beneficiary of the electoral law that the reform communists (renamed the Croatian League of Communists/Party of Democratic Changes) had written for themselves.[21] Based on single-member districts and two rounds, this winner-take-all system translated 41.5 percent into 58 percent of the seats (205 of 356 seats in three chambers, including 54 out of 100 seats, or 67.5 percent of the powerful lower house). The League of Communists in alliance with smaller left-wing parties took 37 percent of the vote, and a centrist coalition took 18 percent. Even so, despite protest from his party's core, Tudjman chose to form a grand coalition of all parties except the Serbian Democratic party, which left the parliament on May 20 after talks to find an accommodation with Tudjman and his nationalist position failed.[22]

Just as the Croatian League of Communists was unable to retain control of a political process engendered by events elsewhere, from Slovenia to Serbia to eastern Europe, the announcement by Slovenia and Croatia that they would hold multiparty elections forced the remaining republics to do the same. Quite apart from their social or political conditions, the process of self-organization, political differentiation, and redefinition of individual and national interests that had been going on at its own pace for a decade in Slovenia now had to occur within months in the other republics. In addition—even before the November–December 1990 elections in Bosnia-Herzegovina, Macedonia, Montenegro, and Serbia—the new Slovene parliament voted on July 2, 1990, to fulfill the campaign promise of the DEMOS coalition and declared complete sovereignty.[23] In an interview three days later with the Italian newspaper *La Repubblica*, the new Slovene foreign minister, Dimitrij Rupel, announced, "Yugoslavia no longer exists."[24]

The Croatian parliament moved quickly as well, immediately amending its republican constitution to ratify its view of the electoral results and declare "political and economic sovereignty" over Croatian territory. It also adopted the historical symbols of Croatian statehood (coat of arms and flag) that had last been used by the fascist state in 1941–45, renamed streets to honor leaders in that state, instituted a loyalty oath required of Serbs holding any public employment in the republic, and made the use of the Latin alphabet obligatory in all official proceedings.[25] In August the new government, under President Tudjman, began to send units of the interior security police (MUP) into districts of mixed Croat-Serb population to disarm and replace local police and reservists of Serb nationality with Croats. In towns of the *krajina* (military border), such as Knin and Glina, shots were exchanged between Croatian government forces and local citizens, among them some autonomists beginning to organize resistance.[26] All this further antagonized relations between the Croatian government and the Serb population, causing tensions that had been brewing for a year to escalate dangerously and Serb militants to intensify their activities to win over local Serbs in areas bordering Serbia and Bosnia. On July 26 the leader of the Serbian Democratic party in the *krajina*, Jovan Rašković, announced that "in the event that Croatia secedes, the Serbs in Croatia have a right to decide in a referendum with whom and on whose territory they will live."[27] The Croatian government declared that any such referendum would be illegal. The Kosovo situation was to become a pattern.

Simultaneously in Serbia, the assembly called a referendum July 1–2 to resolve a conflict between the government and opposition parties in their round-table talks over whether multiparty elections should follow or precede the adoption of a new republican constitution. The government won when 96.8 percent of those voting chose to delay elections, but the result was to escalate the conflict with Kosovo Albanians who responded overwhelmingly to their leaders' call to boycott on the grounds that the government aim was to end Kosovo's autonomy before democratic elections.[28] On July 2, the Albanian delegates in the Kosovo assembly declared political sovereignty for Kosovo as an independent unit of equal status as a nation in the federal system. The Serbian government responded on July 5 by dissolving the Kosovo assembly, beginning a thorough purge of Albanians in government posts and of the media, and at the end of September by enacting the constitution that included the approved revocation of autonomy, reducing the status of its two provinces to little more than municipalities.[29] In preparation for the elections, party leader and Serbian president Milošević abandoned the cadre-based League of Communists in July and created a mass party, the Serbian Socialist party, by joining his faction of the Serbian LCY with its affiliated mass organization (the Socialist Alliance of Working People of Serbia). Like Croatia, Serbia opted for a majoritarian electoral system based on single-member districts instead of proportional representation, with two rounds, and declared the republic sovereign. Serbia also enacted a directly elected presidency, before the election, which would magnify the homogenizing and leader-centered effects of the electoral laws.

Although aware by late spring 1990 that to save his program he would have to join this electoral bandwagon, Prime Minister Marković was one of the last to respond. On July 29 he announced the creation of the only all-Yugoslav party, the Alliance of Reformist Forces of Yugoslavia. Four months later, a coalition of retired army generals and some federal officials of the former League of Communists tried to revive the federal party as well by creating a new League of Communists–Movement for Yugoslavia (*Savez Komunista–Pokret za Jugoslaviju*).

Elections took place in the remaining four republics at the end of the year. In Montenegro and Serbia, communists-turned-nationalists or anticommunist nationalists could not as easily combine the nationalism of republican rights with anticommunism into the negative symbols of Belgrade and Serbs, which had formed the basis for building broad coalitions of opposition forces in the other republics. In both, the renamed communist parties won handily. In Montenegro, the League of Communists won 83 of 125 seats in the parliament, and its leader, Momir Bulatović, won 76 percent of the popular vote for president. Serbian President Milošević combined a call for political change to a "modern federalism" and democratic voting rules with a conservative sedative to ease the pain of economic reforms in the slogan, "With Us There Is No Insecurity."[30] His main rival, the anticommunist Serb nationalist Vuk Drašković of the Serbian Movement for Renewal, won only 16 percent of the vote, and his party, only 19 seats in the parliament of 250. The single-member system gave Milošević and the SPS, like Tudjman and the CDU in Croatia, control of 78 percent of the parliament with votes from only 47 percent of the electorate (although 65 percent of those voting, thus substantially greater support than Tudjman's CDU received). The Albanian population in Kosovo boycotted the election, declaring their opposition to Belgrade policy by refusing to participate. The effect, however, was to hand representation of Kosovo districts to the SPS and Milošević and to increase his majority.[31]

In Macedonia, the electorate spread so broadly over twelve of the twenty parties fielding candidates that it took months to form a coalition government. The electorate split largely into three tendencies: a Macedonian nationalist, pro-independence, right-wing coalition of four parties—the Macedonian National Front—led by a contemporary version of the revolutionary terrorist organization of the first decades of the century (the Internal Macedonian Revolutionary Organization–Democratic Party for Macedonian National Unity [VMRO-DPMNE]), which alone won 37 of 120 seats (31.7 percent) in the unicameral legislature; the pro-Yugoslav, but increasingly pro-independence, center-left League of Communists–Party of Democratic Change, which won 30 seats (25.8 percent). Against the first, Albanians in Macedonia chose to create and vote for separate ethnic parties, the largest of which, the Party for Democratic Prosperity, gained twenty-four seats. And the pro-Yugoslav tendency within the center-left was temporarily strengthened by the nineteen seats (eight in coalition) won by Marković's Alliance of Reform Forces and by the parliament's choice of president, long-time LCY leader Kiro Gligorov.[32]

In Bosnia-Herzegovina, forty-one parties organized. The first to organize was a Muslim party—the Party of Democratic Action (SDA)—led by Alija Izetbegović.[33] The other two constituent nations of the republic, Croats and Serbs, created branches of parties in Croatia—the HDZ, by then the ruling party in Croatia, and the Serbian Democratic Party (SDS), representing Serbs outside of Serbia already active in the Croatian *krajina*.[34] Although the collection of parties formed out of the republic's LCY (the League of Communists—Party of Democratic Change, the Democratic Socialist League, and the Democratic League) and Marković's Alliance of Reformist Forces won seats in the parliament (eighteen and thirteen, respectively), the election results read more like a census of national identities in the socialist period. The three national parties gained votes and seats almost directly proportional to individuals' choices of national identity in the 1981 census (the SDA, 33.8 percent; the SDS, 29.6 percent; and the HDZ, 18.3 percent). They formed a grand coalition to defeat the reform communists and Marković's reformists on the second round, and agreed to govern in a trilateral power-sharing arrangement patterned after the federal government: a collective presidency of two members for each nation and one representative for everyone else (a post revealingly labeled minorities) and the distribution of cabinet and other top positions according to the parity principle of the socialist system based on equal representation according to nation, rather than representation proportional to number.

While democratic elections thus brought to power in each of the republics—except arguably Montenegro—politicians who appealed to voters on nationalist grounds, the substance of that nationalism varied widely from one republic to the next. In each case, it reflected the two layers of the constitutional struggle simultaneously, republic and nation: national self-determination of the republics in relation to the federal government, and the political rights of constituent nations to self-determination regardless of their members' republic of residence. But no party claiming an independent state had a majority; all formed coalition governments. And within a republic there were varieties of nationalists: former communists or anticommunists; those representing the majority nation of a republic, another constituent nation (Serbs, Croats, and Muslims in Bosnia-Herzegovina; Serbs in Croatia), or a nationality seeking political representation as a nation (Albanians in Kosovo and Macedonia); and a range of parties from secessionists to nonnationalists that were republic-firsters, such as the Social Democrats in Slovenia or Croatia.

Because the next elections were not held until after the country dissolved, there is no way to know what voters themselves intended with their vote in 1990. In Croatia, for example, parties spread along the full ideological spectrum. Was the 42 percent vote for Tudjman a vote for right-wing views, a vote expressing Croatian identity, or a vote against Yugoslavia? What was an urban Jew or Serb living several generations in Croatia to choose?

Voting in stable, multiparty democracies is the occasion for individuals to express their economic interests, social identities, and partisan loyalties in a choice for individual candidates or parties. Such identities and interests, however, were anything but stable at the time in Yugoslavia. In fact, the Marković reforms in 1989 had begun to raise questions about people's economic and social identities, which were primarily defined in relation to their landholdings, their coworkers and work communities, and even their social status and standard of living, because these were largely defined in turn by people's employment. The revision of republican constitutions in 1989, even before the promulgation of new constitutions in 1990, had redefined the meaning of national identity and its accompanying political rights, transforming people who were not of a republic's majority nation into the status of minorities. The political rhetoric of economic reform and developments in Europe affected essential parts of individuals' cultural identity independent of their nationality that included transnational sympathies—such as with West, East, or Middle East; more commonly, a mixture of all three; or generally cosmopolitan or locally oriented. And the policies of the economic reform already had very clear implications for local industries and jobs. Even in long-stable democracies where political identities with particular political parties tend to be relatively stable over time and associated with social or community identities, moreover, it is not uncommon for individuals' partisan identities to differ between issues of domestic policy and foreign policy, producing quite unexpected electoral results when a vote is defined specifically in terms of external relations.[35]

A vote in countries with market economies and an extensive private economic and civic sphere is only one of a number of ways of expressing

political preferences. In socialist states the expression of political preferences is a small, relatively insignificant part of individual identity and
public action (outside of the overriding distinction of party membership).
No political parties campaign for individuals to choose among their many
separate loyalties to schoolmates, professional and work colleagues, neigh-
borhood, village or city, region, republic, and country, or, in the Yugoslav
case, factions in workplace economic decisionmaking. The political pack-
aging of such multiple loyalties into a single party identification in democratic systems had not yet occurred. The tally across Yugoslavia in 1990
suggested that most people actually voted in terms of the politically relevant
categories of the socialist system that had shaped their identities, not in
terms of their preferences for the future. They were, after all, presented
electoral choices in terms of the existing system: within the republic of
their residence only; for or against the one political party in which one held
membership—the League of Communists—and its regime; and according
to criteria of economic distribution and social status—employment (occupation, education, and private or public sector), age, and national identity (the other officially recognized political identity next to party membership in the socialist period).

The campaigns in 1990 were largely focused around symbols and
personalities, however. This was a reflection in part of the primary role
played by intellectuals in the politics of the transition (a trait common to
all states exiting Communist party rule). But it also was an inevitable
outcome of the limited amount of time to organize. Not only did voters
not have the time to shape new political identities in terms of the interests
and loyalties appropriate to multiparty, parliamentary democracy, but politicians who might wish to appeal to such particular interests and campaign on specific governmental programs and policies had very little time
to build campaign organizations and learn the skills of electoral competition. They could create associations between individual voters and partisan
identities by means of the labels they chose—liberals, social democrats,
democrats—but the connection between particular policies and constituents' interests was yet to be made. Even those who had access to the
organizational and information network of the Communist party and of
the police had no advantage—and in some cases, a distinct disadvantage—
in making the appeals necessary to win broad-based electoral support.

In a world of competing symbols and personalities at a point of
political transition, nationalism has a particular advantage. The message is
simple and can be largely emotional. It relies on the familiar, using little
time or money to develop a new political language appropriate to the new
times of democratic governance or to communicate and explain the complexities of policy for an entire social and economic transformation. Nationalist appeals thus provide the easiest route to political visibility for

politicians without established constituencies and party organizations and makes no demands on first developing party platforms.

As an alternative to the immediate regime, nationalism reaches into the nonpolitical aspects of contemporary life—cultural identities, historical memories, alternative social networks, and organizations that are already present in society, such as the churches that had established a modus vivendi with the communist regimes. Primarily a political persuasion of the right, it is a ready-made receptacle for an anticommunist juggernaut against the existing regime, gathering into its fold all forms of reaction— from those in genuine opposition, those politically excluded from the previous regime, to opportunists—regardless of their substantive policy positions. Parties of orientation to the left of center, such as socialists or social democrats, can more easily be tarred with guilt by association with the previous regime. In contrast to left-of-center parties, liberals and nationalists have the additional resources of foreign assistance. The rhetoric of the cold war anticommunist campaign and the enthusiastic influx from Western countries of anticommunist émigrés or their money,[36] often with political revenge in mind, were major resources for those running on a campaign against former communists. For Western governments and media, distinctions among the antisocialist forces were not important.

The electoral disadvantage of renamed communists, socialists, and social democrats in this first period of transition away from socialism can also be reduced, however, by adopting a national posture. In the Yugoslav case, where election campaigns occurred first within the republics, it was even necessary to cater somewhat to the nationalism of republican nationalism so as not to be vulnerable to the easy charge of national disloyalty and to compete successfully against the advantages of nationalist rhetoric. Moreover, control over the resources of the state—the courts, police, and army; the power to write electoral laws and define property rights—count most in the revolutionary period. Statist parties, which aim explicitly at these resources, or ally with the police apparatus and local networks of power whether of the left or right, are better placed to win the next election as well.

For all these reasons, the first multiparty elections in Yugoslavia were scarcely a clear mandate for anything. The one clear statement was that of the confusing, halfway house of political transition. Nonetheless, liberals and nonnationalists who supported Prime Minister Marković's Alliance of Reformist Forces were genuinely surprised, even devastated, at its poor showing and the popular vote for nationally defined parties instead. But was this a vote against Yugoslavia?

The problem of the 1990 elections was clearly the lead taken by Slovenia and Croatia in holding elections. Noncommunist parties therefore organized first within the republics, and voters were asked to express a partisan identity first within their republics. Marković's countrywide Alliance of Reformist Forces was created, in fact, to run candidates in federal elections at the end of the year. Nonetheless, decentralized federations and locally based political parties are not incompatible with functioning democracy, as the origins of the U.S. party system demonstrates. The issue was whether alliances would form among political parties from the separate republics, and begin the creation of a new Yugoslav multiparty political arena to replace the League of Communists. Could a genuine political transition take place in which citizens were no longer represented outside their republics by their republican governments and state parties, or would competition over legislation and economic policy remain a matter confined to the republics and mediated by their officials in federal or interrepublican forums? Was the only alternative a political organization along ethnonational lines, such as had begun, or could a rich associational life develop according to many interests that ignored republican frontiers and the vertical hierarchies of the socialist period?

The focus on personalities in the emerging new politics also characterized analyses of its faults and weaknesses. Particularly vulnerable to criticism within the country was Prime Minister Marković, blamed for being too weak a leader. Others focused blame on the Serbian president, Slobodan Milošević, for being too powerful. Far more influential, in fact, on political developments were two characteristics of the process of transition, regardless of personalities: the political aspects of the economic reform package Marković was implementing, and the rapid pace of change once Slovenia moved openly to dissociate with its constitutional amendments of September 1989. This kept the issue of republican rights—national sovereignty—uppermost at the same time that the destruction of institutions and norms—which was moving at a faster pace than their construction—gave greater weight to factors of personality, making even small political missteps or personal weaknesses potentially very costly.

Despite the many hopes attached to the federal reform program within the country and abroad, Marković's precipitate declaration of a new proposal for federal restructuring to accompany marketization in response to Slovenia's confederal proposal in November–December 1989, without preparing the ground politically in advance, was naive. The most solid support for westernization and liberalization in the country for reasons of economic self-interest was in Slovenia (so much so that when Marković's reform began to fail, its primary foreign adviser, Harvard economist Jeffrey Sachs, moved rapidly to advise the Slovenes instead). But it was also in Slovenia that the strongest objections to the political and constitutional aspects of the Marković program were to be found. It was these concerns that were overriding, leaving Slovenia to obstruct the program at every point that one might have expected support. In this constitutional contest between the federal and Slovene governments, moreover, the Slovene leadership had overwhelming popular support within its republic.

The Marković government also had no political base of its own. It bypassed the weak federal party in its constitutional proposals even before the extraordinary congress of January 1990. Its authority depended entirely on its ability to persuade international authorities to support its reforms, and this foreign support was rapidly dwindling toward symbolic gestures with little real economic or political backing. Moreover, sharing the ideology of most economic reformers and their advisers in the post-communist transition period, Marković gave priority to success in the economic realm. In his view economic reform would save the country, and not the reverse. Rather than expend effort on building a party organization, an electoral political coalition, or political reform addressed to new kinds of conflict and perceived injury, his strategy was to use economic policies to lay the social base (such as a middle class and private enterprise) for a market economy and democracy, even though this would take many years to yield political results and, in the short run, implied even greater uncertainty and pain.

But the political consequences of the economic reform, at least in the short run, ran against it. The intellectuals and professionals who might have articulated support for reform held positions on the public payroll, and since the approach to macroeconomic stabilization of the IMF and Sachs required further cuts in public expenditures and upward limits on the federal budget deficit, they would eventually have to orient their activism, choose loyalties, and position themselves politically within the republic and locality that paid their salary. Despite the reform's objective to reduce the ownership role of republican governments in the economy, it did nothing to dismantle their responsibility, or that of localities, for welfare and employment.

To the majority who would face potentially serious social and economic consequences, the federal reforms failed to speak at all. There was no consideration of social policy even though the laws implementing reform instituted managerial prerogatives over employment and wages, the possibility of bankruptcy, and a market for land, and put a precipitate end to worker participation in firms and the solidarity wage funds of the local government. All the social supports for subsistence in the former system were being eliminated, and unemployment continued to rise while incomes fell. Without even a gesture toward short-term safety nets from federal authorities, all citizens would have to depend on the economic policies and budgetary expenditures of their communes and republics and thus focus their political energies and loyalties there.

Anyone with political aspirations or hoping to win a popular following would thus be more inclined to seek power at the republican level, and would focus their fight on controlling the revenue-yielding assets on their territory rather than changing policy at the federal level. Because the jobs subject to unemployment were all public sector jobs—industrial workers in the public sector of the economy, farmers dependent on budget subsidies, and civil employment in administration, services, and government—the incentive was even greater than in market economies to seek political autonomy so as to have power over the key economic resources of the budget, fiscal policy, and investments on a territory.

Moreover, in July 1990, when Slovenia and Croatia declared their sovereignty and intention to pursue a confederation and before he decided to create a political party to represent reform views, Marković even introduced an economic reformers' concept of democratization: a program to give shares in firms directly to managers and workers, which he called privatization from below. But this was recognized for what it was: another way to reduce wages and salaries, in this case by giving workers and employees a share in potential profits down the road, and thus an indirect way to restrict the money supply and aggregate demand further. Furthermore, it was the republican governments that owned all large and medium enterprises slated for privatization, and democratically elected governments were even less inclined to give up such political control over the economy than were their socialist predecessors, preferring to renationalize first and then delay—as Tudjman in Croatia did immediately and Slovenia did in 1992.[37] Nor did giving workers shares in firms erase the real goal of privatization: to give managers the power to decide whom to hire and fire, and to hand the power to evaluate firm insolvency, bankruptcy, and the price of now salable land over to the impersonal forces of market.

Instead of working against the growing assertiveness of economic and political sovereignty by the republican governments, the economic reform gave it additional momentum. Still, as a person, Marković was the most popular politician in all of Yugoslavia during the spring of 1990, above Kučan, Tudjman, and Milošević (see table 5-1). Moreover, there were many pro-Yugoslav liberals, reformists, and undeclared citizens who would immediately benefit from the economic reform, or who could foresee its long-term benefits. They looked increasingly to Marković as their only hope against the republican leaders and parliaments and the consequences of social disintegration. But these people were widely dispersed among urban centers in the various republics, and there was no political avenue to express support for Marković or the federal government until the end of July 1990—after the newly elected governments in Slovenia and Croatia declared their sovereignty.

In the first six months of the shock therapy program, when only Slovene and Croatian elections had occurred, the results were spectacular in bringing down inflation and improving the trade balance. From an

TABLE 5-1.  *Support for Marković, Spring 1990*

| | |
|---|---|
| Yugoslavia | 79 percent |
| Bosnia-Herzegovina | 93 percent |
| Vojvodina | 89 percent |
| Macedonia | 89 percent |
| Croatia | 83 percent |
| Serbia | 81 percent |
| Slovenia | 59 percent |
| Kosovo | 42 percent |

Source: Cited in Robert Hayden, *The Beginning of the End of Federal Yugoslavia: The Slovenian Amendment Crisis of 1989*, The Carl Beck Papers Number 1001 (The Center for Russian and East European Studies, University of Pittsburgh, December 1992), from polls published in *Borba*, July 26, 1990, pp. 1, 12; *Vjesnik*, July 26, 1990, p. 3; and *Borba*, May 21, 1990, p. 7.

annual rate of inflation (consumer prices) in 1989 of 2,714 percent (with a rate of more than 50 percent in December alone), it went to zero in May 1990, bringing glowing accolades for these results from Western creditors and governments.[38] But in June—six months before the remaining elections—economic trends took a turn for the worse: prices accelerated sharply, exports fell, the currency became overvalued, and the policy of real interest rates (at 23.4 percent) and heavy taxation led to massive insolvency of firms. By December, 8,608 enterprises employing 3.2 million persons, in a work force of approximately 6 million at the time, were in serious trouble.[39] Having hitched his wagon to the star of economic results, Marković's popularity began to plummet with the economy after June.[40] There was little time, given the near nonexistence of his party organization, to recover in time for the elections in the remaining four republics in which his party would compete.

Instead of an opportunity to express support for the federal government and reforms, the politics of elections dealt a heavy blow to the reform package and to Marković. In every republic, beginning with Slovenia and Croatia in the spring, governments ignored the monetary restrictions of Marković's stabilization program in order to win votes and buttress slim majorities or coalitions with promises of higher wages or budgetary supplements to declining pensions, farm incomes, and government salaries. Whatever long-term effects the "shock therapy" plan might have had on inflation after June, the free-riding of republican governments on their common currency destroyed its achievements. The one remaining institution to which they remained committed—the dinar—fell victim to the vote-buying of newly forming states. By September inflation had resumed with such vengeance (7.1 percent, followed by 8.1 percent in October, for an annual rate of 121 percent for 1990) that in October Marković had to abandon the project for rapid convertibility. The trade deficit increased threefold in relation to 1989.[41] Slovenia asserted its sovereignty over what it considered "its" foreign exchange—the issue most dear to its antifederalism—by quietly keeping customs duties collected on its international border and ignoring the law obliging the transfer of foreign exchange to the National Bank.[42] In October, a new Slovene currency was being printed secretly in Austria.[43] Still having to negotiate with republican governments over federal policy, Marković made concessions in the second six months of 1990 in response to complaints from republican governments about the hardships of the stabilization program—by loosening some of the monetary restrictions. Republican governments also continued to flout the program's restrictions on wages and budgets, ignore tax obligations to the federal budget, and intensify their economic warfare with each other. The most publicized example was the secret decision of the Serbian parliament on October 23 to impose a tax on all goods from Slovenia and Croatia. Croatia retaliated by levying a tax on all physical assets in Croatia owned by individuals (such as vacation homes) and firms with their primary residence in Serbia. By January 1991 it was learned that a number of republic-level banks had spent their obligatory banking reserves to finance budget deficits, pay wages, and buy convertible currencies, effectively expanding the country's money supply. A major scandal arose over the most visible and egregious instance—Serbian expenditures for state dependents, especially pensioners and farmers, amounting reportedly to $1.5 billion.[44] But the pattern was too general to be halted by exposure alone.

The difficulty of creating a broad political coalition drawn from all parts of the country was compounded by the extent of economic and political transformation at stake, and the fact that Yugoslavia had been attempting marketization and global integration off and on for forty years. This was in stark contrast with eastern Europe; there, the harsh policies for currency convertibility, IMF credits, and stabilization associated with eventual "membership" in Europe came after the Communist party had lost its political monopoly and elections were held. This gave the new eastern European regimes an initial legitimacy and popular support before the economic hardships associated with westernizing reforms were felt. Moreover, the party's monopoly ended only when opposition intellectuals and groups forged heterogeneous political coalitions that cut across social groups and economic interests, or when mass demonstrations erupted with the same broad social membership. The act of establishing such a coalition was profoundly nationalist, but it took the form of a national liberation from a regime associated with Soviet power and isolation in the East and a freed nation's embrace of a forbidden Europe. This initial solidarity was lost to the Yugoslavs because they had experienced their anti-Soviet revolt already in 1948–49. They were not isolated, but had been free to travel, work in Europe, hold foreign currency accounts, and buy imported Western goods since the mid-1950s.

Marković's policies represented a revolt from above within the structure of the old regime, and the elections were taking place after a decade of recessionary contraction, trade reorientation, and structural adjustment of investment and production. Slovenia and Croatia had preempted the role of nationalism in creating a moment of shared purpose and united action, and directed it against the federal government rather than some foreign power. To build a constituency based on the substance of the reforms—without the support of the two republics most likely to benefit from the reforms—and in separate contests in the four poorer republics hardest hit, was extremely difficult. Many argue that Marković's cause was badly damaged by the fact that many of those chosen to build a party organization in these republics were still associated with the League of Communists; however, the same problem in other countries of eastern Europe was not irremediable. Despite the presence of prominent Slovene economists in Marković's federal cabinet, the government in Slovenia (and increasingly Croatia) remained unalterably opposed to reforms that would make it possible to create a democratic system at the federal level and give to Marković or another reform-oriented government the legitimacy of elections.

It also did not help that Serbian President Milošević had mobilized support among the socioeconomic strata and political malcontents most likely to oppose the reforms on their substance under the banner of Serb nationalism. Federal elections could have been structured so as to give citizens a real opportunity to express their views on the reform and the constitution, demonstrating not only the large number of those outside the republics of Slovenia and Croatia who supported the reforms and the real nature of the constituency that opposed the reforms independent of Milošević, but also the large number of Serbs who did not side with Milošević. Nonetheless, Slovene authorities refused to take the risk that Milošević forces would gain a plurality. Whereas in eastern Europe the economic reform programs were accompanied by a breakup of the revolutionary coalition into political parties, the republics in Yugoslavia retained control over the terms of political debate and political forces confronting the federal reform. As long as issues, whether constitutional or economic policy, were defined in terms of republics and nationalism, the federal government had no constituency. It was at a disadvantage in building one as well because there was no external enemy and the republics had already claimed the right to represent what they were calling national interests.

Despite a Slovene veto, Marković and his supporters remained hopeful that federal elections scheduled for December 1990 would be held. They believed that an electoral mandate would reinvigorate his government's reform project and give momentum to antinationalist political forces fighting disintegration. In fact, there never was an all-Yugoslav vote. Yugoslavs found their individual citizenship reduced to that of their republic, and were given no choice in the matter.

## Interregnum

The democratically elected governments of Slovenia and Croatia had wasted no time in announcing their intentions. After declaring their sovereignty in July 1990, they formally proposed that Yugoslavia become a confederation of "sovereign states." Each republic-turned-sovereign state would have its own army and diplomatic missions. Those states meeting the conditions of democratically elected parliaments and guaranteed free enterprise and trade unions would voluntarily recombine into a Yugoslav confederation, linked only by a consultative parliament, council of ministers, and confederal court based on unanimous agreements. Economic relations among these states would be limited to those necessary to meet conditions for EC membership, leaving some doubt about the proponents' long-term commitment to the confederation.[45] The most radical form of Slovene ideas—and what the federal government under Marković, federalists, and international creditors had considered most ineffective economically—was on the table. Indeed, the confederal proposal did away with existing federal institutions entirely, making it unclear even how agreement would be reached to accept, modify, or reject the proposal. Nonetheless, many outside observers and domestic liberals saw confederation as the best way out of the deadlock politically, paying almost no attention to its starting assumption that the republics were equivalent to states with the right to national self-determination and its implications for the composite rights to self-determination in the Yugoslav constitution. Primarily concerned with holding the country together in some way, given the Slovene stand in opposition to anything more, they did not say how this would be negotiated—or by whom—with those who opposed the idea and who would most likely lose as its result, from Serb nationalists to Serb and Albanian autonomists in Croatia and Serbia, to the undefined status of Bosnia and Herzegovina.[46]

Another consequence of the 1990 election campaigns was a breakdown in standards of permissible speech and protections of national rights. What Tibor Várady calls the "civilization-shield" to protect minorities in the socialist period—the constitutional restrictions on free speech to prevent "incitement of national, racial, or religious hatred"—was simply tossed aside.[47] In the interests of electoral success, candidates used ethnic stereotypes to simplify voters' choices and avoid debate on difficult issues, and gave themselves permission to exploit openly a language of intolerance and hate. Most noticeable, because of its historical echoes and because it occurred early in the year of elections and thus could define what was permissible, was the anti-Semitic, anti-Serb vitriol in Franjo Tudjman's campaign in Croatia. But he was not alone. In Macedonia the nationalist bloc and the former communists held diametrically opposite views on Macedonian independence and the idea of Yugoslavia, but in their shared willingness to use prejudice against ethnic Albanians living in Macedonia for political gain there was substantial basis for momentary tactical alliances at the time and in the future. Elections opened the door to a period of acceptable harassment of Albanians and their rights in Macedonia, similar to the attitudes against Serbs that followed elections in Croatia. Albanians in Kosovo boycotted the Serbian elections in December, but this had no effect on Serbs who were exploiting vicious and racist anti-Albanian political language as a way to win the vote of Serb nationalists. The majoritarian appeal of the slogan "all Serbs in one state" replaced the impersonal, administrative slogan of "border rectification" in the campaign of Serbian leader Milošević and his new socialist party, but this appeared as an open threat to leaders in neighboring republics. By giving voice to this goal, forbidden since the Balkan Wars of 1912–13, Serbian nationalists in the opposition, such as Vuk Drašković and Vojislav Šešelj, as well as Milošević and the ruling party, acknowledged that any new Serbian government would be an open supporter of Serbs not only in Kosovo but outside of Serbia, and thus in direct confrontation with the Croatian government and potentially Bosnia-Herzegovina if either chose independence. This claim of protector for Serbs wherever they lived was the logical equivalent of Kučan's identification of Slovenian sovereignty and the defense of Slovene human rights, but in contrast to the parliamentary declarations of republican sovereignty in all republics and provinces in July 1990, this functional equivalent of a declaration of Serb national sovereignty was based on the equally legitimate but alternative concept of a nation in the constitution. If political parties sought votes on national identity (whether Serb, Croat, Muslim, Albanian, Macedonian, or Slovene) and then used electoral victory to claim rights of national self-determination, the constitutional compromise on which stability had depended could bring a disastrous confrontation between nation and republic.

As in 1988–89, the politics within republics could not be isolated as if they were separate states, and their interaction had anything but a moderating effect. While President Tudjman was able to take advantage of Slovene drives for independence against the federal government, he became ever more assertive in using the powers of the state to increase his personal power and that of his party and to move the republic toward full sovereignty by ensuring its monopoly over coercive powers—beginning with the localized system of police, territorial defense, and army. His anticommunist rhetoric in the elections had equated decommunization with getting rid of Serbs, but once Croatian statehood was the goal, it mattered concretely that many Serbs held down police and diplomatic posts, the low status of which turned upside down overnight. Social scientists who were alarmed by the carelessness of the Croatian government's language and insensitivity to the Serb minority in Croatia presented to the Croatian parliament plans for educational programs for cross-cultural and interethnic relations, and development projects to revive local economies in the impoverished interior regions of mixed population in Lika, Banija, and Kordun, where there had been disturbances. The Croatian parliament showed the same cavalier disregard in rejecting their serious consideration. This was more grist for the mill of militant local Serbs who were by then fighting for political autonomy against Zagreb and for Serb nationalists of all camps who believed that Serbs needed protection from Serbia.[48]

Although the issues were still constitutional ones, the confrontation could no longer remain one between republican leaders over constitutional principles alone—as it was between Slovenia and Serbia—once the electoral appeal for voter loyalty was made in terms of individual national identity and the republican parliaments openly identified republics and citizenship rights with single nations. People did not live in nationally exclusive communities as defined by republican borders; moreover, the multiple guarantees of the socialist period had allowed multiple loyalties and identities—to family, culture, town, region, republic, nation, country—to coexist unproblematically. Although Slovene leader Kučan had already "interfered" in Serbian internal affairs, as his views on sovereignty would lead one to describe it when he declared the Slovene-Serbian conflict over the federal constitution an issue of political orders as well as of human rights within republics, the growing confrontation between the Croatian government and Serbia went far more to the heart of the issue of the sovereignty that Slovenia and Croatia had now claimed. This was a confrontation over people, their political loyalties and choice of citizenship, and of borders. Although it remained a latent confrontation at the time, the same was potentially true of relations across the border of Kosovo (Serbia) and Macedonia among ethnic Albanians. Under these new political categories, political autonomy for Kosovo (whether as a province or a republic) would no longer be separable from its basis in the national aspirations of Albanians, or in its source of protection for ethnic Albanians against discrimination from republican governments, even though Albanians were not accorded the status of constituent nation in any of the socialist constitutions. In either case, these principles crossed republican borders. Similarly latent as a political problem at the time was the case of Bosnia-Herzegovina. All three of the governing political parties ruling in coalition as a result of the November–December elections crossed republican borders: the Croatian party was a branch of the ruling party in Croatia; the Serbian party was a party of Serbs in Croatia and Bosnia-Herzegovina; and the Muslim party was active in the Muslim areas of the Sandžak, a region of Serbia and Montenegro, and had many adherents among Bosnian residents of Sandžak origin.

Although the Slovene and Croatian declarations of sovereignty and the proposal to create a federation made these cross-border relations problematic, they could as easily be seen as hopeful signs of common interest. From the point of view of the federal reform program—which required cross-border flows and relations favoring a market economy—and of the cross-republican political parties or coalitions of an all-Yugoslav democratic community that could represent citizens' economic interests and policy preferences, these difficulties could be seen as birth pangs instead. The outcome, however, depended on the capacity in the existing system for statesmanship and for disinterested mediation of these conflicts that would also allow tolerance for cross-border nonnational associations and for alternative political proposals and compromise. The federal government under Prime Minister Marković was an interested party to the constitutional conflict, however. Being perceived as such by Slovene and Croatian politicians, he was disparaged as a political rival of equal stature rather than as the driving force behind a program of common interest. Therefore, the burden of managing the political transition lay heavily on the other two federal institutions, those responsible for the constitutional order and state security—the Yugoslav People's Army and the collective state presidency.

The events of April–July 1990 were precisely what the army leadership had been warning might occur for more than two years and had been most concerned to prevent. The army had attempted to repair the damage of its confrontation with the Slovene public in 1988 by reversing its position on language rights and trying to take a more conciliatory position toward constitutional change. But the move by the new Slovene and Croatian governments to claim full sovereignty over their territorial defense forces (TDFs), in Slovenia full control as well over all units of the YPA, and to create special paramilitary police units as the seed of separate armies posed a far more serious threat to state security. The consequences of the proposal for a Yugoslav confederation, although the details were far more vague than the extensive publicity would suggest, implied the dissolution of the YPA and of the arms industries and research and development that deliberately connected plants throughout the country. The proposal said nothing about the division of YPA assets among the republics or the composition of any collective security arrangements for such a confederation.[49] It was not clear how the army could remain neutral toward such a proposal, particularly given its ultimate responsibility for internal security. Instead, the army's constitutional obligation to guard the civil order as well as territorial integrity of Yugoslavia seemed to require an immediate response to the growing violence and possible armed insurrection in Croatia.

As early as April 1990, when it appeared that parties pledging national independence might win the elections in Slovenia and Croatia, the army general staff began to draw up contingency plans to prevent their secession. Minister of Defense Kadijević declared openly that the army was prepared to defend the territorial integrity of Yugoslavia with all means necessary, and he warned both Slovenia and Croatia against the formation of special police militias.[50] The fact that leaders in Slovenia and Croatia began to appeal to NATO to intervene on their behalf fed directly into the beliefs of the general staff, held since the mid-1980s, that NATO had become Yugoslavia's primary external threat. The army's contingency plans (Rampart-91, or RAM) were based on the assumption of invasion from the West.[51]

At the same time, the army was also an institution with internal divisions, and these were being exacerbated by Marković's economic reform. Cuts in public expenditures threatened the asset most valued by individual officers and veterans—socially owned (subsidized) housing. In an organization with a substantially decentralized command structure, it mattered that this was a local government responsibility, and also that junior officers had been chafing loudly for years at their declining relative incomes and status. While the military journal spoke approvingly in the fall of 1990 of Yugoslavia's orientation toward Europe, there were quarrels between General Kadijević and Prime Minister Marković over army finances and Marković's freeze on a program to develop a new fighter aircraft.[52] Defense producers throughout the country continued to cooperate in their joint production necessary to fill foreign contracts for arms exports without regard to the constitutional quarrel and economic war heating up between the republics (especially Serbia, Slovenia, and Croatia).[53] Kadijević accepted the principle of depoliticization of the army, including the appointment of an army professional as chief of staff, Blagoje Adžić, in the fall of 1989.[54] But he also led a military delegation to Moscow on March 13, 1991, which generated accusations that he secretly had talks with General Dmitry Yazov about purchasing military equipment, including missile systems, helicopters, and airplanes.[55]

Quarrels also erupted during 1990 between the YPA and the governments of Slovenia and Croatia concerning the ownership between them of TDF armaments and equipment. Although the dispute had its origins in defense policy from the mid-1980s, not the declarations of sovereignty in 1989–90, by 1990 the rapidly changing property laws and interpretations of republican sovereignty made it constitutionally unclear whose property was what, and Slovenia's refusal to recognize the legitimacy of the federal courts left in doubt which body would adjudicate disputes. The army was in no mood to risk temporizing in the face of the Slovenian and Croatian plans for confederation, especially given the appointment of Janez Janša as Slovenian minister of defense. On October 4 the YPA moved, under orders from the defense ministry, to take control of TDF and YPA assets in the two republics. It succeeded in taking possession of almost all TDF equipment in Croatia, but seized only 40 percent in Slovenia because of a more alert, premeditative leadership.[56] To replace and build up stocks for independent armies, the two republics began purchasing arms abroad during the fall of 1990. For the most part, these purchases were made surreptitiously through Austrian intermediaries; such transactions were easy because of the huge stocks of arms scheduled for conventional force reduction in Europe (especially in Germany) that were sitting in warehouses of weapons producers in the East, such as in Hungary and the former Czechoslovakia.[57]

The first real test of secession for the army, however, came from the troubles in Croatia between the government and Serbs who were resisting Tudjman's attempts to replace Serbs in police and local administration— whose loyalty he questioned—in border areas with MUP and military personnel and whose efforts to achieve autonomy in response to Croatian moves toward independence were resisted by the Croatian government, leading rapidly to armed confrontations. The army's role in civil order had always been contested, but it also had a checkered history in Croatia. In 1970–71 repeated army warnings to Tito about the danger of the mass nationalist movement developing in Croatia and of its links to groups in foreign countries (especially guest workers and émigrés in Germany) led the president and the highest party circles finally to act in December 1971, and bring the movement to a halt through party discipline on Croatian leaders.

The federal principle of even-handedness in national questions made the army's position more awkward. Any attempt to intervene in armed confrontations between parties to the constitutional conflict would be interpreted as bias. The army's police action in Kosovo (although it had been authorized by the republican representatives in the federal presidency) was generally vilified. In the political climate prevailing in Slovenia and Croatia in 1989–90, whatever the army did was automatically labeled as pro-Serb. To the government of Croatia, the Serb authorities and paramilitary bands forming during the second half of 1990 in the *krajina* were rebels, and its authority to put down this rebellion with arms was legitimate. To others, however, Croatia was not a sovereign state, and Serbs had a right to remain within a Yugoslavia and were in need of protection. Moreover, the first of the serious civil disturbances—those surrounding the attempts by MUP to prevent Serbs from holding a referendum on autonomy in August 1990 and the Serb response of barricading the entrances to their villages and, in some cases, raiding local police stations or TDF stores for weapons—was itself a result of the contest over sovereignty. To the Croatian government, any federal action to restore civil order in Croatia was a violation of its sovereignty. In the bloody shootout between armed locals and MUP in Glina in September 1990, to their attack on Serbs who had seized the police station in Pakrac in March 1991, the army was sent to interpose between the sides and defuse tensions.[58] Air force MiGs intercepted helicopters sent by the secretariat for international affairs to the Knin region two days before the referendum, August 17, 1990,[59] and when armed Serbs killed two security policemen in a detachment deployed to Plitvice National Parks (in the *krajina* region) in an attempt on March 31, 1991, to control it, the YPA intervened again and took control. Thus, as roadblocks, shootouts, and rumors of violence or of approaching tanks proliferated, the confrontation increasingly became one of sovereignty between the Croatian government and the YPA. Although both sides pulled back many times from confrontation, by the spring of 1991 the Croatian government argued increasingly that the YPA was defending Serbs rather than civil order, and the actions of some local YPA commanders—particularly those of Serb nationality and from families that suffered under the fascists in this region during World War II—showed sympathy for Serb fears and in some cases allegedly had permitted thefts of weapons from army depots.

Meanwhile, voter dissatisfaction with the economy was rising in Slovenia. The preoccupation of the ruling DEMOS coalition with nationalist goals and rhetoric and the delays in reaching an agreement on an effective economic program were palpably undermining political support.[60] Sensing this shift and the threat it implied to their objectives, radicals within the DEMOS parliamentary caucus grew increasingly impatient during the fall of 1990 with the pace of dissociation set by President Kučan, leader of the former ruling communists in Slovenia; the Slovene representative to the federal presidency, Janez Drnovšek; and the president of the Slovene parliament, Liberal party leader France Bučar. In an effort to seize the political momentum before it reversed and to refocus attention on the nationalist agenda, they insisted on an immediate referendum on independence. On December 6, 1990, the Slovene parliament adopted a law to hold a plebiscite on December 23, asking Slovene voters to choose yes or no to the question, "Should the Republic of Slovenia become an autonomous and independent state?" If a majority concurred, the parliament would be obliged to adopt within six months, acting as an independent state no longer part of the Yugoslav federation, the constitutional acts and interstate agreements confirming this independence and enabling the republic to join a confederation of the other Yugoslav peoples if they so wished. In a turnout of 93.5 percent of the electorate, it passed with 88.5 percent.[61]

Furthermore, by the end of 1990, the YPA had been placed on combat readiness in Croatia. The Croatian parliament went into continuous session so that it could declare secession if the army moved, and President Tudjman imposed emergency rule by handing effective authority to govern the republic to a special security council, including powers of censorship of the media deemed necessary by "a state of war." At the end of January 1991, the federal military prosecutor ordered the arrest of the Croatian minister of defense, General Martin Špegelj, on charges of treason for allegedly arming paramilitary forces illegally and planning attacks on military installations to kill YPA officers and their families. Instead of challenging federal authority as Slovenia had done, the Croatian government responded by giving Špegelj secret sanctuary.[62]

Constitutional authority over the army, national security, and the constitutional order actually lay, however, with the federal state presidency. Its reconstitution as a result of the elections had to await their completion at the end of 1990. This delay and the fact that the luck of rotation had the Serbian representative in the chair from May 1990 to May 1991 left it unable to act as forcefully on the constitutional quarrel and the rising number of violent incidents during 1990 as one might have hoped. This did not prevent the republics from engaging in bilateral talks, as early as July, such as the secret meeting between Presidents Milošević and Tudjman on July 20–21, arranged by vice-president of the presidency Stipe Šuvar, at which Tudjman apparently conceded Serbian authority over Kosovo and demanded in turn Croatian authority over the *krajina*. The presidency moved rapidly, however, beginning December 25, 1990, to restore constitutional order and to negotiate with the republican presidencies on the future of the country. It began by ordering on January 9, 1991, that all paramilitary groups be disarmed and disbanded. Slovenia and Croatia refused to obey, however, claiming their forces were legal and that the order would imply YPA rights to interfere in their domestic security. The army, in response, refrained from disarming Serbian militias in Croatia. The two republics agreed on January 17 to cooperate on matters of mutual defense and security; nonetheless, Croatia had pulled back from confrontation by the end of the month, and negotiated a mutual reduction in paramilitary and YPA forces with the army leadership.

To attack the constitutional conflict, the presidency also began a series of expanded sessions, held from January 10 to March 31, with presidents of the republics to debate the future of the country, economic policy, and the question of borders, procedures for secession, and the distribution of assets should the country become a confederation.[63] Yet it was not clear what leverage the federal presidency had with the republics other than their mutual commitment to find a solution. The special relationship with the United States and the West was gone. There was no unifying Soviet enemy. Citizenship had devolved to the republics, and budgetary cuts had de facto made it ever more difficult to realize the federal guarantees of all-Yugoslav citizen rights, economic redistribution for national equality, and even their common security.

Leaving prosecution of the cases of economic warfare between the republics up to the constitutional court and ignoring the Slovene plebiscite, the federal government pressed on with its reform. This time—under intense pressure from an IMF concerned that commitment to reform was flagging, and with it the federal government's ability to guarantee repayment of its foreign debt—Marković began in the first days of January to seek agreement among the republics on "minimal functions" of the federal government for managing the "transitional period" that were required for a new arrangement with the IMF.[64]

Nonetheless, on January 25 the Macedonian parliament declared its full sovereignty, catching up with the other declarations of July 1990.[65] On February 21, 1991, the Croatian parliament moved closer to the Slovene position; declaring that it would not implement any federal laws on its territory that were in conflict with a revised Croatian constitution adopted in December 1990 and particularly any emergency measures or use of the armed forces in Croatia without prior approval of the assembly or president, it announced its intention to separate from Yugoslavia as well by June 30. It would consider joining an association of sovereign republics if certain conditions were met—such as the establishment of a new capital city other than Belgrade and a Serbia unable to dominate any Yugoslav confederation. Tensions now escalated between local Croats and Serbs in the ethnically mixed area of Slavonia and Baranja in eastern Croatia, where Croatian police roughed up local Serbs and the Serbian Democratic Party convened a regional assembly and organized protest meetings.

There will long be debates about when the decisive turning point came for Yugoslavia, but the events of March 1991 make it a prime candidate along with the Slovene decision of September 1989. As civil order deteriorated, constitutional challenges escalated, and competing declarations of sovereignty made unclear where federal authority lay, the role of the army and its commander in chief—the collective state presidency— would be critical. But the presidency, as a body representing the republics and provinces, was now split three ways: between independence-oriented confederalists (Slovenia, Croatia, and Kosovo Albanians); those who wanted to retain Yugoslavia but with an even more reduced common state and unclearly specified notions of state sovereignty to its republics (Macedonia and Bosnia-Herzegovina); and those who wanted to retain a united federation (Serbia, Montenegro, and the army). The month began with

the presidency's adoption of a constitutional procedure to regulate secession from the country. It also ordered the YPA to intervene militarily to
stop the armed confrontation between MUP and local Serbs in Croatia,
and appointed a commission of experts from all republics and the province
of Vojvodina to work out a compromise constitutional proposal, which it
presented March 8. On March 6 the nationalist coalition of opposition
parties formed after the election in Macedonia (and 31 percent of parliament)[66] demanded that the YPA leave the republic.[67] The next day Slovenia
stopped sending recruits to the army (although it allowed volunteers to
continue). When the army protested, relations between Prime Minister
Marković and Minister of Defense Kadijević worsened as well.[68]

On March 9, when opposition parties called a demonstration in Belgrade to protest President Milošević's monopoly control of television and
newspapers, Yugoslav president Jović (the Serbian representative to the
presidency) also called on the army to interpose troops between the crowds
and police to protect civil order in Serbia. In this case the general staff first
resisted, but some members (but without the knowledge of others, it
turned out) agreed to intervene when the police reaction was so disproportionate that the protest turned violent, eventually lasting four days, with
two dead and about ninety wounded. Apparently believing that, as in
Croatia in 1971, the demonstration could spread to wider social unrest in
Serbia and challenge the constitutional order,[69] they ordered tanks onto the
streets of Belgrade for the first time since World War II. On March 12 the
army requested the state presidency to declare a state of emergency if, after
forty-eight hours, the Slovene and Croatian governments did not implement the decisions of January 9 and later to disband paramilitary units and
restore YPA authority over the TDFs and army recruitment. In the opinion
of the majority on the presidency, this was a legal attempt at a coup d'état.
Despite the army's attempt to sequester the members in the building, the
presidency refused and the army retreated. Civilian authority prevailed,
but one faction of the army, at least, had also shown its hand in defending
Milošević's rule in Serbia against domestic opposition, as if multiparty
elections in December had not initiated a new era. President Jović resigned
in protest, followed by members from Vojvodina and Montenegro, and
to punish the representative from Kosovo who chose to vote against
emergency powers, the Serbian assembly withdrew his authority. On
March 16, Serbian president Milošević told a television audience that Serbs
also would no longer recognize federal authority in the republic if the army
was not permitted to protect the constitutional order. The same day, Croatian Serbs, who had declared in August 1990 a "Serbian Autonomous
District of Krajina" in the six municipalities around Knin, responded to
Croatia's intention to dissociate from Yugoslavia by declaring its mirror
image: that Croatian laws not in accordance with the federal constitution

were invalid in their region and that they intended to dissociate from Croatia.

The attempted coup failed. Milošević made concessions on the media, Drašković (leader of the March 9–13 demonstrations) backed down from the confrontation, and Jović withdrew his resignation on March 20.[70] Ante Marković survived a vote of no-confidence on his economic program, proposed by Vojvodina on March 27 for a Serbian government that wanted an economic stimulus package instead and that had obtained Tudjman's support. The republics of Serbia and Montenegro and the army proposed a new constitutional formula for a "democratic federation."[71] By the end of the month, all representatives had returned to the presidency, and the presidents of the republics began their own effort at reconciliation at a series of meetings called "Yu-summits." Six summits were held in a progression of cities and republican hosts, beginning in the Croatian port town of Split on March 28, and then moving to Belgrade (Serbia) on April 4, Brdo by Kranj (Slovenia) on April 11, Ohrid (Macedonia) on April 18, Cetinje (Montenegro) on May 29, and Stojčevac near Sarajevo (Bosnia-Herzegovina) on June 6.[72] And on April 18 the presidency's group of experts ended the last obstacle to a countrywide referendum on the country's future to be held by the end of May by resolving the differences among the republics over its wording.

Conflict in Croatia escalated in April, however. The government accused the army of refusing to disarm Serbian paramilitary forces and stop their blockade of Kijevo, a town with a Croatian majority located in Serbian-majority *krajina* in which the MUP had set up a new police station. In May, Croatian President Tudjman issued a call to the people to lift what he called the siege of Kijevo—with the immediate result of a mass demonstration against the army at the naval academy in Split, at which a Macedonian army recruit was murdered, apparently by Croatian interior security forces.[73] Even more ominous was the incident at Borovo Selo on May 2, in which fighting between locals in a Serb-majority village and factory town near Vukovar in eastern Croatia and Croatian police who entered the town to take down a Serb flag eventually led to the killing of twelve Croatian police and three Serb civilians and to exploitation by politicians on all sides who seemed almost to encourage war.[74] Nonetheless, the presidency was able to adopt an action program on May 9 to resolve the interrepublican and interethnic conflicts. The first step was to set up a commission composed of representatives of the Croatian government and elected Serb parliamentarians to investigate the conflicts in mixed areas of Croatia, while federal forces maintained the peace.

Confrontation between the two factions on the presidency flared up again, however, when the annual rotation of the chair of the state presidency came due in mid-May. On May 10 the Slovene, Croatian, and part of the

Kosovo delegation initiated a parliamentary protest to restore the legitimate representative of Kosovo to his seat on the presidency. On May 15 Serbia voted against the pro forma rotation of the chair to the representative of Croatia, Stipe Mesić. Their explanation was that Mesić, the first prime minister of Croatia under the HDZ, from May to August 1990, had proudly declared his platform as president of Yugoslavia to be Croatian independence and the end of Yugoslavia. Without a sitting president, the constitutional status of this collective head of state and commander-in-chief of the armed forces—and thus that of the army—was in doubt.

On May 19 the Croatian referendum on independence—on the question "Do you agree that the Republic of Croatia as a sovereign and independent state, which guarantees cultural autonomy and all civil rights to Serbs and members of other nationalities in Croatia, may enter into an alliance with other republics?"—was approved by 93 percent of the 83.6 percent of the electorate who chose to vote, or, in total, 79 percent.[75] The referendum was boycotted by most Serbs of the *krajina* autonomous region, who had held their own referendum on May 12, approving overwhelmingly the decision to join the republic of Serbia and to remain within Yugoslavia.[76] That same day the Muslims in the Sandžak area of Serbia established their own assembly to represent all Muslims in Serbia.

## Conclusion

The definitive end of the communist regime in Yugoslavia came in 1990, with the collapse of the federal Communist party in January and the competitive multiparty elections held in the republics from April to December. But democratization was not the result. Democratic elections instead became the vehicle for the republics of Slovenia and Croatia to declare popular legitimacy for their assertion of sovereignty for their majority nations on the grounds of their right to national self-determination. This provoked others to do the same, as most other republican and provincial parliaments issued declarations during July, and as persons who found themselves demoted to minority status without rights they had held for forty years also took their turn to claim (as in the case of Serbs in Croatia) or to assert (as in the case of Albanians in Kosovo and in Macedonia) their rights to national self-determination with political autonomy. The declarations of national sovereignty also opened a legal door to extreme Serb nationalists who had revived the dream of a Serbian nation-state and who now could claim the right to redraw borders in the case that the republics followed through on their assertions on the grounds that the right of self-determination in the constitution belonged to nations, not republics.

Because claims to sovereignty are reflexive, the Slovene and Croatian declarations deprived federal institutions of authority in proportion to the gains they demanded in republican sovereignty. Who, then, would manage the political crisis and with what authority in the face of intransigent politicians? The authorities outsiders would expect to take on a negotiating, moderating, or neutralizing role in this interactive spiral had ever fewer political resources, short of calling out the troops. What common ground for agreement and trade-offs was there? The liberalizing and market objectives of the government's economic reform had actually encouraged this emphasis on statehood by focusing on changes in governmental jurisdictions, revenues and budgets, property rights, and the content of citizenship. Republican and provincial politicians had already defined these reform issues as matters of national interest, affirmation, and identity. Moreover, they used the electoral campaigns to make these issues a question of individual identities and political loyalties—to republic or federation and, increasingly, to nationality as a question of survival itself.

The introduction of multiparty elections did not open a democratizing process in the sense of establishing procedures for managing differences and conflict over policies peacefully and regularly by holding officials accountable and guaranteeing individual rights. The elections gave politicians the courage to escalate their demands and rhetoric and to sabotage negotiations. Among citizens there was still much that attracted substantial loyalty to the idea of Yugoslavia, its independence and prestige abroad, the personality of Tito, and even the democratic aspects of the system of workers' self-management, and their voting choices reflected a wide variety of individual grievances with current circumstances, with slights of the Titoist period, or simply their first stab at a new political identity by choosing the one that defined the distribution of government jobs and resources in the socialist period. Politicians claimed their votes as a mandate for change, whether for communist parties, liberal parties, or right-wing nationalists, but the political momentum of national rhetoric, loyalty, and rights over economic assets and territories was moving too rapidly for the construction of genuine alternatives, or even for individual citizens freely to develop political identities and associations appropriate for a post-socialist system.

The federal government continued to believe that more rapid economic reform—on the assumption that it would more rapidly bring recovery and market revolution—was the best solution to the crisis. The federal presidency, handicapped because its members represented their republics and only collectively the country, nonetheless attempted to manage the process—to gain control over paramilitary forces and civil violence, to discuss the practical implications of confederation and dissolution, and to arrange for a federal referendum on the issue and for federal elections. The commodity most needed was time, for alternative civic and political groups to create new political parties and coalitions, to use the courts (long independent) to win protections for individuals against the abuses of the new governments and of groups (official or extralegal) taking the law into their own hands, to build standards of political civility within partisanship, and to develop a public opinion. But these efforts had no support from the outside, and the momentum of the crisis was not solely an internal dynamic.

Foreign influences—from neighboring states, Western bankers, churches, émigrés, and even global powers—also served to escalate rather than moderate the pace of political disintegration in Yugoslavia. Aside from the ongoing influences in Europe, by October 1990 Slovenia and Croatia had begun seeking explicit support in the West for their sovereignty, with some success. The tensions in Kosovo, the Croatian *krajina*, and Slavonia brought U.S. criticisms of Milošević and unspecified warnings to the army not to engage in the internal conflict.[77] External actors began to take sides as they were being defined by republican leaders, while they did nothing to change their policies toward the federal government or to reduce the growing uncertainty in the external environment caused by the end of the cold war and the shifting border within Europe. By March 1991 Western powers began to intervene directly, but not as neutral mediators or with the procedures so patently needed. The rhetoric of the elections and their aftermath posed the choice as one of democracy versus dictatorship, but real democratization was interrupted by confrontation and war.

Chapter 6

# *Western Intervention*

O ne year after the parliaments of the republics of Slovenia
and Croatia declared their sovereignty and right to
secede (in July 1990), they announced their independence from Yugoslavia,
on June 25, 1991.[1] The next day, Yugoslav minister of defense Veljko Kadijević, under the explicit order of the federal parliament, fulfilled his promise of April 1990 to defend the territorial integrity of the country by
ordering federal troops to points along the border with Italy and Austria.[2]
A ten-day war between the Yugoslav People's Army (YPA) and Slovenia
ended with the mediation of the European Community. Fewer than seventy
people had died, giving the impression that the dissolution of a country
was not so difficult after all.

Within two months, however, the armed hostilities simmering between the Croatian government and radical Serbs in Knin since August
1990—which had spread by March-May 1991 to violent local confrontations among police, paramilitary groups, and citizens in towns of ethnically mixed population in the republic of Croatia near its borders with
Serbia and Bosnia-Herzegovina—had become an open war between Croatia and the YPA. The country imploded. The multiple competing nationalisms of the constitutional quarrels, electoral campaigns, and redefinition
of political rights became wars over territory and borders to create separate
states based on the principle of national self-determination.

The war of Croatian independence lasted more than six months, until
a cease-fire in January 1992 brokered by a United Nations envoy, Cyrus
Vance, was considered sufficient to send in UN peacekeeping troops. But
this only produced a stalemate over the contested territory of four UN-
protected areas (UNPAs). Despite warnings that without a comprehensive
political settlement for the whole of Yugoslavia, the tens of thousands of
dead, hundreds of thousands of refugees and displaced persons, and massive destruction of many villages and towns in Croatia would seem a picnic
beside a war in Bosnia-Herzegovina, German Chancellor Helmut Kohl
persuaded his colleagues in the European Community on December
15–16, 1991, to recognize Slovenian and Croatian independence within
the month. He argued that by internationalizing the war, granting recognition of the two republics' right to national self-determination to

signal international protection, they would deter further Serbian aggression (in their view, the cause of the war) and thus bring a quick end to the fighting. U.S. secretary of state James Baker then used the same reasoning to persuade Western allies to recognize Bosnia-Herzegovina as a sovereign state on April 6–7, 1992, so that the United States could join its allies and respond to its Croatian lobby, despite its earlier opposition to recognition.

The isolated instances of barricades, explosions, and local hostilities already taking place in Sarajevo, Mostar, Bosanski Šamac, and Bijeljina during February and March 1992 exploded. The war in Bosnia and Herzegovina created the greatest refugee crisis of post–World War II Europe; widely documented accusations of genocide and the mass rape of women; systematic violation of the Geneva conventions on the treatment of prisoners and of civilians in war;[3] a more than two-year siege of its capital, Sarajevo; and the bombardment by heavy artillery and mortar fire of the majority of towns, villages, mosques, churches, and cultural monuments in the republic.

The longer the agony and horrors went on, the more inevitable and immune to outside intervention the wars seemed. Outsiders labeled them alternately civil wars (ascribed to ancient ethnic hatreds and a history of conflict in the region) and wars of Serbian aggression. They asked whether they should intervene and what interests would justify their engagement, as if they were not already actively involved. Critics of Western governments denounced the ineffectiveness of their diplomacy to stop the fighting with the charge, which began to circulate near the end of 1991, that the crisis was a result of too little, too late. They failed to appreciate that they had been internal players in the story all along.

The interaction between Western intervention and the path of Yugoslav disintegration reinforced the lines of battle as they were drawn in March 1991, as well as the increasingly narrow space left for moderates, nonnationalists, and a democratic transition. Once Western powers began an explicit attempt at mediation in May 1991, they sped up this process by accepting the nationalists' definition of the conflict, undermining or ignoring the forces working against radical nationalists and acting in ways that fulfilled the expectations and reinforced the suspicions of nationalist extremists—exactly the opposite of their stated goals of intervention. Yet this was no concerted policy. Western powers responded piecemeal, in terms of either domestic political calculations and pressures or national interests in their foreign relations with countries they considered significant. The longer the fighting went on, the more involved they became, but they never stopped to alter their original reluctance, reduce their contradictory messages, recognize the role they were playing in the conflict itself, or formulate a policy.

## The End of the Cold War: Differentiation and Preoccupation

In the summer of 1990, when the Slovene and Croatian projects to create sovereign states were on a collision course with the several proposals to redefine the constitutional order of Yugoslavia and when Serbs in the *krajina* (border) region of Croatia and Bosnia were beginning to arm in self-defense, Western powers were in an ebullient mood. The same changes that were creating insecurities and conflicts within Yugoslavia were, from the Western perspective, a new world order of expanding economic opportunities and reduced security threats that confirmed Western values and policy. There were problems—appeals from eastern Europe for membership in the European Community and for new European security arrangements to replace the vacuum left by the collapse of the Warsaw Pact, an unresolved global debt crisis, doubts about the commitment to reform in the Soviet Union, and the Iraqi invasion of Kuwait in August 1990. But these were seen as only transitional phenomena that grew directly from the positive trends of European integration, German unification, the end of the Soviet threat and superpower confrontation, and global liberalization.

The ominous signs after August 1990 of armed clashes in Croatia and of open talk of independence in Slovenia brought warnings from diplomats, scholars, and intelligence agencies about the danger of "Balkanization" and Yugoslavia's violent disintegration.[4] For the most part, these were dismissed out of hand, not because they were unconvincing but because the prospect did not seem to present any threat to the interests of major powers. No longer needed to contain the Soviet Union, not considered capable of sparking a wider war since great power competition in the Balkans was a thing of the past or capable of disrupting Western economies, Yugoslavia and its fate were not significant. But more important than any specific calculations of threat and interest at the time were the general euphoria and self-confidence in the West based on the belief that threats to international security were truly on the decline and that peace dividends and economic interests would define the next period of global order. Only much later did the West's unwillingness to take the threat seriously boomerang, sapping that ebullient mood.

Particularly active in sounding the first alarm was the Austrian foreign minister, Alois Mock. For more than a year before the violence in the spring of 1991, he toured European capitals with ever more urgent appeals to recognize the impending Yugoslav crisis. But those who did not dismiss him as a Cassandra heard his calls for action as part of his country's behind-the-scenes and then increasingly open support for Slovene independence. From the mid-1980s on, both Austria and the Vatican had pursued a strategy to increase their sphere of economic and spiritual influence in central and eastern Europe, respectively. But even within Mock's own government, disagreement prevailed about whether to act on the quarrels in Yugoslavia. Political leaders and bureaucrats in the European Community were so persuaded that the world had changed that they either dismissed the warnings of their foreign offices and intelligence experts or believed that if the Yugoslavs were so foolish as to break apart, even violently, they deserved their fate. While these leaders preferred stability, they saw little threat to European security; any violence could easily be contained.

At the same time, both the Slovene and the Croatian governments were helping to shape Western opinion in their efforts to gain outside support and to prepare the way for independence. The political strategy of the Slovene government elected in April 1990—to win international public opinion over to its position—was to send governmental and parliamentary delegations to Western capitals after mid-1990 to represent the case for independence, to test the waters for likely reaction, and to construct a climate of foreign opinion that would see Yugoslavia as an artificial state that was now irretrievably doomed.[5] Franjo Tudjman's government in Croatia also made preliminary soundings at the time about the best strategy for independence. These included inquiries in Sweden and Norway about how they had managed their separation in 1905 and frequent consultations in Bonn.[6] The Vatican openly lobbied for the independence of the two predominantly Roman Catholic republics, with decisive influence through episcopal conferences on the Bavarian wing of the ruling German party, the CSU, and hence on Kohl's CDU.[7] Jörg Reismüller, publisher of the *Frankfurter Allgemeine Zeitung*, the most influential German newspaper, was particularly sympathetic to the Croatian prospect of independence and waged a campaign against Slobodan Milošević and Serbian nationalism that had a major role in shaping German opinion about the conflict. Whereas Austria was outspoken in its support of Slovenia (a relatively low-risk position since its only common border was with Slovenia), the Hungarian government publicly supported Yugoslav integrity. But Hungary's clear sympathies with the Croatian and Slovene cause could no longer be denied when it was revealed in September 1990 that it had illegally sold 36,000 to 50,000 Kalashnikov rifles to the Croatian government in 1990 (a revelation that unleashed a parliamentary scandal).[8] At the same time, the Hungarian ruling party's campaign pledge to protect the rights of all Hungarians, wherever they lived, had led already to increasing tensions with the government of Serbia over the fate of the Hungarian minority in the province of Vojvodina.[9]

Moreover, the general atmosphere in the eastern and southeastern half of Europe in 1990 was governed by the collapse of the Warsaw Pact and the Council for Mutual Economic Assistance (CMEA) and the requests from east European countries for membership in the European Community and in some pan-European security structure. Neither the EC nor NATO (particularly the United States) welcomed such pressures for fundamental change in the identity, as well as membership, of either organization. Leaving a vacuum in the area of security, the West embarked on a policy of differentiation to manage the pace of closer economic association and eventual incorporation of eastern Europe. Influenced powerfully by the public relations campaigns and western supporters of the central European countries, the EC declared Poland, Hungary, and Czechoslovakia more ready for inclusion because, in their view, they were more committed to economic reform and democratization than the rest. This new policy of differentiation was symbolized early by the singular diplomatic successes of Hungary in the Council of Europe and preliminary EC negotiations, and the initial program of EC economic assistance to Poland and Hungary.[10]

There was much in U.S. policy at the time to support this pattern as well. The decision was made before April 1989, when Ambassador Warren Zimmermann arrived in Belgrade, that the progress of arms reductions talks, achievement of parity, and Soviet leader Gorbachev's "new thinking" on foreign policy had rendered Yugoslavia's independence of Moscow, heavily armed neutrality, and political stability—key elements in NATO's containment policy since 1949—irrelevant to U.S. vital national interests. Although Yugoslavia had never been a member of the Warsaw Pact, this decision created a security vacuum for the Yugoslav army. This decline in U.S. interest in Yugoslavia was not accompanied by a new security structure that would define the rules for Yugoslavs. The United States was, at the time, openly insistent on retaining its role in NATO and NATO's preeminent role in European security. The changes in European security regimes during the 1980s that were the cause of Yugoslavia's declining geostrategic importance as well as improved relations within Europe were the outcome of NATO-Warsaw Pact negotiations. Talks aimed at progress on arms control, the dismantling of cold war armed forces (above all the Treaty on Conventional Forces in Europe, or CFE), and greater transparency and assurance between East and West, although formally convened by the CSCE, left out the neutral and nonaligned powers, including Yugoslavia. NATO continued to resist appeals from central European countries to recognize their vulnerability—due to the security vacuum left after the Warsaw Pact collapsed in spring 1990—until the North Atlantic Cooperation Council (NACC) was created on November 8, 1991. But NACC was limited to members of the former blocs, and NATO continued to define Yugoslavia as "out of area" and therefore ineligible for NATO action until 1993, or even to consider planning what eventually would become military action in Yugoslavia until late in 1992. Thus the Yugoslav armed forces—the defining actor in Yugoslavia's cold war status after the death of Tito—was left intact but in limbo internationally just at the time it faced massive political pressure from citizens, from the governments of Slovenia and Croatia, and from the economic pressure of budget cuts and republican tax revolts.

At the same time, in late 1990 and the first half of 1991, the tide of interest in alternative structures for European security was at its high-water mark. Critics of NATO argued that a post-cold war Europe required a post-cold war institution and that the principles and institutions emerging out of the Helsinki process in the Conference on Security and Cooperation in Europe (CSCE) after 1975—emphasizing transparency, confidence-building, and nonmilitary means of conflict resolution—were more appropriate instruments for all-European security. As recently as January 1989, the Helsinki process to "open" communist countries by obtaining their commitments to human rights had been reaffirmed when the CSCE meeting in Vienna enhanced the mechanisms, and priority, of Basket Three (human rights).[11] Moreover, the Charter of Paris for a new Europe, signed on November 21, 1990, appeared to put institutional force behind this commitment by creating the CSCE secretariat, the Committee of Senior Officials (CSO), an office of free elections, and the Conflict Prevention Center (CPC).[12]

Once U.S. foreign policy placed Yugoslavia in the same category as Eastern Europe and dropped its traditional security priority, in early 1989, it gave more weight to CSCE concerns and its standards on human rights. The appointment of the U.S. ambassador to the CSCE, Warren Zimmermann, as ambassador to Belgrade in 1989 also suggested an implicit, if not explicit, portfolio to exert U.S. pressure on human rights. Joined by members of the U.S. Congress and its Helsinki Committee, Zimmermann paid particular attention to the situation in Kosovo, criticizing the government of Serbia extensively for its violation of Albanian human rights. In fact, Zimmermann was so outspoken against Serbian repression that President Milošević refused to receive him for the first nine months after he arrived. Some argue that Zimmermann's refusal in June 1989 to attend the celebration at Gazimestan of the 600-year anniversary of the Battle of Kosovo (and thus not to listen to Milošević's nationalist diatribe) hardened Milošević further, out of injured pride. Congressional outrage over human rights abuses in Kosovo, led particularly by Senator Robert Dole, had resulted in several fact-finding missions in mid-1990 and, by November, to an amendment offered by Senator Don Nickles to the foreign operations appropriations act that threatened the withdrawal of all U.S. economic assistance and U.S. backing in international financial institutions and markets if improvements did not occur within six months—by May 5, 1991. Thus, at the very same time that Slovene leaders were gaining popular support at home by criticizing Serbia's policies in Kosovo and blurring the lines between collective political rights over territory and individual human rights, there also appeared to be a reversal in Western policy toward Milošević, whose profile as a 1980s-type economic reformer (the combination of economic liberalism and political conservatism discussed in chapter 4) had led many Western diplomats and bankers to see him as an ally and hope for the future. [13]

The pattern of differentiation developing among the republics in Yugoslavia, similar to that toward central and eastern Europe, was repeated in the West's response to the 1990 electoral campaigns in Yugoslavia and their results. Seasoned diplomats like Zimmermann recognized the danger when extreme nationalists became winners in the 1990 elections. [14] The judgment of most Western observers, including members of the U.S. Congress, however, was still under the influence of cold war anticommunism: anyone who opposed the Communist party and communist leaders was, by definition, to be supported. The revolutionary transition in eastern Europe during 1990–91 was being driven by an alliance of long-time Western and relatively new Eastern anticommunist crusaders who created an atmosphere of revenge and retribution against anyone with connections to the former regimes. On the basis of the *stated* objective of ridding eastern Europe of the last remnants of Soviet influence, they in fact displayed a cavalier attitude toward human rights and due process. [15] In the Yugoslav case, this was manifest in a tendency to judge events as described by the new Slovene and Croatian governments, whose ex-communist leaders skillfully portrayed their election results as a victory for democrats in reaction to communist dictators in Belgrade (whether federal officials or officials of the Serbian republic—the distinction was lost) and to ignore or downplay the abuses of human rights and the signs of political repression by elected governments, as in Croatia. [16]

The summer of 1990 was clearly a time when foreign warnings against the violation of human rights wherever it occurred—in Serbia, Croatia, or Macedonia—could have made a difference in establishing legitimacy for the CSCE norms and for individual rights, preventing the escalation of conflict in the *krajina*, and giving support—through even-handed behavior—to moderate forces in Serbia and Croatia that were pressing for dialogue with minorities against their nationalist governments. Instead, the few such warnings were more commonly taken as proof, reinforcing their leaders' rhetoric, that there was a Western bias against Serbs and a re-emergence of fascism in Europe. Despite the prerogatives and commitments of the Helsinki Final Act and the Paris Charter, Europe offered no new standards or conflict-regulating mechanisms in the path of the impending crisis of the spring, leaving its management to the antagonists themselves: to representatives of the republics on the presidency who could not or would not find common ground or to the police action of the federal army.

In fact, U.S. interest in strengthening the CSCE in late 1990 and early 1991 was primarily intended to increase the role and responsibility of Germany for eastern Europe.[17] There were two reasons for this: the task of incorporation was likely to require substantial financial assistance; and the United States was actively engaged in expanding its interests into the eastern Mediterranean (including intrusive support for anticommunist, liberal forces in Albanian and Bulgarian elections).[18] But Germany's economic and political power in relation to eastern Europe—both in the 1930s and in the periods of détente after 1971 and its return after 1982—was being multiplied manyfold during 1990 by its reunification, on the one hand, and the pro-Western policies of Gorbachev that removed the Soviet counterbalance, on the other. While central European states sought German patronage of their applications for membership in west European organizations, there was also a general skittishness—bordering on fear and paranoia—that German power would again look eastward and without restraint.

Moreover, Germany did not share the U.S. priority of human rights within the CSCE, preferring instead to emphasize the stability concerns of the guarantees on post-1945 borders and their inviolability (Basket One). To justify German unification at the end of 1990, moreover, German leaders spoke exultantly about the victory of the principle of self-determination of peoples as an act of democratic will. This fed dangerously into the confusion that the Slovene, Serbian, and Croatian politicians had been allowing to develop. Did this principle give priority to Croatian state interests over the human rights of non-Croats, especially Serbs? Since the Serbian government saw Albanian demands not as an issue of human rights but as a threat of secession on the grounds of self-determination, which ran against the Serbian national right to the same, was it encouraged to continue its repression? Moreover, how did one define a *people* when the issue was the right of people to express their will to self-determination—citizens of each republic in the Yugoslav federation, their majority ethnic group, a constituent nation, regardless of the change in internal borders this implied, or all citizens of Yugoslavia? And what did this shift reveal about the public commitment of both the United States and Germany to Yugoslavia's territorial integrity and unity when doubts on all sides about Western intentions (such as the open enthusiasm in Austria, Switzerland, Hungary, Denmark, and the Holy See for Slovenia's independence or the sympathetic attention to Albanian political rights in Kosovo) were encouraging the competitive positioning of the republics and the federal government?

U.S. policy toward Yugoslavia in 1989–90, particularly within the context of an emerging pattern of differentiation within Europe, also raised doubts about the country's special economic position between the former blocs, and what its demotion to the category of eastern Europe now meant for trade and credit relations.[19] Marković failed to get new commitments from Washington when he sought additional economic assistance to prepare the way for more radical reform and for shock therapy stabilization. In November 1989 an application from Foreign Minister Budimir Lončar for Yugoslav membership in the Council of Europe, in hopes of increasing support in the Yugoslav parliament for the foreign policy of westernization, was meeting with difficulty in both camps.[20] Was Yugoslavia moving precipitously, in Western eyes, from a country far more advanced along the road to reform and Western integration to one outside the inner circle of central Europe—a peripheral, Balkan state?

Of all the elements of Western policy toward Yugoslavia in 1990–91, the one that received explicit attention and priority was concern over the federal government's capacity to service its foreign debt and that of its republics. But this added another element of confusion to Yugoslavia's constitutional quarrels. On the one hand, ever more vocal European support for Slovenia and Croatia and against the Serbian leadership was accompanied by a perceptible decline in symbolic support for the federation by other countries—so critical politically to the federal government and its reform program. On the other hand, the United States, the EC, and Western financial institutions were playing a large role in pushing the federal government's political reforms (which Slovenia and Croatia opposed). This came through most strongly in the actions of the international banking community, which—following the lead of the IMF and the World Bank—considered it vital to the restructuring and repayment of Yugoslav foreign debt that the central government be strengthened and the republican governments act as a group. This was, in part, so the bankers could continue to hold the federal government responsible for its guarantee of that debt and the republican banks for their mutually guaranteed debt. The bankers were particularly concerned, however, about the consequences if the poorer republics were left hanging by the breakup of Yugoslavia. Because these republics had been granted access to credit markets and more favorable interest rates than their own economies justified as a result of the capacity of the wealthier and foreign exchange-earning northern republics, they would surely have to default on their portion of the debt. Bankers also believed that the economies of all the republics were likely to be too small to generate growth sufficient to service current and future lending.[21]

Both western Europe and the United States were far more preoccupied during the summer and fall of 1990 with the events in Hungary,

Poland, and the German Democratic Republic—and with the fate of Gorbachev's reforms and possible instability in the Soviet Union. When, in August 1990, Serb irregulars in the Dalmatian hinterland around the town of Knin disrupted traffic and blockaded the railroad along the main north-south Zagreb-Split route for commerce and tourists and the first shots were fired between them and Croatian police, the United States and its allies were focusing on the Iraqi invasion of Kuwait.[22]

Preoccupied with Moscow and the Middle East, U.S. foreign policy also reflected the belief held in European circles that if the Yugoslavs could not resolve their own quarrels, there was little the United States could do. The people formulating U.S. foreign policy had a penchant for winnable contests and a New World fatalism about Old World nationalism, though they had an unusual expertise, which was notably absent in the European Community and in most European foreign offices.[23] Deputy Secretary of State Lawrence Eagleburger had been ambassador to Yugoslavia in 1977–81 (and second secretary in Belgrade, 1962–65); and the director of the National Security Council, Brent Scowcroft, had been assistant air attaché at the U.S. embassy in Belgrade in 1959–61 and written his doctoral dissertation on the country.[24] If anything, Eagleburger and Scowcroft were inclined to keep some distance from the Yugoslav imbroglio because questions about their private business ventures with Yugoslavia—conducted in the period between their diplomatic careers and their return to governmental service—had already threatened public embarrassment over possible conflicts of interest. Alongside these reasons for the lack of U.S. leadership toward the Yugoslav crisis, the conservative policy toward NATO of the Bush administration led it and its closest European allies to block all initiatives that implied any change in European defense institutions.[25]

Moreover, the great hopes being attached to the CSCE for early conflict resolution did not yet translate into institutional capacity. The CSCE Conflict Prevention Center, to be housed in Vienna with a staff of nine and an emergency mechanism for "unusual military activities," had only been created at Paris in November 1990, opened its doors March 18, 1991, and had no military capacity. At the CSCE summit of July 1991, the United States reversed its veto of CSCE involvement the previous November and rushed a vote to put the emergency mechanism in place. The USSR (which had also vetoed the action in November) agreed to put the mechanism in place as long as decisions continued to be ruled by consensus among the thirty-four, soon to be fifty-two, member countries. A single veto, however—from the United States, the USSR, or the country at issue—would prevent any action at all.

By the time of the Slovene referendum on independence in December 1990, the external environment was thus helping to create and reinforce the political divisions within the country between federalists and supporters of Marković and the confederalists in Slovenia, Croatia, and Kosovo; and between the two blocs that had emerged at the final League of Communists congress in January 1990 and reemerged in the federal state presidency during the spring of 1991. On the one hand, it led Slovenia and Croatia to expect political (and most likely economic) support for independence from their neighbors and Germany, and it encouraged their belief (already strong through the activities of the regional organization, "Communità Alpe-Adria") that they could "join" Europe quickly. On the other hand, it gave Serbia and the YPA general staff further evidence for their suspicions that there was a revival of the World War II Axis alliance and German revanchism against them, exacerbating fears, strengthening the very bases of Milošević's appeal to the Serb population—to act as the nation's protector—and encouraging those who already were inclined to reach for arms and to rely on themselves against a hostile environment.

The West's position toward the federal government was increasingly inconsistent. The preoccupation in the United States and Western capitals with creating market economies in the former communist countries encouraged the Marković administration to expect a continuation of the support that had come with Yugoslavia's special status in the past. But while the West's verbal support for the country's reforms and its territorial integrity remained strong, leading pro-Yugoslav forces throughout the country to assume that the West was siding politically with Marković, financial support was, in fact, dwindling rapidly, and the harsher conditions for credits, just as in 1982, were intensifying the politically destabilizing and contentious consequences of the economic reform.

Moreover, the security vacuum in eastern Europe had led armies and defense departments throughout the former Warsaw Pact region to begin their own search for new alliances. Without any collective conception to override national competition, geopolitical determinants would tend to dominate, and this would encourage revival of historical alignments. And, while excluded from the East-West dialogue on arms control and disarmament, the Yugoslav army naturally joined in this process of regional realignment. Critics of the army's role in the subsequent wars make much of several trips made to Moscow—beginning in early January and continuing into the spring of 1991—by Minister of Defense Kadijević. They argue that he was seeking support from his counterparts for what the federal army considered an increasing threat from the West. Commentaries insinuate that Kadijević also sought Soviet support for an army plan to prevent the secession of Croatia and even to stage a military coup to restore order. There is some evidence that the Soviet-Romanian Friendship Treaty of June 1991, widely criticized by east European countries at the time for restoring Soviet prerogatives in the region, included commitments made to Kadijević on arms deliveries to Yugoslavia.[26] Yet the Desert Storm engagement in the Persian Gulf began on January 16, 1991, with full Soviet concurrence. However Kadijević was actually received in Moscow, it was a reminder to Yugoslavs that changes had taken place in Soviet as well as American strategic thinking and that a new alliance in the East was not to be taken for granted.

At the same time, the army's troop movements in Croatia during January brought a warning from the United States that it would not accept the use of force to hold Yugoslavia together. A little more than a week after the attack on Baghdad, on January 25, 1991, Ambassador Zimmermann made this warning public, reinforcing statements of concern made the day before in Washington by members of the U.S. Congress who had just returned from Yugoslavia (especially Senator Dennis DeConcini, chair of the Helsinki Committee).[27] The United States was in effect telling the Yugoslav army that, in addition to its abandonment of Yugoslavia on the international front, it would consider illegitimate the army's definition of its constitutional obligation to defend the borders of the state from internal threats. By April 4, Representative Frank McCloskey was calling for the use of force against the YPA and the Serb bloc in the presidency that would not seat Stipe Mesić as president.[28]

## Enter Europe: One or Twelve?

The Yugoslav crisis reached its climax between February and June of 1991. In February, Slovenia and Croatia suspended federal laws on their territory, and the collective state presidency intensified meetings with republican presidents and its internal discussions about how the federation could peacefully dissolve—from the division of assets to the partition of Bosnia. In March part of the army intervened on the streets of Belgrade in support of Milošević's government and against popular demonstrations and was deployed by President Jović, the Serbian chair of the state presidency, to quell clashes in eastern Croatia.[29] The call for emergency powers from Jović and the army was rejected by the others on the federal presidency, but the Serbian bloc stalled the regular rotation of the chair to the Croatian representative, Stipe Mesić, an action that left in question the constitutional authority of the federal presidency. In May, Croatia affirmed its intention to separate from the federation with a popular referendum on independence. Predictions of Yugoslav disintegration and the threat of untold violence on the continent of Europe were becoming ever more convincing. The opportunity to demonstrate the European commitment to the peaceful resolution of disputes had arrived.[30]

Quite apart from events in Yugoslavia, the efforts by the U.S. administration since May 1989 to persuade Europe to take greater responsibility for its own security, especially its financial burden, gained unexpected support as a result of the allied actions against Iraq in January 1991. The Persian Gulf engagement revealed sharp disagreements, particularly among France, Germany, and Great Britain, on the nature of Europe's participation in the military action, as well as on fundamental questions of security and a continuing Atlanticist posture after the cold war. The obvious lack of unity was an embarrassment to the Europeanists, who were determined to seek opportunities to demonstrate their capacity for a common foreign policy and their need for and the possibility of a separate defense. For Europe, 1991 was the active phase of negotiations over the Maastricht Treaty before it would be submitted to national referendums and realize its mandate of full financial and monetary integration. Debate focused on the treaty's political implications for common policy among the twelve, including a "common foreign and security policy" (title 5).

The Europeanists' initiative suited the U.S. position on Yugoslavia in many ways, for policymakers were unwilling to commit substantial U.S. resources or any troops to an area no longer of vital strategic interest. Moreover, a core motivation of U.S. urgings for greater European participation was to ensure Europe's responsibility for the transition in eastern Europe. Many saw a more cynical motive to U.S. policy, however, as if it dared the Europeans to prove their ability to go it alone and, in expectation of their inability to do so, served to demonstrate the continuing importance of NATO and U.S. leadership. But the decision to use the UN to organize the military coalition for Desert Storm was even more significant in its negative consequences for the Yugoslav conflict. With Yugoslavia's long history of participation in the United Nations, strong ties with third world countries, and nonmembership in the European Community or in NATO, the UN was the one international organization that could mount an external intervention that all parties in Yugoslavia would most likely accept as neutral and legitimate. UN preoccupation with Iraq and the use of the UN to protect a U.S. vital security interest sent the strong message that no such intervention would occur in Yugoslavia.

But westernization and eventual membership in Europe was one of the driving issues behind the Yugoslav conflict. Both the federal government and Slovene and Croatian politicians had been actively seeking explicit support from European institutions and governments for their separate programs. Slovenia's and Croatia's drives for independence gained a substantial boost on March 13, 1991, when the European Parliament passed a resolution declaring "that the constituent republics and autonomous provinces of Yugoslavia must have the right freely to determine their own future in a peaceful and democratic manner and on the basis of recognized international and internal borders."[31] While most European governments continued to support the federal government and to insist that the Yugoslavs stay together, the apparently uncontroversial nature of this declaration, as if fully in line with CSCE principles, demonstrates how far Slovenia and Croatia had influenced European opinion and how little chance there was that alternatives to republican sovereignty would be heard. Fighting an uphill battle against disappointments with European organizations since 1989, Yugoslav foreign minister Budimir Lončar explicitly sought help in mediating the political crisis from the European Community instead of the United States in the hope that this would energize political support for the federal government's pro-Europe reforms and counteract mounting sympathy for Slovenia and Croatia.

It was by then well known that Germany had already joined the ranks of Austria, Hungary, and Denmark in at least covert support and encouragement of Slovene and Croatian independence. A week after the declaration, on March 20, Slovene president Kučan was in Bonn having talks with German foreign minister Hans Dietrich-Genscher. Austrian support for a breakup became more assertive during the spring. Austrian foreign minister Alois Mock made statements to that effect in early May and began promoting a Croatian proposal to convene a council of elder European statesmen to mediate the crisis.[32] Austrian armed forces were also placed on high alert and moved toward the Slovene border in the second week of May.[33] In an official visit to Belgrade early in May 1991, even EC president Jacques Delors, the prime advocate of EC activism and its reputed insistence on a united Yugoslavia, and his delegation agreed to meet separately with President Kučan.

Italy, by contrast, remained in an ambivalent position. The flight of almost 20,000 Albanians to Italy in early March 1991 had the Italians, as well as other Europeans, sensitized to the prospects of more refugees. The Italian foreign minister, Gianni De Michelis, was particularly active in promoting EC involvement to manage the crisis. Although this included his strong support for a united Yugoslavia, he would not choose Yugoslavia over the EC as the dominant opinion shifted among the EC twelve. In an effort to rein in Austria, De Michelis created a joint group from the two countries to monitor the crisis in May 1991, while he criticized both the United States and Germany for their lack of financial assistance to Marković and argued strongly (against British opposition) for an EC aid package to the federal government. The policies of Alpe-Adria, the tourist, cultural, and economic organization initiated by northeastern regions of Italy, in support of Slovene and Croatian independence were opposed by the Pentagonale, an organization of states rather than regions that De Michelis had created to counteract the influence of Alpe-Adria and the new assertiveness of Germany toward the Balkans.

American actions at this time were particularly confusing. Substantially higher levels of U.S. activity were noticeable in Greece, Albania,

Bulgaria, and the eastern Mediterranean in the spring of 1991, giving the appearance to military planners and politicians in the region that the United States had chosen to divide spheres of influence north and south in eastern Europe with Germany. Despite the U.S. administration's declared abdication to Europe, the U.S. Congress and the U.S. embassy in Yugoslavia continued to try to influence the Yugoslav scene. The Nickles Amendment, which threatened a cutoff of economic aid by May 5 if relations between Serbia and the Albanian population of Kosovo did not improve, was invoked only weeks before the European Community took the opposite tack.[34]

As Foreign Minister Lončar and Prime Minister Marković had hoped, EC president Delors and the prime minister of Luxembourg, Jacques Santer, did visit Belgrade on May 29–30 and made a commitment to the territorial integrity and international borders of Yugoslavia. The week before, and the very day after Croatians voted for independence, the EC had made the Yugoslav-EC association agreement contingent on the country remaining united. Delors also promised to request $4.5 billion in aid from the EC in support of the Yugoslav commitment to political reform.[35] This carrot, however, was to reward the Yugoslavs only on certain conditions: if they implemented the very reforms that were at the heart of their quarrels—a market economy (and its financially centralizing reforms), democratization (at so rapid a pace that it favored nationalists), a peaceful dialogue on a constitutional solution (while cutting the budgets for defense, government programs, and welfare), a respect for minority rights (which was now largely outside federal competence), and the seating of Stipe Mesić as presiding chair of the collective presidency. Without regard for the consequences of these demands on the internal political conflict, the offer included the added condition that Yugoslavia remain united, a "single state."[36]

By early June, Italy's prime minister and president began to reverse Italian policy. They received official visits from the presidents of Slovenia and Croatia and the Slovene prime minister. Italian president Francesco Cossiga made public Italy's sympathy for Slovene and Croatian independence.[37] At the same time the Austrian government issued more cautious statements on Yugoslavia than its foreign office, to accord with those of the EC—reflecting continuing partisan disagreements over the case within the government and the Parliament—and because they were more concerned not to disturb Austria's application for EC membership. The U.S. Congress continued its support for Slovenia and Croatia, with an amendment to the Direct Aid to Democracies Act (the Dole Bill) offered by Representative Dana Rohrbacher (Republican from California) that sought to separate Slovenia and Croatia from Yugoslavia so that penalties for human rights violations in Kosovo did not apply to these republics and they could be sent aid, bypassing the federal government. Then, on June 21, four days before the Croatian and Slovene declarations of independence, U.S. secretary of state Baker—on his way from the first meeting of the CSCE Council of Ministers at Berlin to Tirana to celebrate U.S. recognition of Albania after fifty-two years—made a brief stop in Belgrade, at his staff's request.

This time Baker was in line with the European tactics, since he declared the United States ready to aid Yugoslavia if domestic conditions became normalized. He also declared the United States unwilling to recognize an independent Slovenia and Croatia, calling any "unilateral secession" "illegal and illegitimate." Because he insisted on Yugoslav "territorial integrity and unity," but at the same time reiterated publicly that the United States would not use military force to support this position, Baker was bitterly accused by Slovenes, Croats, and many in the Serbian opposition as well of giving a green light to the army.[38] Yet the very admission that secession could not be unilateral and must be negotiated clearly admitted its possibility. Although Baker extracted a promise (so he thought) from the Slovene and Croatian leaders not to act unilaterally, he also told Serbian president Milošević that if there came a choice between "democracy and unity," the United States would choose democracy. He then declared his open support for the compromise constitutional formula on confederation within a federation put forth June 6 at the sixth Summit of Six meeting outside Sarajevo by President Alija Izetbegović of Bosnia-Herzegovina and President Kiro Gligorov of Macedonia.[39]

Observers of Western policy in this critical period for the Yugoslav crisis, when there was both opportunity for negotiation and its utter necessity, argue that the EC and the United States took a strong and consistent stand against Yugoslav dissolution during the spring, placing their concern for stability in the short run above the only viable option left in Yugoslavia—that of confederation. They said this disapprovingly at the time and were even more convinced of the tragically missed opportunity and of the best political result in retrospect. They criticize this U.S.-EC position for denying the rights of Slovenes and Croats to self-determination and, in ignoring the inevitability of Yugoslavia's demise, encouraging Serbia and the army and thus causing the tragedy that unfolded. But the real problem was that there was no EC position or collective policy in the West. Instead of the clear lines of Western intention and active auspices needed to help negotiate a peaceful outcome, including alternatives not represented by the intransigent nationalists on either side, competing national interests and domestic disagreements among Western states led to ambiguity and mixed messages. The many conflicting signals could have been read in several ways: as support for the Slovene and Croatian cause, for the federal government's policies, for the Serbian suspicions, and for the army's conviction that it needed to prepare a defense and that it would not be deterred by foreign intervention. The effect was to encourage all parties to the conflict to believe their chosen course would eventually win, and thus to become more tenacious.

The idea that Yugoslavia would be the test case of a more unified Europe and of new security institutions in the EC or CSCE arose before those institutions were well in place. Yugoslavia was to serve as a vehicle to create those institutions and force that unity, not as its beneficiary. Rather than provide the means for peaceful resolution of conflict, Western powers would work out a stage in their own global transition on the Yugoslav case. Because national interests and spontaneous sympathies took the lead, outsiders reinforced historically defined perceptions and suspicions among Yugoslavs rather than working to reduce tensions and counteract fears. As the EC became more directly engaged, moreover, the Yugoslav quarrel would become fully enmeshed in the internal politics of Western integration, including the bargaining over the Maastricht Treaty, the competition already emerging among Western countries over potential spheres of influence in eastern Europe, and the heightened sensitivity within the EC to the potential power of a united Germany.

## Intervention and the Use of Force Doctrine: Redefining the Conflict

Four days after Baker's visit (and twenty-four hours before originally planned), Croatia and Slovenia followed through on their intent to declare independence.[40] The Slovene government sent military forces and civilian officials to take over control of eight border controls and customs, replacing signposts for Yugoslavia with ones that read "Republic of Slovenia."[41] The Austrian consul general and several provincial governors attended the Slovene independence celebrations on June 26.[42] The federal government had warned that it would use all means necessary to protect the territorial integrity of the state. However, because the Serbian bloc in the presidency still refused to seat Mesić, the Croatian representative in line for president (their reasons for which—put forth in May—having gained more credibility with the declarations of independence), and no alternative had arisen, constitutional authority over the army remained in doubt. On June 25 the Parliament and the cabinet ignored constitutional niceties and ordered army units based in Slovenia and Croatia to assert Yugoslav sovereignty over its borders with Austria and Italy.

The response of the European Community was rapid. Under its mechanism for intergovernmental cooperation on foreign policy since the

1970s and an Italian proposal, the European Political Cooperation [EPC] of the Council of Ministers, the foreign ministers of the sitting "troika," met on June 28 with Prime Minister Marković, Foreign Minister Lončar, and the republican presidents of Slovenia, Croatia, and Serbia.[43] The EC leaders insisted on a cease-fire and began negotiations to bring it about. In addition, an immediate request from Austria for a meeting of the Conflict Prevention Center of the CSCE (under its rubric for "unusual military activities") and of its CSO resulted in a meeting with Yugoslav parties on July 1.[44] With the agreement of the Yugoslav representative at the meeting, Foreign Minister Lončar, the CSCE called for an "immediate and complete cessation of all hostilities" and a return to barracks of both the YPA and Slovene TDF units. On July 4, its CSO, on the initiative of its chair, German foreign minister Hans Dietrich-Genscher, went to Belgrade, where it joined its "good offices" with an EC mediation mission composed of senior diplomats from its EPC countries. Jointly these parties sought "to facilitate the political dialogue among the parties concerned."[45]

For Europe, the Yugoslav troubles had moved from the category of academic speculation and competing national interests to events constituting a crisis and a potential threat to its collective security. Although 400 deaths had been attributed to the conflict (largely in Croatia) before the army moved to secure the northwestern borders and although the time for political dialogue had been during the preceding twelve months, it was only when the constitutional conflict over competing sovereignties between Slovenia and the federal government moved to military showdown that Europe's mechanisms for a peaceful resolution of disputes came into play.

The unilateral action by Slovenia presented Western powers with a serious dilemma. Their commitment to the right of peoples to self-determination, embodied in the UN Charter and the Helsinki Accords, had several possible interpretations. Did it mean the inviolability of international borders, the territorial integrity of states, and the right of sovereign states to noninterference in their internal affairs? If so, the federal action to protect the territorial integrity of Yugoslavia was legitimate. Did it mean the right of peoples to self-determination, freely chosen? If so, nearly 90 percent of the voting publics of Slovenia and Croatia had chosen independence. Did this constitute an inalienable right of nations to independence, and was the international community therefore obliged to recognize their sovereignty in spite of the sanctity of borders and principle of noninterference? Was this choice a human right, as defined by the Helsinki Final Act and permitting CSCE signatories to abrogate those principles and intervene in its defense? Whose choice should be respected in this case: Did it require a vote of all of Yugoslav citizens? Of those citizens with national rights but in a minority within Slovenia and Croatia, as the federal constitution implied? Or did international obligations extend only to the protection of elemental individual rights within an existing state, and not to the collective right to secede?

Moreover, in the course of the preceding six months, Western powers had spoken in many voices on the subject. The European Parliament had explicitly declared the internal borders of Yugoslavia to be inviolable, effectively accepting the independent rights of Slovenia and Croatia. The German leadership had defined the results of a popular referendum as the deciding criterion for the right of East German citizens to abolish their state and rejoin fellow Germans in West Germany. The delegations of the European Community and the United States had appeared to waver, depending on their assessment of the outcome most likely to promote regional and global stability. The EC had demanded unity in exchange for credits, but its representations had acknowledged contending positions. Its leap to demonstrate its capacity for a common foreign policy regarding Yugoslavia, moreover, was made in response to requests from opposing sides of the conflict—from Slovenia, although it was not a state, and from the Marković cabinet of the federal government.

There were, in fact, two polar positions. The Austrian position, presented by Foreign Minister Mock, was that Yugoslavia was—and always had been—an artificial state, and that denial of the Slovene right to secede threatened war. But this argument patently appeared to be one of national interest, based on Austria's assessment that its border was more secure with an independent Slovenia and with the Yugoslav army at a distance (a position that many read as the continuation of Austria's century-old enmity toward Serbia). The fact that Germany now openly began to call for immediate recognition, however, gave the Austrian position greater weight. The other extreme was represented by the United States. Secretary of State Baker and Ambassador Zimmermann argued that the breakup of Yugoslavia would be highly destabilizing and could not occur without war and horrendous carnage. This position also had strong French and British support. Although many acknowledged Slovene, Croatian, and Albanian aspirations, preoccupations with stability in the Soviet Union and the risks of its disintegration if a precedent were set in Yugoslavia dictated the hope of many that Yugoslavia would remain united.

The EC-CSCE team ignored the political dilemma presented by its contradictory principles of European security and also the inconsistency of its previous positions. Viewing the problem from the perspective of European security, it reduced the entire Yugoslav conflict to a border dispute between two parties, Slovenia and the federal government, and to the limited objective of a cease-fire. In place of the political dialogue it had aimed to facilitate, it applied a procedural rule that obliged CSCE signatories to the peaceful settlement of disputes and defensive use of force alone.

The goal was to stop the fighting, not to establish criteria for judging the right to self-determination among Yugoslav nations and citizens, to reverse the process of a state's disintegration, or to lay the basis for a genuine political negotiation of the conflicts—including borders, if the state did break up.

But the political ascendancy of nationalists willing to use force to achieve their objectives had been a problem for a year. Given the lack of international definition of the practical meaning of self-determination, the introduction of the criterion of force and the distinction between its defensive and aggressive use appeared to give those intent on separation a winning strategy. If they could provoke the Yugoslav army into violent resistance of their moves toward independence and appear to be using force only in self-defense, they could trigger EC and U.S. support for their goal. Indeed, within hours of the army's move, British foreign secretary Douglas Hurd announced a change in policy, saying that the United Kingdom was "obliged significantly to qualify an early statement supporting the 'integrity of Yugoslavia' by adding that this should not include the use of force."[46] On June 30, U.S. deputy secretary of state Eagleburger said that the United States supported "sovereign republics" and the idea of a Yugoslav confederation.[47]

Nevertheless, by defining the outcome in terms of the use of force and leaving untouched the ambiguity over the political issues at stake, these mediators condemned their own efforts to failure. Neither the EC nor the CSCE had the military capacity to act or even to mount a credible threat to intervene with force that might deter those willing to use force in Yugoslavia.[48] The United States had publicly declared its unwillingness to use military power in the case and had insisted as well that NATO should not become involved anywhere "out of area." In addition, the most vocal member state of the EC in support of Slovene independence at the time was Denmark, and the head of the EC negotiating team—Foreign Minister Jacques Poos of Luxembourg—was to be succeeded within days by Foreign Minister van den Broek of the Netherlands. All three countries were adamant supporters of NATO.

This position on the use of force by outside mediators demonstrated, in fact, how unprepared they were for their own intervention. The Serbian leaders had said many times that, if the state broke up, they would insist on redrawing borders to incorporate Serbs currently living outside Serbia. The army had already come to the defense, not only of the Yugoslav border, but also of civil order and of minorities during violent clashes between Croats and Serbs in Croatia in the spring. Leaders in Slovenia and Croatia had also made it clear that their republics' independence would not be complete until the Yugoslav army disintegrated, but that disintegration would make available to others—including those within the army and political circles who opposed the breakup of the state or who hoped to prevent further disintegration of a smaller "rump" Yugoslavia without Slovenia and Croatia—masses of weaponry and reserves. Secretary of State Baker began to speak openly of the threat of Serb aggression, without changing the U.S. policy not to provide a credible threat against this scenario. Officials in both the United Kingdom and the United States even rewrote their analysis of the conflict, as if to justify to themselves and to their publics their rapid policy shift on Yugoslav integrity and their unwillingness to commit force, either to uphold European security or reverse what they now defined as aggression. These same leaders, who had stressed the economic bases for the Yugoslav conflict, now distanced themselves by calling it a consequence of "nationalist passions too long suppressed under the weight of Communism and the cold war."[49]

Slovene minister of defense Janez Janša had prepared well for the possible confrontation, including the illegal purchase abroad of sophisticated weapons and the formation of a network of pro-Slovene military officers and conscripts within the YPA.[50] The Slovene government showed its continuing appreciation of the importance of a combined political and military strategy; its tactics included the shaping of international opinion in their favor.

The military doctrine and division of labor between the YPA and the territorial defense forces (TDFs) of socialist Yugoslavia made it easy to give the appearance of self-defense. In addition, however, Slovenia sought to remind Europe of the threat the conflict could pose to its commerce; for example, the Slovene TDFs used foreign truck drivers and their wagons as hostage barriers against the army on the Yugoslav highway linking the Middle East and Greece to western Europe. Nearly constant air raid sirens in Ljubljana, apparently unrelated to real threats from the air force, served to reinforce Slovene loyalties and portray Slovenes as the weaker party in the face of the army's advantage in air power.[51] The government also recalled all remaining Slovene representatives in the federal Parliament and administration and refused to attend the EC meeting in Belgrade on June 28, arguing that Slovenia was no longer a part of Yugoslavia.

The YPA, in contrast, was not well prepared, as evidenced by its poor organization and its use of conscripts in light summer uniforms only two weeks after they had completed training exercises. Of 20,000 troops stationed in Slovenia, only 2,000 were used.[52] The soldiers were trained to disable an invading enemy by knocking out communications while giving time for territorial defense forces to mobilize for a guerrilla-based defense. Their actions in the face of an internal rather than an external enemy only made them appear to be an invading army to Slovene citizens and played well into Slovenia's propaganda. The army's humiliating performance— Slovene minister of defense Janša crowed at the ease of the fight, saying all

he had to do was blow up a single bridge—led immediately to two interpretations. One was that the army had been planning the fight for many
years, but that its blitzkrieg strategy wrongly assumed no effective popular
resistance.[53] But even if the army miscalculated the strength of anti-
Yugoslav sentiment in Slovenia, the strategic role of the TDFs was to
provide that resistance, and there was surely intelligence about Slovene
military preparations.[54] The other interpretation was that a deal had already been cut between presidents Kučan and Milošević to let Slovenia go,
and that the general staff had accepted this deal and feigned a fight.[55]

A more likely interpretation, however, is the rapidity with which the
conflict had evolved, the absence of policy for such a contingency, and the
general confusion over appropriate action when political disintegration creates doubt about constitutionality and legality.[56] The memoirs of Minister
of Defense Kadijević suggest a clear distinction between the first two days
of YPA action, when it was executing an explicit government policy based
on a court decision that the Slovene actions were unconstitutional, and the
following days, when it began to react to direct attacks on YPA officers
and soldiers (or what Slovenes would call counterattacks) and a blockade
of all YPA units and facilities.[57] Prime Minister Marković denied even the
first mandate, although the Parliament and the cabinet did so decide, by
citing the facts that only the state presidency had authority to order the
army and that it was disabled by the refusal of the Serbian voting bloc to
seat Mesić. The reduced presidency did act, declaring a state of emergency
in Slovenia so as to prevent escalation, but Slovenes ignored the decision.
Kadijević also argues that the general staff had no choice but to act, for if
it "had refused to execute its part of the task of the political decisions of
the Parliament of the SFRY, then that could be the end of the army in the
worst possible way."[58] Evidence of the confusion can be found in the behavior of local commanders, such as those who ignored orders to hold
their fire and the commander at Novo Mesto on the Zagreb-Ljubljana
highway who shot one of his own officers for protesting his engagement
against local units of the territorial defense. Such local showdowns helped
to raise the number of casualties—for the YPA, to 37 killed and 163
wounded, and for the Slovene forces, to 12 killed and 144 wounded—and
to persuade popular and foreign opinion further of YPA ferocity and ineptitude.[59] All of these actions and views suggest ambiguity over whether
Slovenia was still a part of the country, and the goal was to keep it in, or
whether it was lost. The question was settled, according to Kadijević, by
the facts on the ground. The army "found itself in an impossible situation,"
because all Slovenes saw it as an occupation army, which the army did not
want to be. Furthermore, the dispersion of the officer corps to Slovenia,
Croatia, and in part Macedonia and the increasing difficulty with mobilizing soldiers (less than half had reported and the territory for recruitment

was narrowing daily) were threatening the YPA's ability to perform its tasks elsewhere, especially in Croatia. Although the general staff debated three options on how to leave Slovenia, this decision and the dispute within the government were interrupted by the EC intervention.[60]

The day after the army moved, on June 27, Prime Minister Marković called on Slovenia and Croatia to suspend their moves toward independence for three months, although this in effect recognized the legitimacy of their declarations. The next day EC negotiators met in the early morning hours in Zagreb with leaders from Slovenia, Croatia, and Macedonia and put forth Marković's proposals for what was meant as a return to the status quo ante: that the army withdraw to its barracks, that Mesić be seated as president, and that the Slovenes and Croats suspend all activities aimed at independence for three months while talks took place. The Yugoslav presidency concurred on July 1, restoring constitutionality to this collective commander in chief of the army as well as to civilian control by seating Mesić.

The army accepted that authority on July 3, but this did not resolve the original problem. The package agreement attempted to freeze the conflict in place and restore the constitutional authority of the presidency, but this only served as an open rebuke of the Serbian-controlled voting bloc and its view that Mesić intended to use that position to win Croatian independence and dissolve Yugoslavia while the Slovene and Croatian governments ignored the moratorium.[61] The mediators introduced no new parameters to the conflict, and the author of the package they proposed, Prime Minister Marković, used the occasion to continue the federal quarrel between the army budget and economic reform by turning on the minister of defense, Kadijević, on July 4, accusing him and the army of illegal action in Slovenia.[62] On July 5, using one of the few instruments it had to influence the conflict, the EC aimed sanctions at the *federal* government by suspending almost $1 billion in economic aid and imposing an embargo on arms exports to Yugoslavia.[63] The United States expressed its approval.

Moreover, the Brioni Agreement of July 7, named for the island where the EC troika had met with representatives of the Yugoslav federal government and the republics to sign the cease-fire, in effect recognized the Slovene military victory. It also made Slovenia and Croatia the subject, de facto, of international law and cleared the way for the eventual recognition of their statehood.[64] Although foreign journalists at the Brioni meeting challenged Foreign Minister van den Broek to explain how the EC could treat Slovenia in isolation from the rest of the country, the EC troika assumed that the only issue left to the negotiated cease-fire was its monitoring. With a mandate from the CSCE to deploy thirty to fifty observers, named "ice-cream men" by Yugoslavs for the white uniforms they chose, the EC began its first-ever effort at peacekeeping.[65]

The prospects for a military test of Croatian sovereignty were thus dramatically enhanced. By small steps made in rapid succession, the EC and the CSCE were helping to complete the demise of the federal government: withdrawing support from Marković's government, accusing the army of aggression, and taking over the presidency's role as interlocutor among the republics. Despite the tendency in the Western press and among some diplomats to equate Serbia with the federal government, the Brioni Agreement also accomplished the first step of Serbian nationalists' goals—to remove Slovenia and make it possible to redraw internal borders. The EC had ignored the origins of the conflict—the economic decline, market reforms, and quarrels over the political reform necessary to them—and had accepted the representation of the conflict and possible solutions posed by radical nationalist governments in Slovenia, Croatia, and Serbia. It had opened the door to war in Croatia and Bosnia-Herzegovina, and was in the process of depriving the moderates, nonnationalists, southerners, federal government, and majority of the population caught in an ethnically complex situation of any representation or say in the matter. For example, the day after the Slovene Parliament ratified the Brioni Agreement, on July 11, a coalition of peace and civic groups organized a demonstration in Sarajevo of 50,000 citizens in support of a united Yugoslavia. Two weeks later, as fighting escalated in Croatia, massive peace demonstrations were organized by mothers against war and citizens' groups in Belgrade, Sarajevo, and Skopje. The first of five principles established in the Brioni Agreement for future negotiations stated, "It is up to the Yugoslav *peoples* [author's emphasis] to decide their future," as if the individual *citizens* of Yugoslavia, regardless of their nationality or other collective identity, should not decide their own future, or at least have a voice.[66]

Perhaps most decisive of all, the Brioni Agreement struck a serious blow against the authority of the faction within the army leadership that was fighting to hold Yugoslavia together and of those who still hoped to play a mediating, pacifying role in the nationalist quarrels (called the Titoists by their critics on all sides). Forced to choose between loyalty to Yugoslavia or to the new national armies, army leaders at the highest levels began to rethink their role in this political quarrel, and the balance of opinion began to shift toward those who could only see a military solution to border conflicts. The ensuing struggle for power within the army removed the constraints of YPA political traditions in the anti-fascist liberation of 1941–45, the Communist party, or the constitution for many ethnically Serb and Montenegrin junior officers, who long resented the limits on their promotion, salaries, and benefits that national quotas posed for their proportionately greater numbers at those ranks, and for local commanders who sympathized with the fears or aspirations of autonomist Serbs. With the collapse of the state, established lines of authority within the army and between branches of security forces were also being challenged by the growing number of private armies (particularly those attached to political parties), paramilitary formations, and republican defense units, and by the greater demands on local police forces to protect civil order. Myriad possibilities for local and national alliances independent of central command and a growing dependence on irregulars, because the majority of youth subject to conscription did not want to fight such a war, fed the military confusion further.[67] The EC observers sent to Croatia in August refused even to speak to representatives of the federal army.

In contrast to Slovenia, the goal of Croatian sovereignty involved two issues: not only Western recognition of its independence, but also relations with members of the Serb nation within Croatia. The second was already the cause of fighting between Croatian police and Serbian local resistance in the Dalmatian hinterland and eastern Slavonia (Kninska *krajina*, Lika, Kordun, Banija, eastern Slavonia, and Baranja). In some cases this was the result of a Zagreb-directed strategy to consolidate Croat ethnic control over the police and state administration, especially in Knin and its surrounding area. By June 1991 the relative moderates under Jovan Rašković in the Serbian Democratic Party were losing out to militants because of President Tudjman's refusal to consider their demands in 1990 for cultural autonomy, their escalated demands for political representation that followed, and their eventual referendum on territorial autonomy for the Serbian Autonomous Region of Krajina, which he declared illegal. The radical Serbs supporting Milan Babić had political links with the leadership in Serbia and were well armed and organized into multiple militia (the Martićevci of Milan Martić; units trained by the international mercenary Captain Dragan, with aid from paramilitary forces in Serbia and units of the army) to defend their goal of remaining within a rump Yugoslavia if Croatia, which they believed to be a fascist state, actually split.

In other instances, such as the violence in Borovo Selo near Vukovar in eastern Croatia in early May 1991—which electrified ethnic tensions between local Croats and Serbs throughout the region of eastern Slavonia—local power struggles and ambitious police officers, in defiance of a Zagreb agreement for the protection of local Serbs, initiated fighting. This exacerbated fears already stirred up by outsiders—Croat radicals of the ruling Croatian Democratic Union (HDZ)—and the Croatian Party of Right and Serb radicals such as Vojislav Šešelj's Serbian Radical party and the criminal-turned-right-wing nationalist, Željko Ražnatović (also known as Arkan) from across the border in Serbia.[68] Whatever the outcome of these tensions, Croatian authorities would have to face the question of Serb political rights in Croatia and the challenge to its borders if it became independent.

The first issue for Croatia—gaining international recognition—was a matter of strategy. In contrast to Slovene authorities, President Tudjman chose to rely far more on Western diplomatic and military support of what the Croats considered their "moral" rights as members of Western civilization, as democrats, and as victims. He even refused his generals' advice to prepare a serious defense and train soldiers (even while allowing, and in many cases encouraging, military confrontation in ethnically mixed areas) so as to appear defenseless and thereby secure international sympathy and recognition.[69] Although Tudjman was building an army out of the territorial defense forces, internal security police (MUP), and weapons purchased illegally abroad, he was able to portray this as purely a defensive measure. This strategy seemed too passive, however, for militants among local police forces and paramilitary forces of the right-wing Croatian Party of Right (the Croatian Defense League [HOS] under Dobrislav Paraga) who were willing to use military force and took matters into their own hands by engaging in local fights with individual Serbs. Their attempts to force Serbs out of eastern Slavonia and their readiness to match paramilitary gangs from Serbia with equal force made it impossible to separate the two issues of Croatia's sovereignty—human rights and national borders—on the ground. Moreover, the apparent reluctance of the Croatian government to train and arm its conscripts sufficiently, in line with its foreign strategy, contributed to an ever higher casualty rate in eastern Slavonia once the army became involved. As a result, the attractiveness to young soldiers concerned for their own survival of the better-trained paramilitary forces of the HOS increased the number of those fighting offensively and outside governmental authority. Moreover, Minister of Defense Kadijević was sending additional YPA troops and tanks from Serbia and Macedonia into Croatia. On July 18, reacting to Slovene noncompliance with the Brioni agreement, the Yugoslav collective presidency ordered the army to withdraw from Slovenia.[70] The Brioni moratorium on moves toward independence effectively came to an end for Slovenia, the presidency acknowledged its inability to protect YPA troops and their families, and these units were sent to Bosnia-Herzegovina, Serbia, and Montenegro.

Many in Yugoslavia still hoped that a Yugoslavia without Slovenia could be retained. Even President Tudjman's closest advisers believed, in mid-July 1991, that a confederation could be constructed out of the former republics.[71] But because they could only conceive of this as a voluntary act of separate states, they viewed their internationally recognized statehood *and* the disintegration of the last institution of Yugoslavia as a state, the Yugoslav People's Army, as its preconditions. Croatian leaders were no more attentive to the fears, concerns, and interests of the Serb population in Croatia than during the election campaign and revision of the constitution and rights of citizenship, and this arrogance was implicitly approved by the European Community when it treated the Slovene and Croatian declarations of independence equally in the Brioni Agreement and gave no consideration to the consequences in Croatia. Instead the Europeans continued to believe, in agreement with the position held at the time by most political forces in Serbia, that a rump Yugoslavia could be constructed without Slovenia and Croatia. (For example, leaders of the centrist opposition Democratic Party believed that once Croats felt secure in their independence, they would rejoin this new Yugoslavia under some confederal relationship.) Europeans appeared to ignore the threat of Serb nationalists (who differed only on whether this construction of a new Yugoslavia could be negotiated or would require war)—that this Yugoslavia would have to incorporate the geographically contiguous parts of Croatian territory where Serbs lived in the majority.[72] The European response thus ensured that those who accepted the necessity of war would gain the upper hand.

Neither the Croatian leadership nor the European Community seemed to give any thought, moreover, to the consequences for Bosnia-Herzegovina or Macedonia. Croatian president Tudjman's reference point was the Yugoslav idea of 1918 in which the state was formed by three peoples (Slovenes, Croats, and Serbs). Bosnia-Herzegovina, with its delicate balance of three constituent nations—Muslims (44 percent), Serbs (31 percent), and Croats (17 percent)—its Bosnian political identity as a multinational republic, and its many non-Slav minorities, was, theoretically, threatened if either Croatia or Serbia formed a separate state. According to the leaders of Muslim and Croatian communities in Bosnia-Herzegovina, neither group could live with any sense of security in a Yugoslavia without Croatia; leaders of the Serb community felt Serbs would not be safe from this local majority unless the state included Serbia. Tudjman's admission to a London *Times* interviewer in July 1991 that he and President Milošević had met secretly on a number of occasions during March and April 1991 to work out the details of a division of Bosnia between them (which he immediately retracted, but were proved true—except for the fact that they had begun by January 1991 and perhaps as early as July 1990) seemed to confirm the rumors that both had long had advisory commissions of experts to work out territorial divisions and population transfers.[73] It certainly explained why neither leader spoke of Bosnia's fate.

Tudjman had a second reference point, of the borders of Croatia defined by the 1939 autonomy agreement and the wartime independent state of Croatia (NDH), which included much of Bosnia. He made it known on a number of occasions that *his* Croatia encompassed these 1939 parts of Bosnia, and his party's critical constituency in western Herzegovina—and the growing importance in Zagreb political and financial circles of the Herzegovinian lobby—made this historical goal a political imperative.[74] Milošević's advisers also made no bones about their intentions: "We'll deal with Croatia first, then Bosnia," they told me in mid-July 1991. The majority of the Serb population of Bosnia lived in the countryside, and the wish of these people to remain within a Yugoslavia (if the leaders of the Serbian Democratic party [SDS] in Bosnia-Herzegovina are to be believed) provided the basis for a land bridge between Serbia proper and Serb-claimed areas in the Croatian *krajina*—a corridor that had already formed politically between the two branches of the SDS. Even the Yugoslav state presidency discussed the possible division of Bosnia during the spring of 1991, when the hope of a constitutional compromise between Slovenia, Croatia, and Serbia was still alive, but they could reach no agreement on a formula.[75]

Once Slovenia left, the various political struggles within Yugoslavia became focused on the construction of separate states out of the territory that remained. Only the nationalists had organized around this goal and were prepared with concepts and strategy. All others were at an immediate disadvantage, having to regroup and devise a response. The European emphasis on the use of force criterion rather than on the criteria for national self-determination and the drawing of borders where claims conflicted had the effect opposite of that intended, giving a marked advantage to those persons who were willing and had the weaponry to take territory militarily. It also fed a competitive escalation of military force among political parties that perceived themselves as defenders of rights, rather than as aggressors on others' rights. Moreover, the EC missions and negotiations held throughout July and August met only with the leaders of Slovenia, Croatia, and Serbia, whether federal authorities were present or not—as if the fates of Bosnia-Herzegovina, Macedonia, and Montenegro were not also at stake. The EC increasingly treated the federal government as perfunctory, and by November 1991 it was no longer even included. The EC and CSCE had assumed the power not only to define the conflict, but also to decide who would be the players in negotiations over Yugoslavia's future and who would be excluded.

## The War in Croatia:
## Military Intervention or Diplomatic Recognition?

The fighting in Croatia worsened dramatically during late July and August 1991. By the second week of August, the war had claimed 300 lives, and Serbs in Croatia were in military control of 15 percent of its territory. Refugees fleeing the fighting or expelled from their homes in ethnically mixed areas (both Croat and Serb) numbered approximately 79,000 by mid-August. EC negotiators got nowhere with their attempts to obtain a peace accord, as first Croatia refused to sign and President Tudjman walked out, on July 22, and then President Milošević boycotted talks on August 4.

By early July, two alternative tactics had surfaced. The Group of Seven (G-7) powers called for a UN peacekeeping force, and the German Parliament (the Bundestag) voted to recognize Croatia and Slovenia. The first garnered no interest whatsoever in the UN Security Council. Dominant opinion in both the UN Security Council and UN General Assembly at the time was that this was a civil conflict that international intervention would exacerbate. The Soviet Union, which was facing a similar problem at the time with the Baltic republics and in the debate over the constitutional redefinition of relations between the republics (the union treaty), made clear it would veto a peacekeeping force. The United States was also holding back at the time for a number of reasons, the most important of which was its unwillingness to commit its own military resources. But there were also major disagreements among divisions of the U.S. government over whether to become involved (with the National Security Council and the Pentagon opposed, and the State Department in favor), while the secretary of state was reported to be personally piqued at Slovenia and Croatia for blatantly ignoring their promise not to move unilaterally. For the moment, moreover, German foreign minister Genscher was opposed to the idea of using immediate recognition as a diplomatic tool in the war, and the British and French were adamantly opposed, since the precedent might be used by nationalists, such as the Scots or Corsicans, in their countries.

By August 3, EC foreign ministers began to discuss the need for some "interposition forces" if they were to be at all effective in achieving a cease-fire. First suggested by the foreign minister of Luxembourg, Jacques Poos, he was quickly joined by the foreign ministers of the Netherlands (which held the EC Council presidency) and Germany and by the president of France.[76] Yet this required them to confront a fact that they had avoided until then—that there was no force to use. It was obvious to the French, who had been arguing for some time for a European military force as an alternative to NATO, that the time had come to revive talk of a Eurocorps, at the core of which would be a German-French corps.[77] The opposition from the United States, however, was immediate and unambiguous. The French, supported by Italy, then urged the West European Union to begin contingency planning, but it had no troops or equipment. On August 5, France took the issue to the UN Security Council. There, the Soviet Union maintained its opposition, however, arguing that such intervention would escalate: "to enter . . . on one side . . . would mean to come into conflict automatically with others, inside and outside Yugoslavia. And the conflict would grow into an all-European one."[78]

According to the norm of noninterference in the UN charter, more-over, any peace force sent must have the consent of the warring parties—which were identified as the federal government, Croatia, and Serbia. Serbia refused, citing interference in Yugoslav sovereignty.[79] This gave fuel, however, to the German position, as Chancellor Kohl and Foreign Minister Genscher became more assertive on sanctions against Serbia for its "aggression" and on the recognition of Slovenia and Croatia as a means to circumvent the need for consent for an EC interposition force by inter-nationalizing the internal borders. But it also fueled British objections to military force, based on a military staff report concerning the large number of troops that would be required and Britain's own experience in Northern Ireland.[80]

The instruments available to the EC and CSCE in their attempt to influence the Yugoslav conflicts were primarily economic incentives or penalties and moral suasion. The EC was still largely a bureaucracy for economic coordination, and the CSCE a set of voluntary agreements by states to abide by the norms of cooperation, consultation, and human rights that they had established. The effectiveness of both instruments was problematic, however, for they presumed to apply either to a state whose very existence was challenged by their actions (as in the case of the subject of CSCE agreements, as signatory to the Helsinki Final Act—Yugoslavia) or to states that did not yet exist (as in the case of application of punishments or incentives to the republics). On August 6, the EC Council of Ministers (acting as the EPC) requested that the EC Commission recommend economic and financial measures it might take against parties refusing to participate in a cease-fire (at the time identified as Serbia). On August 8–9 the CSCE held its second emer-gency session and demanded the Yugoslav parties respect the cease-fire proclaimed on August 6 by the Yugoslav presidency and urged imme-diate resumption of negotiations on the future of Yugoslavia, repeating its offer of good offices of July 3–4.

In moving from the carrot of economic aid and association with the EC in May to the stick of punitive sanctions and withdrawal of aid during July and early August, however, the two organizations only compounded the division within Yugoslavia between those who saw options outside of Yugoslavia and those who, out of a realist assessment or objection to the consequences of rapid westernization, sought some alternative within an independent Yugoslavia.[81] The EC had no leverage with those convinced (on realist grounds) that it had no intention of incorporating and aiding Yugoslavia anyway (above all Milošević's coalition and many senior army officers), and liberals outside of Slovenia and Croatia once again had no help in counteracting this assumption. The EC also had little leverage over Slovenia and Croatia to convince them to remain within Yugoslavia or even participate in negotiations about its future because they already had assurances of economic assistance if they left.

Reliance on economic statecraft also reinforced the division within the European Community between a powerful Germany and a Britain and France that sought various means to counterbalance it. In place of a common foreign policy and definition of collective interest for a post–cold war Europe, the EC would find unity in common economic interests—the protectionism of a "fortress Europe" against the outside—or else the competition between the twelve members would dominate. Thus, German diplomatic assertiveness could bring closer to the surface for Britain and France a major political subtext of the Maastricht Treaty, that of further constraining German economic power in Europe, and thereby link the Yugoslav crisis to the politics of treaty ratification. Competition would remind all that they were not a single great power able to act in unison with a common foreign policy, but a set of states with different national interests capable of being manipulated to some degree. And it would prevent any decisive and rapid response while member states debated their disagreements. The consequence was most tragic in the debate over military force, as the endless cycles of debate over the next two years gave to all combatants on the ground—whatever the particular Yugoslav engagement of the moment—time to arm, restock, and reconnoiter.

In addition to lowering its effectiveness, the predominance of national interests and the traditional alignments within the EC also reinforced the role in the Yugoslav conflict of perceptions that an older geopolitical divide was reoccurring. The loud support for Slovenia and Croatia from Austria, Hungary, Denmark, Germany, the Vatican, and eventually Italy, on the one hand, and the great reticence about an interpretation of self-determination that would dissolve an existing state on the part of France, Britain, Spain, and Greece, on the other, had the appearance of geopolitical alignments affecting the Balkans at several points in the preceding century. Thus the EC division was likely to revive historical memories within Yugoslav politics and undermine the credibility of EC or CSCE efforts at moral suasion. Beyond the widely shared opinion among Serbs of different political persuasions that they were, in fact, seeing German revanchism, those who were inclined to see the threat of historical geopolitical alignments in the behavior of major powers gained further evidence from the leaderships of Bosnia-Herzegovina and Macedonia.[82] Reacting to their invisibility in the negotiations and lack of European patrons, both began a search for external support in the Middle East. In July 1991, President Izetbegović toured Pakistan, Saudi Arabia, and Turkey and sent envoys of Muslim identity to posts in Islamic states, while Macedonian president Kiro Gligorov went to Turkey; Ankara opened a consulate in Sarajevo soon thereafter. In the face of an impending breakup, Bulgaria and Greece signed a mutual defense pact in response to these overtures to Turkey and to U.S. President Bush's statement made in Ankara that same July that the United States was placing its hopes for stability in the region on Turkey. A year later, Bulgaria and Turkey signed a treaty of military cooperation and force reduction talks, the Sofia Declaration, enabling Turkey to reposition troops on the border with Kurdistan and with Greece.[83]

## The Priority of Other Interests

For the Europeans—and particularly the three powers of Britain, France, and Germany—European security lay with the fate of the Soviet Union and its nuclear arsenal and with the outcome of the Maastricht Treaty, not with conflict in the Balkans. Thus it was a change in these two events that would provide the two key turning points in the EC approach to the Yugoslav conflict.

Until the attempted putsch in the Soviet Union of August 19–22, 1991, the Yugoslav conflict was, for most Europeans, a reflection of the Soviet threat. There were, however, two views of this link. A minority understood the parallels between domestic conflicts in the Soviet Union and Yugoslavia, and thus saw that policies toward the two involved the same issues—just as the Soviet position in CSCE and the UN was taken with this fully in mind. In Germany in early 1991, the head of the foreign affairs committee of the parliamentary caucus of the opposition Social Democratic party (SPD), Karsten Voigt, instructed his staff to prepare an analysis of the Yugoslav quarrels and their lessons for Soviet developments. His motives were twofold: fear of the consequences for Germany if there were serious instability in the Soviet Union, and an effort to regain some SPD influence over foreign policy toward the East after Kohl's bonanza over unification and the four-plus-one (the Four Allied Powers and Germany) talks to negotiate rapid and eventually successful withdrawal of the Soviet army from its eastern *Länder*. On the basis of the staff report, Voigt decided that Yugoslavia could no longer be saved, and so he began a campaign to persuade the German Parliament that recognition of Slovene and Croatian independence would send a signal to Gorbachev: be more accommodating toward the Baltic states and Ukraine, or expect a preemptive strike from Germany.[84] The more common of the views, however, assumed an alliance between the Yugoslav and Soviet armies such that any direct confrontation with the YPA and its objectives threatened to draw in the Soviet army and its nuclear arsenal.

The failed putsch in Moscow made both fears moot, for the Soviet Union began to disintegrate into its separate constituent republics and the Soviet army was (at least temporarily) neutralized. It also removed the obstacle of a Soviet veto in the United Nations and the CSCE and opened a period of transition until its successor, Russia, would reassert this role. Under the leadership of Boris Yeltsin, Russia—like the Yugoslav republics and Germany—needed time to redefine national interests in the new global setting before it was ready to become a major diplomatic player.

With France less concerned, as a result, about maintaining Yugoslav unity and more concerned about EC unity on security matters as the Maastricht summit loomed closer and its prospects for involving the UN (where it could play its role as a major power) improved, the Austrian and German positions became even bolder. On August 24, Foreign Minister Genscher informed the Yugoslav ambassador that Germany would recognize Slovenia and Croatia if the army did not cease its violence. The Austrian vice-chancellor, Erhard Busek, declared that "the collapse of communism in the USSR modifies the situation in Yugoslavia and there is no more reason not to recognize the independence of Slovenia and Croatia."[85] And Hungary lodged a diplomatic protest charging Yugoslav forces with violating its air space. Three days later, on August 27, the EC abandoned its fiction of a commitment to Yugoslavia. The EPC declared the use of force by the Yugoslav federal army "illegal," and that Serbs who opposed their new minority position in the Croatian constitution could not "lawfully receive assistance from the YPA."[86] The EC declaration demanded that Serbia permit EC observers in Croatia, requested a third emergency meeting of the CSCE's Committee of Senior Officials, set up an arbitration commission of international jurists headed by French constitutional lawyer Robert Badinter to arbitrate issues of succession among the republics, and proposed a peace conference.[87] It then threatened further action if there were no cease-fire by September 1.

As for the Yugoslav conflict, the Belgrade Initiative of August 12 was evidence that the rest of Yugoslavia had begun to adjust to European actions. Milošević convened Serbian leaders from Serbia, Montenegro, and Bosnia-Herzegovina (the president of the Bosnian Assembly, Momčilo Krajišnik) to discuss a new constitution for a rump Yugoslavia.[88] On August 16 President Izetbegović announced a referendum on the future of Bosnia within Yugoslavia.[89] In Croatia, fighting had intensified during late August; on August 22 President Tudjman issued an ultimatum to the army tantamount to a declaration of war: leave the republic or be treated as an occupying force. Within days paramilitary Croatian forces and the YPA were in full battle in eastern Slavonia (and its towns of Osijek, Vinkovci, Vukovar, and others). The horror that was to result from the eighty-six-day battle over Vukovar (on the Danube), when the Yugoslav army, local Serbs, and paramilitary Serb groups of various origins eventually leveled the recently reconstructed city and left more than 2,300 dead and thousands wounded, began on August 25.[90]

Even before the peace conference opened in The Hague on September 7, Milošević had rejected its good offices and made it clear that he, along with many citizens in Yugoslavia, did not consider the EC neutral. Even the conference's mandate was decided by the EC rather than the parties to the conflict, and the uncompromising diatribes from both Tudjman and Milošević in their opening remarks cast a pall over European hopes for a rapid agreement. Tudjman called the Serbs war criminals who were engaged in a "dirty, undeclared war," and Milošević accused the Croatians of a "policy of genocide."[91] The next day, Macedonia held a referendum on independence and sovereignty, which roughly 71 percent of the electorate supported.[92] In the mode of the Croatian conflict, the political parties representing ethnic Albanians and Serbs declared a boycott. Bulgaria recognized Macedonian sovereignty on September 16, and Yugoslav president Mesić declared that Yugoslavia had ceased to exist because Minister of Defense Kadijević rejected his ultimatum that the army return to barracks in Croatia (a call repeated on September 15 by the foreign ministers of Germany and Italy). Refusing to convene the state presidency after September 6, Mesić also announced his intention to resign on October 7 when the three-month moratorium agreed at Brioni on Slovene and Croatian independence ran out, and called for peacekeeping forces in Croatia.[93] The Croatian government accused Serbia of masterminding the war and retaliated by turning off the spigot of the Adria oil pipeline that served Serbia (as well as Hungary and Czechoslovakia) from the Dalmatian coast. Imitating the successful Slovene tactics of early July, the Croatian government blockaded army barracks on September 14, seizing control of large stocks of weapons such as tanks and antitank artillery. There was no more doubt that, as Tudjman declared on August 22, Croatia and the army were at war. On September 19, the banned Parliament in Kosovo voted to declare its sovereignty and independence, and to hold a referendum to legitimize the declaration from September 26–30.

Between September 7 and December 15, EC mediation centered on its peace conference; the shuttle diplomacy of its chairman Lord Peter Carrington;[94] and the drafting (by civil servants in the conference's commission in Brussels) of a constitutional document on Yugoslavia's future that could be presented for negotiation to representatives of the republics and parties in conflict. Carrington was later criticized for ineffective methods, particularly for holding plenary sessions of only two hours each, spaced infrequently, and for not permitting debate among Yugoslav parties.[95] But the more fundamental problem was Carrington's mandate, for the EC remained ambiguous about its political objective and competing political principles, inconsistent in its declarations as a result of internal conflict, and unwilling to commit military forces to a situation it had prejudged as aggression by one party against another. Despite explicit

Dutch pressure to mount a force of 30,000 and Croatian requests for foreign troops, the debate in mid-September on using outside force repeated the course of the July discussions; British opposition, based on the belief that the number of troops required would continue to escalate, combined with Serbia's refusal to consent to what would be, in their view, an invasion. Thus the EC pulled back once again and at The Hague Peace Conference meeting on September 19 declared its express exclusion of military intervention.[96]

Without a clear mandate, Carrington also had competition. As early as August 5, the French had begun to explore other avenues of influence, largely through the UN, while Serbia began to pressure for U.S. involvement, believing that it would act as a counterforce to Germany. Austria, as a member of the UN Security Council at the time, doubled its efforts by turning to the UN and, at the request of Austria, Canada, Hungary—and the Yugoslav federal government—the UN Security Council met on September 25.[97]

Invoking Chapter 7 of the UN charter, that the Yugoslav conflict had become a "direct threat to international peace and security," the UN Security Council passed the first of sixty-seven resolutions that would be passed in the subsequent forty months—Resolution 713—which imposed a general and complete embargo on the delivery of all arms and military equipment to Yugoslavia. (The continuing reluctance of nonaligned countries and China to intervene was allayed in this case by the agreement of the Yugoslav representative.[98]) The UN Security Council also called for an immediate cease-fire and gave full support to the diplomatic efforts of the EC, including its position on the inviolability of the *republican and provincial* borders.[99] It then instructed the UN secretary general to begin consultations with the Yugoslav government and to keep the Security Council informed about all interventions to obtain a peaceful solution. In appointing former U.S. secretary of state Cyrus Vance as his personal envoy to Yugoslavia on October 8, UN secretary general Javier Pérez de Cuéllar seemed to confirm the hopes within Yugoslavia that the UN was acting as a proxy for the United States. On October 11, Vance began a series of missions to assess the situation that would soon involve him in full-scale efforts to negotiate a cease-fire, separately from, but in full consultation with, Lord Carrington and the EC.

Yet already on October 2, Slovene president Kučan announced in Paris that French president François Mitterrand had agreed to recognize Slovene independence. In Belgrade—in the name of a Yugoslavia without Slovenia, Croatia, and Macedonia—the Serbian bloc of four within the rump federal presidency declared a state of emergency as it had been demanding since March and assumed the extra powers allowable under the constitution in the case of imminent danger of civil war. The next day an emergency meeting at The Hague between the Yugoslav minister of defense, General Kadijević, presidents Tudjman and Milošević, and EC representatives van den Broek and Lord Carrington accepted in principle a peace plan that took as its starting point confederation and presumed the eventual independence of all republics that desired it.[100]

On October 15 the republican assembly of Bosnia-Herzegovina adopted a memorandum declaring the republic a sovereign and independent state within its existing borders. It also rejected both the Belgrade Initiative to form a new federation of nations and republics choosing to remain within Yugoslavia and a compromise proposed by the non-national, opposition parties in the Bosnian assembly. However, the vote was only by a majority of the assembly, minus the delegates representing Serb political parties. Proposed by the SDA leadership of the presidency, the memorandum was not accepted by its two Serb (SDS) members, and the members of the assembly from the two Serb parties, the SDS and SPO, walked out in opposition before the vote.[101] Claiming the Muslim-Croat alliance to be an anticonstitutional act against the parity principle of consensus of their three-nation, power-sharing coalition, the SDS left the coalition three days later to form its own assembly and announced a plebiscite, for November 9–10, on remaining within Yugoslavia.[102] On October 17, the government of Bosnia-Herzegovina created a new coat of arms and flag for the state and on October 29 informed the federal Parliament that it was a sovereign state. On October 18, the EC's Hague conference proposed a draft convention for a general settlement and threatened sanctions against any party that did not accept it by November 5.[103] The basis for a new settlement was a legal opinion requested from the Arbitration (Badinter) Commission: that since October 8, Yugoslavia was a "state in the process of dissolution."[104]

This legal hedge on the principles in conflict had no standing in international law. By opting against the alternative definition of the conflict, that it was a case of secession, and then recognizing the continuation of a smaller Yugoslavia, the EC took yet another step in support of recognizing Slovenia and Croatia.[105] It also opened the door to independence for the other republics—Macedonia and Bosnia-Herzegovina—that had so declared in the meantime. Although the EC's Brussels draft treaty convention—so called because it was written by EC civil servants in Brussels—was impressive in its construction of compromises that seemed to offer a hope of long-term stability, it contained provisions that were at the core of radical nationalism in the three dominant republics. Therefore the intransigent disagreements stalling negotiations over a cease-fire would also occur over the proposed political settlement. Indeed, even though Slovenia had always said that its proposal for confederation was based on the European Community, it refused even to consider the EC proposal for a customs union and any other post-Yugoslav economic relations among the former republics that would require recreating what it had fought against since 1985–87: that there be no administrative apparatus or institutions in common. Serbia reacted similarly; the EC draft treaty proposed a "special status of autonomy" for Albanians in Kosovo and a restoration of the autonomy of its two provinces, which was the very problem of the 1974 Constitution that Serbia had spent the 1980s attempting to reverse and on which Milošević had based his rise to power. The idea of special status for all territorially concentrated minorities was also not acceptable to the Croatian government or to the *krajina* Serb leadership, who by then controlled almost one-fourth of Croatian territory and had rejected President Tudjman's offer of local self-government to Serbs around Knin on July 31. Croatia by then was interested only in the intervention of foreign troops to assist in its recapture of that territory. Serbia alone openly rejected the plan, giving the reason that autonomy of its provinces was an internal affair that could not be regulated by international treaty and that it could not accept an ultimatum.[106]

Nonetheless, the EC proceeded with its strategy, imposing trade sanctions and threatening isolation on Yugoslavia on November 8 to press Serbia into accepting the plan and both Croatia and Serbia to sign a cease-fire.[107] During November diplomatic activity intensified to negotiate a cease-fire in Croatia and find bases for a political settlement. Britain, France, and Belgium began to push for a UN peacekeeping force to buttress these negotiations.[108] Tensions began to emerge between the EC and the UN over jurisdiction, however, such as the authority to impose the economic sanctions of November 8. Moreover, the German government, under renewed pressure from its Parliament by early November, was also intensifying its drive, along with Austria, for immediate recognition of Slovenia and Croatia.

By this time, world public opinion was beginning to form in response to televised pictures from the war in Croatia and reports by human rights organizations. An assault on Dubrovnik (beginning in early October), which was protected under the UN Educational, Scientific, and Cultural Organization (UNESCO), was particularly significant in creating antagonism toward Serbia and the army; the Croatian government had calculated in using sharpshooters on the Dubrovnik walls to provoke a YPA attack on the city, knowing that Dubrovnik would attract more attention than the more obscure city of Vukovar, which fell to Serbian forces on November 17. The shock effect of the destruction of Vukovar, the shorter siege of Dubrovnik, the first of many reports from Amnesty International and Helsinki Watch of human rights violations, and the beginnings of the refugee crisis became a powerful force for the German side, and its consistent view of Serbia as the enemy and the army and Serbs as aggressors.[109]

## Germany Forces a Choice: Recognition

The original motive for EC engagement in the Yugoslav crisis was to demonstrate its capacity for a common foreign policy under the terms of a closer economic and political union to be signed at Maastricht (the Netherlands) on December 9–10, 1991. As that deadline approached, the EC had eked out an approach to the Yugoslav crisis—to negotiate a cease-fire and try to obtain a political settlement among the republic leaders—but it could not agree on the means to force even a cease-fire. It had not yet recognized the need for a policy on self-determination and, as a result, could not fully confront the necessary link between a cease-fire and a political settlement. Lacking a common policy, unwilling to deploy troops without the consent of all parties on the ground, and more concerned about the Maastricht negotiations and internal EC relations, the EC states became increasingly vulnerable to German assertiveness, which had been on the rise since July. In mid-November, Chancellor Kohl announced that Germany would recognize Slovenia and Croatia by Christmas. Seeing the writing on the wall, Italy did an about-face, and Prime Minister Giulio Andreotti convened talks in Rome to coordinate the common position of Germany, Austria, and Italy, despite the language of the EC plan that recognition could only come "in the framework of a general settlement."[110]

The German argument for "preventive recognition" was that the fighting in Croatia was a result of Serbian and army aggression, against Croatia's territory and its right to self-determination. Therefore denying international recognition of that right was a ratification of the army's "policy of conquest" and invited an escalation of violence. Recognition of Croatian sovereignty would require Serbia to accept the fait accompli, enable international forces to intervene without the assent of the Yugoslav government (now controlled by the Serbian bloc), and therefore lead more rapidly to a cease-fire than would Carrington's negotiations.

The EC peace plan and EC policy, however, accepted the French position that recognition could only come after arrangements for human rights and common relations had been settled, as a reward. Despite fourteen failed cease-fire agreements under Carrington,[111] the Yugoslav army had begun to withdraw from Croatia on November 28, five days after a promising cease-fire negotiated by Vance had been signed at Geneva. Although UN Resolution 724, adopted on December 15, said conditions were not yet ready for a peacekeeping force, Vance had by then made enough progress that the Security Council agreed to send an advance team to prepare the way. So opposed to the German logic were the negotiators, Britain and the United States, that they took the unusual diplomatic step of putting their protests into writing. In letters to Dutch foreign minister Hans van den Broek, as chair of the Troika, and to Foreign Minister

Genscher, Lord Carrington, Secretary General Pérez de Cuéllar, Cyrus Vance, and the U.S. administration pleaded with them not to spoil the genuine progress toward a settlement.[112] In Carrington's letter to van den Broek on December 2, 1991, he warned that premature recognition of Slovenia and Croatia by the EC "would undoubtedly mean the break-up of the conference" and "might well be the spark that sets Bosnia-Herzegovina alight." Even President Izetbegović made an emotional appeal to Genscher in early December not to recognize Croatia prematurely, for it would mean war in his republic.

Despite all this, at the twelve-hour, all-night EPC meeting of foreign ministers in Brussels on December 15–16, Chancellor Kohl refused to budge. Although accused of locking the door and using bullying tactics, Kohl in fact obtained the agreement of Britain, France, and Spain by making two concessions. The first was a set of compromises on the EC monetary union that Britain had been seeking, including its demand to opt out of the treaty's social charter. The second was a compromise to preserve unity among the twelve EC members on Yugoslavia: that all six republics of Yugoslavia were eligible for recognition. The conditions required that the republics request recognition formally by December 23 and meet the criteria established by the Badinter Commission, including a commitment to continue working toward an overall settlement, by January 15, 1992, and UN, EC, and CSCE criteria on the rule of law, democracy, human rights, disarmament, nuclear nonproliferation, regional security, the inviolability of frontiers, and guarantees for the rights of ethnic and national groups and minorities. At 2:00 a.m. during the quarrel in Brussels, Greece inserted an additional requirement: that any state requesting recognition have no territorial claims against a neighboring EC state and not use a name that implied such claims—a blatant reference to Macedonia. Then, without waiting for the decision of the Badinter Commission, Germany recognized Slovenia and Croatia on December 23. "Making a mockery of the EC's joint approach," as John Zametica comments, Kohl portrayed Germany's unwillingness to abide by the agreement and wait until January 15 as "a great triumph for German foreign policy."[113] Ukraine had preceded on December 12, and the Vatican made its recognition formal on January 13.

Germany's policy, which had a decisive effect, was overwhelmingly a response to domestic pressures, however, and had little to do with the Yugoslav conflict. Public sympathies in Germany were already strong for Slovenia and Croatia by the spring of 1991 for many reasons: the leanings of major mass media, particularly newspapers, the public relations campaigns of the Slovenes and Croats that portrayed their actions as a "fight for freedom and democracy," the active propaganda from the Croatian émigré and *gastarbeiter* community and the Catholic Church (particularly in its political stronghold of Bavaria and its wing of the governing party, the Christian Social Union [CSU], but influenced by a Vatican-led campaign beginning several years earlier), and the public's greater familiarity with Slovenia and Croatia through tourism.[114] At the time of the Slovene war, Germany's CDU-CSU-FDP ruling coalition was under severe pressure politically.[115] Chancellor Kohl seized the opportunity of the vote in the Bundestag demanding recognition of Croatia and Slovenia, which was initiated by the opposition SPD, to divert attention abroad to a diplomatic gain and capture the issue for his party. Kohl had the propaganda advantage on this issue, moreover, since he had built the argument for German unification in 1990 on the principle of "self-determination" as the "expressed will of the people." The starkly different consequences of the principle in the case of Slovene and Croatian claims were easy to ignore since they, too, had held popular referendums.[116]

Perhaps the most important factor behind the momentum building under German policy was the personality and political position of Foreign Minister Genscher. Although the foreign ministry, which remained largely a fiefdom of Genscher's liberal Free Democrat party, was staffed with people who continued to oppose the stridently pro-Croatian policy adopted in the course of the summer-fall, Genscher increasingly found himself in a position he most abhorred—trapped as the odd man out between the CSU on the right (with which his party was in coalition) and the SDP on the left instead of leading a policy that they would follow. In this intensified party competition to gain influence over foreign policy in the post–cold war period and reduce the dominance of the liberals, Kohl had already claimed credit for Genscher's initiative on German unification and Soviet withdrawal. Looking to recoup political capital for himself and the Free Democrats, and under pressure from his party, Genscher would accomplish this by asserting his leadership in the EC and CSCE.

Moreover, the issue of Yugoslavia as it presented itself in mid-1991 was, in a sense, tailor-made for the liberals. Although Genscher publicly opposed the Bundestag demand throughout the summer, his moral revulsion at the use of force in Slovenia coincided too well with his political interests, the economic interests of Germany, and the dominant policy line of FDP foreign policy. That policy was based on an ideology that suited German economic power and military restraint, arguing that the world had changed since World War II and that foreign relations and instruments of statecraft should be based on economic rather than military power. This was already apparent in Germany's reluctance toward the use of military force against Saddam Hussein in January and the tensions it caused with the United States. Moreover, Genscher's disbelief, shared with many others, that war and fratricidal hatred could still take place in Europe, was as much a reaction to the real threat of the Yugoslav crisis as much as it was a cultural shock—the proximity of the fighting, the more than 200,000 refugees seeking asylum under Germany's liberal laws by late fall, the threat of internal terrorism from the hundreds of thousands of *gastarbeiter* from Yugoslavia resident in Germany and northern Europe, and the disruption of trade and substantial German investments. The Germans' redefinition of the situation as external aggression on the part of the Serbs fit the antimilitarism of Genscher's Free Democrats and Germany's postwar self-image, making it easy to rationalize their sense of greater affinity for the Slovene and Croatian cause and to ignore the Slovene and Croatian use of military force, including the purchase of German tanks and weapons, in that cause.

It is hard to see how Genscher's threat to use recognition to obtain a cease-fire was likely to be effective—either against the Serbs, who saw themselves as seeking their right to self-determination as well (though it required a change of internal borders), or against Serbia's allies in the army, who knew that the German government could not constitutionally (and, because of World War II, most believed also morally) participate in any military action in the Balkans.[117] The German campaign came through as cultural arrogance—in deciding for the Yugoslavs whose rights were more valid and what use of force was acceptable; in its repeated insistence that the issue was one of *values*, above all "German values" and "European standards"; and in its demonization of Milošević and the Serbs. Unfortunately, this coincided with the propaganda of the Croatian government—that Europe should see the difference between the Croatians and the Serb "barbarians"—and also with the fears among many Yugoslavs that German revanchism was creating its own sphere of influence in the Balkans and redrawing the European divide through its center. Many in eastern Europe at the time saw the region of the former Eastern bloc being redivided into two blocs, one German, the other Turkish. In the *realpolitik* terms of historical memories, it seemed natural to them that Germany would want to neutralize the largest army in the region, the YPA, and the famed Serbian soldiers.[118] If anything, German behavior was as encouraging to Serb nationalists and their army allies as it was to the Slovenes and Croats.

Genscher pushed relentlessly after early July 1991 for recognition of Slovenia and Croatia to be used as a diplomatic tool to threaten Serbia to desist what he called its "aggression" and as a means to circumvent the need for consent from Yugoslav authorities for an EC force in Croatia.[119] From his perspective, this was an uphill battle against an EC majority and with few allies other than Denmark.[120] But because the issue became so important domestically for Germany, it had become, regardless of the consequences for the Yugoslavs, a test of the new German role in Europe and proof of its new form of statecraft. The more opposition the Germans met with, the more they hardened in stubborn support of the line they had adopted. Like the self-fulfilling prophecies they were helping toward realization within Yugoslavia, the more assertive they became, the more fears they aroused that the old habits of *Gross Deutschland* had not died.[121]

German behavior was, in fact, emblematic of the transition taking place throughout Europe. Shifts in power were moving faster than the redesign of supranational institutions, but also faster than domestic strategy. Even the institutions such as the EC, created to defang German power after World War II with bonds of mutual cooperation and functional integration, were undergoing transformation. Yet Germany's understandable ineptness in this new world of learning-by-doing did not reduce the uncertainty it was instilling in those with less power or influence. The political debate over the content of the Maastricht Treaty, for example, was largely about controlling Germany.

Whereas Germany appeared to be pursuing an expansionary strategy eastward, its absence of strategy in fact left it speaking with many voices. At the same time, it was incomprehensible to Germans, and west Europeans in general, that their actions might be contributing to the insecurity and impending chaos in the East. They had no reason to see why their policies of operating out of national interest and adapting rules expediently to new circumstances as they arose would not continue to have the beneficial outcomes of increasing integration, decreasing aggression, and democratic liberation for the region. Able to defend their own security through economic protection and border controls, there was no incentive to see this as contributing to the decline in security in the continent.

This second turning point in European action—Germany's success in its campaign for recognition of Croatia and Slovenia—was, as Carrington warned in his letter to van dan Broek, the death knell to the peace negotiations. The Hague conference was based on the assumption, reinforced by the judgment of the Badinter Commission on October 8, that the issue at stake was the dissolution of a state. The EC declared it was agnostic on the political outcome as long as it was accomplished without force, and The Hague talks assumed that such a peaceful outcome depended on a common framework in which all Yugoslav parties could come to agreement on their mutual relations and the status of all its former parts. Nonetheless, the decisions of the preceding nine months or more had also created a diplomatic fait accompli in favor of independent states and the republican borders, and the Brussels draft treaty had proposed to handle the concerns of those who opposed those borders—such as the enclave Serbs in Croatia—with a special status within the republics. Unwilling to use force to impose this choice, the EC had only the weapon of recognition to obtain a peaceful settlement. As Cyrus Vance implored in his letter to Genscher in December, recognition had to be held out as a reward for a peaceful settlement. To give up that weapon before such a settlement was reached would mean more war.

The cease-fire that he and Carrington were striving tirelessly to obtain in Croatia did not, and could not, contain a political settlement. It was only to stop the fighting and return the parties to the negotiating table, on the recognition that no solution to the conflict in Croatia could occur independently of an overall settlement for the dissolving country. Indeed, because there had been no decisive military victory (and the consequences of waiting for such a victory were too risky), the cease-fire itself could only be achieved if both parties saw it as *not* prejudicing the final outcome. It would create a stalemate "without prejudice," as the Vance Plan for the UN-monitored cease-fire in Croatia declared, until The Hague talks were complete. The EC decision in December to recognize Croatia addressed neither the status of Serbs in Croatia nor the fate of the population in the remaining four republics.[122] To do so at that point, since it preempted the process by which Yugoslav parties would decide with the aid of EC mediation, would have required the EC to make its own decision on the principles at stake—the effective rights of national self-determination, of rights to a state, and of borders. Apparently the implications for other countries (in both western and eastern parts of the continent) were too great to accept the responsibility for the consequences of their decision.

The cease-fire brokered by Vance on November 23, 1991, was only finalized on January 2, 1992, signed at Sarajevo by military representatives of Croatia and Yugoslavia. The first fifty UN monitors arrived in Croatia on January 14, the very day before the EC diplomatic recognition of Croatia contradicted the principle of the UN engagement, that it be without prejudice to the political outcome. Despite grave doubts among senior diplomats at the United Nations such as Marrack I. Goulding, then head of the department of peacekeeping, about the appropriateness of UN peacekeeping troops in this situation, and despite continuing violations of the cease-fire by both the Croatian army and the *krajina* Serbs, the presence of 14,000 UN Protection Forces, or "blue helmets," who began to arrive on March 8, 1992, did keep the cease-fire holding for the most part (with momentary, though significant, breakdowns during 1992 and 1993 and the necessity of a new cease-fire agreement signed March 29, 1994).[123]

Germany thus concluded that its policy had been correct. In maintaining this position in the face of substantial criticism, including accusations that it was responsible for the spread of war to Bosnia-Herzegovina, it raised the policy to the point of principle and therefore precedent. But by denying the legitimacy of the Serb claim for self-determination (in favor of the sanctity of the internationalized internal borders), Germany's policy of preventive recognition of Slovenia and Croatia could not have any effect on Serbia. By denying the legitimacy of the army's constitutional position and its inevitable disintegration into national armies with Yugoslav disintegration, it would similarly have no effect on the army other than to encourage it to fight harder for the remaining territory (with its defense plants, strategic supplies, communications routes, and army housing). Indeed, a reason for the success of Vance's negotiations in contrast to Carrington's, according to members of Vance's team, was his recognition that no cease-fire could occur without the negotiators talking directly to the army. If German policy was to make any contribution to a cease-fire, it would be limited to its effect on the Croatian government. Having fought the war to gain international recognition, however, the Croatian government would have no reason to continue fighting once recognition was granted—and, because recognition alone without a political settlement defining the status of the *krajina* Serbs could not give the Croatian government full control over the territory protected by UN forces, it would at the same time also have good reason to resume fighting as an alternative to negotiations once it felt militarily strong enough to defeat the *krajina* Serbs.

The precedent set by the German maneuver was that the principle of self-determination could legitimately break up multinational states, that EC application of this principle was arbitrary, and that the surest way for politicians bent on independence to succeed was to instigate a defensive war and win international sympathy and then recognition.

## Prelude to Bosnian Tragedy

The conditions that brought about Vance's cease-fire agreement in Croatia, where fourteen prior agreements had not held, were already evident by the time of the December 1991 EC meeting. The army was facing widespread desertions and great difficulty recruiting youth in Serbia and Macedonia. The YPA military prosecutor, Colonel Milan Papić, asserted that by the middle of December approximately 10,000 draftees failed to report to duty. In Bosnia-Herzegovina, President Izetbegović refused to implement mobilization.[124] Winter was coming. The leader in Knin, Milan Babić, opposed the agreement—recognizing that its condition that the Yugoslav army withdraw from Croatia would deprive them of the primary source of security and was a de facto recognition of Croatian sovereignty over *krajina* and therefore their defeat. But moderate forces among Serbs in Croatia were regaining strength.[125] President Milošević intensified his pressure on Babić to accept the agreement by going public. The idea that UN peacekeeping forces would replace the YPA and protect local Serbs in the territory over which they claimed military control and political rights could be presented to *krajina* Serbs as a way to gain time and for Milošević, was a way to save face at home.

The only real dispute for both Croatian and Serbian leaders was where UN forces would be placed. Croatia insisted they locate along the border with Serbia, as international recognition of its sovereign borders and of Serbian guilt. Serbs pressed for stationing along a new border between their territories and the rest of Croatia. Vance proposed—and insisted on—an "inkblot" plan that would station UN forces at points of tension throughout the contested region, which would be divided for administrative ease into four UN protected areas, or UNPAs—Sectors East, West, South, and North.[126]

Contrary to the reasoning of the German policy of recognition, the EC's unwillingness to address the problem of Serb rights alongside those of Slovenes and Croats meant that Germany was pushing for recognition of a state that was not in control of one-fourth of its territory. In order to obtain a cease-fire, the UN plan simply froze the issue of borders and the conflict over principles that the EC refused to resolve. This left each side to believe that the UN presence sanctioned their claims to self-determination over this territory. Eventually, Croatia would break the cease-fire agreement (first in June 1992 on Miljevići plateau and near Drniš) in order to invalidate the Vance Plan and to test the UN and the Serbs on the option of regaining control of its territory militarily.[127]

The ambiguity over territorial rights to self-determination was made worse by German haste to use the issue for domestic political gain. The compromise Kohl maneuvered on the other eleven EC members included the condition that each republic submit to certification by the Badinter Commission on its commitment to CSCE principles of human rights before it was recognized; however, Germany recognized Slovenia and Croatia on December 23, before the commission could meet. According to the commission's ruling in January 1992, only Slovenia and Macedonia satisfied its conditions on specific democratic standards and rights of minorities. Yet the EC refused to recognize Macedonian sovereignty so as to keep the government of Greek prime minister Constantine Mitsotakis in power and buy its affirmative vote on the Maastricht treaty. The commission's ruling found Croatia lacking on its commitment to human rights—including protections for the rights of Serbs and other minorities. To justify recognition, Genscher pushed the Croatian government to revise its constitution to address the Badinter Commission's objections concerning the human rights for Serbs transformed from a nation to a minority. Instead of revising the constitution, the government proposed a constitutional law, which was adopted by the Parliament five months later in May. Moreover, the law had little legitimacy with the Croatian public and did little to dissuade Serbs from their fears of discrimination or worse because it was imposed from the outside and as a matter of some urgency to save face for Germany, rather than the result of negotiation between government and minority and the public debate and popular participation necessary to create commitment to the rights. Particularly important was Germany's rapid retreat from engagement and its resulting demonstration of disinterest in the issue, such as its failure to conduct any oversight to ensure that Croatia was actually implementing the new provisions, which did little to reassure *krajina* Serbs that they were now secure and could therefore reduce their resistance to the Croatian state. Despite the terms of the UN ceasefire, the Serbs continued to believe that they could not safely disarm, while there was nothing to end the SDS alliance that had formed across the republican border linking Serbs in the Croatian *krajina* and Bosnian *krajina* who perceived themselves in the minority in Croatia and Bosnia-Herzegovina and who wanted to remain within a new Yugoslavia. Neither the commission nor the EC ministers, moreover, gave consideration to holding a referendum of the *Yugoslav* population—the equivalent of the federal elections that Slovenia prevented in December 1990 upon which Marković and liberals in his reform alliance (both now irrelevant) had counted, and the normal UN practice of a plebiscite when the fate of a people and a territory are at stake.

The criteria of the Badinter Commission for recognition centered on CSCE principles concerning human rights, democratic rule, and inviolable borders. The return to these principles, which had been cast aside at the end of June 1991 by Western focus on the use of force, should have led to the conclusion that the German argument on preventive recognition applied first and foremost to the republic of Bosnia and Herzegovina. Whereas Croatian sovereignty involved two issues—recognition and the status of members of the Serbian nation—the collapse of the multiple guarantees for self-determination provided by the Yugoslav state meant that sovereignty for Bosnia-Herzegovina required solutions for three. It needed Western recognition of its independence; a constitutional arrangement among its three constituent nations that would give to each its right to self-determination without denying that same right to the other two; and a safeguard against the external threat to its independence and integrity posed by Croatia and Serbia (including their internal influence over Bosnian Croats and Bosnian Serbs).

Had EC members been acting to address the situation in Yugoslavia for what it was and what they acknowledged was about to occur, the German policy should have dictated recognition of the borders of Bosnia-Herzegovina before its fragile but constitutional accommodation of the competing nationalisms of Serbs, Croats, and Muslims collapsed under the weight of those to their north. In Bosnia-Herzegovina the principle of national self-determination could not be realized through territorial sovereignty because people were completely intermixed in marriages, neighborhoods, and towns when it came to ethnonational identities. The real test of the principles on which European security was based would be set, therefore, in Bosnia-Herzegovina. How could Europe guarantee the principle of national self-determination simultaneously with that of inviolable borders in Yugoslavia, and throughout the wider region, when the two were in conflict? Could the contradiction be managed by guaranteeing individual and group rights within a state rather than with separate territorial sovereignties as in the case of Croatia and Slovenia? And what external action would be required to reverse the process that was unfolding rapidly and to implant security guarantees for all those at risk—the state, the nations, and individual citizens?

In place of the confrontation in Croatia, which early recognition had left unresolved, and that between ethnic Albanians and the ruling nationalists in Serbia and Macedonia, which also threatened to erupt in violence, those who had the power and authority to recognize new states needed to realize that declarative recognition of republican independence was not sufficient. They needed to accompany such recognition—or denial of recognition, as Germany was promoting toward Bosnia-Herzegovina—with positive support for the standards on individual human rights, tolerance for ethnic and cultural diversity, and constitutional arrangements to ensure the principle of self-determination that Europeans claimed to uphold and for a procedure to achieve this under the circumstances. If they did not, as the letters of early December to Foreign Minister Genscher warned, the war would necessarily spread.[128] War in Bosnia-Herzegovina would make the problem of Serbs in Croatia appear minor, but war alone could not produce a solution any more than it had in Croatia. The German policy of preemptive recognition could not succeed in ending the war if they recognized Croatia *without* a plan for the remaining four republics and for relations among the three constituent nations of Bosnia-Herzegovina.

The complex political relations of multinationality in Bosnia-Herzegovina were not free to evolve internally after June 1991. Crucial opportunities for peace slipped by unnoticed between July and November 1991 while the EC focused on Slovenia, and then Croatia (despite its definition of the situation on October 8 as "a state in the process of dissolution"). Tensions between ethnic communities had preceded the elections of November 1990 because nationalist political leaders began to mobilize support along communal lines.[129] The leaders of Serbia and Croatia were already working on a secret agreement to divide Bosnia between them should the country fall apart. By March 1991 the issue of partitioning Bosnia had even been discussed by the federal presidency. By April a group of autonomist Serbs in the area fronting on Serb-majority areas in Croatia had declared the formation of a communal (regional) Parliament for *Bosanska Krajina*, with its seat at Banja Luka. On June 24, the two halves of the SDS, radical Serb autonomists in Croatia and Bosnia, signed the first of many agreements to cooperate (and eventually to join in a single state).[130] Once the Brioni Agreement made clear in early July that Yugoslavia as it had been was no more, one of the two elected representatives of the SDS in the Bosnian presidency, Nikola Koljević, appealed to the YPA to "protect Serbs" in Bosnia.[131] Fighting in Croatia spread quickly over the border into northern Bosnia by September 16.[132]

Since the proposal for a constitutional compromise made on June 6 by the leaders of Bosnia-Herzegovina and Macedonia was rejected by the leaders of Slovenia, Croatia, and Serbia (the EC said the proposal formed the basis of the Brussels convention, but the latter leaned far more toward confederation), the two took the next available choice: to declare sovereignty, but within some future Yugoslav federation. As discussed earlier, the Bosnian Parliament debated a memorandum for sovereignty proposed by Izetbegović's Muslim Party of Democratic Action (SDA) on October 15, and an alliance in favor of this proposal formed between the Croatian (HDZ) and Muslim parties. The third party of the power-sharing coalition, the Serbian party (SDS), was adamantly against independence. Its response was to leave the coalition, denouncing the attempt at secession as unconstitutional because their parity agreement required consensus of all three nations, and declare its wish to remain within Yugoslavia. Less than ten days later, these SDS delegates to the Bosnian Parliament declared themselves to be a "Parliament of the Serb nation in Bosnia-Herzegovina." On November 9–10, the SDS held a plebiscite in what they claimed were Serbian areas on the question of remaining within Yugoslavia.[133] At the same time, HDZ leaders demanded the opposite. Setting up two autonomous Croatian regions in Bosnia-Herzegovina, they declared their intention to "recognize the government and elected officials of Bosnia and Herzegovina 'as long as the republic maintains its independence from the former or any future Yugoslavia.' "[134] On November 20, the Bosnian government appealed to the UN for peacekeeping troops.

EC negotiations over the war in Croatia and its sovereignty proceeded with little regard for the consequences in the rest of Yugoslavia. The negotiated withdrawal of the army from Croatia that began November 28, for example, sent the army's largest contingent of officers and professional soldiers to their home in Bosnia. (For both historical and sociological reasons, a majority of YPA officers were from Bosnia, not Serbia, as foreign media tended to confuse. This included the military commander of the Knin corps of the YPA, General Ratko Mladić, a Bosnian Serb who would become commanding officer of the Bosnian Serb army created in May 1992.[135]) Once Slovenia and Croatia had established separate currencies, western Herzegovina (where the large majority of the population were Bosnian Croats loyal to President Tudjman of Croatia and members of the Bosnian branch of his party) adopted the Croatian dinar and was rapidly incorporated into the Croatian economy, while the rest of Bosnia was left with the Yugoslav dinar.

Although Bosnia had thus lost the hope of economic integrity and was dependent on necessities such as food, from Serbia, on December 2 the EC nonetheless chose to lift the economic sanctions imposed in November and restore trade relations with the four republics that accepted their settlement—but to leave them on Serbia and Montenegro. This only gave an excuse to Serbia to continue the economic embargo that it and the Croatian government were also waging against Bosnia-Herzegovina as part of the partition agenda. Bosnia-Herzegovina was reeling from the economic effects of this embargo and near the low point of political relations among its three ruling parties when the EC offer on December 16 to consider recognition (Kohl's compromise) gave the Yugoslav republics one week to apply or lose the opportunity. On December 21, the day after the Bosnian government, without the Serbian party, placed its request, the SDS leadership declared its intention to create a Serbian republic within Bosnia (a statement repeated, with varying claims of autonomy or statehood at intervals over the following nine months).

In place of the German protection given Croatia, the criteria drawn up by the Badinter Commission for recognition of Bosnian sovereignty imposed additional conditions. Ignoring the conflict between majoritarian principles of individual choice and the national conception of self-determination, as the EC had done throughout, the commission adopted the procedural rules set by Germany from its own experience. The Bosnian government had to prove that its request for recognition had popular support by holding a referendum, at which point it could be reconsidered.[136] By the time of this ruling, President Izetbegović was asking the YPA to defend Bosnian integrity.[137] Refugees from the fighting in Croatia (both Serb and Croat) had been flooding into northern Bosnia, villagers were arming (some with the aid of local territorial defense forces), and Croatia had sent armed forces to western Herzegovina.[138]

With the Bosnian Serb party in nearly open rebellion, President Tudjman staged a coup in the leadership of the Bosnian Croats (a wing of Tudjman's HDZ) to replace its elected leader—Stjepan Kljuić—because he stood firmly by Bosnian integrity. Tudjman's appointee, Mate Boban, proceeded immediately to declare a separate Croat state in western Herzegovina, Herzeg-Bosnia.[139] Without its Serbian partner and unsure of Croatian loyalties, the reduced Bosnian leadership now ignored the rules obliging consultation with the parliamentary opposition of delegates from nonethnic parties. Excluding them from further debate on Bosnia's future prior to the referendum, set for February 29–March 1, 1992, it instituted emergency rule.

The capital of Sarajevo had an eerie calm in early February 1992. It had become commonplace in the West to say that if war did spread to Bosnia-Herzegovina, it would be a terrible slaughter. Yet members of the republic's political and cultural elite and the government leadership were still hopeful that war could be averted. Apparently as an attempt to repeat what was by then being identified as the Croatian strategy, Izetbegović's government did not prepare for war.[140] Its predictions that all citizens not under the local control of Serbian nationalists would vote for independence were close to the mark: 63.4 percent of the eligible voters went to the polls and, of the valid ballots, 99.7 percent voted yes.[141] But neither Western arguments that the wars represented Serbian and Yugoslav army aggression nor the rhetoric about popular referendums and self-determination brought the Western support that Izetbegović appeared to expect.

The treatment of Bosnia-Herzegovina encourages the most cynical interpretation of Western policy. Despite Kohl's compromise in December, Germany did not want to recognize Bosnian sovereignty and looked for ways to delay. Once Kohl and Genscher had gained what they could domestically by recognizing Slovenia and Croatia and exhausted the means of foreign influence they were willing to use, more traditional foreign policy concerns reemerged. The Serbs were still the most numerous people in the former country, and if Serbia did win the allegiance of the Yugoslav army it could become a military dictatorship that threatened European security in the long run.

Whatever the outcome of the war in eastern Slavonia, moreover, Serbia controlled a substantial part of the Danube river, which was critical to the German economy. It would not do to allow Serbia's total isolation, German diplomats concluded by late January. It was also a German diplomatic conviction—going back to Bismarck at the Congress of Berlin in 1878, when Serbia gained recognition for its independence from the Ottoman empire after more than seventy years of rebellion, but still held in 1992 by the German ambassador to Yugoslavia, Hansjörg Eiff, and many other European diplomats in Belgrade—that Bosnia could not survive independently without an imperial overlord of some kind. These historical prejudices were nourished by the barrage of propaganda from the Tudjman and Milošević administrations to justify their predatory plans, which fed anti-Islamic fears in Europe that the government aimed to create a fundamentalist Islamic state—for the first time—*in Europe*.

There is some evidence that the propaganda was working, despite the alliance on sovereignty between the Muslim and Croatian political parties within the Bosnian ruling coalition and the fact that the sitting president of the seven-person Bosnian presidency, Izetbegović, had insisted on a united, secular Bosnia. This emboldened most EC countries to consider a rump Yugoslavia made up of the remaining republics the best solution to regional stability, once Slovenia and Croatia became independent. In addition, the refugee crisis, which German leaders claimed was motivating their push for recognition, was, for Germany, actually a relatively simple problem because it could be handled by border controls; but for France and Britain, it was a north African and commonwealth problem, respectively, the prominent Muslim aspects of which were provoking ethnocentrist reaction at home. [142]

Recognition of Bosnia became, in fact, an American cause. Beginning in late January 1992, the United States began a campaign to persuade its European allies to join it in extending sovereignty to Bosnia-Herzegovina and Macedonia. The reasons were many. Now the odd man out on the issue of preemptive recognition, the United States found this disunity within its Western alliance disturbing. Concerned that Germany was "getting out ahead of the U.S." (according to Deputy Secretary of State Eagleburger) and that it had lost any leverage on the Yugoslav situation after the EC's December decision, the United States nonetheless insisted on retaining its position against differential treatment of the republics. Pressure for recognition from the Croatian lobby in Washington was heated. [143] If the United States were to reverse its position on recognition, it could only do so by recognizing all four republics at once and persuading the Europeans to follow suit.

The Europeans countered that political circumstances had deteriorated to such a point that Bosnia was not able to constitute a sovereign state. In the pattern they established toward Slovenia and Croatia, EC negotiators—under their presidency, the Portuguese—now turned their mediating efforts to forestalling war in Bosnia-Herzegovina. A week before the required referendum, Portuguese EC mediator José Cutileiro convened separate EC negotiations on Bosnia-Herzegovina. The stated objective was to gain the commitment of the three party leaderships to existing Bosnian borders, without making any commitment to Bosnian sovereignty at the time. By March 18, the three party delegations, meeting at Lisbon, had agreed on and signed a document outlining the political principles of a republic composed of three constituent nations, each with the right to self-determination, and of the regional cantonization of its territory along ethnonational lines (laid out on a compromise map proposed by the EC). At the same time, apparently influenced by the appeals for recognition from Izetbegović's foreign minister, Haris Silajdžić, Secretary of State Baker was intensifying his pressure on the European capitals. A week after the signing of the Lisbon accord, Izetbegović reversed his position and was joined by Bosnia's Croatian representative, Boban, who also reneged, because the plan gave Croats less territory than they wanted. On April 6, at the NATO meeting in Brussels, and the day after the Bosnian government, preparing for what they called a Serbian onslaught, ordered a general mobilization of territorial defense forces and army reserves, Baker succeeded, persuading his Western allies to recognize Bosnia-Herzegovina as a sovereign state.[144]

The reentry of the United States into the Yugoslav debacle as a part of the balance of power dynamic already in play in Europe added yet another element to the particular way in which Yugoslavia would unravel. The United States, though in competition with Germany, remained primarily concerned with maintaining the Atlanticist posture of the Kohl government.[145] But the one consistency in the U.S. position since spring 1991, other than its refusal to commit soldiers (which Germany shared), had been its interpretation of the conflict as Serbian aggression.[146] Now Germany was shifting its policy to find ways to keep Serbia in the international community and subject to its norms. In place of the confrontation that could have resulted, the United States appeared to move toward a geopolitical division of labor instead, conceding a primary sphere of influence over Croatia to Germany and taking on Bosnia as its responsibility. Yet because the United States remained unwilling even to consider the use of ground forces to back up its recognition of Bosnia-Herzegovina, it reverted to its policy of human rights. Apparently as oblivious as the EC to the local meaning of a nation and of self-determination, it thus attempted to separate the military and political questions of the war from humanitarian concerns for the civilians in the Bosnian wars. And because the U.S. foreign policy objective in reasserting influence over the Yugoslav conflict was to prevent differences between itself and its European allies from causing a rift, it dropped its insistence on recognizing all four republics, deferring to Greek intransigence against a sovereign Macedonia.

No sooner was the principle of preventive recognition applied than it was, once again, subordinated to other priorities. The United States now became preoccupied with the possible spread of war to Kosovo and Macedonia—as the next step in what it viewed as a war waged to create a Greater Serbia. Although it argued that the danger came from Milošević's expansionist policies and Yugoslav army aggression, it also remained unwilling to contemplate military deterrence. Thus it continued to give priority to the issue of Kosovo, to define it as one of Serbian violation of human rights provisions of the CSCE, and to push economic sanctions against and diplomatic isolation of Serbia. This was also in spite of the threat to peace posed by economic damage and its political consequences in Macedonia, which was, like Bosnia-Herzegovina in late 1991, now also reeling from a Greek economic blockade on top of the European sanctions on

Serbia. In keeping with European diplomacy toward Yugoslavia, U.S. policy was an array of mixed messages sufficient to keep all interests on the ground alive.

## Conclusion

Western intervention in the Yugoslav crisis aimed at mediation and crisis management. Instead, it provided the irreversible turning point in its escalation toward nationalist extremism and war. Having ignored the mounting crisis during 1989–90, the international community took actions in 1991 that redefined the origins and myriad aspects of this upheaval as ethnic conflict and nationalist revolution. The result was self-fulfilling.

External intervention continued to reinforce the pressures of the preceding decade that made *states*—political control over territory, its economic assets, and coercive power—the most valuable goal. Nationalist party leaders who had gained legitimacy with the first democratic elections in 1990 but who ruled in shaky coalitions formed out of political expediency and whose programs and performance had not yet been tested by a second election were promoted by EC, CSCE, and UN negotiators to the status of statesmen, leaders of nations struggling for independence. While intervention gave even more authority to the leaders of the republics than in the decentralized federation, it weakened the supports for opponents of their nationalism who considered the creation of democratic procedures, market relations, and guarantees of individual rights *within* states to be more important. By abandoning the Yugoslav federal government, which depended on international support for its economic and political reforms; prejudging the army as nationalist and its actions to restore order in the republics as illegitimate intervention; and ignoring the many citizens' groups working to foster countrywide cooperation, the West deprived Yugoslav citizens of the last of the protections for their individual rights and the last alternatives to nationalist or treasonous loyalties within their republics of residence.

By accepting the principle of national self-determination for the independence of states—without regard to the Yugoslav conditions of multinationality and the shared rights to national sovereignty of the Titoist system, or a willingness to enforce their unilateral decision on borders—Western powers were making war over territory inevitable. The struggle to create new states out of the Yugoslav federation was a struggle to get international recognition; the fight for international opinion had been and would continue to be as important as the fight on the ground.

Chapter 7

# The Right to National Self-Determination

In their attempts to dissuade Yugoslav leaders in May 1991 from their path of dissolution, and then, after June 28, 1991, to put a rapid stop to the use of force in Slovenia, Western diplomats aimed to protect European security and its bases in Helsinki principles—peaceful resolution of disputes, inviolable borders, and human rights. Although clearly intending to influence the outcome of the domestic quarrels, they also sought to draw a firm line between European interests and the internal conflict. They insisted repeatedly, for example, that it was up to the Yugoslavs to find their own solution. Any political outcome was acceptable as long as it was achieved without force. The European Community (EC) was there only to "facilitate political dialogue."

Discussion beginning in July 1991 of interposing European troops or UN peacekeeping troops between armed parties in Croatia, and later in Bosnia-Herzegovina, foundered as much on the norm of consent by sovereign actors as on questions of troop availability and financing. Western powers continued to reject military force for reasons other than humanitarian assistance unless there was an agreement among the warring parties that would permit intervention. The German argument for recognizing Croatian sovereignty was to circumvent this obstacle of obtaining consent by "internationalizing the conflict." By declaring Serbian actions a case of external aggression, Germany could protect the principle of consent as well as its own appearance of nonintervention in the internal affairs of another state. The Conference on Security and Cooperation in Europe (CSCE) was largely immobilized by the Yugoslav government's veto of intervention—even after EC mediation had immobilized the federal authorities working for an internal solution. Its limited power was used only to suspend Yugoslavia's membership in the CSCE on July 8, 1992, as a means of persuading the leadership of Serbia to cease military support for Bosnian Serbs.

Increasing involvement by the United Nations after October 1991 to bring relief and to obtain and observe cease-fires and other political agreements among warring forces in Croatia, and then in Bosnia-Herzegovina, attempted to maintain this distinction between the *causes* of the war and its *effects* on civilians, who should be provided humanitarian assistance. The International Committee of the Red Cross (ICRC) assisted the exchange of several thousand prisoners in both Croatia and Bosnia-Herzegovina beginning in early November 1991; created a safe area around the hospital in the town of Osijek (eastern Croatia) when it was under siege in December 1991; and in the summer of 1992 inspected detention camps in eastern Bosnia-Herzegovina after charges by human rights organizations and journalists that international humanitarian law and the Geneva conventions on war were being violated. The UN Office of the High Commissioner for Refugees (UNHCR) aided persons displaced from their homes by the war, hundreds of thousands of refugees fleeing war or expelled by the war strategy to create ethnically pure territories, and cities and towns subjected to artillery shelling and deprived of basic utilities. Because the UN had never assisted refugees in the midst of war, UN Protection Forces (UNPROFOR) were created to protect UNHCR aid convoys and relief work. But their mandate was limited to self-defense, even when convoys were persistently halted by the warring armies, paramilitary gangs, or civilians' demonstrations, and after the UN responded in August 1992 with a call to states acting nationally or in regional organizations to "take all measures necessary" to ensure the delivery of aid.[1]

Joining the EC in helping to negotiate a political solution in August 1992, the UN agreed to observe political agreements made by the Bosnian parties at the London Conference that month that were designed to "even the playing field" militarily—such as the commitment of Bosnian Serbs to place their heavy artillery under UN supervision and not to use air power for combat. But enforcement of these agreements was limited to UN military observers and NATO overflights, which monitored violations but had no mandate to stop them. In October the United States pressed the UN Security Council to take the next step and impose a ban on military flights over Bosnia.[2] Then in November 1992 and March 1993 it asked for more assertive enforcement, but it continued to limit its own military involvement to monitoring the no-fly zone and economic embargo and making airdrops of food and medicines to besieged towns in eastern Bosnia, which it began in February 1993.

This fine line between protecting the norms of sovereignty without taking sides in a civil war was based on a fiction, however. The EC-negotiated Brioni agreement of July 7, 1991, and the EC's acceptance, on December 16, 1991, of the German policy of preventive recognition, had together ended the sovereignty of the Yugoslav state. The EC, through these actions, had taken sides in the internal constitutional conflict. Whether or not foreign powers wished to remain detached and uninvolved, their actions had a direct influence on political events on the ground.

In recognizing the Slovene and Croatian declarations of independence in the face of substantial opposition from within Yugoslavia—thus accepting without question that the republics were sovereign states and bore exclusively the right to national self-determination—the Europeans, for example, handed a victory to the confederalists. The federalists lost to the EC, not to a domestic vote or an elite political pact. The EC also defeated, by elimination, the third party to the constitutional conflict, the Yugoslav federal government. Prime Minister Ante Marković's resignation in December 1991 in protest against his own government's war budget was a belated recognition of the July 1991 fait accompli. Contrary to the German argument, that Serbian ambition and opposition to Slovene and Croatian freedom was driving Yugoslavia's dissolution, the EC decisions of summer–fall 1991 gave Serb nationalists who hoped also to build a nation-state the unexpected opportunity they needed. Perhaps most decisive was its treatment of the federal army. In treating its presence in Slovenia and then Croatia as an illegitimate aggressor, the EC transformed the Yugoslav People's Army (YPA) into an independent actor in the political contest, moving, with each forced retreat from territory declared sovereign, from trying to hold Yugoslavia together and protect army assets to devising and defending a state-building project of its own.

As a result of the choices made by the EC between July and December 1991, the meaning of votes cast in the 1990 elections was transformed overnight, without new elections to verify the change. Interrupting the process of democratization begun during 1990, the negotiations decided which voters had a right to self-determination and to decide the outcome of their former country. Instead of closing the chapter on Yugoslavia, the decisions opened a new chapter of struggle over territory—a struggle aimed at creating new states out of the Yugoslav federation and gaining international recognition of sovereignty and borders. The principle of national self-determination has many definitions and in a multinational territory does not define borders neatly.

Internal affairs that had been driven by constitutional and economic conflict became driven instead by competition over territory and over peoples to win international recognition for territorial claims. Politicians reoriented their tactics to what mattered: the ability to influence world opinion, to gain foreign patrons or exploit foreign disunity, and to take control of territory militarily. The criteria of the international community and the means of influence in that arena far outweighed citizens' preferences. Even their identities were altered by the judgments and actions of Western powers, which assigned people who had been resolutely pro-Western and culturally European to other spheres of influence or cultural worlds.

## The Problem of "Slovenia First"

The problem began with the EC's definition of the issue. In its decision of June 28, 1991, to negotiate the conflict between the Yugoslav army and the territorial defense forces of Slovenia, the European Community accepted the Slovene claim: that they were fighting for their right to national self-determination, and that any attempt from outside to prevent their realization of that right was an act of aggression and illegitimate. This right, according to the Slovenes, was based in the founding acts of the Yugoslav state in 1943 (the Anti-Fascist Liberation Council of Yugoslavia [AVNOJ] constitutional principles, which nationalist Serbs rejected), whereby each republic, as the embodiment of the right to self-determination of the constituent nations of Yugoslavia, had voluntarily ceded its sovereignty to Yugoslavia and could voluntarily withdraw it. It was the army, therefore, that was acting unconstitutionally.

The European Community accepted that republics were states, and their borders were therefore sacrosanct. The source of their sovereignty was the right of a nation to self-determination (in these cases, of Slovenes and Croats). These rulings seemed unproblematic to the negotiators for a number of reasons. The Slovenes, and to a lesser extent the Croats, had recognized the need to shape Western opinion for more than a year, and had had the assistance of neighbors such as Austria and Switzerland. Despite the almost seventy deaths in Slovenia and much warning about the potential for violence in the rest of Yugoslavia, there was no revival of fighting in Slovenia after the Brioni agreement negotiated the Yugoslav army's return to barracks, after the army withdrew from the republic, or at the end of the three-month moratorium on Slovene independence on October 8, 1991. In judging intra-Yugoslav quarrels motivated increasingly by the desire to be accepted by Europe and the insecurities and costs involved in Europe's criteria, it was particularly significant that the European Community was taking the lead and Slovenia was the westernmost Yugoslav republic.

In Slovenia the potential conflict between citizens' ethnic identities, national rights, and state territory was least apparent. Slovenia was the republic closest to the Western idea of the nation-state. It was also the most thoroughly Western in its orientation, an intermediary between the Yugoslav market and international commerce, and best situated geographically and economically to make the adjustments of global integration. Viewing the Slovene situation in isolation from the multinational and geopolitical context, Western powers were not forced to deal with the violent consequences of applying the principle of national self-determination in the multinational realities of Yugoslavia and much of eastern Europe.

The state preceded the nation in the historical origins of the nation-state in western Europe. These states began as feudal powers. Their sovereign control over territory and subjects was largely defined by their ability to mount armies, to collect taxes, and to gain allegiance of potential rivals, and these varied over time. Not only did their rulers' sovereignty have to be tested and defended with some frequency, but the demarcation of a state's borders remained fuzzy as a result, and authority was not based on rightful representation of a nation. Subjects had loyalties and political identities with their sovereign regardless of language and ethnic identity, and this in turn was sufficient to differentiate them clearly from people in neighboring states long before the borders were clearly defined and marked.[3] Over time, however, the only west European states to survive into the modern era were those able to create nations—to homogenize their populations culturally, developing a sense of one people.[4] All others failed.

The great age of nationalism, the nineteenth century, brought the sovereign, territory, and subjects together through the idea of a nation, and "language became the essential element in the definition of national identity."[5] The primary agents of this process in Europe were military conscription and schools where the state language and patriotic values were inculcated against local languages and loyalties. (Because universal literacy and public schooling are very recent developments, the national identity and allegiance of many of a state's subjects or citizenry are also a relatively recent phenomenon.)[6] But the process of cultural homogenization to create a nation could also be profoundly violent. Where it is still an issue, such as the relation of the French state with Bretons, the Greek state with Macedonians and Turks, or the Spanish state with the Basques and Catalans, we tend to recognize the violence of the process and in some cases refer even to ethnocide. Where ethnic minorities have not been fully obliterated and the conflict between nation and ethnic group has a territorial basis, the process can flare up politically as demands for autonomy or independence rather than as demands for human rights to cultural expression.

European states that were created instead by dissenters from this process of homogenization—whether religious or linguistic—are often said to demonstrate that multiethnic or multicultural harmony is possible under certain constitutional provisions, such as in the Netherlands, Belgium, or Switzerland.[7] Yet they also experienced in the twentieth century major, state-threatening constitutional battles over political rights to language use, the role of the state in schooling, and guarantees of cultural autonomy. The source of their current social peace and stability lies instead in socio-economic processes during the 1960s and 1970s that broke down the parochial boundaries and separate networks of social reciprocity and obligation between citizens that were the basis of ethnic difference: in the Netherlands, through rapid urbanization, and in Switzerland, through greater state management of the economy, which undermined localisms by ever greater economic integration from one end of the country to the other.[8] In Belgium, where economic deterioration revived ethnic conflict and demands for autonomy in the 1970s, the constitutional revisions that stopped just short of the country's division between Flemish and Walloon territories (with separate status for Brussels) appeared to hold because membership in the European Community attenuated—in the broader, multinational environment of Europe—relations among regional sentiment, ethnicity, nation, and state.

The idea that nations have a right to their own state thus turns this west European history on its head. Many historians of eastern and central Europe will argue that a nation is defined as a people whose collective awareness and political identity originate with some historical state and who keep the historical memory of that political community alive in periods when statehood is denied, with the goal of restoring its rights to self-rule.[9] But at the moment when the principle of national self-determination is used to create a modern state, it is reversing the west European process whereby states created nations, not nations states. Some peoples who believe themselves a nation never had states, such as the Slovenes. And as a result of centuries of war and migration, one nation's historical claims can be only one layer of an archaeology of claims by separate nations for the same land, on which now live populations mixed ethnically or with multiple national identities.

Although it is argued that this principle of national self-determination created Yugoslavia after World War I, Western powers sitting at Versailles actually used it only to justify the dissolution of the Habsburg and Ottoman empires—which had ruled the Balkans for five centuries. When these allied powers turned to the task of establishing a new state—faced with the reality of ethnonationally mixed populations, contested borders, the war aims of their ally (independent Serbia) to gather all Serbs into one state, and the danger to regional stability of many potentially warring mini-states in conflict over borders—they adopted the largely Croatian idea that south Slavs were one people (even if they were not a nation in the sense of a common state legacy).[10] Nor did this right to self-determination of the south Slav peoples end constitutional quarrels among them over how to recognize this national complexity or to give that right to the many non-Slavs resident on the territory.[11]

The priority of strategic objectives and political exigencies in the composition of a multinational state based on national self-determination was even clearer after World War II, when the unitary monarchy of the interwar state was replaced by a federal republic that acknowledged the historico-territorial political identities of Bosnia and Herzegovina, Macedonia, and Montenegro as well. Although these three also had identities as separate political communities with a history of administrative self-rule (and even statehood in the case of Montenegro), their republic status served also to create a more even balance of power among the republics (in particular, some would say, to check the power of Serbia) and in the case of Macedonia, to win the allegiance of its population to a Yugoslav state rather than to neighbors.[12]

The effect of defining the Yugoslav question in 1991 as a European problem, one that west European powers and institutions should take responsibility to manage, was to introduce this blind spot about the relation between states and nations and the meaning of national self-determination into the process of conflict mediation. At the height of their self-confidence about European integration, in 1990–91 west Europeans were even inclined to speak of nationalism in the East as a phenomenon of backwardness, of the time needed to "mature" into "civilized" states, instead of as a different set of issues that might require different approaches.[13] The United States contributed an additional blind spot from its perspective as the imperial power on its continent and a land in which immigration and a highly mobile work force had erased the memory of territorial conflicts between nations and the association between ethnic identity and land. These blind spots were particularly apparent when Western powers dismissed Russian criticism of their policy to end the war in Croatia, and then in Bosnia-Herzegovina, with punitive sanctions and threats of military action aimed at changing Serbia's behavior, by accusing Russia of bias as a historical ally of Serbia. This was hardly the case, as both Serbs and Russians would be quick to acknowledge. Russian criticism grew instead from its understanding of the issues at stake as a result of its more similar experiences in the twentieth century and contemporaneously in dealing with the national question. Moreover, the similarity that did exist between the conflict and west European historical experience—that of xenophobic and militant nationalism—led many to question why one would hand to the Europeans the very set of problems which they had not yet solved themselves.

Austria's leadership on the Yugoslav issue, in which it was soon joined by Germany, represented a purist notion of a nation-state. If a Yugoslav nation had not been created sufficient to supplant parochial loyalties and cultural identities, they argued, then Yugoslavia was an artificial state, and if a people freely chose to be independent, they had such a right. Although this was presented as a case of freedom, it was in fact an extension of the

German idea of citizenship through blood alone (*jus sanguinis*) and the impossibility of ethnically heterogeneous states—ideas that had been at the core of fascist ideology.[14]

The reluctance of Britain, France, and Spain to join the rush to recognition was based in large part on their sensitivity to the implications for their own states—given the presence of regional autonomists from Scotland to Corsica and Catalonia—of such criteria and precedent. But from the realist perspective of stability and security, Slovenia did seem to fit, and central European ideology about the difference between "Catholic" or "Habsburg" Europe—of which Slovenia (and Croatia) considered itself a member—and the rest of the country had created a powerful momentum after 1989 that resisted the caution of cooler heads. Nor was the United States able to weigh in effectively on the side of a different principle, for its policies toward the Soviet Union at the time were based on contradictory principles: it held that the Baltic states had the right to *national* self-determination as previously independent states (the United States was silent on the identical case of the USSR autonomous republic of Tuva), but called demands for Ukrainian independence a destabilizing threat to the integrity of the rest of the Soviet Union and thus an unacceptable form of nationalism.[15]

For a Europe and a United States intent on protecting Helsinki norms in its decisions on Yugoslavia, the Slovene case was particularly dangerous, for it fit CSCE criteria in ways that did not easily apply to the rest of the country. The first criterion was a largely (though not wholly) uncontested and ancient border with Slovenia's only Yugoslav neighbor, the republic of Croatia. Once President Franjo Tudjman's election brought Croatia to the same goal, Croatia welcomed the Slovene drive for independence as a part of its own strategy, taking advantage of Slovenia's lead and the smoke screen it might provide for Croatia's very real issues of borders and minorities. The other leading voice among the republics in the federal quarrel, Serbia, also made no objection to Slovene withdrawal. The removal of the most unyielding opposition to a stronger federal government (Slovenia) and the possible shift in the voting balance of the parity system in Serbia's favor—as long as it could maintain unity of the Serbian bloc—could make it much easier for Serbia to achieve its national objectives.[16] If the international community actually rejected the principle of inviolable external borders and Yugoslavia's territorial integrity, it would provide the excuse, perhaps even the justification, for redrawing internal borders to be more in line with Serb settlements.

A second criterion was the effect of Slovene secession on neighboring states. Times had changed since 1918, when Slovenes sought incorporation into Yugoslavia so as not to be absorbed into Italy and Austria and lose identity, although territorial questions over the Yugoslav border with Italy continued as late as 1975. [17] While Austria had helped campaign for Slovene independence, even Italy had made it known for months that it would support Slovene sovereignty, and both appeared not to fear boundary conflicts that would disrupt the peace. In the policies of both Austria and Italy to expand their spheres of economic influence eastward after the mid-1980s, Slovenia was viewed as a part of central Europe.

With the exception of small, autochthonous Italian and Hungarian communities, moreover, Slovene history, terrain, and state policy had collaborated to prevent territorially concentrated minorities. But Slovenia was *not* ethnically homogeneous as is often claimed and as was used by Europeans to justify Slovene independence. More than a quarter of its labor force in the 1980s consisted of non-Slovene immigrants, just as its urban population a century before comprised primarily foreign-born migrants. [18] Instead, its ethnic heterogeneity was not politically relevant because people of non-Slovene ethnicity were not claiming national rights to self-rule. [19] In principle, in contrast to German ideas of citizenship, individuals could have an identity of ethnic origin separate from their Slovene citizenship, which was based most importantly on language and then on residence. The ruling class in the nineteenth and early twentieth centuries comprised German landowners and urban elites who were not Slovene speakers. Slovenes who wrested control after 1918 used their separate language to cement their power and to protect their internal unity and distinctiveness from other Slavic, Austrian, and Italian neighbors and from the threat of cultural dilution due to a continuing history of labor immigration, giving the impression to outsiders that their "state" (as an autonomous republic in federal Yugoslavia) had created a nation, not the reverse. [20] Public opinion polls and the referendum of December 1990 seemed to confirm that the loyalties of the Slovene population were fully behind its local leadership, and even those who still doubted the wisdom of its policy would support independence if it came to that. [21] Pro-Yugoslav Slovenes remained in the federal government through the spring of 1991 but resigned or accepted their recall by June 1991.

The Slovene strategy to win over international opinion took skillful advantage of these regional trends and of the reigning CSCE criteria for countries farther afield, for it did not portray Slovenes' desire for self-determination in nationalist terms, but as a fight for "liberty" and "democracy"—for the right to choose a democratic system of government, which they insisted was no longer possible in Yugoslavia because Serbs and Serbian president Milošević prevented it. [22]

Nonetheless, the dangers inherent in accepting national claims for sovereignty as they are presented by nationalist leaders and without independent evaluation of the domestic situation are particularly great because of the importance of propaganda, mass media, and unconscious sympathies based on history, culture, or personal contact to any campaign aimed at winning international recognition. The advantage in such conflicts lies with those who move early to define external perceptions of the issues at stake, making their claims seem natural. Some are better placed by cultural proximity, financial resources, skills, the presence of mobilized émigré communities in Western countries, or simply recognition of the importance of shaping perceptions, than are others. This was best illustrated by the case of Croatia, where, unlike Slovenia, the conditions of a trouble-free separation on the basis of national rights were not present.

The population of Croatia was not nationally homogeneous. If it became independent, its borders would be contested by some Serbs in Croatia and by Serbia proper. One strand of Croatian nationalism—including that of the ruling party—had its own claims on Bosnian territory, moreover, which gave rise to suspicions about its own commitment to existing internal borders. And while some would argue that it also belonged—through the Habsburg legacy—to central Europe, the EC committee of jurists set up by The Hague conference to advise on legal matters of dissolution and succession, the Badinter Commission, ruled that Croatia did not, at the time, meet European standards on individual and minority rights or free speech.[23] Croatian president Tudjman and his advisers had begun early to portray their conflict with Yugoslavia, which Tudjman nearly always equated with Serbia and Serbs, as a bitter fight between democracy and dictatorship and between civilization and barbarism.[24] Croatia and "democratic Croatia" became synonymous in public speech; Croatia, in effect, offered Europeans a choice between their own kind and an alien darkness. Despite the advice of the Badinter Commission that Croatia did not fulfill the conditions for recognition of democratic protection of minority rights, the fact that it did not control one-quarter of the territory within its republic borders, and serious questions about the consequences of Croatia's independence for Bosnia-Herzegovina, Croatia's repetition of the Slovene theme may well have made it easier for Europeans (more concerned at the time about the Maastricht Treaty for European integration) to accept the German insistence on recognition.

The EC's priority on traditionally defined security considerations and the CSCE consensus against the aggressive use of force also made Europeans vulnerable to a second theme in the Croatian propaganda strategy: the portrayal of Croatians as victims of the Yugoslav army and the requirement, on pain of professional and legal sanctions, that the Croatian media label all Serbs as terrorists and the army as an occupation force.[25] Although Serbs in Croatia, Bosnia, and Serbia also portrayed themselves as victims acting only in self-defense, they did not see any need to develop a propaganda strategy in the West to support their views or to counteract the earlier negative propaganda against them—instead, they prepared to defend themselves and their goals with arms. Yet the mixed results of the propaganda strategy of the dominant Muslim party in Bosnia and the mounting evidence after May 1992 that Muslims might well be the victims not only of a war against them on two fronts but also of a policy of genocide gave fuel to the view of many that the European decisions were not based on principle at all.

## The Problem of National Self-Determination

The primary problem of the European Community decisions accepting the legitimacy of the Slovene and Croatian declarations, and thus granting independence to the republics of Yugoslavia on the grounds of rights to national self-determination, was not so much that they privileged some groups and their claims over others, however, but that they ignored Yugoslav reality. The hopes of the Slovene and Serbian nationalists that Slovenia could exit quietly, without bringing Yugoslavia down, were an illusion. The German argument that independent Slovenia and Croatia could leave behind a viable rump Yugoslavia ignored the very concept of Yugoslavia as a response to east European conditions—that nations aspire to sovereignty in territories that are nationally mixed. The argument also ignored the accusations of many Slovenes and Croats that the army had an explicit plan to create a new Yugoslavia should Slovenia and Croatia secede, but with different borders than the Germans had in mind.[26]

In contrast to its recognition of Slovene and Croatian rights, the EC denied legitimacy to Serbian and Albanian national aspirations and to self-determination on other grounds of all persons who did not accept or have an exclusive national identity and of all areas (including the republic of Bosnia-Herzegovina) that were nationally mixed. Moreover, no one discussed the qualitative difference in requirements between borders separating units of a single state and those that must provide the strategic security of independent states. The creation of new states out of the Yugoslav territory was no simple matter. Unless Western powers were willing to reverse their decision to stay out of the political issues involved, accepting the need to define rights to a state or procedures for resolving peacefully the territorial disputes being created, or were willing to enforce militarily their decision on republican borders, they were inviting more war.

### Republics or People?

The Slovene and Croatian claims to statehood that were recognized by the EC decisions were not made on the basis of abstract principles or historical rights, but on the basis of rights embodied in the constitution of

the Socialist Federal Republic of Yugoslavia (particularly the 1974 constitution). There was no reason to expect other peoples and citizens in Yugoslavia to do otherwise. But this constitutional system, as discussed in
chapter 2, contained a mixture of principles and overlapping rights and
jurisdictions to accommodate the reality mentioned above. To break up
the state without violence therefore required answers to three fundamental
questions.

The first question was, What was a nation, and what rights did
nationhood entail? In the Yugoslav constitution, both the republics and the
constituent nations bore national rights. It was a matter of unresolved
constitutional interpretation whether republics had the right to secede and,
if so, whether individuals who identified with another constituent nation
within these republics had to give their consent. In choosing the republican
borders and the claims of the majority nation for an independent state, the
EC politicians made no accommodation to this second, constitutionally
equal category of rights to self-determination. They referred instead to the
need to guarantee *minority* rights, as if these assurances would be a positive
contribution to peace instead of their repetition in fact of the very cause of
conflict in Croatia (and eventually Bosnia-Herzegovina)—the demotion of
other constituent nations to minority status in the 1990 republican constitutions and therefore their loss of political equality and of a right to self-
determination.

The EC ignored referendums held by autonomist Serbs in Croatia
and Serbs in Bosnia-Herzegovina to remain within Yugoslavia. It also
ignored the applications for recognition of sovereignty sent to the EC by
Serbs in the self-declared autonomous region of Krajina (Croatia) and
Albanians in the province of Kosovo (Serbia) when the invitation to apply
for recognition was issued to the four remaining Yugoslav republics on
December 16, 1991. The EC negotiations conducted by Lord Carrington
at The Hague in 1991 did attempt to address the problem presented by the
referendums of these two territorially compact political communities by
proposing special status (territorial autonomy), but the conference had no
bargaining leverage with which to persuade the governments of Croatia or
Serbia to accept this proposal—it could propose but not impose, as British
Prime Minister John Major insisted at the London Conference on Yugoslavia the next August. It also had no leverage with which to persuade the
Serbs in Croatia and Albanians in Serbia to be satisfied with minority
rights when their rebellions were motivated, in part, by real discrimination
by the governments that would be expected to guarantee them protections.
If international protections had been inadequate to correct the situation in
the preceding years, what confidence could they have that they would now
be secure?

The distinction between republics and constituent nations regarding rights to self-determination created a serious problem for Bosnia-Herzegovina, because the Yugoslav constitution did not recognize a Bosnian nation. Bosnia-Herzegovina was a republic composed of three political (constituent) nations, none of which were in a majority. Many of its citizens identified themselves as Bosnians and spoke a language that mixed Croatian, Serbian, and loan words from Turkish but was identifiably Bosnian.[27] The government elected in 1990 could only represent Bosnians politically, however, if it chose that identity and acted accordingly rather than as separate parties in an expedient coalition. Months before international recognition, the Serb party in Bosnia had left the coalition, and a coup in the Croatian party had left the intentions of Bosnian Croats unclear. The leaderships of Serbia and Croatia had no more intention of letting Muslims speak for Bosnia, challenging the right of President Izetbegović and the Bosnian army to represent the people of Bosnia-Herzegovina as a whole, than had their predecessors who successfully resisted the recognition of a separate Bosnian nation in 1945–63 (when the alternative of recognizing the Bosnian Muslims as a separate nation gained momentum instead).

Thus when the EC and the UN jointly agreed in July 1992 that the war raging in Bosnia-Herzegovina would not cease without a political settlement among what they labeled "three warring factions," they handed an impossible task to the negotiators at Geneva—to find an accommodation between republican and national sovereignty for Bosnia-Herzegovina which had only been possible in Yugoslavia by avoiding a choice. The United States and the EC were unwilling to defend the sovereignty they had recognized, and the UN was unwilling at the time to send peace-keeping troops to the republic without a prior political settlement and the consent of the warring parties. Trapped between the two, the Geneva negotiations set up under joint EC-UN auspices by the London Conference in August 1992 sought a compromise by writing a constitution that granted powers and jurisdictions of governance to the three nations, on parity terms, and by attempting to draw a map to give these *national* rights to self-governance (although usually referred to as ethnic proportions) a territorial basis *within* the *republic*. When the leader of the Serbian Democratic party (SDS) in Bosnia, Radovan Karadžić, refused in January 1993 to sign the constitutional principles of the resulting Vance-Owen peace plan until they revised its preamble to declare Bosnia-Herzegovina a state of three constituent nations, each with the right to self-determination, he was transferring the Slovene precedent (of the right of nations to form states within a state and, if they wish, to secede) from the republics to the constituent nations of federal Yugoslavia. His aim was to legitimize the sovereignty of Bosnian Serbs within Bosnia.[28]

*Territorial Borders*

Although the concept of constituent nation may seem to outsiders an odd irrelevance after national states were created out of the republics and was treated as a nuisance by their new nationalist leaders, it had served a critical purpose in Yugoslavia: of putting a stop to the endless conflict over territorial boundaries that can ensue when national communities and national territories do not coincide. The republics claimed national sovereignty in 1991, but they did not in fact have uncontested national authority over their entire territories. Most often represented by the potential conflict between an independent Croatia and an independent Serbia over their common border, this problem was not simply an old Croat-Serb conflict, as was commonly stated by Western politicians and journalists at the time, or a conflict confined to Yugoslavia alone. This was the existence of multiple and conflicting notions of the nation as a claim to territory.

The second fundamental question raised by the concept of national self-determination and that had to be resolved if the state was to break up nonviolently was: What defined rights to territory? The Balkans contain at least four conflicting concepts of the nation as a right to territory. The *historicist* principle defines a nation and its claim to the right to govern a particular territory as a people who link their common identity to a prior, historical state on those lands. The *democratic* principle states that all who reside on a territory have the right to choose their state, by popular referendum.[29] It accepts that patterns of migration, settlement, and demographic change may have fundamentally altered the national composition of a population since that historical state, although its usual mechanism of numerical majority creates a different set of problems. The *Helsinki* (and United Nations) principle says that all existing, internationally recognized borders are "inviolable" and define states. The *realist* principle accepts the fait accompli of physical control through military force, if not always legitimate authority, and it is the principle on which most European states were actually founded. It need not, however, imply conquest from outside. In countering accusations of external conquest during the war in Bosnia-Herzegovina, moreover, SDS leader Radovan Karadžić appeared to have created a fifth principle for Bosnian Serbs out of the historicist claim. Using a modern (or smallholder's) version of the feudal principle based on land ownership, Karadžić claimed the rights of national sovereignty over 64 percent of Bosnian territory where (he said) Bosnian Serb households held legal title to land and farms.[30]

The difficulty is that there is no agreed-upon lexical priority among these principles, and different principles are at stake in different territorial contests. The historicist claim favored by Croatia was the basis on which republican borders were ostensibly drawn in 1943–45. But the claim cannot resolve conflicts between Croatian leaders, such as Tudjman, and Bosnia-Herzegovina, for they both claim the same territories historically. It also cannot sort out the conflict between Serbia and the Albanian population in Kosovo, both of which claim Kosovo as their historical lands. The historicist principle, moreover, was the basis for Greek opposition to Macedonian sovereignty and to the use of the name of Macedonia if it did become independent; Greece claimed that Macedonian territory was Greek long before Slavs entered the Balkans or Macedonia was a province of the Ottoman empire.

The democratic principle has long been identified with Serbian national aspirations because its state borders, since full independence in 1878, never coincided with the pattern of Serb settlements. This was due to many causes—forced and voluntary migration; imperial invitation (to settle and defend the military border, the *krajina*, between the Habsburg and Ottoman territories, or to repopulate and farm the land in Vojvodina and Slavonia after wars); Serbian colonization (in parts of Macedonia and Kosovo); and Great Power politics (Austrian suzerainty over Bosnia-Herzegovina after 1878, and the creation of Yugoslavia after 1918).[31] According to this principle, Serbs, including Serbian communities in Croatia and Bosnia that voted to remain within a Yugoslav state that would include Serbia, have the right to choose to live in one state. Unlike the historicist principle, the democratic principle makes a particular territory vulnerable to demographic change and to migration that can change its numerical balance. For that reason, nationalists in general tend to be pronatalist, seeking to protect their national rights by numerical preponderance and fearing communities that are more prolific. In Yugoslavia, such fears seemed to produce a particularly emotional prejudice against Muslims. The effect in Bosnia-Herzegovina of demographic changes and emigration in the 1960s and 1970s, for example, was to complete the process begun with the genocidal campaign in 1941–44 of reducing the Serb population from a majority to a minority, ending the national claim they had been making to the area since it had been denied by Austria in 1878; the relative decline of Serbs in the population of Kosovo was even more dramatic. In Macedonia, ethnic Albanians aspiring to national status refused to participate in the 1991 census, so numerical claims to that status and to autonomy could not be refuted.[32]

The Helsinki (international) principle, that existing borders define a nation-state and that any questioning of those borders is an invitation to protracted conflict and instability, was essentially violated by the European Community when it declared the internal borders between the Yugoslav republics international and inviolable. Asked by Serbia in September 1991 to render a judgment on its conflict with Croatia over their common border, the Arbitration (Badinter) Commission reached to third world experience to find a precedent in international law—in the principle estab-lished by the little-known border conflict between Burkina Faso and Mali, resulting from colonial rule, which declared the colonial border to be inviolable on a principle of *uti possidetis*, or "keep what you have."[33] This judgment appeared to acknowledge the historicist claims made by the Slovene and Croatian governments and to reject the democratic claims represented by Milošević's warning in July 1990 that Serbs would have to seek "border rectifications" if Yugoslavia broke apart. It also conceded the Croatian position that the separate referendum of the Serb population in the three areas of large Serb settlements (Krajina, Lika-Kordun, eastern Slavonia and Baranja), in which the Serbs voted to remain within a Yu-goslav state if Croatia became independent, was invalid. Serbia (and many individual Serbs) reacted angrily to the presumption that their circum-stances were equivalent to a postcolonial situation in Africa, while Croa-tian legal scholars ironically claimed that their republic's historical rights had been confirmed. Yet the EC's identification of existing borders with the historicist principle did not clarify the conflict between Greece and Macedonia. On Kosovo, it was inconsistent; the EC seemed to accept the historicist claim that this was Serbian territory and that the Albanian referendum for a separate republic was invalid, but the CSCE seemed to insist that, because it was a separate "federal unit" (a province, though not a republic), the international defense of internal borders applied to Kosovo as well and therefore protected Albanian rights over those of Serbia.

The European position was, in fact, inconsistent. Alongside the in-sistence on Helsinki norms for the sake of European stability in general, it seemed to prefer the democratic principle under the influence of German reasoning that the referendums in Slovenia and Croatia had been the leg-itimizing acts of self-determination—in the same manner as German reu-nification in 1989–90. Not all thought the required referendum in Bosnia-Herzegovina was a good idea, however, and the referendums of groups within the republics (Serbs in Croatia, Muslims in the Sandžak, Albanians in Kosovo)—and the numerous boycotts of the republican referendums—were ignored. By revoking their solution at Versailles but without a con-sistent, principled rationale for the borders of the new states, the European powers opened three specific problems at once: the "Serbian question," the "Albanian question," and Bosnia-Herzegovina.

The Yugoslavia validated at Versailles imposed a compromise on Ser-bian politicians who were the heirs of a foreign policy begun in the 1840s, to create a Serbian national state. Unlike the similar unification projects in Italy and Germany at the time, this task had required liberating areas under Turkish control (such as those in areas now in the borders of Mace-donia and Bosnia-Herzegovina), and it had been frustrated by outside

powers at the Congress of Berlin in 1878, which sanctioned full independence to Serbia but handed Bosnia-Herzegovina over to Austrian control.
The recognition of the Kingdom of the Serbs, Croats, and Slovenes at
Versailles continued this external dictate of sorts with its solution: that not
all Serbs could live in a nationally defined state, but they could live in one
state.[34] To grant Croatia sovereignty in 1991–92 over the territories it
claims historically, therefore, as Vladimir Gligorov puts it, is to "open the
Serbian question."[35] The EC could revoke the Versailles compromise, and
it could define the stated desire of Serbs in Croatia and Bosnia-Herzegovina to unify with Serbia as illegitimate and the armed confrontations
within those areas as aggression against the two new states, but it could
not prevent those armed confrontations or explain with the legitimacy
necessary for a stable peace why it was that Croatian rights to national
self-determination took precedence over Serbian. Instead of acknowledging
the need for discussion on the borders of an independent Serbia, moreover,
the EC's decision to internationalize the internal borders unwittingly fueled
the larger political battle by playing directly into the internal campaign of
revenge against the socialist period, which a number of camps (particularly
in Serbia and Croatia) had come to symbolize derisively by the phrase,
"Tito's borders."

The word Yugoslavia means the land of south Slavs. Non-Slavic peoples had cultural rights but were not considered eligible for constituent
nation status. By combining the principle of Helsinki borders as regards
the federal units and the democratic principle of a referendum on self-
determination, the EC decision made it impossible to ignore the Albanian
position on Kosovo and to continue Western insistence that the solution to
that conflict lay in the realm of human rights. Western powers would have
to decide whether Kosovo was a part of Serbia, and thus an internal matter,
or whether the EC had actually granted international status to the provincial boundaries, giving Kosovars the right to statehood.

In terms of rights to territory, Serbia's relations with Kosovo were
similar to Croatian relations with Serbs in *krajina*: Serbia denied the democratic principle of self-determination to Albanians, asserting its historicist
right to the territory of Kosovo. It had an additional argument not available
to Croatia, moreover, in the Yugoslav constitution that Slovenia and Croatia used to justify independence, but in which Albanians were not a
Yugoslav nation, but rather a nationality without national rights within
Yugoslavia. If external powers recognized Albanian territorial rights to
Kosovo, however, they would create for Macedonia a problem similar to
Croatia's. National status for ethnic Albanians would lead them to use
their numerical majority in some areas of Macedonia to claim, by way of
the democratic principle, a right to autonomous self-governance. It could
only be a matter of time, as people argued would be the case of the

autonomy of Serbs in Croatia, before Albanians in Kosovo and Albanians in contiguous areas of western Macedonia would attempt to unify, with the goal of an eventual union with the republic of Albania.

This democratic principle was even more problematic for Serbia with regard to the Sandžak region because here the Muslim majority population had national status under the Yugoslav constitution; although it did not have territorial autonomy, it did have an administratively autonomous history under the Ottomans in the same way that Slovenia had under the Habsburgs. The Muslims had, in fact, voted in referendum for autonomy on October 25–27, 1991, and for special status on January 11, 1992.[36] Because the region lay partly in the republic of Montenegro, moreover (see figure 7-1), the threat that this could be a prelude to statehood or unification with Bosnia-Herzegovina did not affect Serbia alone.[37]

Nonetheless, the third problem raised by the EC decision, that of Bosnia-Herzegovina, was the most complex. All three claimants to the territory—Bosnians, Croats, and Serbs—could legitimately defend those claims with the historicist principle, because the historical states referred to different periods in time, and with the federal constitution of socialist Yugoslavia. Two—Bosnians and Serbs—could claim the democratic principle. But not one of these three principles led to a territorial solution that could satisfy all three claims. The Bosnian territorial solution and the Croat and Serb solution were incompatible.

For Croatian president Tudjman, the territory of Croatia historically included much of Bosnia-Herzegovina, the borders of which had been confirmed in modern times, in his view, by a 1939 agreement on autonomy under the Yugoslav kingdom and the subsequent independent state of Croatia (1941–45) under Nazi sponsorship.[38] For Serbian president Milošević, the declaration of autonomous self-governing regions in areas of Serb majority settlement during 1990–91 and the results of a referendum among Serbs in these areas against Bosnian independence and in favor of remaining within a Yugoslav state confirmed their pre-Ottoman historicist claims with the democratic principle.[39]

But the agreement between these two leaders of Croatia and Serbia and their counterparts in Bosnia-Herzegovina (at the time, party leaders Mate Boban and Radovan Karadžić) to divide Bosnia between them (as discussed on many occasions between July 1990 and May 1992) would leave the third constituent nation—the Muslims—without a state. The Muslims bore equally the historical right to Bosnian sovereignty although their numerical plurality of 44 percent in the 1980s was not enough to outvote an alliance of the other two. The response of many in Serbia and Croatia was to insist that these Slavic Muslims were really, respectively, Serbs or Croats, while Tudjman and Milošević (and an increasingly vocal Karadžić in Bosnia) attempted to appeal to European audiences with a

FIGURE 7-1.  *The Sandžak and Albanian Majority Areas*

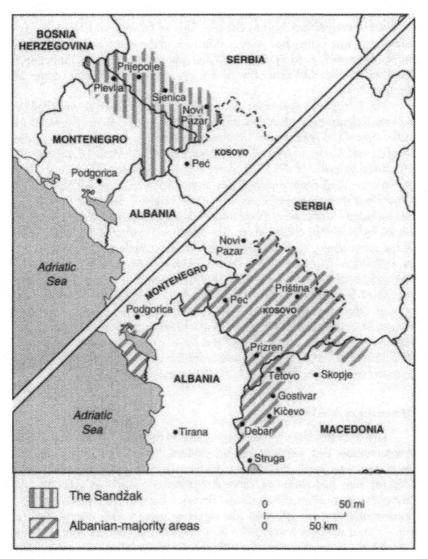

Sources: Patrick Moore, "The 'Albanian Question' in the Former Yugoslavia," *RFE/RL Research Report*, vol. 1, no. 14 (April 3, 1992), p. 9; and Fabian Schmidt, "The Sandžak: Muslims between Serbia and Montenegro," *RFE/RL Research Report*, vol. 3, no. 6 (February 11, 1994), p. 30.

cultural justification. Using identical language, they warned that an independent state of Bosnia-Herzegovina would bring into Europe the threat to Western civilization, and to the very idea of Europe, of Islamic fundamentalism. Just as they had protected Europe in the past from the Ottoman horde, they told visiting diplomats and politicians, Croatia and Serbia remained Europe's ultimate line of defense against the Muslim danger in the East.[40]

The European solution was to require a referendum to certify popular will for independence. But this was no solution in the political conditions at the time. The government by then represented a fragile alliance of the Muslim and Croat parties. The Serbian party had left the coalition; the pro-Bosnian leader of the Croat party—only a branch of the ruling party of Croatia—had been replaced (by Tudjman) with a pro-independence Croat; and the remaining members of the Bosnian collective presidency had excluded—under emergency rules—all representatives of the nonethnic parties from further consultation. The situation is reflected in the language of the referendum, with which the government chose to maximize votes by avoiding a definition of the Bosnian nation: "Are you for a sovereign and independent Bosnia and Hercegovina, a state of equal citizens, the peoples of Bosnia and Herzegovina—Muslims, Serbs, Croats, and members of other nations—living in it?"[41] The European Community also sought to avoid confrontation with the problem and the results of the referendum—which Serbs outside the main cities boycotted and which 99.7 percent of the 63.4 percent voter turnout approved—by delaying recognition until it succumbed to U.S. pressure on April 6.

## Minorities or Irredenta?

The third fundamental question raised by the concept of national self-determination, and which had to be resolved if the Yugoslav state was to break up nonviolently, was: what were the regional or international norms defining who had rights to national self-determination in general? The Yugoslav constitution distinguished between constituent nations and national minorities—people who had rights to protect their ethnic identity but not to a national homeland within Yugoslavia, such as Albanians or Hungarians. Once the state of south Slavs was gone, this distinction could no longer be maintained.[42] The EC and CSCE rulings seemed to equate the two categories under one concept of minority rights, which would apply to all groups not of the majority nationality in the new states. In fact, the rulings removed the limits in the Yugoslav constitution to claims for political autonomy and self-determination of any ethnic group that identified with particular territory throughout the region. The question of who was a nation, with rights to self-determination, could not be contained within existing borders.

Greece was particularly vocal on the danger of a Yugoslav breakup, viewing an independent Macedonia as a threat to its own security and to regional stability in general. Yet, faced with a fait accompli at the EC meeting in December 1991, it reoriented its tactics to focus on whether the principle of national sovereignty applied in the Macedonia case.[43] The Bulgarian government attempted to straddle a fence between its need for external stability during its postcommunist transition, on the one hand, and its need to face the active revival at home of popular sentiments that Macedonians and Macedonia were Bulgarian, on the other. When it chose to manage this threat by forbidding the registration of a resurrected revolutionary nationalist organization of the Balkan-Wars period that had been revived as a political party in Yugoslav Macedonia (the Internal Macedonian Revolutionary Organization [VMRO]), the human rights organization Helsinki Watch took what it considered to be a dangerous violation of human rights to the court of world public opinion and forced its reversal. As in its policy toward Kosovo during 1989–91, the United States saw the question as a case of individual human rights and ignored the threat posed to governments if ethnically based organizations refused such classification and demanded *national* rights to political autonomy instead. Still hoping to avoid the shoals, the Bulgarian government was the first to recognize Macedonian independence (followed one month later by Turkey), but it did so, the Bulgarian president said, not as a "nation" but as a "state."

Serbia was also not immune from external threats. Prime Minister József Antall of Hungary greeted the July 1991 accord at Brioni by warning Serbia that it could not count on its province of Vojvodina (where the largest minority was Hungarian). Alluding to the 1920 Treaty of Trianon, he announced, "We gave Vojvodina to Yugoslavia. If there is no more Yugoslavia, then we should get it back."[44] Like the official policy of Serbia under Milošević, the electoral platform of the ruling party in Hungary (the Hungarian Democratic Forum, MDF) defined Hungarian national interests as including the protection of Hungarians living in neighboring states.[45] After it was revealed that the Hungarian government had illegally sold approximately 36,000 Kalashnikov rifles to the republic of Croatia in the fall of 1990, the ambiguity surrounding the notion of "protection" could not be erased by Antall's public assurances that this meant aid and international attention to human rights concerns, not territorial annexation.[46] This ambiguity was identical to that of Serbian policy and statements toward Serbs in neighboring Croatia and Bosnia-Herzegovina, despite efforts by many to assign responsibility for the Yugoslav tragedy to Serbian national character.

## The Use of Force

Few believe that the European Community or the United States took any of these considerations into account, or even that they consciously accepted the Slovene portrayal of Yugoslavia as an artificial state composed of separate nations and of the right to independence as the pinnacle of political liberty. Their concern was to stop the use of force on the borders of Europe and to demonstrate their capacity for common action. They argued that it did not matter what the Yugoslavs agreed as long as they achieved a political outcome without force.[47] But, in fact, they did take a position. They insisted on "existing" republican (and perhaps provincial) borders and recognized Slovene and Croatian national independence on the basis of both historicist and democratic principles. But because they made no effort to provide alternative guarantees to those whose rights were denied by this decision, or to recognize the genuine conflicts opened by the decision over who had rights of national self-determination, what the bases of such rights were, and what territorial borders they implied, there was no way that an outcome could occur without force.

While refusing to enforce its own rulings or to interpose forces between armed parties, the EC (and then the UN and the United States) nonetheless interposed itself politically. All the while that it insisted on the norms of sovereignty, prohibiting interference in the internal affairs of a sovereign state without consent, the EC had, in fact, stepped into the shoes of that sovereign state. Because it ignored the compromises that Yugoslavia represented in guaranteeing nations the right to self-determination in a nationally mixed area, ignored the security guarantee that Yugoslavia had provided for territories of mixed population, and did little to reassure those relegated to minority status that they would be protected, it could not reverse the downward spiral of suspicion and insecurity that was leading to war. It then assumed the role of mediator to obtain cease-fire agreements as rapidly as possible. But that meant talking to leaders who were fighting because they could not agree, while insisting that no agreement achieved by the use of force would be recognized. It could negotiate cease-fires that froze the disputes over borders and national rights, but it could not persuade parties to disarm without providing a constructive alternative to those whose national rights were denied by the international insistence on the republican borders. To avoid recognizing rights until there was an overall political settlement for the entire country, for example, the Vance plan for a cease-fire in Croatia placed 14,000 UN peacekeeping troops in an "inkblot" pattern at "flashpoints" in four UN protected areas. Sent to monitor the withdrawal of the Yugoslav army, the disarming of Serb militia, and the restoration of control over police and government to local majorities in the UNPAs, the UN operation was viewed by both the

Croatian government and the Serb authorities in *krajina* as legitimating their claims to the territory according to rights to self-determination. Moreover, despite the resort to violence, there was no military solution to these conflicts without the extermination or expulsion of large numbers of people. Military control over territory would still have to return to the constitutional issues of national, ethnic, minority, and citizens' rights.

## Conclusion

Although the war in Croatia produced no military victory, the EC decisions did hand it a victory in the political and propaganda side of the war, which reverberated deeply into the domestic conflict. World opinion accepted the geopolitical and cultural prejudices of the west Europeans— that there was a difference in civilizations between West and East, which ran between Croatia and Serbia; that Macedonians and Bosnians were irrelevant; and that the Serbs throughout what was no longer a country were indeed aggressors, driven by Slobodan Milošević's reported dream of a Greater Serbia. Despite the apparent defeat of the *krajina* militants under Milan Babić in Croatia, who lost the political support of Slobodan Milošević in November 1991, followed by a very public letter in January 1992 for opposing the Vance Plan, the reemergence of the moderate wing of the SDS, under Jovan Rašković, was short-lived. Although invisible to the West, these moderate mayors in Serb-majority towns within Croatia and the far larger number of urban Serbs who had accepted the fait accompli of Croatian independence, viewed themselves as citizens of the new Croatian state, and sought to find their accommodation with it despite antagonism from both Croatian nationalists and Serb radicals. Also invisible with the nationalist spectacles worn by the West were members of the army and local police forces throughout the country still trying to keep peace. World opinion, in fact, delegitimized (and thereby eventually helped to eliminate) army professionals and senior staff who did not support nationalist agendas. Denied support, sanctuary, publicity, or representation by the international community, all these groups had insufficient resources to counteract the process of radicalization. As the stalemate in Croatia and the war in Bosnia made life ever harsher in the border areas, even Serbs from the area of Knin began to leave, and—under cover of worldwide attention to the Bosnian war in the summer of 1992—Babić's radicals were able to revive their power through selected assassinations of moderate leaders.

All of this demonstrated to Serb nationalists that Milošević had been right all along about German and fascist revanchism, foreign victimization of Serbs, Serbs' need to protect each other because no one would come to their aid, and the Serbs' ability to survive, as they had historically, by standing, if necessary alone, against overwhelming odds.

To make the multinational reality of Yugoslavia conform to what both nationalist leaders and Europe said was fact, a truly brutal process had to unfold within the former country. The EC could not find a resolution to the conflicts in the former Yugoslavia; they became more virulent and intractable, and political negotiators weaker. Although most called it a civil war, armed contest did not aim to decide which party should control a state or whether a secessionist region would succeed against the parent state. It was a competition to create wholly new nation-states—citizens and loyalties, strategic assets, and borders defined by the perceived right to national self-determination within the territory of a former state. Defined by the economic and political conditions of the collapse of a state and its ability to provide security and civil order, the contests were a series of wars—sometimes localized, sometimes rolling and interconnected—in which the projects of radical nationalists willing to use force to claim territorial sovereignty and the spontaneous behaviors of people facing this collapse interacted.

# Chapter 8

# *War: Building States from Nations*

As a political force, nationalism is an empty vessel to be filled by all those who see their interests in political independence and states' rights. Its key characteristic is its definition of a political community—its principles of membership, its cultural and territorial boundaries, and also, therefore, its enemies. In contrast to communism, nationalism has no intrinsic substantive goals beyond affirmation of a particular collective bond among people and the creation of an independent state around that identity. Exclusion is as important as inclusion. Nationalist expression may be a positive assertion of commonality in culture, political history, and obligations of social reciprocity. But it is at the same time necessarily a negative assertion of who does *not* belong, of mistrust, fear, even hatred of persons seen as "other," as "foreigner," and of the characteristics of persons who should be excluded.

Nationalism's virulent capacity is not so apparent when it manifests itself as cultural or religious revival and in intellectuals' demands for rights to personal expression, as if to open debate, rather than to draw cultural borders between people. As a vehicle for resolving distributive conflicts by claiming ethnic rights or national ownership over incomes, jobs, economic assets, and tax revenues, it is so familiar to the workings of most societies that it is easily accepted. What society does not seek to defend privilege or wealth as a national right or to organize social roles and patterns of discrimination (positive and negative) in part along cultural lines? When aspiring politicians in countries formerly ruled by communist parties used nationalist symbols and loyalties to maximize votes and popular support, to coopt opposition intellectuals, or to neutralize competitors with charges of being unpatriotic, they did not appear threatening to Western governments that heard the anticommunist language in which it was often cloaked. The ease with which aroused passions could substitute in the short run for ideology and organization and avoid representing individual interests also caused little alarm because it was seen as part of a democratic revolution.

Despite the Jekyll and Hyde potential of nationalism, people tend to distinguish among separate nationalisms, calling some "good" and others "bad" according to the goal sought or the methods used.[1] But this evaluation is always subjective, and it depends on the institutional context within which it appears. In an atmosphere of tolerance and institutionalized pluralism, nationalism can remain a positive expression of cultural or religious identity—ethnic differences—that does not deny the same freedom to others. Even politicized ethnicity, while discriminating against those who do not belong to or identify with officially recognized groups, can exist peacefully under favorable economic conditions if it provides the same rights to members of different groups and ensures institutionalized channels of appeal. But political nationalism defines rights of membership itself: black and white, in or out; on this one defining trait it cannot compromise.[2] Because the goal of nationalist politicians is to use the coercive instruments of the state to enforce that principle, what one thinks about a particular nationalism depends most on whether one is being included or excluded.

Nationalism is often compared with communism as a collectivist ideology, but in fact it defines the membership characteristics of individuals, not the quality of their social interaction. In contrast to communist parties, moreover, its membership is ascriptive and exclusive rather than open to people regardless of racial, religious, and cultural background. And that membership is not only in a party, with its obligations and privileges, but in society itself—as citizen, and with no recourse against others' decision to exclude. But nationalism is compatible with communist rule, either together or as its successor, because both deny (for very different reasons) the need to provide institutional mechanisms to regulate and protect differences (such as permitting an opposition, critical thought, conflicts of interest, or minority rights).

The label of nationalism is not sufficient to describe a situation or predict behavior, however, because of its empty-vessel character—its absence of program outside the insistence on political power for some imagined community. It can therefore ally easily with others, including dispossessed communists who believe in a strong state against international exploitation or who hold bureaucratic positions. Such allies may be ideologically contradictory groups from far left to far right joined only by political expediency. Nationalist parties most often attract individuals when political organizations representing their specific interests are absent or have not sought their support, when individuals—out of a growing rootlessness or anomie—seek a restored sense of community.[3] Because it is a principle of exclusion, however, it tends to surface in conditions that are not conducive to its more benign expression alone. Its potential for violence is ever more manifest as it moves from intellectual expression and economic discrimination to criteria for citizenship and claims for territorial sovereignty. In multinational states such as Yugoslavia, it must destroy while it builds.

This process can be understood not by the labels of historical ethnic hatred or Balkan culture, but by the clash between nationalist goals and Yugoslav reality and by the consequence of translating socioeconomic and political divisions into contests over territory. The wars to create new national states out of Yugoslavia contained many elements: psychological warfare against multiethnic identities and loyalties; the culture surrounding the defense of rights to land; class warfare; the dissolution of the governmental and economic functions of the former state; and the construction of borders, foreign relations, economic infrastructure, and armed forces of defensible, viable, new states.

## Psychological Warfare: Honi Soit Qui Mal y Pense

Despite the claims made by nationalist leaders, the reality of multinational Yugoslavia still existed in the lives of individual citizens in 1990–91—in their ethnically mixed neighborhoods, villages, towns, and cities; in their mixed marriages, family ties across republic boundaries, and second homes in another republic; in their conceptions of ethnic and national coexistence and the compatibility of multiple identities for each citizen; and in the idea of Bosnia-Herzegovina (see figure 8-1). Because people had not expressed their differences politically under one-party socialism, their loyalties were scattered among many associations. These tended to be highly localized and personal—to one's village or town, to school friends, to neighbors, to the town or region of one's origin and parents, to Yugoslavia as an idea and a stature abroad, to workplace colleagues, or to an occupation or profession. A one-time, multiparty election thus was not sufficient to develop partisan identities. The exception to undeveloped political identities was communists—not individuals who had simply been members of a party that had folded, but those who identified broadly with its ideals, traditions, or wartime struggle. But as it was common to say, "I come from a communist family," this had become for most a private identity, however strong it remained.

To legitimize new states on the basis of political loyalty to a nation, nationalist politicians had to draw out the ethnic element in all these social bonds and identities, nationalize it, and win the loyalty of citizens whose allegiances were in doubt. A vote in 1990 for a political party that emphasized ethnonational identity was not the same thing as a vote for a national state, and even a vote for the sovereignty of one's republic was not necessarily a vote for independence, let alone commitment to war, should that be necessary. In Bosnia-Herzegovina, where votes were cast most over-

FIGURE 8-1. *National Composition of Bosnia-Herzegovina by District*

| | % Muslim | % Serb | % Croat | % Yugoslav and Other |
|---|---|---|---|---|
| Sarajevo | 49 | 28 | 7 | 16 |
| Centar | 51 | 21 | 7 | 22 |
| Hadžići | 64 | 26 | 3 | 7 |
| Ilidža | 43 | 37 | 10 | 10 |
| Ilijaš | 42 | 45 | 7 | 6 |
| Novi Grad | 51 | 28 | 6 | 15 |
| Novo Sarajevo | 36 | 35 | 9 | 20 |
| Pale | 27 | 69 | 0 | 3 |
| Stari Grad | 78 | 10 | 2 | 9 |
| Trnovo | 69 | 30 | 0 | 1 |
| Vogošća | 51 | 36 | 4 | 9 |
| Banovići | 72 | 17 | 2 | 9 |
| Banja Luka | 15 | 55 | 15 | 16 |
| Bihać | 67 | 18 | 8 | 8 |
| Bijeljina | 31 | 59 | 0 | 9 |
| Bileća | 15 | 80 | 0 | 5 |
| Bos. Dubica | 20 | 69 | 2 | 9 |
| Bos. Gradiška | 26 | 60 | 6 | 8 |
| Bos. Krupa | 74 | 24 | 0 | 2 |
| Bos. Brod | 12 | 34 | 41 | 13 |
| Bos. Novi | 34 | 60 | 1 | 5 |
| Bos. Petrovac | 21 | 75 | 0 | 3 |
| Bos. Šamac | 7 | 41 | 45 | 7 |
| Bos. Grahovo | 0 | 95 | 3 | 2 |
| Bratunac | 64 | 34 | 0 | 2 |
| Brčko | 44 | 21 | 25 | 9 |
| Breza | 76 | 12 | 5 | 7 |
| Bugojno | 42 | 19 | 34 | 5 |
| Busovača | 45 | 3 | 48 | 4 |
| Cazin | 98 | 1 | 0 | 1 |
| Čajniče | 45 | 53 | 0 | 2 |
| Čapljina | 28 | 14 | 54 | 5 |
| Čelinac | 8 | 89 | 0 | 3 |
| Čitluk | 0 | 0 | 99 | 0 |
| Derventa | 13 | 41 | 39 | 8 |
| Doboj | 40 | 39 | 13 | 8 |
| Donji Vakuf | 55 | 39 | 3 | 3 |
| Foča | 52 | 45 | 0 | 3 |
| Fojnica | 49 | 0 | 41 | 9 |
| Gacko | 35 | 62 | 0 | 2 |
| Glamoč | 18 | 79 | 1 | 1 |
| Goražde | 70 | 26 | 0 | 3 |
| Gornji Vakuf | 56 | 0 | 43 | 1 |
| Gračanica | 72 | 23 | 0 | 5 |
| Gradačac | 60 | 20 | 15 | 5 |
| Grude | 0 | 0 | 99 | 0 |
| Han Pijesak | 40 | 58 | 0 | 2 |
| Jablanica | 72 | 4 | 18 | 6 |
| Jajce | 39 | 19 | 35 | 7 |
| Kakanj | 55 | 9 | 30 | 7 |
| Kalesija | 80 | 18 | 0 | 2 |
| Kalinovik | 37 | 61 | 0 | 2 |
| Kiseljak | 41 | 3 | 52 | 4 |
| Kladanj | 73 | 24 | 0 | 3 |
| Ključ | 48 | 50 | 0 | 2 |
| Konjic | 55 | 15 | 26 | 4 |
| Kotor Varoš | 30 | 38 | 29 | 3 |
| Kreševo | 23 | 0 | 71 | 6 |
| Kupres | 7 | 51 | 39 | 3 |
| Laktaši | 2 | 82 | 9 | 8 |
| Ljištica | 0 | 0 | 99 | 0 |
| Livno | 15 | 10 | 72 | 3 |
| Lopare | 38 | 56 | 4 | 3 |
| Lukavac | 67 | 22 | 4 | 8 |
| Ljubinje | 8 | 90 | 1 | 1 |
| Ljubuški | 6 | 0 | 93 | 1 |
| Maglaj | 45 | 31 | 19 | 5 |
| Modriča | 29 | 35 | 27 | 8 |
| Mostar | 35 | 19 | 34 | 12 |

| | % Muslim | % Serb | % Croat | % Yugoslav and Other |
|---|---|---|---|---|
| Mrkonjić Grad | 12 | 77 | 8 | 3 |
| Neum | 5 | 5 | 88 | 3 |
| Nevesinje | 23 | 74 | 1 | 1 |
| Odžak | 20 | 20 | 54 | 6 |
| Olovo | 75 | 19 | 4 | 2 |
| Orašje | 7 | 15 | 75 | 3 |
| Posušje | 0 | 0 | 99 | 0 |
| Prijedor | 44 | 42 | 6 | 8 |
| Prnjavor | 15 | 72 | 4 | 9 |
| Prozor | 37 | 0 | 62 | 1 |
| Pucarevo | 38 | 13 | 40 | 9 |
| Rogatica | 60 | 38 | 0 | 1 |
| Rudo | 27 | 71 | 0 | 2 |
| Sanski Most | 47 | 42 | 7 | 4 |
| Skender Vakuf | 6 | 68 | 25 | 1 |
| Sokolac | 30 | 69 | 0 | 1 |
| Srbac | 4 | 89 | 0 | 6 |
| Srebrenica | 73 | 25 | 0 | 2 |
| Srebrenik | 75 | 13 | 7 | 5 |
| Stolac | 45 | 21 | 32 | 2 |
| Šekovići | 3 | 94 | 0 | 2 |
| Šipovo | 19 | 79 | 0 | 1 |
| Teslić | 21 | 55 | 16 | 7 |
| Tešanj | 72 | 6 | 18 | 3 |
| Titov Drvar | 0 | 97 | 0 | 2 |
| Tomislavgrad | 11 | 2 | 87 | 0 |
| Travnik | 45 | 11 | 37 | 7 |
| Trebinje | 18 | 69 | 4 | 9 |
| Tuzla | 48 | 15 | 16 | 21 |
| Ugljevik | 41 | 56 | 0 | 3 |
| Vareš | 30 | 16 | 41 | 13 |
| Velika Kladuša | 92 | 4 | 1 | 3 |
| Visoko | 75 | 16 | 4 | 5 |
| Višegrad | 63 | 33 | 0 | 4 |
| Vitez | 41 | 5 | 46 | 8 |
| Vlasenica | 55 | 42 | 0 | 2 |
| Zavidovići | 60 | 20 | 13 | 6 |
| Zenica | 55 | 16 | 16 | 13 |
| Zvornik | 59 | 38 | 0 | 3 |
| Žepče | 47 | 10 | 40 | 3 |
| Živinice | 81 | 6 | 7 | 6 |

Key

Croats above 66%
Croats 50–66%
Croats below 50%
Serbs above 66%
Serbs 50–66%
Serbs below 50%
Muslims above 66%
Muslims 50–66%
Muslims below 50%

Source: Ante Markotić, Ejub Sijenčić, and Asim Abdurahmanović (Bosnia-Herzegovina: Altermedia and NUB, 1991).

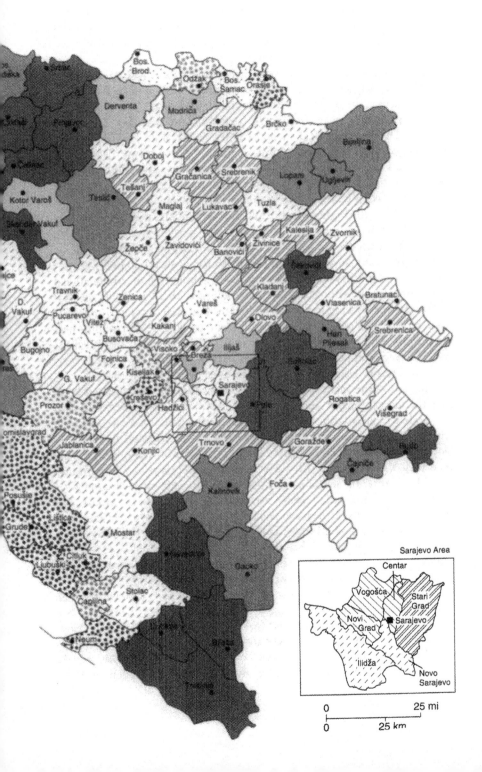

Sarajevo Area

Centar

Vogošca

Stari
Grad

Novi
Grad

Sarajevo

Ilidža

Novo
Sarajevo

0                    25 mi

0          25 km

whelmingly for ethnonational parties, public opinion polls in May and June 1990, and again in November 1991, also showed overwhelming majorities (in the range of 70 to 90 percent) against separation from Yugoslavia and against an ethnically divided republic.[4]

To win against public opinion, nationalist leaders had to engage in psychological warfare. They sought to persuade audiences both at home and abroad that the alternative to national states was no longer viable: in other words, to destroy forever the Yugoslav idea that they could live together. The first stage in the wars of 1991–95, therefore, occurred earlier in the mass media and on the political stump.[5] The domestic objective of various nationalists was to persuade citizens of one nationality that they were under threat from other nations. Accusations of being cheated economically by other nations (in federal taxation or in jobs) or being overcome biologically (by the higher Muslim and Albanian birth rates) and warnings of plots by other groups to create states that would expel citizens from their homes played on a local inclination to conspiracy theories and on growing economic insecurity and rapidly shifting, uncertain political conditions. In a country where everyone was a minority in ethnonational terms, politicians willing to raise consciousness about national survival and the danger of being in a minority had the potential to create a collective paranoia that was self-perpetuating. It was then only a short step to persuade those who accepted this argument that the security of their identity, way of living, and perhaps even person lay with their national group.[6] As terrorists reason, elemental fears were to force people to take sides.

In view of this tactic, the political rhetoric of the 1980s found in debates over the federal budget and constitution from Slovenia to Serbia and in nationalist themes from anticommunist intellectuals therefore became, whether intended or not, a long, psychological preparation for war.[7] In Slovenia nationalists claimed that Slovene standards of living were threatened by federal taxes and that their democracy and pluralism were endangered by Serbia. In Serbia nationalists linked the Albanian demand for a republic in Kosovo with Serbia's 500 years of subjugation to Turkish rule after its defeat in 1389; the nationalist programs of Slovenes, Croats, Muslims, Albanians, and Macedonians in the 1980s, with the progressive splintering of Serbs and Serbia after 1945 and 1974 into ever more separate political units; and the anti-Serb coalition, with a similar alliance of the Vatican, the Comintern, and Germany during World War II.[8]

It was true that in the decade-long struggle over Kosovo between Serbian state power and Albanian demographic power, Albanians had made Serbs and Montenegrins feel unwelcome, persuading them to leave. It was also true that church leaders and intellectuals had given these Serbs and Montenegrins aid in their political campaign with Belgrade to take back political power and property. But the political problem was the hypercharged emotional atmosphere of mutual suspicions within Kosovo, in which rumors of Serbs poisoning drinking water and of Albanians raping Serb women suggested the beginnings of mass hysteria.[9] The Serbian political campaign referred to "genocide" against Serbs and used a "discourse of violence, rape particularly, aiming to spread the fear of communication over ethnic boundaries."[10] It was in this context that Serbian president Slobodan Milošević first gave the war cries, which he repeated often, "No one will be permitted to beat you" and "They will never humiliate the Serbian people again." In some villages, local authorities began to issue permits to citizens to draw arms from the local TDF arsenal "just in case." Croatian leader Franjo Tudjman's revisionist history about the genocide against Serbs, Jews, and Romany under the Croatian independent state in 1941–45 became politically threatening when Tudjman's election as Croatian president was bankrolled largely by right-wing émigrés from that period and brought back its state symbols and a special tax on Serbs from Serbia who had second homes in Croatia (but not on such persons from any other republic).

By 1991 many who might have been expected to fight these developments also had begun to succumb emotionally. Pro-Yugoslav Slovenes began to "recall" unpleasant encounters in Belgrade or in the army. Nonnationalist Croatian intellectuals, who had opposed Tudjman's attempt to deny centuries of communal coexistence and intermarriage between Serbs and Croats or the history of competition between Serbs in Habsburg territories and Serbs in Serbia, began to reassess their own contacts with Serb friends and the stereotypes of ordinary people. Once dismissed by such intellectuals as religious and cultural prejudice, their way of talking about the "other" ethnic group now seemed to reveal a deeper truth—that there was, after all, an ineradicable cultural difference between the two peoples. The cultural revival initiated by Serb nationalist intellectuals from Belgrade in the 1980s in minority areas of Croatia began to appear to non-Serbs as part of a plot to create a Greater Serbia. The discovery in Croatia and Herzegovina of caves and mass graves revealing victims of World War II massacres heightened fears of impending danger and obligations of revenge.[11]

Operating within stable democratic systems, this emotional momentum might have encountered limits even late in the crisis. Instead, those willing to use the extremist language for political ends sought to increase or consolidate their local power in the republics by gaining control over the mass media. The democratic elections in 1990 provided this opportunity, by giving nationalist politicians access to state resources in a system that was constitutionally still the socialist one-party system, and the incentive, because most of them won office with less than a majority and because more than one party claimed to represent each nation's interests.

Censorship of the press and total control of television were essential to the power and wartime tactics, for example, of both Milošević in Serbia and Tudjman in Croatia.[12] As early as December 1990, Tudjman justified such censorship by a "state of war," decreed—as was most other governmental business—by an extraconstitutional security council with emergency powers. When pro-Marković reformers attempted to counteract censorship within the republics with a new all-Yugoslav and antinationalist television channel, YUTEL, Tudjman's government (and the government in Slovenia) gave it an unfavorable slot after midnight. Milošević's strength lay, in particular, in his near total manipulation of television. Without that, it would have been difficult to maintain his portrayal without qualifications of the threats to Serbs in Croatia and Bosnia-Herzegovina and therefore his role as protector and defender of Serb lives and interests, on which so many of his supporters and his leverage with international negotiators came to depend once war had begun.

In Bosnia-Herzegovina the fact that three national parties shared power after the November 1990 election did not prevent all three from collaborating in an attempt to impose state control over the media through legislation whereby each would appoint one-third of the governing boards and editors in TV and newspapers. Although struck down as unconstitutional on appeal, the intention here was the same as in Croatia and Serbia—to hinder rival political parties within the same national community in their access to public opinion and to appropriate for one political party the right to speak and interpret for its particular nation. This was not a case of interethnic conflict, but of intraethnic competition: of consolidating one-party rule within a nation by eliminating competition for the single constituency each was trying to develop and claim to represent. The Serbian Democratic Party (SDS) sought to eliminate the Serbian Movement for Renewal (SPO), the Muslim Party of Democratic Action (SDA) to squeeze out the Muslim Bosniak Organization (MBO), and the Croatian Democratic Union (HDZ) to undermine pro-Bosnian or anti-Zagreb Croats. Yet the voices in danger from these attempts to divide up turf among the three ruling parties were the nonethnic, multinational alternatives and—because the three parties appealed to national identities and crossed republican borders in their search for supporters and organizing activities—also the Bosnian.[13]

Just as in the conflict within the SDS in Croatia, between moderate parliamentarians oriented to Zagreb and radical militants oriented to Serbia, the links with Zagreb of the Bosnian branch of the HDZ and with Belgrade of the SDS meant that the propaganda of partisan struggle within Bosnia-Herzegovina was not confined to the republic. The most active wing of Tudjman's HDZ, including campaign contributions, was the western Herzegovina branch from Bosnia. By the fall of 1991, this area of

Bosnia (which would be proclaimed the state of Herzeg-Bosnia on July 3, 1992) was well integrated into the Croatian state; its Croat citizens had been granted dual citizenship in Croatia in 1990, with the right to vote in Croatian elections, and its local authorities used Croatian educational curricula, currency, state symbols (such as the flag and crest), police uniforms, and car registration plates. As early as 1989–90, Bosnian Serbs in Belgrade (including right-wing radical Vojislav Šešelj, leader of the Radical party) were active participants in the campaign to reshape opinion in Serbia. Given refuge and encouraged by Belgrade publishing houses, they claimed to be in exile from Bosnia after being forced to leave Sarajevo, which they portrayed as a "world of perpetual darkness" (*tamni vilajet*) where Serbs were endangered.[14] A daily feature section, "Echoes and Reactions," running two pages in the main Belgrade newspaper, *Politika* (by then under control of the Serbian Socialist party of Milošević), published carefully selected letters that targeted people who were "anti-Serb," including many members of the Bosnian political and cultural elite.[15]

The struggles for independence in 1991–92 added another audience to this media war—world opinion—and intensified the need to secure loyalties on ethnonational criteria. As the main architect of Tudjman's foreign propaganda policy explained in mid-July 1991, "The West can do a lot for us by seeing the difference between 'us' and 'them,' that we are democrats and they are not." He then specified how the West could help: by "giving Croatia economic aid and technical help" and "intervening firmly to give them the time necessary" to wait for the army and federal idea to fall apart.[16] With war, however, the democratic freedom to present an alternative reality and to oppose the nationalization of all identities had itself become an enemy—its very expression both an act of war and an obstacle to the war effort. In Croatia, the president's office issued a series of state directives, such as forbidding the media from using the terms "Chetniks" and "extremists," requiring them to refer to Serbs exclusively as "Serb terrorists" and to the Yugoslav People's Army (YPA) only as the "Serbo-Communist occupation army."[17] Urban intellectuals whose political identities were not ethnic but philosophical, such as liberal or social democratic, were publicly told instead that their identity was Serb or Croat.

Because the cease-fire in January 1992 did not end Croatia's war for territorial control and a secure independence, but rather shifted the battle back to the domestic political front, Tudjman actually intensified the campaign against independent newspapers and weeklies and harassment of journalists and intellectuals suspected of independent views. The process of property privatization through nationalization and state licensing provided a means and a cover for dismissing editorial boards, closing journals and newspapers, and imposing state control, as well as a way—especially after the middle of 1992—to squelch opposition, ensure Tudjman's reelection, and prevent discussion of policies toward minorities and the UN protected areas (UNPAs) in Croatia. [18] HDZ-nominated administrators at the University of Zagreb began a purge of "suspicious Croats" from its faculty in the fall of 1992, and Croats who showed any sympathy for multiethnic and pluralistic thinking were labeled *Jugonostalgičar* (Yugo-nostalgic) and *Jugozombi*, "for dar[ing] to remember what the country used to be." [19]

Milošević's control over the print media was always less complete than Tudjman's. [20] This control declined when the war in Croatia temporarily energized the opposition in Serbia to try to overthrow him. But the imposition of economic sanctions against Serbia, beginning with the EC and the United States in November 1991 and then the UN (Security Council Resolution 757) on May 30, 1992, worked to restore his control by cutting alternative sources of information and communication with the outside world and making subscriptions to print media prohibitively expensive. The sanctions also prevented his opposition from obtaining the foreign financial support and imported equipment (such as a transmitter with enough power to beam the one truly independent television station, Studio B, beyond Belgrade) that were necessary to compete with Milošević's domestic control through police and customs officials. Thus when Serbia was isolated, it was far easier for Milošević to control information given to the Serbian population about the wars in Croatia and Bosnia-Herzegovina and about world opinion. By late 1994, he was even copying Tudjman, applying the tactics used on *Danas* and *Slobodna Dalmacija* to silence the independent and increasingly critical daily *Borba*.

Nationalists in five of the Yugoslav republics needed only to persuade the majority of their populations and the outside world of the inevitability or desirability of separate national states. The violence of this propaganda war to persuade of the impossibility of nations living together was visible largely where conditions for an alternative view and political opposition existed—in ethnically mixed or ethnic minority areas. But in a sixth republic, Bosnia-Herzegovina, this argument met very different conditions. As a political fact and a cultural ideal, Bosnia-Herzegovina was multiethnic and multinational. The entire territory was ethnically mixed, blatantly defying the argument that national states were inevitable or that people of different national identities could not coexist. Not one of its three constituent nations (Muslims, Serbs, Croats) was a majority, so no one of their separate national projects could dominate the others. In fact, any alliance to create a majority could only be tactical and short-lived, as demonstrated by the SDA-HDZ alliance over sovereignty and national security in the fall of 1991, which placed the Serbs in a minority, or by the many instances of military cooperation between Bosnian Croats and Bosnian Serbs during 1992–94, which squeezed the Muslim party and Bosnian government forces. All the evidence suggested that there was majority support for a Bosnian identity and survival, from public opinion polls on the constitutional debates up to 1990, the civic initiatives, editorial policy in leading mass media, intellectuals' projects for a Bosnia based on individual citizenship and rights, and antiwar rallies in the fall of 1991 and March–April 1992. Because the Yugoslav constitution did not recognize Bosnia as a political nation and because the three ruling political parties represented constituent nations, however, there was no official record of people identifying with Bosnia-Herzegovina, no official desire to gather such data, and few political representatives of such a (potential) majority.

Whatever these trends in public opinion and loyalty during 1990–91 were likely to produce in the long run, therefore, they were preempted by the EC decisions on Slovene and Croatian sovereignty as nations and the breakup of Yugoslavia at the end of 1991 (including U.S. insistence on recognizing Bosnian independence in early 1992). Power-sharing arrangements over voters and state offices would not suffice for *territorial* sovereignty. Slovene, Croatian, and Serbian republican leaders had mobilized domestic sentiment along nationalist lines in order to bargain more effectively over reform and national rights at the federal level, and then parlayed their official position as representatives of the so-called national interests of their republics in talks with international bodies—beginning in the spring of 1991—into national leadership ("fatherhood") of their republics.

In Bosnia-Herzegovina, this same process now played out between its party leaders and international negotiators. These leaders, to retain their position as representatives of their nation, not just in electoral terms but in terms of territorial rights to self-determination, had to go beyond holding a monopoly over an ethnic voting constituency within Bosnia-Herzegovina to destroying the constitutional alternative for an independent Bosnia—the idea of a civic state where ethnic difference was not politically defining and citizens were loyal to ethnic tolerance and multicultural civilization. To secure their monopoly within their national community and also maximize their bargaining position in the EC-sponsored negotiations over a political settlement, they also had to persuade Western negotiators and world opinion that this alternative was no longer viable—that their own citizens believed it was not possible to live together and preferred to live under nationally identified governments. But in contrast to the other republics, Bosnia-Herzegovina had no political force to represent the republic as a whole against outsiders or its idea of multinational identity and civilization, any more than Yugoslavia itself had had. The EC negotiators confirmed this when they began talks in February 1992 with the representatives of the three national parties.

In this new propaganda effort, the HDZ-BH under the Croatian nationalist leadership of Mate Boban (once Tudjman removed the pro-

Bosnian Stjepan Kljuić) had an advantage, because the Croat stronghold of western Herzegovina was relatively homogeneous ethnically, with the important exception of the regional capital, Mostar. Moreover, its only political rival was another party in Croatia (the right-wing Croatian Party of Right [HSP]). The SDA had an initial advantage because the majority of Bosnian citizens who were against ethnic division did not have to be persuaded of its goal to protect an integral Bosnia and because EC and U.S. support for republican boundaries seemed to give it (through its president, Alija Izetbegović) the upper hand with international negotiators and opinion.[21] It did, nonetheless, mount a substantial propaganda campaign at home and abroad, including the creation of new state symbols to demonstrate the venerable historical identity of Bosnia.[22] The SDS had the most difficult task, and was accordingly the most active in its propaganda war, because it was the most actively opposed to Bosnian independence from Yugoslavia and because Serbs lived in communities that were particularly heterogeneous in ethnic composition.

SDS leader Radovan Karadžić was at the forefront of the campaign to persuade all citizens of Bosnia-Herzegovina that it was impossible for Bosnian nations to live together. But it was only when the Bosnian Serbs left the government and prepared for war, setting up headquarters in Pale—a mountain-resort suburb of Sarajevo—that the SDS also created a separate television station, Channel S, and a Bosnian Serb News Agency (SRNA). The difficulty of its task can be measured in the intensity and crudeness of its message. A barrage of commissioned television commercials caricatured Serbian battles against the Ottomans, beginning with Kosovo in 1389, to revive Serbian national myths of heroism and to persuade Bosnian Serbs that it was impossible for them and Muslims to live together. Muslims were frequently referred to as Turks. In an effort to create new national heroes, Channel S televised ceremonies in 1992 in which soldiers were given awards for the number of Muslims they had killed.

The towns and cities of Bosnia-Herzegovina presented a formidable obstacle to the nationalist propaganda aimed at making national states appear the natural condition. With their mixed populations, which were living proof of multiethnic coexistence and multicultural civilization, they could not be taken psychologically. They would also, as a result, put up stronger resistance to military takeover by armies loyal to ethnic parties.[23] Moreover, the rapid urbanization of Bosnia-Herzegovina in the postwar period (from 15 to 36 percent during 1953–81) had loosened ethnic and agrarian identities. Of people choosing Yugoslav nationality in the 1981 census, 83 percent lived in cities, and the majority of them were educated, nonbelieving, often party-member Serbs.[24] As a result, the cities were filled with people who had something to defend, and they were ready to resist an attack on even the idea of mixed communities. Although more villages and towns were ethnically mixed than in Croatia, urban spaces and mixed apartment buildings are far more difficult to identify and separate ethnically than are farmsteads and single-family homes.

The siege of the capital, Sarajevo, drawn out over more than seventeen months—from April 5, 1992, to August 1993, and revived with a vengeance in November 1993 until a cease-fire was negotiated in February 1994—was the most dramatic example, along with Mostar in Herzegovina, of the campaign to destroy the symbol of Bosnian identity and to weaken the physical resistance of citizens still committed to living together. Far more than a military target, Sarajevo stood as a mockery to national exclusiveness. Serb and Croat self-determination, by cantonizing Bosnia-Herzegovina into three ethnic parts, would at best make Sarajevo into a capital of a Muslim canton. Karadžić's map at Lisbon identified "Serbian quarters." By the end of 1993, the Bosnian Serbs' plan for Sarajevo was "twin cities," one Muslim, one Serb. To transform it into separate national cities, they could not destroy it but tried instead to force the Bosnian government to negotiate by progressive strangulation, while its symbolic status served the Bosnian Muslims' strategy so well that it had to be kept a hostage with periodic reminders to the world television audience, if necessary by provoking Serb attacks and preventing the restoration of utilities. Bosnian Croat military forces collaborated with Bosnian Serbs by standing aside when the Serbs took suburbs to the north and northwest of Sarajevo, in exchange for territories such as Stup elsewhere (and reciprocal arrangements for Bosnian Croats when they were fighting Bosnian Muslims in Mostar and elsewhere).[25] Natives of Sarajevo, dwindling from half a million to less than 350,000 during the siege, responded to the essence of the assault by building ever greater resistance on cultural terms and a worldwide campaign to save the "spirit of Sarajevo." At the same time, the lack of world attention to the nearly incessant bombardment of Mostar, which suffered far greater human and physical damage than Sarajevo and had at least as venerable a multicultural tradition, demonstrates the effect of such a campaign and the capacity to manage the media.

The military siege of the cities also reflected the nature of the war as the work of politicians against public opinion, for their bombardment reflected the fact that the balance of resources lay with equipment and not with infantry sufficient to overcome civilian or guerrilla resistance and the cost in human lives of urban warfare. Military tactics were aimed to isolate rather than to defeat: artillery and mortar shelling, the cutoff of food and fuel, and an early attempt to destroy means of communication both within the city and with the outside. Deliberate sabotage of the telephone lines included disconnecting neighborhoods selected by ethnicity.[26] Very early targets were pro-Bosnian media—the television and radio stations, aerial transmitters, and offices of the Sarajevo newspaper, *Oslobodjenje*, which was conspicuously multiethnic and pro-Bosnian. When Bosnian Serb army troops agreed with UN forces to withdraw from their murderous perch on Mount Igman above Sarajevo in mid-August 1993, their parting shot was to blow up the television tower on the highest peak, Bjelašnica. Yet because artillery barrages are far more visible and countable than infantry attacks, parties disadvantaged in heavy weapons but not in infantry could turn that disadvantage into a propaganda victory by provoking firepower and keeping cities vulnerable.

The psychological warfare to justify the creation of national states would be to no avail if diplomatic recognition did not follow. Military engagements aimed not merely at physical control of territory but at foreign support. Military strategists and political leaders chose targets and managed media coverage so as to shape international opinion and local sympathies. The Croatian government, for example, placed sharpshooters on the walls of Dubrovnik to draw fire from the federal armed forces, attracting world attention to that internationally protected city that even the total destruction of Vukovar could not obtain. The Croatian and Bosnian governments placed mortars and artillery batteries within the walls of hospitals (such as at Osijek, Sarajevo, and Goražde) for the same purpose, drawing fire from Serb gunners to gain international reaction. To generate war hysteria, both Serbian and Croatian television stations showed footage of war atrocities by the other side that was as likely to have been taken from their own side, or even from World War II films. All sides used attacks (and mutual recriminations of blame) on cultural monuments, on civilians in breadlines, on wedding and funeral parties, on busloads of orphans, and on international troops to mobilize sympathies and hostility at home and abroad.

## The Right to Land

The source of the conflict raised by the European actions on recognition was the issue of territory. In contrast to ethnic conflict or civil war, national conflict is over rights to land. "Nationalism always involves a struggle for land, or an assertion about rights to land; and the nation, almost by definition, requires a territorial base in which to take root."[27] In the multinational environment of the Yugoslav space, the multiple and incompatible claims on territory of its many nations had been accommodated through constitutional rights. The exclusivity of nationalism, once war over territory and borders began, jettisoned that accommodation. Once leaders justified their goals of national states on the claim, "we can't live together," they had to open a process of defining *which persons* had a right to live on that land. The nationalist argument led to the *physicalizing* of citizenship rights and democracy. The expulsion of persons according to ethnic background, which came to be labeled *ethnic cleansing*, had nothing to do with ethnicity, but rather with securing national rights to land. And because the resulting war is waged to define who can belong to a particular state and its territory, it makes no distinction between soldiers and civilians, between military and civil targets.

Outsiders explained the character of the fighting in Croatia and Bosnia-Herzegovina, including the ethnic cleansing and brutal violations of humanitarian law, by citing ethnic conflict, historical enmities, and—in the actions of Serbs—genocide. But, in fact, these were the results of the wars and their particular characteristics, not the causes. The conditions of breakdown of a state and civil order, on the one hand, and the ideologies and goals of nationalist politicians, on the other, came together in alliance only with war to decide national sovereignty over land.

The advent of war also initiated an element of ethnic conflict. The final collapse of all formal institutions for providing security left individuals and households to provide for their own through informal networks and relations they could trust. In defending land, particularly in villages where the fighting first raged and in a war characterized by *local* battles, there was a natural tendency to rely on older (pre-state) mechanisms of solidarity and insurance adapted to survival—family, kinship, ethnicity.[28] Individuals' resort to family and ethnic bonds and the patriarchal culture of social obligations attached to land created a predisposition to support the distinctions—such as the idea that safety and freedom were only secure in a national state—being made by politicians. The localized, predominantly rural character of the war in border areas, where nationalists could compete because populations were ethnically mixed—regardless of the particular ethnic or national identity of those involved—also tended to revive historical memories of earlier wars for land and who could live there and gave some credibility to the fears of genocide raised by nationalist propaganda.

The essential association between national rights and territorial control was already apparent in the political language of cultural nationalism in the 1980s and the electoral campaigns of 1990, in which the most commonly used word politically, from Slovenia to Serbia, was *hearth* (*ognište/ognjište*). The focal point of a home or homestead, hearth became a metaphor for property, community, citizenship, and patriotism, all in one. But using the symbols of land, even for those who had been urban dwellers for generations, was quite different from fighting for it and for the physical borders of a national community. Once war began, behavior was increasingly governed by the mores associated with land ownership and the social organization built to protect it.

What had been an urban movement shifted its cultural fulcrum to the countryside and its traditions of self-defense. The rural population, less in touch with the pluralist conditions of urban culture, more likely to rely on state-controlled television or radio for information, and having less formal education, had voted in large numbers for ethnonational parties in the 1990 elections. Where people might have been more receptive to the political language of paranoia and threat from the outside, war brought a very real possibility of loss.

The culture of the village contrasts sharply with that of the city, with its moderating forces of cross-cutting associations built on schooling and occupation, psychological and physical mobility, and tendency toward greater religious and political liberalism as a result of the higher education levels of its population and exposure to foreign ideas. The culture surrounding smallholding villagers remained patriarchal, a culture of the Mediterranean type, not necessarily inclined toward ethnic prejudices or nationalist views.[29] Men defended property through soldiering and household unity, maintained through a family's honor and the sexual shame of women. This rural culture is based on obligations to kin, intergenerational transfer of knowledge, the perpetuation of communal rituals and myths focused on the life cycle (especially death), and the social influence retained by clerics in the villages.[30] It did not help that churches remained more influential in villages, despite high levels of reported atheism in society as a whole (with the exception of Croats), because of the strong, shared patriarchal elements in the dogma of all three. Moreover, the strategy for industrialization in socialist Yugoslavia had reinforced the cultural divide between rural and urban residents. Those who sought economic improvement and social mobility left the villages for cities and towns, leaving the countryside disproportionately populated by the elderly or people with little schooling. Although rural in origin, this patriarchal culture was also largely characteristic of the urban underclass of unskilled workers, day laborers, the unemployed, and criminals who were recruited to do much of the fighting when conscripted young people resisted mobilization or deserted.

The character of the wars, particularly as they began, drew out this particular culture. Sites were local, for control of particular settlements. Armies were not yet fully organized or reorganized, and multiple armies, militia, and armed gangs *within* one national camp extended the political party competition to control over turf and citizens' loyalties (voluntary or forced). Where armies at this time pursued a strategy of territorial gain, they nonetheless relied on untrained irregulars, such as criminals released from jails and the urban unemployed who were free or needed pay, and on the "shock troops" of radical paramilitaries and volunteers organized by political parties who did the dirty work of creating interethnic suspicions through terrorizing villagers. As outsiders to the villages and towns where they fought and undisciplined by professional army structure, these two groups had no particular obligation to neighbors, an important social bond in the region.[31] Nor did they have any professional honor to limit the inclination to rape, mutilation, burning, looting, and revenge. Individual motivations differed. To the extent that the fighting involved more than individual aggrandizement, and did aim to identify people as outsiders and exclude them from land, women became particularly vulnerable, regardless of age, because the culture of patriarchy viewed their sexual purity and shame as essential to the honor and unity of the family—to violate women is to destroy the family's ability to resist.

The spontaneous role of patriarchal culture in the fighting was reinforced by political rhetoric. To the extent that nationalist leaders played on religious differences in defining the threat to each national community, they were able to tap a reservoir in rural communities of negative memories or stories of historical conflict between churches, intolerance, and even genocide once that population was exposed to war. The reinforcement was particularly evocative on the Serbian side because the rhetoric of Serb nationalism in the 1980s was based on the same patriarchal themes—the obligation to protect family and community against an external threat, and the reassertion of manhood wounded by perceived victimization, genocide, and the rape of their women.[32] The apparent callousness and insensitivity of Serbian leaders to international accusations—that began in the summer of 1992 in hopes of putting a stop to the violence through publicity and threats of criminal prosecution—of genocide and blatant violation of Geneva conventions in the war in eastern and northern Bosnia can be explained in part by this psychology. While it may well have contributed to more systematic violations of international humanitarian law by Serbs than by other groups, it was simultaneously possible for individuals committing such acts to perceive themselves innocent of genocide and for leaders to insist that they had no such policy.

Alongside the culture surrounding the protection of land and family, the transition from constitutional and partisan conflict to military fights over land introduced elements of historical conflict. The political rhetoric of national assertion by intellectuals and politicians during the 1980s, on all sides, had engaged in historical reinterpretation and a culture of revenge for past wrongs. The politics of the democratic elections and sovereignty declarations had revived symbols and alliances of World War II (the Croatian wartime state and its symbols, the Chetnik regalia of Serbian paramilitaries, the Croat-Muslim alliance in Bosnia-Herzegovina). But once fighting began, the memory of World War II became relevant to ordinary citizens. Even where individuals had come to terms with that war trauma, the revival of such memories in the 1970s and 1980s by writers, historians,

clerics, and political leaders could reawaken sensitivities and mutual suspicions, and predispose many to expect the worst or to reinterpret behavior
in the light of physical danger.[33]

The historical analyses of intellectuals are a far cry from the moral
obligations to avenge the deaths of kin and the tradition of blood revenge
(*krvna osveta*) still practiced in some regions of the peninsula. It is war over
territory that links the two. The previous instance of such life-and-death
choices of political loyalty and the rights to land and settlement for villagers
occurred during World War II and its aftermath. Whole villages had latent
political identities associated with that conflict. Regions in Bosnia-Herzegovina, Montenegro, and Serbia were splintered into Partisan (led by the
Communist party) and Chetnik (Serbian royal army forces) villages; in
Croatia and Bosnia-Herzegovina among Partisan, Chetnik, and Ustasha
(Croatian fascists) villages; in Macedonia among Partisan, Chetnik, and
pro–Bulgarian villages; and in Kosovo between Partisan and the more
common pro-Italian villages. Ethnically mixed villages experienced mass
atrocities, particularly at the hands of the German army and of fascist
collaborators.[34] A mechanism of revenge also played out in the subsequent
revolutionary upheaval of 1945–47 and civil war of 1948–49. The population resettlement programs of the Yugoslav government during 1945–48
attempted to place Partisan soldiers from poor, food-deficient regions in
the Dalmatian hinterland in Croatia and Bosnia-Herzegovina in homesteads in the rich farmlands of Slavonia and Vojvodina of expelled collaborators (Volksdeutsche and Hungarian, Austrian, and Catholic Church
landlords) as a reward for soldiering, and a solution to their lack of self-
sufficiency in food. This settled a loyal class of veterans in vulnerable
borderlands. Such policies created the mixed populations in the border
area contested in 1991–93 between Serbia and Croatia.

Thus, for example, the fears on which Serbian nationalist policy toward Serbs in Croatia and Bosnia-Herzegovina fed had a very real ground-
ing in a recent memory of genocidal atrocities against ordinary Serbs
during World War II. Many argue that President Tudjman could have
undercut the strength of Milošević's appeal to Serbs in Croatia if he had
been willing to dissociate his regime from that period in history with a
public apology, instead of reviving fears by questioning, as he did, the
actual number of Serb victims.[35] Many Serbs felt a moral obligation, at
two levels, to prevent a recurrence; the collective obligation of all Serbs to
say "never again," and the individual, cultural imperative to avenge the
deaths of kin. Both of these obligations required loyalty to other Serbs
(even among those who vehemently opposed Milošević, nationalists, and
war). For some it also obliged rejection of the idea of peaceful coexistence
with Croats and Muslims. But such challenges between national groups
aroused defensive loyalties on all sides; there were more than enough his-

torical memories or myths to be used as justification, to create fears, and to reshape perceptions by politicians aimed at gaining nationally defined support.

One important factor was not national at all, but the economic and cultural divide already present between city and country, for during World War II cities tended to collaborate with the occupying armies. Urban dwellers who joined the resistance did so by escaping to the forests and mountains, whereas villagers had little choice but to take active sides in the civil war that ran parallel to the anti-Axis war of liberation.[36] The pattern of fighting in Croatia in 1991 and in Bosnia-Herzegovina in 1992 could be seen to repeat this past, beginning in towns infamous for World War II atrocities, and distinguishing house-by-house in Slavonian villages between post–World War II migrants and old residents.[37]

Nonetheless, social change had occurred, and people had lived together for more than forty years in spite of their war experiences. The major political trace during the 1945–90 period was the oft-spoken fear that multiparty democracy would bring back ethnically based political competition. Thus the attempt by nationalists to control the mass media and the ability during wartime in 1991–95 to legitimize such control and censorship, were unusually important. Control of the media gave full reign, without opposing views, to the nationalists' myth of "we cannot live together." It made it possible for politicians to connect their message to the world of ordinary people. And it limited the audience of alternative voices—which reminded people that the world had changed, that their history was far more one of coexistence and nonethnic bonds, that their fears were unjustified, and that the moral obligation was not revenge but tolerance—to those who could buy and did read newspapers and journals.

Regardless of the multiple predispositions of culture and memory, the fight to create states out of nations in territories that are ethnically mixed eventually becomes a fight over persons and their rights to live on particular tracts of land. This became known to outsiders during the Serbian onslaught in eastern Bosnia in the spring and summer of 1992 as a policy of "ethnic cleansing." Based on racial beliefs (in the physicalizing of ethnic identity and prerogatives), this policy has had many parallels, such as apartheid in South Africa or the massive population exchanges between Greece and Turkey in 1922, or after the division of India and Pakistan in 1947.[38] Its immediate prelude in Yugoslavia was the exodus of Serbs and Montenegrins from Kosovo—the result of a mixture of reciprocal fears and political tactics during the 1980s in which both the Serbian government and Albanian residents played their part.[39] Nationalist Serb extremists referred loosely to Serb victims of ethnic cleansing and genocide.

The next phase, in 1989, used legal instruments. Republican constitutions redefined citizenship in terms that distinguished between the majority nation and others, and effectively created semi-disenfranchised minorities (in relation to previous rights) most explicitly in Croatia and Macedonia.[40] When war came to ethnically mixed areas in Croatia, mutual fears and local harassment, often provoked by outsiders (paramilitary gangs from central Croatia and from Serbia proper; returned Croat émigrés and mercenaries of Serbian origin), turned the language of endangerment and politics of revenge into invitations to expel unwanted persons.[41]

As a war strategy pursued by Croats and Serbs alike in Croatia and in Bosnia-Herzegovina, however, the association between persons and rights to land became a deliberate policy to clear a territory of all those who were considered not to belong in their national territory and who might be suspected of disloyalty. In Bosnia-Herzegovina, "random and selective killing," detention camps as way stations with "inadequate shelter, food, and sanitation," and even massacres were reportedly used as "tools" to remove populations.[42]

The basis of this policy of ethnic cleansing lay not with primordial hatreds or local jealousies, but with political goals. According to the German criterion on which the Badinter Commission and the EC decisions were made, international recognition of national sovereignty required a referendum of residents in a territory on their choice of a state; where that choice had been ignored, nationalist leaders found their political prejudices vindicated. Military control of territory was not sufficient to recognition; it had to be supplemented eventually by a vote. Thus cease-fires only led to a change in the methods of ethnic cleansing. After the cease-fire in Croatia and in towns of Bosnia-Herzegovina where fighting had ceased, local authorities continued this process by negotiating population exchanges on an ethnic basis between towns. These exchanges were hardly more voluntary because they were peaceable, but their objective—to consolidate ethnically pure territories that would vote correctly in a referendum on sovereignty and in future elections and to justify government administration by their national group—had not been fully obtained by warfare.[43]

Their methods of population transfers varied. In places like the wealthy village of Kozarac in northeastern Bosnia, members of the local Muslim elite who might organize such opposition were first murdered or brutally expelled. Serbs in the Croatian *krajina*, such as the village of Pod Lapača, appealed to the UN forces sent to protect them to help them leave the area instead out of fear after a Croatian army scorch-and-burn attack on three neighboring villages just outside the UNPA in September 1993. Elsewhere, local rivalries were encouraged to play out, perhaps given a boost by the terrorizing tactics of outside extremists and then fed by a cycle of revenge between neighboring villages. One measure of the level of resistance by many local leaders and citizens to such cleansing and of the strength of commitment to mixed environments and nonnationalist political preferences is the fact that the process gained momentum in later stages of the war. Official exchanges of minorities between villages of different majority ethnicity to create overwhelming national majorities and justify government administration by their national group became systematic after the Washington agreement for federation of March 1, 1994, was signed by Bosnian Croats and Muslims. Local radicalization, as those who opposed ethnic partition of the republic became ever weaker or had left, brought renewed expulsions in the spring and summer of 1994, such as the forced expulsions by Serbs of Muslims from Banja Luka and Bijeljina areas or the voluntary exodus of Croats and Serbs from Tuzla the same year. Whatever the method, however, ethnic cleansing was a particularly extreme reminder of the conflict between the goal of national states and Yugoslav reality.

The victimization of Muslims through ethnic cleansing was also a result of the political contest behind the wars, not ethnic or religious hatreds. Claiming a unified Bosnia as its base instead of a separate national enclave, the SDA could not win with a policy of ethnic cleansing. Its political difficulty in settling on a consistent strategy for national sovereignty (see chapter 9)—against the two other parties, the SDS and the HDZ—extended to this tactic. A referendum confirming the national sovereignty of Bosnia had to be supported by more voters than those who identified politically with the SDA as Muslims, and depended, therefore, on maintaining mixed communities. When relief agencies of the Office of the UN High Commissioner for Refugees (UNHCR) and the International Committee of the Red Cross (ICRC) chose to help evacuate Muslims from towns in eastern Bosnia, such as Srebrenica and Konjević Polje, in order to save lives in April 1993, they were not only accused of being accomplices to Serbian ethnic cleansing, but were in many towns blocked by local Muslim (SDA) officials and Bosnian government army commanders who knew that once people left, they had lost political control over that territory (whatever military objectives they might accomplish).[44] Similarly, in withholding support from the peace plan drawn up by the Geneva international conference on former Yugoslavia in October 1992–January 1993 based on creating mixed communities and provinces and an integral Bosnia-Herzegovina (the Vance-Owen plan), on the grounds that it did not guarantee enough land to Muslims and rewarded the "aggression of Serbs," the Clinton administration in January–February 1993 doomed the Muslims as well to a policy of ethnic cleansing.

Whether the failure of a political agreement on the Vance-Owen plan was a result of military gains and ethnic cleansing on the ground that were impossible to reverse, as some claimed, or a result of U.S. encouragement of Izetbegović to bargain for more Muslim territory, as those seeing the parallels with the failed Lisbon Accord the previous March claimed, the appearance of ethnically based massacres and fighting between Croat and Muslim forces in central Bosnia was not an attempt to realize the Vance-Owen plan. Many observers argued that the plan legitimized the assignment of territories ethnically and that armies were fighting between December 1992 and May 1993 to take those territories militarily, but it in fact only acknowledged national rights to form governments and territorial administrations over provinces that would remain ethnically mixed and a part of a sovereign Bosnia. It was the failure of international support for the plan—in the same manner as the EC decision in December 1991 on recognition was made without first obtaining agreements on borders and principles of national self-determination—that led politicians and armies to settle the question of territorial rights on the ground. In the face of territorial losses and without a political settlement, the Bosnian government in December 1992 had begun a temporarily successful campaign to take back areas of eastern Bosnia and to control central Bosnia. As Bosnian Croats, through ethnic cleansing, extended their territory in the fall of 1992 beyond western Herzegovina into mixed towns in central Bosnia, such as Prozor at the end of October, Muslim militias (not Bosnian government forces) also began to expel Croats.

The move from nationalist psychological warfare to nationalist warfare over land on territory that was multinational had predictable outcomes in the character of that warfare. The political goal of creating national states made little distinction between military and civilians, either as fighters or as targets.[45] What would seem only to be a matter of military doctrine, in which the YPA held preponderant power with artillery designed to delay an attacker and then to hit invaders' supply routes with ambushes, land slides, and artillery, and the TDF in rural villages would swing into guerrilla warfare in a long war of attrition, if necessary, was reinforced by the sharp urban-rural divide within the country's social and political structure. Heavy artillery shelled population settlements and had to make up for the refusal of urban young people to fight. Cities were encircled by artillery, using supply depots intended for repelling invaders. Guerrilla warfare in urban settings comprised snipers from all political sides and commando raids by small groups of disciplined soldiers in the early mornings to demoralize soldiers of the other side. The objective of such tactics and the threat of death by starvation, disease, and cold, however, was to persuade civilians of a different ethnicity to leave without putting up a fight. Psychological and economic pressure to force capitulation of cities to ethnic definition and loyalties included destruction of the physical infrastructure on which urban life depends—electricity, heating plants, kiosks selling newspapers, TV and radio transmitters, the communal bakery—but one of the first objects of attack in cities as well as towns and villages was also the church or mosque of the "other" group.

The goal of national control of land meant that male civilians of any age but of the "wrong" nationality were sent to detention camps on the assumption that they were potential soldiers for the enemy or were forcibly conscripted to the front line to dig trenches or initiate assaults on armies of their own ethnicity. Bosnian Serbs in Banja Luka and Bijeljina were accused by the ICRC and UNHCR of forcibly separating non-Serb men from their families during waves of ethnic expulsions to do "work detail" on the front.[46] Even the Croatian government—in violation of the Geneva conventions—forcibly returned Bosnian men of all ages who had taken refuge from the Bosnian war in camps across the border in Croatia.[47] Women of any age were victims of rape, in part for reasons always associated with warfare and in part to demoralize armies composed not of professionals but of fathers, sons, and brothers from the region. Because the purpose of the warfare was largely defense of village and land, even if a particular military engagement were classified as offensive, the armies were largely composed of people from the region. Except for small elite units, army units were not mobile, were locally recruited among farmers and villages of all ages, tended to be led by commanders from the area, and were known to be fiercely loyal to that local commander, even if doing so meant that they disobeyed orders given higher up the normal chain of command.

Even if political leaders wish to reverse course and sign cease-fire agreements in good faith and citizens desperately want an end to the fighting, the momentum of such wars becomes increasingly difficult to stop. The limit on ethnic expulsions begun with local quarrels or as a result of political rivalry between radicals and moderates within a political party is only reached when there are no more people of that particular category to be expelled. The political rhetoric that prepared the way for war by emphasizing group danger tended to perpetuate the practice in conditions of anarchy and ever further unraveling of legal and moral standards and stable social organization. Localized fighting for the territory and soul of a village, and then between villages as refugees fled or as fighting fanned out, eventually drew in villagers who had tried to stay out of politics but found they had to fight or be killed or expelled. Those who did not flee sought to ensure their own security by turning on those from the threatening group and torching their homes, cultural monuments, and places of worship to discourage their return.

Among soldiers, the horrors alone and the fact that "many of them didn't understand what they were fighting for, or didn't approve of a war in which people from two nations with the same language and origin were killing each other" led to the emergence of what was called the "Vukovar syndrome," in which psychological breakdown turned them not away from war but into "uncontrolled killers." The explanation offered by a clinical psychologist for the "Bijeljina (Bosnia) case"—a twenty-three-year-old reservist mobilized by the army who "gunned down three other soldiers from the Bijeljina barracks and then his girlfriend's family" on February 1, 1992—was the psychological pressure of this particular type of war: "it's neither war nor peace, they've been living for months in trenches, their position as well as their mission is unclear, they lose their nerves and they drink heavily."[48]

On all sides of the war, the expulsion or execution of rival local elites and the exodus as refugees of moderates repelled by the war meant that, as the war went on, an ever larger proportion of those who remained or reappeared ready to fight in other towns were militant radicals most committed or bound to that land. By committing atrocities to clear that land, engendering the likely revenge of the ethnic group of its victims, these radicals had even more reason to continue fighting for fear of retribution and no honorable exit. This was particularly the case for Serbs in eastern Croatia and in Bosnia-Herzegovina, who aroused global condemnation and outrage because they were accused, as a result of reports by human rights organizations and by UN inquiries, of a systematic policy of genocide and mass rape and blamed for the overwhelming portion of the wars' atrocities. In other cases, such as the fratricidal fighting in central Bosnia in the summer of 1993 between Croatian and Muslim forces that had remained at peace or fought side by side during the previous eighteen months, the continuation of war created its own momentum in the rising numbers of displaced persons who had lost everything (often including families) and who had little left to do but to fight for some other land or take revenge.

## Civil War

In the course of the constitutional struggle of the 1980s, nationalist politicians at the republic level had channeled social unrest and economic grievances into demands for national rights. This did not, however, remove those grievances. As the above discussion of urban-rural differences implies, the characteristics of these wars for new states owed as much or more to the social and economic divisions that existed within Yugoslav society before the war as to the ethnic conflict proclaimed by nationalist elites and outside powers.

In interrupting the process of democratization begun with the elections in 1990, the Slovene and Croatian declarations of sovereignty and the European response in 1991 taking these declarations at face value prolonged representation throughout the region in terms of national self-determination and ethnic political rights. Instead of a change in the organization of economic life and interests in the socialist period toward organizations like class-based political parties and interest groups more suited to parliamentary democracy and market economies, the political organization of elections by republic and by ethnonational parties therefore reinforced the territorial, vertical, and state-based organization of the socialist regime. The regionalized specializations, relative immobility of labor and capital, and geopolitically influenced economic policy characteristic of all socialist countries created a pattern of economic advantage and disadvantage that was defined by territorial (including urban-rural) lines. Thus national movements were subject to few if any checks and balances that might dampen political escalation once they mobilized grievances and interests in the political and economic transition.

When the European Community and the United States ignored the difference between Slovenia and the rest of the country and the likelihood of conflicts over borders and land, they exposed to territorial dispute those very areas most threatened by the policies of the liberal economic reformers and less privileged in economic development. In the Croatian *krajina*, central Bosnia, the "Serbian corridor" of northern Bosnia, Kosovo, and Macedonia, deindustrialization and declining demand since the mid-1970s had led to severe economic decline largely as a result of economic policy or global change outside the immediate control of these areas.[49] Dominated by extractive industries (minerals, timber, transport) or military production with uncertain demand in foreign markets and in government contracts, these areas had been hard hit by the reform policies favoring export-oriented manufactures to convertible currency countries. They also tended to have declining per capita income in the 1970s and 1980s, so that local budgets for services and welfare were increasingly dependent on federal subsidies; they were therefore also hurt more by the drastic cuts in government budgets under policies of stabilization and liberalization. Local industries were more dependent on sources of investment capital that were being sharply curtailed—the development funds of their republican budgets and the investment and services of the army and military industries financed by the federal budget. Unemployment in these areas was rising and income falling far faster than in the rest of the country.[50]

These were areas that traded more with the markets that collapsed in the Council for Mutual Economic Assistance (CMEA) and the Middle East. In the line being drawn through the country's center between Europe and the Balkans, moreover, there was increasing uncertainty over the fate of the areas of the former military border between Habsburg and Ottoman empires, the Danubian region, and Bosnia-Herzegovina. Were they West or East?[51]

Individual prospects also had a pronounced territorial dimension. Upward social mobility in the socialist period through education eventually required a move to the cities, leaving poorer interior areas with people of lesser prospects, lower status, and a sense of cultural inferiority. Although poverty and open unemployment were increasingly urban phenomena in the 1970s and 1980s, urban areas retained their association with the privileges of public sector employment, social welfare, and opportunities not dependent on the land. Rural communities retained a secondary status, where those who had no opportunities to leave (whether through lack of education, urban relatives, or cash incomes) remained tied to the rural or semirural community of their birth. Decentralizing reforms to reduce federal expenditures and favor the TDF in national defense had also had the effect of concentrating security forces and retired soldiers in localities in these areas, for reasons of World War II experience and poverty.

Patterns of migration, because they followed routes laid by family and by schooling, also had an ethnic dimension, particularly in Bosnia-Herzegovina. Overall, studies for the 1960s–80s show that emigration occurred in economically declining villages and regions, and was greatest in ethnically mixed communes.[52] This pattern created more ethnically homogeneous villages within districts (opštine/općine) that remained heterogeneous (a pattern more common in Croatia). In particular, Serbs left for other republics and cities (primarily in Serbia) and Croats most frequently went abroad. Both poor and elite Muslims, on the other hand, tended to stay "at home" in Bosnia-Herzegovina. Migration and the relative differences in birth rates between these groups had reversed the numerical preponderance of Serbs over Muslims.[53] Bosnian Serbs and Bosnian Croats were thus more likely to be those left behind by their own ethnic group.

This situation may have made these people receptive to politicians who, in the 1990–93 period, encouraged resentment against new elites of a different ethnicity, particularly Muslims, who were at earlier, more assertive stages of national consciousness. The 1990 elections had not yet replaced at the local level the single-party system of the previous forty years, except for takeover by the ethnonational party corresponding to the local political elite. Politicians often used the excuse of an anticommunist purge to expel members of other political parties, but because the main electoral victors were identified with the nation, this process had left interethnic emotions occasionally raw.[54]

The actual characteristics of the fighting on the ground, however, reflected the socioeconomic basis of these politics far more than the ethnic coloration and historical revenge that characterized politicians' rhetoric. For many, war became a rare opportunity for enrichment, through theft or smuggling, in a period of serious economic decline. Early pictures in the war in Bosnia-Herzegovina show soldiers looting VCRs and stereos, urban furniture and appliances, and foreign automobiles such as BMWs—most originally bought with the enviable foreign hard currency. Illiteracy and mobilized resentments over who were the "rightful owners" of land help to explain the destruction of cultural monuments, razing of prosperous farms, and crowds of village women who prevented aid convoys from reaching their destinations.

Although soldiers were frequently paid two to three times more than they were earning in civilian jobs, the actual pay was still meager and was often given in alcohol and cigarettes instead of cash. The incentive for class-based revenge was high. The recruitment of soldiers when the state collapsed also reinforced this class division, because more urban and better educated youth could escape the draft, often by leaving the country. The unemployed, poorer village youth, and industrial workers, unpaid for months, were more vulnerable to the draft and promises of pay and veterans' benefits. In the first stages of the war in Croatia, the promise in Serbia of significant discounts on the price of electricity and fuel for households was sufficient for many heads of households to enlist.

War closed schools and factories in many areas, either because of the fighting or because of the interruption of transport and supplies in other areas, compounding the number of people left idle. Paramilitary forces, in particular, were filled with teenagers faced with the choice either to leave the country or to join a military organization, but under little organized command or adult standards of behavior. Evidence also suggests that those who felt excluded in the socialist period, such as unskilled workers or troubled young people, tended to volunteer to fight; war presented an opportunity for them to achieve a certain status and honor unavailable in peace or to get revenge for their previous impotence and discrimination. They were also more inclined to the culture of patriarchy and protection than to the norms defining the Geneva conventions on war.[55] At the same time, like the right-wing teenagers rampaging against foreigners in west European countries, the war attracted "weekend Chetniks" from a lost generation of educated youth with meager prospects in Serbia. These unemployed high school or university graduates, living on the outskirts of big cities, went on shooting sprees with Kalashnikov rifles from Friday night to Sunday in villages of little consequence to them over the border in Croatia or Bosnia.[56]

As in the events leading up to war, independent forces became mutually reinforcing in ways that accelerated violence. Class-based resentment and revenge legitimized as national liberation and anticommunism were a potent force. Those who took up arms to defend their land and communities were also incited and led by people who saw themselves as outsiders—dissidents against communism (from Franjo Tudjman to Alija Izetbegović to Vojislav Šešelj), urban migrants from poor regions (such as Radovan Karadžić), in many cases actual criminals (the most infamous was Željko Ražnatović, or Arkan). This self-perception was reinforced by the language of combat, such as the labeling of all Serbs as barbarians and the urban professionals' derision of Bosnian Serb leader Karadžić for his "village" speech. Given the Western judgment that Slovenes and Croats were democratic and peace-loving whereas Serbs were aggressors in Slovenia, Croatia, Bosnia-Herzegovina, and, potentially, Kosovo and Macedonia, it was doubly unfortunate that the Slovenes had captured the liberal space in the Yugoslav political spectrum and that Serbian nationalism under Milošević had come, accurately or not, to represent the fears or reaction of the less privileged and the political forces under attack.

## Dissolution of a State

In recognizing Slovene and Croatian independence, the European Community was not only creating new states but dissolving an existing one—Yugoslavia. It approached this problem ad hoc, with the result that the primary mechanism became an arbitration commission of jurists with advisory authority only, set up at the request of the Slovene government in August—almost two months before the end of the moratorium on moves toward independence—for an independent, European body to deal with the economic questions of succession. Skeptical about their ability to resolve such questions without outside arbitration, the Slovenes also argued that they could not participate in the setting up of some new "Yugoslav" institutional forum, however temporary it first appeared. The Badinter Commission soon found its effective mandate expanded, under the auspices of the EC peace conference at The Hague, from arbitrating disputes over the allocation of federal economic assets and obligations among the republics to advising on border disputes and the criteria for recognition.

Even this minimal regulation of the process of dissolution fell victim to the diplomatic recognitions in December, January, and April, however, and the deadly pause of ten months before the second peace conference was set up at Geneva in September. The work on economic issues of succession was handed to one of the conference's six standing commissions, which remained in Brussels for continuity. Its authority depended on that of the Geneva conference and its cochairmen, who rapidly became preoccupied by the work of another of its standing commissions, that on Bosnia-Herzegovina, in its efforts to negotiate a political agreement that would end the Bosnian war. Like the European decision that the republican borders were legitimate international borders, moreover, the issues of dissolution were also colored by their assumptions regarding economic accounts—that the assets and debts of the former state belonged to the republics and that the only issue was what proportions would govern their distribution among the six.

The question of state succession was, in fact, decided in May 1992 by Western policy aimed at ending the war in Bosnia-Herzegovina. As part of its strategy to hold Serbia and the YPA responsible for the war and to exert pressure on the Serbian leadership to end its military aid and political support to the Bosnian Serbs, the UN Security Council denied successor status to the Federal Republic of Yugoslavia (created between Serbia and Montenegro on April 27, 1992). Declaring that it could not continue "automatically the membership of the former Socialist Federal Republic of Yugoslavia in the United Nations," the UN rejected the argument of the new Yugoslav leadership that it bore the right of successor, in the way that Russia had since been accredited the UN seat of the Soviet Union, because the other republics had seceded. Thus the Security Council let the question of state succession die on September 19, 1992 (SCR 777), in a way similar to the EC's de facto usurpation of the federal presidency and cabinet during the summer and fall of 1991 by its mediating intercession.

But the reality was that this had been a country, not only a confederation of states—however autonomous the republics had been. There were not only psychological interdependencies that needed to be broken, but also economic interdependencies and an entire structure of security—local police, internal security police, territorial defense forces, federal army, and all-Yugoslav laws and standards—protecting civil order and external defense. In line with its incorrect assumption that there was no conflict between the independence of the republics and the right to national self-determination, the EC in particular paid no attention to the disposition of the armed forces and security apparatus or to the consequences for the security of citizens if it removed the last vestiges of authority from the common procedures and guarantees of the entire structure of civil order.

## The Disintegration of Internal Security and Civil Order

The country's system of territorial defense and security could not be rearranged neatly in accordance with the republics, as if they were already states in which the loyalties and authority of police, TDFs, intelligence agencies, and army were not in doubt and the only issue was to expel aggressors from other states. The federal army was a significant political actor in its own right, which could not succumb to the lack of quorum and simply disperse among republics, as the federal parliament chose to do after months of debate. It was not simply a body representing the republics, but an independent, coequal partner representing Yugoslavia as a whole and its multinational ideal and antifascist origins. In contrast to other federal institutions, such as the central bank, its fate and the distribution of its assets could not wait for decades of diplomatic wrangling. As an integral part of the constitutional and then the political-military contest, the YPA would have to undergo a process of reorientation: from its defense of Yugoslavia, through disorientation as an army without a state, to a state-building project of its own. Moreover, military districts had not coincided with republican borders since the reorganization of the mid-1980s. Just as troops in Croatia were part of the Slovene operation, troops from the Banja Luka (5th) Corps in Bosnia participated in the Croatian conflict over the border in Slavonia and in the Dalmatian hinterland.[57] The war in Bosnia-Herzegovina reflected, in part, the YPA's division between eastern Herzegovina—which fell under the command of the fourth military district headquartered in Podgorica (Montenegro)—and areas of central and eastern Bosnia, which were in the first military district headquartered in Belgrade and encompassing parts of Serbia proper and Vojvodina.[58]

There was no reason, moreover, for the territorial defense forces to become automatically national armies of the separate republics. Although nominally under republican authority in the previous order, the TDFs were simultaneously integrated into the central command and control structure of the federal armed forces and under the administrative jurisdiction of the local governments. Local politics were most decisive, therefore, in the role and loyalties of TDF units. Whereas Slovenia had constructed its national army on the basis of the TDF in the course of its conflict with the federal army over several years, the Croatian army evolved only after the elections held in the spring of 1990 as a result of two conflicts—one with the army over federal or republican rights to TDF assets and the other with local Serbs over "national" (Croat) control of local police and TDF units. In part because the YPA was quicker than the Croatian government to take control of some TDF assets and in part because Serbs had sought to defend themselves in Baranja-Slavonia and in the Dalmatian hinterland and around Knin with civil defense units (and later paramilitary groups) using local TDF weapons and facilities, Croatia built its national army instead on the basis of internal republic-level security forces called MUP and their counterinsurgency activities during 1990–91. President Tudjman held the first public parade of this National Guard Corps (ZNG), which would later become the core of a standing Croatian army (HV), in March 1991, and it had active and reserve motorized brigades poised in the field against Serb militia by May.[59]

The disposition of the TDF in Bosnia-Herzegovina followed the same, though more complex, political evolution: from interrupted democratization through national self-determination to armed conflict. When power changed hands with the elections of December 1990, most local TDF units became instruments of local political elites, their political ambitions, and the consolidation of power behind their political party. Along these political party (and therefore ethnic) lines, these units began to combine into militia beyond the local level. TDF units in western Herzegovina were active, through HDZ politicians, in helping form the HV, and the HV then sent troops and equipment to organize Croat units in Bosnia (eventually the HVO), for example. Local officials and SDS party leaders in the Bosnian *krajina* lent logistical and economic support to Serbs in the Croatian *krajina* and were aided later in turn. The war in Croatia thus sped up the preparation for war in Bosnia-Herzegovina through these reciprocal networks among political parties in forming armies and also through refugees who poured over the border (both Croats and Serbs) for sanctuary and who kindled tensions along partisan, ethnic, and military lines.[60] This earlier formation of military and partisan paramilitary links between Bosnia-Herzegovina and Croatia, among Croats and among Serbs, meant that the Bosnian government army would be built largely on the basis of internal resources in Bosnia-Herzegovina among local SDA (Muslim party) elites. President Izetbegović created a National Defense Council on June 10, 1991, as an arm of his party, and was illegally purchasing weapons from Slovenia during the fall.[61] Despite the political alliance between Croatian and Muslim parties, in fact, a defense alliance appeared necessary between Bosnia-Herzegovina and Croatia in June 1992 to gain access to arms through HVO-controlled supply routes and Croatian ports on the Adriatic. The Bosnian army was eventually built on the basis of TDF units—in addition to a separate militia called the Patriotic League—largely from areas outside Croatian and Serbian strongholds where the SDA governed or the town was indisputably ethnically mixed. The continuing predominance of the local character of military formations meant that, while armies were primarily organized by ethnonational parties, their soldiers were often of a different ethnicity, such as the thousands of Bosnian Muslims fighting in the HVO, for example, or the Bosnian Croats and Bosnian Serbs who fought in the Bosnian army.[62]

Local leaders who commandeered the Bosnian TDF, with its stockpiles of weapons and civil defense units of all-citizen training, were called warlords after war came officially to the republic in April 1992, but they remained preoccupied largely with local power. The system of civil order at the local level had already begun to disintegrate as a result of the 1990 elections. The shift from Communist party oversight of judgeships and police to that of a nonpartisan, independent branch of government had also been interrupted—no longer communist but still controlled by the local party or preoccupied with an intense battle between types of judicial systems. Police forces tended to take partisan sides, form their own paramilitary groups with criminals released from jails, and often exploit "business opportunities" in league with mafia trafficking in lucrative contraband in drugs and illegal arms.

At the time of the Slovene and Croatian declarations of independence, the primary source of rising tensions and armed confrontations was not the armies based in the TDF or the YPA but the paramilitary groups formed by political parties. In Serbia the powerful internal security police supported Milošević and the Socialist party.[63] All the major parties and renegades created their own armies: the Chetniks of Serbian Radical party leader Vojislav Šešelj; the Serbian Guard of Vuk Drašković's Serbian Movement for Renewal; and the White Eagles, Dušan Silni, and the Serbian Volunteer Guard (also known as Arkanovci or Tigers) organized by Željko Ražnatović-Arkan, a criminal wanted in Europe for political assassinations and drug trafficking. In Croatia the interior police (now National Guard) were similarly attached to Tudjman's party, while Ustasha units of the Black Legion, the Zebras, and the 5,000-strong Croatian Defense League (HOS) of the Croatian Party of Right of Dobroslav Paraga all operated in both Croatia and Bosnia-Herzegovina.[64] The SDA organized its Green Berets. Five separate militia were operating in the *krajina* region of Croatia alone by June 1991, and there were twenty such paramilitary groups in Bosnia-Herzegovina.[65]

The military wings and activities of political parties were no more confined within republican borders than were their electoral activities. With the internationalization of the political contest, however, the purpose of these military wings changed as the determinants of interparty competition shifted from the size of voting constituencies and ability to form local alliances to the willingness to use armed force to control persons and territories. It also gave rise to a new struggle within political parties and between political parties claiming to represent the same nation: that between moderates who believed in or counted on international support and peaceful negotiations for their national goals and radicals who believed in the inevitability of an armed contest and prepared for military confrontation—the diplomatic versus the war option. Citizens reoriented their loyalties from political identities and preferences to physical survival and therefore to those parties, leaders, and identities they thought most likely to win in the end. The conditions of anarchy and territorial contest favored the armed radicals.

Thus by the fall of 1991, paramilitary gangs, foreign mercenaries, and convicted criminals roamed the territory under ever less civil control.[66] Shady deals between the police and black marketeers confirmed that the line between what was legal and what was not had evaporated. Republican intelligence agencies were offering their services to political parties. Engaged in their own fight for political control locally, civil authorities were not inclined to restore order if it required collaboration with political enemies. Rising criminality, local shoot-outs and armed provocations in contested areas, as well as politically aroused fears about the neutrality of the law and police and the untrustworthiness of other national groups, left many citizens with the impression that the only true security was ownership of a firearm. Locals also raided army barracks. In some areas local police and army units have been charged with distributing weapons from official stocks to villagers and militia of the same ethnic group.[67]

## The Federal Army

The federal army was simultaneously engaged in this local process, since its actual command structure was substantially decentralized, and in the high politics of state formation taking place. While the assets of the TDFs and arms purchases from abroad (despite the embargo) were falling into various hands, a complex internal struggle over the YPA's political identity, goals, and appropriate strategy was taking place, paralleling the path of European mediation of the Yugoslav dissolution.

The army's evolution began, as described in chapters 4 and 5, in the contest with Slovenia. The growing antagonism between the YPA and Slovenia in the 1980s culminated in March 1991, when Slovenia withheld its conscripts and confirmed the impossibility of reconciliation. The Croatian government paraded its new army (still based legally on the rights of the TDF and the MUP) that month as well and, like the Slovenes, rejected any suggestion of negotiation with the YPA. (Some generals, such as Generals Martin Špegelj and later Anton Tus in Croatia, had defected early from the YPA to command national security in their republics.) In the view of the Croatian government's top strategists, the sovereignty of the republics was not achievable until the army, as the last remaining Yugoslav institution and the one most committed to the Yugoslav idea, succumbed to internal disintegration from the contest between what they called Titoist elements still committed to Yugoslavia and Serbian elements which, like the Slovenes and Croats, were nationalists committed to an independent state. The nationalist momentum was such, in their view, that Serb nationalists had to win and the Titoists had to concede defeat. The events of March 1991, when the Serbian bloc in the presidency and the minister of defense pushed for emergency rule and when one section of the army general staff agreed to assist Milošević by sending tanks into the streets of Belgrade against opposition demonstrators, seemed to fit their scenario. The fight between the army and Prime Minister Ante Marković came to a head in July, when Marković turned on Defense Minister Kadijević, accusing the army of illegal action in Slovenia.[68] Then, in early July, with the collective presidency, the prime minister, and the president of Croatia gathered in the presidential palace in Zagreb to attempt negotiation of Croatian independence, someone faked an air attack on the palace and blamed it on Kadijević.[69] The intention apparently was to end any possibility of reconciliation between the military and civilian authorities of the federal government. Moreover, monitoring of the cease-fire negotiated by the federal presidency in Croatia during July and August was assigned not to the army but to representatives of the Federal Secretariat of Internal Affairs (although by August 30, the republican governments of Bosnia-Herzegovina and Macedonia, which had agreed to share this task with federal authorities, decided not to participate, and they withdrew their representatives from the monitoring groups on September 4).[70]

Nonetheless, the army did not dissipate on demand. While the republican declarations of independence in June 1991 forced Slovene and Croatian recruits and officers to choose between competing loyalties, their cohorts from other republics continued to be conscripted and to fight into 1992. The senior officer corps, the composition of which had followed the strict application of the rule of national parity (the *ključ*), did not reflect Croatian propaganda. One of the three generals in the supreme staff at the time of the Slovene war was a Slovene (Admiral Stane Brovet). The army was led by the representative of Croatia on the supreme staff, Veljko Kadijević, a Yugoslav born in Croatia of mixed Croat-Serb parentage, minister of defense, and commander of the army. He resigned in January 1992 when he accepted full responsibility for the air force attack on an EC helicopter monitoring the cease-fire in Croatia that killed its five crewmen (and which appeared to be another stage in the rivalries internal to the armed forces). General Zvonko Jurjević, the chief of the air force, obliged to resign because of the same attack, was also Croatian. At the time of the Bosnian declaration of sovereignty, in October 1991, Kadijević promised President Izetbegović to do everything possible to prevent war from spreading to Bosnia-Herzegovina. This promise was honored until April 1992, when those working throughout the fall and early winter to keep the peace (such as Generals Nikola Uzelac in Banja Luka and Milutin Kukanjac in Sarajevo—both Serbs) lost to those seeking to escalate fighting (officers of Serbian ethnicity—Ratko Mladić and Momčilo Perišić—and of Muslim ethnicity—Colonel Vehbija Kadić, who then left to command the Bosnian territorial forces).[71] The purge of the Titoists, or Partisan faction, of the YPA began only after Kadijević's resignation: twenty generals in February 1992, thirty-eight in March. It continued over the next eighteen months, even after the army's small residual officer corps and employees originating from Serbia and Montenegro had been renamed the Yugoslav Army and the internal struggle (favoring the air force) interacted with the political struggle in Serbia.[72]

The stages of the YPA's transformation and its reassessment of political goals were driven, however, by international decisions. The army's apparent military strategy in Slovenia, to combine surprise and overwhelming force in a blitzkrieg assault, on the assumption that there would be little local resistance, had no political objective other than its constitutional duty to defend Yugoslav integrity. According to James Gow, a British specialist on the YPA, the YPA's backup strategy to begin a slow, calculated escalation was foiled by the unexpected intervention of EC mediators; "confused and constrained," it hesitated.[73] The Brioni Agreement of July 7, 1991, obliging the army to return to barracks and leveling accusations from both the EC and Prime Minister Marković of illegitimate and aggressive use of force, was the first step of a process by which the army was forced to retreat, step by step, from each republic that had declared independence. As the violence increased in Croatia, but long before the army had adjusted politically to events, the EC and the United States began to call it a Serbian army and to view the fight as some old Croat-Serb conflict played out between the Croatian government and the army. The policy question in July and early August 1991 was whether to interpose forces (whether Western European Union [WEU], Eurocorps, or UN) between them or to enable Croatia to build up its army and air force legally by recognizing its sovereignty. In fact, the army had been attempting for some months already, and continuing into September 1991, to provide such a neutral buffer between Serbs and Croats, particularly in eastern Croatia, so as to dampen the fighting and create cease-fires. Like Slovenia and Croatia, the EC monitors (ECMM) refused to speak to the army and by early fall of 1991 had joined Croatia in labeling the YPA an occupation force. Still, UN envoy Cyrus Vance began to have greater negotiating success during November 1991 than his EC counterpart, Lord Carrington, in part because he included the Yugoslav minister of defense. When Kadijević resigned, Vance considered it a serious blow to his efforts.

By the second month of the Croatian war, however, this Western response forced the army leadership to reassess totally its political and strategic position. Critical to this reassessment, according to Gow, was the Persian Gulf war, which YPA analysts saw as a "true paradigm for the use of modern technology and a credible model for the use of force in a hypothetical war in similar military-political circumstances, something which (with reference to our crisis and its possible internationalisation) cannot leave us indifferent."[74] That war demonstrated the "instrumentalisation of the UN, as a system of global security, serving to realise the global strategic interests of the greatest world powers," and thus the necessity of U.S. leadership and international consensus for any armed intervention in cases such as Yugoslavia. The United States at the time was preoccupied with Iraq and thus unlikely to back the EC militarily. Consensus in the UN Security Council was also unlikely, particularly if the fear of another Vietnam could be sown. Intervention seemed improbable if the army accepted that Yugoslavia was no longer salvageable and moved to secure the strategic quadrants of a new state—what was being called, by August–September 1991, a rump Yugoslavia (*krnja Jugoslavija*)—without Slovenia and without most (but not all) of Croatia. In Gow's estimation, the consequences of this reassessment could be seen in Croatia by October in the army's participation in the siege taking place for Vukovar, on the Danube, and the campaign in Konavli, south of Dubrovnik, in the Montenegrin military district, to ensure control of the Prevlaka peninsula and therefore its naval base on the Adriatic and the most strategic point on the entire coastline. But Miloš Vasić, the military expert of the independent Belgrade weekly, *Vreme*, saw the army floundering, without "any proper political aim" and a "resulting strategic confusion," into the end of December (and long after the "Pyrrhic victory" of the fall of Vukovar).[75]

Whether a YPA strategy existed at the time, the political path of dissolution continued. The UN-negotiated cease-fire in Croatia required the YPA to withdraw, which it did beginning November 29, and to be replaced by UN troops. The Macedonian government accompanied a request for recognition of its sovereignty to the EC in December 1991 with negotiations for the army to leave (redeployed to Kosovo). UN troops would remain in Croatia, at the behest of the Secretary General and Security Council, until the rebel Serbs disarmed and political negotiations resolved the contest between the two in a political settlement for the country as a whole.[76] This agreement not only met with opposition from the Serbian leader in the *krajina*, Milan Babić—against the public reprimand of his former patron Milošević—but also meant a loss of territories in Slavonia for the faction within the army fighting to create a new, smaller Yugoslavia.[77] Although it still did not include the army in its negotiations, now over Bosnia-Herzegovina, the EC began to demand on April 11, 1992—only five days after Bosnian sovereignty was recognized—that the army withdraw from the republic. In "alarm over the rapid deterioration of the situation" in Bosnia-Herzegovina, the UN Security Council declared in its resolution of April 10 that it would demand on April 24 that "all interference from outside cease." UNSCR 752 (May 15, 1992) demanded that "JNA [YPA] or Croatian Army units in Bosnia-Herzegovina be withdrawn or subject to Bosnia-Herzegovina government authority or disarmed and disbanded with weapons under international supervision." While repeating the same demand in Resolution 757 on May 30, the Security Council also imposed "wide-ranging sanctions" against the new federal republic of Yugoslavia (Serbia and Montenegro) because of the "failure of Serbia, Montenegro and JNA [YPA] authorities to meet Resolution 752."[78]

Despite this foreign view that the army was an external aggressor on Bosnian sovereignty, a primary reason for concern if war erupted in Bosnia was the intimate bond between the Yugoslav People's Army and that republic. The fate of the army would not be determined before the fate of Bosnia-Herzegovina, for the relationship between the two was of a different order altogether than the question of political loyalties or of obtaining diplomatic recognition of sovereignty. For geopolitical, geological, and historical reasons, Bosnia-Herzegovina had been the heart of the country's defense. Located in the interior of Yugoslavia with the natural resources of mountainous terrain, Bosnia-Herzegovina was ideal for the location of military production—coal, iron, timber, metallurgy, steel, hydroelectric power, armaments, and industrial crops. The industrialization of Bosnia-Herzegovina under the Habsburgs after 1878, the removal of strategic industries from borderlands into the interior after 1938 (before World War II) and again in the quarrel with the Cominform in 1948–49 (leading the army to call Bosnia its "Dinaric Fortress"), and the massive federal investment in Bosnian industry in 1948–52 were all consequences of Bosnia-Herzegovina's military significance. Even in the 1980s, when the army was being substantially downsized, 40 to 55 percent of the Bosnian economy was tied to military industries; 50 to 55 percent of its industry was federally mandated investment for that reason; and 40,000 people were employed directly in military production. Sixty to 80 percent of the army's physical assets (armaments factories, supply routes, airfields, mines and basic raw materials, stockpiles, training schools, oil depots) were located in Bosnia-Herzegovina. On the eve of the war, 68 percent of the federal army's 140,000 troops were stationed in the republic.[79] To the extent that the Yugoslav army was fighting a war for its own integrity and state, it could not easily be a neutral party in Bosnia-Herzegovina or abandon its own economic foundations.

Even if the army's identity is equated with its permanent personnel alone, it was inextricable from Bosnia-Herzegovina. Because the primary site of Partisan fighting against Axis powers in World War II was in Bosnia-Herzegovina, an estimated 80 percent of the officer corps originated there. Early accusations of Serbian aggression in Croatia and Bosnia were commonly supported with the allegation that the army was 70 percent Serbian. It is not fully clear how these data were compiled, since a large portion of the officer corps identified their nationality as Yugoslav, and reliable statistics on the ethnic composition of the army were not publicly available. Moreover, the army experienced substantial turnover for political and natural reasons. To obtain such an estimate, Serbs, Montenegrins, and Yugoslavs would have to be equated as Serbs; the data would have to represent only the professional corps of officers and its civilian employees and not the entire army or armed forces; and the differences between ethnic Serbs from Serbia proper and from outside Serbia would have to be ignored. The full active component, including conscripts, reservists, and reserve officers, was far more representative of the ethnic composition of the population. This was even more true if one assessed the total armed forces, which included the TDFs of each republic. The senior officer corps and assignment of commands strictly followed the legal requirement—the key (*ključ*)—of national proportionality.

More important, the labeling of the YPA as a Serbian army, with all its implications, accepted the nationalist argument that ethnic origin was equivalent to political loyalty and partisanship. In the hands of outsiders who were insisting on borders and sovereignty as defined by the former republics, the label was also confusing, if not hypocritical, for like the nationalists, it seemed to deny the difference between ethnic origin and republic of origin or residence. But the army was ideologically a communist institution, dogmatically antinationalist.[80] To the extent it had a Serbian "character" in terms of ethnicity, these Serbs came largely from Bosnia-Herzegovina and Croatia as a result of the army's origins during World War II, when ethnic Serbs in the areas of the former military border between Austria and Turkey took sanctuary with Partisan units against the fascist Ustasha campaign of genocide against them. Along with many officers of the royal army from Serbia proper, they chose to join the Partisans under Tito rather than the Serbian Chetniks.[81]

Relations between the army and the Bosnian government nonetheless deteriorated as the country dissolved. At the time of the Slovene and Croatian independence declarations, the Bosnian government and Parliament had made no particular effort to communicate with the army, in part because of internal divisions among the parties. From the beginning, the Croatian party took the position of its Zagreb superiors that the YPA was an army of occupation. Bosnian Serb party leaders issued calls to the YPA as early as mid-July to protect the Serb minority, just as its other SDS branch had done in Croatia. While preparing actively for armed conflict like the others, the SDA leadership under Izetbegović began to talk as a state-building party about transforming the army within Bosnia-Herzegovina into the republic's national army in a future Yugoslav confederation. The declaration of Bosnian sovereignty by the Croat-Muslim alliance on October 15, 1991, however, was a direct reaction to the army decision to mobilize troops in the Bosnian *krajina*, as part of the intensified fighting in Croatia during September. Although President Izetbegović ordered draft boards to ignore the order for mobilization, he was sensitive enough to the Slovene and Croatian precedents and to the YPA's commitment to some form of a Yugoslavia that included Bosnia to issue a warning to all sides not to do anything against the army. Minister of Defense Kadijević promised to do everything necessary to prevent the war's spread to Bosnia.

Such a commitment in the midst of a rapidly deteriorating and shifting political scene depended, however, on the ability of these two men to maintain a consistent position and keep control over their own forces. Izetbegović's mandate as president expired in November 1991 and the means used to extend it a second twelve months were not universally considered legitimate. Kadijević felt obliged to resign in January 1992. Officers loyal to both the YPA and Bosnia who tried to play a neutral and pacifying role faced a rise in incidents requiring damage control during the fall. In September 1991, within days after the Belgrade Initiative issued its proposal for a new Yugoslavia, reservists from Serbia went on a shooting spree in Tuzla, the truly multiethnic city in northern Bosnia, and cross-border raids began to terrorize citizens in eastern Bosnia into ethnic factions. Refugees from the war in Croatia brought with them the polarizing epithets of Chetniks (for all Serbs) and Ustasha (for all Croats) and provoked clashes with local army units. Officers unsure of which way the political wind would blow maneuvered their own local alliances and provocations to test the waters, which had the effect of exacerbating tensions.[82]

Also during the fall, while the YPA was preparing to leave Croatia, Izetbegović sought to negotiate a political accommodation and partial demobilization, promising that officers and their families could keep their apartments and receive their pensions, and that the government would assist their transition to employment in the civilian sector. Yet it was not at all clear where he would find the funds necessary to make the promise credible. The economy had already begun to collapse as a result of the country's dissolution and of an economic embargo imposed on Bosnia-Herzegovina during the fall by Croatia (on transportation routes) and Serbia (on most trade in food and fuel).

Izetbegović appealed to German foreign minister Genscher in early December to wait to recognize Croatia until Bosnia's political relations were more settled, but he also showed his hand by requesting UN peace-keeping troops to guard the border on December 6. The EC decisions on recognition in December and the decision of the Croat-Muslim faction within the Bosnian government to request recognition and of the Serb party to declare in response that it would create its own republic within Bosnia-Herzegovina appeared to force YPA units and officers toward an alliance with Serbs wishing to remain within Yugoslavia and TDF units in Serb majority localities. All other territorial defense forces began to mobilize on the side of the Croat-Muslim alliance. Yet the period between Kadijević's resignation in January 1992 and the EC demand of April 11, 1992, that the YPA leave Bosnia-Herzegovina still presented opportunities for reversing the polarization and for preventing open war. The confrontation mounted only after April 4, when the Bosnian government, assured that recognition was coming on April 6, called up the national guard to fight Serb insurrection and declared the YPA untrustworthy and on the side of the Bosnian Serbs. Following the tactics chosen earlier by Slovenia and then Croatia, it blockaded YPA barracks and insisted on the army's retreat under UN supervision.[83]

Although President Milošević had been resisting for over a year calls from the Serbian parliament and nationalists for the formation of a Serbian national army, he acknowledged the fait accompli on May 8 when the new Yugoslav army (VJ) retired thirty senior officers known as Titoists. Života Panić, who had been commanding officer at Vukovar, was appointed the new state's minister of defense. Only a week after Panić claimed that the YPA would remain in Bosnia-Herzegovina at least five years, he ordered its withdrawal from the republic.[84]

The YPA project for a rump Yugoslavia disappeared with the YPA. But the retreat of the YPA from Bosnia-Herzegovina May 4–10 meant in fact the departure of the 20 percent of its personnel who originated from Serbia and Montenegro, the two remaining republics of the former federation that joined into a new Yugoslavia on April 27. Left in Bosnia were two-thirds of the YPA's ammunition, much heavy artillery and equipment, and 80,000 troops who were Bosnian citizens. These were largely transferred to the territorial defense forces of the "Serb Republic of Bosnia and Herzegovina," the core of a new Bosnian Serb army formed on May 13.[85] Bosnian loyalist Milutin Kukanjac was replaced by General Ratko Mladić, the openly pro-Serb militant from Bosnia who had been commander of the Knin corps of the YPA.[86] Mladić's military campaign to keep eastern and northern Bosnia within Yugoslavia so as to create a corridor between Serbia and the areas claimed by Serbs in the Croatian *krajina* and a strategic buffer along the Drina River had become explicitly Serb nationalist in its motivations, attached to the Bosnian Serb party (SDS) leadership and its political aims. At the same time, the forced retreat of YPA officers from Croatia and Bosnia-Herzegovina had been to Belgrade; the senior ranks of the new Yugoslav army were former colleagues of Mladić, veterans of the campaigns in Croatia and Bosnia, and in many cases, exiles from their origins in these republics. In contrast to the moderate Panić, for example, was General Nikola Uzelac, responsible for arming Serb irregulars in the Banja Luka region, who was appointed to the general staff and commander of the third army (of three) with jurisdiction over Kosovo.[87] Moreover, on June 16, Bosnian president Izetbegović announced that he had signed a formal military alliance with Croatian president Tudjman.

## The Proliferation of Weapons

In addition to the influence of EC and UN diplomatic negotiations to recognize republican sovereignty and obtain a cease-fire, the UN arms embargo imposed in September 1991 in response to the war in Croatia contributed to further chaos in the system of defense. It gave impetus to political groups throughout the country to seize local stockpiles of weapons and ammunition (such as the move by Croat forces in Herzegovina to secure TDF assets and keep them from the YPA) and to plan the relocation of assets in preparation for war (as appeared to be the motivation of YPA troop movements out of Bosnian cities during the fall of 1991). It made control over Bosnia and sites of domestic defense plants and installations more critical and led governments (especially Croatia and Serbia) to begin war production from the substantial domestic arms industry.[88] Such production, however, did not interrupt cooperation between Croatian and Serbian tank and arms producers even while Croats and ethnic Serbs were at war in Croatia.

The embargo gave an initial advantage to those who had built up armies during 1990–91, those who had taken the early initiative over TDF assets, and those aided by the army from existing stocks. Slovene territorial defense forces used Armbrust rocket launchers and antitank weapons from Germany in the ten-day war; in Croatia and Bosnia, Serb irregulars used new German submachine guns and sniper rifles sold to an arms buyer in Belgrade; and the Croatian government had little difficulty purchasing west European antitank weapons, east German AK-47 and Argentine self-loading rifles, Stinger missiles, and west German light arms and, apparently, even Leopard tanks.[89] The initial disproportions in access to domestic stocks and the uncertainty and higher risks and cost attached to foreign supplies encouraged a local arms race. Croatia captured arms in September 1991 by blockading YPA barracks and by seizing about thirty ships and all bases of the former Yugoslav navy.[90] The YPA supported some Serb groups in Croatia. Slovene war booty was transferred to Croatians, and YPA equipment, including heavy artillery and planes, to Bosnian Serbs. This led to the development of new arms industries, such as Croatia's construction of a fully equipped army, navy, and air force of 110,000 troops by November 1992 from its own plants—the Djuro Djaković tank factory, Zmaj aircraft center, and shipyards.

The primary source of continuing disadvantage, in fact, was physical location and the dependence of some areas—above all, central Bosnia—on others within the former country for access to supply routes and transport. The UN embargo thus reproduced the effects of economic reform and westernization and the EC decisions on recognition and aid. In its early stages the embargo largely affected the Bosnian army, Muslim paramilitaries, and special forces created by Albanians in Kosovo. Able to purchase or receive from foreign patrons, émigrés, and arms markets abroad substantial imports of light arms and ammunition, they could not overcome their disadvantage in access to heavy weapons (artillery, tanks) and aircraft of the Slovenes, Croats, and Serbs, because supply routes were controlled by their potential or real enemy. Thus President Izetbegović's military alliance with Croatia aimed to gain access to the sea for arms, fuel, and supplies. When Croatian war aims extended beyond their political stronghold in western Herzegovina, during the fall of 1992, Croatian forces that controlled those routes began to insist on a 50 to 70 percent cut of all weapons traffic, if they let any through at all (which they did less and less after September 1992).

The Bosnian government's dependence on Croatian cooperation to allow arms and refugees to flow prevented President Izetbegović, in fact, from calling for international sanctions on Croatia, even when it was clear that the alliance meant little to the fighting on the ground and that the Croatian army (HV) was an active participant against Bosnian forces. Indeed, it led Izetbegović to protect Tudjman by muting international criticism on numerous occasions. At the same time, the borders between Serbia and Montenegro and areas of Bosnia-Herzegovina claimed by Bosnian Serbs were so permeable and its legitimacy as an international border so rejected by locals that Serbian assistance of weapons, fuel, supplies, and "weekend warriors" were easily provided and difficult to interdict. Landlocked Bosnian forces and Albanians in Serbia thus had to rely more than the others on attracting international sympathy to obtain the foreign military assistance, such as air cover for their ground troops or actual attacks on enemy heavy artillery, that the embargo was designed to make unnecessary.

### Economic Disintegration and the Collapse of Trade

Inseparable from the collapse of civil order and the protracted process of transformation from a single Yugoslav to many separate armies and paramilitary groups that characterized the fighting was the dissolution of their common economy. Also not obedient to republican borders, economic relations and the flow of goods and transport necessarily were casualties of the political conflict—in part, a spontaneous breakdown and, in part, deliberate destruction of the economic interdependencies of the former state. But the fact of these interdependencies also provided weapons of war. Thus the Serbian attempt to boycott Slovene goods after December 1990 had little effect on the Slovene economy. But when Serbia and Croatia both imposed an embargo on goods going into Bosnia-Herzegovina during the fall of 1991, in order to sabotage the Bosnian economy and facilitate their respective war aims, the effect was devastating.[91] The economy of Bosnia-Herzegovina not only was fully integrated into the Yugoslav economy, but also particularly depended on the import of food. While Bosnians reeled from the inflationary effects, the areas claimed by militant Bosnian

Croats (their state of Herzeg-Bosnia) had an important buffer of stability from their early economic incorporation into Croatia proper, Croatian currency, and Dalmatian trade routes. This also helped to facilitate the payment and therefore loyalty of soldiers and local administrations that were critical to the Bosnian Croats' war aims.

The persistent efforts during 1991 and again in mid-1992 by the leadership in Montenegro to distance itself from Serbian policies and be more independent were also futile without international support, because Montenegro's transportation routes, energy grids, and similar lifelines were connected to Serbia and because the republic's dependence on federal budgetary subsidies had been transferred to Serbia after the collapse of Yugoslavia. The Croatian decision on September 11, 1991, to shut off the Adria oil pipeline feeding Serbia (and central Europe) and the war's disruption of links with Croatia and Slavonia meant that Serbia could not easily afford to lose its access to the sea through Montenegro. Each Montenegrin move, therefore, was met by some form of economic pressure, such as an overnight rise in the cost of electricity or a blockade of fuel oil, from Serbia. Unable to gain even international acknowledgment of its separate interests, the Montenegrin liberals had nowhere to turn, and the Montenegrin government had to find accommodation with Milošević (particularly after December 1992, when its support for the campaign of Yugoslav prime minister Panić to end the war was defeated along with Panić in the Serbian presidential election). The UN economic sanctions on Serbia and Montenegro after May 30, 1992, imposed to stop the war in Bosnia, not only made Serbia's alternative routes in the east more risky, but also caused serious hardship for Macedonia. Macedonia was landlocked and nearly all of its road, railway, energy, power, and telecommunications links went through Serbia. Macedonia sold about two-thirds of its agricultural and manufactured goods to Serbia.[92]

The actual path of the dissolution of the state had a direct consequence on the character of those wars. The first stage of fighting (seen in both the wars in Croatia and Bosnia-Herzegovina, when the world was least attentive or prepared to react) was not a calculated military strategy between contending armies or between the Yugoslav army and republican militias. The situation was, instead, chaotic. Competing militias and gangs marauded, only loosely linked to centers of command and control or fully freewheeling, and paramilitary extremists escalated small confrontations to force political leaders to greater militancy. The declining number of regular troops and difficulty finding conscripts willing to fight led to supplementation with militant extremist volunteers and criminals released from jails, who were more often motivated by the invitation to loot and plunder than nationalist fervor. The worst excesses of reported massacres, rape, and mutilations emerged because of such conditions.

Local interests and alliances predominated, giving a very different character to warfare in different regions and municipalities. To the extent that battles had a strategic character, each commanding officer also faced a choice among competing loyalties (based on a calculation of the probable fate of the army itself as well as personal sentiments and bonds of obligation).

The political conflict within national and military organizations over political goals and strategy, the absence of appropriate equipment for communication among local units, and the continuing dominance of local loyalties interfered throughout the period with efforts to impose central control or enforce negotiated agreements. Events such as the shelling of Dubrovnik at the end of October 1991 and the attack on an EC monitoring helicopter that killed five airmen in January 1992 appear to have been the result of policy disagreements within the YPA senior command and the branches of the armed forces. It remains unclear whether there would have been a three-month siege (August 24–November 17, 1991) and destruction of Vukovar, the worst battle of the Croatian war, had renegade forces from the Croatian National Guard (called the Wolves of Vukovar) and neofascist Ustasha bands such as the Zebras, who were loyal to local politicians (particularly the right-wing radical in the HDZ, Tomislav Merčep), not chosen to ignore Zagreb authority and put up a stiff resistance—in order to draw the government into a more aggressive strategy.[93] They succeeded in escalating the war because they were matched on the Serb side by right-wing radicals from Serbia, such as Šešelj, who had attempted to make eastern Slavonia a Chetnik base through radicalizing campaigns during the spring. In similar fashion, these irregulars were also outside much control but had allies within the army among officers who were attempting to drag Belgrade into the war.[94] The army, for its part, faced increasing problems of recruitment and desertion. Two units of the TDF refused to fight; morale was declining and there were insufficient soldiers in a location of major geopolitical significance. The commanding general, Života Panić, assessed that there would be no YPA left within two months unless he turned to artillery. Each fighting their own battles as much as each other, they continued until there was nothing left to destroy.[95]

In Bosnia-Herzegovina, lack of communication affected the command and control of both the Bosnian Serb and Bosnian government armies and emphasized the dominance of local territorial forces in their origins and the psychology of defending home territory. The Bosnian government tended to fight many battles with small units of 1,000 to 2,000. Even after December 1992, by which time the organization of a new army made it possible to launch serious campaigns, they continued to have difficulty concentrating forces and creating mobility. Local alliances and local commanders held sway for the Croatian HVO and even the Bosnian Serb army, despite the Serbs' mobile elite units and slightly higher proportion of former YPA officers.

Moreover, the dissolution of the country erased the security guarantees for most individuals and families. The bases of self-restraint and mutual trust that make civil order possible without massive coercion were already fragile after a decade of economic depression and social disintegration. The tactics of outside terrorists, the mass media propaganda, and the political interests of ethnically pure local administrations or police were additional assaults. The many recorded examples of heroic neighborliness across ethnic lines and in village solidarity against outside radicals could only provide for many a temporary protection against displacement or voluntary exile once the last vestiges of trust were destroyed by the unexpected hostility of other neighbors.[96]

## State-Building

Perhaps the most negligent element of the European policy to recognize the republics of the Yugoslav federation as separate nation-states was its disregard for the characteristics of states, as opposed to nations. States are more than communities of political identity. In addition to legitimacy and citizens, they require strategically defensible borders, economic assets sufficient to survive against external threats, and a monopoly on the use of force over territory claimed. The borders of the republics had never had to satisfy the needs of independent states. Once nationalists turned to state-building, there was an additional reason on many sides for contesting existing republican borders. While political rhetoric and propaganda continued to emphasize ethnic criteria, the actual goals of military activity would be driven by strategic objectives.

Therefore, although Europeans had argued that recognition of Slovene and Croatian sovereignty—and the invitation to recognize Bosnia-Herzegovina and Macedonia—would stop the use of force, its consequence was to up the ante instead. Once it was clear that Yugoslavia was no longer salvageable and that separate states would ensue, the strategic requirements of statehood fueled war.

In this aspect of the Yugoslav conflict, too, the Slovene case deceived those who thought that the creation of new states, state powers, and foreign relations would be unproblematic and peaceful. Its economy had long been more integrated internationally (especially with Western markets) than domestically. Slovene firms adjusted rapidly to war and international sanctions, maintaining their contracts and markets in Serbia by redirecting routes, through friendly Hungary where necessary, in spite of the UN embargo.[97] The availability of Austrian capital and the central

European trade and tourist organizations such as Alpe-Adria provided Slovenia with a buffer, in the short run, against the collapse of the Yugoslav market. Because Slovenia had the highest proportion of export producers, it could reassure international financial organizations and credit markets that it could reliably assume its portion of the Yugoslav foreign debt and guarantee new loans. Membership in the United Nations for Slovenia came easily and quickly, in May 1992. By December 1992, long before there was any hope of discussion over the economic questions of the Yugoslav succession, Slovenia had been admitted to the IMF and to the Council of Europe.

Slovenia's Alpine terrain provided a natural line of defense as long as the policy it chose during the 1980s to repopulate the uplands could be maintained. It had succeeded in taking control over most of the military assets of the Yugoslav army, establishing a national monopoly over the use of force, and gaining foreign assistance in purchasing supplementary arms even before its declaration of independence. Reconstruction of war damage was minor, in contrast to the effects of the war on its border. With borders and international relations stable, a parliamentary vote of no confidence over failing economic policies brought down the center-right government that had waged the war, and an election six months later resumed the prewar trend back to the liberals.

In contrast to Slovenia, war in the other republics reflected, in part, the process of creating the coercive instruments and borders of states. Armed clashes began when police forces moved in to challenge local control by national minorities, as in Glina, Plitvice, and Borovo Selo in Croatia in 1990–91. A critical moment in the consolidation of control over Herzeg-Bosnia, the state within Bosnia-Herzegovina being created by the Bosnian Croat branch of the HDZ, occurred when its armed forces succeeded in assassinating Blaž Kraljević, the regional commander of rival Croatian forces, the right-wing HOS, in Trebinje in August 1992. Although the military alliance between the Croatian and Bosnian governments had broken down after September 1992, it did not lead to open warfare between Bosnian Croats and Muslims until the end of January 1993, when Bosnian Croat leader Mate Boban began to disarm Bosnian government police and army personnel in areas of central Bosnia that he claimed for Herzeg-Bosnia. Brutal massacres carried out by both forces in mixed Croat-Muslim towns of central Bosnia beginning with Vitez in April 1993 were triggered when Croatian defense minister Gojko Šušak visited Bosnia and ordered the Croatian state flag raised over these towns.

War in the other republics also concerned strategic assets, in contrast to Slovenia's natural, and largely uncontested, borders and its linkup with European transportation and communication routes. Ethnically defined territories are not by and large defined by natural borders, and the fact of war between ethnically defined armies heightened sensitivity to the need for defensible borders between national states that might be hostile.[98] Access to the sea, ports, and international transportation routes became necessities for landlocked areas which aimed to become independent states. One aspect of the fight for Vukovar was geopolitical, made more immediate by the increasing importance of the Danube River as an international waterway for commerce and defense in the continental expansion of European trade with the end of the cold war.[99] Although Croatia claimed western Herzegovina on both historicist and ethnodemocratic principles, its importance was strategic: as an essential cordon protecting the Dalmatian coast tourist trade and its thin, long, vulnerable line of north-south communications of an independent state of Croatia.[100]

Montenegro (and therefore Serbia, with which it was allied in one state) could not defend itself without control over the Prevlaka peninsula, and the fishing industry that was critical to its economy could not afford the Croatian claim of territorial waters that it extended from the Prevlaka it controlled. Regardless of international recognition for the former republican borders, the strategic significance of the Prevlaka peninsula for Montenegro, of the Drina and Danube rivers for Serbia, and of the Dalmatian hinterland for Croatia required subsequent negotiation.

Perhaps the greatest confusion for foreign observers was the debate over maps that seemed to derail all political negotiations over Bosnia-Herzegovina. The more war continued in Bosnia-Herzegovina, the more armies fought for routes, defensible corridors, and contiguous territories. Outsiders continued to talk of *percentages* of territory in ethnic terms and of what they considered to be a just solution, including their aim of not "rewarding aggression." Neither had much resonance in the behavior of military forces, whose leaders were thinking in strategic terms of independent survival and natural lines of defense and stable borders. Although leaders continued to lay claim to territory on national grounds, including the criterion of the majority ethnic identity of residents in the 1991 census, claims to territory on grounds of national rights did not mean they would be limited to ethnic-majority or historically national territories.

When international mediators, for example, ignored Karadžić's insistence on the cantonization of Bosnia, with his claim of Serbian rights to 65 percent of Bosnian territory on the grounds that Serbs held legal title to this much land in Bosnia even if their percentage in the population was lower, the Bosnian Serb army under General Mladić pushed instead to fill in the patchwork quilt of these landholdings to make contiguous, statelike territory and to build a land corridor between Serbia proper and the Serbian-claimed areas in the Croatian *krajina* that was intended to ensure the survival of Serbs as a nation in this area.[101] Even cities that were considered clearly Muslim territory by population and historical tradition became military targets because of their military assets (airfields, oil depots, hydroelectric power plants, armaments factories, communication lines for supplies).[102] Similarly, when Bosnian government forces took the offensive at the end of 1992, some of the most vicious fighting of the war (in terms of atrocities and ethnic cleansing) occurred in central Bosnia. Whereas journalists argued that this fight between predominantly Muslim forces and their former Croatian allies occurred because the Bosnian government could not penetrate Serbian-held territory, the fact was that Bosnian Muslim goals were strategic: the industrial heartland and above all the armaments factories in towns such as Vitez.

The importance of economic assets to new states, moreover, was behind the prolonged refusal of Bosnian Serbs to sign on to the map part of the Vance-Owen plan. Whereas the international community accused the plan of appeasing aggression (for assigning the Bosnian Serbs majority control over 43 percent of the territory—a rollback from the 70 percent they held militarily at the time of the negotiations but more than their approximately 33 percent of the population), the Bosnian Serbs were calculating not only the percentage of territory given each constituent nation in relation to its percentage of the population, but also the proportional value of industrial and mining sources, energy sources (thermal, coal, hydroelectric power), and railways per province and "per ethnic group." In this calculation, the Vance-Owen map was leading to the economic destruction of their territory "with the stroke of the pen" because it "deprive[d] them of energy sources and industrial plants" and made them "dependent in energy and therefore economically submitted [sic]" to Muslim and Croat provinces and "condemned to permanent economic inferiority and dependence."[103] The same calculation of economic values by nationality became a key bargaining document of the Bosnian Muslim leadership in the summer of 1994 when the map at issue was one formulated by the Contact Group. A stumbling block in the one in between, the Invincible plan, was the Bosnian government and Bosnian Muslim demand for access to the sea and to the Sava River.

## Conclusion

Had the Western view that Yugoslavia was an artificial creation of separate nation-states been correct, there would have been no reason for war. Moreover, the characteristics of the ensuing wars were defined by its causes rather than by some historical predilection to war and to the particular form of brutality witnessed in Yugoslavia. Because the EC left it up to partisans in Yugoslavia to decide which justifications for territory would prevail in defining new states and borders, the constitutional methods of combat during 1989–90 (national claims through constitutional preamble, citizenship rights, and loyalty oaths) were replaced by the methods, social organization, culture, and weapons associated with land and its defense.[104]

Regardless of ethnic differences, the process of justifying a nation's sovereignty over territory became embodied in persons and their rights to live on that land. It was this association, of this link between particular persons and land with past wars, that made historical memories relevant to the conflict and opened thoughts of revenge that had been laid aside. And the EC's insistence on referendums to legitimize these rights, while accepting the validity of only some, provided the impetus—whatever the spontaneous reasons (envy, hatred, competition)—to expel people from their homes and jobs on the basis of their ethnicity and to create ethnically pure areas through population transfers and expulsions as a prelude to a vote. The goal was not territorial acquisition but statehood. For that, only international recognition would complete the task.

Contrary to the distinction made by the international community between humanitarian and political objectives, there can be no distinction between soldier and civilian in such wars. The goal is to claim territories *for* a particular people and to resolve questions of membership and political loyalties through war. As in a referendum, the size of the turnout is as important as the size of the vote—but neutrality is even less of an option. Whatever the methods used, the fight to establish national rights to land has a genocidal aspect. According to the myth of right-wing nationalism, ethnicity is pure and a *natural* basis for state rights. Those who refuse to accept an ethnically defined political loyalty are reclassified as enemies of their people. The conflict is not ethnic, in other words, but national: ethnic Croats who protested exclusive Croatian nationalism or President Tudjman's policies, ethnic Serbs who opposed Slobodan Milošević or argued for intellectual dissent, Serbs and Croats in Bosnia-Herzegovina who identified themselves as Bosnians rather than side with Bosnian Serb or Bosnian Croat nationalists were all classified with the enemy and vulnerable to treatment as traitors.

Moreover, contrary to those who argue that these wars represent a clash of civilizations—between civilized and barbarian, Western and Balkan, Roman Catholic and Eastern Orthodox, Christian and Muslim—the real clash is social and economic. Territorial war for new states does not put an end to the political, economic, and social conflicts raised by the policies of global integration but that lost out to the nationalist juggernaut; they are simply played out under the guise of ethnic conflict. The war became an opportunity for a revolt of the disadvantaged, for individual enrichment, for political aspirations, and for revenge against the communist regime. The character of the fighting itself is best explained by the socioeconomic background of those leading the fight and doing the soldiering. Thus the element of revenge is far more social and generational than historical, although the two can come together. Right-wing nationalists in Serbia and Croatia did revive the names, symbols, and even uniforms of right-wing nationalists from World War II—the monarchist Chetniks and fascist Ustasha—for their paramilitary forces.

The description of the Yugoslav wars as ethnic conflict is most misleading, however, as a predictor of military activity. Military strategy in this case was not driven by ethnic hatred, class conflict, or historical aspirations for territory, but by the geopolitical and institutional preconditions of sovereignty: obtaining the strategic and economic assets and borders of a secure future state, destroying those of one's enemies, and building (in the course of war) the armies and foreign alliances of a new defense. Strategically defensible territories may have little relation to the borders defined by medieval states (as proclaimed by the historicist principle of a nation), by the patterns of migration and settlement of individuals and households (leading to the claim of the democratic principle), or by the administrative units of a former state (and the Helsinki principles); but short of such security, a state is incomplete. Like the social conflicts defining loyalties and fighting, this strategic objective is part of the longer process of the disintegration of one state and transformation of its assets and institutions to new states in the process of formation. The local organization of territorial defense in the previous Yugoslav system, the massive stockpiles of weapons, the armaments factories, and the organization of the federal army contributed substantially to the pattern of fighting. And as an actor in its own right in the constitutional battle, the army also had a political project: first, to hold a Yugoslavia together and to protect its particular assets and people, and then, as the political reality shifted, to create a state (a different state, depending on which officers and conscripts) to serve. Because the multiple elements and conflicts creating the wars in Croatia and Bosnia-Herzegovina were part of a prewar and postwar political continuum encompassing all of former Yugoslavia, however, they also characterized politics and calculation in areas that were not yet at war.

# Chapter 9

# *Stopping the Bosnian War*

The war in Bosnia-Herzegovina posed a severe test for the international community. It did not fit any of the categories for which international and regional organizations were designed. Two sets of problems were overriding in revealing this lack of fit and preparation and in thwarting a more adequate response.

The first was the dilemma posed by the decision of the major powers on the one hand that Bosnia-Herzegovina had no strategic significance and the ability of the republic and its people on the other hand to mobilize nearly continuous pressure on the major powers from the global mass media and international public opinion to act. The absence of vital interest for major powers meant that they would not become engaged militarily in the war, but the pressure from the media and the public acted as a moral campaign, reminding the world that international conventions and moral law were being violated and demanding that the major powers take decisive military action. This dilemma made concrete the proverbial identification of Yugoslavia—and particularly Bosnia-Herzegovina—as a "crossroads." It was, but it also was not, a part of Europe. The compromise was to send UN peacekeeping forces to deliver humanitarian assistance to civilians in the midst of a multisided war. The predictable effect of such a policy was to satisfy no one, to build in constant pressure for more assertive action, and to endanger seriously the credibility of the United Nations and peacekeeping in general.

The second set of problems, arising from the issue of national sovereignty, plagued the multiple rounds of political negotiations aimed at bringing an end to the war. The European Community's willingness to break up multinational Yugoslavia on the principle of national sovereignty showed little regard for the consequences for multinational Bosnia-Herzegovina. This mistake was compounded by U.S. insistence on recognizing Bosnia's sovereignty before its ties with other parts of the former country (particularly Croatia and Serbia) were clarified and before some negotiated arrangement had been reached among the three ethno-"national" political parties (each claiming the status and rights of "constituent peoples" or "nations") governing the republic in coalition. The result was an artificial dilemma over the cause of the war—was it a civil war or external aggression from Serbia?—and appropriate actions to end it. This problem, never resolved, prevented Western powers from addressing the actual nature of the conflict and formulating an appropriate policy toward it. Instead, having recognized Bosnian statehood and membership in the UN, the international community had to behave as if Bosnia was a state besieged by both rebel forces and external aggressors. In practice it treated the war as a civil war. The goal of international negotiations was, therefore, to obtain a political settlement among the three former coalition partners whose aim, however, was to create separate national states on contested territory.

This second dilemma interacted, therefore, with the first. The decision of the major powers not to act militarily in the conflict meant that they would not defend the Bosnian state they had recognized. The confusion about, or lack of understanding for, national as opposed to civil conflict created a self-made trap for the types of intervention used by the international community. Good offices, humanitarian relief to civilians, and political negotiations all became instruments of the conflict that the warring parties used to achieve their goal of separate states.

## The Failure to Prevent

The most serious failure of existing international and regional institutions with regard to the war in Bosnia-Herzegovina was their inability to prevent it—either by putting an early stop to the war in Croatia before it could spread to Bosnia-Herzegovina, by persisting in the negotiation of a comprehensive settlement for the entire country, or by not repeating earlier mistakes when the Bosnian war did explode. This is particularly important to emphasize because the perception that the war was inevitable grew as the ferocity and duration of the war increased and as outsiders sought to absolve themselves from any responsibility.

During 1992 Europeans still acknowledged this failure, but they explained it as the consequence of unfortunate timing, coinciding, as it did, with their own transition to the post–cold war era. If the events in Yugoslavia had occurred a few years earlier or later, European security institutions would have been up to the task, but post–cold war institutions were not yet ready. By this they meant that the crisis-management mechanisms of the Conference on Security and Cooperation in Europe (CSCE) were only being voted at the time. The EC, as its president, Jacques Delors, said in the fall of 1991, was still in its adolescence.[1] In addition, the transition away from cold war stability and institutions had caused an explosion of new demands that overloaded the ability of states and existing institutions to deal with them. It was, they insisted, unrealistic to expect an effective response.

This thesis of transition does not stand up very well, however, in the face of international action that did take place. It assumes that there would be some learning over time or a change of policy as institutions did make the transition. Instead, the approach of Western governments to Bosnia-Herzegovina was nearly identical to the failed approach toward Croatia, and that approach reflected a continuity in thinking from the cold war period. Moreover, there was little change in approach over the course of the more than two years recorded in this book. This is all the more remarkable because the conflict itself was changing as a result of the war and of international negotiations.

Just as in Croatia, events outside Bosnia-Herzegovina moved faster than the political development within the republic that was needed to avoid war. But Western action regarding Bosnia-Herzegovina, even more than Croatia, was a result of decisions concerning other areas of the former country. By ignoring developments within the republic and the effect as well of actions in other republics or internationally on Bosnia, Western governments and actors repeatedly reinforced the factors leading to war and eventually to ethnic partition.

Thus, just as the Croatian leadership was not obliged by its own sense of consequence or by external actors to provide a remedy for the problem it was creating for the Serb population in Croatia before it jumped on the bandwagon of Slovene "dissociation" in July 1990, these events caught the political leadership of Bosnia-Herzegovina in total disarray. When Slovenia walked out of the federal party congress in January 1990, the Bosnian Communist party leadership was still reeling from the political effects of the Agrokomerc financial scandal of 1989. Ethnic political parties were only beginning to form out of small circles of nationalist intellectuals and personal or ideological opponents of the regime when Slovenia and Croatia announced multiparty elections for the spring of 1990. The Slovene and Croatian campaign—between July 1990 and the publication of their draft proposal in October 1990—to transform Yugoslavia into a confederation of independent states had already established one of the two options for Yugoslavia's future months before multiparty elections for parliaments and executives in Bosnia-Herzegovina and Macedonia were held in late November and December. The effort of new leaders from these latter two republics to propose a compromise constitution between the confederal and federal options bore fruit only six months later, on June 3, 1991. By this time, the European Community had deprived Slovene and Croat leaders of any incentive to compromise by acknowledging de facto their right to self-determination (and thus independence).

Sarajevo, the capital of Bosnia-Herzegovina, became the symbol of Yugoslavia's efforts to stop the momentum toward breakup and war during the first half of 1991. The Yugoslav state presidency chose Sarajevo as a neutral ground to begin its expanded sessions with presidents of the republics in January aimed at finding a way out of the constitutional crisis. The Round Table of Authorities and Opposition in Yugoslavia—a gathering of representatives from the Parliament of Yugoslavia (from about thirty political parties and movements) and from republican and federal officials and parties (government and opposition) that aimed at stopping the armed conflict and opening new lines of political communication—held all its meetings in 1991 and 1992 in Sarajevo.[2] Although the elections in Bosnia-Herzegovina had produced a government coalition of three ethnic parties, groups committed to a multiethnic Bosnia-Herzegovina and to the process of democratization had begun to challenge successfully the attempts by these three parties to create a trilateral ethnic condominium over political life; for example, the attempts to revert to the socialist procedure for controlling the mass media by government (now three-party rather than one-party) control over appointments and editorial policy were successfully challenged in the courts and declared unconstitutional. Even while EC mediators were beginning to take over the role of the federal presidency in negotiating a political solution to the crisis, starting with the Brioni Agreement of July 7, 1991, the peace movement staged an all-Yugoslav rally in Sarajevo (on July 10), where the antiwar constituency was particularly large. Within weeks, a similar demonstration took place in Skopje, the capital of Macedonia.

No external attention was in fact paid to the republic until December 16, 1991, when EC ministers accepted German chancellor Helmut Kohl's compromise in order to gain recognition for Slovenia and Croatia. The EC agreed to entertain requests for recognition of independence from all the republics within one week. The EC had until then ignored developments in Bosnia-Herzegovina just as it had in Croatia before June 1991. The momentum toward Bosnian independence had been artificially hastened already by the consequences for Bosnia-Herzegovina of Slovene and Croatian independence and by the war in Croatia. Since early September, paramilitary gangs from Serbia had stirred up interethnic conflict in towns of eastern Bosnia such as Bijeljina, Foča, Višegrad, and Bratunac. The war in Croatia had also spilled over its borders, with Croatian paramilitary attacks in the area of Banja Luka in the north of the republic and fighting between the Croatian army and the federal army in villages around Trebinje, in Neum, and in Mostar in the southwest. In preparation for its plan to annex those parts of Bosnia that it claimed as Croatian, the Croatian government was helping to create an army (the Croatian Defense Council, or HVO) among autonomist Croats in western Herzegovina. Autonomist movements of Serbs in the Banja Luka region and subsequently in four other areas, beginning with Serbs around Sarajevo (which they called "Romanija"), also proclaimed regional governments during the fall of 1991.

Apart from the ambitions of nationalists in Croatia and Serbia toward their conationals in Bosnia-Herzegovina, moreover, the Bosnian government had to make a choice when Slovenia and Croatia created independent currencies. Because local authorities in Croatian-majority towns of western Herzegovina adopted the Croatian currency, the Sarajevo government found itself trapped between dependence on a Yugoslav currency that would increasingly be defined by Serbian monetary policy (as the new economic center of a rump Yugoslavia) and the state's virtual economic partition. The alternative would have meant a step toward its own independence by creation of an independent coin.

In October, the delegates of the Croat and Muslim parties in the parliament had allied to declare Bosnian sovereignty, and the Serbian delegation had left the parliament in protest. Villages in eastern Bosnia had been subjected for a month to ethnic violence from terrorist gangs, and the Yugoslav leadership (now dominated by Serbia) urged the UN to send about 400 monitors immediately to the republic. This appeal was repeated frequently during the fall of 1991 by the president of the Bosnian collective presidency, Alija Izetbegović, and ignored just as frequently. In December, Serbia imposed a ban on the exports of foodstuffs to Bosnia, and Croatia banned exports of raw materials and energy, apparently with the aim (whether coordinated or not) of crippling Bosnia to facilitate its partition. But the government response was to prohibit Bosnian firms and individuals from selling to Serbia and Croatia any of a list of essential Bosnian goods (such as coal, lignite, coke, iron, steel, nonferrous metals, principal chemicals, lumber, detergents, cosmetics, foodstuffs, sugar, oil, rock salt, and poultry).[3]

Albeit with some ambivalence, the Sarajevo leadership did attempt during the fall of 1991 and winter 1992 to avoid the fate of Croatia's war with the Yugoslav People's Army (YPA) by negotiating with the military leadership in the republic. But in the face of economic warfare, it had declining resources to make good on the commitments on apartments and pensions it was offering the army and to retain the confidence of the population in the impending struggle over statehood and political allegiance.

Peace negotiators from the EC Hague Conference and the UN were sufficiently aware of the situation in Bosnia to refer to violent consequences for the republic if Germany refused to budge on its intention to recognize Croatia, when they appealed to German foreign minister Hans Dietrich Genscher in early December—a warning against what UN envoy Cyrus Vance, in an uncharacteristically judgmental moment, came to call "Genscher's war"—but to no avail.

In this context, the offer of less than one week to request recognition from the European Community was hardly enough time for the government of Bosnia-Herzegovina (which was already in an unclear constitutional position because of the boycott of the Serb coalition partner) to make so momentous a decision. It could not possibly negotiate differences among politicians, seek compromises, or fully canvass opinion on a decision that should be made by the entire people, not just a portion of the political elite. The remaining two party elements of the government coalition did not even consult with sitting members of parliament from the opposition parties.

Chancellor Kohl's tactical compromise at the EC meeting on recognition was a rapid shift from his government's position toward the Yugoslav conflict—that the most stable outcome (and preferable for Germany) was to create three states in place of one. Kohl had to conceal Germany's patronage of Slovenia and Croatia by conceding that each republic, in theory, had the same right to national self-determination. But this was the very principle (the right of self-determination and therefore secession for each of the three constituent nations) that was being contested in Bosnia-Herzegovina and that would lead to war. Moreover, the EC decision was reached at the same time that the separate activities in Croatia of UN envoy Cyrus Vance were bearing fruit in a negotiated cease-fire. The primary condition of the cease-fire agreement signed November 24, but with details not specified until the military accord of January 2, 1992, was that the federal army withdraw from Croatia. Just as the federal army had been required by the Brioni Agreement to move from Slovenia to Bosnia-Herzegovina, Serbia, and Montenegro, it would now have to retreat further into Bosnia-Herzegovina.

## The Dilemma of National Sovereignty

Of the two problems that most severely beset international efforts to deal with Bosnia-Herzegovina, the principle of national sovereignty in a multinational environment created the greatest damage on the ground and greatest difficulty for negotiators. The choice of the international community would largely sidestep the theoretical and legal problems at issue as it had for a century, substituting other principles and the role of mediator instead of dealing with the problem head on and devising solutions.

### Negotiations as Prelude to Recognition

The EC response to Bosnia's request for recognition was a set of conditions presented in early January 1992 on the advice of the Arbitration

(Badinter) Commission—the panel of judges giving advice on legal matters to the Hague conference, on the request of Slovenia, to arbitrate the disposition of economic assets of a dissolving Yugoslavia. The conditions proposed were based on the same Council of Europe and CSCE principles for European membership being applied at the time to the other republics as well as to the states of central and eastern Europe: constitutional guarantees for human rights and a referendum of citizens on independence (which had not yet been held in the case of Bosnia-Herzegovina). The question was not the viability of the republic as an independent state, which many openly questioned at the time, but democracy.

EC foreign ministers had to be aware by early February 1992 that the Serbian Democratic party (SDS) in Bosnia had declared a boycott of the referendum; that barricades were going up in Mostar and in villages of western Herzegovina; that an explosion on the bridge at Bosanski Šamac had disrupted all transport on the northern border between Croatia and Bosnia; that Serb and Croat refugees from the Croatian war had incited numerous violent clashes with the army or local militia in the republic; and that rapid mobilization for self-defense was occurring in the villages. The decision to recognize Croatia without a previous political settlement on the "Serb question" and on guarantees for Serb rights within the republic not only created a stalemate in Croatia, but also provided no precedent for the place of Serbs in Bosnia-Herzegovina or to counter the goal of the SDS leadership of Radovan Karadžić, Nikola Koljević, and Biljana Plavšić of "not becoming a minority in an independent Bosnia-Herzegovina."

At the same time, the recognition gave Croatian president Tudjman the green light he needed to proceed with the Bosnian part of his national vision. One week after the independence decisions went into effect on January 15–16, 1992, Tudjman staged a coup in the leadership of the Bosnian wing of his Croatian Democratic Union (HDZ), the ruling party of Bosnian Croats, replacing its pro-Bosnian elected head (Stjepan Kljuić) with a Herzegovinian Croat nationalist (Mate Boban).[4] It became clear that the Muslim-Croat alliance favoring Bosnian independence after October 1991 had been for the HDZ only the first step necessary to the separation of "Croatian national territory" from Bosnia-Herzegovina and its annexation by Croatia. By early February, President Izetbegović was making open appeals to citizens of all national identities to resist the nationalist propaganda of those who aimed to divide the population and to heighten social tensions.[5]

The conditionality for recognition would presumably force the EC to turn its attention to the Bosnian internal conflict. Instead, the EC did nothing on Bosnia during January and February, losing an invaluable opportunity for political negotiations. And just as Germany ignored the

Badinter Commission's advice that Croatia did not meet its conditions for recognition, so the EC ignored a crucial ruling by the Commission on Bosnia-Herzegovina—that a vote on independence would be valid only if respectable numbers from all three communities of the republic approved. As it turned out, one-third of the population—the overwhelming majority of one of the constituent nations, the Serbs—refused to vote. On March 1, the second day of the referendum, shots fired at a Serb wedding party as it wound through a Muslim-majority section of central Sarajevo (perhaps because they were waving Serbian flags) killed a member of the wedding party and wounded the Orthodox priest. The atmosphere of tension, anticipation, and probably fear was immediately evident when this shooting sparked incidents in Sarajevo and many towns and barricades went up in neighborhoods and on village roads throughout the republic.[6] On March 3, the rump government declared independence.

As chapter 6 discussed, despite the government request and the referendum, many (including Germany) still had doubts about whether an independent Bosnia-Herzegovina was viable. They sought ways to delay recognition—much as Greece had convinced the EC to delay recognition of Macedonia, although the Badinter Commission had actually judged it (along with Slovenia) ready for immediate recognition. Although the reasoning was different, the EC delay in effect forced a waiting period on independence for Bosnia-Herzegovina—similar to the three-month moratorium on Slovene and Croatian independence contained in the Brioni accord—while negotiations took place. Although some might view this as a breathing space, the delay instead raised uncertainty about the outcome and encouraged all three parties to mobilize for war, as a means to negotiate from a position of strength and prepare to defend territorial claims—a result similar to that of the previous summer in Croatia. Although the EC decision on immediate diplomatic recognition for Slovenia and Croatia in December had abrogated the principle of The Hague conference, that a comprehensive political settlement was necessary, the conference was kept as a framework for separate talks on Bosnia beginning in early February 1992 under the auspices of the EC troika and its current chair, negotiator Cutileiro from Portugal.

But these political negotiations also repeated the earlier pattern. The leaders of the three ethnic political parties that had won the most votes in the 1990 elections, the three ruling parties—the SDA (Party for Democratic Action), SDS, and HDZ—were treated as legitimate interlocutors for all citizens of Bosnia-Herzegovina (to invite others was apparently seen as interference in internal affairs). The objective was to find a political settlement upon which the three party leaderships could agree that would establish Bosnian stability and sovereignty. Thus, instead of establishing a constitution for Bosnia-Herzegovina, or a constituent assembly to write one, or even inviting constitutional experts or other leaders to the talks, the EC negotiators accepted that the internal conflict was ethnically based and that the power-sharing arrangement of the coalition should translate into a triune state in which the three ethnic parties divided territorial control among them.[7] Stjepan Kljuić, president of the Bosnian Croat HDZ (before his resignation in February 1992), had proposed on October 22, 1991, to divide the republic on ethnic criteria.[8] By the time of the Lisbon conference in March 1992, all three parties spoke of ethnic cantonization of the republic into three parts—a "Balkan Switzerland" in the words of SDS leader, Radovan Karadžić.[9]

The obvious problem of cantonization among ethnonational parties, however, was its linkage of ethnicity and national rights to territorial governance and its denial of a separate Bosnian national identity and political representation. The problem was immediately evident in the fact that the primary dispute among the three leaders was over the lines of such a cantonal map.[10] Because the nonethnic parties were not represented in the talks, there was no discussion of rights and identities that could exist independent of territorial administration. Moreover, no attention was apparently paid to the fact that this concept provided no defense against those, such as Croatian and Serbian nationalists, who viewed Bosnia as either Croatian or Serbian territory.[11] As the EC had done for Slovenia and Croatia, the negotiations presumed to be able to find a settlement to Bosnia-Herzegovina independent of the rest of the country—either in defense of Bosnia against external claims or in recognition of the fact that the constituencies of all three governing parties and their national claims did not coincide with the borders of the republic.

The Lisbon agreement was signed on March 18, 1992. Cutileiro's committee appears to have been unaware that the party leaders' acceptance of the principles of the plan did not resolve fundamental differences of opinion about the meaning of cantonization, its implications for Bosnian sovereignty, and its specification in maps.[12] (See figure 9-1.) Whether emboldened by the growing U.S. pressure on Europe for immediate recognition of Bosnian sovereignty, as many argue, by promises of support from Middle Eastern leaders, or by the negative implications of the accord for Bosnia and the Muslim nation, President Izetbegović reneged on his commitment to the document within a week.[13] He was followed by the Croat leader Mate Boban, who saw the opportunity to gain more territory in a new round of negotiations.

The collapse of these talks did not, however, create an opportunity to reconceptualize a political settlement for Bosnia-Herzegovina. By late March the republic was at war. The intention of the Croatian party under Boban to create a separate state of Herzeg-Bosnia that would join Croatia and the disillusionment of the Serb leadership with the collapse of the

FIGURE 9-1. *The EC (Lisbon) Proposal*

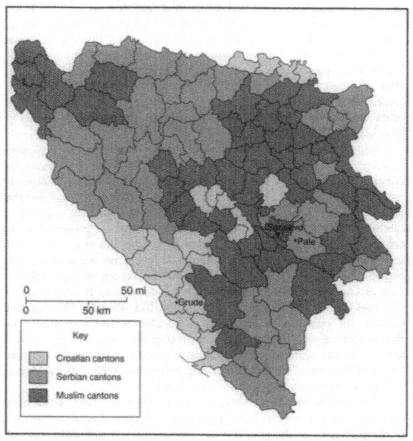

Source: Lee Bryant, "Bosnia-Herzegovina," *WarReport*, November/December 1992, p. 12.

Lisbon Accord led both parties to shift tactics. Territorial control on the battlefield and a media campaign to persuade those at home and abroad that the peoples of Bosnia could not live together, because of fear and hatred, would present the international community with a fait accompli. But more important at the time, these negotiations—like those at The Hague on a comprehensive settlement—were interrupted before their conclusion by another precipitate act of recognition.

### Recognition

This time the decision was the result of a U.S. campaign with its European allies, begun in January 1992 and particularly active in the month of March, to recognize Bosnian sovereignty. But, in line with most actions toward Bosnia-Herzegovina until this point, the purpose had far more to do with Croatia. During the fall of 1991 the United States had resisted German pressure to recognize Croatia, arguing that if one republic was recognized all others should be, if they wished. But the United States lost this fight and thus lost leverage over events in former Yugoslavia. So the United States needed to find a way to recognize Croatia and quiet the Croatian lobby at home without losing face. The solution was to recognize Croatian sovereignty only as a part of a package that granted recognition to the four republics requesting it. In fact, the Bush administration recognized only three, in deference to Greek objections on Macedonia, thus defying its own insistence on equal treatment to excuse its recognition of Croatia, a reversal of principle that it made no effort to defend. Just as the EC countries had reversed their opposition to Germany in December, so their view that recognition for the remaining four republics should be delayed also gave way on April 6, 1992, to American pressure.

This eliminated the last hope of a comprehensive settlement—such as an association of the remaining four Yugoslav states with some confederal relationship with Croatia—that could prevent further war. This, too, was reminiscent of the opportunities rejected at Brioni and again in December 1991.[14] Moreover, the purpose of recognition—in the case of Slovenia and Croatia, for Germany, and in the case of Bosnia-Herzegovina, for the United States—was not to end the violence that had already erupted or to influence the situation in Yugoslavia, but to accede to domestic pressure in support of Croatian sovereignty, to win accolades for their foreign ministers (Genscher and Baker), and to assert power and leadership within the Euro-Atlantic alliance.[15] Therefore, recognition did not bring security guarantees from either country. The German proposal for recognition in July 1991 had been posed as an alternative to sending interposition forces between the warring parties in Croatia, and both countries remained adamantly opposed in April 1992 to military intervention in the Yugoslav conflict. As in the case of Croatia, recognition of Bosnia-Herzegovina was assumed to be a sufficient warning to outsiders not to interfere in Bosnia's sovereign space.

The Lisbon talks had foreclosed options in one direction by assuming the conflict in Bosnia-Herzegovina to be ethnic and then negotiating only with nationalist leaders of ethnonational political parties. The recognition of Bosnian sovereignty before these talks were complete foreclosed options in another direction—by assuming an independent state. Excluded by the actions of outside powers were the range of nonethnic options for Bosnia's internal governance, such as a civil state based on individual rights, and the range of options for incorporation of Bosnian territory into a larger association, such as a new association of some Yugoslav republics or newly configured states for which new territorial borders were drawn through negotiation rather than war. Equally serious, the two options that outside powers did leave open were mutually incompatible.

If it had not been clear before recognition that, of the three parties claiming national rights of self-determination, two wished to join with conationals in neighboring states of the former Yugoslavia and would not accept a sovereign Bosnia-Herzegovina unless their rights of self-determination were *first* guaranteed, then it was clear shortly thereafter. On April 7, 1992, the two representatives of the Serbian party on the Bosnian collective presidency, Biljana Plavšić and Nikola Koljević, resigned. The "assembly of the Serb nation in Bosnia-Herzegovina," composed of the SDS and SPO parliamentarians who had left the parliament in protest at the memorandum on sovereignty in October, proclaimed the independence of a Republic of Serbia of Bosnia-Herzegovina.[16] The same day, the YPA "liberated" the strategic town of Kupres (lying between majority Croatian areas of western Herzegovina and ethnically mixed central Bosnia) from the Croatian army, which had seized it the previous week. Two days before the recognition, on April 4, the Bosnian government issued a general mobilization of national guard and reserve troops saying that it expected a Serb onslaught; the next day, the mobilization was answered by attacks on Sarajevo from the hills. Fighting intensified also in the north around Bosanski Brod, where Serb and Croat villages had united in January to prevent war, and in eastern Bosnia around Bijeljina. On April 10, Jewish organizations began an airlift, evacuating 127 Jewish and 273 non-Jewish refugees on the first flight, followed by 200 to 250 more Jews the same day (of a total population of Jews in Sarajevo in 1992 of approximately 1,000).[17] By April 22 the bridge over the Sava to Croatia at Bosanski Šamac, badly damaged on February 5, was destroyed. The leaders of the Bosnian Serb and Bosnian Croat parties met at Graz May 7 to agree to a cease-fire between them and to negotiate the details and proclaim publicly a pact to divide Bosnia, as agreed secretly the year before by the presidents of Serbia and Croatia, and on July 2, Mate Boban declared the formation of a Croatian state to be called Herzeg-Bosnia, although it had been operating de facto since September–October 1991.

## Civil War or External Aggression?

Recognition of Bosnian sovereignty was an attempt by the West to shut this Pandora's box. Perhaps because the distinction between ethnic and national rights was still lost on outsiders, the granting of independence led them to view the escalation of fighting as a civil war. The Bosnians would be lucky—they were not, it turned out—if this incompatibility between an ethnonational perspective and a Bosnian state led to a stalemate of the kind created in Croatia by the Vance plan for UN-protected areas and international recognition of Croatian sovereignty over this contested territory. Western powers, above all the Americans and British, were even less ready to send ground troops to Bosnia-Herzegovina than they had been to Croatia. And even if they had understood what they had created, it was expedient and in their interest to view the conflict as a civil war. Using arguments applied to Croatia the previous year, that the hostilities were the result of ancient ethnic and religious hatreds unleashed by the end of communist rule, and a problem separate from other areas of the disintegrating country, the West was again able to justify not deploying troops.

Also as an extension of their activities in Croatia, and similar to the parallel tracks of the EC and UN negotiations in Croatia, UN envoys Cyrus Vance and Marrack Goulding had held multiple meetings with leaders in Sarajevo to see whether a cease-fire or political agreement could be reached that would justify sending UN peacekeeping troops. There had been calls from various parties during the fall and winter of 1991—including from the Yugoslav government and Bosnian president Izetbegović—for UN troops to protect the peace in the republic. In fact, as soon as the breakup of Yugoslavia appeared imminent in 1991, knowledgeable Yugoslavs and some Western diplomats and scholars had warned publicly, and made proposals to the responsible authorities, that there would have to be, in such a case, an interim international protectorate for Bosnia-Herzegovina. This could take the form of the state treaty with which the Allied powers protected Austrian integrity and neutrality until 1955, guaranteed therefore by Europeans, or a revival of the UN concept of trusteeship (the more common proposal). Adherents of the idea became more numerous once the war in Bosnia began. They were convinced that only a UN protectorate that would place a bell jar over the republic could save Bosnia's sovereignty, hundreds of thousands of innocent civilians, and Muslim rights of national self-determination. Nonetheless, a new UN secretary general in January 1992, Boutros Boutros-Ghali, accepted the advice of his deputy, Goulding, that conditions were not appropriate to UN involvement in Bosnia. In addition, as he was to make a matter of principle by June, he asserted that conflict management in the post–cold war period should be foremost a responsibility of regional organizations.[18]

The choice instead repeated the choice the Europeans made at Brioni when they sent unarmed monitors to Croatia. The UN chose to place its headquarters for the Croatian peacekeeping mission, the United Nations Protection Forces (UNPROFOR), in Sarajevo as a *symbolic presence* to protect the republic from the spread of war. But even this decision was, in fact, addressed to the situation in Croatia, where UN authorities wanted to distinguish their peacekeeping forces from the EC mission, particularly from the EC's failure to remain neutral. UN staff members and statesmen with long experience at peacekeeping were sharply critical of EC novices who refused to seek UN advice before they attempted peacekeeping work in Yugoslavia. To make clear its commitment to neutrality, the UN would establish headquarters in Bosnia-Herzegovina, but it would have no mandate to act in the republic. These troops only began to arrive in Croatia in March because of delays in putting together the mission that occurred when states did not want to assume the financial obligations.[19] As a result the UN opened shop in Sarajevo not long before the war was full blown. Moreover, the UNPROFOR commander, General Satish Nambiar, actually requested permission to pull out of the city even before the recognition decision of April 6–7 because the administrative and communications headaches he encountered in Sarajevo had proven too great to make the Croatian operation effective.[20] The speed of events and spreading violence instead caught him with a peacekeeping operation in the midst of a war.

As a result, the only foreign personnel on the ground when the war exploded in Bosnia-Herzegovina were international relief organizations—primarily the International Committee of the Red Cross (ICRC) and the United Nations Office of the High Commissioner for Refugees (UNHCR)—and UNPROFOR for the peacekeeping operation in Croatia. By April 28, UNPROFOR was forced to extend humanitarian operations into Bosnia-Herzegovina as a result of the flood of refugees being expelled by the Bosnian Serb campaign in eastern Bosnia. The UN mandate in Croatia provided for the deployment of 100 military observers (UNMOs) from the Croatian theater into Bosnia-Herzegovina as a preventive measure, once demilitarization had been accomplished in Croatia, but the deteriorating conditions made such a precondition unrealistic. On April 30, forty-one military observers were sent to the Mostar region. France urged the EC and the UN to coordinate humanitarian relief and increased pressure during May for more active involvement in assisting the citizens of Sarajevo, who had been under siege from Bosnian Serb heavy artillery in the surrounding hills since April 5.

But neither UNPROFOR, with its peacekeeping mandate, nor the humanitarian organizations were prepared for war. The UNMOs were withdrawn from Mostar on May 14, and UNPROFOR pulled the majority of its headquarters staff from Sarajevo on May 17, leaving behind 120 to lend their good offices toward a cease-fire in Bosnia-Herzegovina. Conditions became so dangerous by May 20 that the ICRC also decided to pull out of Bosnia-Herzegovina.[21] By July 29, the UN High Commissioner for Refugees, Sadako Ogata, was pleading for assistance.

Throughout April and into May, the staff within the office of the UN Secretary General and its office of peacekeeping pushed hard for the resumption of political negotiations over Yugoslavia in the form of a UN-sponsored peace conference at Geneva in June. Their idea was to bring together a wide range of representatives from Yugoslavia and from the major powers (including Russia, which had begun to take a more assertive role in the Yugoslav conflict in response to domestic pressures). They failed, however, to persuade the secretary general. The UN activities remained confined to humanitarian assistance and the principle of noninterference in the internal affairs of a sovereign state under pressure from France, Britain, and the United States—all of which, as in the case of Croatia, preferred to use the UN to avoid greater involvement. At the same time that such action presumed the fighting to be a civil war, however, the United States and the EC simultaneously resumed their position (as they also did in July toward Croatia) that this war was the result of external aggression from Serbia. In addition to international conventions on the rights of sanctuary and humanitarian assistance, therefore, European norms on the inviolability of existing international borders and human rights guarding their collective security had to be protected.

The EC had ended trade sanctions against Serbia along with its recognition of Bosnia on April 6, but warned it would reinstate them if fighting did not cease in Bosnia by April 29. On April 11, the EC told the army to leave the republic and threatened to recall its ambassadors from Belgrade; the United States warned the rump Yugoslavia that it would not be recognized as successor state and would be denied membership in international organizations, such as the IMF and the UN, if the YPA did not leave by the end of the month; and Austria and Hungary proposed expulsion of Yugoslavia (by which they meant Serbia) from the CSCE. Facing a fait accompli, Serbia and Montenegro joined forces alone to create a federal republic of Yugoslavia on April 27. Diplomatic activity continued to seek a political settlement for Bosnia along the dual tracks established for Croatia: the EC held another round of talks in Brussels on March 30 and 31, in Sarajevo on April 12, and in Lisbon at the end of April, while UN secretary general Boutros-Ghali had dispatched Cyrus Vance on April 10 to assist and, on April 29, Marrack Goulding to canvass conditions for peacekeepers.[22] But the United States also appeared to accept the need for political leadership, when Secretary of State Baker called leaders of the EC, Britain, France, Germany, and Portugal on April 15 to discuss ways to end the fighting, but this lasted only until May 4, when the administration retreated because it saw no solution. By the end of the month, the EC had accepted a French proposal to increase collaboration with the UN, humanitarian relief, and negotiating efforts.

Despite the retreat of UNPROFOR headquarters from Sarajevo, the UN Security Council became increasingly assertive in the crisis during May, although it was simultaneously following the lead of France on a humanitarian and negotiating strategy and the lead of the United States and the EC on a strategy to hold Serbia responsible for the war by economic and diplomatic isolation.[23] On May 15, the Security Council gave all parties involved in the war in Bosnia-Herzegovina (in which it included the YPA and the Croatian army) two weeks to end the fighting and ethnic cleansing, cease all foreign assistance, and stop interfering with UN agencies engaged in humanitarian relief.[24] Hoping for more universally binding authority behind the economic sanctions in place, the United States, Britain, and France tried once again to obtain a UN resolution. UN sanctions, like the arms embargo imposed in September 1991 (SCR 713), had to invoke the norms of the UN charter and surmount the reluctance of most states to permit intervention unless there was a clear threat to international peace and security. The granting of UN membership to Croatia and Slovenia on May 18 (Resolutions 753 and 754) and Bosnia-Herzegovina on May 20 (Resolution 755) made this possible. On May 30 the Security Council voted (SCR 757) on the grounds of chapter 7 of the UN charter—a threat to regional and global security—to impose mandatory economic sanctions on the federal republic of Yugoslavia (Serbia and Montenegro) for interference in Bosnia-Herzegovina. By the end of May, Serbia was being transformed into a pariah state, isolated from diplomatic, scientific, sports, and economic exchange until the fighting ceased in Bosnia-Herzegovina.[25]

The same resolution established a security zone around the Sarajevo airport to enable an airlift of humanitarian relief to the city. On the basis of an agreement negotiated by UNPROFOR on June 5 between the Bosnian government and the Bosnian Serbs to withdraw antiaircraft weapons from the airport and to hand control of the airport to the UN for humanitarian purposes, the Security Council voted on June 8 (SCR 758) to redeploy 1,100 UNPROFOR personnel from Croatia to supervise the airport agreement's implementation. It also began to discuss the creation of military escort for humanitarian convoys on the far less expensive overland routes. Almost four months had elapsed between the cease-fire agreement in Croatia and the arrival of peacekeeping troops while the financing and troop commitments were cajoled and extracted from member states. Similarly, these resolutions brought no action until French president François Mitterrand, facing the possibility of defeat on the referendum on the Maastricht Treaty, flew unannounced into the undefended Sarajevo airport on June 28 for a seven-hour visit to the city.[26] The embarrassment to all those responsible for delay succeeded.[27] The next day 300 of the redeployed 1,000 troops (French and Canadian) began what would become an UNPROFOR mission to Bosnia-Herzegovina. Four French planes brought food, bottled water, and medicines to "save Sarajevo" on June 30, and the airport opened to C141s and C130s on July 3.

## The Dilemma of Strategic versus Moral Significance

By May–June 1992, the issue of national sovereignty was beginning to confront Western governments with a dilemma between their assessment of the strategic nonsignificance of Bosnia-Herzegovina and a growing humanitarian crisis that all the world could see. People in all of the Western and Islamic countries engaged were becoming increasingly vocal about the flood of refugees, the massacres, and the attacks on civilian populations being reported in the press and on television. The pressure created by public opinion mounted during the summer of 1992, but was already sufficient to put Bosnia-Herzegovina on the agenda at the annual meetings of the Group of Seven (G-7) economic powers, the Western European Union (WEU), and the CSCE, all being held in July. President Izetbegović and his foreign minister, Haris Silajdžić, made urgent personal appeals at the CSCE meeting at Helsinki for military aid and for the placement of troops along the border of Bosnia-Herzegovina. At the same time, the Bosnian Serbs were asking UN troops to guarantee a cease-fire and to establish a protectorate for Sarajevo.

Although President Bush began to adopt a belligerent tone toward the conflict, he held steadfast to the U.S. position of no intervention, insisting at both CSCE and WEU meetings that those bodies should deliver humanitarian aid "no matter what it takes."[28] The United States was joined by the British in this adamant opposition to sending military force for any other than humanitarian purposes. Rather than denying it had vital interests at stake, as the United States did, however, the British reasoned that this was a civil war and the cycles of animosity and revenge had to be left alone to run their course. As the NATO summit in Oslo on June 4, 1992, had declared, the Euro-Atlantic partners would "not be dragged into the conflict." After multiple failed cease-fire agreements in April and May, moreover, the likelihood that there would be UN peacekeeping troops faded rapidly as the Bosnian government suspended talks, declaring its refusal to negotiate with aggressors and war criminals—the Serbs. On June 20, the Bosnian government declared a "state of war" against the army and the Serbs and six days later signed a military alliance with Croatia. (Less than a week before the July meetings at Helsinki, Bosnian Croats declared independence for their state of Herzeg-Bosnia.)

### Sanctions

The obvious solution to this dilemma of moral pressure without strategic interest—between the major powers' refusal to become militarily involved and the growing pressure for action from domestic publics outraged by their countries' apparent indifference to the particular immorality and injustice of the war—was to impose economic sanctions. Sanctions gave the appearance that governments were taking appropriate action because of their punitive aspect and their response to the portrait of the war developing in the media of ethnic hatred and guilt. Sanctions particularly suited the Bush administration approach to the war—that Serbian president Milošević was responsible and that the appropriate regional security organization for dealing with the Yugoslav crisis was the CSCE. But sanctions also suited the view most often associated with Britain—that this was instead a civil war, and that although little could be done to prevent or stop it, its end could be hastened, by analogy to a wildfire, by depriving it of fuel and ammunition from the outside. In this sense, the sanctions could be seen as a continuation of the policy that motivated the imposition of a generalized arms embargo the previous September.

This capacity of economic sanctions to serve many masters, providing not only an alternative to decisive military action but also the lowest common denominator among competing views of the war, meant that the sanctions also protected major powers from having to formulate a policy for the war's conclusion. The sanctions merely worsened the dilemma regarding national sovereignty by identifying the problem with Serbia and Serbs and by handing its resolution to Milošević. By allowing the major powers to avoid the contradiction between their recognition of the right to national self-determination and their insistence on Bosnian sovereignty, sanctions could hardly be an instrument of policy aimed at ending the war itself.

Thus economic sanctions were said to be a complement to political negotiations. By making it too costly for Milošević to aid the war in Bosnia-Herzegovina, sanctions would compel the Serbs in Bosnia-Herzegovina to agree to a cease-fire and to the republican borders. Certainly, the removal of sanctions from the federal government and their reimposition on Serbia and Montenegro identified clearly which borders the international community considered legitimate international frontiers. But the basic assumption of Europe's negotiations was that the war was an internal conflict that would end when the warring parties reached a political agreement of their own creation on the territorial division of governing rights within the republic. Putting pressure on Serbia and its president contradicted this assumption by viewing the Bosnian Serbs not as independent actors with goals and minds of their own but as puppets of a Belgrade-sponsored aggression to create a Greater Serbia. This in turn seemed to legitimate the Serbian nationalist view that the right to self-determination belonged not to the republics but to the nations, that all Serbs should live in one state if they wished. This underlying ambiguity about national sovereignty became clear later in the course of 1993–94 after multiple rounds of unsuccessful negotiations. The sanctions aimed to overthrow President Milošević and his policy, but negotiators became increasingly dependent on keeping Milošević in power as the primary interlocutor and the primary lever of pressure with the Bosnian Serbs. And their differential treatment of the Croats—such as ignoring the Croatian role in Bosnia and the links between Bosnian Croats and Zagreb—led them to set precedents in rights for Bosnian Croats that they did not intend to offer Bosnian Serbs but had no principle to defend.

In fact, the imposition of sanctions reflected a shift away from the EC approach of political negotiations to the particular crisis in Bosnia-Herzegovina to a CSCE approach to the problem of European security in general preferred by the United States and Germany. The issue was to assert the existence of a community of norms to which states made commitments, enforced by the threat of sanctions against those who deviate. But after winning recognition for Croatia, Germany seemed to abandon the strong stand on norms expressed by Foreign Minister Genscher and adopted a more realist—or national interest–oriented—policy, which aimed to prevent the total isolation of Serbia as a potentially major military power in the Balkans and as a possible gatekeeper of significant stretches of the Danube River, which was so vital to much of Germany's commerce. The United States, therefore, took the lead as the primary proponent of the sanctions regime and of the broader European security approach to the conflict.

For the same reasons that economic sanctions had not had any effect in their intended direction against the federal government in the spring of 1991 and again in the summer, however, this approach to European security and the application of economic and diplomatic sanctions were misplaced, based on faulty assumptions about political behavior when sovereignty itself and membership in Europe were at stake in the conflict. The idea was that Milošević would be forced to change his policy in order to regain international recognition. But the international recognition that the warring party—the Bosnian Serbs—wanted was sovereignty; and this was a condition for membership in the international communities of norms. Until the dissolution of Yugoslavia was complete, assets and debts were distributed, and the new states attained membership in international economic and security organizations, the moral pressure of such membership was tenuous at best.

Moreover, treating Serbia as a pariah state and the Bosnian Serbs as outlaws only reinforced the perception fostered by earlier EC actions and their position on political negotiations: that the Western powers were drawing a new border of European insiders and outsiders through the former Yugoslavia. By ascribing the cause of war to Serbs, regardless of where they lived, the rhetoric of the sanctions appeared to make that European border even more impenetrable and invulnerable to influence by specific behavior than before. And by replacing the instrumental goal of exclusion with a cultural identity of guilt, they were bound to be counterproductive, reinforcing the very loyalties and political appeals they were aiming to deny.

The sanctions regime depended particularly on the behavior of the army, whose interests in Bosnia-Herzegovina were discussed in chapter 8. But it is difficult to see how the general staff would feel bound to uphold Helsinki norms when the state it served (and which was the Helsinki signatory) had ceased to exist. The YPA had not been adopted by the new Yugoslavia; those of its officers who had not gone to their home republic were being further purged by Milošević to create a more malleable instrument. It had already been judged the aggressor for defending the borders of Yugoslavia against rival armies on its soil; it had not been invited into any of the evolving forums for international cooperation or arms control within Europe, or offered any assistance with the difficult task of demobilizing a cold war army and converting defense industries. And while the distinct military advantage of the Bosnian Serbs in heavy artillery had come from the YPA, this was the consequence of the dissolution of the army with each international negotiation on a republic's sovereignty. Most YPA officers, YPA equipment and supplies, and defense industries were not from Serbia but from Bosnia, where they remained after April 1992. One portion formed the new Bosnian Serb army.

As a solution to the problem posed by the dilemma of national sovereignty for Bosnia-Herzegovina, sanctions sent a signal that military gains would not be deterred, and this message was the opposite of what they intended. Their identification of the Serb nation as a political entity rather than as a people living in different states with different political allegiances was the goal of Serb nationalists who insisted on material support to the Bosnian Serbs, the very behavior that the sanctions intended to punish and reverse. The imposition of sanctions on Serbs (in Serbia, Montenegro, and eventually even the *krajina* of Croatia) seemed to concede the very point for which Milošević was most criticized—his claim that it was in the national interest of Serbia to protect Serbs wherever they lived and the antidemocratic motto emblazoned on Serb nationalist banners: "Only unity can save the Serbs." Moreover, the assumption that a different leadership in Serbia would adopt a different policy toward Serbs in Croatia and in Bosnia-Herzegovina misunderstood the nature of nationalism and its loyalties. The sanctions were imposed for behavior that a majority of Serbs themselves saw as both praiseworthy and obligatory, aiding their conationals to survive. Most Serbs, therefore, viewed the sanctions as a punishment rather than as an incentive to change behavior. The behavior of sanctioning countries reinforced this response. The actual criteria for the lifting of sanctions were unclear from the start, and efforts by Milošević to do international bidding, at great political risk, such as pressing the Croatian Serbs and Milan Babić to accept the cease-fire agreed in November 1991 and the Vance plan in January 1992 or the Bosnian Serbs to accept the Vance-Owen plan in spring 1993, received no recognition.[29]

Sanctions, by imposing economic hardship, were intended to create an angry public opinion that would turn against Milošević and demand a change in policy toward Bosnia, or, if necessary, overthrow his rule altogether. But economic hardship had nurtured nationalist sentiments and feelings of being endangered in the first place. Further economic hardship would require individuals to spend more time on daily survival and less on political action. It would reinforce the informal economic networks and social obligations that define ethnicity—family, cousins, godparents—or crime. The sanctions, instead of undermining the sitting regime, increased the power of the government and of Milošević personally, because the resulting supply shortages and inflation (which reached 1 billion percent for Serbia and Montenegro in 1993) required the state to act. In rationing necessities and imposing anti-inflationary restrictions, the government could determine which enterprises would gain subsidies, which workers would therefore become unemployed, and whether farmers, veterans, pensioners, and the army would have income.

While Milošević could be considered to govern within a state defined by the borders of the republic in the Yugoslav federation, this was not a stable state, let alone a functioning democracy. The assumption that people could organize to express their views and vote freely, on the basis of a free flow of information, was also not correct. Even if it had been, there was no clear and uniform message about the reasons for the sanctions, either from those who imposed them or from the state-controlled media in Serbia.

While the sanctions undercut the prospects of democratic and antiwar pressures, they increased the ability of the ruling party and nationalist militants to Milošević's right (those with police connections or the kind of wealth that only criminal networks and sanctions-runners could amass) to control the mass media and to interpret the meaning of the sanctions. The sanctions regime made newspapers prohibitively expensive, reduced the sources of information from outside the country, and cut the funds of opposition forces. Concerned that popular unrest over the sanctions might develop, Milošević added 20,000 men to the police in 1992 and equipped "special units with armored vehicles and helicopters as well as rocket launchers and other weaponry."[30] By 1993, there was one policeman for every seventh person in Serbia. But popular anger could just as easily be directed at the democratic opposition if its anti-Milošević arguments sounded like those of foreign powers; for many apolitical Serbs who might oppose Milošević, the sanctions violated their sense of fair play because other Yugoslavs were also guilty of the charges made. Still other Serbs considered the sanctions just punishment, interpreted in religious terms of shame or guilt, but this required accepting the pain of absolution, not acting politically to get them removed by ousting Milošević.

In fact, the economic elite of Serbia and Montenegro who stayed at home chose to wait out the sanctions, to demand subsidies, or to make huge profits by running the embargo. The vast network of criminals, go-betweens, and bribed officials that sprang up to circumvent the embargo actually gained an interest in keeping the sanctions in place. The consequence was a substantial redistribution of wealth that did not favor those who would oppose the Bosnian war. The reaction of members of the political elite was to believe, as they had in 1986–90, that the primary issue was a matter of persuasion; once the world learned of the truth of their case, the sanctions would be lifted. Realists argued that the sanctions could not last once Europe realized the costs and that some accommodation with the largest power in the Balkans would have to be made. The groups in Serbian society most capable of political action—the urban and professional middle class, particularly in Belgrade, and university students—reacted to the sanctions by leaving the country. In the first year of the sanctions, hundreds of thousands were reported to have emigrated.

For reasons discussed in chapter 10, the sanctions were more likely to exacerbate the causes of war and its escalation and expansion. Even if they did lead the government to reduce support for the Bosnian Serbs over time, their effect would move too slowly to make much difference in the course of the war in Bosnia-Herzegovina.[31] Nor would they have any effect on the external support flowing to other warring parties, such as the Bosnian Croats, who were also supplied with soldiers, arms, and ammunition from outside.[32]

## Containment

Despite persistent arguments in favor of economic sanctions as an alternative to military force, the fact that sanctions do not make an impact quickly makes them particularly inappropriate as an instrument to *stop* a war over national sovereignty—that is, if they are imposed only after the conflict has deteriorated so far as to be a question of territory.

It was not long before the war in Bosnia-Herzegovina had surpassed the worst predictions for its level of violence, speed of escalation, and capacity to spread from one village or city to the next, engulfing the entire republic. By the summer of 1992, there were also revelations of atrocities committed by Serbs in eastern Bosnia—beatings and executions in detention camps, accusations of mass rapes and a network of forced bordellos, killing by mutilation—and Western governments were beginning to feel the heat from citizens and editorialists shocked by the violence.[33] The pressure on governments to act to stop the "humanitarian nightmare," as U.S. secretary of state Baker began to call it as early as April 1992, mounted rapidly as the mass media increased its coverage and as refugees began to flow at a rapid pace into Europe.

The moral pressure did not lead Western governments to alter their view that they had no vital, strategic interests at stake, but they did begin to think in terms of the war spreading to areas where they did have such interests. The role that the republican borders of the Yugoslav federation had played for outsiders in the case of Slovene and Croatian independence—to clarify sides between antagonists and decide which party had sovereign and which had minority rights—was replaced with a new function: that of containment.

Bosnia's fate was a consequence of its interior location at the geopolitical and cultural heart of the former Yugoslavia—cordoned off from Europe by the republics of Croatia and Serbia, with no external border except a tiny outlet to the Adriatic Sea at the cluster of fishing huts, tourist inns, and villas for Sarajevo politicians called Neum—so its war could not spill over *Western* borders. There was still no cause to defend Bosnia's borders with military force, but if war occurred in Kosovo or Macedonia, it would have international implications. A war in these areas could threaten to involve Albania, Bulgaria, Greece, and perhaps Turkey and oblige a NATO response, including intervention between two NATO members. On July 8 the CSCE sent unarmed monitors to the province of Kosovo. Their purpose was to look for signs of escalating tensions and to give notice to President Milošević that Europe was watching. By December 9 the UN secretary general had recommended—on the basis of a request made on November 11 by the government of Macedonia and the report of an assessment team sent November 28—authorization of an UNPROFOR presence along the Macedonian border with Serbia and Albania to monitor conditions and to report any threatening movements.[34]

Of more immediate concern for Europeans, however, was the direct effect the war was beginning to have on them through the flow of refugees. Germany, the primary foreign host, began to demand after mid-July that European countries set quotas for the number of refugees they were willing to accept. This, too, called forth a containment response: to beef up the work of UNHCR and humanitarian relief to keep those displaced by war from becoming refugees. As one of the prime targets of German criticism for not accepting a fair share of refugees, Britain proposed that safe havens for civilians be established within Bosnia-Herzegovina, based on the program designed for the Kurdish population in Iraq after Operation Desert Storm had dramatically worsened their situation. On July 23, the UN high commissioner for refugees, Sadako Ogata, called for a conference in Geneva on July 29 of eight-six countries to obtain pledges to finance aid and refugee work.[35]

Also in the summer of 1992, televised pictures and firsthand accounts of the horrors sought to shock international public opinion into taking a principled stand against the reappearance of genocide in Europe. Congressional hearings elicited accusations of administration callousness from individual members of Congress, at the height of the nominating conventions for the presidential campaign.[36] The U.S. government was particularly influenced by the entrance of its interests and allies in the Middle East. The Organization of the Islamic Conference (OIC) was becoming more vociferous in its condemnation of Western disregard for Muslim victims and its calls to exempt the Bosnian government from the arms embargo and to supply it arms. Moderate states such as Egypt, Turkey, and Saudi Arabia appealed for action, claiming that U.S. inaction was strengthening the position of Islamic fundamentalists in the region.

Still unwilling to alter its fundamental policy against sending soldiers, the United States began to push through resolutions of the UN Security Council to strengthen enforcement of the sanctions on Serbia and Montenegro and to supplement this by helping to defend the Bosnian government indirectly by reducing the military imbalance on the ground that favored the Bosnian Serbs. The United States thus argued for a naval blockade of NATO ships in the Adriatic Sea to tighten enforcement of the embargo on goods arriving at Montenegrin ports and for a no-fly zone against military flights over Bosnian airspace patterned after the one imposed over Iraq after the Desert Storm operation to protect Kurds and Shiite rebels, but with less authority to act. The United States also began to argue for lifting the arms embargo on the Bosnian government on the basis of Article 51 of the UN charter—that a member had a right to self-defense—and for the use of NATO air power to threaten air strikes against Serbian heavy weapons and supply routes.

Although the U.S. approach conflicted with the approach underlying the UN protection forces on the ground—that this was a civil war and the only action that should be taken was to aid the civilian victims—the task of implementing these initiatives was handed to those troops. To the initial UNPROFOR mandate for Bosnia-Herzegovina—to open the Sarajevo airport for humanitarian aid flights and to protect UNHCR convoys with infantry battalions in five separate sectors of the republic, working under peacekeeping rules of engagement—was thus added a monitoring role at airfields (in Bosnia-Herzegovina, Croatia, and the federal republic of Yugoslavia) to implement the "no fly zone" and at 123 crossing points along the Bosnian border to observe violations of the arms embargo and economic sanctions. Alongside the enhanced mandate was a rapid escalation of troop size (authorized by SCR 787 of November 16, 1992) and a dramatic increase in the potential military capacity of those troops with the addition of NATO air assets.

But the effect of these U.S. initiatives was to transform in part the role of sanctions against Serbia and Montenegro into a weapon of quarantine for Bosnia-Herzegovina and to harden the distinction between the "internal conflict" and "Europe." In addition, the expansion of UNPROFOR led to increased reluctance, because of dwindling finances, on the part of Secretary General Boutros-Ghali for UN involvement. Since January 1992, he had balked at more involvement in the Yugoslav conflict, citing the need to save scarce resources for the many relief and peacekeeping needs of poorer countries (Western states cared more for "rich" and "white" Muslims, he complained)—including impending operations in Africa—at a time when the UN was badly strapped for funds because of U.S. nonpayment of dues in a campaign to force UN reform.[37]

The U.S. and the European approaches to the war were now potentially in direct conflict. Countries contributing troops to UNPROFOR in Yugoslavia—particularly France and Britain, both of which had initiated UN involvement and lobbied for more humanitarian action—now had an interest in preventing decisive military engagement in the war because they had troops on the ground that would be at risk. The result was that, from July through November 1992, they objected, stalled, and weakened each resolution being pressed by the United States that involved greater use of military power.[38]

In addition, in Russia, where post-Soviet domestic politics were beginning to take shape, the West's policy of demonizing and punishing Serbia had become the lightning rod around which opposition forces within the Russian parliament would organize their criticism that the Russian government was bending too far to Western economic influence and political pressure. In protesting what they called the world's—and particularly the U.S.—duplicity on human rights when it was a matter of Serbs outside Serbia, the Russian right and nationalist groups actually had in mind the disregard they saw for the human rights of Russians outside Russia, the Western support for Baltic independence without regard for the plight of Russian minorities, and the freedom to change borders if one had the right patron internationally. The symbolic power of the parallel was strong enough to push the Yeltsin government from a "policy in shambles," due to intense factional conflict within foreign policy circles, toward an active policy of abstention and even the threat to veto in the UN Security Council measures that singled out Serbs as aggressors rather than simply as one of three parties in a civil war.[39]

Instead of its sponsors' call for more assertive action to defend the Bosnian government, moreover, the media campaign tended to confirm the war's fratricidal character and to motivate people to distance themselves from it, as much from self-protection as from repulsion at the horrors. Seeking to understand the atrocities, people were drawn to historical novels and historicist journalism on the region, and this added an air of inevitability to the war. Novels by Ivo Andrić (Yugoslavia's only Nobel Prize winner for literature, and a Bosnian), which chronicled atrocities during Ottoman rule, experienced a revival and were taken as evidence that the Bosnian war was "true, Balkan" behavior. Thus the idea that this was a civil war peculiar to Bosnia that should (and could) be contained was further strengthened. Even President Bush and his chairman of the Joint Chiefs of Staff, after six months of pressuring Europeans to act, admitted in separate interviews in September and October 1992 that they had yet to be persuaded that there was any political objective or strategic interest for engagement in the Balkans.[40]

### Bosnians or Muslims?

Perhaps the most tragic and certainly the most consequential result of this developing response by the international community to the Bosnian war was that the world lost sight of the Bosnian people. The monumental confusion over the difference between ethnic and national conflict in the European approach (such as was blatant at the failed talks at Lisbon) was perpetuated by another confusion: the ease with which outsiders seemed not to realize the difference between Bosnians—citizens of the recognized state of Bosnia-Herzegovina, regardless of their ethnic identity—and Muslims—people of one of the republic's three ethnonational communities. The two words became interchangeable for many, although the political meaning of each was quite different and the institutional arrangements for protecting the rights of each group were potentially in conflict. This misunderstanding was compounded by another kind of confusion represented by the equally careless inattention to the distinction between Croats and Bosnian Croats, and that between Serbs and Bosnian Serbs. By emphasizing Bosnian sovereignty and CSCE norms on borders, the United States was in principle in a better position not to make these confusions than those who saw ethnic conflict and civil war. Instead, this focus on the territorial integrity of the state seemed to lose sight of the people who were to occupy this space and the basis of their right to do so. Even those most sympathetic to and supportive of the human lives at stake, the human rights/antigenocide lobby, did little to reduce this confusion or its effects with their rhetoric, without explanation or clarification, calling simultaneously for support of the "Bosnian" president (Izetbegović) and of "Muslim" victims.

The fate of those committed to the idea of Bosnia-Herzegovina (pro-Bosnian Muslims, Croats, and Serbs; people of mixed marriages or parents; people who identified themselves as Bosnians; and those who believed in a nonracial, nonexclusivist, or multiethnic state) was reminiscent of the fate in 1991 of Yugoslav prime minister Marković and the proreform forces. The interruption by Slovene and Croatian independence of internal political development after the first elections of 1990, when ethnic parties won, meant that there was no interested party to propagandize for Bosnia any more than there had been for Yugoslavia. Parties that could claim neutrality on the national question and legitimately defend Bosnian interests without suspicion from a particular national community of favoring the interests of another were minority parties in the opposition and increasingly excluded as such from participation. Although rhetorically committed to Bosnian sovereignty, the international community vacillated on whether to consider President Izetbegović the president of the main Muslim political party (the Party of Democratic Action, SDA) or the president of Bosnia-Herzegovina. They therefore ignored the fact that he was only the rotating chair of the seven-person Bosnian presidency, and they rarely distinguished his actions taken as political party leader from those taken as head of state.

Once the tri-party coalition fell apart (depending on one's view, when either the Croat-Muslim alliance broke it apart or the Serbs defected), there was no politician or party that could represent Bosnian interests, apart from the abstract principle of the government's constitutionality, and that was even more difficult to defend when war required extraordinary measures. But just as with Marković, this defense of a set of institutions rather than a person (the government rather than the government of X), seemed beyond the capacity of major powers and international institutions to understand. Political negotiations assumed the conflict to be "ethnic" and addressed nationalist politicians in their role as political party leaders, not making the distinction between this role and their claim to represent nations (as if all Croats were of the HDZ, all Muslims were of the SDA, and all Serbs were of the SDS). In such talks President Izetbegović was considered to be only one leader of three warring and negotiating parties of equal status. At the very same time, he was treated in all diplomatic relations with the Bosnian government, including all activities by UN forces, as the country's head of state and the representative of all Bosnians.

This conflict between the state and party, its confusion between Bosnian and Muslim, and the eventual equation of the two groups in the minds of many outsiders prevented major participants in the international community from recognizing the incompatibility between the two options that their approach to the conflict had left open: an ethnonational definition of political rights and an independent state of Bosnia-Herzegovina. Instead of attempting to redress the military balance on the ground to ensure a "fair fight," outsiders therefore might have redressed the political and diplomatic imbalance—to which they contributed—of pitting disadvantaged "Bosnians" against nationalists of all sides. Nationalists, who clung to their idea of national survival on a patch of land, had the same advantage as single-issue pressure groups in a democratic system—the ability to mobilize and maintain fierce loyalty around a single cause without having to compromise or take time to build coalitions around multiple interests and abstract principles that characterize most political parties. The idea of "Bosnian" in an outside world that perceived only ethnic conflict and unidimensional concepts of national self-determination was too complex.

The SDA and Muslim nationalists were also in a difficult political position as a result of international decisions to insist on the sanctity of the republican border and on Bosnian integrity, but through action more suited to civil war. The fact that their rights to self-determination as a Muslim nation could not easily be realized except through an integral Bosnia-Herzegovina made their devotion to this goal inevitably suspect in the eyes of nationalist Serbs and Croats. To these groups, the prospect of an integral Bosnia-Herzegovina was a guise for eventual Muslim domination, and they made the most of this in propaganda. It did not help that President Izetbegović was simultaneously the president of the main Muslim political party (the SDA) and treated as the head of state in foreign capitals, or that he had made his political fame with religious activism and had been jailed in 1983 for writings and activities of pan-Islamic sentiment.[41] Once diplomatic negotiations dealt with the leaders of national political parties, the common bond of a single Bosnian language became a liability for these three political communities, and their need for differentiation led ultimately to religion.

The existence of a common language as the prerequisite of a modern nation was not sufficient protection of sovereignty in the Bosnian case. Unlike Slovenes, Albanians, and Macedonians, who could protect and defend their national distinctness from Croatia and Serbia through separate languages, the Bosnians had a language that was an amalgam of Croatian and Serbian, and both scripts—originally, Latin for Catholics and Cyrillic for Orthodox—remained in use. Whereas the Croat-Serb national conflict fine-tuned arguments of linguistic difference, the two nations focused on religion as the basis of their identity in Bosnia-Herzegovina because of the common bond it represented between them and their respective mother states of Croatia and Serbia. And although it was religion—Roman Catholic versus Eastern Orthodox—that largely defined who was Croat or Serb in Bosnia-Herzegovina, they turned this into a common bond of Christianity against a common threat of fundamental Islam (heard frequently in the rhetoric of Tudjman and Milošević), and occasionally even averred to their common historical enemy of Turkey when it was in their interest to ally temporarily against Muslim (or "government") forces. Thus, contrary to those who saw the war in Bosnia-Herzegovina as an extension of the Croat-Serb conflict, secessionist Serbs and Croats had a common interest in playing up the issue of religious identity in order to deny the veracity of President Izetbegović's commitment to a secular Bosnian state, and his claim to represent all Bosnians.[42]

Izetbegović reflected this tension through a damaging inconstancy in speech and action. He and his SDA could never decide what constitutional arrangement would best serve the Muslim nation once Croatia declared independence—an alignment with the federal government in Belgrade, with Zagreb as an independent state and against Bosnian Serbs, or with Serbs in a downsized federal Yugoslavia. They also gave varying impressions of the meaning of Bosnia itself—as a former federal unit of Yugoslavia with a legitimate historical state legacy of its own; as a state of the Muslim nation; or as a convenience on the road to a larger Muslim unit to include areas such as the Sandžak in Serbia and Montenegro, which were numerically majority Muslim areas and one-time Ottoman provinces.[43] This made consistent propaganda difficult, left those who identified themselves as Bosnians without a reliable protector, and allowed the international community to be inconsistent in its approach also.

The political advantage held by domestic nationalists with their simpler and more extreme concept of nationhood had an analog in the international community that also influenced the political direction of the conflict. Early support for the SDA came from religious Islamic countries such as Iran, Pakistan, and Saudi Arabia. Leaders of secular Islamic countries, such as Turkey, found it far more difficult to be effective defenders of Bosnian rights because they were engaged in a war against Islamic fundamentalism at home. They had to respond to popular pressure at home to support Muslim victims of the war and denounce Western callousness without appearing to support a Muslim political party. The simpler ideology of ethnic incompatibility—"we cannot live together"—similarly served the military objectives of both Bosnian Serbs and Bosnian Croats to create territorial enclaves for their nations. Even the theme of the SDA's campaign to gain international military support by arousing moral outrage at the slaughter of innocents undermined its "Bosnian strategy." Because both Bosnian government forces and Muslim paramilitaries had to fight a war on two fronts, they would inevitably have more dead, injured, and displaced. As an indirect result of their larger numbers and as a direct result of Bosnian Serb and Croat policy, Muslim civilians were the most numerous victims of the war. But this judgment also required calculating in ethnic terms and ignoring the many non-Muslims who were also victims. The consequence was that foreign reporters, official investigations, politicians, and human rights organizations expressed outrage at the genocidal policy of the Bosnian Serbs (similar Bosnian Croat tactics were said to be in self-defense) and thus focused attention increasingly on the rights of Muslims, not Bosnians. Those who needed the greatest international support received ever less.

## Repetitive Cycles of International Action

The first half of 1992 had repeated the pattern of 1991. Despite the growing recognition of a need for international leadership toward the Bosnian war, jockeying continued between the United States and the European Community over who should take the lead and with what approach. The United States rhetorically favored Bosnian territorial integrity (as they did Yugoslav territorial integrity the previous year), but it would not commit military force to defend that integrity. It also reverted to the position that the conflict was a European problem. The EC continued to put stock in mediating a political agreement among the parties, but any new initiative introduced after the United States had preempted the Lisbon talks depended on overcoming EC internal disunity and establishing the capacity for a common foreign and strategic policy, the original goal of its mediation efforts. The prevailing view—that the problem lay largely with the absence of leadership—appeared to put any serious action on hold as they awaited turnover of the EC presidency to Britain in June 1992. Many appeared to assume that a British presidency (as a major power) would be more active. In addition, British prime minister Major was said to be in search of a diplomatic victory and British leverage in the Maastricht process of EC integration. The U.S. Congress also resumed pressure on the White House, in light of media reports from the escalating war, to show more leadership against what it called EC ineptitude. The result was the decision to convene a second peace conference to find a comprehensive settlement for the territory of former Yugoslavia.

Despite the sense of urgency in public debate, however, the idea floated for more than a month before it was announced by British foreign secretary Hurd on July 25, and another month passed before it convened in London on August 26–27. British preference for UN involvement—seen first in the discussion of interposition forces for Croatia the previous August as an alternative to French and German proposals to enhance EC foreign and security policy—with its implications for a force separate from NATO and for the balance of power in Europe, combined with behind-the-scenes U.S. pressure to join the forces of the EC and the UN in the joint sponsorship of the conference.

This joint sponsorship provided an opportunity for greater coordination among Western powers and international organizations and a face-

saving shift away from the EC's failure in the previous rounds of negotiations. It did not lead, however, to a change in the underlying flaws in their
approach to the conflict. According to the organizers of the London meeting, the prime accomplishment was its statement of *principles*. But these
principles contained all the contradictions and equivocation on the problem
of national self-determination and the collapse of a state that had characterized Western action during the previous fourteen months. Prime Minister Major emphasized three of the thirteen principles in his closing remarks: 1) to deliver humanitarian aid from the international community,
using armed escorts where necessary; 2) to protect human rights by stopping all violations of humanitarian law, granting humanitarian agencies
immediate access to and then closing detention camps, and warning leaders
that they would be held personally responsible for the commission of war
crimes; and 3) to establish a peace process based on two principles—"that
frontiers cannot be altered by force" but only by mutual consent and
negotiation, and "that within those fixed frontiers minorities are entitled
to full protection and respect to their civil rights . . . whether in Bosnia,
Croatia or Serbia." Major then concluded, "The different former Yugoslav
delegations, and in particular I think those from Serbia and Montenegro,
must ask themselves this question: Do you wish to be considered as part
of Europe? Do you wish to belong to the world community? If so, good,
but that does mean accepting the standards of the rest of Europe and of
the world community."[44]

Western powers thus continued their inconsistent approach to the war:
the London meeting reasserted the international commitment to the sovereignty and territorial integrity of Bosnia-Herzegovina. The principles of
CSCE norms of human rights and inviolable borders were given priority.
Only the presidents of the former Yugoslav republics were seated at the
front table, infuriating SDS leader Radovan Karadžić (among others), who
was shunted into the role of observer. Serbia and Montenegro were condemned. The new peace conference established (in permanent session) at
Geneva in September 1992, the International Conference on the Former
Yugoslavia (ICFY), also resumed negotiations among the ethnonationalist
leaders of the three "warring factions." Insisting that it would be illegitimate interference to "impose a political solution," the conference handed
the task back to those who could not generate one before the wars.[45] The
great public attention to Presidents Tudjman and Milošević, as if the HDZ
and SDS leaders from Bosnia-Herzegovina were under their tutelage,
seemed to contradict the firm declaration of Bosnian independence. The
United States (which was particularly vocal on this matter) and the EC
and the Geneva negotiators repeated that they would support and even help
to enforce *whatever* agreement the parties reached, on the condition that the
parties were sincere and honored agreements signed. The purpose of ne-

gotiations was to end the fighting as quickly as possible, to obtain a cease-fire. And, despite the joining of EC and UN forces, their original division of labor was retained; the use of force would remain under UN auspices, confined to the implementation of agreements and the protection of a humanitarian mission to assist civilians and displaced persons with food and shelter while the war and simultaneous political negotiations played out.

The Geneva conference (the ICFY) revived the Hague conference idea of a comprehensive settlement and created six working groups (including one dedicated to Bosnia-Herzegovina) to that effect. The working group on issues to decide on the disposition of assets and debts among republics remained seated at Brussels, continuing work from the Hague conference, and the working group on ethnic and national communities and minorities focused its attention on Albanians and special status for Kosovo. But, like Lord Carrington before them, conference cochairmen Cyrus Vance and David Owen quickly found themselves preoccupied with the goal of the working group on Bosnia and Herzegovina—to formulate a political agreement that would achieve a lasting cease-fire.[46] By October they had formulated a peace proposal consisting of a constitutional agreement and a map (see figure 9-2).

The Vance-Owen plan for Bosnia-Herzegovina made a heroic effort to move away from the presumption of ethnic partition in the Lisbon Accord and to reconstitute the idea of Bosnian sovereignty. The territory of the republic was laid out into ten provinces, drawn on the basis of geographic and historical criteria as well as the ethnic mix of the local population. The constitution established a power-sharing agreement among the nations on local and central government, and a weak, decentralized state. Formulated by civil servants from the EC and the UN, the constitution drew substantially on the earlier Brussels treaty proposed by Carrington's conference, and the map drew on proposals for ten provinces based on mixed criteria that were made by the Izetbegović-led Bosnian delegation to the London conference.[47] Nonetheless, the negotiators' mandate was still to obtain a cease-fire as rapidly as possible. This meant negotiating with those who commanded armies and who were fighting for national rights—the same three party leaders. By the time of Geneva, groups of Bosnian intellectuals had organized to promote alternative constitutional proposals, but as independents with no military leverage, they could not get a serious hearing.[48]

The incentive for all parties to negotiate from the strength of a military and psychological fait accompli on the ground was even greater after London than it had been after Lisbon. Within days of the London conference, the military alliance between the Bosnian government and Croatia began to break down and officially ended on October 24. The consequences of this were clear by November: Bosnian Croat forces that controlled the

FIGURE 9-2.  *The Vance-Owen Plan*

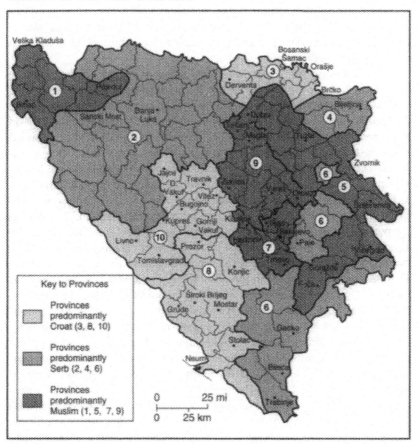

Source: Mladen Klemenčić, *Boundary and Territory Briefing*, vol. 1, no. 2 (International Boundary Research Unit, Department of Geography, University of Durham, United Kingdom, 1994).

main supply route to the Bosnian government were taking a cut of supplies (up to 70 percent) and blocking all arms deliveries. A Bosnian government offensive begun in earnest the same month made inroads against Bosnian Serbs in Sarajevo and eastern Bosnia, and also against Bosnian Croats in central Bosnia. The Bosnian Serbs took the London conference as a final defeat of their hope to negotiate cantonization. The result was that there were no more political restraints on the military plans of General Mladić's Bosnian-Serb army.

Western action was still on its own timetable rather than one adapted to the war on the ground. The U.S. initiatives in the UN Security Council during the summer to toughen sanctions against Serbia and Montenegro and to impose a no-fly zone were not adopted until November. On December 27, 1992, one month before he would leave office, U.S. president Bush informed Serbian president Milošević that if Serbia began a war in Kosovo, the United States would consider it a direct threat to U.S. national interests and would be obliged to act.[49]

The following year, 1993, was a close repeat of 1992. Cochairmen Vance and Owen had good reason to believe in the third week of January that the Bosnian parties would sign their peace plan, and they were encouraged by an EC declaration of support. Bill Clinton, in his campaign for president, had made much of the moral failure of the Bush administration's policy toward defenseless Muslims.[50] Calling it a "process," instead of a "plan," that would be impossible to implement, the United States refused to support the Vance-Owen plan on the grounds that it gave insufficient land to the "Muslims." The U.S. State Department even accused Vance and Owen of "appeasing" the Serbs and demonstrated its lack of confidence by appointing a U.S. envoy to the negotiations to help gain "improvements" in the plan along lines sought by President Izetbegović. To undercut possible Russian obstruction in the UN Security Council in support of Serbs, the United States also insisted that there be a Russian representative to the talks.[51] Like the division of labor between Germany and the United States regarding Croatia and Bosnia-Herzegovina the year before, the effect of this was to favor national interests and bilateral patron-client relations over multilateral initiatives and a norm-based approach.

Moreover, although as a presidential candidate Clinton had appeared to commit his administration to forceful action to defend Muslim victims and end the war, his arrival in Washington ushered in a period of costly delay, similar to the EC's dallying twelve months earlier, as his administration conducted a month-long policy review. This culminated in a reaffirmation, announced on February 10, of his predecessor's approach. Washington's on-again-off-again threat of lifting the arms embargo on the Bosnian government and aiding its struggle with air power against Serb heavy weapons and supply routes was given a label—"lift and strike"— and more effort was to be put into implementing economic sanctions and prosecuting war criminals. The result was a substantial increase in tension between the United States and its European allies, who had thought that a peace plan was near and who continued to object to an escalation of war while they had troops on the ground. The policy also represented what Russia most opposed, reviving the possibility of its veto in the Security Council. To the Clinton administration argument that this policy would level the playing field, British foreign secretary Douglas Hurd retorted that it would "[create a] level killing field."[52] U.S. secretary of state Warren Christopher toured Europe and found support lacking. The United States again retreated and Secretary Christopher replaced talk of Bosnian sovereignty and its status as a symbol of multiethnic coexistence with talk of

Muslim victims and ancient ethnic hatreds. Within a month of announcing a change in policy to make Bosnia "a test case of America's ability to nurture democracy in the post–cold war world," Christopher was describing Bosnia as "an intractable 'problem from hell' that no one can be expected to solve. . . . less as a moral tragedy . . . and more as a tribal feud that no outsider could hope to settle."[53]

Negotiations over the Vance-Owen plan continued during January–May 1993, but they stalled repeatedly over the same problem as in Lisbon: the lines on the map. Breaking the plan down into its parts—the constitutional principles, a peace agreement to cease hostilities, the delineation of provincial boundaries, and an interim constitution—the cochairmen obtained signatures from all three parties on only the constitutional principles. All other parts obtained no more than two signatures, in shifting combinations over the course of three months. But by March 25, the Bosnian government and Bosnian Croats had signed all four documents, while the Bosnian Serbs refused to sign the map and the interim constitution. The solution was to put pressure on the Bosnian Serbs by turning again to President Milošević: if the Bosnian Serbs did not sign by April 26, the sanctions on Serbia and Montenegro would be substantially extended and tightened.

At the same time, the UN Security Council decided on March 31 to strengthen its enforcement of a no-fly zone over Bosnia-Herzegovina, and NATO planes began overflights—Operation Deny Flight—on April 12. The French resuscitated the British proposal of the previous year for safe havens, turning it into an explicit defense of civilians in Muslim-majority towns besieged by Serbian shelling. The occasion arose from the fury of the French commander of UNPROFOR in Bosnia-Herzegovina, General Philippe Morillon, at Bosnian Serbs' violation of a settlement he had negotiated with them to demilitarize the town of Srebrenica in eastern Bosnia. The citizens of Srebrenica were being shelled from outside by Bosnian Serb artillery and at the same time were prevented from leaving by local SDA leaders who feared losing the town if the population fled. The concept of a "safe area," as the safe havens of the Iraqi campaign were renamed, gave international protection under Chapter 7 of the UN charter to specified cities under attack by Serbian artillery. UNPROFOR would supervise the withdrawal of Bosnian Serb military and paramilitary units to create demilitarized areas. This arrangement was first established for Srebrenica by UNSCR 819 of April 16, 1993, and then extended to Sarajevo. On May 6, the UN Security Council (SCR 824) set up four other safe areas for the "Muslim towns" of Tuzla, Žepa, Goražde, and Bihać.

President Milošević also intensified pressure on the Bosnian Serbs. With the assistance of Greek prime minister Mitsotakis, Milošević convened a meeting at Athens on May 1–2 of the ICFY cochairmen and

Yugoslav, Croatian, and Bosnian leaders—Ćosić, Bulatović, Tudjman, Izetbegović, and Karadžić. The direct appeal to Bosnian Serb leader Radovan Karadžić appeared to succeed, and, having obtained his signature to the Vance-Owen plan, the group moved on to a meeting of the Bosnian Serb assembly at Jahorina to ratify it. At this meeting Milošević again made public his support for the plan.

Karadžić had been able to negotiate solo as a political party leader at Lisbon, but a year of war aimed at creating a separate state had transformed the political conditions he had to meet. The assembly of Bosnian Serb delegates to the Bosnian Parliament had been acting as an independent parliament for more than a year; they represented the districts at war to create a Serbian republic. Military victories had substantially strengthened the radicals and made them and the army ever more determined not to compromise on territory. The popularity of General Mladić—now commander of a separate Bosnian Serb army—was on the rise, not only in Serb-held areas of Bosnia and his previous command, the *krajina* of Croatia, but also in Serbia proper. As a former YPA officer trained to view NATO as the enemy, Mladić was beginning to consider the possibility of war against NATO itself because of the U.S. administration's rhetoric and the rising number of UN Security Council resolutions to introduce NATO air power in support of the Bosnian government, defend what it called "Muslim civilians and towns," and redress the military advantage held by Serbs. Despite his ties to Belgrade through officers of the new Yugoslav army, Mladić took the floor of the assembly late at night to speak against the Vance-Owen plan and Milošević's appeal to support it. As a result of this "midnight coup," as it came to be called, against Karadžić and Milošević, the assembly rejected the plan. To preserve his political position, Karadžić proposed that a popular referendum on the plan be held at the end of the month. At the same time, Milošević, who held Karadžić responsible for the assembly's vote, began to withdraw his support and to wage a media campaign to destroy Karadžić's reputation by revealing his expensive habits and gambling addiction. The referendum returned a resounding no.

While the United States continued to push its contradictory approach to the war, putting pressure through sanctions on Milošević to force Bosnian Serbs to sign a peace plan while insisting on a "just" territorial settlement and "leveling the playing field" militarily for the Bosnian government, the Russians argued that the deadlock over the Vance-Owen plan during February–April 1993 was a result of insufficient support by the major powers and its focus on Bosnia-Herzegovina alone. In March 1993, Russian foreign minister Andrei Kozyrev took up the theme of the need for unity among the major powers and global leadership toward the crisis and began to float the idea of a new global conference. In May he called a joint meeting of the UN Security Council and Western foreign ministers in New York to coordinate and devise a new plan of action. The result was to bring the United States back from its other preoccupations in order to prevent Russia from getting "out in front," as the previous administration had referred to its similar response to initiatives by France in 1991 and Germany in 1992. Secretary of State Christopher refused to attend the meeting, inviting foreign ministers from the major troop-contributing countries of UNPROFOR (Britain, France, Spain, and Russia) to Washington instead. One week before the Bosnian Serb referendum, on May 22, Christopher announced a "joint action program" outside UN auspices that was, in effect, a restatement of the U.S. approach. He did, however, also reiterate President Clinton's commitment to send U.S. troops to Bosnia in the event of a peace agreement.

The negative result of the Bosnian Serb referendum saved the U.S. government from sending troops just as a sharp turn for the worse in the humanitarian mission in Somalia was having negative reverberations in Washington that seemed to close the door on any possible action in Bosnia. Within days of the vote, on June 4, the Security Council authorized the use of air power to defend the safe areas; *close air support* from NATO planes would protect UNPROFOR personnel and the threat of NATO *air strikes* in retaliation for any shelling on the safe areas would protect its civilians. The use of air power in turn required deployment of additional troops, which were authorized on June 14 to increase by at least 7,500. Nonetheless, the Bosnian Serbs renewed the bombardment of Sarajevo, and overland aid convoys to the city were blocked by Bosnian Croat offensives in central Bosnia—just as the annual meeting of the G-7 powers convened in Tokyo. While UNPROFOR commanders were already working out the details of the June 4 resolution on safe areas, President Clinton demanded air strikes against Serb forces to "stop the strangulation of Sarajevo." General Morillon, commander of UNPROFOR in Bosnia-Herzegovina, called for NATO to provide close air support to his troops, and in August the North Atlantic Council (NAC) met to approve his request and definitively commit NATO assets to a UN peacekeeping mission.[54]

This steady ratcheting-up of air power—the preferred weapon of the United States—together with the U.S. commitment to contribute troops if a peace agreement were actually signed generated a new source of conflict, however, between the United States and its allies, and between the United States and the UN. Just as in Somalia, the refusal by the United States to subordinate its troops to the command and control of any other country and its pressure for assertive use of NATO air strikes against Bosnian Serbs were direct slaps at the institution of UN peacekeeping and its principles of neutrality and consent. The threat of air strikes also brought the United States into conflict, once again, with its European allies who actually had troops on the ground.[55]

By the third week of May, conference cochairman Owen had acknowledged the failure of the Vance-Owen plan, and he and Norwegian foreign minister Thorwald Stoltenberg (who replaced Cyrus Vance in May) set about negotiating a new plan. The attempt to preserve a sovereign Bosnia-Herzegovina had failed in all but name only. Between June and September a new peace plan was formulated (variously called the Owen-Stoltenberg plan, after the cochairmen, and the Invincible package, after the British battleship on which the revised version was discussed on September 20) that returned to the ethnic principles of Lisbon and divided Bosnia into a confederation of three ethnic states.[56] (See figure 9-3.) Based on a draft written by Croatian president Tudjman and approved by Serbian president Milošević, the plan reflected the military gains of Bosnian Serbs and Bosnian Croats and appeared to confirm the victory of the alternative scenario for Bosnia-Herzegovina looming in the background since the Tudjman-Milošević discussions of July 1990–March 1991 to partition the republic. The state proclaimed by Bosnian Croats—Herzeg-Bosnia—would eventually make official its de facto incorporation into Croatia. The Republic of the Serb People of Bosnia-Herzegovina proclaimed by Bosnian Serbs would presumably join with the federal Yugoslavia of Serbia and Montenegro. The first step toward a state of the whole Serbian nation was usually seen to be union with the Republic of Serbian *Krajina* in Croatia, an intention proclaimed frequently and made official at a meeting in Prijedor, northeastern Bosnia, on October 31, 1992, when the first steps toward unifying armies and currencies were decided. They were voted on in a referendum among *krajina* Serbs on June 19–20, 1993. Yet Karadžić now appeared to abandon the *krajina* Serbs as demanded by President Tudjman so that he could obtain from Croatia the territorial guarantees of access to the sea south of Dubrovnik and a corridor linking Serb-claimed lands through the Croatian Posavina that the Bosnian Serbs considered essential to their own state.

Like the Lisbon agreement, this plan was supported by the Bosnian Serbs and Croats and opposed by the Bosnian government. The Bosnian government focused during the summer of 1993 on securing access to the Adriatic and to the Sava River in the north, through what would become Croatian territory, and on the recovery of (prewar) Muslim-majority towns held by Serbs, but it appeared to have lost hope for a sovereign Bosnia. President Izetbegović finally gave up on his dual role on July 31, 1993. In a radio broadcast of the meeting to the Bosnian population, he announced that the Muslims would now have to fight for territory to ensure their survival as a nation. In August, a separate parliament of Muslim representatives and intellectuals—the *Muslimanski Sabor*—met in

FIGURE 9-3.  *The Owen-Stoltenberg Plan*

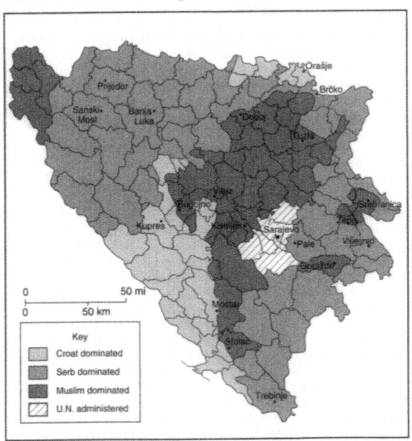

Source: Mladen Klemenčić, *Boundary and Territory Briefing*, vol. 1, no. 2 (International Boundary Research Unit, Department of Geography, University of Durham, United Kingdom, 1994).

Sarajevo to vote on the plan before the remaining members of the Bosnian Parliament convened; the answer was no. On August 30, 1993, the Bosnian government rejected the plan and brought negotiations to a standstill. The Geneva conference cochairmen proposed a new global peace conference for Yugoslavia on the argument that no peace would result until the conflicts in all parts of the former country were settled.

Despite strong evidence that public opinion favored an end to the war, the Izetbegović-Silajdžić leadership insisted it had no choice but to shift from diplomatic to military means and to continue the campaign to reclaim territory lost to Serbs and Croats.[57] With the failure of negotiations during 1993 and simultaneous military gains by Bosnian government and Muslim militia forces, Muslim politicians gave up on their Bosnian identity and began to create a Muslim state, expelling non-Muslims from villages and towns. Muslim schools sprang up to give children religious training, and circles within the government demonstrated increasing radicalism. By October the Sarajevo leadership was engaged in a fierce battle with Muslim autonomists, led by Fikret Abdić in northwestern Bosnia around Cazinska krajina. Abdić had signed a separate peace with Bosnian Serbs. His company, Agrokomerc, and the Croatian government in Zagreb had extensive trade contracts.[58]

The war intensified during the late fall of 1993. The Bosnian army and the Muslim militia were gaining territory against the Bosnian Croat Army (HVO) and expelling Croats in what was an increasingly brutal war in central Bosnia, while the Croatian Army (HV) openly intervened to reverse those gains. At the same time the Bosnian Serbs returned to military means with the failure of the Invincible package, renewing their campaign against Sarajevo and Muslim enclaves in Serb-held areas, such as Tuzla, to achieve the military division of Sarajevo into twin cities (Muslim and Serb) that it had sought diplomatically and to force the Bosnian government into signing a peace plan and ceasing hostilities. Croats continued their merciless siege of Mostar, willfully destroying its sixteenth-century bridge, a symbol of Bosnian unity and culture, on November 9.

At the same time, Western officials were congratulating themselves for success in keeping the Bosnian war contained. Efforts by the ICFY cochairmen to raise the idea again of a global conference for all representatives of the former Yugoslavia and the major Western powers directly engaged in the conflict fell on deaf ears. During November Clinton administration officials declared their policy in Bosnia a success because the media battle had been won: the war was fading from the airwaves.

During November and December 1993, however, two essential elements of the Western approach to the Bosnian war began to unravel. Under increasing pressure from front-line states, particularly Hungary, to relieve the costs of the sanctions to their economies and political stability, the EC began to discuss terms under which sanctions on Serbia and Montenegro might be gradually lifted. With no end to the war and to the UN operation in sight and facing rising attacks on their UNPROFOR soldiers and a seriously deteriorating military situation in Bosnia-Herzegovina, the French and British began threatening to withdraw their troops from Bosnia altogether.

Although the European Union backed down when the United States refused to budge on the sanctions, France began a more consistent campaign to obtain a substantial change on the ground. It pressured the United States to help obtain signatures on a peace agreement to counter the opposition of the Bosnian government, but the United States refused to alter its objections to a plan that the Muslims found unacceptable.[59] The Clinton administration, in fact, showed no interest in resuming engagement in the Bosnia crisis. It was preparing a major policy initiative for eastern European security, the Partnership for Peace, to be unveiled at a NATO summit for January 10–11, and it did not want to dilute the plan with any discussion on Bosnia. Nonetheless, the French insisted on raising the issue. Turning the tables on the United States, France now demanded more assertive use of NATO air strikes; a reticent Clinton replied that it was too late for such action. The French response was to mobilize the UN secretary-general, Boutros-Ghali, persuading him to reverse his position of mid-January and agree by January 26 to permit air strikes to open Tuzla airport and to force a rotation of UN troops in Srebrenica (from Canadian to Dutch) that the Bosnian Serb army was blocking.

By late December, Secretary General Boutros-Ghali had also appointed a senior UN diplomat, Yasushi Akashi, as his special representative for the former Yugoslavia to be in residence as head of UNPROFOR and to provide a diplomatic capacity and policy presence for the mission. The ICFY cochairmen, meanwhile, had shifted to a "two-track" approach: to continue negotiations on the Invincible package with the parties in Bosnia-Herzegovina while seeking to create more options for a peace settlement by "tackling certain problems in the former Yugoslavia together."[60] Contrary to the insistence of the international community that the republican borders of the former country were internationally sacred and that each state was sovereign, they argued that the limits to negotiations within these borders had been reached and instead sought to gain a way out of the deadlocks over some intractable issues by negotiating between republican leaders, such as to provide access to the sea in Croatia for the Bosnian government.

This new ICFY tactic yielded an areawide cease-fire among all three parties in Bosnia-Herzegovina, and also between the Croatian government and *krajina* Serbs—a "Christmas truce"—from December 23, 1993, to January 15, 1994. By mid-January, the cochairmen appeared to have resolved disagreements on all but about 5 percent of contested territory in Bosnia-Herzegovina. A joint declaration between presidents Tudjman and Milošević on January 19 to normalize relations between Croatia and Serbia, negotiated also at Geneva in November, appeared to return the diplomatic task to the hopeful status quo ante of January 1992 in relations between Croatia and *krajina* Serbs. Also in January, a new UNPROFOR commander for Bosnia-Herzegovina, British Lieutenant-General Michael Rose, committed himself to build on the diplomatic progress of his predecessor in Sarajevo, Belgian Lieutenant-General Francis Briquemont, with a "robust" approach to implementing its mandate.

Against this background of mounting impatience in Europe with the war and Serb shelling of Sarajevo, which had resumed serious proportions at the end of December and escalated during January 1994, on the one hand, and the myriad diplomatic endeavors on the ground and in foreign capitals, on the other, came an opportunity in the guise of tragedy on February 6. A 120-millimeter mortar fired into a central market in Sarajevo killed at least 68 people and wounded 197, providing the psychological shock necessary to mobilize diplomatic efforts from many sides.[61] The civilian and military leaders of UNPROFOR in Zagreb—Yasushi Akashi and General Jean Cot, together with General Rose in Sarajevo—began to negotiate a cease-fire for Sarajevo. Aided by a NATO ultimatum to the Bosnian Serb army issued by the North Atlantic Council on February 9 to "end the siege of Sarajevo" by withdrawing, or regrouping under UNPROFOR control, all heavy weapons from an exclusion zone around Sarajevo of twenty kilometers within ten days or be subject immediately to air strikes, the first of three negotiated cease-fires over the next six weeks appeared to create a momentum of peace "from the bottom up."[62] The Sarajevo cease-fire was followed on March 1 by the Washington Framework Agreement, which had been negotiated over the previous six months under U.S. auspices in Vienna on the basis of local initiatives, to create a federation of two states between the Bosnian Muslims and Bosnian Croats on the land they claimed by principle of ethnic majority in 1991.[63] On March 29, ICFY negotiators and the U.S. and Russian ambassadors to Croatia negotiated a total cease-fire between Croatia and the *krajina* Serbs, also on the principle of a demilitarized zone of separation between them monitored by UNPROFOR. During April NATO again threatened to use air power—and for the first time actually carried out two separate bombings—to defend a safe area (in the eastern Bosnian town of Goražde) against Bosnian Serb attack.

These three cease-fires created a momentum toward peace on the basis of coordination at all levels and organizations—from civil and military leaders of UNPROFOR, the joint EU-UN conference cochairmen, diplomats from the United States and Russia, and NATO—and of patient negotiating in foreign capitals and preparation on the ground during the preceding months. Building on the approach to the conflict followed by ICFY since the previous June, the package of cease-fire agreements had created a new political approach. The idea was to create step-by-step, with patient confidence-building and negotiation on the ground, aided by the judicious threat of air strikes, general cease-fires—what SRSG Akashi began to call a "piecemeal peace." The absence of hostilities would provide the first step in a three-step process that would move to economic negotiations, building on mutual interests to restore communications and trade.

On that basis the difficult political negotiations necessary to a final settlement could be confronted.

Nonetheless, from the point of view of Washington, the Washington Agreement was a reversal of this approach and that of ICFY. Its goals were, once again, to adjust the military balance in favor of the Bosnian government against the Bosnian Serbs—by ending the war between Croats and Muslims so that forces could be redeployed fully against the Serbs. With the federation the Bosnian Croats would permit supplies to flow again to the Bosnian government (including weapons and material for the army) along routes they controlled, and joint operations could be encouraged between the HVO and government forces. The agreement also supported the Bosnian government goal of recreating a unified Bosnia-Herzegovina. Symbolizing this victory with a change of names, the Muslim prime minister in the Bosnian government, Haris Silajdžić, took over the label "Bosniak" (in place of Muslim) from the SDA's rival party, the Muslim Bosniaks' Organization (MBO) of Adil Zulfikarpašić.

At the same time, in order to win the support of Croatia, although the agreement was in the military interest of the Bosnian Croats who had begun to lose militarily to the Muslims in central Bosnia and of many Bosnian (as opposed to Herzegovinian) Croats who were actively behind the original idea, the agreement included eventual confederation of this federation with Croatia. According to President Tudjman, there had to be guarantees—provided by an association with mother Croatia—that the Bosnian Croats would survive as a nation. In consequence, if not in policy, therefore, Washington had thus come around to the view of the Lisbon talks and the European nations, lowering its expectations to a de facto acceptance of Bosnia's ethnic partition into a confederation of three states and institutionalizing this outcome in a way that nothing else had. The primary consistency with its earlier positions was in its attitude toward the Bosnian Serbs, for the agreement did not concede the same right of Bosnian Serbs to guarantees for their nationhood by confederation with Serbia.

While providing a welcome cease-fire and the revival of commerce through the opening of routes in areas controlled by the federation, the Washington agreement thus encouraged an intensification of the Bosnian government military offensive during the spring, confirmed General Mladić's interpretation of the NAC decision of August 1993 that Serbs were at war with NATO, and returned negotiations on a peace agreement to the situation that existed before May 1993. Now Bosnian Croats and the Bosnian government were inclined to sign peace plans, and the Bosnian Serbs were again in the opposition. To ward off what appeared to be a death blow to ICFY from U.S. initiatives and to avoid the fate of the Hague conference in December 1991 and the Lisbon negotiations in March

FIGURE 9-4. *The "Contact Group" Plan*

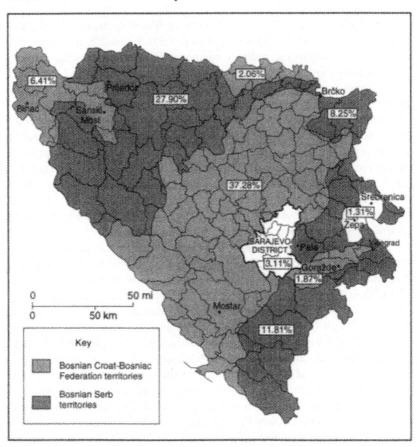

1992, the cochairmen proposed to set up a negotiating group of the major powers—a Contact Group composed of representatives from the United States, Britain, France, Germany, and Russia—to work out the missing ingredient to a general peace, of an agreement between the new Bosniac-Croat federation and the Bosnian Serbs. The UNPROFOR-ICFY momentum of February–March then went on hold until July, while yet another peace proposal was constructed (see figure 9-4).

## Conclusion

This chapter began by identifying two sets of problems that emerged from the international approach to the war in Bosnia-Herzegovina (and the conflicts throughout the former Yugoslavia) and that, in their interaction particularly, help to explain its inadequacy. Those were: a choice of methods to solve the conflict based on a distinction between places that major powers considered of vital national interest or of significance to global security, on the one hand, and those which only justified humanitarian assistance, on the other; and the lack of understanding of the pursuit of national self-determination and its implications for international intervention, which resulted in a constant tension between the view that the war in Bosnia-Herzegovina was a *civil* war among *ethnic* groups and the view that this was a war of aggression by its neighboring republics of Serbia and Montenegro (neither view being correct). These problems reflect above all the application of instruments designed for a different set of problems and a different era—the cold war, in brief—that were not appropriate to this conflict. The paucity of ideas about how to approach the problem and the inadequacy of those first applied out of habit or availability were demonstrated in the increasingly ad hoc character of the international response—trying out elements lifted from other engagements that were considered successful and repeating in one part of the country approaches that were used in another, regardless of the difference or similarity between them and of the success or failure of the first instance.

The experience of attempts to stop the war in Bosnia-Herzegovina in its first two years, from April 1992 to April 1994, suggests three conclusions in particular. One is that the current distinction between humanitarian concerns and security interests and the form of intervention appropriate to each is unsustainable in such wars. At a minimum, such conflicts require an understanding of threats to international security that is different from that which dominated thinking during the cold war. The second is that political negotiations over conflicts of national sovereignty can only produce a complex Cyprusization, when the major powers behind those negotiations are unwilling to define and agree on a policy concerning the right to a state and perceive no vital interest to do anything more than to contain the conflict. The third is the fallacy of containment. Let us examine each briefly.

## The Misplaced Distinction between Humanitarian and Security Interests

The one consistency in international action toward the conflict in Bosnia-Herzegovina was that the interests at stake did not justify military action except in support of humanitarian goals; this included the refusal of the United States to send any soldiers to the ground at all. The overriding objective was to do as much as possible to aid the war's victims and to assist the Office of the UN High Commissioner for Refugees in implementing its global mandate, but without becoming engaged in the war itself. This suited the majority conviction in Europe that this was a civil war in which Europeans should not mix, and it suited the United States, which remained guided throughout its policy shifts by the priority of upholding prevailing norms of European and global security that Yugoslavs should obey (primarily those embodied in the Helsinki Accords concerning borders and human rights) rather than address their problem. But even the interventionists used moral arguments, demanding military action to defend a system of values and a class of "victims." No more than their governments, they never argued the more compelling motives of economic or national interest because that would have required substantial rethinking on all sides to recognize the fundamental security interests for nations, Europe, and the international order in the type of conflict represented by the Bosnian war.

The humanitarian mission undertaken by the thousands of brave peacekeeping forces and staff workers of UNHCR and other humanitarian organizations such as the International Committee of the Red Cross and nongovernmental charities clearly saved lives and assisted in innumerable ways the right to asylum, safe transit, and food and shelter necessary to winter survival of the populations at risk. The question remains, however, whether there was an alternative. Would there have been such a need for this assistance and could even more deaths have been prevented if the political and security issues had been confronted more directly? The course of the war itself was influenced by the presence of a humanitarian mission and this international approach, which makes the counterfactual question even more difficult to answer. But was this the most effective way to approach this conflict?

Whereas the UN peacekeeping forces did not enter Croatia until a cease-fire had been signed and had held for nearly three months, the humanitarian organizations and peacekeeping forces sent to protect them entered Bosnia-Herzegovina in the midst of a war. The very organization that had opposed action during 1991 as interference in the internal affairs of a sovereign state was introduced into the conflict when that state had ceased to exist. The organization most constrained by the norms of sovereignty and neutrality was chosen to deal most immediately with warring parties who were fighting to achieve separate recognition of their own sovereignty and its rights of non-interference within their claimed borders. Peacekeeping principles require neutrality, consent of the parties, and rules of engagement that allow the use of force only in self-defense. These principles were irresistible resources for nationalist leaders aiming to create a state and to gain international recognition. In implementing these principles, the UN organizations on the ground became vehicles of their state-making, in effect not observers but integral parts of the political struggles that included war. This in turn constantly interfered in the ability to implement the UN mandate.

Any humanitarian operation is based on the distinction between civilians and warriors, but civilians in this war were not inadvertently trapped by fighting: they were its intended subject. The humanitarian agencies and the UN force providing them essential protection and assistance were inadvertently trapped into a Hobson's choice between protest to attract international attention and acting the accomplice. Because they were obliged to ensure refugees' right of asylum, for example, they were accused of facilitating the combatants' policies of population transfer or expulsion to create national states that excluded from their territory all those of the wrong ethnicity or those who opposed the policy of ethnically pure areas. The obligation (and prudence) to request consent of a warring party for passage of relief convoys through the territory it controlled left the relief forces little choice but to accept the terms of passage, such as what they could and could not transport and when. Seen as concessions to their opponent, however, this then risked compromising their appearance of neutrality to the other side. Government forces criticized them harshly for assisting the aggressors and war criminals. Others accused them of covertly delivering arms and ammunition to Government forces. In a war to define the populations as well as the territories of new states, any aid to those populations was perceived by the other sides as aiding their enemy.

The rule of consent was at the same time a golden opportunity for each warring party to have its authority over a territory recognized as legitimate. Bosnian Serbs, in part because they had the fewest alternative sources of recognition from an international community that labeled them the aggressors, were particularly inclined to subject UNHCR and UNPROFOR convoys to endless inspections and restrictions on their freedom of movement. More than half of all humanitarian aid went to support the war effort by feeding and supplying soldiers. Control over the distribution of aid was a primary basis of local power; rivals deprived of this source of patronage (not only across ethnonational lines but especially within one camp) could not survive for long. Because supply routes (roads, railroads, and rivers) were among the most important strategic objectives of military offensives, there was a necessary conflict between warring parties and the UN organizations over the control of routes, a conflict between the war and the humanitarian goals.

Performing the tasks of peace in the midst of a war for competing rights to self-determination thus made this UN mission vulnerable to two kinds of criticism for ineffectiveness. On the one hand, the war and the principle of consent limited the freedom of movement without which it could not function—to deliver aid and to report on violations of international conventions, signed cease-fire agreements, and mandated weapons-

exclusion zones. Major powers were not willing to create a peace-enforce-
ment mission, so the mandate could be implemented only to the extent
that the parties gave their consent. On the other hand, the Bosnian government and its SDA leadership expected, because Bosnia was a recognized member state, that the UN should protect its sovereignty against
the Bosnian Serbs. Many Bosnians and Bosnian supporters believed that
the principle of neutrality was totally inappropriate because it assumed a
legal, military, and moral equality between them and the heavily armed
Bosnian Serbs that they did not accept. Simple logic told them that the
UN's neutrality meant it was in fact siding with the Serbs. Explaining the
distinction between a humanitarian mission and one aimed at the defense
of a nation's borders and sovereignty only brought out the incongruity of
such a mission under the circumstances and a cynical response about
fattening lambs for the slaughter.

In responding, through the Security Council, to the real and the
perceived ineffectiveness of the UN mission, the major powers in effect
admitted that part of the problem was their own unwillingness to commit
sufficient military force to implement the principles they proclaimed, for
they added more and more peacekeeping troops and more and more military assets. But this ratcheting up of the meaning of "all necessary means"
applied to the humanitarian goals. It did not alter the other source of the
problem—the major powers' unwillingness to state an objective other than
containment with charity. Their response did nothing to remove the contradictions in the mandate or between the mandate and the nature of the
conflict. Instead, they expressed dissatisfaction by adding more and more
tasks to the original mandate and making it ever more difficult to fulfill.

The most blatant case of the contradiction embedded in most Security
Council resolutions on the conflict was the concept of safe areas. This was
the quintessential humanitarian task in motivation: to protect civilians in
six Muslim-majority towns that were largely within Serbian-held territory
and encircled by Serbian artillery by declaring them demilitarized and
threatening the use of air strikes against those heavy weapons if they fired
into the town. In two cities, Sarajevo and Goražde, this protection was
extended to the creation of weapons-exclusion zones, activating the principle of demilitarization with commitments of NATO air power and operating procedures that delegated to the UNPROFOR commander and
civilian head the authority to call in close air support to defend UN
personnel or air strikes on weapons in violation.

An additional tactic of warfare was thus encouraged. The Bosnian
government turned the safe areas into bases for rest, recuperation, and
resupply of troops within "enemy" territory that it hoped to regain and
for bases from which to fire out of their enclave into Serbian-claimed
territory. The aim of the latter was to provoke Serbian artillery fire to

invoke the use of air power against the Serbs and to use the media attention and test of UN and NATO credibility that safe areas would attract (unlike other cities and towns similarly at risk from shelling by all sides, such as Mostar) to reinforce their propaganda strategy of being the victims of Serb aggression and deserving military assistance. To Bosnian Serbs, the purpose of these enclaves was not humanitarian but strategic, a tactic of the Bosnian Muslim government to gain international protection for pockets of land that would break up into an indefensible patchwork the contiguous territory Serbs claimed in order to deprive them of a viable state. In targeting the safe areas, however, they found an excuse within the humanitarian concept—that if a safe area was not in fact demilitarized but rather an active Bosnian government military installation, they could attack it to provoke international attention. Even if they risked being bombed, they could thereby exert pressure on the UN to create an exclusion zone that would be more likely to demilitarize the area in fact; they could hope to force movement on the diplomatic front to obtain not only a local but a general cease-fire and pressure for a political settlement to end the war that would give them recognition of their statehood; and in the worst case, that of no international attention, they might succeed in expelling the Muslim civilians and taking the territory.

The creation of safe areas, motivated largely by the humanitarian objective, thus made possible an escalation of the war and further exposure of civilians to bombardment. Because the safe areas were created explicitly as havens for Muslim-majority towns and against Bosnian Serb attack, protecting them with air strikes risked compromising the neutrality of the UN mission. The more that air power was used, the more it moved the UN mission toward war against the Bosnian Serbs, risking not only retaliation against its personnel but also a fundamental change in the mandate from a humanitarian to an offensive or enforcement operation that required different rules of engagement and statement of mission. This view was reinforced by the fact that the primary proponent of assertive use of air power, the United States, had no troops on the ground in Bosnia-Herzegovina and held to the view that this was not a civil war but a war of Serbian aggression. But the result was also constant pressure on UNPROFOR officials to activate air power, threatening a shift from decisions that carefully weighed the costs and benefits of a particular air action in relation to the humanitarian tasks throughout the republic and the efforts to bring the war to an end by negotiation and cooperation among the parties to a contest of wills and relative power between NATO and the UN and between the United States and its allies with troops on the ground.[64]

The humanitarian objective of international intervention in Bosnia-Herzegovina also included upholding international and European conventions on humanitarian norms. This goal was a priority for the United States in its approach to the conflict as significant only in terms of broader norms, but it was also the main focus of those actively promoting military intervention on the side of the Bosnian government and of Muslims. It led as well to contradictions in practice as a result of the humanitarian-security distinction. The primary method of defending these norms was transparency: monitoring violations of international law and UN resolutions so as to shame the parties by public attention, or its threat, into observing the norms. But fighting interrupted the freedom of movement necessary for UN military observers or the ICRC to perform this task, whereas no warring party preparing a military offensive or activities that violated the norms would be likely to give consent to observe violations of those norms—expulsions, massacres, rapes—unless they wanted to be seen. Those parties who already had widespread international support were more vulnerable to international opinion but less likely to be exposed, whereas those who were most accused of such atrocities and on whom media attention focused—the Bosnian Serbs in the case of Bosnia-Herzegovina—were far less susceptible because they had little international support to lose or to try to maintain. In fact, the conditions in which publicity and shaming were most likely to have their desired effect (stopping such violation) were those that promoted the outcome the United States and the Bosnian government supporters also opposed—the further creation of states on ethnic bases and the consolidation of power for nationalist leaders, such as when it gave leaders an excuse to dismiss local rivals (as occurred with the exposure of the Bosnian Serb detention camps in summer–fall 1992 and their eventual closing).

The problem lay not in the goals but in the methods. The primary policy was to declare that warring parties and regional leaders obey existing norms regardless of their actual effect on civilian lives or the continuation of war and with little attention to the means necessary to enforce. The recording of numbers of atrocities, artillery and mortar rounds, flights of soldiers and supplies, and deaths was of no use without external action, for the observers themselves did not have the mandate or the rules of engagement to prevent them. The U.S. government pressed for an international war crimes tribunal on the model of Nuremburg, apparently intending that this would deter violations of the Geneva conventions on conduct in war and against genocide by holding leaders accountable for "serious violations of humanitarian law" and would force leaders to negotiate.[65] Many argued that it was one thing to look the other way at a Pol Pot or an Idi Amin, but when the threat of genocide reached Europe, the procedure had to be revived. Otherwise, the world community would lose the instrument itself for lack of legitimacy.[66]

But threats that pushed warriors further into a corner and that increased incentives to create a separate state and the sanctuary inherent in national sovereignty were unlikely to stop the war. Investigations into abuses caused by ethnic cleansing in both Croatia and Bosnia-Herzegovina were taking place at the same time as new, intensified campaigns of forced expulsion and exchange of populations, under cover of cease-fire and military peace. Accusations of war crimes and threats of prosecution after the war against political leaders who claimed to be acting to protect the nation tended to induce fiercer loyalty among their followers rather than rejection. By ignoring this counterproductive result—encouraging the conditions that led to violations—supporters of the War Crimes Tribunal appeared to give priority to defending the norms rather than to preventing conditions that would result in more victims.

A threat depends on its credibility. The fact that the war was in part the result of a process of political disintegration and the destruction of one state and creation of others meant that the conditions for upholding norms without external force did not exist.[67] Political and military leaders unaccountable to a stable legal order are unlikely to have the "paper trail" necessary for legal proceedings.[68] Moreover, because the procedure was pushed largely by the United States, the accusations became a servant of American policy toward the conflict itself, which required a conspiracy of silence about atrocities committed by parties who were not considered aggressors. Such atrocities by Bosnian Croats were acknowledged at Mostar, Stupni Do, and Ahmići. Timed when Bosnian Serb forces were pressing in August 1992 for a political settlement and again in December 1992 when opposition forces in Serbia had realistic hopes of defeating President Milošević in Yugoslav elections, a war crimes prosecution was given priority over the goal of a political settlement. UN envoy Madeleine Albright intensified pressure for the tribunal and its financing during 1993, arguing that the U.S. policy was following two separate tracks, one seeking negotiations and one aiming toward a tribunal. The British insisted that the two were in conflict. The original proponents of a war crimes tribunal, in fact, were antiwar activists within the country (particularly from Belgrade but also from Sarajevo) who believed that a tribunal would interrupt the cycle of revenge that kept the conflict going. It would take the obligation of vengeance out of the hands of local communities and citizens and hand the task of judging and punishing to an international body of neutral, respected professionals, enabling all victims to begin the healing process.

The humanitarian focus was also seriously constrained by its reliance on the categories of victims and victimization. Focusing on the defense of victims instead of on the military or constitutional protections necessary to prevent their victimization created more victims. This was most noticeable, as discussed above, in the American defense of Muslim victims rather than Bosnian sovereignty. Without a nonethnic definition of citizenship, Muslims would lose their claim to an integral state against Croats and Serbs. When the U.S. Congress and the Clinton administration derided the Vance-Owen plan for "appeasing Serbs" and rewarding "land grabs," they withdrew support from the one remaining effort to protect a multiethnic state and to constitute Bosnian integrity. One could not defend Muslims without consistently defending Bosnia as a concept. When the Bosnian army went on the offensive to control or to retake land, foreign support for the Bosnian Muslims waned. When they no longer acted like victims, the basis for defending them was difficult to sustain. Indeed, reports of atrocities and ethnic cleansing by Muslim militia as well seemed to affirm the judgment that military intervention was not wise and that this was in fact a civil war after all.

The most problematic consequence of the focus on humanitarian needs, moral arguments, and the need to uphold universal norms instead of arguments based on vital security interests was the role it gave to the mass media, the most sophisticated weapon of the late twentieth century. Monitoring and recording abuses of norms depended on publicity and media attention. The image of victim, particularly within Europe, was unusually telegenic and was well suited to the "human interest" and (perversely) "entertainment" approach of television news in the 1990s that abhors complexities and emphasizes the fast-moving "sound bite" measured in seconds. The country was far more accessible to journalists and to their audiences than many other places. Twenty-two journalists were killed in the first nine months of the war; four more were missing and presumed dead.[69] The traditional Balkan portrait is of backward peoples, but they are not only fully Europeans but also highly educated in communications technology and sophisticated in its manipulation. Just as nationalist intellectuals and politicians had used the mass media to encourage war at home, they also built it into their external strategies.[70] It was the most successful weapon of the Bosnian government. Whenever attention to Bosnia's plight lagged, the government provoked incidents around Sarajevo and other safe areas. These incidents were immediately reported live by ham radio operators employed by the government. The resulting public pressure was so persistent that even the Bosnian government's most consistent supporters began to complain. In the fall of 1993, for example, members of the U.S. administration berated the dangerous role of the global media in stimulating humanitarian impulses for action that was not in the interest of the United States. The administration referred to this phenomenon as the "CNN curve" of public opinion.[71] "Television images," Secretary of State Warren Christopher told the Senate Foreign Relations Committee, "cannot be the North Star of America's foreign policy."[72]

Classifying action toward Yugoslavia as "humanitarian" did just that. By denying any political or strategic objective, Western governments gave their publics no other option but to pressure policymakers on humane and ethical grounds. But humanitarianism is rarely sufficient motive for sustained political action or effective policy. When the Bosnian war was entering its second winter and citizens had far fewer reserves of fuel and fat than the previous year, European donors had committed only 20 percent of the food and funds necessary for UNHCR to sustain the population— even though UNHCR was there to protect European states from an even greater refugee flow by assisting displaced persons within Yugoslav borders. Because moral outrage is organized within individual countries, cultures, and media networks, it even exacerbated the tendency of Western leaders to address their policies on the Yugoslav crisis toward the attention span of domestic audiences and a voting cycle.

Moreover, this was a false humanitarianism. Channeling moral concerns into humanitarian relief while refusing to confront the political causes of the conflict (both within the country and among foreign powers) was creating more war, more casualties, and more need for humanitarian assistance. The humanitarian approach was only a way for the EC and the United States to avoid defending the choices they had made and defining a political objective in intervening. There was a particular irony, in fact, in the offer of humanitarian aid after Western creditors and leaders had demanded welfare cuts, unemployment, an end to socialist securities, and an absence of safety nets other than land ownership and family protection in the austerity to repay foreign debt and implement economic reform in the 1980s. The cost to the United States alone of military operations to enforce the no-fly zone and economic embargo and to drop aid packages from the air during 1993 was far in excess of $300 million.[73] Bosnian medical doctors criticized UNHCR in the first year of the war for delivering medicines appropriate to diseases and conditions in a third world setting but not to those in Europe. But the organization was transformed by the magnitude of the conflict, and it managed to provide supplies such as orange juice and toiletries that would never be delivered to third world populations.[74] European governments spent fabulous sums on the spectacular evacuations of children for medical care in their capitals when the medical skills were available locally and the repair of damaged equipment would be far less costly.[75]

### Cyprusization?

The delivery of humanitarian assistance was meant to last only as long as it took to achieve a political agreement that would justify a true peacekeeping operation and permit reconstruction. UNHCR depended on voluntary contributions from donor governments for which the high commissioner often had to appeal. After its first twelve-month mandate, the UNPROFOR mandate was never renewed for longer than six months at a time. But the political negotiations, which operated parallel to this intervention (the original division of labor between negotiations and peace-keeping had survived the organizational linkup at Geneva of the EU and the UN), suffered from the unsustainable distinctions in the approach to that intervention. The consequence was to prolong the end of the war and to fill the vacuum with cease-fires that threatened a complex form of Cyprusization.

The primary problem was that the political negotiations were based on the principle of "good offices"—Western leaders repeated frequently that it was up to the people of Bosnia to decide their fate—but that they also intended an outcome (as a principle of European security) that was not neutral. Commitment to the sanctity of the republican borders and to a minority-rights concept of national rights favored some warring parties (in Croatia, the Croatian government, and in Bosnia-Herzegovina, the SDA leadership) over others. Negotiations were also based, however, on the goal of avoiding military action, including peace enforcement. Since Western powers refused to enforce these nonneutral choices, negotiators had to obtain a voluntary agreement among warring parties to commit them to enforce it themselves.[76] The EC and CSCE idea of good offices presumed that the parties could compromise through negotiation, but the negotiators refused to entertain the compromises that might have ended the war in Bosnia sooner and prevented its spread, compromises with their own positions such as exerting pressure on the SDA leadership to negotiate when they did not militarily control land they claimed, redrawing republican borders, or permitting special relations among Serbs caught on different sides of international borders as a guarantee of the security and national rights they sought (the same applies to Croats, but that was conceded by the Washington Agreement in March 1994).

Europeans declared that they would not accept an outcome in Bosnia-Herzegovina that was not coincident with their commitment to pluralism.[77] At the same time, however, they encouraged ethnic partition to avoid military commitment in March 1992 and to obtain a cease-fire—any cease-fire—in the fall and winter of 1993–94. U.S. President Clinton declared for more than a year beginning in January 1993 that the United States would only accept a political agreement that was fair and that the Bosnian government considered just. Even though he continued his predecessor's insistence that no U.S. ground troops be deployed to enforce such an agreement, his policy delayed a settlement because the Bosnian government had no incentive to negotiate any compromise, when the United States offered air strikes against Bosnian Serbs, a lifting of the arms embargo, and covert—and eventually overt—military aid to win back control of all Bosnian territory.

One result of this contradiction between the declared neutrality of the negotiations and the actual choice about admissible and inadmissible outcomes was that negotiations went around in endless circles. Political negotiations could not question the recognized republican borders, while warring parties increasingly created a reality of national territories, including their resident populations. The German policy of recognition to legitimize the republican borders for Croatia in place of interposing troops prevented acknowledgment that states were not yet fully sovereign, that their fates were linked, and that a more rapid end to the war might be reached if territories were negotiable or compensations were required where they were not.

By treating Bosnia-Herzegovina as separable from the rest of the former country, not only were negotiators limited dramatically in their options, but proposals alternated between those that acknowledged the emerging partition on the ground by recognizing three ethnonational entities and those that insisted on denying such entities (at least to the Bosnian Serbs) to recreate an integral Bosnia-Herzegovina. Recognition of the Bosnian Muslim leadership gave it the public relations advantage in its media strategy, but this meant that political negotiations became a part of the media war to put pressure on international public opinion and from there on foreign governments. Geneva negotiators found frequently that the Bosnian government had reached the media with privileged information even before it had briefed the secretary general and the Security Council—making serious negotiating extremely difficult. But all leaders used the negotiations to enhance their own visibility, stature, and authority in power struggles at home, to gain time for military advances, and to consolidate their national political entities rather than a Bosnian state. Signatures were not commitments so much as ways to delay while military forces regrouped and built up their strength and to sway international opinions to one's own side as peacemakers and against one's opponents who did not sign. Since the momentum of negotiations lagged behind the momentum of the military situation, the maps and the constitutional proposals within peace packages were also inevitably behind, based on government goals and the relative bargaining position of the various sides that had prevailed months before. All this made the Geneva process appear ineffectual and undermined the authority of the cochairmen.

The same contradiction undermined the authority of the UN forces on the ground. Two aspects of this contradiction generated the dominant criticism. One was the result of sovereignty norms: was the UN there to protect Croatian and Bosnian sovereignty or to protect the norm of sovereignty through neutrality and consent? The other was the conflict between ends and means arising from the norm of sovereignty: that the UN was not enforcing (or equipped to enforce) the particular outcome approved by the international community. But the actual cause of the declining authority of UN forces was the contradiction in their mandate itself as a result of conflicts among Western powers on the best policy. In Croatia, peacekeeping forces were sent to monitor a cease-fire agreement before Croatia became a member of the UN. That subsequent decision granted Croatia sovereignty over the territory protected by UN forces in direct contradiction to their mandate in the Vance plan to protect the peace "without prejudice to the final political settlement." Although humanitarian assistance and UN protection arrived in Bosnia–Herzegovina after its admission as a UN member state, the mandate also was not to interfere in the political and military conflict but to provide humanitarian aid to all civilians regardless of ethnicity while political negotiations took place elsewhere. Until those political negotiations came to a conclusion or Western powers chose to intervene militarily, the UN would be trapped in contradictory requirements: to give preference to the government of a member state in all political dealings (in practice, the SDA leadership of President Izetbegović) and to give preference to neutrality among the three parties of that government (SDA, HDZ, and SDS).

The contradiction was embedded in all Security Council resolutions after May 20, 1992, which reemphasized the humanitarian mission and principle of consent while simultaneously attempting to support the Bosnian government leadership's fight for sovereignty. It invaded the entire peace process at Geneva under ICFY beginning in September 1992. It led to conflicts and tensions between UNPROFOR and the different forums of major power engagement—the Security Council, the UN Secretariat in New York, and ICFY. Many of the tasks assigned UNPROFOR could not be implemented, in part or in full, because they were contradictory. Limits were imposed on what UNPROFOR could do to promote peace on the ground while political negotiations stalled. Persistent and harsh criticism from the political authorities in Zagreb and Sarajevo for not implementing their expectations of the UN presence combined with popular anger of citizens who were told that the UN forces were there to guarantee their sovereign borders against aggressors contributed to the image of ineffectiveness emanating from the difficulties in Geneva.

Since both these contradictions and the similar ones plaguing the negotiating process contained within them the conflict in interpretations of the war and possible outcomes between the United States and Europe, the repeated attempts of major powers to present a united front toward all warring parties was not in fact able to reduce the tensions between them over a permissible political solution, the best means to terminate the war, and the vulnerability of troops on the ground to the U.S. policy of "lift and strike." The growing frustration of the leaderships in Sarajevo and Zagreb with the presence of UNPROFOR was matched by that of their strongest patron, the United States. The United States, responding to its frustration against UNPROFOR for not taking a more assertive posture against the Bosnian (and Croatian) Serbs, increasingly criticized its civilian head, Yasushi Akashi, and UN peacekeeping in general.

Outsiders insisted that they could do little other than assist civilian victims while the conflict played itself out. Yet the continuing delays at the bargaining table and limitations on the ability of UNPROFOR to implement cease-fire and demilitarization agreements to the letter led to a growing impatience at the cost of the UN operation. This was the costliest peacekeeping operation in UN history, as well as the largest—its annual budget of $1.6–1.9 billion was almost half the entire peacekeeping budget of the UN.[78] The priority on containment also encouraged impatience because it seemed that the longer the war continued, the greater was the risk that it would spread. Impatience became the defining factor in negotiations, rather than the goal of achieving a realizable outcome. The warring parties were increasingly under pressure to sign a peace agreement— by July 1994, the Contact Group peace proposal made a take-it-or-leave-it demand of the Bosnian Serbs—rather than to change their approach. Moreover, this toughened bargaining stance on the part of the international community conveyed a lingering doubt about U.S. support, since that would require President Clinton to follow through on his commitment to send ground troops to implement a true peace agreement.

As a result of the various limitations on a political settlement, negotiators from ICFY and in UNPROFOR returned time and again to the more limited objective of achieving cease-fires. They made the reasonable assumption that as long as there were active hostilities, the conditions for a settlement would continue to deteriorate. Bilateral agreements were far easier to negotiate than the multilateral deals necessary for the republic, as were cease-fires that froze territorial gains without acknowledging political rights. Localized cease-fires in particular did not have to prejudice the overall outcome, and local security interests were not always the same as those of the republican or federal government.

UNPROFOR officials thus began to focus on building a peace, piecemeal, "from the bottom up," which created stalemates on the political issues and allowed each side to buy time to further its goals, but which also provided conditions in which mutual interests might redevelop. But for all their benefits, such cease-fires are bought at the price of frozen lines of confrontation, partial but unlegitimized autonomies, and a continuing sense of personal insecurity that the absence of a comprehensive political agreement on territory and sovereignty would bring a resumption of hostilities and the use of military force to hold, take, or regain territory if the cease-fire broke down. Because they are technically created by drawing lines of separation and interposing peacekeeping troops in place of heavy weapons between warring parties, they recognize and protect the ethnic partition sought by national armies. Far from stopping the process of ethnic cleansing, they facilitate a more silent, less violent form of population exchange, providing the occasion for completion of the goal of ethnically pure territories, as illustrated by one of the effects of the Washington Agreement between Bosnian Croats and Bosniacs. The partition being negotiated at Geneva in August 1993 had been expected to require resettlement of nearly 1 million persons.[79] And because such cease-fires reflect the absence of political agreement and of alternatives to a territorial division, like Cyprus, they can institutionalize the presence of UN peacekeepers for a very long time.

## The Fallacy of Containment

The international community had two reasons to insist on the territorial integrity of Bosnia and Herzegovina. One was to protect European security and stability by protecting the Helsinki norm on existing borders. The other was containment. Allowing the partition of Bosnia-Herzegovina would only open the door to a domino effect and raise the likelihood of war in adjoining areas. It would raise more questions about borders than it resolved and would double the number and effect of refugees and displaced persons.

For example, if Bosnian Serbs could create a national state and international negotiations could recognize the principle, what legitimacy did Milošević's claims that Kosovo and Vojvodina were parts of Serbia have? What principle would restrain radical forces on both sides of the national conflicts in each region (Serbs for republican boundaries, Albanians or Hungarians for independence) from war?[80] Many in Serbia had been arguing for some years that the only solution to Kosovo was its partition, giving to Serbia the areas of historical significance—such as the main Byzantine monasteries, the Peć archbishopric (center of the Serbian Orthodox Church), and the Kosovo Polje (where the Serbian medieval kingdom went down to defeat by the Ottoman Turks)—and leaving the rest to Albanians. The idea had grown in stature from a suggestion given little serious attention in 1991 to the most realistic outcome by late 1993. But the process of applying this Solomonic choice to Kosovo could be at least as bloody and contested as the partition of Bosnia-Herzegovina—unless negotiators took it in hand explicitly to manage, renouncing their previous position on borders, and than confronted its possible consequences for the territorial integrity and stability of Macedonia.

If President Tudjman could participate in dividing Bosnia and incorporate territories of Bosnia and Herzegovina into Croatia, what claim did he have to the lands in Croatia held by the Serbian minority, which remained militantly opposed to citizenship in Croatia? The Owen-Stoltenberg plan elicited an immediate outcry from five main opposition parties in Croatia, which joined forces in August for that purpose and published a declaration on August 27.[81] They decried the plan as "collusion" with Serbian president Milošević, damaging to Croatia's image abroad, and a threat to the territorial integrity of Croatia. Even a large faction of Tudjman's ruling party, the CDU, supported the declaration. By mid-April 1994, this faction had formed a new party, the Croatian Independent Democrats, in protest at Tudjman's Bosnia policy.

Moreover, if a greater Croatia and greater Serbia could be negotiated between these two leaders, on the basis of the bloodiest forms of forced population movement, what was to stand in the way of greater Albania, greater Hungary, and so forth? What was to prevent the partition of Macedonia among Albania, Bulgaria (for which Macedonians are actually Bulgarians), and Greece, with Serbia stepping in to take a piece?[82]

At the same time, the constraints on finding a political solution of this commitment to the republican borders of Bosnia-Herzegovina discussed above had led through military fait accompli to the internal partition of the republic into three nationally exclusive ministates. This included the right to secede agreed by the parties to the Owen-Stoltenberg (Invincible) plan, and the right to confederate with Croatia for Croats in the Washington Agreement. The ICFY cochairmen, moreover, acknowledged that they had come closest to a territorial settlement on the infamous maps in December 1993–January 1994 when they had abandoned the straitjacket of republican borders and reached for bargaining leverage by negotiating tradeoffs with neighboring republics. The interconnectedness of the battles and principles at stake and the futility of treating each former republic in isolation were even more vivid to the commanders of UNPROFOR. Despite UNPROFOR's division into three separate commands—Croatia, Bosnia-Herzegovina, and FYROM (former Yugoslav Republic of Macedonia)—the commanders understood that Croatia and Bosnia-Herzegovina were one theater of war. This was particularly clear in the strategic pockets and political alliances that overlapped borders in the Bihać area of northwestern Bosnia bordering the UN protected zones and Croatia; the strategic split of the Prevlaka peninsula bordering Montenegro and Croatia; the Drina valley dividing Serbia from territory claimed by Bosnian Serbs; or the Posavina corridor dividing Croatia from areas of Bosnian Croat population and ethnically mixed towns through which ran the primary route needed to connect Serb areas in Bosnia-Herzegovina, Croatia, and Serbia.[83] In the third week of January 1993, the ICFY cochairmen Cyrus Vance and David Owen were hopeful that signatures on their peace plan for Bosnia-Herzegovina were only a matter of days away. These expectations were precipitously dashed when the negotiations unraveled as a result of the military incursion at Maslenica, Zemunik, Peruča, and the surrounding area in Croatia on January 22. The response of the SDA leadership, particularly President Izetbegović, to the July 1993 proposal to partition Bosnia-Herzegovina into three states was to seek to expand. Having lost their project of a Bosnian state and concerned about the strategic and economic viability of their "piece," they began to assert that the Muslim-majority area of the Sandžak in Serbia and Montenegro had originally been part of Bosnia and that they would seek, either militarily or politically, to link up with it.

If the principles of transparency and internationally declared borders, implemented by unarmed or lightly armed monitors, were insufficient to prevent the war from spreading to Croatia and then to Bosnia-Herzegovina, what would make them work in Kosovo and Macedonia? The official answer was that these warnings were accompanied by economic and diplomatic sanctions against Serbia and Montenegro and that, although they had not seemed to stop the wars in Croatia and Bosnia-Herzegovina, this was because the sanctions had needed time to work. By July 1994, the diplomatic efforts of the newly created Contact Group to end the war in Bosnia-Herzegovina by imposing a peace proposal on the Bosnian Serbs came to depend entirely on the ability of President Milošević to isolate the Bosnian Serbs in exchange for a gradual lifting of the sanctions.[84] Act one, in the Washington Agreement between the Bosnian government and Bosnian Croats, similarly centered on support from President Tudjman to exert pressure on Bosnian Croats. The question remained whether this diplomatic strategy to use the leverage of the two presidents would bring a settlement or whether it would only keep alive the national bases of political formations that were being created in the Balkans. Accepting that there was no legitimate reason to deny to the Bosnian Serbs the same right granted Bosnian Croats to confederate with Croatia, French foreign minister Alain Juppé publicly contradicted the U.S. policy in early September 1994. The result, however, was an immediate announcement by the elected president of the Kosovo Albanians, Ibrahim Rugova, that they too, therefore, had the right to confederate with Albania.[85]

The policy of containment had allowed the major powers to ignore the political questions at stake, but if they did not confront these issues directly and seek solutions that transformed incompatible goals into acceptable compromises and provided security guarantees for individuals and nations instead of for states, the conflict could not be contained.

# Chapter 10

# The Dynamic of Disintegration and Nationalist War

F ew inside or outside Yugoslavia had believed the dire predictions in 1990 or earlier that the country would disintegrate in bloodshed, or even the forecasts in 1991 that violence would spread. The European Community mediators and foreign ministers from the more active states such as Germany and Austria assumed that they could negotiate Slovene and Croatian independence with minimal violence, leaving the rest of the country to form a rump Yugoslavia. There would thus be three states where there had been one. In July 1991 many people in Yugoslavia also believed this would happen.

Even in February 1992 many in Sarajevo could not conceive of war in Bosnia-Herzegovina. They saw no will to war, and they felt protected by the complete intertwining of the lives of individuals from different national communities and by the multicultural tradition that defined Bosnian culture. The same refrain—"it can't happen here; we've lived together forever"—could be heard during 1992–93 among leaders of multiethnic states in the former Soviet Union. The Soviet Union had also dissolved in spite of the conviction in Western capitals during 1991 that the policy signals that they were sending from the Yugoslav case would be enough to prevent the breakup.

This failure to predict and to prevent was a failure to understand the real causes of the wars. The views underlying Western policy toward Bosnia-Herzegovina, as discussed in chapter 9, made this worse. One view was that this was a civil war, ingrained in the history and temperament of the Balkans, particularly Bosnia, and inclining its populations inevitably toward ethnic conflict and war over territory whenever an imperial or dictatorial protection collapsed. The other explanation—expansionist aggression by a revanchist Serbia—accused leaders in Serbia (often only President Slobodan Milošević) of having a deliberate plan to annex territory where Serbs lived and create a Greater Serbia. According to this view war would break out in these areas as military opportunity arose, independent of other national projects in the area.

The first view led to a policy of containment, aimed at keeping the war from spreading over Bosnian borders. But the longer the war went on, the more the "ethnic" assumption became a self-fulfilling prophecy: three separate national states were being created. Negotiators increasingly had to look beyond the republican borders of Bosnia-Herzegovina to find a political solution to the territorial conflict. The second view was based on the assumption that the Serbian military machine would move to Kosovo or Macedonia when the war in Bosnia-Herzegovina ended.[1] The response in this case aimed at prevention through the deployment of Conference on Security and Cooperation in Europe (CSCE) monitors to Kosovo, issuance of a warning against Serbian military action in Kosovo from two U.S. presidents, and the deployment of UN peacekeeping soldiers as monitors along the border between Serbia and Macedonia.

But none of these actions addressed the delicate and unstable cease-fire in Croatia and the continuing threat that war would resume there. Nor did they address the increasing internal instability of Macedonia, exacerbated by pressures from all four neighbors, above all Greece.[2] In fact, if either of these explanations had been sufficient for Bosnia-Herzegovina, no one would have been unprepared or surprised when war occurred. The great and understandable concern with whether the war in Bosnia-Herzegovina would spread could not be answered without reverting to the causes of war and to the particular political dynamic of unchecked nationalism. The same factors were operating in 1994 as in 1991—only they had intensified.

First, the borders and the sovereignty of states succeeding the former Yugoslavia had not been settled, with the exception of Slovenia. The international community was helping to prolong the insecurity by not noticing the difference between the right of republics and the right of nations to a state and through its unwillingness to defend militarily its choice of republican borders. The Serbian leadership in Belgrade was only one of the participants aiming to create national states in a territory that was nationally mixed and contested. Nor were the Serbs as unified as their slogan proclaimed.[3] In conflict with the idea of containment, moreover, all national claims to territory in the region overlapped.

Second, the areas that first achieved independence had greater economic and political resources to maneuver this process than those left hanging when their common state collapsed. The latter were already less prepared for independent political and economic life and faced greater economic difficulties and insecurity as a result of their new environment of war, interrupted trade, and challenges to their sovereignty.

Third, the conditions leading to ever greater internal instability and a radicalization of demands for political autonomy, and then sovereignty, were growing rather than diminishing. Parties to specific conflicts became more stubborn as they paid the costs of war but did not achieve their original political goals. Proponents of exclusivist, territorial nationalism increasingly prevailed against political ideas and groups whose goals might have been achievable without war.

The longer war continued, moreover, the more present in the region were factors that fed it—refugees, arms, youth unemployment, and economic decline. In place of a system of law and order that would counteract the insecurity, distrust, and resort to arms that had made war possible, entire networks of criminals, sanctions-busters, war profiteers, gun runners, gangs, and local paramilitaries arose. Even as populations tired of war, more and more people had a vested interest in its continuation.

The wars were part of a process that had begun with economic reform and constitutional conflict. Its metamorphosis into nationalist politics and focus on territory had depended on the interaction of many other factors. Nonetheless the process itself had the tendency to escalate rapidly from small events or confrontations that triggered a chain reaction of responses in the prevailing conditions of extreme insecurity and nationalist rhetoric.

One cause of this process of escalation was the interaction between competing nationalisms. The character of exclusive nationalism is that it lives off antagonism to other nations. Interaction and defensive perceptions on all sides, as discussed in chapter 7, keep it alive. But this tendency to escalate was also fed by political competition within national communities and by the vacuum of civil order created by the process of forming new states. Uncontrolled and rebel elements were not only free to develop but could be encouraged in this political free-for-all, while individuals took actions to defend themselves that would not have been necessary in an established system. The choices of international action were particularly influential in feeding this escalation, for they tended to reinforce rather than to dampen the conditions and opportunities that had led to war. War did not need inexorably to continue or to spread to new areas, but the political leadership necessary both at home and internationally to prevent that from happening continued to be absent.

The world's focus on the war in Bosnia and containing it there tended to lose sight of the more general phenomenon from which it was inseparable. The trend of further radicalization and disintegration would continue until the causes of the conflict were confronted and its path reversed.

## Overlapping Claims to Territory

The mixture of rights that defined national self-determination in the Yugoslav constitution was written to avoid a unidimensional association of those rights with territory. With the breakup of the state on the basis of national self-determination, political action did not focus on transforming the rights of the socialist system to rights associated with private property, free enterprise, civil rights, and competitive political regimes, but on national sovereignty. This focus on statehood and territory, however, had no national limits—no point at which it could stabilize—because all the human issues at stake overlapped the borders of the federal units—national identities, sympathies and moral obligations, political party constituencies, productive activities, and legitimate claims to territory. Western powers were flying in the face of reality when they insisted that the republican borders were international borders. Outsiders' declarations, without force to back them up, that these borders were sacrosanct were not sufficient— not only for some Serbs, but also for some Croats, Albanians, Muslims, and possibly others.[4]

The primary difficulty lay with the identification of nations with territory, since national claims to territory overlapped each other in current population settlements and in layers of historical states. The borders of a Croatian national state and of a Serbian national state were broader than their republic borders, although these broader borders were also opposed by some political parties within each nation. The partition of Bosnia-Herzegovina into three national states, even if nominally in one federal union, opened the way to the expansion of Muslim claims to a national state. President Alija Izetbegović and Vice-President Ejup Ganić openly demanded during 1994 the creation of such a state, to include Muslim-majority areas in the Sandžak region, which overlapped the border between Serbia and Montenegro. Albanians in Kosovo had sought a separate republic in the 1980s, but with the breakup of Yugoslavia they aimed to secede and to join up with neighboring Albanians in Albania and in towns and villages of western Macedonia, where they formed the majority ethnic group. Just as the Serbian question cut across three republics—Serbia, Croatia, and Bosnia-Herzegovina—the Albanian question hung like a sword of Damocles over Serbia, Macedonia, Montenegro, Albania, and, potentially, Greece. The territory of Macedonia was claimed by not three nations, but four. The scenario of Serbian aggression guiding Western preventive diplomacy had no territorial justification in Macedonia, where the community of Serbs numbered 2 to 4 percent of the population and had had only a fleeting flirtation with autonomy. But the Federal Republic of Yugoslavia (Serbia and Montenegro) continued to insist into 1995 that the borders of Macedonia were only administrative borders, and Greece continued to refuse to recognize Macedonian statehood.[5] Any attempt to partition Macedonia or an internal explosion of ethnic violence could cause another war. If such violence involved the Albanian community, war could begin in Macedonia and spread to Kosovo, instead of the opposite scenario that had led to the deployment of UN troops.[6]

The lack of coincidence between borders and nations applies to moral communities as well. When states are stable and borders unchallenged, outsiders recognize the rights of sovereignty, which include the right to noninterference in a state's internal affairs. But when sovereignty is contested, law has collapsed, and civil order comes to depend on informal obligations, then the juridical borders do not confine those obligations. The threat of war's spreading from one region to another within Yugoslavia and then across its borders included the unplanned consequences of a largely spontaneous process of national identification.

This potentially uncontrollable psychological mechanism derives from the culture of nationalism. National identities define political loyalties and, even more profoundly, moral obligations. Violence against conationals in a neighboring state or province arouses sympathy and requires response. The essence of an ethnic or national bond is its moral obligation to protect, defend, and avenge kin. Where the culture of collective security is defined by this norm, the public pressure on other governments to act cannot be easily deflected, and armed volunteers may rush to take matters into their hands. At the same time governments can more easily mobilize citizens for war if they can make the case that it is in defense of "their people."

In Kosovo province, serious violence of any origin threatens to embroil the government of Albania, where public sympathy for Kosovar Albanians had reached fever pitch by the summer of 1991. The new president of Albania (who happened to be from a village near the Kosovo border) was already inclined to use nationalist arguments for popular support in his nascent democracy. Three years later, economic hardship in Albania and its citizens' poverty relative to that of Albanians in Kosovo had dampened this sympathy. Yet Albanians also admitted that if fighting occurred, or if their government declared Kosovars in danger, they would have no choice but to respond. This was even more the case for Albanians in western Macedonia, who had both family and political ties to Kosovar Albanians. Their stockpiling of weapons for "communal self-defense" in the early days after Macedonian independence, however, became an increasing point of conflict with the Macedonian government. By mid-1994 criminal charges of arms smuggling and forming a paramilitary organization had been filed involving members (including a former general secretary and two deputy ministers, one for health, the other for defense) of the moderate branch of the largest Macedonian Albanian party. Convictions in the arms scandal, as it was called in the blowup this caused, led to unusually long prison sentences.[7] But even the 25,214 Bulgarians living in Serbia, scarcely .3 percent of the population, began defensive self-organization in 1992 with calls to the government of Bulgaria for protection against the possibility of discrimination.

One defining element of national identity in this region is religion, which is the basis for the old idea of Yugoslavia as a crossroads—regimes representing three of the world's major religions confronted each other territorially in the Balkans in the periods of Byzantine, Ottoman, and Habsburg rule. The mechanism of sympathetic response can therefore spread even more widely afield among people who identify with the same faith. The global networks of religious organizations and the prominent role of propaganda and mass media in nationalist warfare move this process rapidly. Thus the view spread by belligerents and onlookers alike that the conflict in Bosnia-Herzegovina was a war of religion (and that this would also be the case if war erupted in Kosovo and Macedonia) was an open invitation to volunteers of *mujahedin*, who joined the battles of Bosnian Muslims within five months of their start.[8] The Organization of the Islamic Conference was actively involved in the conflict, particularly in formulating resolutions in the UN Security Council and convening debates in the UN General Assembly, and arms, monies, and supplies flowed from Muslim countries such as Iran, Pakistan, and Saudi Arabia. In January 1993 a prominent Muslim cleric of Saudi Arabia declared the Bosnian war a *jihad*. Thousands of Russian volunteers reported to be fighting on the side of Serbs in Croatia and Bosnia were said to be motivated by bonds of Eastern Orthodoxy. The Greek clerics' exclusion of all non-Greeks at the annual Istanbul summit of church leaders in March 1992 was interpreted as a direct attack on Macedonia through its church. All doomsday scenarios for the escalation of war in Bosnia-Herzegovina envisioned a global confrontation of two religions, with Muslim countries rushing to the aid of the Bosnian government and Orthodox countries (Greece, Romania, Russia, and others) obliged to defend the Serbs.

A common assumption is that these conflicts have historical origins. Certainly each national community has individuals who harbor political ambitions to recover territory they believe is historically theirs and to retrieve their national minorities from a neighboring state. Such historically defined ambitions are often nurtured most in émigré communities, where people use them to maintain a sense of collective identity and individual importance in a foreign land or to criticize the government of the country they left many years and even generations earlier. Their political activities tend to influence thinking in Western capitals where they are citizens far more than the actual conflict. If such people return to their national homeland to realize these ambitions, the influence of their money can be disproportionate to local incomes.[9]

Once a contest takes on territorial dimensions, moreover, memories of previous conflicts and wars can be revived to fuel fears and mobilize support for nationalist leaders who claim to protect them. Villages in Macedonia took opposing sides in World War II, just as did villages in Bosnia-Herzegovina and in Croatia. If war erupted in Macedonia, memories of fratricidal atrocities and obligations for revenge could be revived there also, creating ethnonational hostilities in a pattern similar to the Bosnian war. Between nurtured ambitions and the escalation of violence lie historically influenced perceptions of governments. The mere existence of national projects at some time in the past or in the dreams of small minorities can be sufficient to create the perception of threat, leading officials to view any demands by autochthonous minorities for cultural or administrative autonomy as the first step toward secession.[10] If governments react with repression, contemporary conflicts can appear to be historical and can escalate rapidly.

But the more important causes of such conflict are not old feuds but current rights and protections and the relation between such rights and protections and the territorially defined state. The most significant political development in former Yugoslavia was the equation of individual rights with national rights, a process that occurred simultaneously in Slovenia and Serbia in the 1980s. The shift from a conception of security in terms of human rights to demands for territorial autonomy and sovereign rights can be treacherous, particularly if groups (nations in this case) are identified as the legitimate claimants of rights. The demand for ethnic group rights teeters dangerously between the demand for human rights that can be granted to individuals as members of a group and the argument that such rights can only be secured by the people themselves through the right to govern a particular territory.

The attempt to create national states in this environment, therefore, only opened the door to additional claims. When the breakup of Yugoslavia relegated to minority status people who once had equal rights, they responded, where they were able to dominate a particular territory, by seeking to create their own state rather than lose basic rights and suffer discrimination. The Serbs in Croatia and in Bosnia-Herzegovina each had begun to mobilize in a defensive posture out of fear of becoming a minority in new states. Once those states were recognized and the Serbs' rights as an equal nation were denied (retracted in Croatia and ignored in the coalition politics of independence in Bosnia-Herzegovina), the Serbs escalated their goals, aiming for a separate state. Even the Slovene government, however—acclaimed a success because it was ethnically homogeneous—

negotiated rights for autochthonous Hungarian communities in Slovenia in a reciprocal arrangement for Slovenes in Hungary but denied such rights to other south Slavs, mainly Croats and Serbs, on the grounds that they were not autochthonous.[11]

The result was growing ethnic tensions during 1992–93 between the Slovene government and citizens of other Yugoslav national identity who were experiencing discrimination on ethnonational grounds but had no equivalent legal protections.[12] These communities presented no threat to Slovene security because they were not territorially concentrated, but the Italian community (granted autochthonous status) was. The fact that this community also overlapped the Slovene and Croatian border, and thus found itself divided into separate countries when the republics became independent, had led to a movement for secession from both republics that had growing support (with historical echoes) in Italy; to demands by the summer of 1994 for dual citizenship with Italy; and to tensions between the governments of Slovenia and Croatia and of each with Italy.[13]

The reverse process also took place. Groups that in Yugoslavia had had minority status (nationalities) with cultural rights seized the opportunity to claim national status and its political rights. Albanians in both Kosovo and Macedonia began to insist that they had always been a constituent nation and therefore had the same right of self-determination as had Serbs in Serbia or Macedonians in Macedonia and, therefore, the right to govern themselves.

In fact, Albanians in Kosovo based their national claims, like the Slovenes and the Croats, on the autonomy granted federal units (provinces as well as republics) in the 1974 (socialist) Constitution. They argued that constitutional rights to provincial self-government, together with their numerical majority (by 1981 they composed approximately 78 percent of the population), gave them the right to the status of a separate republic. When the existing republics gained independence as nations, they claimed the right to independence, too. Because they were highly organized into an entirely parallel society to fight for autonomy and then against Serbian repression on the basis of ethnonational loyalty—who would deny their case? But according to the principle of republican borders, Kosovo was a province of Serbia. It was also controlled fully in 1991–92 by Serbian police, military, and civil administration. As war raged in neighboring Bosnia-Herzegovina, however, the Serbian government reacted to the realization that it might, in fact, have lost Kosovo by tightening police control, harassing and arresting Albanians with little regard for legality.

For instance, in early September 1993 they attempted to prevent schoolchildren from attending the underground system of Albanian schools used by 85 percent of the population. They also replaced the directors of the largest state enterprises and utilities with members of

Milošević's socialist party, and took over relief organizations (such as the local Serbian Red Cross offices) and local administrations where Albanians were still employed.[14]

Kosovo, the center of medieval Serbia and of Serbia's historical identity as a nation, was a litmus test for Serbian nationalists. Albanians could not claim national rights there, they argued according to the same 1974 (and preceding) Constitution, because they had a mother state in Albania. Moreover, domestic critics of Milošević argued that he could not survive politically if he gave up Kosovo because he had built his career since 1987 defending Serbian rights to a Serbian state in the contest with Albanians over Kosovo. The U.S. government, CSCE human rights monitors, and human rights organizations demanded that Serbia restore Albanians' human rights and end police repression. But the Serbian government and the Albanian minority both considered the issue to be one of collective political rights of national aspiration rather than one of individual human rights. As in Croatia, the contest had evolved, becoming ever less subject to compromise between two groups with incompatible claims over territory that each considered rightfully its own. The experience of Serbian repression and the deterioration in relations between the two communities had only cemented the determination of ethnic Albanians not to settle for individual human rights alone, leading many to believe that the Albanian demand for territorial rights was irreversible. Moreover, Serbia proper was not immune to the conflict. As long as Albanians could boycott every election, democracy in the republic, which many considered a precondition to any solution, would be stunted.

The options for Albanians in November 1993, according to Ibrahim Rugova, the elected president of their Republic of Kosovo, were "neutrality, independence in some arrangement with the Albanians in Macedonia, or union with Albania."[15] By 1994 both Serbian and Albanian leaders in Serbia entertained the idea of a territorial partition of Kosovo as a possible alternative to the outcome in Bosnia-Herzegovina. But even if the sensitive negotiations this required could survive the protest of more radical nationalists in both camps, the side effect might be to destroy Macedonia.[16]

The Albanian community in Macedonia is only one of more than twenty-five ethnic groups, but it is the largest, composing approximately 23 percent of the population.[17] One-third live in a concentrated area in western Macedonia, adjacent to Albanian areas in Kosovo and Albania. The conflict between the Macedonian government and ethnic Albanians in 1991–92 bears strong similarities to the pattern in Croatia between its government and *krajina* Serbs. During the 1980s discrimination and government carelessness toward Albanian human rights increased. Macedonian Albanians mobilized for political action in the atmosphere generated by the constitutional revisions of citizenship rights in 1989, forming com-

munal political parties in the democratic opening during 1990. Their political activity was fueled by Albanians from neighboring Kosovo, refugees
or politicians, who aimed at arousing anti-Serb and autonomist opinion
among their fellow nationals in Macedonia. But Macedonian nationalists
did not win in the 1990 elections, and President Kiro Gligorov and his
center-left coalition government remained loyal far longer to the former
federation and the idea of Yugoslavia than did Croatia. Nonetheless, the
breakup of Yugoslavia and unresolved Albanian and Macedonian questions
put Gligorov's government in a vise, trapped between radical Macedonian
nationalists (especially the main parliamentary opposition party, the Internal Macedonian Revolutionary Organization–Democratic Party for Macedonian National Unity, VMRO-DPMNE) and Albanians demanding
national status. Forced to think of winning elections, Gligorov and his
party tended to respond to its main voting constituency among Macedonians by forming a united front with other Macedonian political parties
against Albanians. At the same time concerned to prevent internal destabilization, the government attempted to prevent Albanians from demanding national rights by coopting Albanian political moderates, offering
them political representation in the government (in 1992, four ministerial
portfolios went to the Party for Democratic Prosperity, PDP) and meeting
some cultural demands regarding education and mass media. When a
police crackdown on smuggling activities in the Bit Pazar led in November
1992 to the arrest of ethnic Albanians and reports that one young Albanian
from Ljuboten had been beaten to death in the police station, angry crowds
proclaiming their innocence and protesting government discrimination
threatened to explode in violence. The situation intensified fears that there
would soon be armed confrontation.

By late 1992 Macedonia was negotiating group rights for Serbs and
for the large population of Romany with some success. But Albanian
politicians were rapidly radicalizing in their demands for group-based political rights to territorial autonomy for *Ilirida*, as they called their proto-
state in the western counties. Macedonian leaders, like their counterparts
in Croatia and Serbia, resisted such demands on the grounds that they
were a Trojan horse of eventual separation in a Greater Albania campaign
aimed at joining western Macedonia, Kosovo province, and perhaps parts
of Montenegro to Albania.

The distinction between human rights and national rights, which all
governments in the former republics were struggling to maintain, was not
aided by the intervention of international actors. In the name of human
rights for minorities and of a stable solution to internal communal conflicts,
the two international conferences on former Yugoslavia, the CSCE, the
United States, and other European organizations paid substantial attention
to the rights of Albanians, in particular in both Serbia and Macedonia. All

sides saw these activities as giving encouragement and even legitimation to Albanian national aspirations. The special status proposed by The Hague Conference, in October 1991, in effect, reaffirmed Serbian authority over the land while restoring the autonomy provided by the thoroughly discredited 1974 Constitution, with international guarantees. At the same time, however, CSCE documents adopted the line of the antifederalists that all of the former federal units had rights to independent statehood, including Kosovo. This was also the dominant international rhetoric. As the war in Bosnia-Herzegovina dragged on, however, external powers increasingly leaned toward the view that the republics were the state entities. Therefore, Kosovo was an integral part of Serbia and under the jurisdiction of its internal affairs, as Milošević insisted when his government refused on July 2, 1993, to renew visas for the twenty CSCE monitors sent the previous August. But the continual attention to Kosovo—particularly the U.S. insistence by 1993 that the economic sanctions against Serbia and Montenegro not only applied to a resolution of the war in Bosnia-Herzegovina but also would not be lifted until a resolution of the Kosovo problem—left open the ambiguity over the status of Kosovo's borders and over the grounds for Albanian political rights. Given that international attention to Kosovo was in part aimed at preventing what had occurred in Bosnia-Herzegovina, this ambiguity was particularly surprising. This was the trap that was stalling all political negotiations aimed at ending the war in Bosnia—the simultaneous insistence on ensuring the sovereignty and territorial integrity of Bosnia-Herzegovina and on talking to warring parties as if this were a civil war rather than a struggle by each for national rights.

In their policies toward Macedonia during 1993, international actors appeared to be on the road to the same error. They assumed that interethnic conflict was a prime source of internal instability, which could escalate into armed hostility and war, so they focused on the human rights of the Albanian minority. They did so without, apparently, noticing that Albanian politicians were already demanding the status of constituent nation and its attendant rights. Nor did they make the connection that any guarantee of human rights would have to be based on constitutional and political provisions that applied equally to all individuals and all minority groups. Singling out the largest for special treatment was in complete contradiction of this principle.[18] By early 1994, however, observers already took for granted that Albanians in Macedonia had the right to territorial autonomy in the western counties and that denying this right would deny their human rights.[19] Not only were they keeping alive ambiguity over the legitimacy of Serbian rule in Kosovo and signaling support for the Albanian project of separate statehood, but they also appeared to be helping this project along in its goal of linking with Albanians in Macedonia and Albania.

This ambiguity was particularly destabilizing because of the international inconsistency on Macedonia and the basis of its right to independence. The Greek refusal to recognize Macedonia under that name, and the deference of the European Union (EU) to this position of its member, despite the legal advice of its own Arbitration (Badinter) Commission in January 1992 that Macedonia met the conditions for recognition, was not in itself a challenge to the republic's borders, but it was a challenge to the national status of its inhabitants. Bulgaria, another neighbor with historical claims to Macedonia's people and territory, took the opposite approach by recognizing Macedonian statehood, but it also refused to recognize the existence of a Macedonian nation. On what political basis, therefore, was a Macedonian state legitimate? On what basis could it defend its territorial integrity, particularly if Albanian aspirations continued to gain encouragement as well?

The Greek government, acting for all the world like nationalists within former Yugoslavia, refused to recognize the republic of Macedonia under that name, arguing that the use of the name implied the country had territorial ambitions to parts of Greek Macedonia. For Macedonians, this point of view had a history going back to the Balkan Wars and several forced expulsions of 200,000–300,000 Macedonians from Greece. For contemporary Greeks, historical memory focused on the second Greek civil war (1944–49), when the rebel Democratic National Army had strong support among Macedonians in northern Greece and was aided by the Yugoslav communists. But far more immediate and problematic to the Greek government was the domestic consequence of recognizing a Macedonian national state. If the Greek government recognized a state on the basis of a Macedonian nation, it might have to recognize the ethnic identity of the large Macedonian population still living in northern Greece, to admit that Greece was not nationally homogeneous but multinational in fact, with all the potential political consequences, and to subject itself to European regulations on the treatment of minorities and protection of their cultural rights. Moreover, the intensity aroused by the issue of Skopje, as Greeks insisted on calling Macedonia, was expressed repeatedly over more than two years in demonstrations that drew more than a million people in Athens and Thessaloniki and in the slogans printed on large numbers of Greek products and correspondence. Macedonia excited such emotion because of its link to Greek security and the popular sense that Greek borders were insecure. Greeks also feared the ripple effect of a precedent in Macedonia. Far more important than Macedonia was the security of two other border regions that might be threatened by ethnic minorities: Thrace, the easternmost region, bordering Turkey, where autonomists might be encouraged by Macedonian success; and Albania, where historical disputes over northern Epirus threatened to reignite through irredentists of Greek origin living just over the border in Albania, and of Albanian origin living just over the border in Greece.

The pressures for territorial governing rights opened up by the breakup of Yugoslavia did not emanate solely from nationalists. Regionally identified political parties that could have no hope of winning electoral control of the government created movements for autonomy. Politicians who could claim allegiances on a particular territory had a better chance of wielding power, controlling patronage, and implementing their own choice of policies if they fought for autonomy rather than for electoral victory and influence over central policy. The dynamic of disintegration was stronger than the dynamic of nationalism.

In Croatia, opposition to the centralizing tendencies of the government of Franjo Tudjman and hopes that local self-government would make possible an escape from the economic consequences of the war in Bosnia-Herzegovina and of the government's economic policy fortified autonomist sentiments during 1993–94. Regional political parties in Istria (the Istrian Democratic Alliance), a peninsula on the Adriatic coast, and in Dalmatia (Dalmatian Action) had intensified the struggle for autonomy from Zagreb.[20] Even the Croatian Social Liberal party (HSLS) was pushing "regionalism" because its voters were regionally concentrated. Major differences among the four sectors of the UN protected areas—in geopolitical position, economic traits, and political parties—although claimed as parts of one Serbian state of *krajina*, became increasingly manifest as the status of the *krajina* remained unsettled for a third year and as the international community attempted to force Serb compliance with the republican borders by disrupting cooperation among them in Croatia, Serbia, and Bosnia-Herzegovina. By mid-1994, a process of what the former president of *krajina*, Goran Hadžić, called "localism," suggested that the conflicts, at least, between the government in Knin and the easternmost sector of Baranja and eastern Slavonia, and their very different relations with Belgrade, would lead Sector East to go its separate way politically from Sectors South and North.[21]

War in Bosnia-Herzegovina, on supposedly "ethnic" grounds, did not prevent autonomists from developing within areas of particularly mixed population where interethnic alliances were a matter of survival and of political commitment. Best known were those in Muslim-majority areas, such as the Autonomous Region of Western Bosnia led by Fikret Abdić in *Cazinska Krajina*, and groups active in the region of Tuzla in north central Bosnia. The Sarajevo leadership would not tolerate such autonomists and sought to eliminate them, calling their activities acts of treason during wartime. In Serbia the Parliament of the Muslim National

Council of Sanjak (Sandžak) voted on January 11, 1992, to demand special status for the area along the lines of the Brussels treaty convention proposal for Kosovo.[22]

Demands for autonomy need not raise the problem of borders that are created by national movements, for they are compatible with a more encompassing political structure. They can even provide a realistic avenue to self-determination without igniting territorial war. But this is not a foregone conclusion unless explicit efforts prevent them from taking the same path of escalating aspirations, which can lead to confrontation over territory. The Istrian regionalists in Croatia began as a political party, moved to a regional platform, and soon thereafter declared not autonomy but sovereignty. What this would eventually mean depended in part on the outcome in other parts of the country and on the peninsula in general, just as the outcome of a similar escalation by Sandžak activists in Serbia would depend not only on relations with Belgrade but also on the political resolution of the Kosovo conflict and of Muslim goals in Bosnia-Herzegovina.

Croatia contradicted the view that this process had some natural endpoint, that in contrast to an "artificial Yugoslavia," national states were natural, and that negotiating territorial divisions would put an end to the process of disintegration and the threat of war. Croatia was ostensibly at peace by the time war broke out in Bosnia-Herzegovina, but the cease-fire produced only an unstable stalemate between the Croatian government and the Serbs in the UN-protected areas. Just as the revolving-door diplomatic negotiations to end the war in Bosnia-Herzegovina remained preoccupied with finding a political agreement on the map, Croatian president Franjo Tudjman and government members from his ruling party spoke of a resolution of the conflict with *krajina* Serbs only in terms of the "reintegration of occupied Croatian territories," as if there were no people in question.[23] International recognition of Croatian sovereignty over the contested territory appeared to define the "natural" unit and to solve the problem by identifying the Serbs as rebels, occupiers, and a minority that must find accommodation with the Croatian government. Zagreb took this recognition to mean that the UN peacekeeping forces sent to monitor the Vance plan and to provide the conditions for a real peace were obliged to restore Croatian authority over its territory. International representatives, such as U.S. ambassador to Croatia Peter W. Galbraith and German foreign minister Klaus Kinkel, repeatedly told the Serbs that their insistence on a separate state (and their intention to integrate with Serb lands in Serbia and Bosnia-Herzegovina) would never be recognized. But if anything the conflict was more entrenched three years later than it was at the time of the war, and the cease-fire had not stopped hostilities or prevented the Croatian government from launching military offensives against the Serbs on four separate occasions. In fact, the only way to unblock the standoff was to reverse the process of disintegration, moving away from exclusive claims to territory and back to the question of civil and political rights. Despite the gruesome sacrifices of territorial war and involuntary population resettlements to achieve territorial control, there was no stable solution in any part of the region as long as everyone remained focused on borders and land.

In summary, despite the belief in containment (which seemed, ironically, to restore some authority to the borders of the former Yugoslavia even after they had been dissolved), the potential for further disintegration, for escalation of conflict to war over territory, and for long-term instability did not stop at the Yugoslav borders. Throughout the region, existing political borders divide national communities. All the borders are artificial, contested, and imposed by outside powers or by political compromise, shaped in modern times by war and imperial dissolution. Once one border is challenged on grounds of national self-determination, it sets up a chain reaction in which each successive border is open to revision. Friendly relations between neighbors (within countries or between them) can become subject overnight to doubt, suspicion, and defensive military build-up. Because there are also few natural borders that are at the same time uncontested, there is no stable solution without a willingness to negotiate an explicit compromise or to create binding international rules that are then enforced. The international community demonstrated its unwillingness in the case of Yugoslavia to ensure the first or to answer the questions necessary to the second. Governments learned that they should aim to become the stronger local power and use strong-arm tactics against an opposing nation, and this lesson threatened to increase the likelihood of military confrontation.

The principles of the momentum moving from northwest to southeast within former Yugoslavia apply equally going northward. Just as Albanians and Macedonians are not confined to one state, but spill over political borders, so Hungarians live in Vojvodina province within Serbia, in the Transylvania region of Romania, in Slovakia, and in Ukraine.[24] Serious conflict already existed in Transylvania between the Hungarian minority and Romanian nationalists (including democratically elected officials), and by 1995 the issue of autonomy was being confronted directly and angrily. Tensions were rising perceptibly between Hungarian political groups and the Slovak government as Slovakia moved toward independence. The delicate balance in these two countries could be upset by an incident between Hungarians and Serbs in the province of Vojvodina that encouraged Hungarian nationalism in response, whether popular or official, and fed a cycle of escalation through reciprocal suspicions and fears.

The confusion between ethnic conflict and national rights (that individuals have rights by virtue of their membership in an ethnonational group rather than as citizens alone and that those rights adhere to a particular territory) raises the question not only of the treatment of residents who do not belong to the majority national group (minorities). Self-consciousness as a nation also creates a new category of foreign policy—the identification of and interest in nationals living elsewhere. All the nationalist parties that came to power in eastern Europe after the collapse of communist regimes included in their definition of national interest the protection of their diaspora populations. For example, the platform of the first postcommunist Hungarian governing party, the Hungarian Democratic Forum (MDF), identified the national interest of the Hungarian state with protection for Hungarians in Yugoslavia, Romania, Slovakia, and Ukraine. These four countries perceived this platform as a threat to their territorial integrity just as Greece feared Macedonia. From Poland to Slovenia, the new regimes created state ministries responsible for their nationals in other lands. The Italian government elected in 1994 did the same. Although such ministries may only encourage private cultural activities to protect a language or seek investment from faraway emigrants, closer to home they tend to watch for threats to their minorities in neighboring states and to demand their protection.

Even if a government does not take on the nationalist project as policy, groups within countries throughout the region are actively advocating such a project. Politicized ethnic tensions within Vojvodina, Slovakia, and Transylvania, for example, are inseparable from the activities of human rights organizations based in Hungary that press for the autonomy of Hungarians in these three lands and that mobilize international opinion in support of their goal.

Other conflicts that involve territory but cross state borders, such as conflicts concerning natural resources, can become identified with the ethnic or national group resident in the area and be perceived as part of a neighbor's coordinated nationalist strategy to destabilize their government. An example is the Slovak perception of the Hungarian position and propaganda in western Europe on the joint Danube project, the Gabčikovo-Nagymaros Dam.[25] Another example is the stimulus given to Macedonian nationalism in the 1980s when Greece interrupted the water supply to Macedonian fields, affecting export crops several years in a row.

The general tendency is for such conflicts to radicalize, as in Yugoslavia. A parallel to the Croatian case could be seen developing in Slovakia. Serbian militants in *krajina*, a minority among Serbs in Croatia and even in their own region, continued to battle moderates among fellow Serbs after the war in Croatia. Similarly, Hungarian autonomists in Slovakia were the least popular of four Hungarian organizations at the time of the division of Czechoslovakia. The independence of the Slovak republic, alongside attempts by neighboring Hungary to draw international attention to the "plight" of Hungarians in Slovakia, and the policy of the Slovak government against the threat of autonomy and secession together gave that minority increasing visibility and political weight. Within a year local autonomy (with unknown consequences for the political development of Slovakia) became accepted as the natural course.

## The Cascade from West to East

Certain conditions were necessary to turn ethnic differences into ethnic conflict and ethnic conflict into national conflict and war over territory. Those conditions applied throughout the former Yugoslavia. The breakup of the country did not lead to improvements; instead, economic deterioration and psychological insecurities were exacerbated by the prolongation of uncertainty over sovereignty and borders and by war itself. The disintegrating effects of these conditions on the social fabric and on the governmental and political capacity to manage the postcommunist transition without radicalization and to resolve border disputes without war were more powerful than those favoring integration and moderation. In calculating the risk that war would spread, it was critical to recognize that this process of disintegration and national formation was moving geographically from areas with economic reserves and international patrons to areas far less equipped economically and politically to manage the consequences.

The dynamic of disintegration in Yugoslavia followed a pattern seen in all the European cases in 1989–91: in order of occurrence, the Soviet bloc, Yugoslavia, the Soviet Union, and Czechoslovakia. The process of economic reform was initiated by central governments, foreign creditors and advisers, and liberal economists. Although nationalist politics emerged among many different groups for a variety of reasons, the first group to move toward national independence and exit from each of these constituted orders comprised politicians who had reason to think that they could win and sustain this independence. The collapse—of the socialist bloc and of individual countries—actually occurred when the most Western-oriented and wealthiest areas chose independence. Hungary, Slovenia, Estonia and Lithuania, and the Czech lands set the pace, even if their exit was made possible in part by actions initiated by others—for example, in these cases, by Poland, Serbia, Gorbachev, or Slovakia. The process of breakup was begun by politicians in wealthier regions located nearer to Western markets, with closer communication and cultural links to Western and central Europe, and with less dependence on the internal economy and greater integration into foreign trade, investment, and capital flows. These were also areas with influential Western patrons who promised support.

But this challenge to the authority and laws of the former state (or intrastate alliance) and then to the borders defining new states moved from places originally better able to cope with economic austerity and Western-oriented liberalization to areas with far fewer independent resources and higher costs of transition. There the personal insecurities and social anomie that can find expression in nationalism and ethnic antagonisms and that provide the early raw material for nationalist political entrepreneurs are also more severe. In these cases the agrarian sector tends to be larger, and the economic importance of land and of natural resources greater. As a result, ethnic bonds are stronger in the villages, and more people have identities attached to the land. Unemployment is higher, and a smaller proportion of the population comprises urban dwellers with their multiple allegiances and moderating attachments. With greater insecurities on the ground, political polarization escalates faster, and forces for moderation and compromise are more easily marginalized.

Those governments that seize the initiative and succeed are far better prepared politically and economically than those for whom independence is a second-best choice or on whom independence is forced. They are often at an earlier stage of developing national consciousness and consensus and must provide a political response for which economic conditions and political development are not ready. Often they must respond in the context of largely external events that have achieved a momentum that is beyond their control. Caught in the path of a collapsing political order, they must adjust. But they must do so with less interest from external powers, with less advance political preparation for independence and national assertiveness, and with a greater need for an external substitute for the security umbrella, as was provided by the former Yugoslavia.

The reasons that independence movements developed later in Bosnia-Herzegovina and Macedonia, and similarly in Azerbaijan, Georgia, and Tajikistan, are also reasons that violence—once it began—spread with far greater speed and intensity. Borderlands of former imperial regimes, these regions had populations that were particularly mixed ethnically and nationally. Created by outside powers as international compromises to achieve a regional balance of power, the former Yugoslav republics of Macedonia and Bosnia-Herzegovina and the former Soviet republics in the Caucasus are not easily able to achieve political autonomy. Even where their leaders pushed for their own greater autonomy within the overarching state, these lands and peoples caught in between the policies of a reforming center and those of nationalist separatists supported the multinational state longer because their territorial and multinational security depended on it.[26]

A second reason is that these areas tend to be poorer and more oriented toward domestic production of raw materials, semifinished goods, and capital goods for sale to manufacturers in the wealthier and more trade-oriented areas of the same country, which are often (as in Bosnia-Herzegovina) also the site of defense industries. Their economic profile is

therefore less suited to export orientation to the West and rapid liberalization. The structural adjustment of global reorientation was far more costly
economically and therefore socially and politically for Bosnia-Herzegovina,
Macedonia, Montenegro, Slovakia, Azerbaijan, and Central Asia, and all
were affected more severely by the collapse of foreign markets in the Middle
East and in the Council for Mutual Economic Assistance (CMEA). More
dependent on government subsidies, investment, and welfare transfers to
their economies, and far more integrated into and dependent on the economy of their common state, they stood to lose substantially from its
disintegration. Already poorer or experiencing more precipitous economic
decline during the 1980s than other areas of their former countries, these
regions had an economic interest in finding a compromise with the pace
or policies of extreme liberalizers to protect some central redistribution
and investment and some links with markets in the east and developing
countries. When those economic links were broken by economic warfare
among republics, when even their common currency was destroyed, these
regions had to choose separate statehood. Even then the meaning of this
independence was constrained by their economic vulnerability to other
parts of the former state.[27]

The effects on Bosnia-Herzegovina were described in chapter 9. But
Bosnia-Herzegovina was not alone. The republic of Montenegro had to
alter entirely its original strategy for westernization, and this meant shifting political power and economic resources away from liberals and stunting
the development of a stronger liberal party.[28] Montenegro's economic dependence on Serbia for energy, communication and transportation links,
and food reduced substantially its independent room for maneuver when
Yugoslavia dissolved. Montenegrin leaders attempted several times—in the
summer of 1992, around the Yugoslav elections in December 1992, and
again in the fall of 1993—to object to Milošević's policies and to pursue
liberal and peace-oriented initiatives. These attempts were dismissed as
unserious or inconceivable by the international community, which had
assigned Serbian nationality and war guilt to Montenegrins.[29]

Political evolution in Macedonia was also seriously affected by the
economic consequences of the republic's geographical location when Yugoslavia collapsed. The Macedonian government found itself trapped between the trade sanctions imposed by the United Nations on neighboring
Serbia and Greek attempts to obtain political concessions by squeezing
Macedonia economically. (Macedonia's only port was in Thessaloniki.)
The Macedonian government thus had to proceed with democratization
and marketization under extremely harmful and destabilizing conditions.
The secret economic boycott by Greece in its campaign against Macedonian sovereignty during 1992–93 and the U.S. pressure to tighten enforcement of the sanctions on Serbia after July 1993 both exacerbated Mace-

donia's difficulties.[30] A second Greek economic blockade on all traffic through Thessaloniki and along the Greece–Macedonia border imposed on February 17, 1994, gradually sent the economy into a nosedive and increased social and interethnic tensions dramatically.

Third, new political forces in areas in the wake of a collapsed state are often at earlier stages of maturation. With a proportionally smaller middle class and much higher unemployment, political pressures for the democratic and civil restraints appropriate to a multiparty democracy and market economy are far weaker. At the first manifestations of nationalism among alternative elites and in the population, the governing elites in these ethnically mixed areas did not tend to perceive any political interest in nurturing that nationalism for a fight against central power or the status quo. They saw it as profoundly dangerous to civil order, and they tended to react accordingly, with a mix of conservative and repressive policies at home.[31] Without the socioeconomic foundations of centrist politics, leaders faced extremists in an atmosphere that was already highly polarized socially and economically. They chose the more immediately pragmatic, but in the long-run risky, tactic of playing off radicals against each other or of delaying any change as long as possible.

The enormous real difficulties of managing this triple transition—to multiparty democracy, market economies, and independent statehood— require a rare combination of leadership skills. The fact that its timing was set by political developments elsewhere reduced substantially the probability that the available leaders would have what was necessary. At the same time, the collapse of established political procedures and the political instability placed a premium on individual leadership. Politicians who rode the nationalist tide to power had to shift roles rapidly with little preparation. They moved almost overnight from Communist party sinecures or from the political isolation of individual dissent (including prison) to positions that required organizational talents and statesmanship, to build party organizations and to keep the newly independent state from further breakdown of civil order and war. The disadvantage of their region in the strategic balance of power is thus compounded by the inexperience of their leaders, which increases the probability of costly and even tragic tactical mistakes. Despite this, not one political entity in former Yugoslavia had turnover in its executive branch; those elected president in 1990 were in every case still president in 1994.[32]

## Political Radicalization

Many observers expected that international recognition of the requesting republics' sovereignty would bring an end to war because it would satisfy national aspirations, but it only removed the antifederalist step. Except in Slovenia, the process of creating states did not end. Far from abandoning the ideology of nationalism, leaders found more uses for it— and it was now legitimate, accepted by the international community as the cause of conflict and by most citizens as the goal. Indeed, the paranoia about threats to the nation that politicians manufactured for the purpose of bargaining on federal policy (and the fight for states' rights) among the republics became more plausible when the enemy was a neighboring state and army or a community within the state claiming national rights. The worsening existential and psychological insecurity created by deteriorating economic and political conditions and unresolved issues of sovereignty also intensified the defensive psychology common to all sides: each felt that it was the underdog, the minority in need of protection. The constraints on nationalist expression and its interactive dynamic under the former state were gone, and the nationalists refused to replace that state with international agreements of cooperation and mutual security among them that could dampen the tendency to radicalize further. This tendency for political radicalization was a significant third factor contributing to the escalation rather than the cessation of hostilities and to the possibility that the conflict would continue to spread.

Two separate processes were pushing political escalation. One was the conditions of war and extreme uncertainty. Under such conditions individuals, rather than making rational calculations based on mutual interest and compromise, were more likely to react to some small, local event or confrontation in ways that could escalate rapidly out of control and a "downward spiral of mutual hostage-taking . . . following the logic that 'what they are doing to our people, we are entitled to do to their people.' "[33] The second was the politics of political competition within national communities, which interacted and fed this spiral. The process of nationalist revolution against members of the former regime and to build nation-states had only begun in 1990–91 and was nowhere near completion.

The breakup of the country interrupted a process of democratization when it had only begun—one election and only six months of political organizing by civic groups. Elections did not automatically produce democratic institutions and the electoral and judicial constraints on power that are the essential characteristics of democracies. Elected leaders in the new states and potential states placed priority on consolidating their own political power and that of their political party by taking control of state assets such as the mass media, the military, and the police. The continuation of war, the threat of war, or uncompleted projects of national sovereignty provided the pretext for extraordinary executive power and, de jure or de facto, emergency rule. The greatest influence over affairs of state was thus wielded by the most militant and hard-line nationalist faction within ruling parties.

As long as war or unresolved borders and unstable external relations continued, politicians who addressed serious economic and social problems with flag-rallying patriotic fervor and invitations to ethnic discrimination had the political advantage. The most notorious, perhaps, was the successful electoral campaign of paramilitary Serbian gang leader and accused war criminal Željko Ražnatović to be the representative of his newly founded Party of Serb Unity from Kosovo to the Serb Parliament in December 1992. Running on the slogan "I promise you nothing," he posed a real danger of igniting a local campaign of terror and expulsions of Albanians with his campaign "extol[ing] the virtues of family, the Orthodox Church, and patriotism." In a speech to one such audience of Serbs in Kosovo he explained, "I don't promise you new telephone lines. I don't promise you new highways. But I pledge to defend you with the same fanaticism that I've used so far in defending the Serbian people."[34] But it was not to the advantage of many leaders to hurry the process toward peace, because peace would require them to do something concrete about internal problems rather than avoiding these more difficult tasks through war and external scapegoating.[35] Nationalist rhetoric was a particularly effective means to keep the opposition on the defensive. By frequent reminders that the survival of the nation remained at stake, leaders could cast any hint of internal opposition as a threat to the nation and the critic's questionable loyalty. In fact, so useful was such rhetoric to remaining in power within their own communities that it seemed to become a habit, as if the incumbent leaders would not know how to govern without it.

But when this nationalist rhetoric, whose message was directed outward at enemies, was used for domestic political advantage, it interacted with the same politics in other communities, keeping alive mutual hostilities and heightening the possibility of war where neighbors were not already at war. President Tudjman was particularly inclined to manipulate war fever against Serbs in the UN protected areas (UNPAs) and to use military adventures to win votes. On January 22, 1993, three days before elections for the upper house of the Parliament, he violated the Vance plan and ended the progress of UN forces toward demilitarizing the UNPAs by ordering serious military incursions into a pink zone to retake Maslenica bridge, a vital communication link between Zagreb and Dalmatia, Peruča dam, under UN supervision according to the Vance plan, and Zemunik airport, and into the UNPA Sector South to take villages nearby.[36] He repeated unilateral military action to rebuild and reopen the bridge in July of that year, just before elections in August, and on September 9–11, before the party congress, the Croatian army invaded the Medak area in the UNPAs, seizing three Serb villages.[37] As they were withdrawing under pressure from the UN Protection Forces (UNPROFOR), the troops destroyed the houses and massacred the inhabitants of the villages. Although each instance won Tudjman votes, it also pushed Serbs in the *krajina* to take back their weapons, to slow efforts at dialogue and cooperation, and to be more convinced than ever that they needed their own state.

Even when nationalist leaders did not stir up nationalist fervor, they were not easily able to escape the role they had created. Establishing their credentials as national protectors, nationalist politicians had to respond in kind when challenged by more extreme nationalists in order to keep their constituency. They were particularly vulnerable to pressures from groups on the right that had the same goals and the same language but differed on pace and means, insisting on speed or on the use of unconstitutional methods as an assertion of states' rights. In Serbia the opposition nationalists, despite (or perhaps because of) their weakness from internal divisions and personal quarrels, challenged Milošević's leadership in terms, largely, of nationalist goals and whether he was measuring up to his claim to speak for the Serb nation. Their primary focus on a reconstitution of the Serbian state that would give an advantage to their own party and bring a change of government more quickly, although an internal matter, could not easily be separated from the national question and borders. Serbs living outside of Serbia were pawns in this competition, in which any commitment to republican borders and guaranteed minority rights for Serbs in other states—the terms necessary to end war in Croatia and in Bosnia-Herzegovina according to the approach adopted by the international community—was declared a betrayal of the Serb nation. Whenever Milošević attempted to separate the national question from the fate of Serbs in the diaspora, even if only for short-term international legitimation, such as his public rejection of *krajina* leader Milan Babić in January 1992 for not signing the Vance plan for Croatia, opposition nationalists took the opportunity to demonstrate their purer national credentials by continuing support of Serbs in Croatia, in Kosovo, or in Bosnia-Herzegovina.

Both Serbian president Milošević and Croatian president Tudjman encouraged the presence of right-wing radicals, both within their parties and further right, so that they could appear the more moderate and stabilizing factor to the international community and to undercut other nationalist parties in their opposition. Milošević, for example, used his party organization and the police network to help elect Vojislav Šešelj, the extreme right-wing nationalist founder of the Serbian Radical party, to Parliament in 1990 and to build up his power base in Serbia. Šešelj was a more extreme anticommunist than those who originally motivated Milošević's nationalism. He had usurped the Serbian Chetnik tradition for a neofascist ideology, putting Milošević's main rivals, Vuk Drašković and the Serbian Movement for Renewal (SPO), so much on the defensive by his rhetoric and his violent activities in Croatia and Bosnia that it forced Drašković to change his line, while giving a bad name to the Chetnik legacy and the social forces of Church, nation, monarchy, and tradition associated with it. Even when Šešelj began to use his dominance of the parliamentary opposition during 1993 to attempt to bring down Milošević's government and to challenge Milošević's leadership directly with his defiant defense of Serbs outside of Serbia (such as the Bosnian Serb refusal to adopt the Vance-Owen plan) and his control over supply networks across the border, Milošević used him again for the next step in his campaign to destroy Drašković (and to send a message to other rivals).[38] Šešelj's ruffians staged an altercation in Parliament against SPO delegates, and their protest, which included mass public demonstrations, provided the police with a pretext to arrest Drašković and his wife, in June 1993, beating, torturing, and putting them on trial. Milošević then turned on Šešelj. Preempting his call for a no-confidence vote in September by dissolving the Parliament and calling an election for December 1993, Milošević arrested forty of Šešelj's local party bosses on charges of war crimes in Bosnia-Herzegovina, ended his media coverage, and beamed the light of favor further right onto Ražnatović instead.

But the consequence of this tactic of domestic power politics was to create, keep alive, and tolerate—even use—groups that pursued terrorist, semilegal, and criminal activities in Croatia and in Bosnia-Herzegovina, including campaigns of "ethnic cleansing" that continued into 1994. There were very clear parallels, with similar results in Croatia and in Bosnia-Herzegovina, in President Tudjman's use of extreme right-wing organizations—such as the Croatian Party of Right; its paramilitary wing, the Croatian Defense League (HOS); and Tomislav Merčep's Association of Croatian Volunteers for Defense of the Fatherland—and of right-wing elements within his party (the HDZ) in Croatia and in Herzeg-Bosnia. The result of this apparent necessity of domestic political contest in such regimes would be to revive hostilities even where they appeared to be over. The political game in Zagreb, for example, reactivated hostilities between the Croatian government and the Serbs of *krajina* during 1994 that threatened a progressive collapse of the global cease-fire signed March 29, 1994, and explained much of the fragility of the cease-fire between Bosniacs and Croats created by the Washington Agreement the same month. Even in Bosnia-Herzegovina the government's invitation to *mujahedin* warriors during 1992 and the use of these forces for terrorist, illegal, and shock-troop activities had produced a situation over which the government appeared to have less and less control. By 1994 this was becoming a matter of serious concern. These *mujahedin* were increasingly influential, and their inclination to disrupt negotiated cease-fires and teach fundamentalism seemed to work directly against peace. Local populations had become ever more fearful of their bullying.[39]

By retaining the initiative in the use of nationalist tactics, incumbent leaders not only put opposition parties continually on the defensive, but also kept them weak. The center of the political spectrum moved toward the right. Members of opposition parties who had been explicitly anti-nationalist found they could no longer gain a hearing if they did not adopt a position on their particular national question and some version of nationalist rhetoric. Those with a different approach to the national question and therefore toward minorities or enemies, such as an approach focused on rights rather than on territory, found it difficult to penetrate the controlled television and press and were not able to increase votes or retain influence long. In their effort to defeat the incumbent leader, opposition parties became more royal than the King, adopting more extreme and militaristic proposals in their attempt to demonstrate their more genuine national credentials. Instead of the moderating social forces, political cross pressures, and restraining institutions of democratic governance that give democracies a reputation for peace, parliaments tended to be more radical than leaders.[40] Governmental policy appeared to remain intransigent, or to move further away, from the policies necessary to bring an end to the conflict. Even where there was movement toward rapprochement behind the scenes, the public posturing and its domestic political uses were the face seen by adversaries, who remained defensive.

The nonnationalist president of Macedonia, Gligorov, had been brutally criticized during 1990 and 1991 by Macedonian nationalists for failing to campaign for independence along with Slovenia and Croatia in 1990. Even he moved from a position in early 1992 that admitted, in exchange for Greek recognition, a range of possible options for the name of the state to an increasingly uncompromising position on Macedonian national symbols (such as the star of Vergina chosen for its flag) and the name of the state and phrases considered objectionable in the constitutional preamble. Although Greek economic and diplomatic pressure did not help Gligorov to maintain a more flexible stance, the primary motive for his increasingly nationalist position was domestic competition from an increasingly vocal and extremist opposition (led by VMRO-DPMNE) and even from former centrists such as Petar Goshev, who made more openly nationalist appeals, during 1994, apparently calculating that it would increase their votes.

At the same time the government faced radicalization within the Albanian community in Macedonia. Like the Macedonian nationalists, the Albanians were responding with impatience to the delays in government implementation of promises. The nationalist radical wing within the Party for Democratic Prosperity, the largest of the Albanian parties in Macedonia, confronted the leadership of Nevzat Halili at its party congress on September 2, 1993, for failing to "obtain either autonomy or the status of a 'people of the state' in Macedonia."[41] The party split in two. By the spring of 1994 even the more moderate wing (although still coalition partners of Gligorov's SDSM) had adopted the radicals' position on the demand for "constituent nation" status in Macedonia. And while Greek opposition to Macedonian statehood and the first economic embargo had arisen under the conservative government of Constantine Mitsotakis, pressures for even more militant policy from a nationalist right wing within his party brought his government down. Although the Greek elections in October 1993 brought the socialists to power, the new prime minister, Andreas Papandreou, declared immediately that Greece would close the border with Macedonia if it did not drop its claim to the name in some form.[42]

The question that remained in this rightward shift and radicalization of the political spectrum was whether it necessarily led to war. Were these uses of nationalism in domestic politics and in creating nation-states out of autonomist movements legitimized by nationalism part of a process of democratization, or were they only anticommunist reaction? In Slovenia the process had seemed to lead to electoral democracy. A rightward shift did occur. Then in the summer of 1993 Defense Minister Janez Janša attempted to destabilize the subsequent coalition government so that he could justify his campaign to purge the state bureaucracy of all persons associated with the old regime, social democrats and former communists who had nonetheless remained significant players. Nevertheless, the country remained at peace.[43]

Where the nationalist revolution had been explicitly anti-communist—in Croatia and in Bosnia-Herzegovina—there was war. Whichever tendency turned out to be the stronger—anticommunism or democratization—and whether its association with war or peace followed the same pattern, it was far from completion in the areas of the country in the northwest-to-southeast path of disintegration.

The conflict among Serbs by 1994 as a result of the wars in Croatia and Bosnia-Herzegovina—personified by Socialist party leader Milošević and right-wing nationalist Radovan Karadžić—had brought this ideological confrontation to the surface. The issue was the acceptance or not of Western proposals for a peace plan in Bosnia (the Vance-Owen plan in 1993 and the Contact Group plan in 1994). But the confrontation was portrayed as a battle royal over the future leadership of the Serb nation, playing out in the Serb *krajina* between Milošević loyalists Milan Martić and Borislav Mikelić and Milan Babić, and in Serbia between Milošević and right-wing nationalists from Drašković to Vojislav Koštunica to Šešelj. If, as a result of international pressure on the Bosnian Serbs to accept the

Contact Group's proposals, this confrontation led to full-scale war in Bosnia-Herzegovina, the path would lead not to institutionalization of democratic competition but to civil war among Serbs.

As a result of such civil war or of its own internal development, the same question was becoming an issue in Kosovo by 1993. In the first years of nationalist conflict in the rest of the country, the Albanian leadership in the province had had an advantage: that the Serbian party purges of Albanian communists during the 1980s had done the work of the anticommunist revolution for Albanian nationalists such as Ibrahim Rugova. Serbian policies to counteract Albanian autonomism and the Albanians' boycotts after 1988, by removing from formal positions the entire political, economic, and cultural elite, had built extraordinary cohesion and parallel organization around anti-Serbianism and Rugova. But this unity could not be maintained in the changed conditions of the breakdown of Yugoslavia, the opportunity for full independence provided by international condemnation of Serbia, and the growing impatience at delays in achieving their goals. By 1993 a process of radicalization threatened the lives of Albanian moderates. The growing resentment at international negotiators for not according the Kosovo Albanians full status at Geneva had begun to shift the balance within Rugova's movement toward radical militants who preached a military solution.

In addition to the inadvertent dynamic of nationalist politics and the ideological commitment toward the more militaristic, violent solutions of right-wing nationalists, impatience was a powerful force driving toward war. The international approach to the conflict in former Yugoslavia had created a stalemate in Croatia, prolonged the war in Bosnia-Herzegovina, and reinforced uncertainty about what rights and borders in the rest of the country would eventually gain recognition. Impatience with these delays was galvanizing radical youth and officials who favored the war option over prolonged negotiations, making them more vocal on the need to choose the military option to resolve the issues (as if they could be resolved this way once and for all), from Croatia to Kosovo. Military commanders became more powerful and popular, and paramilitary extremists moved from the fringe to legitimate politics. The balance of power seemed to move toward those who had been willing to contemplate and prepare for war and whose historical definition of the conflict gave them staying power for the long haul. Moreover, at the same time that militants gained legitimacy in all communities, the shifting balance of military power among combatants—by which decisive gains of territory without reversals were rare, and build-up on one side led to compensatory build-ups on the other—prolonged the possibility of war and its spread.

The perpetuation in power of nationalist leaders—indeed of the same nationalist leaders—and the absence of moderating forces from within society were strongly influenced by the actions of the international community. Active international negotiations and shuttle diplomacy gave continuing publicity and prominence to leaders such as Milošević, Tudjman, Izetbegović, Haris Silajdžić, Ganić, and even Karadžić, enhancing their stature far more than they could have hoped for from domestic policy. International negotiators, treating these individuals as the representative of their nation rather than of a political party or transitory government, supported their ambitions and even created the illusion that these people were indispensable, in the belief that a change in leaders would require starting anew and might harm the country's interests in these diplomatic relations. This advantage in domestic political competition prolonged their power beyond what would have been its natural life in normal circumstances and delayed democratization and the consequent development of internal checks and balances.

The two moments after independence when President Tudjman was facing challenge in the polls and when the parties and social groups (such as the Church hierarchy) opposed to his policy in Bosnia-Herzegovina overcame their differences to cooperate for change, were the moments when international negotiations restored his stature: in August 1993 when his proposal for Bosnia-Herzegovina was adopted as the basis of the Owen-Stoltenberg plan and in February 1994 when the Washington Agreement was negotiated.[44] Growing divisions within the Bosnian Serb camp during the fall of 1991 had culminated in a major challenge to Karadžić's leadership from the original base of Bosnian Serb autonomy at Banja Luka, but the EC-mandated referendum for the republic and the Lisbon negotiations gave Karadžić new authority as their representative with international negotiators.[45] While Milošević mounted a coordinated strategy to replace Karadžić with a more pliant leader during the spring of 1994, negotiations over the consequences of the Washington Agreement and over the Contact Group peace proposal gave Karadžić renewed attention and leverage. Efforts by the international community to intensify the isolation of the Bosnian Serbs until they accepted the proposal only strengthened support for Karadžić within his community. A similar situation existed with respect to the Bosnian Muslim leaders. Whereas a group of more secular, centrist Muslims that had broken away from Izetbegović's party in 1990 had created competition for the Muslim vote, the breakup of the state and Bosnian independence gave Izetbegović authority to represent both the Muslim nation and the Bosnian people. International recognition of the country while Izetbegović was president gave him international backing over the coming years for his domestic struggle against opponents within his party (the best known being Fikret Abdić).

The most striking example of a nationalist whose political career was furthered by the international community is Milošević. Although the world portrayed Milošević as nearly omnipotent in 1988–91, he had a long way to go in consolidating his position as leader of the Serbs and in transforming the coercive institutions of the socialist regime to his instruments of power. In fact, public opinion polls showed that nationalism was supplanting both anticommunist and prosocialist sentiments in Serbia just as the Western campaign to isolate and punish Serbia's nationalism was beginning.[46] But the sanctions fed the brand of nationalism associated with Milošević, as protector of Serbian national interests against external enemies, while foreign rhetoric blaming Milošević personally for the wars reinforced his stature as national martyr. How far his salvation was due to the economic sanctions and diplomatic isolation against Serbia is difficult to assess, but those factors clearly facilitated his task of governing.

Far from deterring the spread of the war, the sanctions exacerbated its causes by worsening economic hardship, intensifying a sense of paranoia against the outside, and undercutting the ability of opposition forces to compete. International behavior also vindicated radicals who were Milošević's instrument against the more centrist opposition, such as Šešelj. His predictions that Western powers would oppose Serbian interests and claims that only military force would prevail helped Šešelj gain ever more mainstream voter support during 1993.

After the recognition of Bosnia–Herzegovina left Serbia and Montenegro no option but to create a new state in April 1992, Milošević again combined his goals of international legitimation and of preempting opposition nationalists through formation of a new federal government that made the patriarch of Serbian anticommunist nationalism, Dobrica Ćosić, president and Milan Panić, an American businessman of Serbian birth who had U.S. support and public relations skills, prime minister. But the two turned against him and joined with an alliance of opposition forces formed temporarily in response to growing popular discontent over the war. The group comprised members of the Orthodox Church hierarchy who defected from Milošević's camp, an antiwar splinter group from his Socialist party, and some who hoped to bring back the monarchy with Crown Prince Alexander Karadjordje III. Public opinion polls at the time of the London conference in August 1992, when Panić publicly attacked Milošević, found that only one-third of the electorate supported Milošević. His willingness to use a parliamentary maneuver to manipulate the electoral laws in his favor, electoral fraud, and the police to win elections called for December 1992 reveals how close a call he knew it to be. But once again, the international community (and his opponent, Panić) played into his hands. The U.S. State Department delayed for months, until it was too late, the approval of an exception to the sanctions regime that would provide a television transmitter for independent stations that could counteract Milošević's state monopoly with alternative sources of information and campaigning. Quixotic and seen by some as an American plant, Panić campaigned on a standard program of liberal economic reform and westernization, as if Milošević had not built his popular constituency in 1989–91 largely from persons fearing the unemployment necessitated by such reforms. Such a platform revived these fears at a time of mass unemployment (compounded by war refugees) and hyperinflation. Far from providing an alternative to Milošević's use of Serbian nationalism, it gave Milošević a renewed opportunity to blame economic troubles on UN sanctions and to direct popular attention to national pride, underlining the unfairness of condemning the Serb nation as an international outlaw and as the agent responsible for the wars. This task was then actually performed by U.S. secretary of state Lawrence Eagleburger, who named Milošević a war criminal four days before the election in order to appear more militant than U.S. policy actually was and to regain stature at a meeting called in Geneva December 16 between ICFY cochairmen and the foreign ministers of 29 countries to find an end to the Bosnian war. This hurt the antiwar opposition by reinforcing Milošević's national appeal to voters, but the real gainer was the right, because a significant number of votes shifted to Šešelj's Serbian Radical party.[47]

Nonetheless, the failure of the sanctions to stop the war in Bosnia-Herzegovina led Geneva negotiators to depend increasingly during 1993 and 1994 on Milošević's assistance in pressuring Bosnian Serbs. President Tudjman continued throughout 1993, and explicitly in the Geneva agreement between the two presidents with ICFY negotiators of November 30, 1993 (a declaration normalizing relations between the two states, signed on January 19, 1994), to insist that Milošević was the key to the integration into the Croatian civil order of the UN protected areas under the control of local Serbs. Even before the Contact Group placed its entire strategy beginning in August 1994 for ending the war in Bosnia-Herzegovina on Milošević's willingness and ability to isolate the Bosnian Serbs, eventually rewarding him (and thus elevating further his popularity in Serbia) with a staged lifting of the economic sanctions, UN and EU negotiators visited Belgrade for nearly every issue affecting Serbs in Croatia or Bosnia-Herzegovina. The incalculable consequences of civil war in Serbia also made Milošević's apparent ability to maintain control of the situation look ever more attractive to Europeans.

In their own impatience to have an end to the post-Yugoslav conflicts but without committing soldiers to the task of imposing their decisions on borders, external powers also looked to the leaders of warring factions to demonstrate the capacity and authority to implement and enforce the agreements made. They were being treated, in other words, as if they had already achieved the goal of their continued fighting, to be recognized as national leaders of independent states. The international community was even tolerating extensive police repression in Serbia (most egregious in Kosovo province), and also in Croatia and Macedonia, as a means of keeping order and containing the conflict under current conditions, although such repression actually gave greater power to extremist elements in local police or military units and made it more likely that small incidents would aggravate the situation and their consequences would spread.

## The Weapons of War

Finally, war itself contributed new fuel for nationalist extremism and for war to spread. Economies continued to decline as a result of war and of sanctions, leading the distributive conflicts, insecurities about survival, and mutual suspicions to worsen. The primary tactic to influence behavior, whether by Croatia against Knin authorities, Greece against the Macedonian government, Serbia against Albanians in Kosovo, or the international community against Serbia and the Bosnian Serbs, was a negative pressure to bring populations to their knees economically, on the assumption that this would compel a change in policy. The continuing flow of refugees, major shifts in population balances, the influx of arms and ammunition, increasing unemployment, and the opportunities for war profits and crime provided by the UN sanctions all perpetuated war unrelated to sovereign borders.

The successes of government forces in central Bosnia during 1993 owed much to the troops composed of people flooding into the area who had nowhere to go after they were expelled from their villages in other areas of the republic (most numerous from Serb-held eastern Bosnia, but also from Croat-run neighboring villages). The fighting was generating hundreds of thousands more Muslim displaced persons, since Croats and Serbs could more easily enter (or transit) Croatia or Serbia as refugees.[48] Migrants expelled from their homes, whether by violence or by official exchanges, had no ties to their new environment. Even towns and cities that had for two years maintained their commitment to multiethnic existence and culture, such as Sarajevo and Tuzla, were becoming more ethnically homogeneous and overrun by newcomers. The restraints moderating against the politicians who proclaimed "we can't live together" were rapidly evaporating. There were ever more people who had reason to seek revenge and to fight to defend or recover their homes, land, towns, and national identity.

While the refugee flow continued, refugees were increasingly bottled up in areas at war or where war might spread. Slovenia and Croatia closed their borders to refugees in August–September 1992 (and therefore passage outside former Yugoslavia to the north). Croatia reversed its practice, but not its decree, during 1993 to admit Croat refugees only.[49] Most of the 500,000 to 700,000 refugees in Serbia were housed in family homes, becoming a source under the deteriorating economic conditions in Serbia of increasingly open tensions.[50] In April–June, 1993, Serbia began to force the refugees to return home by disqualifying anyone from Serbian areas in Bosnia (fifty-six communes) or the Croatian *krajina* (twenty communes) as refugees, unless they were eligible for Red Cross aid. In a mobilization aimed at plans to escalate war in Bosnia-Herzegovina in January 1994, both Serbia and Croatia were forcibly rounding up refugees from Bosnia to be sent to the front. Germany began in February 1994 to require most refugees from Croatia to return home, and in March it began deporting all illegal refugees from the federal republic of Yugoslavia, the majority of them ethnic Albanians.[51] Sweden, a major depot for Yugoslav refugees, refused in 1993 to accept asylum applications from Albanians (largely from Kosovo) in order to save limited spaces for refugees from Bosnia. Kosovo Albanians denied asylum by West European governments were being deported to Macedonia rather than to Serbia because of the transport obstacles imposed by the UN sanctions. On top of the illegal flow of Albanians from Kosovo into northern Macedonia and the influx of Bosnian Muslim refugees from the war, this flow was a serious threat to interethnic relations and the question of who was and who was not a citizen and what rights of citizenship entailed at the heart of political stability in Macedonia.[52] Bilateral relations between Albania and Greece were seriously strained in 1991–93 over Albanian refugees in Greece, and then by Greeks from Albania wishing to enter Greece. Should fighting erupt in Macedonia, refugees would be trapped there or would rush to safety in Albania, Bulgaria, or Serbia. By arousing political tensions and organizing armies, this would sharply increase the probability of war in neighboring states, just as refugees from the war in Croatia had helped to instigate war in Bosnia-Herzegovina.

Another consequence of war, which complicated hopes for an end to hostilities, was astounding unemployment, affecting all areas from Slovenia to Macedonia. In the early stages of the conflict, the unemployed provided ready fighters because they were promised wages and benefits. Outside immediate war zones, they vote for xenophobic, right-wing radicals and exacerbate ethnic tensions with gang fights, terrorizing minorities, and crime, preparing the soil for war. Even in Slovenia, increasing unemployment (below 2 percent in 1988, it was at 14 percent by mid-1993) and the influx of refugees from Bosnia-Herzegovina led to a rise in hostile acts against foreigners, the birth of new parties to the right of the ruling nationalist coalition, and sufficient votes for one far right party to put it over the 5 percent minimum in the parliamentary elections held on December 6, 1992.[53] By September 1992 the government was using unabashedly nationalist justification to close its borders against refugees, and ever more Serbs were finding it expedient to change their identifying surnames and find sanctuary against open hostility and economic discrimination in a Slovene or German pedigree drawn from names on their maternal side of the family.[54] In Macedonia by mid-1994, official unemployment was 28 percent, and 23 percent of those who were employed had not been paid for over four months.[55] Because this unemployment was primarily in the formal economy, Macedonians were far more affected than Albanians who congregated more in the informal sector, and resentment at this difference was contributing to interethnic tensions and a rise in support for Macedonian nationalist political parties.

Cease-fires without a political solution in Croatia and Bosnia-Herzegovina exacerbated this problem of unemployment, for there was no way to restore normal life and work. The town of Srebrenica in eastern Bosnia, subjected to periodic shelling from Bosnian Serb artillery surrounding the town from April 1992 to April 1993, began to explode with social problems after the cease-fire and the UN Security Council declared it a safe area, in May 1993. Life in the town was characterized, according to visiting journalists and UN officials, by theft, black market activities, prostitution, and total boredom, particularly among youth.[56] In Banja Luka, a regional capital of the "Republic of Serbia," the Bosnian Serb army general Ratko Mladić was able to incite soldiers to rebellion in September 1993 against "war profiteers," miserable living standards, and the high cost of food and necessities so as to send a warning to the civilian leadership of Radovan Karadžić that he had this power.

Although displaced persons and the unemployed provided a pool of soldiers to replace those who had fled the country, refused to fight, or deserted, these were not soldiers trained to show restraint and obey a chain of command above their local commander. Because armies no longer had the option or the resources to screen for recruits who were psychologically unsuited, incidents that could escalate into armed confrontations were on the rise (including in Serbia) in 1993.[57] The vacuum created by the collapse of production, currencies, and legal trade was filled by black marketeers, arms and drug smugglers, sanctions-runners, and criminal syndicates—an entire underground economy based on war profit in guns, petroleum, liquid fuel, military supplies, cigarettes, and food.[58] It was difficult to see why armed citizens and groups should disband, disarm, or withdraw under such insecure conditions.

The aim of the arms embargo imposed by the UN Security Council on the region on September 25, 1991, was to staunch war by reducing its ammunition. Croatia, however, had no difficulty circumventing the embargo.[59] Serbs had little need to be concerned about the embargo because they had received large portions of ex-Yugoslav army stocks. Bosnian

Croats and Bosnian Serbs continued throughout the war to be supplied from their mother states of Croatia and Serbia. Heavy weapons could not be easily transported through Croat or Serb lines, but the Bosnian government and Muslim forces received substantial light arms and ammunition from émigrés and sympathizers in the West and from Islamic states such as Iran and Pakistan (although these caches fell in part to Croat forces which controlled the main supply routes).[60] And all warring parties sold each other weapons across battle lines in Bosnia-Herzegovina.

Moreover, the production of arms sufficient to make Yugoslavia one of the largest arms exporters in the developing world in the 1980s was at best slowed by the war.[61] While constant talk of lifting the arms embargo in the international community gave permission to an increasingly blatant violation of the embargo, Bosnian Serbs were developing whole new series of weapons. The longer the war went on in Bosnia-Herzegovina and the longer the stalemate continued in Croatia, the more weapons were produced and the more the international arms trade flourished in the area. The process of reorganizing and consolidating armed forces, of taking control of paramilitary forces, and of obtaining new sources of arms and fuel takes time.

This meant that the capacity for war was growing alongside political radicalization. Muslim forces in Bosnia-Herzegovina not only grew more radical as the war proceeded, but they also had the means to be more radical. The Croatian capacity to retake control over territory held by rebel Serbs increased, and as they demonstrated this capacity in more frequent military exercises, they provoked Serbs to enhance their military assets and readiness, to resist demilitarization as prescribed by the Vance plan, and to develop military cooperation with Bosnian Serbs. Negotiated cease-fires in both republics served the primary purpose of preparing for the next offensive. Radicalization among Kosovo Albanians was commensurate with their buildup of arms. Croatia and Serbia devoted substantial budgetary resources to building new capacity and weapons systems, paying the high cost for illegal imports of armaments, bombers, or strategic raw materials, and enhancing their arms industries to make them independent of the regionally integrated defense production in the former Yugoslavia. The trend in further militarization was even acknowledged by the Geneva negotiators when the Owen-Stoltenberg (Invincible) plan for an ethnic partition of Bosnia-Herzegovina abandoned a key plank of the Vance-Owen peace plan prescribing the republic's demilitarization.

The possession of arms was also a problem of civic order. Attempts by new governments to establish a monopoly over the legitimate use of coercive force, which is the precondition of any stable state, was an increasing cause of internal conflicts that could flare up into major confrontations without warning. The repressive use of Serbian police control over Kosovo beginning in 1988 was hardly within this realm of legitimacy, but the problem of relations between the Macedonian government and its ethnic Albanian population also showed worrisome signs of escalating conflict. The November 1992 crackdown by Macedonian police on smuggling and black market activities in the Bit Pazar mentioned earlier led to confrontation with Albanian youth and charges of anti-Albanian behavior. The Macedonian government crackdown on illegal possession of firearms by members of the Albanian community in November 1993 and subsequent trial and conviction of several deputy ministers of government in the summer of 1994 nearly led to a parliamentary crisis. Tensions in Vojvodina during the spring of 1992, which many feared presaged war, rose when Serbian police began to collect weapons house to house in mixed villages. One of the first acts of Milan Panić, in his six-month tenure as prime minister of Yugoslavia, was to fire the deputy minister of the interior, Mihalj Kertes, on the charge of instigating terror campaigns in Vojvodina in preparation for ethnic cleansing against Hungarians and other minorities (largely by Šešelj's Chetniks), but the response of Serbian authorities (it is assumed, from President Milošević) was to challenge his authority by barricading the interior ministry building. The crisis was later resolved, but only by Panić's defeat at the polls.

International action to contain the conflict in Bosnia-Herzegovina presumed an aggressive move on the part of Serbia toward Kosovo, but it was only one of a number of scenarios by which conflict could spread. Internal tensions within Macedonia, which could be sparked by events in neighboring Kosovo or Serbia, continued to rise without reversal between 1991 and 1994. A police crackdown in Kosovo or Vojvodina could trigger mass demonstrations and loss of life or the kind of local violence and reciprocal ethnic expulsions that began wars in Croatia and Bosnia-Herzegovina. The lobby favoring a military reintegration of *krajina* into Croatia could revive war in the republic at any moment. This would require the Bosnian Serb army to deploy troops immediately—because of military agreements and the obligation to provide fraternal assistance—and Croats would be likely to volunteer by the thousands. In the event of an escalation of war in Bosnia-Herzegovina or in Croatia in border areas of the federal republic of Yugoslavia, the Yugoslav Army would be likely to intervene on the grounds of vital interest. Such a war, the growing impatience of countries contributing troops to the UN forces, or the simple lifting of the arms embargo would oblige UNPROFOR to withdraw, with the likely collapse of existing cease-fire agreements. Radical nationalists among Serbs, Croats, Muslims, or Albanians could seize the occasion to create their vision of national states by military victory.

## Regional Instability

The question of whether the war in Bosnia-Herzegovina could be successfully contained, as major powers contended by late 1993, was based on a direct and exclusively military concept of spillover. But there were already externalities from the wars in 1991–93 that were having destabilizing effects in the Balkans and in Europe more generally. They received little attention because they did not constitute a classic case of war, but their cumulative effect in the long run would be just as serious, not precluding the outbreak of war.

The first of these externalities chronologically was the flight of refugees into central and western Europe, largely along previous paths of economic migration that promised networks of sanctuary—to Austria, Germany, and Sweden, for example. As the greatest flow of refugees *in Europe* since World War II spilled out of Croatia, Bosnia, and Serbia, or as foreign workers in European countries asked for resident asylum, the numbers began to threaten economies and political balances in otherwise stable European countries (see table 10-1).[62]

The danger of political instability began in Germany in 1992, where political discontent over the economic and political costs of German unification was already rising and migrants from all of the former communist bloc were flocking toward its liberal right of asylum (but not citizenship). Right-wing gangs intensified attacks on foreign residents, set fire to migrants' hostels, and rioted in east German towns, where unemployment of 50 to 70 percent provided receptive audiences for their xenophobic message of hate. Similar attacks against foreigners, riots by neofascist groups, and a surge in popularity among extreme right-wing political parties occurred in Britain, France, and Austria, where citizens were already concerned about the consequences of neo-Nazi revivals in Germany. Despite tighter laws on refugees in 1993, anti-foreigner extremists in Austria sent ten letter bombs in the first week of December 1993 to people who were working with immigrants and refugees, especially from former Yugoslavia. One of these people was the mayor of Vienna, Helmut Zilk, who was seriously wounded.[63]

The response came within the first year of the Yugoslav wars, when countries tightened border controls and moved to narrow or to reverse rules on amnesty and sanctuary that had been created to deal with the refugee crisis after World War II. Austria acted early to protect its borders by negotiating agreements with Hungary to keep migrants there, in camps, or to send them home. A petition drive initiated in January 1993 by Jörg Haider, the leader of the right-wing Freedom Party of Austria (FPOe), sought a national referendum to end further immigration. Hungary and Greece closed their borders with Yugoslavia in the fall of 1992.

TABLE 10-1. *Refugees from Yugoslavia by Country of Destination, Selected Countries, 1992–94*

| Country | As reported 7/29/92 | As reported 8/13/92 | As reported 11/12/92 | As reported 12/4/92 | As reported 7/16/93 | As reported 4/94 |
|---|---|---|---|---|---|---|
| Austria | 50,000 | 50,000 | 57,500 | 73,000 | 89,739 | 55,000 |
| Belgium | 870 | 870 | 1,800 | 3,371 | 5,420 | 4,865 |
| Czech Republic | 1,500[a] | 4,000[a] | 4,000[a] | 10,000[a] | 3,300 | 2,730 |
| Denmark | 1,637 | 1,637 | 6,412 | 7,323 | 7,078 | 20,128 |
| France | 1,108 | 1,108 | 1,108 | 4,200 | 5,524 | 15,918 |
| Germany | 200,000 | 200,000 | 235,000 | 250,000 | 340,200 | 309,449 |
| Hungary | 50,000 | 50,000 | 50,000 | 40,000 | 128,700 | 8,886 |
| Italy | 7,000 | 7,000 | 17,000 | 16,500 | 23,483 | 33,902 |
| Luxembourg | 1,000 | 1,000 | 1,200 | 1,618 | 1,280 | 2,535 |
| Netherlands | 6,300 | 6,300 | 6,300 | 7,000 | 2,648 | 42,253 |
| Norway | 2,331 | 2,331 | 3,674 | 3,720 | 2,173 | 18,563 |
| Poland | 1,500 | 1,500 | 1,500 | 3,000 | 3,170 | 675 |
| Portugal | n.a. | n.a. | n.a. | 144 | 159 | 150 |
| Russia | n.a. | n.a. | n.a. | n.a. | n.a. | 8 |
| Slovak Republic | n.a. | n.a. | n.a. | n.a. | 1,930 | 2,400 |
| Sweden | 44,167 | 55,000 | 74,141 | 62,202 | 92,047 | 76,189 |
| Switzerland | 17,573 | 17,573 | 70,450 | 80,000 | 72,380 | 32,102 |
| Turkey | 15,000 | 15,000 | 15,000 | 18,060 | 20,270 | 33,817 |
| United Kingdom | 1,100 | 1,300 | 4,000 | 4,424 | 8,640 | 8,027 |
| Total | 432,068 | 445,731 | 581,425 | 594,645 | 819,815 | 692,611 |

Source: UNHCR estimates.
n.a. not available
a. Represents all of Czechoslovakia.

And the ease with which some states could use border controls only increased the potential for regional instability as a result of squeezing refugees along paths less easily barricaded. Central European countries such as the Czech Republic worried increasingly about instability resulting from increasing numbers of refugees trapped in the east.[64] More immediately measurable were the increased presence, from Prague to Zurich and Amsterdam, of Yugoslav migrants and refugees in illegal drug trafficking networks and the violence accompanying their activities.[65] The fear of creating a new Gaza within Europe itself led many officials to argue strongly for an international commitment with UN or NATO troops to ensure the existence of Muslim areas in a partitioned Bosnia or to protect the continuity and integrity of Bosnia-Herzegovina. Giving to Islamic fundamentalists "a chance they never had in Bosnia-Herzegovina," there would be "in the heart of Europe" generations of uprooted Muslims aiming to prevent the death of their community, avenge their losses, and reconquer homeland.[66]

The Yugoslav wars had already during 1991–93 contributed directly to domestic political strains in many countries in the region. Their influence spread from Greece, where a splinter party broke from the New Democracy party on an anti-Macedonian platform and was defeated in the elections in 1993, to Russia, where Russian nationalists gained leverage in the parliamentary struggle with President Boris Yeltsin in late 1992–early 1993 with persistent pressure on the Serbian question. Yeltsin's coup against the Russian Parliament in September–October 1993 succeeded in replacing delegates elected in the Communist regime who were most vocal on the question, only to have the new parliament elected in December 1993 assert this position even more strongly and continue to use it to mobilize opposition to Yeltsin.[67] While insisting on political rather than military solutions to the national question in eastern Europe and the Balkans, they also argued for a greater Russian willingness to act militarily in conflicts in neighboring states of the former Soviet Union.[68]

The more Serbian and Croatian war propaganda portrayed the conflict in Bosnia-Herzegovina as a religious war, in which Serbs and Croats were playing their historical role in defending Christian Europe against the Muslim infidel, the more Islamic countries felt obliged to become involved and respond to their public's outrage at the slaughter of Muslims.[69] Secular Muslims in western Europe warned their compatriots that Islam was the second largest religion in Britain, France, and Germany, while neighbors such as Bulgaria with large Muslim minorities feared the destabilizing consequences of transforming the conflict into a religious war.

Four of the seven frontline states—Hungary, Romania, Bulgaria, and Albania—were attempting the same economic transition as former Yugoslavia within fragile democracies with particular dependence on an expansion of trade and foreign investment as engines of growth. Within less than two years of the 1989 revolutions, the war in Croatia and stalemate in the UNPAs had interrupted the main transportation route between the Middle East and the Balkans. Between July 1991 and July 1992 there was a slight diversion of both east-west and north-south traffic through Serbia and Hungary. Six months later the sanctions regime imposed a full halt. Five days on average were added to every trucker's route; the damage to roads in Bulgaria, Romania, and Hungary not built for trans-European traffic was costly; and traffic on the Danube River—Europe's water lifeline— was stalled for months at a time as a result of confrontations between Serbian barge captains and a Romanian government attempting to enforce the sanctions. The corruption of customs officials and border guards contributed to the general increase in lawlessness in regional trade and incentives to profit from war. West European subcontractors shifted production away from the Balkans, including Slovenia and Croatia, to other areas considered more politically stable such as the Baltics, and foreign investors waited for greater stability. The case of Bulgaria was particularly severe. The effect of the economic sanctions against Serbia came at the point of greatest austerity in Bulgaria's IMF macroeconomic stabilization program. The government claimed a loss of $1.5 billion in trade revenues in the first ten months of the sanctions.[70] The very trade and open market economies that the region was trying to achieve were blocked by war, which coincided with growing protectionism in western Europe. Alongside the direct costs of peacekeeping and humanitarian assistance, the indirect costs of enforcing the economic embargo and of constructing new roads through the Balkans (east-west through Macedonia and north-south through Bulgaria) mounted.

Although governments in neighboring Bulgaria, Romania, and Hungary labored to resist popular demands to assist conationals on the other side of the Yugoslav border, in part because they understood the radicalizing and uncontrollable potency of a mass-elite nationalist alliance, they were less able to control the economic consequences of the security vacuum that Western policy toward the Yugoslav conflict made abundantly clear. The fate of their postcommunist, westernizing reforms depended on cutting military budgets and forces and on demonstrating to those who controlled vital economic assistance and organizational memberships that they were trustworthy partners, stabilizing forces in their area, and secure places for foreign investment. As new governments without long-established legitimacy, however, they were more vulnerable to the danger of losing the army's loyalty in the face of inaction and to the apparent lack of Western support for liberal forces that was expressed in disinterest by Western powers in the consequences on their attempts to westernize. While there appeared to be somewhat more caution in official speeches in their nationalist language about borders and minorities during 1991, liberal parties from Bulgaria and Hungary to Russia had become more nationalist by 1993, preoccupied more with their diaspora and with the threat of minorities than with open borders and individual freedoms.

Even if the hostilities in former Yugoslavia did not become a catalyst of greater instability outside its borders, the failures of the Western response and the inadequacy of European security arrangements clearly heightened the perception of external insecurity throughout the region. Urgent appeals for NATO membership or other Western security guarantees to fill the security vacuum in eastern Europe came from presidents, prime ministers, and defense ministers in all countries of the former eastern bloc during 1993, pushing the Euro-Atlantic allies faster than they wanted to be pushed toward their incorporation and creating tensions within the alliance and between it and a more assertive Russia.

A series of interlocking security dilemmas also appeared to escalate closer to home. Sharp disagreements over foreign policy played a role in escalating tensions between the president of Bulgaria, Zhelyu Zhelev, and the new government coalition led by the Bulgarian Socialist party. Active Turkish diplomacy in Croatia and Macedonia during 1993 under the late President Turgut Özal, the arrival of Turkish troops to participate with the UN peacekeeping forces in Bosnia in the spring of 1994, and a pattern of U.S. policy perceived as solicitation of Muslim populations in the Balkans in general led to increasing nervousness in Greece. As a result of the unstable military situation in the Balkans, the reluctance of NATO to become involved militarily, and the insipid reactions of the CSCE to its responsibility for crisis management and conflict-regulation, states began to see military buildup as their only secure bargaining tool.

The ease with which Western governments had reimposed border controls, ignoring the unavoidable economic costs for neighboring states of the disruption of trade, the sanctuary to refugees, the relocation of production, and the implementation of sanctions against Serbia and Montenegro, also contributed to a growing anxiety on the part of the new regimes of central and eastern Europe that the processes of economic integration in Europe could be reversed. This potential for renewal of Fortress Europe struck a very bleak note at a moment of rising unemployment, voter dissatisfaction with reform that returned former Communist parties to government in Poland and Bulgaria, and renewed censorship or police surveillance and right-wing extremism in Hungary and Romania.

Moreover, the west European concept of security since the 1960s had been based primarily on a sense of belonging to a cultural community that was defined by common values and psychological predispositions. Thus many felt the barbarity of the war in Bosnia-Herzegovina, the many publicized images of atrocities within Europe, and Europe's failure to take an effective stand against a revival of ethnic purification, expulsion, and racial final solutions in the late twentieth century as a direct attack on their own security—perhaps on the idea of Europe itself. Far more insidious than the threat of military spillover was the sense, expressed often during 1992–93, that the wars in the Balkans were a violation of the European soul. Despite attempts to explain the atrocities by defining Balkan peoples as culturally different, many suggested that similarities between a European past and the Balkan conflict might not be a matter of history and that even if there was no reason to fear revival in central and western Europe, the idea of a European civilization was nonetheless tainted by the reappearance of nationalist hatreds and genocidal policies on European soil. The demoralizing effect of more than two years of nearly constant televised coverage of detention camps, bombed-out villages, mass killings, mutilations, and forced marches of persons expelled for reasons of ethnic background was not likely to show up for some time.[71]

The mutual recriminations and defensive bickering within the Euro-Atlantic alliance suggested more longer-term threats as a result of declining self-confidence and failure of nerve because of the inability of the international powers to manage the Yugoslav conflict successfully. Some within the NATO alliance questioned the purpose of military forces that cannot protect innocents in Europe against the threat of genocide. By November 1994 the role assumed late by NATO in Bosnia-Herzegovina had led to a genuine crisis of the alliance between the United States, which was pushing for ever-more assertive use of air power against the Bosnian Serbs, and those with troops on the ground in the UN protection forces—particularly Britain, France, Canada, the Netherlands, Denmark, and Russia, which insisted on a diplomatic solution to the war. EU diplomats had defined the Yugoslav challenge as a test of European unity and leadership and had just as publicly failed to meet that challenge. And by seeing the new threats to security in wars of civilization instead of those of ideology, and in culturally defined arcs of instability on their periphery where the West had better prepare to protect its civilization against this threat, Western politicians were instead giving encouragement to the very xenophobic, nationalist hatreds and suspicions that they were convinced had caused the Yugoslav wars.[72]

# Chapter 11

# *Conclusion*

A t the end of 1994, more than three years after the international community intervened explicitly to mediate the
Yugoslav conflict, there had been no progress on any of the issues raised
by the dissolution of the country in mid-1991. In Sarajevo, the cease-fire
of February 1994, which had brought to its residents the first rays of hope
that at least for them the war was over, had begun to break down. The
cease-fire in Croatia signed on March 29 had ended active hostilities but
was highly unstable without daily efforts by UN forces to keep both sides
to their agreements. The political stalemate between the Croatian government and the *krajina* Serbs when UN forces were approved was more
entrenched. Angry impatience on the Croatian side was channeled into
regular calls for the UN forces to leave and for military action, while an
atmosphere of fear on the Serb side sustained the impulse to seek protection
from Serbs elsewhere and from their own arms. The cease-fire between
Bosnian Croats and Bosniacs in Bosnia-Herzegovina also appeared to
depend on the presence of UN forces, for both sides found reasons to delay
or obstruct implementation of the political arrangements of cantonal organization, elections, and a joint army that would make their March 18
agreement to federate a reality. The long-term goals of both parties—
the Sarajevo government to reconquer militarily all territory in Bosnia-
Herzegovina and the Bosnian Croats to ensure their long-term security as
a nation—remained incompatible. At various times beginning in July, the
UN secretary general, the main troop-contributing countries, and
UNPROFOR officials threatened (with increasing credibility) simply to
withdraw the forces if cease-fires were not honored, additional cease-fires
signed, and more progress made toward a political settlement.

Although there were occasional rumors of progress in negotiations
between the Serbian government and Albanian leaders in Kosovo, President
Slobodan Milošević had made it a condition of assisting international
negotiators with Serb leaders in the Croatian *krajina* and in Bosnia-
Herzegovina that the two issues not be handled together. The Kosovo
question was to be kept separate and a matter of Serbian internal affairs.
Leaders from Macedonia and Greece remained at loggerheads. Slovene
progress toward association with the European Union was blocked by

Italy over disputes regarding Italian properties (about 300 houses) in Slovenia. New quarrels between Slovenia and Croatia over their border at the Adriatic (the Slovene Parliament claiming three villages outright from Croatia) had interrupted their initial steps toward rapprochement in the summer of 1994. The leaders responsible for the wars were more firmly established in power than they had been in 1990–91, and they appeared not to have changed any of their goals.

At the same time the best options for a solution to the crisis of 1990–91 had already been lost. Fundamental changes had taken place in the human and physical landscape that directly affected any political settlement. Mass population movements—by forced displacement or voluntary migration—had transformed the character of cities by flooding them with thousands of rural refugees. The longer the war went on and insecurity prevailed, the less likely it was that the displaced would ever return to their homes, despite the constant demand from politicians in Zagreb and Sarajevo that the UN accomplish this international commitment. The countryside in Bosnia-Herzegovina and Croatia was nearly shorn of its multiethnicity, and a brain drain of serious proportions was threatening the long-term prospects for recovery from central Bosnia to Serbia. Where there were tentative steps toward a negotiated peace, such as the federation between Bosnian Croats and Bosniacs, the inducement offered Croats of a confederal arrangement with neighboring Croatia was roundly attacked in Croatia as the beginning of a re-creation of the old Yugoslavia. The specter grew when diplomatic efforts to fill in the third piece of the Bosnian puzzle (the Contact Group proposal) made no headway until consideration was given to the same right for Serbs to confederate with Serbia. Those who had held the opinion since mid-1991 that the only stable solution to the crisis was a re-creation of links among the Yugoslav nations—their de facto restoration if not the creation of a new state itself—had gone silent for fear of retribution.

But whether as fear or as conviction, even these expectations were short-lived. Diplomatic efforts seemed once again at a dead end, and the tragedy stumbled on. In fact, local observers argued that if such a solution were found, the political fallout would be enough to prevent it from being accepted. Delay, that renowned Balkan method of conflict resolution, would be used to protect politicians from the inevitable moment when they would be forced by their constituents to answer the searing question, Why had there been war?[1]

## Quicksand

External powers had been correct in one element of their condemnation of the Yugoslav actors in mid-1991: in opposing the resort to armed force to achieve their political objectives, including a change in borders. A part of the ongoing tragedy was that military victory was still seen by most insiders in 1994 as the only solution to their particular conflict. The war option remained sufficiently popular that armies were actively being built up and supplied, despite the existence of a UN embargo on arms. But now this view was shared by many outsiders.

One impulse came from impatience. Abandoning hope that external intervention could assist, a new consensus was growing that it was necessary to withdraw the UN protection forces (and with them, humanitarian agencies and nongovernmental organizations) and leave the parties to fight it out on their own. A second impulse came from a shift in the view of interventionists and supporters of the Bosnian government to the theory of just war.[2] The Bosnian Muslims had not only the right (by UN Charter, Article 51) to self-defense, but also the moral right to reverse the territorial gains of Bosnian Serbs and to expect the world's assistance in avenging Serb aggression and crimes against humanity.[3]

Whatever their other objectives, however, neither of these proposals had much prospect of providing a solution to the war in Bosnia or to the other Yugoslav conflicts. The defeatist impulse to withdraw the international presence was once again resisted at the last moment for fear of the alternative.[4] The war would not only escalate and erase the cease-fires that had been reached but would also spread. And according to most military experts, the just war impulse—to exempt the Bosnian government from the arms embargo, withdraw UN forces, and support the Bosnian government army with air strikes against Bosnian Serb military capacity and with training in the use of the tanks and heavy artillery they would receive—would not lead to a decisive military victory. In fact, it could lead to a preemptive strike by the Bosnian Serbs and a re-creation of the Croat-Serb alliance to partition Bosnia that together could defeat the Bosnian Muslims decisively.[5] Neither proposal would begin to solve the other conflicts in Croatia, Serbia, or Macedonia, but both would certainly lead to an expansion of the war beyond Bosnian borders.

More to the point, these attempts by outsiders at extrication were no longer possible. The definition of tragedy introduced in chapter 1 had deepened. The actors continued to play the roles they had set out; the onlookers continued to think this was not worth the trouble or importance to become fully engaged; and the fate of the two were increasingly intertwined. Leaders continued to insist that national self-determination was a question of territory, not of people and rights. Onlookers defined the problem as one of military aggression, but they were unwilling to use military force to stop that aggression. They insisted on one set of borders for the new states on the grounds that international norms were at stake, but they were unwilling to defend those borders militarily or to accept that the role of mediator with the governments of these new states was insufficient.

Instead, the international approach to the Yugoslav conflict had become like pesticides—each application seemed to strengthen the resistance of those it aimed to defeat, requiring ever heavier doses and tougher formulas for ever less effect. But this approach had not been abandoned in favor of a real alternative by the end of 1994. Instead, each crisis was met with efforts to strengthen the means of leverage over the parties rather than to reconsider the strategy and solution. The instruments chosen—such as economic sanctions against Serbia and Montenegro, safe areas for Muslim cities, and the use of air power against Bosnian and Croatian Serbs aimed, it was said, at bringing the Serbs to the bargaining table—were exhausting their effectiveness, and the world community seemed to be running out of instruments.

In fact, for analysts in major capitals and international organizations engaged in the Yugoslav crisis, the issue of intervention had become focused on the use of force. Should it have been used and when? Who should have intervened? The UN mission failed, many said, because it was not given sufficient force and robust rules of engagement to implement its tasks in conditions of war and to roll back aggression and prevent ethnic cleansing. NATO faced its Dunkirk in the first week of December 1994, according to the response of its core governments and its new secretary-general, because the UN prevented it from using sufficient force against Serb forces in the Bihać pocket.[6] The harshest criticism was reserved for UN generals on the ground (particularly those in command in Sarajevo) and for defense establishments (particularly the Pentagon) for obstructing military engagement for fear of falling into a quagmire and of losing soldiers' lives.

Nonetheless, the unity that major powers agreed to preserve in the spring of 1994 was based on their consensus that there was no military solution to the crisis but only a negotiated, political solution. The crisis of credibility for NATO and the UN was averted in December by a reaffirmation of the humanitarian and peace-facilitating role of UNPROFOR *and* the need to give it more forcefulness. The reluctance to use military force therefore remained a cover for major disagreements among the major powers about their objectives in the Balkan peninsula and their continuing absence of a policy toward the conflict itself. This has been transparently clear when decisions *were* made to use military force, such as air power to defend safe areas, because the use was reactive, crisis-driven, motivated almost by pique at Bosnian Serb defiance. It was simply added to the existing approach, with all its contradictions. Thus UN commanders saw air power as extending their means of self-defense, protecting the lives of their soldiers and other UN personnel aiding civilians no matter which warring party was the offender, whereas some governments behind the UN Security Council resolutions and NATO decisions, particularly the United States, intended air power to support the sovereignty of a UN member state by helping the Bosnian government defeat the Bosnian Serbs. Moreover, to judge the effectiveness of additional military force would have required explicit definition of and consensus on the political goals of such military action.

However, the reluctance to use military force also reflected what had been the dominant view only five years earlier, in 1989–90, that a pan-European reduction in troops and weapons was a positive goal. The reluctance of comfortable citizens in wealthy states and urban environments to go to war certainly had not changed. The issue of force was far larger than the question of Balkan significance, such as the redesign of militaries to meet post–cold war tasks and the question of whether the assumptions and methods of diplomacy and of existing multilateral institutions depend too much on the threat of military force that will not be forthcoming.

Finally, the cause of the Yugoslav conflict was the collapse of the Yugoslav state. For Yugoslav citizens, the collapse of the state did not mean exposure to external invasion but the collapse of internal security guarantees. The stable expectations of other peoples' behavior that make possible survival by what Europeans were calling civilized norms evaporated, and the shared rules of the game and political culture that are necessary to communicate in resolving differences, regardless of linguistic differences, dissolved. But this was now a problem for international negotiators as well. The same chaos undermined negotiations that were meant to be cumulative and to depend for their enforcement on the accountability of leaders who signed agreements. In place of the expectations on which negotiations were based, there was a breakdown of command and control within military hierarchies; a refusal by many ordinary citizens to treat the republican borders as international frontiers or to accept their legitimacy; an illegal flow of arms and strategic resources such as fuel across international borders; and the priority of local interests, personal connections, and criminal networks across warring factions over central command. Moreover, the collapse of the state and fight for new states faced negotiators with onerous tradeoffs, particularly in instances where paramilitaries, terrorists, and local rebellions were tolerated or even used by political leaders to pursue their goals. To get political agreements or to put a stop to abuses of international norms, international negotiators must concede the legitimacy (and even require that its authority be strengthened) of persons who have been condemned for defying those norms. To hold leaders accountable for implementing arrangements and obeying norms, these negotiators have to contend with the limits of political authority in this stateless chaos. Though negotiators may themselves risk condemnation from their own governments, they risk undermining the small existing accountability and political control in the environment if they do not allow leaders to obtain compliance from followers and soldiers in ways that permit them to save face with their constituents.

## Political Capacity and the International Context

The use of force in the Yugoslav crisis, and the call for the international community to use force, reflect a failure of political capacity on both sides to resolve conflicts peacefully. The international context was critical to the process of disintegration in Yugoslavia. International action during the 1980s contributed to an erosion of the existing constitutional order and political capacity for managing the transition. By 1989 the last elements of international security and stability on which the Yugoslav government had calculated its policies for forty years were gone. And while one can assume that up to 1991 these international influences were largely unintended in their political consequences, the actions of EC and CSCE officials as mediators in early July began a process by which major powers and international negotiators and organizations assumed the functions of the Yugoslav state.

Whether in its more unintended phase or in its interventionist phase, actions coming from the international community undermined the Yugoslavs' capacity for autonomous resolution of their internal conflicts. But having taken over the function of the Yugoslav state temporarily—as conflict mediators, police forces, rulemakers, standard bearers, watch dogs, and charity organizations—the international community was not helping the various political communities and citizens of former Yugoslavia to rebuild that institutional capacity. UN forces were able to give them the time needed, saving lives in the meantime, but they could not intervene to help build that capacity or to require that it be built.

The impulse behind the two proposals for international action at the end of 1994 cited above, to hand the task back to the former Yugoslavs themselves, was not in principle a bad idea. But it was irresponsible at this point to abandon the people to more war because the failure was shared. Outsiders had not even begun in 1994 to provide the conditions in former Yugoslavia's external environment that would enable them to find a nonviolent solution. Negotiators and major powers were expecting leaders and citizens to respond to their demands, incentives, and disincentives in what they considered a rational calculation of their best interests, but they were not providing the coherent context necessary for such strategic behavior. The opposite, in fact, was intended; the bases of deterrence as a substitute for military force are uncertainty and risk. And, in some cases, the major powers were demanding what parties perceived to be not in their best interests.

In the absence of a more secure and benign external context, nationalism and the calculation of national interest were the logical response of political leaders. As long as outsiders defined the problem as ethnic conflict or took sides with particular ethnonational groups (whether as victims or victors), they would see an ethnically defined result such as was being crafted in every peace proposal for Croatia and for Bosnia-Herzegovina. The problem was not ethnic conflict but the collapse and rejection of an overarching legal authority and of a capacity to tolerate and manage difference. The particular means chosen for accommodating differences in socialist Yugoslavia (including, but not only, ethnonational differences) had been rejected, and outsiders had helped to disable and diminish the natural constituencies within the country for the values they claimed.

## Democratization

A question frequently posed about Yugoslavia is whether a democratic country would have gone the same route, and therefore whether the source of the problem was dictatorship. The answer is that democracy is another way of saying the same thing: it is that political capacity to manage conflicts, even as polarized and uncompromising as the positions taken on economic and constitutional reform in the 1980s, without violence. But that does not mean that to have democracy is a matter simply of wishing, or that democracy and dictatorship are the only alternatives. Democracy comprises institutions and procedures that have to be built, and the early stages of democratization in Yugoslavia led to violent conflict.[7]

Nationalism became a political force when leaders in the republics sought popular support as bargaining chips in federal disputes. The insistence on majoritarian rule for national communities in a system where all nations were minorities led to legitimate fears of majority tyranny and defensive mobilization rather than alliance-building to protect political rights. Nationalist politicians were able to mobilize support with the opportunities provided by the process of democratization—the organization of social movements and protest demonstrations, the revival of assertive parliaments, freedom of speech and press, competition for votes, and revisions of citizenship rights. The speed with which hostilities escalated was in part due to the unrestrained freedom of speech and press, which allowed the media to play to current fears with historical memories and emotive symbols to build a popular base.

Western powers and organizations enthusiastically welcomed the appearance of competitive elections in 1990 and even the revival of right-wing, exclusionary, ethnic nationalism when it came in the guise of anti-communism. But their apparent commitment to elections and to individual freedoms was not strong enough, when republics began to press for independence, to insist that citizens have a chance—through a federal election or a special referendum or plebiscite—to register their preferences on the breakup of the country before it was dissolved. In the decisions made in 1991, Europe accepted without question that the people who had the right to self-determination were the majority nations within the republics, not the Yugoslav people as a whole. They then became more concerned to support the leaders who had been elected, as if this would promote stability, than to develop democracy and the genuine stability it can bring.[8]

The primary protection of minority rights in the socialist system—the proportional distribution of government jobs and the budgetary outlays for cultural rights—could not be sustained economically in the face of deep fiscal cuts or politically in the face of the confrontation between rich and poor over taxation and federally mandated redistribution that economic crisis brought. The increasing openness and belligerence of political rhetoric among the political and cultural elites forged the political link necessary in democracies between the antipolitical responses of average citizens and the politics of elites in the defense of privilege or the righting of wrongs. Absent were institutionalized and professional restraints on the media, political organizations based on economic interests that cut across national identities and can moderate debate, and accepted procedural safeguards for those whose rights were being abused. The primary mechanism of holding governments accountable for protecting of rights and freedoms during the liberalizing period of the 1980s was the country's extensive political decentralization. It created multiple political arenas in the various republics: journalists who could not publish in one republic could get an audience in another; people facing discrimination in one republic could emigrate temporarily to another; and social movements repressed in one republic might hope for publicity and outside pressure in another. While far from satisfactory as a means of protection, this form of competition ended when Slovenia and Croatia chose to leave the federation and those outsiders negotiating the country's dissolution failed to insist on conditions that would foster alternative protections in the new states. Persons threatened with a loss of rights and status mobilized faster and more effectively than those who were poorer and had less power, but international support continued to favor the majority nation in each case of conflict and to accept their labels of minorities and rebels (except, for a short time, Albanians in Serbia, and possibly Albanians in Macedonia).

The human rights mandate of the CSCE was used to press for defense of anticommunist intellectuals—including the dissident Vojislav Šešelj, who turned into a neofascist promoter of ethnic cleansing by violence and terror—but not for the defense of individuals expelled from their jobs because of their ethnic identity or for the representation in some way of individuals who voted against their republic's secession, for political autonomy within the republics, or for constitutional alternatives to ethnic partition. In the one exception—U.S. opposition beginning in April 1989 to repression against Albanians in Kosovo based on CSCE principles and authority—the policy had the opposite result. It focused publicity on the republican government of Serbia to press for respect for Albanian human rights. The federal government had final authority over human rights, however, and it was federal decision to send a police action into Kosovo, declare martial law, and accept Serbian revisions of its constitution to reduce Kosovo's (and Vojvodina's) autonomy. When pressure did focus on the federal government at the end of 1990 and early 1991 it took the form of economic sanctions that further undermined its dwindling authority. This cumulative pressure therefore favored the nationalist rather than the civic, nonnationalist definition of the Kosovo problem, bypassed the arena where a nonnationalist, democratic approach was possible, and strengthened the trend of European states to ignore the federal government and talk directly to the leaders of the republics.

Even if such pressure had not been counterproductive toward Kosovo, by improving Milošević's standing with Serbs who saw this as illegitimate interference in their internal affairs, the policy contributed to the weakening of the federal government and to the victory of the nationalist agenda. The policy to protect Albanian rights needed more backing than declaration of CSCE principles because it was in direct contradiction to the pressures from the IMF and the banking consortium organized by the U.S. State Department to recentralize monetary control and create more effective economic administration—a primary reason for the Serbian constitutional revision reducing its provinces' autonomy. This was even clearer when outsiders retreated on even this exception in the face of Kosovar referendums on sovereignty beginning in 1990 and when the republican principle, as in the similar case with *krajina* Serbs in Croatia, took precedence over popular expressions of self-determination through elections.

## Economic Reform and Incorporation

On the face of it, IMF macroeconomic stabilization programs and credit ratings are clearly inadequate and inappropriate as the primary method of transforming socialist countries into market economies and certifying eligibility for membership in the West. In their development in the immediate postwar balance-of-payments crises of 1947 and the stabilization reform programs of the Marshall Plan, they were applied to economic and political circumstances very different from the postsocialist transformation of the 1990s, and they were only one part of a comprehensive political and strategic framework for West European integration under U.S. leadership. Though these stabilization programs had revolutionary consequences in socialist countries in the 1980s and the postcommunist transition, their aim and the goal of the policies toward Yugoslavia at the time (particularly of the United States and Great Britain) was profoundly conservative. In fact, the primary interest in holding Yugoslavia together in its crisis days of 1990 up to the late spring of 1991 came from the international banking consortium concerned about debt servicing and repayment. Terms for loans had been based on the export-earning capacity of the richer republics, which served as a kind of collateral for the others, which would likely have to default if the country dissolved.

The primary problem, however, lay in the lack of recognition and accommodation for the socially polarizing and politically disintegrating consequences of this IMF-conditionality program and approach to Westernization. The austerities of policies of demand-repression led to conditions that could not easily foster a political culture of tolerance and compromise. Instead, the social bases for stable government and democratization were being radically narrowed by economic polarization between rich and poor, fiscal crises for most government budgets, deindustrialization without prospects of new investment in poorer regions, growing uncertainty and individuals' resort to nonmonetary means of obtaining necessities because of rising inflation, and serious unemployment among young people and unskilled workers that began to affect even the secure jobs and incomes of public-sector professionals, skilled workers, administrators, and their children.

The architects of the programs of macroeconomic stabilization and economic austerity ignored the necessity of creating not only social safety nets but even more important a political capacity to recognize and manage these conflicts. The system had been structured around substantive and participatory rights that depended on budgetary expenditures and public ownership, not the procedural rights of market-oriented democracies. Instead, the insistence that welfare should be provided either through free-market forces or by lower-level governments made average citizens more dependent on their local and republican governments and on nurturing informal networks of loyalty and support than on organizing around collective economic interests and Yugoslav-wide solutions. Both reinforced the tendency to disintegration of their common legal order. This attack on welfare in a system designed to guarantee subsistence and institutionalize protection also gave republican governments even greater reason to resist federal taxation and authority, encouraged localisms where the politics of capital cities neglected poorer regions or ethnic minorities, exacerbated the gap between those with relatively secure public employment and an insecure, disenfranchised private sector, and made it even more difficult for those who wanted to create cross-republican and society-wide political organizations and communication to counteract the appeals of nationalists to themes of national exploitation and protection.

The political effects of economic reform were equally important and also neglected. The common view that priority should be given to economic reform in the transition from socialism and that faster economic change is better (as in shock-therapy stabilization, for example) ignores the fact that such reforms cannot succeed without institutional changes. And these changes fundamentally alter the existing distribution of rights and power. Economic reform, far from providing a solvent of political conflict, creates new conflicts. The technocratic assumption behind the political and administrative reforms that international creditors and domestic economic reformers promoted led, in fact, to a fateful confrontation over the nature of the state. The program—restoring financial discipline by recentralizing control over monetary policy, allocating foreign exchange through market mechanisms instead of exporters' privileges, insulating central bankers from parliamentary debate and political choice, making the federal government more administratively effective in implementing economic decisions and imposing sanctions, and transferring the burden of adjustment to economic decline onto fiscal policy and parliaments—was not politically neutral. But the federal prime minister, his government, and his advisers did not appear to recognize the need to dedicate time to selling the program politically or to building a governing capacity in addition to more effective administration. In fact the economic program and its legitimating rhetoric of free enterprise and property rights encouraged autonomist demands by regional or local governments and by politicians who could exploit the exclusionary language of nationalism and its narrowing definition of those entitled to rights in a time of cuts.

### The International Context of Domestic Calculation

The change in U.S. policy as a consequence of Soviet reforms after 1985–88 also contributed to destabilization of the federal government because it brought a rapid, unilateral end to the implicit guarantees of financial assistance and of Yugoslav independence and integrity that had accompanied Yugoslavia's strategic role for the Western alliance over four decades. At the same time, NATO's posture in the eastern Mediterranean and the U.S. focus on developing high-tech weapons systems seemed to increase the threat to Yugoslav independence and security. This expressed itself in the quarrels in 1989–91 between Prime Minister Ante Marković and Defense Minister Veljko Kadijević and the army general staff over what constituted minimal defense preparedness at a time when the defense budget was under attack as a result of the stabilization policy and the tax rebellions of republican parliaments.

To the extent that the European Community attempted to influence the Yugoslav crisis before the declarations of Slovene and Croatian independence on June 25, 1991, it was in response to the federal government's effort to substitute Europe for the retreating United States. The EC agreed to Yugoslavia's request for $4.5 million in credits in support of its shock-therapy stabilization program, but with additional conditions: not only that it show further progress on reforms but also that the country hold together. At the same time, however, the U.S. government was pulling further in the opposite direction, withdrawing existing economic assistance from the federal government and promising reinstatement on condition that the country remain together. Moreover, because Yugoslavia had not been party, as a neutral, nonaligned country, to the strategic- and conventional-arms reduction talks, confidence-building measures, and growing cooperation on East-West security, neither the Europeans nor the United States did anything to fill this vacuum in security. In fact, reversing the logic of security regimes, Europeans adopted an explicit policy in 1992–94 that no discussions about incorporating the former Yugoslav states into European forums of military cooperation and confidence-building on the continent could begin while they were at war.

Like the IMF before it, the EC mission appeared to believe that economic reform was primarily a matter of sufficient political will and that politicians would be guided by an economic rationality that would override nationalism in the republics. Yet economic reform and IMF conditionality had become issues of constitutional (called "national") rights by 1987–89. In the conflict between confederalists and federalists over the reform of government and over the budget, economic interest and nationalism could not be separated. Moreover, those most in need of persuasion to keep the country together were not federal officials but the Slovene and Croatian governments, and they opposed key elements of the economic reforms. The issue was not political will but political authority.

The decisions of nationalists, particularly in Slovenia and Croatia, were also being made within an international context. That context included more than the EC mission and offers of aid. Encouraged by outsiders (from neighboring states to the European parliament) to believe that they could more easily and rapidly enter Europe as independent states, the Slovenes and Croats had already calculated that it was in their economic interest in the long run to separate.[9] Serbian nationalism was also not vulnerable to economic persuasion because the Serbian leadership had determined that its economic interest would be unaffected by Slovene secession. The increasing discussion in the wider region after 1985 about "natural economic regions"—in particular by Austria, Italy, Switzerland, Germany, and Greece (and even by the United States after 1989 as regards the role of Germany towards central and eastern Europe)—was also sending signals of economic options to Slovene and Croatian leaders (and as a fall-back position, also to Serbia) that challenged the Westerners' assumption that it was economically more rational to remain united.

Although the leverage of economic incentives in new credits or restoration of aid was insufficient to keep the country together, Western powers chose the same approach to obtain a political agreement in the fall of 1991. They repeated it to stop the war in Bosnia-Herzegovina. But in these cases, the economistic approach was reduced to punishments and disincentives. The reasoning behind economic sanctions on the federal government in the fall of 1991, to the extent that there was any government left, is difficult to fathom. Economic sanctions against Serbia and Montenegro did do serious damage to their economies, as intended, but they did not achieve peace in Bosnia more quickly. Although the role of sanctions independent of other factors is difficult to measure, it is clear that sanctions worsened the economic decline and competition over economic resources that had led originally to a disintegration of civil order and a rise of radical nationalists in Yugoslavia. The political consequences for the new Yugoslavia were therefore counterproductive, as a result of intensified class warfare, a fortress mentality against the outside, and the resort to familial systems of support and the resources of rural households and landholdings outside the cash economy that entail the social obligations and patriarchal culture tied to defense of the land and nation.

The sanctions, by isolating areas inhabited by Serbs from outside sources of information and commerce, weakened the external pressures for and internal causes of a policy of peace. By contrast, forcing the Serbs to rely more on their own resources required nationalist policies. Applying sanctions to Serbs wherever they lived made them feel one people who had to support each other.[10] Sanctions encouraged expenditure on new weapons systems and military buildup, provided an excuse for expanding police forces and ruling by fiat, and fostered overall lawlessness at home and in foreign trade. These developments also were not likely to be easily reversed with a lifting of sanctions. The sanctioning countries were counting on being able to propel into political action against the war and Serbian nationalism certain groups in particular, such as those with liberal economic interests and cosmopolitan identities. These people responded to the sanctions by leaving the country or becoming more nationalist out of outrage at their one-sided application. Although the sanctions increased opposition to Milošević's rule, it was a more nationalist opposition committed ideologically to Serbs outside of Serbia. This, together with the direct effect of sanctions on the economy and society, gave Milošević further reason to delay democratic change and normalization, and at the same time gave outsiders reason to keep Milošević in power.

The effects on Macedonia were increasingly difficult to assess as they moved from the consequences of an embargo against its main trading partner (not only of final goods but also of stages of integrated production) to the effects of the transfer southward of illegal trade through its borders after sanctions were tightened on Danube traffic. Was it disruption of the path to marketization, privatization, and a law-based state, or the impending disruption of their primary source of economic growth by 1994 in sanctions-busting, that was more destabilizing?

The ineffectiveness of economic pressure to reverse nationalist policies is perhaps better seen in its local versions. The Croatian government chose to gain leverage over the *krajina* Serbs by weakening them through, among other instruments, economic sanctions. Aided by the international community in its sanctions policy against all Serbs, the intent was either to starve the leadership into submission to Zagreb so as to achieve "reintegration of occupied Croatian territories,"[11] or to force individual Serbs through economic deprivation to leave Croatia and thereby clear the territory for Croats to return home or to resettle.[12] Greece also used economic pressure against Macedonia through two trade embargoes that included blocking its only access to the sea at Thessaloniki to force Macedonian leaders to change their position on the country's name, flag, and constitutional preamble. In both cases, these tactics appear to have made their targets more stubborn. In Croatia, they only confirmed Serb fears about their fate in a national Croatian state, making them more intransigent about seeking political independence. When the Contact Group succeeded in persuading Milošević to increase pressure on the Bosnian Serbs to sign their peace proposal by closing the Yugoslav border on August 4, 1994, to all nonhumanitarian goods and aid to Bosnian Serbs, the consequence was also to squeeze the *krajina* Serbs and to intensify the effect of Croatian policy. Despite expectations that both *krajina* Serbs and Bosnian Serbs would be forced into accepting rule from Zagreb and Sarajevo, respectively, the result was political chaos in Knin, as leaders recalculated alliances and national interest and intensified bonds of sympathy and interest between the two groups of Serbs that overcame remaining resistance to their joint military activity.[13] The immediate result was an escalation of war in Bosnia-Herzegovina and the most significant shift in the strategic situation in more than a year. In Macedonia, the embargo and European reluctance to punish Greece interrupted negotiations and quiet moves toward concessions on the part of Macedonia, worsened economic conditions that were feeding radicalization of Albanian and Macedonian nationalists and interethnic conflict, and bred alienation among average citizens in Macedonia against the international community and what they began to call a new colonialism.

## Codes of Conduct without Membership

The international community also sought leverage over the conflict in Yugoslavia with moral instruments. This was both a rationale for intervention and an objective of intervention: to impose a code of conduct on political leaders and on warring parties. The code of conduct was based on CSCE principles: the inviolability of existing borders, human rights, and the peaceful resolution of disputes. The leverage was membership—access to association agreements with the European Union, eligibility for European assistance programs such as PHARE, membership in the Council of Europe, and, for the federal republic of Yugoslavia (Serbia and Montenegro), restored membership in the CSCE and admission as a member state (but not successor to Yugoslavia) in the United Nations.[14] As British Prime Minister John Major concluded at the London conference in late August 1992, "The different former Yugoslav delegations, and in particular I think those from Serbia and Montenegro, must ask themselves this question: Do you wish to be considered as part of Europe? Do you wish to belong to the world community? If so, good, but that does mean accepting the standards of the rest of Europe and of the world community."[15] The economic sanctions were also based in part on the incentive of membership, telling the leaders in Serbia and Montenegro that they would be isolated from European forums until they practiced the community's norms.

The difficulty with this moral sanction was credibility. For those who were the object of sanctions, European actions had been duplicitous. Europeans told Yugoslavs to honor the sanctity of international borders while they were themselves violating the norm of sanctity by applying it to the republican borders instead of Yugoslav and after some European nations had counseled secession and helped secretly to supply alternative national armies in the republics. In offering good offices to facilitate dialogue in June–July 1991, the EC and CSCE delegations acted as if the conflict between the Slovene government and the federal government was a border dispute between independent states. They thus showed that the moment for mediation had passed, not because it was too late in the Yugoslav conflict, as is generally argued, but because the mediators had already drawn conclusions. The irony for those who regretted the loss of their country or the unnecessary deaths and destruction as a result of the way it was dissolved was that principles originally designed to be subversive— the right of national self-determination in the case of the empires in 1918 and the right to intervene in defense of human rights in the case of the communist bloc in 1975—were used to defend European security and stability.[16] The community of norms that the United States and Europe were demanding members respect presumed reciprocity, but in practice it appeared still to be based on the assumption of a divided Europe.

The real issue of membership was the definition and geographical scope of Europe by west Europeans. The imposition of sanctions against Serbia and Montenegro reinforced their leaders' perception that the recognition of Slovenia and Croatia and the anti-Serbian agenda at home and abroad was part of a larger policy to divide the country in two, between a "European" north and a "Balkan" south, in which residents of the southeastern half would not in any case be eligible for the European membership they sought. Had not the Europeans already signaled their inclination with their policy of containment toward the Bosnian war, with their refusal to send troops in defense of the European norms they insisted that Yugoslavs obey except under the cover of the United Nations and a humanitarian and peace-keeping mandate, usually reserved for the third world, and with their priority in December 1991 to the issues of the Maastricht treaty for deepening current EC integration over their disagreements with Germany on early recognition of Croatia? These decisions strengthened the camp within Serbia that either forecast or favored European preference for deepening before widening its integration and that asserted that Serbia must expect to create its own position of strength in the Balkans. This camp took the position that countries such as Austria would not continue to have so much influence over Serbia's fate if Serbia was *not* constrained by membership in common European institutions but became a regional power instead.

Economic and moral sanctions therefore reinforced the *realpolitik* calculations of President Milošević. Each U.S. threat to extend the conditions and prolong the date for lifting the economic sanctions—an end to the war in Bosnia-Herzegovina, then a recognition of Croatian sovereignty and resolution of the *krajina* conflict, and then a resolution of the conflict with ethnic Albanians in Kosovo—gave Milošević further reason to continue behaving as he had until then, with cold calculation of Serbian national interest. This calculation, moreover, included the judgment that European states would choose eventually to traffic with Serbia and Montenegro because of their own perceived national interests and that this required a Belgrade policy of securing as much geopolitical and economic strength in the Balkans as the contest at any particular moment would bear.[17] Although major powers had imposed the sanctions to obtain Serbian cooperation, this long-term strategic perspective, in turn, limited what Milošević could do in resolving the conflicts on his border in Croatia and Bosnia-Herzegovina and gave him the short-term tactical advantage.

The threats of exclusion and promises of inclusion as a means of influencing the behavior of all parties in the conflicts not only depended on more convincing commitments that membership was possible; they also ignored a fundamental precondition of membership for the parties themselves, which was statehood. Only states can be members. Each national leader would do first what was necessary to obtain sovereignty and to establish the borders of a viable, defensible state.[18] If the choice was between behaving in ways that would in the short run receive condemnation and exclusion but in the long run, statehood, national leaders would risk exclusion. If the consequence of that choice to put the security of their people first was prosecution as a war criminal in the future, that would only occur after they had succeeded, or definitively failed. In either case, they would have become heroes to their nation. That status might even rise if they were actually condemned.

## Borders and Human Rights

The difficulty for outside powers seeking ways to defend the CSCE principles and their goal of European security lay in their attempt to keep separate the issues of borders and human rights.[19] The Yugoslav conflict after mid-1990 was not an ethnic conflict but a struggle for national rights. Insofar as citizens identified as members of nations, in a country where all nations were numerically a minority they perceived their survival in the constitutionally defined equal status of those nations. This equality protected them from being treated (and even being perceived) as a minority. This sense of entitlement had not dissolved with Yugoslavia but had instead intensified in the face of necessity and opportunity. Although the international community did not accept the right to create national states for all those who claimed it, this did not diminish the strength of conviction among many that their very survival was at stake. Outside powers could not insist on inviolable borders without an accompanying policy on human rights for those who felt unsafe or unwelcome in their new country.

Evidence from Croatia, moreover, demonstrated that such an accompanying human rights policy had to be assertively interventionist. The fears of Serbs in border regions of Croatia, who sought remedy through an independent state after the republic declared its independence, grew from actual treatment in Croatia in 1989–91, when their constitutional status was demoted from that of equal nation to ethnic minority. Discrimination against Serbs throughout the republic in jobs, schools, and citizenship rights led them to believe they would never be secure as Serbs in Croatia. This did not excuse their resort to arms, as many within the Serb community of Croatia also argued at every stage of the escalating conflict.

But their resort to arms also does not excuse others from denying the problem of rights and protections, if for no other reason than the reality of their situation.

The turning point in the dissolution of Yugoslavia as it affected endangered individuals, according to their own reports, was when they saw the necessity as families or localities to resort to guns in self-defense. For the international community also, reversal of the imbalance in weaponry that was so decisive in the terror unleashed on cities such as Sarajevo and Mostar became the primary object of military involvement: to reduce the intensity of the possible violence and to create a more balanced contest militarily with the no-fly zone, the heavy-weapons exclusion zones around safe-area cities, the arms embargo, and the use of sanctions to deter military assistance from the outside. This initial military advantage or disadvantage was largely the result of who was able to seize control of weapons stocks and eventually to obtain heavy artillery, tanks, and planes from the withdrawing federal army (the YPA). Yet there would have been no reason for the federal army to hand over its weapons to political parties in Croatia and in Bosnia-Herzegovina if it had not been required to withdraw by international negotiations on Croatia and the UN Security Council in the case of Bosnia. Accused by Croats and by Bosnian Muslims of siding with Serbs, the army was accused by Serbs of standing by in an effort to remain neutral. The task assigned the YPA by the federal presidency in early 1991 was similar to that of a peacekeeping force—separation of forces, disarming paramilitaries, and a holding action until political talks could resume—and there is evidence that it was attempting to do just that long into 1991. Incentives to those activities and leaders could have been employed. The Bosnian representatives on the Yugoslav presidency in July 1991 opposed the withdrawal of the YPA from Slovenia because of its implications, and the Bosnian government and the YPA negotiated during the late fall to find a way to prevent war in the republic. International mediators rejected the option of working with the army or using it as a neutral force, for that would presume a continuation of the state. But the leaders of the *krajina* Serbs rejected the Vance plan primarily because they saw the withdrawal of the YPA as leaving them with no protection other than their own arms.

The ruling of the Arbitration (Badinter) Commission on Croatian recognition, German pressure for constitutional amendments and a human rights court to redress Croatian failure to meet European standards, and declarations of CSCE norms did not bring improvements in the human rights of urban Serbs (those living outside the border regions and whose status as citizens of Croatia was carefully watched by *krajina* Serbs), despite the gradual incorporation of Croatia into the European family of states during 1992–94. Continuing discrimination against employment of

Serbs, an official campaign during 1994 to evict all Serbs from publicly owned apartments without due process, and the failure to set up the promised human rights court did not bring condemnation by European human rights institutions such as the Council of Europe or its patrons Germany and the United States.[20] Yet insistence on Croatian sovereignty within republican borders meant there was no other option. The United Nations forces could do little, moreover, to promote human rights in Croatia and reduce the need for their presence because that would have constituted interference in Croatian sovereignty.

In Bosnia-Herzegovina, the Bosnian Croats would only sign the Washington Agreement for federation with Bosnian Muslims, within the internationally recognized borders of Bosnia-Herzegovina, when its constitutional agreement guaranteed their rights as a constituent nation, declared the federation to be an alliance between two national entities, guaranteed their survival as a nation by means of confederation with Croatia, and allowed them to keep the institutions of their separate state, Herzeg-Bosnia, until the political institutions of the new federation were fully agreed and established. These demands were made (and won) in spite of the fact that Bosnian Croats had more or less been militarily defeated by the Muslim-led Bosnian government forces at the time of the agreement. Bosnian Serbs, working from a position of military strength, refused to sign the Contact Group peace proposal because it did not guarantee them the constitutional status of constituent nation and the defensible territorial configuration that they too considered essential to survival as a nation. In their view, this military advantage was only short-term. The facts of international military support for the Bosnian government and demographic trends made them vulnerable in the long run, they believed, along with Bosnian Croats, without political power. When the members of the Contact Group from Britain, France, and Russia suggested amendments to the proposal to accommodate these requirements, while insisting on the territorial integrity and international legitimacy of the state of Bosnia-Herzegovina (all elements granted in the Invincible [Owen-Stoltenberg] plan the previous September), it became another source of allied disunity. The policy of the United States and Germany was that such adjustments were an act of appeasement toward Serbian aggression, but they offered no alternative reassurance on Serbian rights within a Bosnian state. Indeed, the clauses on political representation, individual rights, the court system, the Ombudsman for human rights, and the rights of refugees to return in the Bosniac-Bosnian Croat constitution referred in each case to "Bosniacs, Croats, and others," although Serbs constituted 17 percent of the federation population at the time, the same percentage as Croats composed of the entire republic when the war began. Ethnic quotas for all political positions—the cabinet, government administration, and local police—demonstrated the monopoly that the two national parties had achieved raising serious concerns about what protections there would be for all others who were not loyal to the SDA and HDZ or who were identified in the constitution as "minorities" (instead of citizens).[21]

In regard to Serbia, the dissolution of Yugoslavia led the CSCE to retreat from its human rights agenda of the cold war period to its preoccupation with intrastate questions and a definition of conflict prevention as issues of spillover. Willing to condemn Serbian repression of Albanians' human rights in Kosovo and periodically requesting a return of its monitoring mission, the CSCE respected the borders of Serbian sovereignty, agreeing not to interfere in Serbia's internal affairs without consent.

At the same time in Macedonia the attention to the Albanian minority in the republic by a CSCE mission to prevent spillover of the conflict, aided by ICFY negotiators, suggested no lessons had been learned from earlier mistakes on the relation between borders and human rights. The idea was to deter two scenarios by which war could erupt and spill over borders. One was to prevent linkups between the Albanians in Kosovo and in Macedonia by putting pressure on the Macedonian government to guarantee minority rights for Albanians within the republic. The other was to prevent internal destabilization through interethnic conflict between the majority Macedonians and the largest of the minorities, ethnic Albanians. Instead, outsiders' privileged attention to Albanians was having the opposite effect. It encouraged radicals among Albanians to pursue their claim of national rights with a territorial foothold in the Macedonian portion of a cross-border political community. This pushed the political moderates in the Albanian community who had preferred a civil rights approach to hold on to their voters with an electoral platform demanding the status of a constituent nation in Macedonia. Moreover, resentment at the international pressure appeared to be increasing interethnic hostilities. Majority Macedonians resented the special attention to Albanians and the expenditure of monies at a time of economic crisis to protect Albanian ethnic identity in education and the mass media and for employment quotas in army, police, and government office. They took special offense when Europeans were not also willing to require Greece to end the blockade that had brought serious unemployment, which affected Macedonians especially, in the formal economy. Concerned to prevent these resentments from increasing support for opposition nationalists, the centrist government made promises regarding Albanian rights but then delayed implementation. This led to growing resentments among minority Albanians. As in the other republics, a focus on particular ethnic groups rather than on stable democratic political institutions was counterproductive. The greatest threat to both internal and cross-border stability in Macedonia was not ethnic conflict but incomplete sovereignty and fragile governments without the external stability and domestic resources to find their own solutions to ethnic relations and economic decline that were self-sustaining.

## Political Solutions

Outside powers and negotiators had three choices in solving the conflicts of Yugoslavia after mid-1991. One was to impose a solution, as they had done in all previous territorial wars of the century. Their solution was the same: to reduce the territory of defeated powers and accept the creation of transborder minorities. But they were unwilling to deploy military force to achieve those defeats, or go beyond the role of mediators in the internal affairs of states they recognized. This was not the era of the Balkan wars. Without credible reassurances of rights to those placed at risk in a minority position and without political alternatives offered to those who opposed the new state they saw imposed on them, there would be no relinquishing of weapons and no stable solution, even with lasting cease-fires. Moreover, such intervention could not simply repeat the mistakes that occurred after World War I, when the new states of eastern Europe—Poland, Czechoslovakia, Greece, Romania, and Yugoslavia—were obliged to sign on at the Paris Peace Conference of 1919 in Versailles to minority treaties guaranteeing transborder minorities rights. Their more established neighbors that were home states of these minorities were not similarly obliged, however. Impressive documents of rights to self-determination and minority protection against national tyranny, they led to a "thicket of litigation . . . around school and language issues, local government, citizenship options, and property rights."[22] They failed, however, because they depended on the response of outsiders: a minority could be defended only by the petition of a League of Nations member. German (and in some cases Hungarian) nationalists were able to use this prerogative to destabilize neighboring states, and no international actor was willing to enforce the rights against resistant governments.[23] In 1991–95, major powers were also not yet willing to interfere or work out alternative political arrangements to the failed solutions of the previous eighty years.

The second choice was to accept the consequences of outsiders' mistakes in 1990–92 and to become true mediators in helping the parties negotiate alternatives. But this meant admitting that borders could be changed if the result was a more stable and legitimate outcome. A less acceptable version, given the arguments made about aggression and Helsinki norms, was that borders had in fact been changed and were only awaiting international acknowledgment. This second choice was unacceptable, although it was rapidly becoming the most likely outcome. Moreover, it was unacceptable even to prepare for such a contingency in the unresolved conflicts over sovereignty in other parts of the former country, however unlikely, so that border negotiations and population movements could be done peacefully with international assistance.

The third choice was to move away from the trap of ethnic partition. The focus on national control of territory and negotiations over maps had only made territory more important as a bargaining chip rather than more subject to compromise, and bargaining could be prolonged indefinitely by the shifting alliances and demands of parties on the ground. It was leading into a trap that would result in the reestablishment of one-party states, but along ethnic lines. Individuals in a minority position (ethnically or politically) who were not territorially concentrated would lose representation and protection. These were hardly stable political solutions. The acceptance at face value of nationalist party leaders' arguments had prevented outsiders from taking advantage, in the way that insiders had, of the useful weapons of the cold war, such as the mass media and domestic opposition, but with the objective of breaking the information blockade and propaganda within communities and of supporting internal solutions against war and ethnic exclusivism.

This third choice was to assist, not hinder, the people in the former country in developing the capacity to solve the problem themselves. This choice is not the same as the decision to provide humanitarian assistance alone, not to interfere in a civil war, and to accept whatever outcome the parties reached themselves, such as was behind the principle of consent that caused anger and frustration at the UN forces and delayed negotiations. This requirement of impartiality was necessary because outside powers were unwilling to enforce agreements and depended on the parties providing enforcement themselves. But it was the political capacity that had been destroyed. To find lasting, stable solutions to the Yugoslav crisis, outsiders would have to think instead about supporting the development of the political institutions and a political climate within the area that could enable the people themselves to generate solutions. But such a capacity required a more conducive and predictable external environment than existed in 1994.

## U.S. Policy

The lack of progress in the Yugoslav conflict since mid-1991 reflects the lack of change in the European and U.S. definition of the problem and their respective interests. The United States necessarily bears a heavy responsibility in the Yugoslav tragedy, for its hegemonic role in defining Europe in the cold war period was particularly influential in the Yugoslav case. And while the Bush administration chose to abdicate leadership in the early stages of the Yugoslav conflict, both the Bush and the Clinton administrations were also unwilling to remain uninvolved, leaving the situation entirely to Europeans. Whenever developments toward the Yugoslav conflict seemed to challenge the U.S. leadership role in Europe, it stepped in.

The most commonly accepted assessment of international action toward the former Yugoslavia is that it was too little, too late. The lesson drawn is that the world needs better systems of *early warning*. But the reality is that there was plenty of early warning about the Yugoslav case and not enough incentive to act. Europeans threw away valuable resources to influence the outcome, such as the enormous leverage held by the European Community in 1989–90, when alternative paths to European membership were critical factors in the behavior of Yugoslav politicians, or in 1991 when the EC chose to recognize Slovenia and Croatia—spending its most powerful weapon—and to ask almost nothing in return. They also wasted time when there was little time to waste. In January–March 1992 a golden opportunity to find political solutions for Bosnia-Herzegovina, Macedonia, and Serbia presented itself but was squandered. Each of three presidencies of the European Union of Great Britain (July–December 1992), Greece (January–June 1994), and Germany (July–December 1994) began by publicly promising diplomatic initiatives and results, but in the end were passive. When action came, it tended to be out of date, suited to an earlier stage of the conflict. Even diplomatic proposals that emerged from a greater sense of urgency tended to reflect a situation on the ground that had long passed. Parties on the ground who had chosen paths that seemed to require external mediation, either by seeking international recognition for independence or by resorting to arms, retained the initiative. The lesson is that prevention requires sustained leadership, or prepositioned institutional capacities suited to these types of conflicts, which swing into play automatically.

Criticism of outsiders for contributing to the path of Yugoslav dissolution and for failing to prevent its violent outcome or to defend the values that they proclaimed were at stake can justifiably be considered harsh, however, when the timing of the Yugoslav crisis is set in its global context, in the early transition after the cold war. Institutions designed for conflict prevention and resolution during the cold war were based on one of two sets of premises, neither of which applied: cooperation on the basis of mutual interests and reciprocal trade-offs; or containment on the assumption that conflicts were too great to reconcile. Facing a case characterized instead by irreconcilable conflicts and incompatible interests, mediators and powers did not seek to restructure interests or to create incentives for cooperation but demanded compliance to principles they chose. When that did not work, they resorted to containment.

This frame of obedience and containment was particularly unreceptive to the possibility of independent action by Yugoslav actors, who, by habit of many centuries, saw international action as a resource to exploit. International publicity, recognition, humanitarian assistance, and peacekeeping forces became endogenous elements of their political strategies. The difficulty this created for obtaining compliance, intended results, and effective implementation was exacerbated by the multiplicity of actors, lack of co-ordination, and largely reactive postures that characterized international action.

Neither U.S. administration facing the Yugoslav conflict considered it a matter of U.S. vital interests, although the Clinton administration did refine its categories in response to the war in Bosnia to allow a middle category of national interest. This category did not justify risking soldiers' lives but was sufficient to justify diplomatic attention.[24] The debate over policy from the spring of 1991 focused primarily on whether the conflict was a European problem or a situation requiring U.S. leadership. The Bush administration answer was codified in a policy called the new regionalism according to which the United States (as sole remaining superpower) would "pick and choose" among conflicts and regions according to its vital interests and those of global security.[25] The premise of this post–cold war principle was that regional organizations had the most direct incentive to prevent violent escalation of a conflict within their area and also had the greatest leverage over parties because of the immediacy of moral sanctions and economic ties binding members. The concept was also the centerpiece of UN Secretary General Boutros Boutros-Ghali's *Agenda for Peace* proposed in June 1992 and the declaration of the annual meeting in July 1992 of the G-7 economic powers.[26]

With the reversal in NATO's position on out-of-area action during the autumn of 1992, in staffing the UNPROFOR headquarters in Bosnia-Herzegovina with the Northern Army Group to provide a framework for command and control and in enforcing the economic embargo at sea, U.S. policy had extended the geographical scope of Europe. At the same time, however, it redefined the conflict as a question of universal principles rather than of regional security. The Bush administration was intent on retaining the humanitarian conception of policy and avoiding the obligations of a security conception. Its developing alliance at the time with Islamic countries—in the UN Security Council and in support of the Bosnian Muslim leadership of Bosnia-Herzegovina on the grounds that the Muslims were the victims in the Bosnian war, not only of Serbian aggression but also of genocide, also contributed a geographical dimension to the U.S. policy that extended beyond Europe. But these changes (flowering under the Clinton administration) were not accompanied by a change in the original Bush administration position that it would not commit soldiers, either as combatants or as ground troops in the UN peacekeeping forces (at least, President Clinton added, until a peace agreement was signed).[27] U.S. efforts to take a position on the conflict in terms of systemic norms—that borders not be changed by force and that fundamental human rights not be violated—while not viewing its national interest as sufficiently implicated in this particular case to contribute soldiers to defend these norms, demonstrated the particular difficulty of exercising global leadership when the institutions appropriate to a post–cold war regime had not been created.

Nonetheless, the means by which the Europeans trapped the United States into taking a role of leadership toward the conflict, although many argued that it came too late to salvage the long-term consequences of the U.S. loss of moral leadership in Europe, was through NATO as a European security organization.[28] The U.S. government had to recognize that European problems in the realm of security *were* American problems. Maintaining the alliance was in its vital national interest. But the arrival in March 1994 of U.S. diplomatic leadership, which all considered necessary to end the conflict, only produced momentary commitments to unity, not a consensus on objectives that could be sustained. By the end of 1994, the expansion of the European Union and the expansion of NATO had been linked.[29] But the conflicts among NATO allies over Balkan policy and the war in Bosnia, which appeared to bring NATO itself to the brink by December 1994, were once again patched up temporarily by a retreat to the more narrow, humanitarian conception of intervention in former Yugoslavia and rhetoric about giving more forcefulness to the UN protection forces in performing its original tasks. The United States asserted its leadership by accepting NATO responsibility for any withdrawal of UN forces and insisting that, because the United States would commit ground troops, command and control would shift from the UN secretary general and force commander to the United States. But allied reconciliation did not produce a policy toward the Balkans.

American leadership had initiated the Truman Doctrine in 1947 and Yugoslavia's special status outside the East-West blocs beginning in 1949; but these policies had also imposed a cold war division on the Balkans. Neither was a basis for the regional economic cooperation and security— in the Balkans or in Europe—that was necessary to support peace and democratization in place of war and the economic bases of stable governments in the area. The conservative impulses of U.S. policy in 1990–91 were still intact.

The absence of any conception of a postwar settlement or regional solution to the Balkan conflict was especially apparent in the case of Kosovo (and by implication Macedonia). Although both the Bush and Clinton administrations were criticized for not specifying under what conditions and with what means they would act on their warnings to Serbian president Milošević, this tactic of deterrence was not the problem. Rather it was the absence of a policy coordinating the separate commitments to existing state borders (of the republics) and to fundamental human rights that remained unresolved in the other conflicts in the former country. The issue for both ethnic Albanians and the Serbian government was not individual rights but collective governing rights over territory. Would the borders of Serbia take precedence over Albanian demands for the right to self-governance on the basis of national self-determination? U.S. policy had quietly shifted to the position that Kosovo was an internal affair of Serbia, just as it accepted that the independence movement in Chechnya was a Russian internal affair. Efforts to defend the aggrieved and abused human rights of Albanians remained declarations only. Was the conflict moving toward military measures, and if so, what then would be the policy toward this largely Muslim population whose disadvantage in weapons would surely lead to a blood bath that would challenge Bosnia?

The issues of Bosnia and former Yugoslavia could not be isolated from those affecting U.S.-Russian relations, the expansion of NATO, and stability in eastern Europe. The tendency to revert to historical explanations of the Yugoslav conflicts revealed a lack of understanding about the persistent element of territorial and strategic insecurity in parts of the world that are not geopolitically free from conflicts over land, borders, supply routes, and vital physical resources such as water in the way that North America and western Europe have been, more or less, for some time. In the absence of stable international conditions, such sensitivity, even hypersensitivity, about external threats in a region exposed to frequent invasion and occupation as recently as World War II and about border conflicts in a region where borders do not follow ethnonational lines but contain substantial irredenta, is neither ancient nor modern but part of the landscape.[30] It was outside powers and neighbors, in fact, that were acting historically in their repeat of interests, alignments, and means of influence toward the Yugoslav tragedy and that were insensitive to its demands.

As western European integration since World War II has proven, even in conditions of relative prosperity and stable political institutions, the potential in such conflicts and insecurities for violent confrontation and deteriorating relations that cannot be reversed can only be interrupted if they are subordinated to a different mechanism. Supranational institutions that provide mutual reassurance and that require sustained interaction and cooperation among peoples and among sovereign states make that possible. The outcomes of political disintegration, territorial fragmentation, tolerance for intolerance, and nationalist self-reliance in the region are not inseparable from the conditions imposed by major powers for financial and military assistance, access to credit markets, trade, and membership in regional alliances. If the primary burden for human rights and security for a population will remain with the sovereign state, outsiders cannot remain oblivious to their role in undermining the capacity to provide security and rights nor miss opportunities to help strengthen governing capacity, without which there can be neither stability nor justice.

Appendix

---

# United Nations Security Council Resolutions and Presidential Statements on Yugoslavia, September 1991 to January 1995

**Resolution 713 (1991), September 25, 1991**
The Council fully supports the collective efforts for peace and dialogue in Yugoslavia under the auspices of the member States of the European Community (EC) with the support of the States participating in the Conference on Security and Cooperation in Europe (CSCE), invites the Secretary-General to offer his assistance without delay and to report as soon as possible to the Security Council, and decides under Chapter VII of the Charter of the United Nations that all States immediately implement a general and complete embargo on all deliveries of weapons and military equipment to Yugoslavia.

**Resolution 721 (1991), November 27, 1991**
The Council, considering the request by the Government of Yugoslavia and the findings of the mission of the Personal Envoy of the Secretary-General to Yugoslavia, approves the efforts towards the possible establishment of a United Nations peacekeeping operation in Yugoslavia, and urges the Yugoslav parties to comply fully with the agreement signed in Geneva on November 23, 1991.

**Resolution 724 (1991), December 15, 1991**
The Council endorses the view expressed in the Secretary-General's report that the conditions for establishing a peacekeeping operation in Yugoslavia still do not exist, endorses his offer to send to Yugoslavia a small group of personnel, including military personnel, to prepare for possible deployment of a peacekeeping operation, decides to establish a committee to ensure that the general and complete embargo imposed by Resolution 713 (1991) is effectively applied, and encourages the Secretary-General to pursue his humanitarian efforts in Yugoslavia.

### Statement by the President, January 7, 1992

The Council condemns an attack by Yugoslav aircraft on unarmed helicopters of the EC Monitoring Mission, killing five members of the Mission.

### Resolution 727 (1992), January 8, 1992

The Council welcomes the signing of an Implementing Accord in Sarajevo on January 2, 1992, to implement the cease-fire agreed to on November 23, 1991, and endorses the Secretary-General's intention to send 50 military liaison officers to promote maintenance of the cease-fire.

### Resolution 740 (1992), February 7, 1992

The Council approves the Secretary-General's proposal to increase the authorized strength of the military liaison mission to a total of 75 officers, expresses its concern that the United Nations peacekeeping plan has not yet been fully and unconditionally accepted by all in Yugoslavia, reaffirms that the plan and its implementation are in no way intended to prejudge the terms of a political settlement, and calls upon all States to cooperate fully with the committee established by Resolution 724 (1991), including reporting any information brought to their attention concerning violations of the embargo.

### Resolution 743 (1992), February 21, 1992

The Council decides to establish a United Nations Protection Force (UNPROFOR) as an interim arrangement to create conditions of peace and security for an initial period of twelve months, requests the Secretary-General to deploy immediately those elements of the Force which can assist in developing an implementation plan for the earliest possible full deployment of UNPROFOR, reaffirms that the peacekeeping plan and its implementation is in no way intended to prejudge the terms of a political settlement, and decides that the embargo imposed by paragraph 6 of Resolution 713 (1991) shall not apply to weapons and military equipment destined for the sole use of UNPROFOR.

### Resolution 749 (1992), April 7, 1992

The Council decides to authorize the earliest possible full deployment of UNPROFOR, urges all parties to maximize their contributions to UNPROFOR, urges all parties to take all action necessary to ensure complete freedom of aerial movement for UNPROFOR, and calls upon all parties not to resort to violence, especially where UNPROFOR is to be based/deployed.

## Statement by the President, April 10, 1992

The Council reiterates its appeal in Resolution 749 (1992) to all parties in Bosnia-Herzegovina to stop fighting immediately, and invites the Secretary-General urgently to dispatch his Personal Envoy to the area.

## Statement by the President, April 24, 1992

The Council notes with deep concern the rapid and violent deterioration of the situation in Bosnia-Herzegovina, welcomes the recent efforts of the EC and the Secretary-General aimed at prevailing upon the parties to respect fully the cease-fire signed on April 12 under the auspices of the EC, demands that all forms of interference from outside Bosnia-Herzegovina cease immediately, and urges all parties to respect immediately and fully the cease-fire.

## Resolution 752 (1992), May 15, 1992

The Council demands that all parties concerned in Bosnia and Herzegovina stop the fighting immediately, that all forms of interference from outside, as well as any attempts to change the ethnic composition of the population, cease immediately and that those units of the Yugoslav People's Army and elements of the Croatian Army either be withdrawn or be subject to the authority of the Government of Bosnia and Herzegovina, or be disbanded and disarmed with their weapons placed under effective international inventory.

## Resolution 753 (1992), May 18, 1992

The Council recommends to the General Assembly that the Republic of Croatia be admitted to membership in the United Nations.

## Statement by the President, May 18, 1992

The Council extends congratulations to the Republic of Croatia on the occasion of the Council's recommendation to the General Assembly that the Republic be admitted to membership in the United Nations.

## Resolution 754 (1992), May 18, 1992

The Council recommends to the General Assembly that the Republic of Slovenia be admitted to membership in the United Nations.

## Statement by the President, May 18, 1992

The Council extends congratulations to the Republic of Slovenia on the occasion of the Council's recommendation to the General Assembly that the Republic be admitted to membership in the United Nations.

**Resolution 755 (1992), May 20, 1992**

The Council recommends to the General Assembly that the Republic of Bosnia and Herzegovina be admitted to membership in the United Nations.

**Statement by the President, May 20, 1992**

The Council extends congratulations to the Republic of Bosnia and Herzegovina on the occasion of the Council's recommendation to the General Assembly that the Republic be admitted to membership in the United Nations.

**Resolution 757 (1992), May 30, 1992**

The Council condemns the failure of the authorities in the Federal Republic of Yugoslavia (Serbia and Montenegro) to take effective measures to fulfil the requirements of Resolution 752 (1992), and decides under Chapter VII of the Charter of the United Nations to impose comprehensive mandatory sanctions on that country.

**Resolution 758 (1992), June 8, 1992**

The Council notes the agreement of all parties to the reopening of Sarajevo airport for humanitarian purposes under the exclusive authority of the United Nations, decides to enlarge the mandate and strength of UNPROFOR, strongly condemns all those parties and others concerned that are responsible for violations of the cease-fire, and demands that all parties and others concerned create immediately the necessary conditions for unimpeded delivery of humanitarian supplies to Sarajevo and other destinations in Bosnia and Herzegovina.

**Resolution 760 (1992), June 18, 1992**

The Council, acting under Chapter VII of the Charter of the United Nations, decides that certain prohibitions contained in Resolution 757 (1992) shall not apply, with the approval of the Committee established by Resolution 724 (1991) under the simplified and accelerated "no objection" procedure, to commodities and products for essential humanitarian need.

**Resolution 761 (1992), June 29, 1992**

The Council authorizes the Secretary-General to deploy immediately additional elements of UNPROFOR to ensure the security and functioning of the Sarajevo airport and the delivery of humanitarian assistance, and calls upon all States to contribute to the international humanitarian efforts in Sarajevo and its environs.

### Resolution 762 (1992), June 30, 1992

The Council urges the Government of Croatia to withdraw its army to the positions held before the offensive of June 21, 1992, and to cease hostile military activities within or adjacent to the United Nations Protected Areas (UNPAs), recommends the establishment of a Joint Commission to consult with the Belgrade authorities on relations with UNPROFOR, and authorizes the strengthening of the Force by the addition of up to 60 military observers and 120 civilian police to perform additional functions in certain areas ("pink zones") in Croatia.

### Resolution 764 (1992), July 13, 1992

The Council authorizes the Secretary-General to deploy immediately further additional elements of UNPROFOR to ensure the security and functioning of Sarajevo airport and the delivery of humanitarian assistance, and reaffirms that all parties are bound to comply with the obligations under international humanitarian law.

### Statement by the President, July 17, 1992

The Council welcomes the agreement between the parties in Bosnia and Herzegovina, signed that day at London, and decides in principle to respond positively to the request that UNPROFOR supervise all heavy weapons in accordance with this agreement.

### Statement by the President, July 24, 1992

The Council concurs with the Secretary-General's view that conditions do not yet exist for the United Nations to supervise the heavy weapons in Bosnia and Herzegovina as envisaged in the London agreement, and invites the Secretary-General to contact all Member States to ask them to make urgently available information about the personnel, equipment, and logistic support which they will be able to contribute to the supervision of heavy weapons in Bosnia and Herzegovina.

### Statement by the President, August 4, 1992

The Council condemns violations of international humanitarian law in the territory of the former Yugoslavia and especially Bosnia-Herzegovina; demands relevant international organizations, particularly the International Committee of the Red Cross (ICRC), be granted immediate, unimpeded, and continued access to camps, prisons, and detention centers; and calls on all parties, States, international and nongovernmental organizations to make immediately available to Council any further information that they might possess regarding camps.

### Statement by the President, August 4, 1992
The members of the Council condemn the attack on UNPROFOR positions in Sarajevo resulting in loss of life and injuries among the Ukrainian servicemen; express their condolences to the family of the officer killed and to the Government of Ukraine, and express their condolences to the families of the two French officers of UNPROFOR killed in Croatia and to the Government of France.

### Resolution 769 (1992), August 7, 1992
The Council authorizes the enlargement of UNPROFOR's mandate and strength to enable it to perform immigration and customs functions on the international borders in Croatia, and resolutely condemns the abuses against civilian populations, particularly on ethnic grounds.

### Resolution 770 (1992), August 13, 1992
The Council calls upon States to "take nationally or through regional agencies or arrangements all measures necessary" to ensure the delivery of relief supplies to Sarajevo and other parts of Bosnia and Herzegovina and demands that unimpeded and continuous access to all camps, prisons, and detention centers be granted immediately to the ICRC and that all detainees receive humane treatment.

### Resolution 771 (1992), August 13, 1992
The Council strongly condemns violations of international humanitarian law, including those involved in the process of "ethnic cleansing," demands that all parties in the former Yugoslavia and all military forces in Bosnia immediately desist from such violations, demands that relevant international humanitarian organizations be granted immediate, unimpeded, and continued access to prison camps, calls on all parties to do all in their power to facilitate such access, and calls on States and international humanitarian organizations to collate substantiated information relating to breaches of humanitarian law.

### Statement by the President, September 2, 1992
The Council expresses its full support for the Statement of Principles adopted, and other agreements reached, at the London Conference, held on August 26-27, 1992.

### Statement by the President, September 9, 1992
The Council invites the Secretary-General to inform it on the findings of the inquiry into the circumstances of the attack which cost the lives of two French soldiers of UNPROFOR near Sarajevo, as well as other similar incidents.

## Resolution 776 (1992), September 14, 1992

The Council authorizes the enlargement of UNPROFOR's mandate and strength in Bosnia and Herzegovina to provide protection to UNHCR-organized humanitarian convoys, and asks for States to contribute everything in their power (including funding) to the ongoing UNPROFOR operation.

## Resolution 777 (1992), September 19, 1992

The Council considers that the Federal Republic of Yugoslavia cannot continue automatically the membership of the former Socialist Federal Republic of Yugoslavia in the United Nations, and therefore recommends to the General Assembly that it decide that the Federal Republic of Yugoslavia (Serbia and Montenegro) should apply for membership in the United Nations and that it shall not participate in the work of the General Assembly.

## Resolution 779 (1992), October 6, 1992

The Council authorizes UNPROFOR to assume responsibility for monitoring arrangements agreed for the complete withdrawal of the Yugoslav Army from Croatia, the demilitarization of the Prevlaka peninsula, and the removal of heavy weapons from neighboring areas of Croatia and Montenegro.

## Resolution 780 (1992), October 6, 1992

The Council requests the Secretary-General to establish, as a matter of urgency, an impartial Commission of Experts with a view to providing him with its conclusions on the evidence of grave breaches of the Geneva Conventions and other violations of humanitarian law committed in the territory of the former Yugoslavia.

## Resolution 781 (1992), October 9, 1992

The Council decides to establish a ban on military flights in the airspace of Bosnia and Herzegovina, and undertakes to examine without delay all the information brought to its attention concerning the implementation of the ban and, in the case of violations, to consider urgently the further measures necessary to enforce it.

## Statement by the President, October 30, 1992

The Council strongly condemns attacks on civilians in the Republic of Bosnia and Herzegovina, which constitute grave violations of international humanitarian law, and reaffirms that persons who commit or order the commission of grave breaches of the Geneva Conventions are individually responsible in respect of such breaches. The Council expresses its wish that such violations be brought to the attention of the Commission of Experts mentioned in Resolution 780 (1992).

### Resolution 786 (1992), November 10, 1992

The Council allows for the enlargement of UNPROFOR by 75 to monitor the ban on military flights in the airspace of Bosnia and Herzegovina implemented in Resolution 781 (1992), and allows for UNPROFOR and EC ground teams to observe Yugoslav, Croatian, and Bosnian airfields.

### Resolution 787 (1992), November 16, 1992

The Council strongly reaffirms its call on all parties to respect strictly the territorial integrity of the Republic of Bosnia and Herzegovina, condemns the refusal of all parties in the Republic, in particular the Bosnian Serb paramilitary forces, to comply with its previous resolutions, and demands that all forms of interference from outside the Republic, including infiltration into the country of irregular units and personnel, cease immediately, acting under Chapters VII and VIII of the Charter of the United Nations calls upon States to halt all inward and outward maritime and Danube shipping in order to verify their cargoes and destinations and to ensure strict implementation of the provisions of Resolutions 713 (1991) and 757 (1992), and invites the Secretary-General to study the possibility of safe areas for humanitarian purposes.

### Statement by the President, December 2, 1992

The Council expresses deep concern about and outrage at the increasing number of attacks against United Nations personnel serving in various peacekeeping operations, including UNPROFOR. The Council condemns these attacks and demands that all parties concerned take all necessary measures to prevent their recurrence. It considers the abduction and detention of United Nations peacekeeping personnel as totally unacceptable and demands the immediate and unconditional release of all of the UNPROFOR personnel concerned.

### Statement by the President, December 9, 1992

The Council strongly condemns the renewed offensive by Serb militia in Bosnia and Herzegovina, and in particular against the city of Sarajevo, and demands the immediate cessation of these attacks and of all actions impeding the distribution of humanitarian assistance and forcing the inhabitants of Sarajevo to leave the city.

### Resolution 795 (1992), December 11, 1992

The Council authorizes the Secretary-General under Chapter VIII of the Charter of the United Nations to establish a presence of UNPROFOR in the Former Yugoslav Republic of Macedonia to monitor its borders with Albania and the Federal Republic of Yugoslavia and urges the UNPROFOR presence to coordinate closely with the CSCE mission there.

### Resolution 798 (1992), December 18, 1992
The Council condemns the detention and rapes of women in the Balkans, especially Muslim women, demands that all detention and/or prison camps be closed, especially those housing women, and calls for support of the EC investigation team in Bosnia.

### Statement by the President, January 8, 1993
The Council strongly condemns the killing by Bosnian Serb forces of Mr. Hakija Turajlić, Deputy Prime Minister for Economic Affairs of the Republic of Bosnia and Herzegovina, while he was under the protection of UNPROFOR, and requests the Secretary-General to conduct a full investigation of the incident and to report to it without delay.

### Statement by the President, January 8, 1993
The Council fully supports the efforts of the Co-Chairmen of the Steering Committee of the International Conference on the Former Yugoslavia (ICFY), and fully endorses the view of the Secretary-General that all the parties involved in the conflict in the Republic of Bosnia and Herzegovina are duty-bound to cooperate with the Co-Chairmen in bringing this conflict to a swift end.

### Resolution 802 (1993), January 25, 1993
The Council demands the immediate cessation of hostile activities by Croatian forces in UNPROFOR protected areas, strongly condemns Croatian attacks against UNPROFOR, demands that heavy weapons seized from UNPROFOR storage areas be returned immediately to UNPROFOR, and demands that all parties comply strictly with the cease-fire arrangements already agreed and cooperate fully and unconditionally in the implementation of the UN peacekeeping plan.

### Statement by the President, January 25, 1993
The Council reaffirms its demand that all parties and others concerned, in particular Serb paramilitary units, cease and desist forthwith from all violations of international humanitarian law being committed in Bosnia and Herzegovina, including in particular the deliberate interference with humanitarian convoys, and warns the parties concerned of serious consequences if they continue to impede the delivery of humanitarian relief assistance.

**Statement by the President, January 27, 1993**
The Council expresses its deep concern at reports that the offensive by Croatian armed forces continues unabated in flagrant violation of Resolution 802 (1993) at a crucial time in the peace process and demands that military action by all parties cease immediately.

**Statement by the President, January 28, 1993**
The Council expresses its concern about a flagrant violation of the mandatory economic sanctions it had imposed against the Federal Republic of Yugoslavia (Serbia and Montenegro), and reaffirms its support for vigorous enforcement of the relevant resolutions.

**Statement by the President, February 10, 1993**
The Council, on the basis of a report about the detention of Romanian vessels by the authorities of the Federal Republic of Yugoslavia (Serbia and Montenegro), condemns any such retaliatory action, and demands that the Yugoslav authorities release the vessels and desist from further unlawful detentions.

**Statement by the President, February 17, 1993**
The Council condemns the blocking of humanitarian convoys and the impeding of relief supplies, which place at risk the civilian population of Bosnia and Herzegovina and endanger the lives of personnel delivering such supplies, and reiterates its demand that the parties and all others concerned allow immediate and unimpeded access to humanitarian relief supplies.

**Resolution 807 (1993), February 19, 1993**
The Council demands full compliance with the UN peacekeeping plan in Croatia, demands that the parties refrain from positioning their forces in the proximity of UNPROFOR's units in the UNPAs and pink zones, demands that the parties respect fully UNPROFOR's unimpeded freedom of movement, decides to extend UNPROFOR's mandate for an interim period terminating on March 31, 1993, and invites the Secretary-General to strengthen the security of UNPROFOR with the "necessary defensive means," in order to reinforce its self-defense capability.

**Resolution 808 (1993), February 22, 1993**
The Council decides to establish an international tribunal for the prosecution of persons responsible for serious violations of international humanitarian law committed in the territory of the former Yugoslavia since 1991 and requests the Secretary-General to submit a report on the matter within 60 days.

### Statement by the President, February 24, 1993

The Council endorses the statement of February 23, 1993, by the President of the United States and the United Nations Secretary-General, calling on the leaders of the parties involved in the peace talks in Bosnia and Herzegovina to come to New York immediately to resume discussions aimed at the early conclusion of an agreement to end the conflict.

### Statement by the President, February 25, 1993

The Council strongly condemns once again the blocking of humanitarian convoys and reiterates its demand that the Bosnian parties grant immediate and unimpeded access for humanitarian convoys and expresses its strong support for the use of humanitarian air drops in isolated areas of Bosnia and Herzegovina that are in critical need of humanitarian supplies and cannot be reached by ground convoys.

### Statement by the President, March 3, 1993

The Council condemns the continuing military attacks in eastern Bosnia and Herzegovina and the resulting deterioration in the humanitarian situation in that region and demands that the leaders of all parties to the conflict in that Republic remain fully engaged in New York in a sustained effort with the Co-Chairmen of the ICFY to reach quickly a fair and workable settlement.

### Statement by the President, March 17, 1993

The Council demands from the Bosnian Serbs an immediate explanation of the violations of the "no-fly" zone and particularly of the aerial bombardment of villages in Bosnia and Herzegovina, and requests the Secretary-General to ensure that an investigation is made into the reported possible use of such air strikes.

### Statement by the President, March 25, 1993

The Council welcomes the signature by President Alija Izetbegović and Mr. Mate Bòban of all four documents of the peace plan for Bosnia and Herzegovina and calls on the remaining party to sign without delay the two documents of the peace plan that it has not yet signed and to cease its violence, offensive military actions, "ethnic cleansing," and obstruction of humanitarian assistance.

### Resolution 815 (1993), March 30, 1993

The Council demands full respect for international humanitarian law in UNPAs, decides to reconsider within one month, or at any time at the request of the Secretary-General, UNPROFOR's mandate in light of developments of the ICFY and the situation on the ground, and decides, in this context, to extend UNPROFOR's mandate for an additional period terminating on June 30, 1993.

### Resolution 816 (1993), March 31, 1993
The Council decides to extend the ban established in Resolution 781 (1992) to cover flights by all fixed-wing and rotary-wing aircraft in the Republic of Bosnia and Herzegovina, and authorizes Member States to take all necessary measures to ensure compliance with the ban on flights.

### Statement by the President, April 3, 1993
The Council demands that the Bosnian Serb party cease and desist forthwith from all violations of international humanitarian law, including in particular the deliberate interference with humanitarian convoys, and to allow all such convoys unhindered access to the town of Srebrenica and other parts in the Republic of Bosnia and Herzegovina.

### Resolution 817 (1993), April 7, 1993
The Council recommends to the General Assembly that the "Former Yugoslav Republic of Macedonia" be admitted to membership in the United Nations under this provisional reference pending settlement of the difference that has arisen over the name of the State.

### Statement by the President, April 7, 1993
The Council welcomes the efforts of the Co-Chairmen of the Steering Committee of the ICFY to set up a mechanism to settle the difference which has arisen over the name of "the Former Yugoslav Republic of Macedonia" and to promote confidence-building measures in the region.

### Statement by the President, April 8, 1993
The Council expresses concern at the ICRC report, according to which 17 detainees lost their lives in Bosnia and Herzegovina, condemns all violations of the Geneva Conventions, and requests the Commission of Experts to carry out an investigation of the practices and to make a report.

### Resolution 819 (1993), April 16, 1993
The Council demands that all parties treat Srebrenica and its surroundings as a safe area, demands the immediate cessation of armed attacks by Bosnian Serb paramilitary units against Srebrenica and the immediate withdrawal of these units, demands that the Federal Republic of Yugoslavia immediately cease the supply of military arms, equipment, and services to Bosnian Serb paramilitary units in Bosnia, and requests the Secretary-General to increase the UNPROFOR presence in Srebrenica and to arrange for the safe transfer of the wounded and ill civilians from Srebrenica.

**Resolution 820 (1993), April 17, 1993**
The Council commends the peace plan, declares its readiness to take all necessary measures to assist in the implementation of the plan, denounces the Bosnian Serb refusal to endorse the plan, and decides to tighten sanctions on the Federal Republic of Yugoslavia and to disallow transshipment of commodities through UNPROFOR occupied parts of Croatia and Bosnian Serb occupied parts of Bosnia until the Bosnian Serb party accepts and implements the plan.

**Statement by the President, April 21, 1993**
The Council strongly condemns the new outbreak of violence in Bosnia and Herzegovina, demands that Bosnian governmental forces and Bosnian Croat paramilitary units cease immediately those hostilities, and calls upon all the parties to cooperate with the current efforts in this regard by UNPROFOR and Lord Owen.

**Resolution 821 (1993), April 28, 1993**
The Council reaffirms that Serbia and Montenegro cannot continue the United Nations membership of the Socialist Federal Republic of Yugoslavia, and that they thus cannot participate in the Economic and Social Council.

**Statement by the President, May 3, 1993**
The Council welcomes the signature of the Vance-Owen peace plan in its entirety by all the Bosnian parties.

**Resolution 824 (1993), May 6, 1993**
The Council demands that any taking of territory by force cease immediately; declares that Sarajevo, Tuzla, Žepa, Goražde, Bihać and Srebrenica and their surrounds should be treated as safe areas by all the parties concerned and should be free from armed attacks and from any other hostile act; and declares its readiness, in the event of the failure by any party to comply with the present Resolution, to consider additional measures necessary with a view to its full implementation, including to ensure respect for the safety of UN personnel.

**Statement by the President, May 7, 1993**
The Council reaffirms its position that the basis for a peaceful solution to the conflict in Bosnia and Herzegovina is the Vance-Owen peace plan and that the Bosnian Serbs must return to it.

**Statement by the President, May 10, 1993**
The Council condemns the new military offensive launched by Bosnian Croat paramilitary units, demands that the attacks against the areas of

Mostar, Jablanica, and Dreznica cease and that Bosnian Croat paramilitary units withdraw immediately from the area.

### Statement by the President, May 14, 1993
The Council expresses its indignation and grief at the tragic death of a member of the UNPROFOR Spanish battalion.

### Resolution 827 (1993), May 25, 1993
The Council establishes an international tribunal for the purpose of prosecuting persons responsible for serious violations of international humanitarian law committed in the former Yugoslavia beginning January 1, 1991. The Council urges states, intergovernmental and nongovernmental organizations to contribute funds, equipment, and services to the international tribunal. The work of the tribunal will be carried out without prejudice to the right of the victims to seek compensation for damages incurred as a result of the violations.

### Statement by the President, June 1, 1993
The Council learns, with distress, of the killing of two UNHCR Danish civilian drivers in Bosnia and Herzegovina, and declares the targeting of humanitarian convoys by the parties to the conflict totally unacceptable.

### Resolution 836 (1993), June 4, 1993
The Council decides to extend the mandate of UNPROFOR to enable it to protect the safe areas of Sarajevo, Tuzla, Žepa, Goražde, Bihać, and Srebrenica, and to use force in self-defense or in deterring attacks against the safe areas. The Council also authorizes Member States to take all necessary measures, through the use of air power, to support UNPROFOR. UNPROFOR forces are to monitor the cease-fire, promote the withdrawal of military and paramilitary units other than those of the Government of Bosnia-Herzegovina, occupy some key points on the ground, and participate in the delivery of humanitarian aid.

### Statement by the President, June 8, 1993
The Council expresses deep concern over the failure of the Krajina Serbs to participate in talks on the implementation of Resolution 802 (1993) which were to be held in Zagreb on May 26, 1993.

### Resolution 838 (1993), June 10, 1993
The Council reinstates its demand with respect to Resolution 819 (1993) that the Federal Republic of Yugoslavia immediately cease supply of military arms, equipment, and services to Bosnian Serb paramilitary units and requests, in order to facilitate the implementation of the relevant Se-

curity Council resolutions, a report on the options to deploy international observers on the borders of Bosnia-Herzegovina as indicated in Resolution 787 (1992).

### Resolution 842 (1993), June 18, 1993
The Council welcomes the important contributions of the existing UNPROFOR presence in the Former Yugoslav Republic of Macedonia to stability in the region and decides to expand the size of UNPROFOR accordingly.

### Resolution 843 (1993), June 18, 1993
The Council confirms that the Committee established pursuant to Resolution 724 (1991) is entrusted with the task of examining requests for assistance under the provisions of Article 50 of the Charter of the United Nations, welcomes the establishment by the Committee of its working group to examine requests for assistance, and invites the Committee to make recommendations to the President of the Security Council for appropriate action.

### Resolution 844 (1993), June 18, 1993
The Council authorizes an additional reinforcement of UNPROFOR by an initial 7,600 troops and reaffirms the use of air power in and around the declared safe areas in Bosnia and Herzegovina to support the force. It also calls upon Member States to contribute forces, including logistic support and equipment, to facilitate the implementation of provisions regarding those safe areas—Sarajevo, Tuzla, Žepa, Goražde, Bihać, as well as Srebrenica, and their surroundings.

### Resolution 845 (1993), June 18, 1993
The Council calls on Greece and the Former Yugoslav Republic of Macedonia to continue to cooperate with the cochairmen of the Steering Committee of the ICFY in order to arrive at a steady settlement on the different issues affecting both countries. The Council requests that the Secretary-General keep it informed of progress toward the objective of resolving differences by the start of the 48th session of the General Assembly.

### Draft Resolution (Not Adopted), June 29, 1993
The Council would have decided to exempt the Government of the Republic of Bosnia and Herzegovina from the arms embargo, imposed on the former Yugoslavia by Resolution 713 (1991), with the sole purpose of enabling that Republic to exercise its inherent right to self-defense.

### Resolution 847 (1993), June 30, 1993

The Council calls on all parties to comply with the cease-fire arrangements already made, and to agree to confidence-building measures in Croatia including: the opening of the railroad between Zagreb and Split; the highway between Zagreb and Županja, and the Adriatic pipeline; securing the uninterrupted traffic across the Maslenica Straits; and to restore electricity and water to all regions in Croatia, including the UNPAs. The Council requests the Secretary-General to report within one month on progress toward the peacekeeping plan in Croatia and to reconsider in light of that report UNPROFOR's mandate in Croatia and decides, in this context, to extend UNPROFOR's mandate for an interim period terminating September 30, 1993.

### Statement by the President, July 15, 1993

The Council expresses its deep concern at the reported hostilities in the UNPAs including in particular by the Krajina Serbs, considers the planned unilateral reopening of the Maslenica bridge and of Zemunik Airport would jeopardize the objectives of the Council's resolutions, and urges the Government of Croatia to refrain from this action.

### Statement by the President, July 22, 1993

The Council demands an immediate end to the offensive by the Bosnian Serbs on Mount Igman and to all attacks on Sarajevo, to all violations of international humanitarian law, to the disruption of public utilities by the Bosnian Serb party, and to the blocking by both the Bosnian Serb and the Bosnian Croat parties of the delivery of humanitarian relief.

### Statement by the President, July 30, 1993

The Council demands that the Croatian forces withdraw from the area of the Maslenica bridge and permit the immediate deployment of UNPROFOR, and that the Krajina Serb forces refrain from entering the area.

### Resolution 855 (1993), August 9, 1993

The Council calls upon the authorities in the Federal Republic of Yugoslavia to cooperate with the CSCE by taking the practical steps needed for the resumption of the activities of its mission in Kosovo, Sandžak, and Vojvodina, and to agree to an increase in the number of monitors.

### Resolution 857 (1993), August 20, 1993

The Council establishes the list of candidates for judges of the International Tribunal.

## Resolution 859 (1993), August 24, 1993

The Council affirms that a solution to the conflict in Bosnia and Herzegovina must be in conformity with the Charter of the United Nations, the principles of international law, the continued membership of the Republic of Bosnia and Herzegovina in the United Nations, and the principles adopted by the London Conference on former Yugoslavia, calls for an immediate cease-fire and cessation of hostilities, demands the unhindered flow of humanitarian assistance, in particular to the safe areas, and declares its readiness to consider taking necessary measures to assist the parties in the effective implementation of a fair and equitable settlement once it has been freely agreed by the parties.

## Statement by the President, September 14, 1993

The Council expresses its profound concern at the reports of recent military hostilities in Croatia, calls on the Croatian Government to withdraw its armed forces to positions occupied before September 9, 1993, and calls on the Serbian forces to halt all provocative military actions.

## Statement by the President, September 14, 1993

The Council expresses its profound concern over recent reports that Bosnian Croats have been holding Bosnian Muslims in detention camps under deplorable conditions and reiterates the principle that ICRC must be given access to all detainees in Bosnia and Herzegovina.

## Resolution 869 (1993), September 30, 1993

The Council decides to extend UNPROFOR's mandate for an additional period terminating on October 1, 1993.

## Resolution 870 (1993), October 1, 1993

The Council decides to extend UNPROFOR's mandate for an additional period terminating on October 5, 1993.

## Resolution 871 (1993), October 4, 1993

The Council declares that continued noncooperation in the implementation of the relevant resolutions of the Council or external interference in respect of the full implementation of the United Nations peacekeeping plan for the Republic of Croatia would have serious consequences, and decides to extend UNPROFOR's mandate for an additional period terminating on March 31, 1994, with a report by the Secretary-General in two months to reconsider UNPROFOR's mandate in light of progress.

## Statement by the President, October 13, 1993

The Council condemns the blocking of the Danube river by two Serbian nongovernmental organizations, expresses concern that the authorities of the Federal Republic of Yugoslavia continue the illegal imposition of tolls on foreign vessels, and reaffirms the unacceptability for that Republic to take retaliatory measures in response to action by a State in fulfillment of its obligations under the United Nations Charter.

### Resolution 877 (1993), October 21, 1993
The Council appoints Mr. Ramón Escovar-Salom, Attorney-General of Venezuela, as Prosecutor of the International Tribunal.

### Statement by the President, October 28, 1993
The Council, after having heard an initial report concerning the massacre of the civilian population in the village of Stupni Do by troops of the Croatian Defense Council, accounts of an attack against UNPROFOR by armed persons bearing uniforms of Bosnian Government forces and an attack on a humanitarian convoy in central Bosnia, unreservedly condemns these acts of violence, and requests the Secretary-General to submit a complete report on the responsibility of these acts.

### Statement by the President, November 9, 1993
The Council expresses its deep concern at the reported deterioration of the situation in central Bosnia, where increased military activities are seriously threatening the security of the civilian population, and at the overall humanitarian situation prevailing in the Republic of Bosnia and Herzegovina.

### Statement by the President, November 9, 1993
The Council expresses its shock at the report of an incident in which two persons were taken hostage by Bosnian Serb forces, while members of a delegation headed by the Archbishop of Sarajevo, traveling to the city of Vares on a mission of peace under UNPROFOR protection. The Council strongly condemns this act, demands the immediate release of these hostages, and requests the Secretary-General to conduct a thorough investigation of the incident and to report to the Council without delay.

### Statement by the President, January 7, 1994
The Council expresses its deep concern at the continuing widespread hostilities in Bosnia and Herzegovina, deplores the failure of the parties to honor the agreements they have already signed, condemns the flagrant violations of international humanitarian law, and condemns any hostilities in the United Nations-designated safe areas, in particular the continuing military pressure on and the relentless bombardment of Sarajevo by Bosnian Serb forces.

**Statement by the President, February 3, 1994**
The Council demands that the Republic of Croatia withdraw all elements of the Croatian Army along with military equipment and fully respect the territorial integrity of the Republic of Bosnia and Herzegovina, and expresses readiness to consider other serious measures if the Republic of Croatia fails to put an immediate end to all forms of interference in the Republic of Bosnia and Herzegovina.

**Resolution 900 (1994), March 4, 1994**
The Council requests the Secretary-General to appoint a senior civilian official, who will act under the authority of his Special Representative for the Former Yugoslavia, to draw up an overall assessment and plan of action for the restoration of essential public services in the various opštinas of Sarajevo, other than the city of Pale, invites the Secretary-General to establish a voluntary trust fund for the purpose, and requests a report on the feasibility of extending protection defined in Resolutions 824 (1993) and 836 (1993) to Maglaj, Mostar, and Vitez.

**Statement by the President, March 14, 1994**
The Council most strongly condemns the flagrant violation by the authorities of the Federal Republic of Yugoslavia of the relevant Security Council resolutions prohibiting the shipment of commodities and products to that Republic.

**Statement by the President, March 14, 1994**
The Council strongly condemns the indiscriminate shelling of the civilian population of Maglaj by the Bosnian Serb party and demands that the siege of that city be ended immediately, and also demands that the Bosnian Serb party and the Bosnian Croat party allow passage of all humanitarian convoys.

**Resolution 908 (1994), March 31, 1994**
The Council extends the mandate of UNPROFOR for an additional period ending September 30, 1994, approves the UNPROFOR plan to reopen the Tuzla airport for humanitarian purposes, decides that member states may take, under the authority of the Security Council and in close coordination with the Secretary-General and UNPROFOR, all necessary measures to extend close air support in defense of UNPROFOR personnel in Croatia, and authorizes an increase of UNPROFOR's strength of up to 3,500 troops.

**Statement by the President, April 6, 1994**
The Council strongly condemns the shelling and attacks by Bosnian Serb forces against the safe area of Goražde and expresses its concern at the

recent acts of violence and terror, including reported acts of ethnic cleansing in Banja Luka and Prijedor.

### Statement by the President April 14, 1994

The Council expresses its deep concern at recent incidents in Bosnia and Herzegovina affecting the safety and freedom of movement of UNPROFOR personnel and demands that all parties, and in particular the Bosnian Serb party, allow UNPROFOR unimpeded freedom of movement and refrain from further actions which could threaten the safety of UNPROFOR personnel.

### Resolution 913 (1994), April 22, 1994

The Council condemns the shelling and attacks by Bosnian Serb forces against the safe area of Goražde and demands force and weapon withdrawals, demands an immediate release of all UN personnel held by Bosnian Serb forces, and also demands the unimpeded freedom of UNPROFOR in the fulfillment of its tasks.

### Resolution 914 (1994), April 27, 1994

The Council authorizes an increase in UNPROFOR personnel of up to 6,550 additional troops, 150 military observers, and 275 civilian police.

### Statement by the President, May 4, 1994

The Council expresses its concern at recent indications of increasing tension in the Republic of Bosnia and Herzegovina, in particular the Posavina "corridor," welcomes the arrangements to establish an UNPROFOR presence in the region, and warns the parties of the serious consequences of any offensive military action in or around the Posavina "corridor."

### Statement by the President, May 25, 1994

The Council reiterates the urgent need to intensify efforts toward an overall political settlement of the conflict in the Republic of Bosnia and Herzegovina and calls on the parties to resume, without preconditions, serious efforts to reach a political settlement.

### Statement by the President, June 1, 1994

The Council expresses its support for the efforts by the Secretary-General's Special Representative and the UNPROFOR Force Commander to negotiate a cessation of hostilities in the Republic of Bosnia and Herzegovina and welcomes the decision to convene a meeting with the parties in Geneva on June 2, 1994.

### Statement by the President, June 30, 1994

The Council underlines its support for the June 8, 1994 Agreement of the parties to the conflict, in which they agreed to observe a cease-fire for a period of one month starting June 10, 1994, and expresses its grave concern at the parties' failure to comply with the Agreement to date.

### Resolution 936 (1994), July 8, 1994

The Council appoints Richard J. Goldstone as prosecutor of the International Tribunal for the prosecution of persons responsible for serious violations of international humanitarian law committed in the territory of the former Yugoslavia since 1991.

### Statement by the President, August 11, 1994

The Council expresses its deep concern of reports of blockades of UNPROFOR traffic into UNPAs in Croatia by demonstrators and considers such impediments on the freedom of movement of UNPROFOR are inadmissible.

### Statement by the President, September 2, 1994

The Council expresses its deep concern at continuing reports of acts of ethnic cleansing by the Bosnian Serb party in the Bijeljina area, condemns this practice, and demands its immediate cessation. It further notes with dismay the restrictions on UNPROFOR's freedom of movement in Bosnia and Herzegovina, in particular Banja Luka, Bijeljina, and Sarajevo.

### Resolution 941 (1994), September 23, 1994

The Council condemns all violations of international humanitarian law, in particular the unacceptable practice of "ethnic cleansing" perpetrated in Banja Luka, Bijeljina, and other areas of the Republic of Bosnia and Herzegovina under the control of Bosnian Serb forces, and demands that the Bosnian Serb authorities immediately cease this practice and allow immediate and unimpeded access for the Special Representative of the Secretary-General, UNPROFOR, UNHCR, and ICRC to these areas.

### Resolution 942 (1994), September 23, 1994

The Council strongly condemns the Bosnian Serb party for its refusal to accept the proposed territorial settlement (Contact Group plan), demands that that party accept this settlement unconditionally and in full, and resolves to reinforce and extend the measures imposed by its previous resolutions with regard to those areas of the Republic of Bosnia and Herzegovina under the control of Bosnian Serb forces as long as that party has not accepted the proposed settlement in full.

### Resolution 943 (1994), September 23, 1994

The Council decides to suspend the restrictions on travel and sports imposed by its resolutions on the Federal Republic of Yugoslavia (Serbia and Montenegro) for an initial period of 100 days from the receipt by the Council of a report from the Secretary-General that the authorities of the Federal Republic of Yugoslavia (Serbia and Montenegro) has effectively closed its international border with the Republic of Bosnia and Herzegovina with respect to all goods except foodstuffs, medical supplies, and clothing for essential humanitarian needs.

### Resolution 947 (1994), September 30, 1994

The Council decides to extend UNPROFOR's mandate for an additional period terminating on March 31, 1995, and requests the Secretary-General to report no later than January 26, 1995, on progress toward implementation of the peacekeeping plan in Croatia and to reconsider UNPROFOR's mandate in light of that report.

### Statement by the President, September 30, 1994

The Council expresses its deep concern at the deteriorating security situation in the safe area of Sarajevo and elsewhere in Bosnia and Herzegovina, which has included increased levels of armed violence, deliberate attacks on UNPROFOR troops and on humanitarian flights, severe restrictions on public utilities, and continued restriction on the flow of transport and communications.

### Statement by the President, November 13, 1994

The Council views with alarm the escalation in recent fighting in the Bihać area and the flow of refugees and displaced persons from it. It strongly urges all parties and others concerned to refrain from all hostile actions and to exercise the utmost restraint.

### Statement by the President, November 18, 1994

The Council condemns in the strongest possible terms the attack on the safe area of Bihać by aircraft belonging to the so-called Krajina Serb forces as a violation of the territorial integrity of the Republic of Bosnia and Herzegovina and relevant Security Council resolutions and demands an immediate end to all military activity which endangers the lives of the UNPROFOR personnel deployed in the Bihać area.

### Resolution 958 (1994), November 19, 1994

The Council decides that the authorization given in Resolution 836 (1993) to Member States to take, under the authority of the Security Council and subject to close coordination with the Secretary-General and

UNPROFOR, all necessary measures, through the use of air power, in and around the safe areas of Bosnia and Herzegovina, to support UN-PROFOR in the performance of its mandate shall apply to measures taken in the Republic of Croatia.

### Resolution 959 (1994), November 19, 1994
The Council expresses its grave concern over the recent hostilities in Bosnia and Herzegovina and condemns any violation of the international border between the Republic of Croatia and the Republic of Bosnia and Herzegovina and demands that all parties and others concerned, and in particular the so-called Krajina Serb forces, fully respect the border and refrain from hostile acts across it.

### Statement by the President, November 26, 1994
The Council condemns in the strongest possible terms all the violations of the safe area of Bihać by whomsoever committed, and in particular, the flagrant and blatant entry into the safe area by the Bosnian Serb forces.

### Statement by the President, November 29, 1994
The Council notes with satisfaction the proposal put to the parties by United Nations officials for an immediate and unconditional cease-fire in the Bihać region to be followed by a cease-fire throughout the territory of the Republic of Bosnia and Herzegovina, welcomes the acceptance by the Bosnian Government of this proposal, and calls on the Bosnian Serb party also to accept it.

### Statement by the President, December 13, 1994
The Council strongly condemns the deliberate attack on Bangladeshi United Nations peacekeepers on December 12, 1994, in Velika Kladusa in the region of Bihać, expresses its outrage at this incident of direct attack on UNPROFOR personnel, and demands that such attacks do not recur.

### Resolution 967 (1994), December 14, 1994
The Council decides to permit, for a period of thirty days from the date of the adoption of this Resolution, the export of 12,000 vials of diphtheria anti-serum from the Federal Republic of Yugoslavia (Serbia and Montenegro) with payments for such authorized shipments to be made only into frozen accounts.

### Resolution 970 (1995), January 12, 1995
The Council welcomes the measures taken by the authorities of the Federal Republic of Yugoslavia (Serbia and Montenegro) to maintain the effective closure of the international border between the Federal Republic of Yugo-

slavia (Serbia and Montenegro) and the Republic of Bosnia and Herzegovina and decides to suspend for a further period of 100 days the restrictions and other measures referred to in paragraph 1 of Resolution 943 (1994). The Council reaffirms the requirement of paragraph 12 of Resolution 820 (1993) and requests the Secretary-General to submit a report every 30 days that the border remains closed.

Sources: *The United Nations and the Situation in the Former Yugoslavia* (United Nations Department of Public Information, 1994); "UN Resolutions on the Balkan Crisis," *WarReport*, no. 28 (September 1994), pp. 16–17; and published texts of Security Council Resolutions and Presidential Statements.

# Notes

## Chapter 1

1. The German constitutional court ruling that permitted use of German combat forces out of the NATO area came only in July 1993. The German government would not go so far, however, as to provide six to eight Tornado fighter bombers to the no-fly ("Deny Flight") operation when requested by NATO at the end of November 1994, even though Germany was the only NATO country with planes available that were equipped with the capacity to suppress or destroy the antiaircraft missiles that the Bosnian Serbs activated in mid-November to deter further NATO air strikes.

2. In contingency planning in late 1994 to assist the extraction of the UN protection forces from Bosnia-Herzegovina, should their withdrawal under less than benign circumstances be necessary, NATO also intended to employ its Rapid Reaction Corps, created in 1991 but not yet fully operational. This as yet untested corps represents the primary structural change made by NATO to adapt its military capacities to post–cold war circumstances. Ann Devroy and Bradley Graham, "U.S. to Send Forces if U.N. Quits Bosnia," *Washington Post*, December 9, 1994, p. A1.

3. For example, Stipe Mesić, *Kako Smo Srušili Jugoslaviju: politički memoari posljednjeg predsjednika Predsjedništva SFRJ* (How we destroyed Yugoslavia: Political memoirs of the last president of the presidency of the SFRY) (Zagreb: Globus International, 1992); Veljko Kadijević, *Moje Vidjenje Raspada: Vojska bez Država* (My view of the collapse: An army without a state) (Belgrade: Politika, 1993); Dobrila Gajić-Glišić, *Srpska Vojska: iz kabineta ministra vojnog* (Serbian army: From the cabinet of the defense minister) (Belgrade: Narodna biblioteka Srbije, 1992); Mario Agnes, ed., *La Crise en Yougoslavie: Position et Action du Saint-Siège (1991–1992)* (The crisis in Yugoslavia: Position and action of the Holy See) (Vatican City: Librairia Éditrice Vaticana, 1992).

4. A useful short synopsis is in Robert Lee Wolff, *The Balkans in Our Time* (New York: W. W. Norton, 1967), pp. 92–95.

5. Paul Lewis, "U.S. Seeks Tougher Sanctions on Yugoslavia," *New York Times*, April 7, 1993, p. A15.

6. The title of Misha Glenny's account of the 1989 revolutions, *The Rebirth of History: Eastern Europe in the Age of Democracy* (London: Penguin, 1990), captures the mood expressed widely at the time. A recent example of the "history as destiny" school concerning the Balkans is Robert D. Kaplan, *Balkan Ghosts: A Journey through History* (St. Martin's Press, 1993). The argument was so often repeated as to become nearly irrefutable; U.S. President Clinton generalized it to characterize the entire era that was closing in a speech to the graduating class of the U.S. Naval Academy on the eve of the fiftieth anniversary of D-Day: "The Cold War's end 'lifted the lid from a cauldron of long-simmering hatreds. Now, the entire global terrain is bloody with such conflicts.'" Cited in Ann Devroy, "President Cautions Congress on 'Simplistic Ideas' in Foreign Policy," *Washington Post*, May 26, 1994, p. A31.

7. U.S. Senator Daniel Patrick Moynihan calls this "neo-Wilsonianism," in his book *Pandaemonium: Ethnicity in International Politics* (Oxford University Press, 1993), p. 147.

8. Nonofficial supporters of the Muslims in Bosnia-Herzegovina insisted that they were victims of genocide and that conventions against genocide required the most vigorous action to give them aid, from military intervention to exempting Bosnian government forces from the arms embargo imposed on the former Yugoslavia and providing them with weapons, training, and auxiliary air strikes. Governments, however, held back from officially proclaiming Serb atrocities against Muslims (Croat actions were rarely discussed) as genocide.

9. In the United States this view was pushed most publicly by John J. Mearsheimer and Robert A. Pape, "The Answer," *New Republic*, June 14, 1993, pp. 22–29.

10. Indicative of this problem was the Clinton administration's request for assistance from the United Nations High Commissioner for Refugees, Sadako Ogata, and her office, in managing the refugee outflow from Haiti in mid-May 1994. At the same time it was taking a strongly critical position against the UN operations in former Yugoslavia, including UNHCR, and the special representative of the UN Secretary General for former Yugoslavia (SRSG), Yasushi Akashi.

11. This view became more consequential after the victory of Republicans in the U.S. congressional elections of November 1994 and the shift to Senate leadership of one of the antimultilateralists, Robert Dole. In response to NATO air action he considered insufficient in the northwestern part of Bosnia-Herzegovina called the Bihać pocket, Dole said, "The UN should get off NATO's back and let NATO take care of Serbian aggression," and "I don't see any reason for their [NATO's] existence if they have to take orders from the UN." Cited by Bruce Clark, Laura Silber, and Nancy Dunne, in "UN Force On High Alert As Serbs Head For Safe Area," *Financial Times*, November 21, 1994, p. 1.

12. The phrase used for this process in March 1994 by the head of the UN Protection Forces, SRSG Yasushi Akashi.

13. For the important distinction between an ethnic group and a nation, see chapter 7.

14. A particularly eloquent representative of this school is Moynihan, *Pandaemonium: Ethnicity in International Politics.*

15. Interviews with Croatian and Yugoslav officials, July 1994.

16. Based on confidential interviews.

17. Interview with Sergei Stankevich, Aspen Institute conference, Vienna, August 1992.

18. Croat journalist and novelist, Slavenka Drakulić, writes in her anger at Europe's perception of the war as "ethnic conflict" and an "ancient legacy of hatred and bloodshed": "In this way the West tells us, 'You are not Europeans, not even Eastern Europeans. You are Balkans, mythological, wild, dangerous Balkans. Kill yourselves, if that is your pleasure. We don't understand what is going on there, nor do we have clear political interests to protect.' " *The Balkan Express: Fragments From the Other Side of War* (W. W. Norton, 1993), pp. 2–3.

# Chapter 2

1. Two examples are the political theorist Robert A. Dahl [see *Dilemmas of Pluralist Democracy: Autonomy vs. Control* (Yale University Press, 1982)] and the historian Charles Tilly on the West European experience. See "Reflections on the History of European State-Making," in Charles Tilly, ed., *The Formation of National States in Western Europe* (Princeton University Press, 1975), pp. 3–83.

2. Mark Thompson's wonderfully evocative book about the last three years of Yugoslavia, interspersed with much historical commentary, *A Paper House: The Ending of Yugoslavia* (Pantheon, 1992), is nonetheless a good example of this rejectionist mentality about Yugoslavia and its socialist system, in which the myths were "delusive" (p. 2) and the idea of Yugoslavia "fantasy" and "illusion" (preface).

3. It is true that one could hear this more commonly in Bosnia-Herzegovina, Macedonia, or Serbia than in Slovenia and Croatia, where the new legitimizing myths about their independence had fully taken hold.

4. See Samuel P. Huntington, "The Clash of Civilizations," *Foreign Affairs*, vol. 72 (Summer 1993), pp. 22–49.

5. For the full analysis of the Yugoslav socialist system on which this sketch is based, see Susan L. Woodward, *Socialist Unemployment: The Political Economy of Yugoslavia, 1945–1990* (Princeton University Press, forthcoming 1995).

6. Few works are more useful as introductions to the mentality of the period than Oscar Jászi's *The Dissolution of the Habsburg Monarchy* (University of Chicago Press, 1929).

7. See Ivo J. Lederer, *Yugoslavia at the Paris Peace Conference: a Study in Frontiermaking* (Yale University Press, 1963). For an introduction to the origins of Yugoslavia, see Aleksa Djilas, *The Contested Country: Yugoslav Unity and Communist Revolution, 1919–1953* (Harvard University Press, 1991).

8. Ivo Banac, *The National Question in Yugoslavia: Origins, History, Politics* (Cornell University Press, 1984), is best on this issue, where he argues that the fundamental flaw of the first Yugoslavia was an irresolvable conflict between two state ideologies, one Croat, one Serb.

9. The classic study by Albert O. Hirschman, *National Power and the Structure of Foreign Trade* (University of California Press, 1945), on the role of German economic power in eastern Europe in the 1930s included the Yugoslav case. On the interwar period in general, see Joseph Rothschild, "Yugoslavia," in *East Central Europe Between the Two World Wars* (University of Washington Press, 1974).

10. Stalin did nothing to oppose the Tripartite Agreement of February 1948 to hand Trieste and Zone A to Italy, leading Yugoslav Communists to view it as yet another example of Stalin's betrayal after the 50–50 deal that so infuriated Tito.

11. On its role in mobilizing anti-Soviet sentiments and eventually revolutionary action in the 1980s in Poland, see Neal Ascherson, *The Polish August: The Self-Limiting Revolution* (Viking Press, 1982). Of course, the symbol of Yalta could also represent betrayal by the West, and its sellout at these meetings of their future as a security band and sphere of influence for the Soviet Union in exchange for Soviet entrance into the war in Asia.

12. This is the theme of the film by Bosnian director Emir Kušturica, *When Father Was Away on Business* (Cannon Films, 1985). This highly mixed group was tarred with the single label of "Cominformists" (*ibeovci*, from *Informbiro*), as people siding with the June 28, 1948, letter of expulsion of the Yugoslav Communist party (CPY) from the Communist Information Bureau, or Cominform. Ivo Banac analyzes this group and its place in the political factions of the CPY in *With Stalin Against Tito: The Cominformist Splits in Yugoslav Communism* (Cornell University Press, 1988); see also Stephan Clissold, *Yugoslavia and the Soviet Union, 1939–1973: A Documentary Survey* (Oxford University Press, 1975).

13. See John R. Lampe, Russell O. Prickett, and Ljubiša S. Adamović, *Yugoslav-American Economic Relations Since World War II* (Duke University Press, 1990) for data on U.S. aid to Yugoslavia and the history of the relationship established in 1949.

14. Tito asked for Marshall Plan assistance at several points beginning in July 1948 and into 1949 but was refused, and they were not even invited to the founding meeting of Comecon in February 1949, although the Yugoslavs claimed to have initiated the idea for it. The nonaligned movement was created by Tito, Indonesian president Sukarno, Indian prime minister Jawaharlal Nehru, and Egyptian president Gamal Abdel Nasser in 1955, with the first meeting in Belgrade in 1961. See Alvin Z. Rubinstein, *Yugoslavia and the Nonaligned World* (Princeton University Press, 1970).

15. An example of the consequences of this is discussed in Michael Palairet, "Ramiz Sadiku: A Case Study in the Industrialisation of Kosovo," *Soviet Studies*, vol. 44 (1992), pp. 897–912; despite warfare among Slovenia, Serbia, and Croatia during 1991–92, producers of military equipment such as tanks in the three republics continued to cooperate and to produce for both domestic and export markets.

16. Yugoslavs had a long tradition of self-defense and of bearing personal arms; in 1989, an estimated 1.6 million Yugoslavs, or 7 percent of the total population, owned private firearms legally. David C. Isby, "Yugoslavia 1991–Armed Forces in Conflict," *Jane's Intelligence Review*, vol. 3 (September 1991), p. 394–403.

17. Useful summaries are Isby, p. 394–403, and Anton Bebler, "The Military and the Yugoslav Crisis," *Südosteuropa*, vol. 40 (1991), pp. 127–44. See also James Gow, *Legitimacy and the Military: The Yugoslav Crisis* (St. Martin's Press, 1992).

18. William Zimmerman argues, in *Open Borders, Nonalignment, and the Political Evolution of Yugoslavia* (Princeton University Press, 1987), that Yugoslavia's openness was even more important for its political stability, such as through the safety valve for social discontent of temporary foreign labor migration, than for economic flexibility and growth.

19. Michèle Ledić, "Debt Analysis and Debt-related Issues: the Case of Yugoslavia," *Economic Analysis and Workers' Management*, vol. 18 (1984), pp. 35–64. The debt continued to rise until the late 1980s when the government succeeded in lowering the debt to the 1981 figure ($19.3 billion) by 1990. World Bank, *World Debt Tables, 1990–91, External Debt of Developing Countries*, Supplement (World Bank, 1991), p. 242.

20. A still useful economic geography for former Yugoslavia is F. E. Ian Hamilton, *Yugoslavia: Patterns of Economic Activity* (Praeger, 1968).

21. See Banac, *The National Question in Yugoslavia*, on the national question as it influenced the first Yugoslavia, and the conflicts between, especially, Croats and Serbs. The Communist party's answer to the "national question" was composed during the 1920s and 1930s, as a result of Comintern tactics, the party's original federal structure cemented by separate Slovene membership in the Comintern in 1936 (followed by the Croats in 1937), and the leaders' adoption of Leninist (not Stalinist) political principles in general. Similarities in the breakup of the former Soviet Union, the Czech and Slovak Republic, and potentially, contemporary Ethiopia can be attributed in part to their common adoption of the Leninist program. For an excellent introduction to the national question after 1945, see Paul Shoup, *Communism and the Yugoslav National Question* (Columbia University Press, 1968).

22. See the useful discussion in Frits W. Hondius, *The Yugoslav Community of Nations* (The Hague and Paris: Mouton, 1968), pp. 129–32.

23. Hondius, *The Yugoslav Community of Nations*, p. 246. This is Article 1, Part One, of the 1963 Constitution; there was no substantive change in the phrasing in the 1974 Constitution.

24. Hondius, *The Yugoslav Community of Nations*, p. 252.

25. Muslims were not listed originally in the federal constitution as a founding nation, but citizens had the right to identify themselves as Muslims in the 1961 census—establishing what Hondius calls a "quasi-national status"; the constitution of one of the republics, Bosnia and Herzegovina, identified this republic as formed by three constituent peoples—"Serbs, Moslems and Croats, allied in their past by a common life"; they entered the list of constituent nations in the federal constitution of 1963; and the 4th congress of the League of Communists of Bosnia-Herzegovina in the spring of 1965 granted Muslims the right to national self-determination. See Hondius, *The Yugoslav Community of Nations*, pp. 130, 247–48.

26. Originally called national minorities, this label was seen to imply inferiority and so was abandoned for the more neutral term, nationalities.

27. See Hondius, *The Yugoslav Community of Nations*, pp. 250–52, and Walker Connor, *The National Question in Marxist-Leninist Theory and Strategy* (Princeton University Press, 1984), pp. 128–71, and especially pp. 158–63 and 224.

28. Greg Englefield, *Yugoslavia, Croatia, Slovenia: Re-emerging Boundaries*, Territory Briefing 3 (Durham, U.K.: International Boundaries Research Unit, 1992), especially pp. 9–14, provides a succinct summary. Milovan Djilas chaired the

boundary commission held in 1945 on the Croatian-Serbian border; see articles by Milovan Djilas, Mladen Klemenčić, Ivan Pauletta, and Branka Prpa-Janović in *WarReport*, no. 9 (December 28, 1991), and for debates within the communist leadership at the time, Shoup, *Communism and the Yugoslav National Question*.

29. Milorad Pupovac, "Manjine–Ključ mira ili uzrok rata?" [Minorities–the key to peace or the cause of war?"] (unpub. ms. 1993).

30. See Paul Shoup, "The Future of Croatia's Border Regions," Radio Free Europe/Radio Liberty, *RFE/RL Research Report on Eastern Europe* (November 29, 1991), pp. 26–33, for a careful statistical analysis of the ethnic composition of communities in the border regions of Croatia, including the *krajina*.

31. Steven L. Burg and Michael L. Berbaum, "Community, Integration, and Stability in Multinational Yugoslavia," *American Political Science Review*, vol. 83 (June 1989), pp. 535–54, studied this group, which "increased 4 1/2-fold, from 273,077 to 1,219,024 persons, or from 1.3% to 5.4% of the population" between 1971 and 1981. In a 1987 survey cited by Burg and Berbaum, "15% of Yugoslav youth declared Yugoslav identity and some 36% expressed a 'preference' for declaring it in place of their ethnic identity," p. 535.

32. Silvano Bolčić, "Citizens sans Frontiers," *WarReport*, no. 9 (December 28, 1991), p. 7.

33. There were four constitutions—1946, 1953, 1963, 1974—before the constitutional reforms began again in the 1980s, and they differed in the details of voting systems, distributive rules, and governmental jurisdictions; for example, the national key in some periods required parity representation by republic and in others by nation.

34. 1991 census figures show ethnic Hungarians composing 22 percent of the population of Vojvodina. See Edith Oltay, "Hungarians Under Political Pressure in Yugoslavia," *RFE/RL Research Report* (December 3, 1993), p. 43.

35. Article 170/3 of the 1974 Constitution, cited in Tibor Varady, "Collective Minority Rights and Problems in Their Legal Protection: The Example of Yugoslavia," *East European Politics and Societies*, vol. 6 (Fall 1992), p. 263. For some, this constituted repression; for others, it was the line drawn for civilized societies in John Stuart Mill's *On Liberty*.

36. Varady, "Collective Minority Rights," p. 265; this paragraph is drawn from his concise summary, pp. 263–65, of widely recognized characteristics of the system. He adds: "With the collapse of the social system that mandated this notion [equality], the concept of postulated equality also disappeared; and so did the confines halting the escalation of ethnic hatred, discrimination, and violence."

37. The word *samoupravljanje* is usually translated as self-management, but in the pre-socialist period, it was just as likely to be used for self-government; the governing role was shared by independent managers, elected councils of workers, and annual assemblies of all employees.

38. Consensus and parity were commonly said (by all non-Serbs, but also in criticism, by Serb nationalists) to be the primary protection against any possible resurgence of Serbian dominance, as the largest nation numerically. But this assertion assumed that Serbs outside of Serbia would always choose to vote their national identity as an ethnic people rather than their identity as a member of the territorial people of a republic, an assumption that had no basis in historical experience,

where Serbs from Croatia or Vojvodina, for example, were most often in conflict with Serbs from Serbia proper. It also assumes that there are no competing forms of power, such as economic dominance, in the country.

39.  It is often said that this "contractual" or "bargaining" system characterized the economy in the 1970s only, but in fact it was the dominant system in the public sector throughout the period after 1949. See Woodward, *Socialist Unemployment*.

40.  For example, the absence of independent capital or bond markets and a requirement for government budgets to balance, which put severe restraints on the political choices of distribution; the territorialized and segmented banking system and markets; the relative openness to world market prices while being supply-dependent on imports, making frequent devaluation an inflationary instrument in practice; and the strict limits on wealth from private assets, which made individuals vulnerable to inflation. On the difficulties of reforming socialist economies with inflation, see Simon Commander, "Inflation and the Transition to a Market Economy: an Overview," *The World Bank Economic Review*, no. 1 (1992), pp. 3–12.

41.  Donna Bahry, "Perestroika and the Debate over Territorial Economic Decentralization," *Harriman Institute Forum*, vol. 2 (May 1989), pp. 1–8. She also describes the same pattern of decentralization and some of the same consequences in the Soviet Union after 1985.

42.  The question of introduction first asked was not "what do you do?" but "in whose house do you live?" This policy of resettlement as well as the mutual suspicions of ethnic favoritism accompanying it predates the socialist period, however. (Interviews with Yugoslav sociologists.)

43.  Two examples are Radovan Karadžić, leader of the Serbian Democratic party in Bosnia-Herzegovina, and Slobodan Milošević, president of Serbia and leader of the Socialist party of Serbia.

44.  Between 1950 and 1975, the Yugoslav economy (GDP) grew at a rate of 6.6 percent annually. In per capita terms, growth was 5.7 percent, "which more than doubled Yugoslav GDP per capita relative to the world's average." In the period 1980–85, the average annual growth rate was 0.7 percent. James H. Gapinski, Borislav Škegro, and Thomas W. Zuehlke, *Modeling the Economic Performance of Yugoslavia* (Praeger, 1989), p. 12.

# Chapter 3

1.  An excellent introduction to the political environment of 1980–85 is Steven L. Burg, "Elite Conflict in Post-Tito Yugoslavia," *Soviet Studies*, vol. 38 (April 1986), pp. 170–93.

2.  See Branko Milanović, *Poverty in Poland, Hungary, and Yugoslavia in the Years of Crisis, 1978–87*, PRE Working Paper 507 (World Bank, September 1990), and Susan L. Woodward, "Orthodoxy and Solidarity: Competing Claims and International Adjustment in Yugoslavia," *International Organization*, vol. 40 (Spring 1986), pp. 505–45.

3.  People working temporarily in northern and western Europe came to be called, regardless of where they were employed, by the euphemism *guest workers*,

which Germans devised to avoid association with the forced foreign labor of the Nazi period.

4. The articles in Pedro Ramet, ed., *Yugoslavia in the 1980s* (Westview Press, 1985), give a very good sense of the atmosphere as well as useful data on 1979–83.

5. Ritual kinship, found in many of the world's cultures, was similar in former Yugoslavia to the institution of godparenthood in the United States, except that it need not have religious connotations, and it created immensely stronger bonds between a person and his or her *kum* and obligations on the *kum*. Different occasions would give rise to the appointment of a *kum*, such as birth and marriage, which would be denoted in the title. The institution of *kumstvo* was also much stronger among Serbs and in rural environments than in the northwest, where it either never existed or had long been dying out. On the importance of solidarity networks in time of austerity, see Marcel Fafchamps, "Solidarity Networks in Preindustrial Societies: Rational Peasants With a Moral Economy," *Economic Development and Cultural Change*, vol. 15 (October 1992), pp. 147–74.

6. Pedro Ramet, "The Dynamics of Yugoslav Religious Policy: Some Insights from Organization Theory," in Ramet, ed., *Yugoslavia in the 1980s*, p. 173.

7. Young people tended to rebel in apolitical ways, however; see Pedro Ramet, "Apocalypse Culture and Social Change in Yugoslavia," in Ramet, ed., *Yugoslavia in the 1980s*, pp. 3–26. See chapter 2, "Slovenian Spring," in Mark Thompson, *A Paper House: The Ending of Yugoslavia* (Pantheon, 1992), pp. 3–59.

8. In 1977, for example, to improve financial discipline over foreign exchange and the capacity to service the foreign debt, the government allocated half of federal customs revenues to republic-level associations of enterprises engaged in foreign trade. In dividing the country's balance of payments into republican accounts, the government made each republic responsible for its portion of the trade deficit and foreign debt. Enterprises were given a right to their foreign exchange earnings.

9. The Federal Assembly debated three days and two nights before it adopted the program. One night was spent waiting for the Slovene delegation to consult its base in Ljubljana before conceding to the article authorizing the National Bank to prohibit any payment to a business bank with outstanding foreign obligations, in effect agreeing to the rule of solidarity among republics on foreign debt repayment, should it be necessary.

10. Chaired by a leading Slovene economic liberal (Sergej Kraigher), this commission and its five working groups of economists, politicians, and delegates from party and economic organizations followed the principles of representation from organized official interests (the party, producer associations, governments, research institutes) and of decisionmaking by compromise and consensus that was political practice in the socialist period.

11. The more common labels for federalist and antifederalist in Yugoslav public debate were "integrationists" and "confederalists."

12. The process of dismantling the federal budget and replacing "state" financing with social self-management had by 1986 created 8,500 independent, socially managed agencies providing services with public funds, the so-called self-managed interest communities, in fields of roads, education, science and technology, employment, housing, foreign economic relations, and so forth; these were still strongly influenced, however, by local and republican governments. Božidar

Raičević and Dejan Popović, "Fiscal System and Fiscal Policy," *Yugoslav Survey*, vol. 15, no. 3 (1990), pp. 27–52.

13. From confidential interviews by the author.

14. A conflict over this land for most of the century burst open again in 1981.

15. Industrial policy, largely a system of indicative planning, was called the "social planning system." The draft law introduced in February 1985 to reform it was, according to Vojvodina, both "statist" and "unconstitutional," and the Slovene party leadership found it "incomprehensible that the Federal Executive Council [the cabinet] could [bring to the Assembly] such an unsuitably drafted bill." See Dr. Miha Ribarič's comments in "Slovene LC Body on Constitutional Court's Role," *Borba*, March 19, 1985, p. 3, in Foreign Broadcast Information Service, Daily Report: East Europe, March 22, 1985, p. 14 (hereafter FBIS, *East Europe*). It was nonetheless adopted by majority vote at the end of August 1985.

16. Croatia won autonomy in 1939 from the interwar central government (the Cvetković-Maček Agreement); in 1967–71, a multisided movement among the republic's politicians, independent intellectuals, church groups, and cultural associations—merging into what became identified as a nationalist mass movement, or *MASPOK*—pressured for Croatian rights and greater control of its economic resources and foreign affairs (including demands by some groups for separate membership in the United Nations). This movement occurred also at a time of economic reform, was preceded by Slovene and Bosnian pressures on federal economic policy, and worried military leaders about the implications for state security.

17. Such conflicts often erupted over language policy because of the similarity between Serbian and Croatian and a long-standing debate over whether the two languages, Serbian and Croatian, were variants of one literary language, Serbo-Croatian, or two distinct languages. The answer had implications for the national distinctiveness of the two peoples, which the Slovenes, by carefully protecting the survival of their language, did not have to confront.

18. Author's interviews with economists in the Slovene planning bureau in October 1982. See Susan L. Woodward, *Socialist Unemployment: The Political Economy of Yugoslavia, 1945–1990* (Princeton University Press, forthcoming 1995), chapters 7–10, for more details.

19. Milica Žarković Bookman, "The Economic Basis of Regional Autarchy in Yugoslavia," *Soviet Studies*, vol. 42 (January 1990), pp. 93–109.

20. Many Austrian firms had built plants along the Austrian-Slovene border during the 1970s to take advantage of the high technical skills but relatively low cost of Slovene engineers and workers who could live at home while employed in Austria.

21. The following discussion and data are drawn from Woodward, *Socialist Unemployment*.

22. These debates were cast in terms of the "true meaning of AVNOJ," referring to the provisional government led by the Partisans during the war and its declaration of a federal republic (renouncing the Serb monarchy). As early as the 12th Party Congress of 1982, one alternative to revise economic policymaking along more functional than territorial lines by a leading Belgrade politician was rejected. The politician was removed from his post, but the party established a commission to examine political reform alongside the economic reform program

under way. There was a fascination during this period among constitutional theorists in Belgrade, such as Kosta Čavoški and Vojislav Koštunica, who became politically active later as Serbian nationalists, with the Articles of Confederation of the United States and *The Federalist Papers*.

23. This was largely the migration zone of ethnically mixed communities (primarily Serbs and Croats, but also minorities such as Vlachs) of the former imperial borderland, the military frontier (*krajina*). This policy occasioned debate about whether the area's poverty and inherited underdevelopment had been conscious political choice of discrimination after the war as well.

24. This area, especially the Dalmatian coast, was usually seen as Croatian treasure for the value of its hard currency earnings and led occasionally to conflicts with firms from outside the republic attracted to its potential for high profits. But see N. L. Karlović, *Croatia and its Future: Internal Colonialism or Independence?* reprinted in *Journal of Croatian Studies*, vol. 22 (1981), pp. 49–115, for a nationalist criticism of the federal government for this policy.

25. Although this investment followed patterns common in many countries during the 1970s in response to the shifts in global terms of trade, public opinion in Croatia identified it with a political attempt to buy back loyalty of the Serb population in the poorer hinterland, especially in Lika and Knin, after the "mass movement" of Croat nationalism in 1967–71 had been so threatening to Serbs in Croatia.

26. In 1984, Jovan Mirić published *Sistem i Kriza: Prilog kritičkoj analizi ustavnog i političkog sistema Jugoslavije* (System and crisis: contribution to a critical analysis of the constitutional and political system in Yugoslavia) (Zagreb: CeKaDe, 1984) criticizing the decentralization and ineffectiveness of the federal government and political system in general; in 1985, Zvonko Lerotić published the first open defense of legal reform for a truly confederal system, *Načela federalizma višenacionalne države* (Principles of federalism for a multinational state) (Zagreb: Globus, 1985).

27. By 1983, "80 percent of Yugoslavia's arms requirement was developed and produced domestically," and during the 1980s defense industry exports (arms, but especially engineering services) exceeded imports at an ever higher ratio, from 2.5 to 4 times by 1985, in value terms. James Gow, *Legitimacy and the Military: The Yugoslav Crisis* (St. Martin's Press, 1992), p. 103.

28. The failure to integrate the various imperial and state systems during the interwar period had bequeathed substantial variety in transport and infrastructural systems, and they had been under the separate administration of republican jurisdiction since 1950.

29. See Gow on the misperceptions of the army's behavior, in *Legitimacy and the Military*. Garden-variety paranoia about a military coup commonly surfaced in Yugoslavia when economic troubles threatened.

30. At the same time, inflation thereafter increased revenues from the sales tax. See Neven Mates, "Inflation in Yugoslavia: Specific Form of Public Deficit Caused by Parafiscal Operations of the Central Bank," unpublished ms., February 4, 1990.

31. The reform argued for market determination (and eventually privatization) of expenditures on roads, schools, health care, insurance, and the like, which had until then been under local or republic jurisdiction in the independent but public "self-managed communities of interest."

32. Zoran Jasić, *Budžet i Privredni Razvoj* (The budget and economic development) (Zagreb: Narodne Novine, 1980), p. 247.

33. Financing for the journals (such as *Nova Revija* and *Mladina*) and youth groups where this was clearest came from the Socialist Alliance, the party's mass organization, leading many to assume that the Slovene party leadership intended to nurture such expression as part of its bargaining for republican prerogatives without having to admit responsibility should it get out of hand. A good source on pluralist developments are writings by Tomaž Mastnak, such as "Civil Society in Slovenia: From Opposition to Power," *Studies in Comparative Communism*, vol. 23 (Autumn–Winter, 1990), pp. 305–17.

34. See *Raspad Jugoslavije: Produžetak ili Kraj Agonije* (Zbornik) [The collapse of Yugoslavia: prolongation or end of agony (symposium)](Belgrade: Institut za Evropske Studije, 1991), pp. 129–30.

35. The man who later became president of an independent Croatia entered political life first in the nationalist movement of 1967–71 on the basis of his Ph.D. dissertation (begun as an officer in the army and required for promotion), which reassessed the death toll of the Croatian fascist regime during World War II. This sparked a long debate, still alive in 1990–93, which characterized the spirit of this 1980s reexamination. For a taste of this debate on the victims of the concentration camp at Jasenovac, Croatia, see Ljubo Boban, "Notes and Comments: Jasenovac and the Manipulation of History," *East European Politics and Societies*, vol. 4 (Fall 1990), pp. 580–92, the comment by Robert Hayden, "Balancing Discussion of Jasenovac and the Manipulation of History," and Boban's reply (to which Hayden was not permitted a response by the journal's Croatian-American editor) in vol. 6, no. 2, pp. 207–17.

36. An association working to promote political, economic, technical, and cultural cooperation initiated by the Italian foreign minister, Gianni Di Michelis, the Pentagonale was formed in Budapest on November 11, 1989; Czechoslovakia joined in May 1990, and Poland on July 27, 1991; the name was changed in 1992 to the Central European Initiative.

37. In a series of writings and public speeches, including those to the national assembly, particularly in November–December 1985 and January–February 1986, Mamula referred to the new arms race, the maneuvers in the southern European theater, the fact that Yugoslavia was the only country in the region cutting its military budget, to internal disintegration, excessive import dependence, and the need to strengthen the League of Communists in the face of rising fascism in the world. See, for example, records in FBIS, *East Europe*, January 7, 1986, p. 110; also February 12, February 25, and March 6. Mamula's book, published in 1985, is *Savremeni svijet i naša odbrana* (The contemporary world and our defense) (Belgrade: Vojnoizdavački zavod, 1985).

38. Personal communication from Anton Bebler.

39. This change was said to make it possible to outvote representatives of the less-developed republics who would favor more expansionary policy and subsidies. This is only one example of the strange results of economic reform if viewed uncritically as made of clear interests for and against reform, for it was primarily Slovenia and Croatia who opposed most vigorously any shift from consensual to

majoritarian voting on the argument that as "smaller nations" they needed the protection of consensus. James Madison's arguments in 1789, especially *Federalist No. 10*, are instructive in this regard.

40. By May 1986, President Tito's official birthday had passed without notice by the major news magazines, which had until then devoted cover and issue for more than forty years to the ritual and man.

41. "Dolanc on Responsibility, Debts, Nationalities," *Delo*, January 26, 1985, p. 2, in FBIS, *East Europe*, February 4, 1985, pp. 116–17. On these developments in Slovenia, chapter 2, "Slovenian Spring" in Mark Thompson, *A Paper House: The Ending of Yugoslavia* (Pantheon, 1992), pp. 3–59, captures the period well.

42. In 1972, Croatian right-wing émigrés from Australia did cause some trouble in an attempt to stage a popular uprising in the republic of Bosnia-Herzegovina.

43. A particularly interesting exchange of ideas on political reform among intellectuals representing Slovenia, Croatia, Serbia, and Macedonia, including people politically active in the post-1989 changes such as Vojislav Koštunica, Zvonko Lerotić, and Vasil Tupurkovski, occurred at a conference at the Wilson Center, the Smithsonian Institution, in Washington, D.C., September 4–6, 1986. Its published product is Dennison Rusinow, ed., *Yugoslavia: A Fractured Federalism* (The Wilson Center Press, 1988).

44. Mark Thompson provides a gory and helpful portrait of this "delirium," as he calls it, in *A Paper House*, pp. 129–30, and writes, "A Croat journalist investigated the many allegations that Serb and Montenegrin women were being raped in Kosovo. Records showed no disproportion among Albanian and Slav criminality in the province, and a lower than average number of rapes. Researchers in Belgrade bore the journalist out; but by the time their dull book of statistics was published in 1990, who cared?"

45. One of the most prominent of these groups, headed by Alija Izetbegović, was put on trial for "hostile and counterrevolutionary activity from positions of Muslim nationalism." The trial began on July 18, 1983, and the Izetbegović group was sentenced on August 20 of that year. Sentences for the group totaled 90 years, in sentences ranging from six months to fifteen years. Izetbegović himself was sentenced to fourteen years. Other prominent figures in the group included Omer Behmen, Hasan Cengić, Ismet Kasumagić, Edhem Bicakičić, Huso Živalj, Salih Behmen, Mustafa Spahić, Džemal Latić, Melika Salihbegović, Derviš Djurdjević, and Djula Bicakičić. ("Sarajevo Trial of Muslim Nationalists Ends," TANJUG *Domestic Service*, August 20, 1983, in FBIS, *East Europe*, August 22, 1983, p. 13.)

46. Cited in Bogdan D. Denitch, *Limits and Possibilities: The Crisis of Yugoslav Socialism and State Socialist Systems* (University of Minnesota Press, 1990), p. 30.

47. Mikhail Gorbachev, as a typical reform communist, used the same phrase and concept frequently, including in his swan song before parliament after the failed army coup of August 1991 and his return from Crimea, where he attempted to revive support for his path of reform and the political system adopted by Yugoslavs after 1949.

48. The commission was established as a task force of 216 scholars and politicians by the 13th congress of the LCY (June 25–28, 1992), in response to a letter from Dr. Najdan Pašić, distinguished political scientist, member of the Supreme Court of Serbia, and long-time party leader. Originally labeled the Vlaškalić Com-

mission after its chair, Tihomir Vlaškalić, the commission worked for three years until its public report, *A Critical Analysis*, was issued in November 1985 and eventually became known colloquially for its final chair, Josip Vrhovec, party leader from Croatia.

49. A still incomplete copy of the full memorandum was published only in 1989; see "Memorandum SANU, grupa akademika Srpske akademije nauka i umetnosti o aktuelnim društvenim pitanjima u našoj zemlji," (Memorandum of SANU, a group of academics of the Serbian Academy of Sciences and Arts on contemporary social problems in our country [Yugoslavia]), *Duga* (Vanredno izdanje, June 1989), pp. 19–47, of the "nedovršeni dokument" (incomplete document) of Belgrade, September 1986. A book with the full text and critical commentary of its now magnified role, including documents showing the opposition at the time from the Serbian party (LCS) leadership, was published in Belgrade in 1993.

50. Ivo Banac, "The Fearful Asymmetry of War: The Causes and Consequences of Yugoslavia's Demise," *Daedalus*, vol. 121 (Spring 1992), pp. 141–74.

51. The party presidency was a collective body of nine representing each of the eight federal units (republics and provinces) and the army.

52. Conversation with Vasil Tupurkovski, Wilson Center conference, September 4–6, 1986.

## Chapter 4

1. Foreign trade fell sharply during 1986, leading to a deficit 25.7 percent higher for 1986 than 1985 and the decline in the value of the dinar by 73.1 percent against a basket of hard currencies. See *Keesing's Record of World Events*, vol. 34 (February 1988), p. 35732, citing data published by the National Bank of Yugoslavia on April 4, 1987. The second phase of a debt rescheduling agreement, signed in April 1986 with the Paris Club of donor countries, was agreed on March 30, 1987, but the difficulties with foreign trade continued during the year on repayment of the $4 billion to $5.5 billion due for repayment in 1987. In September, Prime Minister Mikulić asked Western banks for a three-year moratorium on payment of principal until a long-term restructuring plan could be developed and for a reduction in its debt service from 40 to 25 percent of foreign exchange earnings, without which, in the words of the deputy prime minister in December, Yugoslavia faced "total economic collapse in the immediate future." Ibid., p. 35733.

2. Ibid.

3. Eugenio Lari, of the World Bank, speaking at a December 1988 conference of the U.S.-Yugoslav Economic Council in New York. This is "essential," he said, and "I have told the Yugoslav government." "The track record of the next few months will be very important for the Bank's actions toward Yugoslavia."

4. See, for example, "KP-SK-?" *Ekonomska Politika*, November 21, 1988, p. 5, a journal representing the views of liberal economic reformers and business similar to *The Economist* (London) after which it was patterned.

5. Branko Smerdel, "Constitutional Developments in Croatia and Yugoslavia 1989–1991," a preliminary report prepared for the Constitutionalism in Eastern Europe Project, University of Chicago Law School, February 1991.

6. *Keesing's Record of World Events*, vol. 34 (February 1988), p. 35732, citing the Yugoslav news agency TANJUG report of January 4, 1988, noted 900 recorded strikes in 1986. Of those 900, 140 strikes involving 23,042 workers and 202,245 working hours lost were in Macedonia, which set the republican record during 1986 for the number of workers on strike.

7. "Hronologija Krize Jugoslovenske Države" (Chronology of the crisis of the Yugoslav state), *Raspad Jugoslavije: Produžetak ili Kraj Agonije (Zbornik) [The breakup of Yugoslavia: prolongation or end of agony (symposium)]* (Belgrade: Institut za Evropske Studije, 1991), p. 131.

8. Personal communication from Croatian sociologist Silva Mežnarić in 1992.

9. Personal communication from Belgrade economist Ivan Vujačić at Aspen Institute conference on the crisis in Yugoslavia, Berlin, March 1992.

10. Sabrina Ramet evokes the mood of youth particularly well, in "Apocalypse Culture and Social Change in Yugoslavia," in Pedro [Sabrina] Ramet, ed., *Yugoslavia in the 1980s* (Boulder, Colo.: Westview Press, 1985), p. 9; so also does Mark Thompson, *A Paper House: The Ending of Yugoslavia* (Pantheon, 1992).

11. James Gow, *Legitimacy and the Military: The Yugoslav Crisis* (St. Martin's Press, 1992), p. 76.

12. That is, the newspaper of the Socialist Alliance of Working People, the mass organization responsible for implementing party policy and for establishing links between the LCY and the rest of the population (not the party's organ, *Komunist*).

13. The main director, Fikret Abdić, became a local hero as a result, and later retired to his home region of Cazinska Krajina, where he played the leading role in keeping it fed and largely at peace during the war in Bosnia-Herzegovina, until the fall of 1993 when he declared autonomy and conflict began with the Sarajevo-based leadership of the Muslim political party, the Party of Democratic Action of President Alija Izetbegović, and the fifth corps of the Bosnian army. Hamdija Požderac, then vice-president of the country, was not indicted but felt compelled to resign. A brief account can be found in *Keesing's Record of World Events*, vol. 34 (February 1988), pp. 35730–31.

14. According to observers concerned with the threat of disintegration and the exacerbation of north-south conflict between rich and poor by the economic reform, the growing links between Slovene and Bosnian enterprises were the most significant countertrend. Slovene firms seeking access to Middle Eastern markets began recruiting Bosnian engineers in the 1970s and establishing direct contracts in production and trade with firms in Bosnia. This grew in the 1980s. These observers were prophetic, for it was probably the most important link working against the breakup in 1991. Many saw in this political massacre of the Bosnian, pro-Yugoslav and federalist, political elite a conspiracy of high-ranking Slovenes and Serbs. The full story remains to be told.

15. The first organized protest of Serbs from Kosovo was a petition signed by 2000 citizens of Kosovo Polje denouncing Albanian nationalism and separatism and published in *Književne Novine* on January 15, 1986. A month later, on February 26, a group of about 100 Serbs from Kosovo began to arrive in Belgrade in what became a series of secret visits and appeals to the political leadership of Serbia and Yugoslavia over the coming years. In Serbia they received ever greater attention,

while in Slovenia these protest visits came to be called "wagons (*vozovi*) of nationalism." See "Hronologija Krize Jugoslovenske Države," *Raspad Jugoslavije*, p. 130.

16. The example of the National Socialist party (Nazis) of Germany and its unexpected name, for a fascist party, is often cited because it began as a socialist party of radical industrial workers and gained early support from the rising numbers of unemployed in the devastated German economy of the 1920s–1930s; the reason is that it was the Nazis, not the left-wing parties as one might expect, who sought to organize them. F. L. Carsten, *The Rise of Fascism* (University of California Press, 1967). This is a major theme of Hannah Arendt's masterly study *On Revolution* (Viking, 1963); revolutions may be initiated by myriad grassroots activity and protests against authority, but it is the political party that organizes these spontaneous and scattered acts of rebellion behind its agenda and leadership that wins.

17. The draft amendments sent in February 1987 to the lower house of the parliament for debate, which began March 30, were adopted December 8; of those, amendments 9–48 were adopted, on November 29, 1988, when the presidency chose to cut short the debate. During this period of February 1987 and November 1988, discussion on the federal amendments took place within the republics and provinces; after November 1988, the process of amending the republican constitutions began. Branko Smerdel, "Constitutional Developments in Croatia and Yugoslavia 1989–1991." Although there is some discrepancy on the date for adopting the draft amendments, Mijat Šuković (citing December 29, 1987), "Constitutional Changes in Yugoslavia," *Review of International Affairs*, vol. 39 (January 20, 1988), pp. 1–6, provides an overview of the original ninety-six articles of the constitution proposed for change and sixteen proposed additions.

18. The campaign for the right to conscientious objection was initiated by a group of Jehovah's Witnesses in the second city of Slovenia, Maribor. At this point the Slovene government did not support their demand, taking the position of established law and the YPA. When the young journalists around *Mladina* took up the call as part of their broader campaign against the army and for social and political change, the government switched, seeing it as a convenient addition to its own antifederal campaign (see below). See Gow, *Legitimacy and the Military*, pp. 76–88.

19. These were published by two *Mladina* journalists, Janez Janša, who later became Slovene minister of defense, and David Tasić.

20. "Milošević Address," Belgrade Domestic Service, April 25, 1987, in Foreign Broadcast Information Service, *Daily Report: East Europe*, April 27, 1987, p. 14. (Hereafter FBIS, *East Europe*.)

21. The many who would draw a sharp distinction between the two would be likely to add that the League of Communists of Serbia (LCS) had, already in 1986, adopted the symbol of a fist for its flag.

22. See Ivo Banac, "The Fearful Asymmetry of War: The Causes and Consequences of Yugoslavia's Demise," *Daedalus*, vol. 121 (Spring 1992), pp. 141–74.

23. An expert on the Kosovo cycle and myth provides a particularly insightful analysis of its political power after the wars began in 1991 in Thomas Emmert, "Why Serbia Will Fight for 'Holy' Kosovo; and the Peril for Western Armies Approaching the Balkan Tripwire," *Washington Post*, June 13, 1993, p. C1.

24.  See *Raspad Jugoslavije*, p. 131. A literary journal, *Nova Revija* gathered around it the older opposition (*Mladina*, the younger) composed primarily of traditional intellectuals placing emphasis on conservative social values and the nation and attempting to revive the tradition of a dominant political party of the interwar tradition, the Slovene Christian Socials. See Branka Magaš, *The Destruction of Yugoslavia: Tracking the Break-up 1980–92* (Verso, 1993), p. 132.

25.  Personal communication with Paul Shoup, February 22, 1991.

26.  See Branka Magaš, *The Destruction of Yugoslavia*, pp. 140–46, who emphasizes the importance to the mobilizing effect of the trial of the concurrent rumors in Slovenia of army plans for widespread arrests of Slovene intellectuals and political activists. See also James Gow, *Legitimacy and the Military*, pp. 78–88; Mark Thompson, who was *Mladina*'s London correspondent, *A Paper House*, pp. 44–47; and Lenard J. Cohen, *Broken Bonds: The Disintegration of Yugoslavia* (Westview Press, 1993), p. 86.

27.  The primary reason was the claim that inflation was largely due to demand push wage pressure from worker-managed firms; in fact, wages had not been keeping pace with prices since 1981. See Christopher Martin, "Public Policy and Income Distribution in Yugoslavia: A Case for Arrested Market Reform" (Ph.D. dissertation, University of California, Berkeley, 1989); and International Monetary Fund, *International Financial Statistics*, vol. 39 (IMF, December 1986), p. 530. A second reason was the insistence by foreign investors that they be allowed to manage firms without consulting workers.

28.  International Monetary Fund, *International Financial Statistics*, vol. 45 (November 1992), pp. 566 and 748–49.

29.  Nonetheless, an LCY central committee plenum in October 1988 had mounted an impressive political alliance against Milošević, according to Paul Shoup (seminar at George Washington University, February 22, 1991) consisting of "ideological conservatives in Serbia such as Vidoje Žarković; the strong man of Montenegro, Marko Orlandić; Hamiltonians such as Stipe Šuvar [then president of the LCY, from Croatia]; Red Flag Titoists such as patriots of Bosnia-Herzegovina; the Army [concerned about the internal security implications of Serbian demonstrations]; and the Slovenes." All but Milan Kučan, LCY leader of Slovenia, however, were about to rotate out of these positions.

30.  V. P. Gagnon, Jr., "Yugoslavia: Prospects for Stability," *Foreign Affairs*, vol. 70 (Summer 1991), p. 35.

31.  Slovenia also rejected a number of key provisions, including the removal of restrictions on agricultural property, and voted to introduce a multiparty system in Slovenia.

32.  The foreign minister of Slovenia after April 1990, Dimitrij Rupel, admitted at a conference in Berlin in March 1992 that Slovene nationalists had "used Kosovo" to achieve their goal.

33.  See, for example, Ivo Banac's discussion of the exchange emanating from Taras Kermanauer's "Letters to a Serbian Friend," in Banac, "The Fearful Asymmetry of War," p. 160.

34.  The situation has a parallel with the Northern Ireland conflict in this difference of perceptions: that the politically dominant but numerically smaller Protestant forces viewed their position as a minority within a Catholic island while the

numerically larger but politically subordinate Catholic forces viewed themselves as an oppressed minority within Ulster. There was no persuading Slovenes of their actual economic and political power in the Yugoslav federation once they viewed themselves as a small nation in relation to Serbia, nor any persuading most Serbs that their political power before 1945, their increasing preponderance in official positions in the 1970s, and their numerical plurality made them the greater threat to the state when they saw themselves as a beleaguered, partitioned minority in a declining economy and holding onto vilified, less-well-paid political positions.

35. Smerdel, "Constitutional Developments in Croatia and Yugoslavia, 1989–1991."

36. Marković is by origin, like Mikulić, a Bosnian Croat, but he had moved to Croatia long before.

37. Smerdel, "Constitutional Developments in Croatia and Yugoslavia, 1989–1991."

38. Frits W. Hondius, *The Yugoslav Community of Nations* (The Hague and Paris: Mouton, 1968), p. 302.

39. Cohen, *Broken Bonds*, pp. 55–57. Cohen also quotes Janez Stanovnik, state president of Slovenia, at a press conference in Washington, D.C., in November 1988, at which he predicted civil war and singled out Milošević for criticism, to the same effect: "There are no significant differences when it comes to the economy. The views of Mr. Milošević with whom I disagree on political issues do not differ from mine on economic matters. He is just as liberal as I am when it comes to economic matters." p. 61.

40. Even before the constitutional changes, the republic of Macedonia substantially reduced the cultural rights of its Albanian minority in the field of education (see Magaš, *The Destruction of Yugoslavia*, p. 140); by the fall of 1989, the nationalist fervor had materialized in signs posted around the capital, Skopje, demanding a united Macedonia and reading, "Solun je naš [Thessaloniki is ours]." Proposals to make the Serb-majority region of Lika within the Croatian *krajina* an autonomous region began to appear. (Personal communicaton from Steven Burg, December 1989.)

41. This definition of national interests to include those of diaspora where states and nations were not coterminous is common throughout the region: it is part of the platform of the ruling Hungarian party (the Hungarian Democratic Forum) and of the Macedonian nationalists (Internal Macedonian Revolutionary Organization-Democratic Party for Macedonian National Unity, VMRO-DPMNE), and it was also part of the Polish constitution of 1990.

42. There was intense debate in the construction of the federal system after World War II over whether this region, like Vojvodina and Kosovo in Serbia, should be given autonomous status within Croatia. It was also an area where Croatian fascists were particularly active during World War II, and their policy of genocide against Orthodox Christians led many to flee for protection into the Partisan army and as a result, after the war, to emigrate to Belgrade into political positions.

43. Not all persons thrown into a minority and discriminatory position by these changes could express their grievances through a demand for autonomy; for example, two-thirds of the Serbs in Croatia are integrated into urban life and occupational ties that make it nearly impossible to retreat into the forests or interior,

who did not wish to emphasize their ethnonational identity until Croatian nationalists did it for them, depriving them of other identities or a multiplicity of identities they preferred, and who continued to argue that participation within the Croatian state was a better route to their rights than the path taken by Serb autonomists in the *krajina* and eventually Slavonia and Baranja. Views of this group can be had from the writings of Milorad Pupovac and Slavko Goldstein.

44. Slovenia is an exception here because autochthonous minorities—Italians and Hungarians—had not had national rights in Yugoslavia whereas Serbs, Bosnians, and Albanians experiencing discrimination and a loss of status could not claim territorial rights.

45. Vladimir Gligorov, "Is What's Left Right? (The Yugoslav Heritage)," in János Matyás Kovacs, ed., *Transition to Capitalism? The Communist Legacy in Eastern Europe* (New Brunswick, N.J.: Transaction Publishers, 1994), pp. 147–72.

46. A typical example of less than careful data analysis to make this point is N. L. Karlović, "Croatia and Its Future: Internal Colonialism or Independence?" *Journal of Croatian Studies*, vol. 22 (1981), pp. 49–115.

47. The language of the interwar period, identifying all those who supported federal power as "unitarists" and all Serbs by definition as unitarists was also useful once Slovenia began to push for confederation. Dispassionate analysis of the proportion of Serbs in police, army, and local government is hard to find, but it varies substantially according to the period that is chosen and according to the republic and region within it. No study has been made of the assertion that one's ethnic identity necessarily means biased rather than professional behavior or preferential treatment to one's group, or that political office meant power (it certainly did not mean wealth, and it meant only some forms of privilege, even though such privileges were simultaneously devalued in general and of greater value to those who kept them in particular under austerity in the 1980s). This is important to emphasize because the argument was available to many groups: not only by Slovenes and Croats against Serbs, but also by Serbs against Muslims in Bosnia-Herzegovina where their proportions in political positions rose in the 1980s (largely due to the outmigration to Croatia and Serbia of upwardly mobile Croats and Serbs from poor or declining areas in Bosnia-Herzegovina). More significant than the facts was the political link made between budget-cutting economic reforms and *collective and individual* national rights in the both reform and electoral campaigns.

48. Robert M. Hayden, *The Beginning of the End of Federal Yugoslavia: The Slovenian Amendment Crisis of 1989*, The Carl Beck Papers, Number 1001 (Pittsburgh: The Center for Russian and East European Studies, University of Pittsburgh, December 1992), analyzes this event. See also Cohen, *Broken Bonds*, p. 63 and n. 41. Other amendments included the identification of minority rights only for "autochthonous" minorities of Hungarians and Italians, and any federal action in Slovenia which did not use Slovenian had no legal effect. The federal state presidency declared the measures unconstitutional, which required approval by the Slovene assembly of any action based on the federal provision on emergencies and which declared the republic's right to secede. The federal-level LCY Central Committee voted, 97 to 40, prior to the assembly's action that Slovenia should postpone its vote on the amendments.

But when the Constitutional Court heard the case (despite Slovene refusal to accept its constitutionality), between December 1989 and February 1990, it found provisions in all republican constitutions except Montenegro's that were against the federal constitution. In its opinion submitted to the federal assembly in January 1990, the Constitutional Court particularly emphasized the unconstitutionality of the amendments in 1989 to the constitutions of Slovenia, Bosnia and Herzegovina, Macedonia, Croatia, and Vojvodina that ended the obligations of firms in the so-called "large systems" of electric energy, railway transport, and postal, telephone, and telegraph networks to organize their operations so as to maintain them as unified technological systems for the entire territory. For this and the opinions on each republican and provincial constitution, see Djordje Djurković and Dragana Kušar, "The Opinion of the Constitutional Court of Yugoslavia on Conflicts between Amendments to the Constitutions of the Republics and Autonomous Provinces and the Constitution of the SFRY," *Yugoslav Survey*, vol. 31, no. 2 (1990), pp. 59–70.

49. See "Motion for the Adoption of a New Constitution of the SFRY," *Yugoslav Survey*, vol. 31, no. 1 (1990), pp. 3–24.

50. The Slovenes began to refer to socialist Yugoslavia as having been created as a "free association of nations," ironically adopting the Marxist language of the Communist party for the socialist organization of the economy around self-governing enterprises that were "free associations of workers."

51. One such warning came from no less than the state president of Slovenia, Janez Stanovnik, at a November 1988 press conference in Washington, D.C., at which he stated that Yugoslavia was on the verge of civil war.

52. Paul Shoup, "Crisis and Reform in Yugoslavia," *Telos* (Spring 1989), p. 144.

53. Adam Przeworski, *Democracy and the Market: Political and Economic Reforms in Eastern Europe and Latin America* (Cambridge University Press, 1991) argues this generally, pp. 180, 187.

# Chapter 5

1. Marković was holding the position of prime minister as representative from Croatia, but of origin, a Bosnian Croat.

2. Also like the Polish program, Marković's policies were assisted by and identified with Harvard economist Jeffrey Sachs. The hope of economic liberals was that an outsider would be more able to obtain consensus and override continuing domestic quarrels over the wisdom of such an approach (in part because they could shift the blame onto Sachs). An alternative program was being developed by economists outside the government with the advice of Israeli economist Michael Bruno.

3. Retired Minister of Defense Admiral Branko Mamula first began this push in 1986. Interviews with Anton Bebler, and see James Gow, *Legitimacy and the Military* (St. Martin's Press, 1992), pp. 93 and 98–99.

4. See Robin Alison Remington, "The Federal Dilemma in Yugoslavia," *Current History*, vol. 89 (December 1990), p. 407; and Ivo Banac, "Post-Communism as Post-Yugoslavism: The Yugoslav Non-Revolutions of 1983–1990," in Ivo Banac ed., *Eastern Europe in Revolution* (Cornell University Press, 1992), p. 179. The extent to which psychological antagonism, fear, and misunderstanding (even mutual paranoia) was now contributing to the political dynamic is illustrated by this event. It came to represent the essence of the Milošević threat in the eyes of Slovenes, in the sense captured by studies about the fear of the crowd in France in the 1880s. Slovenes viewed it as an act of violence and against the constitution. Many neutral Serbs, on the other hand, insisted that the march was a bluff and found it hard to understand Slovene hysteria. Any realistic assessment would, of course, have noted the lack of popular support such demonstrations would have found in Slovenia, and the minuscule chance of destabilizing the Slovene government in such a way, given the strength by then of Slovene civil society, of proto-democratic institutions, of popular support for the Kučan leadership, and of cultural distance from Serbia and Kosovo.

5. The SAWPY originated in revolutionary and wartime days as the popular front. It was responsible for nonparty political activity, such as organizing elections, nominating candidates, and funding civic action, protopolitical, and party-affiliated groups.

6. Manufacturers in the Serbian province of Vojvodina complained loudly that this cut them off from their suppliers in Slovenia and could halt production. Serb liberals argue that this was the moment when the U.S. Embassy should have acted forcefully because Marković's lack of response was simultaneously the crucial signal to President Milošević that he could act accordingly and the real end of hopes for the economic reform (Personal communication with Vladimir Gligorov).

7. See Peter Ferdinand, "Yugoslavia—Beyond the Beginning of the End?" *The Journal of Communist Studies*, vol. 6 (September 1990), pp. 99–104, esp. p. 101.

8. Marković's delay in introducing the program until January 1, according to his critics, gave encouragement to Serbia to continue what they saw as part of a deliberate Serbian plan to sabotage the economy.

9. Cited in Lenard J. Cohen, *Broken Bonds: The Disintegration of Yugoslavia* (Westview Press, 1993), p. 84.

10. Cohen explains this Slovene idea, halfway on the road from federation to confederation, succinctly: "the notion of federal asymmetry referred to an arrangement whereby each republic would negotiate its own terms of power sharing and power distribution with the central government in a federation," making possible separate arrangements between the center and particular republics. Cohen, *Broken Bonds*, pp. 62–63.

11. See Jonathan C. Randal, "Yugoslav Communist Party Splits Over Pace of Reform," *Washington Post*, January 23, 1990, p. A1.

12. The coup de grace came the next month, when the Slovene League of Communists declared its independence from the Yugoslav League and then dissolved, changing its name to the Party of Democratic Renewal. For these events, see Dennison Rusinow, "To Be or Not to Be? Yugoslavia as Hamlet," *Universities Field Staff International Field Staff Reports*, no. 18 (1990–91), pp. 5–6; also Cohen, *Broken Bonds*, especially pp. 79–85.

13. The Slovenes began the withdrawal on February 4. See TANJUG, February 4, 1990, in Foreign Broadcast Information Service, *Daily Report: East Europe*, February 7, 1990, p. 76 (hereafter, FBIS, *East Europe)*; see also Branko Smerdel, "Constitutional Developments in Croatia and Yugoslavia 1989–1991," a preliminary report prepared for the Constitutionalism in Eastern Europe Project of the University of Chicago Law School, February 1991.

14. The state presidency, by a majority of votes, ended the state of emergency in Kosovo after three months, on April 18, 1990, on the argument that "public order and peace in Kosovo has stabilized" and that "reform and democratic processes, which created the opportunity for Kosovo's problems to be resolved in a democratic fashion and under peaceful circumstances, have begun in the country." See "Presidency Ends Kosovo State of Emergency," TANJUG, April 18, 1990, in FBIS, *East Europe*, April 19, 1990, p. 37.

15. Robert A. Dahl, *Political Oppositions in Western Democracies* (Yale University Press, 1966).

16. There were of course popular pressures for political change, and the Croatian communist leadership agreed to elections in response to a petition signed by 25,000, but the decision on elections still reflected the lack of democratic conditions within the country and the prevailing combination of antipolitics and political alienation among the population and an oppositional political space dominated by intellectuals.

17. Adam Przeworski, *Democracy and the Market: Political and Economic Reforms in Eastern Europe and Latin America* (Cambridge University Press, 1991), pp. 15–37.

18. See chapters 4 and 6.

19. See Juan J. Linz and Alfred Stepan, "Political Identities and Electoral Sequences: Spain, the Soviet Union, and Yugoslavia," *Daedalus*, vol. 121 (Spring 1992), pp. 123–40, on the critical issue of political transitions in federal systems of whether elections take place first at the federal or the regional level; if they occur first at the regional level, they are likely to be destabilizing.

20. The Christian Democrats (13 percent), Farmers' Alliance (12.6 percent), Democratic Alliance (9.5 percent), Greens Alliance (8.8 percent), Social Democratic Alliance (7.4 percent), and Craftsmen's Party (3.5 percent). The seventh DEMOS party, the Alliance of the Society of Pensioners of Maribor (Grey Panthers), did not surpass the required 2.5 percent margin to gain a seat in the Chamber. See Milan Andrejevich, "Preliminary Results in Slovenia's Elections," *Radio Free Europe Report on Eastern Europe*, vol. 1 (April 27, 1990), pp. 35–37. The motto of this ruling coalition, according to Branka Magaš, was "who is not with us is against the nation!" See Magaš, *The Destruction of Yugoslavia: Tracking the Break-up 1980–92* (Verso: 1993), p. 254.

21. Like many of his contemporaries, Tudjman joined the partisans during World War II as a youth, but remained within the army after the war, reaching major general in 1960. Eight months later he retired and became a professor of history on the basis of the doctoral thesis required of all candidate generals in the YPA (awarded in 1965 by the regional university at Zadar, after the University of Zagreb rejected the thesis). He was expelled from the Communist Party in 1968 for signing a declaration on Croatian language rights, with which intellectuals in

Croatia in 1967 initiated the Croatian nationalist movement of 1967–71, and in the political purge that followed of Croatian nationalist leaders, Tudjman received a two-year prison sentence (of which he served ten months). His nationalist credentials, however, derive largely from the Ph.D. thesis, later published as a book, in which he attempted to prove that the communists had deliberately exaggerated the number of Serbs, Jews, and others who died in Ustashe (Croatian fascist) concentration camps in World War II (particularly Jasenovac) and that the number was only about 35,000. Created illegally in June 1989, the HDZ had offices in 116 Croatian municipalities and branches among Croat communities in Vojvodina and Bosnia-Herzegovina and in many cities in the United States, Canada, and Australia. See Cohen, *Broken Bonds*, p. 95 and nn. 45–46.

22.  The occasion for their walkout was an assault with a knife, allegedly by an HDZ member, on the president of the local branch of the SDP in Benkovac, a town in the northern Dalmatian hinterland between Šibenik and Knin. See Mark Thompson, *A Paper House: The Ending of Yugoslavia* (Pantheon, 1992), p. 260, and "CDU Condemns Assault on Serb in Croatia," TANJUG, in FBIS, *East Europe*, May 23, 1990, p. 56. See also the chronology in Predrag Simić, "Civil War in Yugoslavia: From Local Conflict to European Crisis," Institute of International Politics and Economics, Belgrade, mimeo., chronology, p. 1; on the number of seats, see Remington, "The Federal Dilemma of Yugoslavia," p. 429n.

23.  The "Declaration of the State Sovereignty of the Republic of Slovenia," adopted by a vote of 187 to 3 (with two abstentions), declared the federal constitution and all federal laws and regulations valid in Slovenia only insofar as they "do not conflict" with the constitution and laws of the Republic of Slovenia, included the republican government's assumption of full control over units of the YPA on Slovene territory, and established a procedure to adopt a new constitution within a year. At the same time, the assembly endorsed a proposal "in the spirit of the declaration" that the Slovene delegates to the federal assembly no longer attend its sessions. See "Slovene Assembly Declares Republic's Sovereignty," Zagreb Domestic Service, July 2, 1990, in FBIS, *East Europe*, July 3, 1990, p. 62.

24.  Zagreb Domestic Service, July 5, 1990, in FBIS, *East Europe*, July 6, 1990, p. 71.

25.  See TANJUG, December 20, 1990, in FBIS, *East Europe*, December 21, 1990, pp. 43–4. The amendments were published on July 4, 1990, and adopted on July 25. See "Amendments to Croat Constitution Published," *Borba*, July 4, 1990, in FBIS, *East Europe*, July 10, 1990, p. 87, and "Croat Assembly Adopts Constitutional Amendments," TANJUG, July 25, 1990, in FBIS, *East Europe*, July 26, 1990, p. 61. On the loyalty oath, see Brian Hall, *The Impossible Country: A Journey Through the Last Days of Yugoslavia* (David Godine, 1994), pp. 17 and 95. See also Cohen, *Broken Bonds*, pp. 130–33.

26.  See the thorough description of confrontations and growing violence in Knin in Misha Glenny, "The Massacre of Yugoslavia," *New York Review of Books*, January 10, 1992, pp. 30–35.

27.  The address followed a *slava*, or celebration in honor of a saint, for St. Archangel Gabriel, in Zemun, a town across the Sava from Belgrade. TANJUG, July 26, 1990, in FBIS, *East Europe*, July 27, 1990, p. 36. Lenard Cohen provides evidence that the Serb leaders in the *krajina* made an important distinction in goals,

that Rašković and others accepted Croatia as their "homeland" but also saw the continuation of the Yugoslav state as essential to their sense of security; thus, if the Yugoslav federation continued, Serbs in Croatia would only need the rights of cultural autonomy (which the Croatian government was willing to grant), but if Croatia became independent, they would seek political autonomy. See Cohen, *Broken Bonds*, pp. 130, 132.

28. There was cause for this interpretation, since escalating Kosovar political mobilization had led the government in June to institute direct rule over security and militia in the province and, on June 26, to adjourn the assembly on a technicality. See Cohen, *Broken Bonds*, p. 122.

29. In the meantime, the Albanian delegates to the dissolved provincial assembly began to meet secretly as a separate assembly and on September 7, 1990, adopted a constitution for a "sovereign republic of Kosovo" and laws permitting the formation of political parties. See Cohen, *Broken Bonds*, p. 125. Perhaps in part as a result of their common front at the time against Albanian political mobilization, but in direct response to the declaration of Slovenia that it would only remain within a Yugoslavia reconfigured as a confederation, delegates from the republics of Serbia and Macedonia also met on July 5, 1990, to declare that Yugoslavia should become a "democratic federation" of six, free and equal, republics. See "Serbian, Macedonian Officials Urge Federation," TANJUG, July 5, 1990, in FBIS, *East Europe*, July 10, 1990, p. 88.

30. Quoted in Misha Glenny, *The Fall of Yugoslavia: The Third Balkan War* (Penguin Books, 1992), p. 41. However, Glenny translates *neizvesnosti* as insecurity, whereas it means uncertainty.

31. For the final election results see Belgrade Domestic Service, December 12, 1990, in FBIS, *East Europe*, December 13, 1990, p. 45. On the composition of the Serbian parliament, see TANJUG, December 25, 1990, in FBIS, *East Europe*, December 26, 1990, p. 44. Whereas Milošević's party gained 65 percent of those who voted, this was only 47 percent of the electorate. See Dennison Rusinow, "Yugoslavia: Balkan Breakup?" *Foreign Policy*, no. 83 (Summer 1991), p. 150.

32. See "Four Parties to Share Power in Macedonia," TANJUG, December 12, 1990, in FBIS, *East Europe*, December 13, 1990, p. 55.

33. Disputes within the party over a shift from a Bosnian, historico-cultural emphasis to Islamic and clericalist forces associated with Alija Izetbegović and the other defendants in the trial of 1983 against "Islamic fundamentalists," led to a split two months before the elections when a liberal, secular wing led by a returned émigré, Geneva-based businessman Adil Zulfikarpašić, formed the Muslim Bošnjak (hereafter Bosniac) Organization (the MBO). See Milan Andrejevich, "Bosnia-Herzegovina: Yugoslavia's Linchpin," in *RFE-Report on Eastern Europe*, vol. 1 (December 7, 1990), pp. 20–27.

34. By June 1990, the SDA, like the HDZ and SDS, had extended its organizing beyond the republican borders of its home base, holding rallies and establishing party branches in the predominantly Muslim-majority area called the Sandžak that overlapped the republics of Serbia and Montenegro and arguing, like the Serbs in Croatia, that should Serbia and Montenegro unify as sovereign republics in a future federation or confederation, the SDA would demand cultural and political autonomy for this area. See Cohen, *Broken Bonds*, p. 144.

35. This was most clearly revealed in the voting studies done by Stein Rokkan of the first (defeated) Norwegian vote on possible European Community membership, where predictions based on partisan alignments in regular domestic elections proved wrong, and the partisan alignments last seen at the time of Norway's separation from Sweden reemerged. See Stein Rokkan, "Geography, Religion, and Social Class: Crosscutting Cleavages in Norwegian Politics," in Seymour H. Lipset and Stein Rokkan, *Party Systems and Voter Alignments: Cross-National Perspectives* (New York: The Free Press, 1967), pp. 367–444.

36. For example, Croat émigrés in North and South America, Australia, and Germany, especially those from western Herzegovina in Bosnia, reportedly gave an estimated $8.2 million to the HDZ and its president, Franjo Tudjman, for the campaign of 1990 in Croatia. See Thompson, *A Paper House*, p. 269. Prominent among them was Toronto businessman Gojko Šušak, who was rewarded with the ministry of defense in the new government. The Herzegovinian lobby remained as powerful in Zagreb in 1994, or more, as it was in 1990. See Patrick Moore, "Croatia," *Radio Free Europe/Radio Liberty Research Report*, "The Politics of Intolerance" (April 22, 1994), p. 81.

37. In the case of Slovenia it was more a slowdown of privatization than an all-out renationalization. See DNEVNIK, February 18, 1992, in FBIS, *East Europe*, March 10, 1992, p. 45.

38. See Milica Uvalić, "How Different Is Yugoslavia?" *European Economy*, no. 2 (1991), pp. 202 and 208; see also Remington, "The Federal Dilemma in Yugoslavia," pp. 407–408.

39. For the economic indicators, see IMF, *International Financial Statistics*, vol. 43 (November 1990), pp. 576–79. For the insolvency of firms, see Remington, "The Federal Dilemma," p. 430.

40. See Gow, *Legitimacy and the Military*, pp. 133–34. The pace of decline varied among republics, so that in September, a retreat by Milošević toward more moderate rhetoric, even downplaying nationalism, was attributed by many to the competition he perceived in Marković's popularity. See Milan Andrejevich, "Milošević and the Serbian Opposition," *RFE/RL Research Report on Eastern Europe* (October 19, 1990), p. 44. Polls in Bosnia-Herzegovina on upcoming elections had Marković and his reform alliance at the top of the list with 25.9 percent. See "Sarajevo Poll Shows Marković's Party in Lead," *Oslobodjenje*, September 21, 1990, in FBIS, *East Europe*, September 28, 1990, p. 60. Nonetheless, his popularity not only continued to decline but also was not sufficient to win elections, despite the emphasis of political commentary on personality.

41. See Uvalić, "How Different Is Yugoslavia?" p. 209.

42. It acknowledged this practice publicly in a note to the federal presidency January 10, in which it claimed to have a right to do so in retaliation for Serbia's "attack on the monetary system" of the SFRY.

43. Eventually, after international recognition in 1992, the government chose a British printer and extremely beautiful but very expensive notes that continue to show its appreciation for foreign public relations. Interview with Slovene government official, Berlin, March 1992.

44. For the sum quoted, see Slovene political scientist Bogomil Ferfila, who calls it "the robbery of the century," in "Yugoslavia: Confederation or Disintegra-

tion?" in *Problems of Communism*, vol. 60 (July–August 1991), p. 26, note 12. For a more nuanced analysis, see Uvalić, "How Different Is Yugoslavia?" p. 209. There are many rumors about the currency and banking irregularities of this period, and much informal knowledge is not yet fully a matter of public record. Some U.S. government officials made much of the Serbian actions as a deliberate attempt to destroy the country. More to the point of the economic reform at stake was that it was part of a widespread pattern of abuse related to the new democratic politics of vote buying and to the particular composition of budgetary expenditures (for example, in the Serbian case, the large proportion of pensioners and farmers in its population) that orthodox stabilization policies require be slashed.

45. The draft document for this confederation was presented October 5. See "Documents on the Future Organization of Relationships in Yugoslavia," *Yugoslav Survey*, vol. 31, no. 4 (1990), pp. 3–60, which includes the conclusions of meetings by the state presidency with all republican leaderships in June–July 1990 aimed at resolving the political crisis at which, among other decisions, it was agreed that "each people in Yugoslavia should have, as an expression of its sovereignty, the right to national self-determination up to and including the right to secede" (p. 5), and an analysis presented October 19 of the resulting political situation by then president of the state presidency, Borisav Jović, in which he clearly lays out all the political options facing the country. See also Milan Andrejevich, "Crisis in Croatia and Slovenia: Proposal for a Confederal Yugoslavia," *RFE/RL Report on Eastern Europe*, November 2, 1990, pp. 28–33, and Bogomil Ferfila, "Yugoslavia: Confederation or Disintegration?" pp. 24–26.

46. A countrywide opinion poll published by *Borba* on October 8 showed 21 percent favoring a confederation, 64 percent favoring a federation, 7 percent something else, and 8 percent with no opinion. See "Poll Says Federation Favored Over Confederation," *Borba*, October 8, 1990, in FBIS, *East Europe*, October 15, 1990, p. 64.

47. Tibor Várady, "Collective Minority Rights and Problems in Their Legal Protection: The Example of Yugoslavia," *East European Politics and Societies*, vol. 6 (Fall 1992), pp. 263–65; and chapter 2. Tibor Várady was a professor of international law in Serbia, became minister for justice in the Milan Panić government in July 1992, which lasted until December, and later joined the faculty of the Central European University in Budapest.

48. The same day that the Croatian parliament adopted the constitutional amendments which were opposed by the Serbs led by the Serbian Democratic Party and Jovan Rašković, July 25, 1990, the Serbs in the *krajina* region adopted a "Declaration on the Sovereignty and Autonomy for the Serbian People," and announced their intention to hold a referendum between August 19 and September 2, 1990, of all Serbs in Croatia on this declaration and its demand for autonomy. In the growing confrontation with the Croatian government over this referendum (President Tudjman stated that the government would not allow the referendum to be held and Serbs began to form armed self-defense units and to place barricades on the approach to towns so as to prevent interference by Croatian militia), Rašković requested federal protection at a meeting he arranged with federal president Jović (unfortunately for the nationalist dynamic, the representative of Serbia happened to be in the chair of the presidency at the time). See Cohen, *Broken Bonds*, pp. 132–35; also, Glenny, *The Fall of Yugoslavia*, pp. 7–27.

49. "Draft of the Treaty of the Yugoslav Confederation—the Alliance of South Slavic Republics" (Zagreb, October 11, 1990), *Review of International Affairs* (Belgrade), vol. 41 (October 20, 1990), pp. 17–22. Moreover, Mamula's reorganization of the YPA in the mid-1980s meant that military districts and control of assets did not correspond to republics but cut across those boundaries; he did this furthermore to prevent regional officers' coalitions and just such a threat to the army's integrity and its command and control (interview with Anton Bebler).

50. Remington, "The Federal Dilemma," p. 430n, citing *Narodna Armija*, July 5, 1990.

51. Željko Krušelj, "The Yugoslav People's Army: From Liberation to Liquidation," *East European Reporter*, vol. 5 (March–April 1992), p. 32. Rampart-91 later became a prime source for the argument—put forth during the wars in Croatia and Bosnia-Herzegovina—that the army intended to create a Greater Serbia.

52. See Gow, *Legitimacy and the Military*, p. 139.

53. See Paul Beaver, "Yugo-Arms: Enough to Export," in Anthony Borden, Ben Cohen, Marisa Crevatin, and Davorka Zmiarević, eds., *Breakdown: War & Reconstruction in Yugoslavia* (London: Institute for War and Peace Reporting, 1992), pp. 45–46.

54. Critics of the role of the army in 1991 would strongly dispute the characterization of Adžić as a professional, citing his disputes with vice-president Stipe Mesić over policies to restore order in Croatia in January 1991 and his criticism of civilian authorities for the fiasco in the army's actions in Slovenia after its declaration of independence. Aided by the emphasis of most commentaries on his Serb ethnicity and the fact that nineteen members of his immediate family were killed by Croatian fascists during World War II, they assume he was a Serb nationalist and accuse him of independent actions in defense of Serbs. This is both an anachronistic reading backward from 1991 to conditions in 1989 and a simplistic understanding of the dilemmas faced by the army in 1991 and the positions taken as the country and federal civilian authority began to dissolve, particularly by those such as Adžić who were pro-Yugoslav. At the time of the appointment, Kadijević emphasized that his choice reflected the transition away from the communist army to a professional profile, and many others lauded the appointment because Adžić was so regarded within the officer corps—as a soldier's soldier. See Gow, *Legitimacy and the Military*, pp. 141–44, and on Adžić's disputes with Mesić, see Cohen, *Broken Bonds*, p. 52.

55. These accusations were made by Prime Minister Marković in explaining his demand on September 18, 1991, that they resign. See "Marković Threatens to Replace Kadijević, Brovet," Belgrade radio, September 19, 1991, and "Marković Asks Army to Explain Moscow Arms 'Deal'," TANJUG, September 19, 1991, in FBIS, *East Europe*, September 20, 1991, pp. 29–30; "Marković Seeks Kadijević, Brovet Resignations," *Borba*, September 20, 1991, pp. 1, 7, in FBIS, *East Europe*, September 24, 1991, p. 29; and "Ministry Denies 'Secret Contacts' With Yazov," TANJUG, September 20, 1991, in FBIS, *East Europe*, September 23, 1991, p. 29.

56. See Gow, *Legitimacy and the Military*, p. 140, and Andrejevich, *RFE/RL Report on Eastern Europe*, October 19, 1990, p. 52.

57. See James Gow, "Arms Sales and Embargoes: The Yugoslav Example," *Bulletin of Arms Control*, no. 3 (August 1991), pp. 2–7.

58. See Glenny, *The Fall of Yugoslavia*, pp. 89–93, and "The Massacre of Yugoslavia," pp. 30–35. Ivo Goldstein, in "Serbs in Croatia, Croatia in Yugoslavia," *East European Reporter*, vol. 3 (1990), p. 66, introduces the critical element of inexperience and resulting clumsiness on the part of the Croatian government in reacting to what "was really no more than an informal party opinion poll" in the case of the referendum and in confiscating weapons from reserve police units (around Knin in July and August and around Petrinja in September) and removing signs in Cyrillic ("the straw that broke the camel's back") in the region around Knin, in his analysis of the events of the second half of 1990.

59. According to the federal secretariat for defense, they were only responding to radar alerts of aircraft straying off their flight path. See Cohen, *Broken Bonds*, p. 133.

60. Rusinow, "Yugoslavia: Balkan Breakup?" pp. 154–55.

61. "Slovene Assembly Adopts Plebiscite Law," DELO, December 7, 1990, p. 1, in FBIS, *East Europe*, December 17, 1990, p. 68, and "Slovene Voters Choose Independence, Autonomy," TANJUG, December 26, 1990, in FBIS, *East Europe*, December 26, 1990, p. 39. While the president of the parliament, France Bučar, proclaimed the republic an "independent state" in announcing the results to a joint session of all three chambers on December 26, and the plebiscite debate specified that Slovenia was no longer a part of the federation, a major, unresolved dispute arose between the Slovene and federal governments and within the country over whether this meant secession. A sample of that debate can be read in the excerpts printed in FBIS, *East Europe*, December 19, 1990, pp. 71–72.

62. The charges were dramatized by the showing of a videotape on Belgrade television said to document the plotters' discussions. See the dramatic description of the resulting confrontation between the army and Croatia on January 25–26, including President Tudjman's resulting appeal to U.S. President George Bush for defense of the "young democracies," Slovenia and Croatia, in Branka Magaš, *The Destruction of Yugoslavia*, pp. 267–68. While Špegelj denied the charges, he also revealed the heightened uncertainty after the July 1990 parliamentary declarations about the new meaning of republican sovereignty when his defense was that he "could not be arrested for doing his job, which includes his duties to defend Croatia." See Cohen, *Broken Bonds*, p. 191.

63. The meetings were held January 10, February 13, February 22 (at which the presidency agreed, in Sarajevo, to consider procedures for secession at the next meeting), March 1, March 21, and March 27 (the communiqué for which stated that the presidency was so paralyzed for lack of a quorum and then boycott by some members that it was unable to perform its constitutional obligations). At the same time, the tendency for bilateral meetings between delegations of the republics and their presidencies to replace the presidency as a medium of conflict resolution, developing since July 1990, became stronger, with eleven such meetings in this period, as if the confederal model of sovereign states were becoming a reality. See "Documents on the Future Regulation of Relations in Yugoslavia," *Yugoslav Survey* vol. 40, no. 1 (1991), pp. 3–26, and "Activities of the SFRY Presidency in Relation to the Political Future of the Country," *Yugoslav Survey*, vol. 40, no. 2 (1991), pp. 11–38.

64. Smerdel, "Constitutional Developments in Croatia and Yugoslavia, 1989–1991," p. 19.

65. Sovereignty was defined as independence, territorial integrity, and the right to self-determination, including the right to secession, as a "sovereign state," but they differed from the Slovene acts in accepting federal authority as long as it was with the consent of republican authorities and as long as the future of the country was defined by "consensus and in a democratic manner" with the other "sovereign republics of the SFRY." See "Declaration on the Sovereignty of the Republic of Macedonia," *Yugoslav Survey*, vol. 40, no. 3 (1991), pp. 57–58.

66. Computed from results quoted in Gow, *Legitimacy and the Military*, p. 122.

67. See *Borba*, March 6, 1991, in FBIS, *East Europe*, March 8, 1991, p. 56.

68. The defense secretary responded with changes in the Law on National Service, adopted by the federal assembly (by a majority of those present) on April 26, that handed back to the YPA responsibility for army recruitment (including assignment of where conscripts serve, the primary source of dispute) from the local, provincial, and republican governments, to which it had been given in 1987. "Assembly Adopts Changes to National Service Law," TANJUG, April 26, 1991, in FBIS, *East Europe*, April 29, 1991, p. 36. It is unclear what legal authority the assembly had by then, however; its mandate had expired in May 1990, the two prolongations of that mandate pending adoption of a new electoral law had not produced such a law, and Slovenian and Croatian delegates were no longer participating (and the disbandment of the Kosovo assembly and institution of direct rule from Belgrade had left the legal status of Kosovo delegates unclear).

69. In December 1971, although the army's intervention then was political, not military. The Croatian nationalist resurgence in 1967–71, under very similar circumstances as the Serbian resurgence in the 1980s—an economic reform program leading to unemployment and growing inequality and including constitutional reform, a nationalist party leadership looking to change Croatia's position in the federation, and a revolt of opposition intellectuals together linking up with mass nationalist sentiments—had appeared so threatening to the entire constitutional order and the possibility of keeping social unrest within tolerable limits that it pressured President Tito to clamp down. It was only when the students in several faculties of Zagreb University went into the streets in massive protest (at the "exploitative" character of the foreign exchange regime) in December 1971 that Tito was persuaded by these warnings. Because the authority of Tito and the coalition he built with anti-liberal and pro-federal elements of the Communist party were sufficient to reimpose party discipline on the Croatian scene, the army did not have to participate directly in restoring order. In March 1991, the absence of Tito and collapse of the Communist party had left only the federal presidency and the army as the guarantors of the constitutional order.

70. Misha Glenny provides an eyewitness account of the March 9–13 events in Belgrade, in *The Fall of Yugoslavia*, pp. 45–61; see also the analysis of Cohen, *Broken Bonds*, pp. 201–15, and Branka Magaš, "Youth Rebel Against Milošević," in *The Destruction of Yugoslavia*, pp. 281–86.

71. See "Serbian-Montenegrin Talks on Democratic Union," TANJUG, March 27, 1991, in FBIS, *East Europe*, March 28, 1991, p. 43.

72. At the last meeting, the presidents of Bosnia-Herzegovina (Izetbegović) and Macedonia (Gligorov) presented their compromise proposal for a future Yugoslavia (which they sent simultaneously to the federal assembly and had unveiled on June 3); it combined more confederal elements of republican sovereignty (aimed at Slovene support) while retaining the continued existence of Yugoslavia, an armed forces, and powers of defense and finance. See "Activities of the SFRY Presidency in Relation to the Political Future of the Country," in *Yugoslav Survey*, vol. 40, no. 2 (1991). See also Chuck Sudetic, "Yugoslavs Push Compromise Plan," *New York Times*, June 7, 1991, p. A5.

73. In demonstrations in Skopje and Kavardžc in June 1991, the crowd yelled "Tudjman is a murderer" and demanded all Macedonian soldiers be pulled from the army.

74. For example, Vojislav Šešelj's broadcast claim that his Chetniks were responsible when in fact they were not present, and the Croatian government accusations of mutilations that did not occur but became a liturgy. Brian Hall begins his elegant portrait of the period, *The Impossible Country*, with the statement "the current period of civil war more or less began with the massacre at Borovo Selo" (p. ix) and then presents (pp. 14–16, 75–79) multiple versions of the incident as told by ordinary Yugoslavs he meets to illustrate that "the idea that people of good will could disagree on important issues is foreign to [citizens and 'even intellectuals in Yugoslavia {who} tend to think the truth is not only knowable, but obvious']. If you disagreed, you had a motive. . . . An irony here was that I had never been in a country where the truth was more complex, more fundamentally unknowable, than in Yugoslavia" (pp. 5–6). But the different versions also demonstrate the tragic extent of miscommunication and disinformation that had permeated society by this time. On the incident, see also Glenny, *The Fall of Yugoslavia*, pp. 75–77.

75. Branko Smerdel, "Republic of Croatia: Three Fundamental Constitutional Choices" (ms., August 8, 1991), Zagreb University, p. 21. The referendum's meaning was not clear at the time, however. A second question was also posed: "Are you in favor of the republic of Croatia remaining in Yugoslavia as a federal state?" This was rejected by 92 percent of those voting, while 5.4 percent said yes. See "Croatian Referendum Shows Independence Favored," TANJUG, May 22, 1991, in FBIS, *East Europe*, May 23, 1991, p. 24. Some regional leaders cast doubt on the official results on turnout, citing, for example, the boycott in municipalities where Serbs were in the majority; the few voters in nationally mixed towns; and the boycott called by a number of parties in Istria and which openly disputed the government's figures. See TANJUG, May 21, 1991, in FBIS, *East Europe*, May 22, 1991, p. 39.

76. SDS leaders said that the referendum was in response to the scheduling by the Croatian government of its referendum on independence for May 19 (as the Croatian assembly's resolution on separation February 21 specified that it was taken upon receipt of the Slovene resolution for an agreed division of Yugoslavia), and it demonstrates how much the Serb leaders in the border region were reacting piecemeal to events elsewhere, largely on initiative in Zagreb and in federal Belgrade, rather than executing a planned goal, as some assert. The referendum took place only in seven of the municipalities in the area of *Kninska Krajina*, and the

level of organization and of coordination among Croatian Serb-majority communities was still quite low, for the original notice had included five other municipalities in central Croatia (including Petrinja) and it was not until May 15–18 that Serbs from 34 villages in eastern Croatia (Slavonia, Baranja, and western Srem) in which they were a majority chose to hold a similar referendum. See "Large Turnout for Krajina Referendum," and "Seven Municipalities Back Unifying With Serbia," TANJUG, May 12, 1991, in FBIS, *East Europe*, May 13, 1991, pp. 53–54, and "Slavonia, Baranja, Western Srem Plan Referendum," Radio Belgrade, May 15, 1991, in FBIS, *East Europe*, May 16, 1991, pp. 29–30.

77. See David Gompert, "How to Defeat Serbia," *Foreign Affairs*, vol. 73 (July/August 1994), pp. 11–18.

## Chapter 6

1. The declarations and accompanying acts can be found in "Acts of the Republics of Slovenia and Croatia on Sovereignty and Independence," *Yugoslav Survey*, vol. 32, no. 3 (1991), pp. 47–56.

2. "Federal Chamber Adopts Conclusions on Slovenia," Belgrade RTV, June 25, 1991, and "Federal State to 'Take Over' Slovene Borders," TANJUG, June 26, 1991, both in Foreign Broadcast Information Service, *Daily Report: East Europe*, June 26, 1991, pp. 44, 46 (hereafter FBIS, *East Europe*). In his memoirs Kadijević defined the YPA task as implementing the decision of the federal cabinet to ensure execution of all federal regulations concerning border crossings in Slovenia on the basis of the federal chamber's decision that the Slovene takeover of all such federal functions (both internal affairs and customs) and intention to establish a state border with the rest of Yugoslavia were unconstitutional; also, that within forty-eight hours, they had taken control of 133 out of 137 border installations. See Veljko Kadijević, *Moje Vidjenje Raspada: Vojska bez Država* (My view of the collapse: an army without a state) (Belgrade: Politika, 1993), p. 117. Representatives of Slovenia and Croatia to the federal assembly had already withdrawn, although members of the federal cabinet were ordered back to Ljubljana or Zagreb only at the time of the declarations, late on June 25.

3. See *The Geneva Conventions of August 12, 1949* (Geneva: International Committee of the Red Cross Publications, April 1991), and *Protocols Additional to the Geneva Conventions of April 12, 1949* (ICRC Publications, July 1991).

4. Agencies assigned to be concerned, such as the United States Central Intelligence Agency and the desk officers of Western departments of state and foreign affairs, were well informed of events and tried to draw public attention to the dangers during 1990. On the leaked November 1990 report of the Central Intelligence Agency, see John Zametica, *The Yugoslav Conflict*, Adelphi Paper 270 (London: Institute for International and Strategic Studies, 1992), p. 58.

5. For example, a visit by a Slovene parliamentary delegation to Vienna at the invitation of the Austrian parliament on June 27, 1990, was, according to France Bučar, president of the Slovene parliament, "very important for Slovenia's statehood and sovereignty" and "confirmed that Slovenia had been accepted as a partner for

cooperation." (See "Slovene Parliamentarians on SFRY Confederation," TANJUG, June 27, 1990, in FBIS, *East Europe*, June 28, 1990, p. 71.) A mixed parliamentary and governmental delegation visited Washington in the early days of October 1990.

6. John Newhouse, in "Dodging the Problem," *New Yorker*, August 24, 1992, p. 64, quotes Ambassador Warren Zimmermann, when he was urging the Slovenes and Croats to stay in Yugoslavia: "We discovered later that Genscher [the German foreign minister] had been in daily contact with the Croatian foreign minister. He was encouraging the Croats to leave the federation and declare independence, while we and our allies, including the Germans, were trying to fashion a joint approach." The Croatian government also employed public relations firms in the United States to influence opinion.

7. According to Gianni De Michelis, Italian foreign minister at the time (interviews in Italy, 1994).

8. "Army General Interviewed on Arms Trade," January 3, 1990, in FBIS-*East Europe*, January 4, 1990, pp. 14–15; Donald Forbes, "Hungary: Pressure Grows for Dismissal of Hungarian Ministers," Reuter Newswire, February 8, 1991; and Andrej Gustinčić, "Yugoslavia: Yugoslav Presidency Warns of Rebellion, Confiscates Weapons," Reuter Newswire, January 9, 1991, on the story in *Politika Ekspres* (Belgrade). The Hungarian interior minister, Péter Boross, authorized the sale (of which the first installment in September 1990 was from 36,000 to 80,000 rifles, depending on the account), the foreign minister admitted to knowing of it, and some argue that the Hungarian ministry of foreign affairs also informed Yugoslav intelligence, which means that the Yugoslav federal army knew of the sale from September on but chose to do nothing about it until January (ostensibly, the argument goes, because the army was looking for a new role and could justify helping arm Serbs in Croatia if it let the Croatian government arm, and thereby then create for itself a role as a peacekeeping force; by this reasoning, the army changed its mind in March when it struck a deal with Milošević to defend Serbs).

9. The Hungarian Democratic Forum, whose policy toward diaspora Hungarians was a special personal interest and part of the official portfolio of the foreign minister, Géza Jeszenszky.

10. The EC program, known as PHARE (Pologne-Hongrie: Actions pour la Réconversion Économique), was initiated in July 1989 and extended in April 1990 to the other East European countries.

11. Mihailo Crnobrnja, a Yugoslav economist and ambassador to the European Community (1989–92), in *The Yugoslav Drama* (Montreal: McGill-Queen's University Press, 1994), p. 136, refers to this policy of using human rights as a way to intervene in the East after 1975 as a Trojan Horse, a characterization with which East European dissidents who benefited would likely concur.

12. The secretariat was established at Prague, opening February 20, 1991; the CSO first met in Vienna on January 28–29, 1991; and the CPC was set up in Vienna, opening March 18, 1991.

13. The consequences of his nationalist policy once the wars began in Croatia and especially in Bosnia led many to make an agonizing reappraisal of the role they might have played in encouraging Milošević, or at least to question the source of their mistake. See, for example, the Barbara Crossette interview of August 22, 1992, with Larry Eagleburger, "Baker's Deputy, Now Acting Secretary, Presses

Ahead With a Full Schedule," *New York Times*, August 23, 1992, p. A18: "Mr. Eagleburger has acknowledged that he may have misjudged the Serbian President, Slobodan Milošević, whom he remembered as a more reasonable man before Yugoslavia slid into chaos." While the moral question is fully appropriate, the personalization of the Yugoslav tragedy with the demonization of Milošević ignores the disregard for human rights by most Pinochet or Reaganite types, the ways that Western policy supported them, and the many ways that such leaders reflected the conditions that made possible their rise to power.

14. In a speech to the Center for Strategic and International Studies, in Washington, D.C., on June 9, 1992, Warren Zimmermann referred to the elections as a "double-edged sword," for American policy had to support democratic elections, but in all cases they brought "intolerant leaders to power" and "polarized nationalism."

15. The widespread policy of lustration, for example, focused many political energies at the time, and even had official U.S. government encouragement (interview with Peter Fridner, journalist, *Národná Obrada*, Bratislava, Slovakia, June 5, 1992). Studies of specific cases can be found in early issues of *East European Constitutional Review*, such as Poland [see Wiktor Osiatynski, "Agent Walesa?" *East European Constitutional Review*, vol. 1 (Summer 1992), pp. 28–30].

16. This was not true in the early days of Ambassador Zimmermann, who also earned President Tudjman's ire, but the question of policy remains unresolved as a result of continuing to focus on violations by Serbia and Serbs rather than adopting a nonnational criterion; and if the distinction being made is that of a threshold of what is tolerable, should not that principle be communicated instead? This became relevant to Western policy toward Russia by 1991, when Russian nationalists saw a pattern in Western differentiation between the Baltic states and Russians that was similar to that between Croatia and Serbia, choosing to protect some claims for national rights above their commitment to all human rights (in this case dismissing the rights of Serbs and Russians caught outside their "national" states).

17. President Bush made the case for German leadership initially in his "partners for leadership" speech in Mainz on May 31, 1989. The U.S. position that Germany (and indeed the EC as a whole) should take the lead in Eastern Europe was echoed by Secretary of State Baker in a speech to the Berlin Press Club in December of 1989. He argued, "The promotion of political and economic reforms in the East is a natural vocation for the European Community." See "A New Europe, A New Nationalism," *Vital Speeches of the Day*, January 15, 1990, p. 197. In a speech delivered to the American Council on Germany in New York on June 5, 1990, Chancellor Kohl, on the other hand, tried to stress from the outset that assistance to the East should be a shared responsibility. He called on the United States to recognize "its legitimate position in Europe and . . . its share of responsibility for the future of the Old Continent." "A United Germany in a United Europe," *Vital Speeches of the Day*, July 1, 1990, p. 548.

18. Interviews in Bulgaria, July 22–24, 1991, and in Greece, August 28–30, 1992; see also Misha Glenny, *The Fall of Yugoslavia: The Third Balkan War* (Penguin Books, 1992), p. 178.

19. A critical element of Tito's foreign policy had been to gain recognition of Yugoslavia's exceptional status, deserving of special treatment in its own category or as a part of western or southern Europe in foreign offices and international organizations, or in related forums in the United Nations as a leader of the non-aligned countries.

20. Yugoslavia had successfully negotiated association agreements of various kinds with the European Community beginning in 1955 with the Organization for European Economic Cooperation. It established formal relations with the EC in 1967, worked out a trade agreement in 1970, opened a diplomatic mission in 1973, and negotiated a comprehensive cooperation agreement beginning in 1975. The agreement completed in 1982 was better than the agreement that the central European three (Poland, Hungary, and Czechoslovakia) obtained in 1991, but the Yugoslav-EC association agreement being negotiated in 1989–91 was in serious trouble, in part because Greece blocked it beginning in July 1990.

21. Although Croats and Slovenes retorted that Europe knew many smaller but economically viable states such as Luxembourg, their argument ignored the preconditions to such viability of regional economic integration.

22. The area centered on Knin became known by the historical label its rebels adopted for their autonomous region, *krajina*.

23. German diplomats complained later that, as late as January 1992, there were only four persons in the German foreign ministry with any knowledge and responsibility for all of Yugoslavia; according to Stefan Schwartz, a deputy to the Bundestag actively concerned about Bosnia-Herzegovina, they did not then even have telephone numbers for government officials in Sarajevo. A similar absence of expertise was said to be true of the EC.

24. "Congress and Foreign Policy: An Examination of Congressional Attitudes toward the Foreign Aid Programs to Spain and Yugoslavia" (Columbia University, 1967). See the discussion by John Newhouse in "Dodging the Problem," pp. 60–71.

25. For example, the new secretary general of the West European Union (WEU), Willem van Eekelen, wrote a report in December 1990 that urged immediate action toward Yugoslavia and proposed that the WEU organize a division based on national brigades. This plan had won support from all of the WEU foreign ministers except Hans van den Broek by February 1991, when van Eekelen took the plan to Washington. The result was the Bartholomew letter to the WEU ministerial in which the United States laid out every possible objection (interview with van Eekelen in December 1994). On the letter, also called the Dobbins Démarche, see Catherine Kelleher, *The Future of European Security* (Brookings, forthcoming 1995), in which she states that the letter laid out U.S. "preconditions for cooperation" on European defense based on the Bush administration's "clear goal of preventing an independent European security organization that would undermine NATO."

26. From conversations with Misha Glenny in Davos, Switzerland, January 31–February 2, 1992. The argument continues that the failure of the attempted putsch in Moscow in August 1991 prevented deliveries and may even have nullified the agreement. When the evidence to assess these trips becomes available, it will be necessary to dis-

entangle Kadijević's search for an alternative source of weapons and funding in his by then bitter conflict with Prime Minister Marković from plans of the general staff to protect Yugoslav territorial and constitutional integrity against Slovenia and Croatia and against the possible consequences of the breakup of the country.

27. Senator Dennis DeConcini (Democrat of Arizona) and Representative Steny H. Hoyer (Democrat of Maryland), chair and cochair of the U.S. Helsinki Commission, sent the following telegram to the president of Yugoslavia, Borisav Jović, on January 24, 1991: "There are numerous reports of threatening movements by the Yugoslav Army in Croatia and especially in the Zagreb area. We are deeply concerned about the possibility that military force will be used in that republic, which, as Co-Chairmen of the U.S. Commission on Security and Cooperation in Europe, we would consider to be counter to the aims of the Helsinki Final Act and other CSCE documents, including the Paris Charter for a New Europe which you signed last November. Military force cannot provide a just and lasting solution to Yugoslavia's crisis. We therefore urge you to order a halt to any planned military action in Croatia or any other republic, to reaffirm your commitment to a peaceful and serious dialogue, and to call upon all those concerned to do the same." "Commission Urges Yugoslavs to Refrain from Violence," *CSCE News Release*, January 24, 1991. On March 13, 1991, Zimmermann also warned of a cutoff in U.S. aid if the military "enforced a crackdown." Blaine Harden, "Yugoslav Army Wavers on Civil Role," *Washington Post*, March 15, 1991, p. A33.

28. Communication from Representative McCloskey during hearings of the House Armed Services Committee on the Use of Force in the Post–Cold War Era: The Situation in Bosnia-Herzegovina and Croatia, May 26, 1993.

29. See Stephen Engelberg, "Belgrade Sends Troops to Croatian Town," *New York Times*, March 3, 1991, p. A3; Engelberg, "Serb-Croat Showdown in One Village Square," *New York Times*, March 4, 1991, p. A3; and David Binder, "Head of Yugoslavia's Government Resigns in Dispute on Army Role," *New York Times*, March 16, 1991, p. A1.

30. Most scholars insist that it had long since passed, at the very latest by March.

31. European Parliament resolution on Yugoslavia, clause 8, cited by James Gow, "Deconstructing Yugoslavia," *Survival*, vol. 33 (July/August 1991), p. 308. This reference to internal borders in particular, suggesting that Helsinki principles would apply to the borders of the republics as well, was a momentous decision. Some argue that the European Parliament is an insignificant body, but this mistakes the reality of power within western Europe for the symbolic power of any signal to those outside who hope for inclusion or even the closeness with which any sign of support for one's cause among those with the power to realize it actually is read.

32. This proposal for a "Council of Wise Men" was rejected by Yugoslav foreign minister Budimir Lončar.

33. As many Bulgarians put it at the time, "The neutral Austria showed its horns in Yugoslavia." Interviews in Sofia, July 22–24, 1991.

34. Marc Weller, "The International Response to the Dissolution of the Socialist Federal Republic of Yugoslavia," *American Journal of International Law*, vol. 86 (July 1992), pp. 570–71; David Binder, "U.S., Citing Human Rights, Halts Economic

Aid to Yugoslavia," *New York Times*, May 19, 1991, p. A10. The Nickles Amendment, a vehicle "to penalize the government of the Serbian Republic in particular and Yugoslavia in general for the repression of ethnic Albanians in the Kosovo region," said that economic aid must be halted "if it is determined that there is a pattern of systematic gross violations of human rights in Yugoslavia," to be certified by the secretary of state. The Zagreb daily *Vjesnik* quoted a *New York Times* story on the suspension of aid that ascribed the "main driving force behind the moves" to "Senator Bob Dole." See "Daily Accuses U.S. of 'Political Punishment,'" TAN-JUG, May 19, 1991, in FBIS, *East Europe*, May 22, 1991, p. 40.

35. This was the sum requested by Marković as essential to continue debt repayment and thereby succeed with the stabilization program. Yugoslavia had been seeking this amount from international financial institutions (through negotiations with the IMF, an appeal to the Paris Club of creditor governments for debt rescheduling, and others) during the spring. Judy Dempsey, "Yugoslavia Seeks \$4.5bn to Help Its Economic Reforms," *Financial Times*, May 23, 1991, p. 2. Great Britain, however, blocked the aid package.

36. David Gardner and Laura Silber, "Brussels Warning to Yugoslavs on Aid," *Financial Times*, May 21, 1991, p. 2.

37. Gow, "Deconstructing Yugoslavia," pp. 304–05. The Italian ambassador to Bonn, Marcello Guidi, notes the great irony of this policy shift for Italy, because in the 1940s and 1950s, Slovenia and Croatia were seen as Italy's greatest enemies, far more than the USSR, because of the border conflicts over Trieste, Istria, and the Julian Alps. In fact, these actions reflect the presence of competing currents toward the Yugoslav crisis within Italian politics and government as well as competing goals. This characterized all the major external actors and explains much about the mixed signals that were being sent.

38. David Gompert, "How to Defeat Serbia," *Foreign Policy*, vol. 73 (July/August 1994), pp. 30–42. Some knowledgeable observers also charge that the U.S. government gave explicit instructions to the federal army about how to defend those borders, but government sources insist instead that the United States opposed any military intervention to prevent secession. Confidential communications.

39. The proposal combined republican sovereignty with a continuation of Yugoslavia, including a common defense and financial integration. See chapter 5 and "Platform Concerning the Future of the Yugoslav Community," *Yugoslav Survey*, vol. 32, no. 2 (1991), pp. 39–44.

40. The Croatian Parliament chose to preempt Slovenia's declared date of declaration of June 26 and declare independence a day earlier without warning, forcing the Slovenes to do the same. As it was, many believed (and still believe) that Slovene independence was not problematic as long as Croatians, in very different circumstances, did not insist on the same; this act infuriated the Slovenes, revived memories of 1967–71 when Slovene pressures for greater republican sovereignty backfired because Croatia also followed suit but then pressed the limits so far that even the Slovenes supported federal reaction, and exacerbated growing tensions between the two governments that were only relieved temporarily in the first half of 1994.

41. In the first hours, however, they were without a new flag, because its design was still the subject of heated controversy in the sitting Parliament. There is some

dispute about how many border posts were taken: eight, sixteen, or all sixty-seven [the latter figure is from Lenard J. Cohen, *Broken Bonds: The Disintegration of Yugoslavia* (Westview Press, 1993), p. 219]. Kadijević states that within forty-eight hours, the YPA had taken 133 of its intended 137 border facilities. The main external routes were clearly most critical to both militaries, the Slovene and the YPA, but see Mark Thompson, *A Paper House: The Ending of Yugoslavia* (Pantheon, 1992), pp. 3–5, 8, and 63, for a more intimate sense of what was taking place, such as his discussion of the border through Istria, which "as with all Yugoslav borders . . . was invisible, until 1991, when Slovenia erected border-posts along backroads to mark the limits of its new sovereignty." The army also encircled the capital, Ljubljana, and the president of Slovenia repeated Slovenia's intention to "defend by all means their sovereignty." See *Calendrier de la crise Yougoslave*, p. 2. France Bučar, president of the Slovenian Parliament, explained the move as a protection against "drugs and third world immigrants," on a BBC radio broadcast in June 1991.

42. Gow, "Deconstructing Yugoslavia," p. 308. Paul Shoup, in a speech at George Washington University on February 2, 1991, reported that the most enthusiastic supporter of Slovene independence in Ljubljana was the Swiss Consul General.

43. Formalized in the Single European Act of 1986, the EPC "troika" represented the state holding the presidency, its predecessor, and its successor. Its composition, rotating each six months, was about to change on June 30. The first two missions comprised Gianni De Michelis of Italy, Jacques Poos of Luxembourg, and Hans van den Broek of the Netherlands. In the third and in those until December 30, 1991, Italy replaced Portugal, and van den Broek of the Netherlands replaced Poos of Luxembourg as chair.

The irony of the selection of this date was lost on the Europeans. June 28, Vidov Dan (St. Vitus' Day), the feast day of the patron saint of Serbia, was the date of the infamous Battle of Kosovo in 1389; the day on which Archduke Franz Ferdinand was assassinated in Sarajevo in 1914; the date of the 1921 Constitution, called the Vidovdan Constitution, which Slovenes and Croats opposed; and the date of the letter (the Cominform Resolution) expelling the Yugoslav Communist party and its leadership under Tito from the Communist International and the developing eastern bloc in 1948.

44. At the time some countries, including France, considered this a violation of principle VI of the Helsinki Act, noninterference in internal affairs. Personal communication from Eric Remacle, December 1994.

45. See Weller, "The International Response to the Dissolution of the Socialist Federal Republic of Yugoslavia," pp. 570–73.

46. Ibid., p. 572.

47. See Gow, "Deconstructing Yugoslavia," p. 309, for Eagleburger interview on CNN, June 30, 1991.

48. Some would argue that this ignores the EC's capacity for collective military action in the WEU, which under the leadership of Secretary General van Eekelen began ever more vigorously after December 1990 to design and push for a WEU-initiated intervention force. The mediation efforts of the EC and CSCE, therefore, could not be separated from the issue of European defense and the Bush administration policy to prevent alternatives to NATO.

49. Aide to British prime minister John Major, cited in Craig R. Whitney, "Spur to Summit Action: Yugoslav Crisis Brings New Pressure for Rich Nations to Help the Soviets," *New York Times*, July 5, 1991, p. A1.

50. Janša was a former youth leader who featured in the army's campaign to restore its authority in 1988 by arresting and trying him and two others for revealing military secrets; his immense popularity now spread because of his militant stand (as did that of other leaders of the radical wing of the Christian Democrats, including many clerics, who appeared in fatigues on television and militarized political language).

51. The air force did eventually bomb the Ljubljana airport at Brnik (Gow, "Deconstructing Yugoslavia," p. 309).

52. According to Misha Glenny, the YPA had 20,000 troops in Slovenia and 2,000 special forces from the Niš military region, but only 2,000 were deployed in the war, of which 1,000 were brought from bases in Croatia (in Varaždin, Zagreb, and Karlovac). The explanation given is that the army planned only to intimidate Croats and to exploit the good offices of the European Community to do the task of separating Slovenia from Yugoslavia. See Glenny, *The Fall of Yugoslavia*, p. 96.

53. See James Gow, "The Role of the Military in the Yugoslav War of Dissolution," paper prepared for the international conference, Armed Conflict in the Balkans and European Security, on April 20–22, 1993 (Ljubljana, Slovenia: Ministry of Defense–Center for Strategic Studies, June 1993).

54. Lenard Cohen writes that General Blagoje Adžić, the YPA chief of staff, "was stunned by the ferocity of Slovene military moves against the JNA [YPA]. He added that 'having been brought up over decades in the Yugoslav spirit, we could not believe that so much evil and hatred could accumulate in one place and be expressed in such terrible terms.' " See Cohen, *Broken Bonds*, p. 218.

55. This interpretation was still held three years later by many ex-Yugoslavs, who argued that Milošević wanted Slovenia to leave because he could then control the state presidency and therefore the army. Although this assumes that there would have been no constitutional changes in the existing system if Slovenia left and that the army general staff, various federal authorities, and other republican leaders did not have separate interests, the behavior of President Kučan also lends credence to this interpretation.

56. The real story will not be known for some time. General Konrad Kolšek, the commander of the Fifth Army District of the YPA, which was based in Zagreb and covered Croatia and Slovenia, and a Slovene, was interviewed in the daily newspaper of Maribor (Slovenia's second city) on August 3, 1993. He admitted (under "immense pressure from unnamed officials and anonymous death threats") that "he prevented the Yugoslav army from deploying special units to Ljubljana and obstructed air strikes on the Slovenian capital and other towns" against general staff decisions, thus helping Slovenia to break away. Milan Andrejevich, "Ex-Yugoslav General Says He Helped Slovenian Independence," *RFE/RL Daily Report*, August 5, 1993. Minister of Defense Veljko Kadijević acknowledges that many "worked to paralyze the YPA" by "interfering with mobilization or interfering with the movement of mobilized units toward places they were needed," which he saw as "very synchronized, on a wide scope, obviously directed from a single center." Kadijević, *Moje Vidjenje Raspada*, p. 119.

57. Ibid., pp. 116–25.

58. Ibid., pp. 122–23.

59. Cohen, *Broken Bonds*, p. 224. According to Christian Wegger Strommen, Norwegian diplomat at the International Conference on Former Yugoslavia, there were sixty-eight deaths in the Slovene war: sixty-four YPA soldiers and four Slovene TDF soldiers.

60. The three options were: 1) defeat Slovene military formations and then withdraw, an operation requiring six to eight days and using supplementary infantry and substantially more airpower; 2) use all available military force to coerce compliance to the rulings concerning the border, and accept the possibility of substantial civilian casualties; or 3) combine political means with the threat of YPA resources to achieve the political goals. The general staff preferred the first option and excluded the second. Kadijević, *Moje Vidjenje Raspada*, pp. 120–21.

61. In his memoirs, *Kako Smo Srušili Jugoslaviju* (How we destroyed Yugoslavia), Mesić denied that he had said this was his intention, although he was widely quoted at the time to this effect and he told the Croatian Parliament in early December, "I have fulfilled my duty—Yugoslavia no longer exists." Quoted by Cohen, *Broken Bonds*, p. 228.

62. Marković told the press on July 4 that the "decision by the staff of the Supreme Command was made which, I must say, had no connection with and was not in the service of the FEC [Federal Executive Council] and its president. This was an autonomous decision by the staff of the Supreme Command in a situation in which the Supreme Command had not been set up and was functioning, that is, the SFRY Presidency was not functioning." See "Marković Holds News Conference," Radio Belgrade, July 4, 1991, in FBIS, *East Europe*, July 5, 1991, p. 28.

63. Note that it was only at the end of May that they were extending the carrot of economic assistance to the federal government. The aid cutoff represented a suspension of the EC's "second and third financial protocol" with the country. See "Declaration on the Situation in Yugoslavia, 5 July, 1991," in *Review of International Affairs*, vol. 42, no. 995–97, p. 19.

64. Perhaps ironically, Brioni was the island retreat off Croatian Istria favored by President Josip Broz Tito for international guests and matters of diplomacy and when he gathered party leaders to resolve a particularly thorny internal quarrel. When the federal presidency attempted to meet the next day in Belgrade, the Slovene and Croatian representatives refused, feigning illness and fears of personal danger (which incensed citizens of Belgrade), but when it attempted then to accommodate them by meeting in Brioni on the 16th, four others—from Kosovo, Montenegro, Serbia, and Vojvodina—reciprocated and refused to attend.

65. The EC refused advice offered by the United Nations from its decades of peacekeeping experience, leading to some mistakes over the next months that can be ascribed to inexperience.

66. *Calendrier de la crise Yougoslave*, p. 7. See also "Brioni Declaration," *Yugoslav Survey*, vol. 32, no. 2 (1991), pp. 45–48.

67. The problems of recruitment, of conscripts sent unknowingly from other republics to fight in Croatia, and of growing desertions and attempts to evade the draft were already serious (see Kadijević, *Moje Vidjenje Raspada*, p. 119) and became

the subject of growing reports and concern. For consequences in the war in Croatia, see Glenny, *The Fall of Yugoslavia*, p. 24.

68. On Knin and Borovo Selo, ibid., pp. 7–27, 75–77. The "Chetniks" of Vojislav Šešelj began to form in February–March of 1991 with the help of Serb nationalists in the army and particularly the Serbian security police (ŠUP) and masterminded by the interior minister of Serbia, Radmilo Bogdanović, whereas Ražnatović specialized in organizing criminals. As later reports of the massacre in Borovo Selo on May 2, 1991, revealed, however, Šešelj or his gangs were not always where he boasted to have been.

69. This included putting a stop to the military preparations of General Martin Špegelj (see chapter 5 on the YPA attempt to expose these preparations and to charge him with treason). Even during the horrors of the Slavonian war and siege of Vukovar, youth drafted into the Croatian Territorial Defense Forces were neither trained nor properly armed, causing far higher casualties than necessary and growing defections to right-wing paramilitary forces, which claimed to be doing the real fighting for Croatia under Dobrislav Paraga.

70. Weller, "The International Response to the Dissolution of the Socialist Federal Republic of Yugoslavia," p. 574. The decision, signed by President Mesić, declared that "The regimen on the borders existing before June 25, 1991, has not been restored. The blockade of all the units and facilities of the Yugoslav People's Army has not been lifted, supplies and free communication are being hampered. The impounded matériel and equipment of the Yugoslav People's Army have not been released. Territorial Defence units of the Republic of Slovenia have not been de-activated and demobilized. Recruits are not being sent to serve their army terms with the Yugoslav People's Army. The elementary human rights of army members and their families have been grossly violated." "TANJUG Carries Presidency Statement," TANJUG, July 18, 1991, in FBIS, *East Europe*, July 19, 1991, p. 29.

71. Interview with Zvonko Lerotić and Mario Nobilo in the presidential palace in Zagreb, July 16, 1991.

72. Interviews in Belgrade, July 12–17, 1991, with the leader of the Serbian Democratic party and with chief advisers to Slobodan Milošević. Even the Serbian opposition believed at the time, however, that the army would have to "pacify" the border between Serbia and Croatia, and that at the time "the JNA [YPA] was protecting Croats more than Serbs, even though Croatia won't recognize this."

73. Their meeting at Karadjordjevo (a royal hunting lodge favored after 1945 by the late President Tito for crisis meetings of the federal and republican Communist party leaders) in March 1991 was announced in the media, but the subject of the discussion remained secret at the time; others, actually beginning in July 1990, were secret; the agreement to divide was revealed by President Tudjman in an interview with the *Times* of London in July 1991 (and confirmed by the actions of Bosnian Croat and Bosnian Serb leaders at many times during 1992). "The partition of Bosnia-Herzegovina is the best solution to the Yugoslav conflict, according to Dr. Franjo Tudjman, the Croatian president. Dr. Tudjman said he had agreed with Slobodan Milošević, the Serbian leader, that 'the major issue regarding a peaceful solution is demarcating the borders between Croatia and Serbia and solving the Muslim problem there'. Asked if that meant setting up a Muslim state, Dr. Tudjman replied 'In some way, yes.' "

74. For example, in an interview to the German weekly *Der Spiegel*, Tudjman apparently said, "One does not have to be a historian to realize that Bosnia and Croatia are a geopolitical unit." See "Bosnian Socialist Alliance Rejects Tudjman Claim," *Borba*, June 22, 1990, in FBIS, *East Europe*, June 27, 1990, p. 84.

75. Janez Drnovšek, prime minister of Slovenia, in a speech at the Center for Strategic and International Studies, Washington, D.C., September 17, 1992. Drnovšek was at the time the Slovene representative on the Yugoslav presidency.

76. It is not clear whether van den Broek actually changed his mind or gave verbal obeisance to a shifting mood within the EC, for only six months earlier he had led an effective opposition to WEU proposals to compose such a force from among EC states.

77. This French-German joint army corps, of from 35,000 to 50,000 soldiers, which could grow into a Eurocorps if other members of the Western European Union chose to contribute troops, was being floated as the basis of an EC common defense policy independent of NATO at the time of the Persian Gulf War, mid-February 1991. Plans were announced October 16, 1991, to give Europe the capacity to respond to "crises such as the Yugoslav civil war." Friction with the U.S. administration over the relation between such a corps and NATO arose at the NATO meetings in November 1991 and May 1992. Escalating U.S. lobbying against it with other Europeans led by December 1992 to a joint memorandum from France and Germany that the corps could come under NATO command in the event of a peacekeeping force outside of NATO area or an attack on the alliance. An accord to that effect was signed January 21, 1993, increasing the prospects that other NATO members (for example, Belgium, Spain, and Luxembourg) would join.

78. Weller, "The International Response to the Dissolution of the Socialist Federal Republic of Yugoslavia," p. 575. David Gordon and Judy Dempsey, "Soviets Warn Over Yugoslavia," *Financial Times*, August 7, 1991, p. 1.

79. According to the explanation given the next March by the Serb leader Borisav Jović, president of the presidency and leader of the Serbian bloc, the Yugoslav presidency had ordered the army to be that neutral force. During July there was strong evidence that the army was in large part (but not entirely) playing this role in Croatia, although it was so essential to the Croatian strategy that this not be the case (the government ordered the news media to refer to the YPA as an army of occupation) that a dispassionate analysis will take a long time. Miloš Vasić, military expert for the independent Belgrade weekly *Vreme*, emphasizes the *process* by which the army lost its mission, subdividing into competing groups with different objectives, each of which was seen to represent the army as a whole, and then deteriorating into many local commands and a rump army of the new Yugoslavia (primarily Serbia) in May 1992. See Aleksandar Ćirić and Miloš Vasić, "No Way Out: The JNA and the Yugoslav Wars," *WarReport*, no. 17 (January 1993), pp. 3–5; and Miloš Vasić, "The Federal Army and the Agony of Change," in Anthony Borden, Ben Cohen, Marisa Crevatin, and Davorka Zmiarević, eds., *Breakdown: War & Reconstruction in Yugoslavia* (London: Institute for War and Peace Reporting, 1992), pp. 43–44.

80. Steven L. Burg, "The International Community and the Yugoslav Crisis," paper prepared for the Workshop on International Organizations and Ethnic Conflict at Cornell University, April 16–17, p. 12.

81. The CSCE joined the EC embargo on the supply of arms and transfer of weapons "for the duration of the crisis in Yugoslavia" on September 4, 1991. See "Documents of the CSCE," *Review of International Affairs*, vol. 42, no. 995–97, p. 17.

82. Interviews conducted by the author in many parts of the country during the third week of July 1991; also, Glenny, *The Fall of Yugoslavia*, p. 44, reports this mood.

83. See Paul Beaver, "Militarisation: Shifting Alliances in the Balkans," *YugoFax*, no. 13 (August 1, 1992), p. 4.

84. Estonia's path of dissociation from the Soviet Union followed nearly identical steps as the Slovene; observers in eastern Europe long drew parallels between Ukraine and Croatia, including their essential role in their respective states: the USSR could not survive the secession of Ukraine, nor Yugoslavia the secession of Croatia. Moreover, for several years after 1991 some in Russia held on to the idea that Ukraine would rejoin Russia, as some in Serbia felt Croatia would do.

This unusual alignment on the Yugoslav case, from the point of view of the cold war, between the left (Social Democratic Party-SPD) and the right (Christian Social Union-CSU), and which the ruling party would attempt to preempt, was also occurring in the United States—between foreign policy liberals in the Democratic party (known usually as "doves" on the use of military force) and right-wing anticommunists in the Republican party (known as "hawks," usually on the opposite side of the aisle from the liberals).

85. *Calendrier de la crise Yougoslave*, p. 15.

86. Weller, "The International Response to the Dissolution of the Socialist Federal Republic of Yugoslavia," pp. 575–76. But see Weller's discussion, pp. 576–77, on the continuing ambiguity in EC declarations about whether Yugoslavia did or did not exist.

87. The commission consisted of five jurists, one each from France, Germany, Spain, Belgium, and Italy. It was originally proposed by Slovenia, which wanted an outside body to help it negotiate *economic* disputes over the distribution of assets and debts of the former federation so that it did not have to deal directly with any Yugoslav body.

88. The initiative was "based on the fact that throughout the entire Yugoslav crisis no decisions on seceding or independence from Yugoslavia were either passed or proclaimed in Bosnia and Herzegovina, Serbia, and Montenegro." It committed its organizers to preserve Yugoslavia on the basis of the summits of republican presidents, the proposal of Serbia and Montenegro at the meeting in Kranj, "the Izetbegović-Gligorov Platform, and on the Muslim-Serbian Agreement [between Adil Zulfikarpašić and Radovan Karadžić]." See "Document From the Representatives of Serbia, Montenegro, and Bosnia and Herzegovina," *Yugoslav Survey*, vol. 32, no. 2 (1991), p. 50. They agreed to send their proposal to the assemblies of their three republics, to the constitutional commission of the Yugoslav Parliament, and "to the republics of Slovenia, Croatia and Macedonia, with an invitation to participate in the discussion of this Initiative on an equal footing." See "Belgrade Initiative—Bases for the Determination of Relations in Yugoslavia," *Yugoslav Survey*, vol. 32, no. 3 (1991), pp. 43–44.

89. On August 22, however, he made a public speech accusing Milošević of "[wanting] the whole of Bosnia."

90. Cohen, *Broken Bonds*, p. 226.

91. Cited in Steven L. Burg, "The International Community and the Yugoslav Crisis," p. 12, from Paul L. Montgomery, "Yugoslavs Joust at Peace Meeting," *New York Times*, September 8, 1991, p. A8.

92. The referendum asked for an affirmative or negative vote on an independent and sovereign Macedonian state, which included the possibility of joining a union of independent states in Yugoslavia. Turnout was 71.85 percent of the 1,495,626 registered voters, of which 95.09 percent voted in favor (reported by "'Official' Referendum Results Released," TANJUG, September 10, 1991, FBIS, *East Europe*, September 11, 1991, p. 39). The Albanian and Serb populations (comprising about 23 percent and 2.3 percent, respectively, of the population) did boycott. President Gligorov claimed that this was not a vote for secession but a "national and historic act" expressing the "centuries-long strivings of the Macedonian people." Skopje radio report of a speech given August 29, 1991, in FBIS, *East Europe*, August 30, 1991, p. 43.

93. *Calendrier de la crise Yougoslave*, p. 60, and "Croat Resigns as Head of Belgrade Presidency," *New York Times*, December 6, 1991, p. A9. Mesić did not, in fact, resign until December 5, 1991, so that, as he told a Hungarian interviewer on November 20, "he could freeze Yugoslav funds abroad and not let the money 'get into Serb hands.' " See Cohen, *Broken Bonds*, p. 255, n. 15.

94. Former British foreign secretary and secretary general of NATO, Carrington had successfully negotiated the Rhodesian conflict that brought majority rule and independence in Zimbabwe.

95. Brian Urquhart, former United Nations under secretary general for political affairs, in an interview with the author May 8, 1992, noted the similarity between the United Nations at its start and the European Community in 1991: a collection of states rather than the collectivity embodied in its charter; the need for a statesman to define a common policy and authority and a secretariat for foreign and security policy with experience in peacekeeping. He also noted that the EC (some would say in arrogance) refused to seek or accept advice from those with long experience in conflict mediation and peacekeeping, such as persons in the UN secretariat, but preferred to learn by doing. One symbol of their naïveté became the white clothing chosen for its observers and their equipment.

96. John Zametica reports that the meeting was particularly "acrimonious" and that it was British foreign secretary Douglas Hurd who "finally quashed the plan" to send WEU troops to establish peace, in Zametica, *The Yugoslav Conflict*, p. 66.

97. The foreign ministers of France, Britain, and Belgium were preparing on September 23 to sponsor a resolution permitting the right of intervention by the international community without consent of the Yugoslav government. Because some members of the council (Zimbabwe, India, China, Cuba, Zaire) would have opposed discussion on what they considered an internal affair, Weller reports that "the federal presidency's support for a meeting was elicited from the central authorities in Belgrade at the very last minute." See Weller, "The International Response to the Dissolution of the Socialist Federal Republic of Yugoslavia," p. 578.

98. The draft resolution was submitted by Austria, Belgium, France, the USSR, and the United Kingdom. The initial request for an arms embargo against

Yugoslavia, however, came from its own representative. See Weller, "The International Response to the Dissolution of the Socialist Federal Republic of Yugoslavia," pp. 578–80, for an analysis of the debate within the council, including substantial concern about the application of chapter 7 to what some still considered largely an internal conflict.

99. The UN accepted the judgment of the EC's Badinter Commission that the doctrine of *uti possidetis* applied to Yugoslavia's internal borders—the first time it was used outside a colonial situation. Weller, "The International Response to the Dissolution of the Socialist Federal Republic of Yugoslavia," p. 580. See also Crnobrnja, *The Yugoslav Drama*, pp. 206, 223, on UN support for the work of the Badinter Commission.

100. The three conditions established for recognition were: 1) guarantee of minority rights, including special status to certain regions; 2) no unilateral change of borders; and 3) participation in negotiations within the peace conference over creation of an alliance of independent or sovereign state (that is, that independence of individual states be recognized only in the framework of a general agreement).

101. A Belgrade Islamicist, in an interview to the weekly NIN, suggested that Izetbegović pushed through the memorandum in urgent procedure in order to seize the moment when European attention through The Hague conference was available to bring international pressure to bear. Izetbegović calculated, Tanašković argued, that "a unified B-H within its present borders cannot survive outside of Yugoslavia (the Serbs would not accept that), but neither could it survive on the principles of the Belgrade initiative (the Croats would not accept that). His expectations are bound up with the survival of Yugoslavia with all six republics." The Hague conference formula, similar to the Izetbegović-Gligorov proposal, would "ultimately be accepted even by the Serbs under international pressure and the pressure of reality." See "Professor Interviewed on Serb-Muslim Relations," NIN, October 25, 1991, pp. 18–20, in FBIS, *East Europe*, November 26, 1991, p. 53.

102. The SDA leadership requested of the Serb leaders that there be instead a joint referendum of citizens and peoples, as a compromise between Izetbegović's insistence that there be a vote of all citizens and Karadžić's insistence on a vote of nations. At the same time, in an interview to *Novi List*, Stjepan Kljuić, the leader of the Bosnian Croat HDZ, announced that the "Serbs in the republic must separate their territories and their people" and the "Croats will propose to the Moslems to remain to live with them in the remainder of the republic which could be completely independent or could join in a confederation with Slovenia and Croatia." "Croatian Party Leader Urges SFRY's Division," TANJUG, October 18, 1991, in FBIS, *East Europe*, October 21, 1991, p. 43.

103. The first draft of the convention, issued October 23, 1991, identified the "new relations between the Republics" as "a) sovereign and independent republics with an international personality for those which wish it; b) a free association of the Republics with an international personality as envisaged in this Convention; and c) comprehensive arrangements, including supervisory mechanisms for the protection of human rights and special status for certain groups and areas" (Article One). See "Treaty Provisions for the Convention," *Review of International Affairs*, vol. 42, no. 995–97, p. 33. The "corrected version" of November 4, 1991, added the possibility, between paragraphs b and c, that a new, rump state would also be

formed: "c) a common state of equal Republics for those Republics which wish to remain a common state." See "Treaty Provisions for the Convention," ms.

104.   The EC first threatened sanctions—suspension of cooperation agreements and trade concessions, escalating toward complete economic isolation—in order to obtain a cease-fire on October 6, postponing the threat each time parties signed a cease-fire document. Twelve had been signed by November 5.

105.   See Vojin Dimitrijević, "The Yugoslav Precedent: Keep What You Have," *Breakdown*, pp. 62–64.

106.   In fact President Milošević was working hard behind the scenes to pressure the Croatian Serbs to accept the EC plan that all now identified as a loose association of independent republics (although paragraph five of Article One did admit the possibility of a change in borders: "in the framework of a general settlement, recognition of the independence, within the existing borders, unless otherwise agreed, of those Republics wishing it." See "Treaty Provisions for the Convention," p. 33). He covered the opposition of Milan Babić to "a completely unacceptable plan" by accusing the EC plan of leaving "the 2m Serbs living outside Serbia in an independent Croatia or Bosnia-Hercegovina in which their status could be undermined," but Milošević apparently gave an ultimatum to Babić to accept the plan by November 2 (before the next Hague meeting on November 5). See Laura Silber, "Serbian Leaders Divided Over How to Respond to EC Threat of Sanctions," *Financial Times*, November 1, 1991, p. 2.

107.   The sanctions included immediate suspension of the EC 1980 trade and cooperation agreement with Yugoslavia and of General System of Preferences trade benefits, restoration of EC quantitative import limits on Yugoslav textiles, and suspension of PHARE food and economic assistance. The country was not invited to the meeting of the Group of 24 on November 11, and the EC urged a UN embargo on oil exports and a tightening of the arms embargo. Compensatory measures for "parties which do cooperate in a peaceful way towards a comprehensive political solution on the basis of the EC proposals," such as Bosnia and Macedonia, were discussed. Robert Mauthner and Laura Silber, "EC Puts Sanctions on Yugoslavia," *Financial Times*, November 9–10, 1991, p. 24.

108.   The first request for UN peacekeeping forces in Croatia came in September from the Croatian Stipe Mesić, acting as president of Yugoslavia but without the knowledge, it turned out, of the other members of the collective presidency. The rump Yugoslav presidency of Serbia, Kosovo, Vojvodina, and Montenegro, whose authority to act for Yugoslavia was not recognized, requested troops on November 11. The cease-fire agreement brokered by Cyrus Vance in Geneva on November 23 between the presidents of Croatia and Serbia and the minister of defense presumed the deployment of UN forces, and although both Tudjman and Milošević alternately dickered on the terms—especially their location and its implications for the border between Croatia and Serbia—the question after mid-November was only a matter of details and of who would fund the operation.

109.   Amnesty International, "Yugoslavia: Torture and Deliberate and Arbitrary Killings in War Zones" (London, November 1991). According to Jacques Delors, "Community action was disappointing in the eyes of those who would have liked to achieve the impossible." See Crnobrnja, *The Yugoslav Drama*, pp. 203–04.

110.   Article I:e.

111. See "Decisions and Agreements on the Suspension of Armed Conflicts in Croatia," *Yugoslav Survey*, vol. 32, no. 4 (1991), pp. 25–34.

112. Secretary-General Javier Pérez de Cuéllar also wrote, on December 10, to express Cyrus Vance's report of the "widely expressed apprehensions about the possibility of premature recognition," including those of the leaders of Bosnia-Herzegovina and Macedonia, of the "possibly explosive consequences" of a "potential time bomb" and to Hans-Dietrich Genscher, on December 14, to note his omission in a letter in reply of "the common position adopted by you and your colleagues of the Twelve" on November 8 that "the prospect of recognition of the independence of those Republics wishing it, can only be envisaged in the framework of an overall settlement." Confidential correspondence.

113. Zametica, *The Yugoslav Conflict*, p. 65. At the time a young scholar in England of mixed Bosnian Serb and Bosnian Muslim parentage, Zametica later joined Radovan Karadžić as a political adviser in Pale during the Bosnian war. Kohl would likely have agreed with Zametica, for the very day after the EC decision, December 17, was the opening of the CDU-CSU party congress at Dresden, at which Kohl announced the triumph in his opening address, that Germany would recognize Croatia and Slovenia on December 19, and added "the Croats will not be left alone." John Tagliabue, "Kohl to Compromise on Yugoslavia," *New York Times*, December 18, 1991, p. A3.

114. Also as a result of the pervasive campaign mentioned earlier by the preeminent German newspaper, the *Frankfurter Allgemeine Zeitung*. A standard joke in Yugoslavia was that the country comprised not six republics, as people thought, but seven, the seventh being the Federal Republic of Germany, because there were so many cars with German license plates on the roads, as tourists along the Adriatic and as returned *gastarbeiter* in the poor Dalmatian hinterland. There were officially 700,000 Yugoslavs then working in Germany, and although many argue that the group comprised more Serbs than Croats, the Serbs were a more recent migration, were less organized, and did not have the autonomist or fascist traditions that mobilized the political action of many Croatian émigrés. There is no evidence that these Serbs supported Milošević, whereas the Croatian community had been well-organized on national lines since the early 1960s, in part to ensure cultural continuity with Croatia and to provide education for their children (funded in part by the Croatian government), and actively supported independence and Tudjman. Moreover, although Austrians and Germans were most inclined to explain xenophobic and nationalist outbursts in Yugoslavia and eastern Europe during 1990–91 as a consequence of their "isolation" from Western civilization under the communists, it was their own publics that betrayed evidence of isolation. According to Klaus Becher, formerly of the Research Institute of the German Society for Foreign Affairs, Germans educated after World War II (particularly those who were in their thirties in 1991) had not been told about the Ustasha regime in Croatia during the war or its atrocities toward Serbs, Jews, and Romany, so that their sympathies for Croatia and acceptance of the line that this was a fight between "democracy and dictatorship," victims and aggressors, met no cognitive dissonance from knowledge about the context of historical memories in Yugoslavia.

115. The Christian Democratic Union, led by Helmut Kohl, its Bavarian wing, the Christian Social Union, and its coalition partner, the Free Democrats.

116. So, too, had the Serbian community in the Croatian *krajina* and the Albanian community in Kosovo.

117. The same applied to Austria: although persistently active in attempting to influence the outcome in favor of Slovene and Croatian independence and in defining the conflict as a case of Serbian aggression, it stated clearly that it could not use military force, not because it was a former Axis power but because it was a "neighbor."

118. This opinion was expressed too frequently in the summer of 1991 and into 1992 not to be taken as a serious concern, from Bulgaria to Slovakia.

119. See Weller, "The International Response to the Dissolution of the Socialist Federal Republic of Yugoslavia," p. 575.

120. Newhouse, "Dodging the Problem," p. 66.

121. As one sympathetic Western ambassador stationed in Bonn at the time told me, "*Gross Deutschland* is second nature to them, it is part of their makeup; they can't do anything about it, but it is a problem for others."

122. Genscher did press the Croatian government to respond to the Badinter Commission ruling on this matter to specify the rights of minorities (Serbs included) and to institute a human rights court. But the government refused to amend the constitution, adopting instead a "constitutional law" months later, in May 1992, in which no affected domestic groups (including the Serbs of *krajina*) had any say. It had not created the required human rights court as of January 1995.

123. See chapter 9.

124. The effects were already being reported in early November. Local leaders in what were by then Serb-claimed areas of "Bosnian *krajina*" around Banja Luka did, however, implement the mobilization, leading to charges in Sarajevo that men in the area had three choices: accept conscription, face unemployment, or go to prison. Elsewhere, draftees and reservists were trapped between the army's order and their citizen's military obligation, on the one hand, and the instructions of the municipal authorities not to respond, on the other.

125. Largely elected mayors for whom representation in Croatian political institutions, such as their parliamentary seats and local assemblies, was the better route to Serbian rights and who were in competition politically with those who based their power on paramilitary bands and the new local armies.

126. The plan was the idea of his deputy, Ambassador Herbert S. Okun.

127. "Croatian President Franjo Tudjman said Monday he was confident the U.N. peacekeepers would help his republic regain territory lost in the war. He told the Reuters news agency that if the United Nations cannot ensure the return of the territory, then Croats themselves will take it back." Blaine Harden, "Unarmed U.N. Officers Begin Yugoslav Mission," *Washington Post*, January 15, 1992, p. A20.

128. Izetbegović told this to Genscher even earlier, in November, but his message was not as clear as it could have been (see chapters 8 and 9 for a possible explanation). While Izetbegović was opposed to international recognition at the time, he inexplicably failed to present the arguments against it that the German ambassador to Yugoslavia, Dr. Hansjörg Eiff, had prepared for him when he met with Foreign Minister Genscher in Bonn. See Newhouse, "Dodging the Problem," p. 65.

129. Survey results of public opinion show a sharp disjuncture between 1988 and 1991, where socioeconomic characteristics largely differentiate opinions in 1988. By 1991, however, differences fall most clearly along ethnonational lines. This means that there had to be substantial political organizing to make ethnicity politically salient in this short period. Based on a discussion between Silva Mežnarić and Vladimir Goati at a workshop on peace in Bosnia-Herzegovina held at the Woodrow Wilson International Center for Scholars, Washington, D.C., February 10–11, 1993.

130. This "Agreement on economic, cultural and informational cooperation of Bosanska and Kninska Krajina" between the Serbian Autonomous Region (SAO) of Krajina and the Alliance of communes [localities] in Bosanska Krajina was to integrate "economic, political, cultural, educational, health, social welfare and policy, transportation and communications, information, defense 'as well as other fields of life and work in which the need for integrative cooperation is demonstrated'." They agreed to retain their separate political and legal identities "until the general political circumstances in Yugoslavia, and the processes of integration between them, require and make possible otherwise." The next step in this process was seen to be a referendum, to be held no later than January 9, 1992, on joining the five Serbian autonomous regions declared in Bosnia-Herzegovina into a Republic of the Serbian people of Bosnia-Herzegovina and on their decision to remain within Yugoslavia. Cited by Paul Shoup, "Uloga Domaćih i Medjunarodnih Aktera Bosanskohercegovačke Drame [The Role of Domestic and International Actors in the Bosnian-Herzegovinian Drama]," *Bosna i Hercegovina izmedju Rata i Mira* (Bosnia and Herzegovina between war and peace) (Belgrade: Institut Društvenih Nauka, 1992), p. 89.

131. Quoted on National Public Radio, July 7, 1991.

132. See also "Bosanska Krajina Authorities Protest Croatian Attacks," TANJUG, October 14, 1991, in FBIS, *East Europe*, October 15, 1991, p. 56.

133. Of the 800,000 Serbs eligible to vote, 85 percent went to the polls. Of those who voted, 98 percent voted for an independent Serbian republic within the current borders of Bosnia-Herzegovina. The referendum was declared unconstitutional by the remaining members of the Bosnian government. See Milan Andrejevich, "Bosnia and Herzegovina: A Precarious Peace," *RFE/RL Research Report*, February 28, 1992, p. 9.

134. Andrejevich, "Bosnia and Herzegovina: A Precarious Peace," p. 9. On November 12, the Bosnian Sava Valley (*Posavina*) community of eight communes was set up in Bosanski Brod, and on November 18, eighteen communes formed Herzeg-Bosnia in western Herzegovina. A third community of four communes in central Bosnia was established January 27, 1992.

135. Figures vary. See Gow, *Legitimacy and the Military*, pp. 56–59. See the revealing portrait of Mladić written by Misha Glenny in 1991. Glenny, *The Fall of Yugoslavia*, pp. 26–29.

136. See Weller, "The International Response to the Dissolution of the Socialist Federal Republic of Yugoslavia," pp. 591–93, for the reasoning of the Badinter Commission, and how it was coming to define the right to self-determination in relation to the sanctity of borders by means of the doctrine of *uti possidetis*. See also

the discussion by Vojin Dimitrijević, "The Yugoslav Precedent," p. 63, on this principle (meaning "keep what you have"), based on a legal precedent from a conflict between Burkina Faso and Mali.

137. The appeal as early as July 1991 from Nikola Koljević, one of the two Serbian representatives on the Bosnian presidency, was ignored, although many would argue that local commanders began then to arm Serb civilians in preparation for war. By January, there were 100,000 YPA personnel, 30,000 Bosnian interior ministry troops (MUP), and 250,000 others organized by the three national parties. See James Gow, "Military-Political Affiliations in the Yugoslav Conflict," *RFE/RL Research Report*, May 15, 1992, pp. 16–25. By this time many refugees from the fighting in western Slavonia, Croatia, had fled to northern Bosnia-Herzegovina as well.

138. The numbers of the "substantial military formations of the Republic of Croatia" in war operations in Bosnia-Herzegovina, particularly on the Herzegovinian front, are in dispute (See Janjić, "Civil war and the possibilities for peace," in Palau and Kumar, *Ex-Yugoslavia*, p. 288). The distinction between soldiers of the Croatian army (HV) and the Bosnian Croat army (HVO) was also not always clear, with much moving back and forth. The most common figure given for the troops of the Croatian Defense Councils (HVO) in Bosnia-Herzegovina by late 1991 is 50,000. Particularly active in Croatian-claimed areas of Herzegovina also were the paramilitary forces of the right-wing Croatian Party of Right (HSP) led by Dobroslav Paraga, and the Croatian Defense League (HOS), which had gained notoriety in its decision to go on the offensive in Vukovar, against Tudjman's policy. In January 1992, there were 16,000 HOS troops in western Herzegovina, and by March, 45,000. See Gow, "Military-Political Affiliations in the Yugoslav Conflict," pp. 19, 24.

139. This was made official on July 3, 1992, but it was stated publicly at this time and repeated many times until July, in the same way that Serbs in Croatia and Serbs in Bosnia-Herzegovina repeated declarations of their autonomy, then sovereignty, over many months. On May 7, 1992, in the Austrian city of Graz, Boban and Karadžić also met publicly to affirm the agreement between Tudjman and Milošević to divide Bosnia-Herzegovina and to determine the military strategy necessary to achieve it.

140. Unconfirmed reports at the time argued that the Turkish foreign minister, Hikmet Cetin, told Izetbegović in the first week of February, when they formally recognized Bosnian sovereignty, not to prepare militarily, although the quid pro quo was not specified. The assumption is that the United States was involved.

141. Commission on Security and Cooperation in Europe, *The Referendum on Independence in Bosnia-Hercegovina: February 29–March 1, 1992* (Washington: March 12, 1992), p. 23.

142. Kohl's treatment of the right-wing, domestic backlash against foreigners in 1992 seemed another example of his use of foreign issues for domestic political gain, for his government was able to negotiate a forced return of all Romanians illegally in Germany (estimated at 50,000 to 100,000, of whom 60 percent were Romany [Gypsies] claiming asylum on political grounds) for $20 million across the table with the Romanian government, agreed September 24,

1992. "Germany and Romania in Deportation Pact," *New York Times*, September 25, 1992, p. A7.

143.  According to Ambassador Nedzib Sacirbey, President Izetbegović's life-long friend and colleague (and father of the man chosen to represent Bosnia-Herzegovina in the United Nations), who was serving as the representative of Bosnia-Herzegovina to Washington before recognition, the first telephone call placed to announce Bosnian recognition was actually to President Tudjman to congratulate him on what was the primary reason for the decision—recognition of Croatia.

144.  Fighting had already begun in several places, including the Croatian attack on Kupres (see chapter 8). Two-and-one-half months after recognition of Slovenia and Croatia, and thirty-six days after the Bosnian referendum, the Europeans granted recognition April 6. The United States waited another day in response to pleas from Serbian diplomats not to create even greater political difficulties than necessary by announcing recognition on the anniversary of the German bombard-ment of Belgrade that started World War II in Yugoslavia (April 6, 1941). Baker's behavior suggests a strikingly similar dynamic to that of Hans-Dietrich Genscher: first wanting to get back into the action to regain leverage in Europe; under increasing pressure from politically influential commentators and a coalition of Republican conservatives, Reagan Democrats, and human rights liberals; and re-acting increasingly over the next months out of his own or (reportedly) his advisers' (such as Tutweiler) moral revulsion at the reports of Bosnian foreign minister Haris Silajdžić beginning in a meeting on April 14, 1992.

145.  There will be some dispute on this. Some active in the policy argue that the United States could not go against Germany and was careful to make this clear, while observers have suggested that the United States proceeded to pull the rug out from under them at this point, leaving the Germans to feel alone again and later (in August) even creating a potential parliamentary crisis when the United States insisted that Germany participate in the blockade of Adriatic ports to enforce the UN embargo.

146.  Note, for example, its early position in the UN Security Council debates, on the first Resolution, 713, where "The United States delegation, uniquely, con-tinued to classify the situation as one of 'outright military intervention against Croatia' by the JNA [YPA]." This argument was based, according to Secretary of State Baker, on the direct transfer to Croatia by Serbia of its policy toward Kosovo. See Weller, "The International Response to the Dissolution of the Socialist Federal Republic of Yugoslavia," p. 579.

# Chapter 7

1.  United Nations Security Council, Resolution 770, S/RES/770, August 13, 1992.

2.  UN Security Council Resolution 781, S/RES/781, October 9, 1992.

3.  In his study of identity and territory in the Pyrenees, *Boundaries: The Making of France and Spain in the Pyrenees* (University of California Press, 1989), p. 7, Peter

Sahlins writes, "The history of the boundary between 1659 and 1868, then, can hardly be summarized as the simple evolution from an empty zone to a precise line, but rather as the complex interplay of two notions of boundary—zonal and linear—and two ideas of sovereignty—jurisdictional and territorial. The two polarities can be found at any given moment in the history of the boundary, although the dominant but hardly unilinear tendency was the collapse of separate jurisdictional frontiers into a single territorial boundary line. The French Revolution gave to the idea of territory a specifically national content, while the early nineteenth-century states politicized the boundary line as the point where national territorial sovereignty found expression."

4. Charles Tilly, "Reflections on the History of European State-making," in Charles Tilly, ed., *The Formation of National States in Western Europe* (Princeton University Press, 1975), especially pp. 38–46.

5. Sahlins, *Boundaries*, p. 268.

6. Eugen J. Weber, *Peasants into Frenchmen: The Modernization of Rural France, 1870–1914* (Stanford University Press, 1976). This was a theme of Italian cinema in the 1970s, particularly the incorporation into Italian nationality through military conscription of southerners who still spoke a different language.

7. Particularly useful for the modern origins of nationalism and the different forms it took in the West is Benedict Anderson, *Imagined Communities: Reflections on the Origin and Spread of Nationalism* (London: Verso, 1983).

8. Arend Lijphart, *The Politics of Accommodation: Pluralism and Democracy in the Netherlands* (University of California Press, 1975), on the Netherlands; Aristide R. Zolberg, "The Making of Flemings and Walloons: Belgium: 1830–1914," *Journal of Interdisciplinary History*, vol. 5 (Summer 1974), pp. 179–235; and Benjamin Barber, *The Politics of Communal Liberty: The History of Freedom in a Swiss Mountain Canton* (Princeton University Press, 1974). The Swiss cantonal system is cited frequently as the model for multicultural societies, but the historical origins of the cantons and the decline of autonomy with economic modernization are the opposite of what most of its imitators think they see in it.

9. Ivo Banac makes this argument well in *The National Question in Yugoslavia: Origins, History, Politics* (Cornell University Press, 1984). A different approach to the fundamental differences in the process of state building between western and eastern Europe is in Perry Anderson, *Lineages of the Absolutist State* (London: New Left Books, 1974). See also Miroslav Hroch, "How Much Does Nation Formation Depend on Nationalism?" *East European Politics and Societies*, vol. 4 (Winter 1990), pp. 101–15. Particularly instructive of the complexity of the dynamic and malleable relation between states and nations in the region is the analysis of Romania in Katherine Verdery, *Transylvanian Villagers: Three Centuries of Political, Economic, and Ethnic Change* (University of California Press, 1983).

10. The "triune" people, called the "Kingdom of Serbs, Croats, and Slovenes," or colloquially, as the "Triune Kingdom," of "three peoples in one," until the King renamed it Yugoslavia in his period of dictatorship after 1929. See Aleksa Djilas, *The Contested Country: Yugoslav Unity and Communist Revolution, 1919–1953* (Harvard University Press, 1991), for a broad and informative history of Yugoslav national conflicts and harmonies.

11. Most leaders in Croatia, Slovenia, and Dalmatia saw this composite state in strategic terms, as a means of security against predator neighbors, especially Austria and Italy, while Serb leaders were compensated for their perceived loss of a national state with political power—that the country would be a constitutional monarchy under the Serbian royal house. For the negotiations at Versailles, see Ivo J. Lederer, *Yugoslavia at the Paris Peace Conference: A Study in Frontiermaking* (Yale University Press, 1963), and for the different conceptions of nation and debates over the constitution of the first Yugoslavia, see Ivo Banac, *The National Question in Yugoslavia*.

12. A quarrel between the Communist party in Macedonia and the Yugoslav party leadership over the meaning of the national question (whether Macedonian peasants had a right to land and Serbs—considered "colonists" by these Macedonians—did not) led the Macedonian communists to side with Bulgaria during the war and to be replaced by Yugoslavs sent from Tito's headquarters to organize a separate party organization. In the Greek civil war of 1944–49, 200,000–300,000 Macedonians fled from Greece (especially from Greek Macedonia) to Yugoslavia.

13. Interviews in Europe, 1991–92.

14. See E. A. Hammel, *The Yugoslav Labyrinth* (Institute of International Studies, University of California at Berkeley and Anthropology of East Europe Review, 1992). Whether these ideas can be separated from the willingness to use violence, if necessary, to maintain the distinction between citizens and foreigners necessary to pure-race principles is being tested currently in Germany, where anti-foreigner riots in 1992–93 led to calls for a revision of their liberal asylum laws instead of a revision of citizenship rights (so that, for example, even Turks living and working into the second and third generation in Germany could not become citizens, and those awaiting an asylum ruling could not get the papers to work).

15. For supporters of Ukrainian independence at the time, this contradiction was symbolized most by the speech in Kiev on August 1, 1991, by President George Bush.

16. Some observers insist that Milošević's tactics after 1988 were designed to push Slovenia out, and even most members of the Serb opposition parties by mid-July, 1991, admitted that they were "not unhappy" to see Slovenia go.

17. The final stage of the Helsinki Final Act, settling the border conflicts raised by World War II (1939–45), was the Treaty of Osimo of October 1, 1975, settling the Trieste question by accepting the temporary settlement of 1954 that gave Zone A to Italy and Zone B to Yugoslavia as permanent and creating a free industrial zone of twenty square kilometers of duty- and tax-free imports and rights to work freely on both sides. Nonetheless, Italians concerned about the fate of Italians in an independent Slovenia and Croatia demanded reconsideration of the treaty in 1991–95, and a border dispute between Italy and Slovenia (and then Croatia) over territorial waters and land borders had not been resolved by early 1995. Italy and Austria settled their border conflict over South Tyrol only in June 1992.

18. According to the 1908 census which Slovene sociologists have extensively analyzed. On Bosnians in Slovenia, see Silva Mežnarić, *"Bosanci": A kuda idu Slovenci nedeljom?* ("Bosnians": And where do Slovenes go on Sundays?) (Belgrade: Filip Višnjić, 1986).

19. This does not mean that the concept of "outsiders" and "foreigners" was absent; indeed, many were made painfully aware of their status, and there were many tensions over the application of citizenship rights. In the December 6, 1992, parliamentary and presidential elections, 10 percent of the electorate voted for the far right Slovene nationalist Zmago Jelinčič, who ran on the platform Slovenia for Slovenes and who accused Bosnian refugees of having fled economic deprivation rather than war. Laura Silber, "Slovene President Set For Re-election," *Financial Times*, December 7, 1992, p. 3; and Silber, "Slovenia's Voters Reject Balkans Diet of Nationalism," *Financial Times*, December 8, 1992, p. 2.

20. One of its latest manifestations was the refusal to consider discussions among the other republics in the mid-1980s about establishing a countrywide core curriculum for primary and secondary education (schooling in federal, socialist Yugoslavia was under local and republican jurisdiction only), including selections from all national literatures, to develop mutual awareness and appreciation of Yugoslavia's cultural differences and to break down the educational barriers to labor mobility. That Slovene objections prevented what even the Croatian leadership was willing at the time to contemplate (given its greater vigilance about maintaining separate cultural identity through linguistic distinctions from Serbs—a much more difficult task because of the closeness of Croatian and Serbian, and the reason that their confessional differences as Roman Catholic and Eastern Orthodox remained more important even in a socialist era of privatized religion). This meant that the primary means that made Western states into nations—education—was being denied Yugoslavs by those who had already achieved it.

21. See Dennison Rusinow, "To Be or Not to Be? Yugoslavia as Hamlet," UFSI [Universities Field Staff International] *Field Staff Reports*, no. 18 (1990–91), p. 7.

22. The large majority of Slovenes had come to believe this to be the case and the reason they "had to leave"; Tomaž Mastnak argues that those who label this flight to liberty as nationalism are the real nationalists, in Tomaž Mastnak, "Doing Good That Evil May Come: The Nationalism of Anti-Nationalists," unpublished manuscript.

23. But Croatia was without the legacy of individual rights and local self-government of the Austrian crownlands as in Slovenia, because its landed class joined the sphere of feudal reaction to Austrian reforms and belonged to the Hungarian half of the Dual Monarchy. Much of twentieth-century Croatia, including the area that was most ethnically heterogeneous, had actually belonged to the former military border (the *krajina*) protecting the Habsburg territory from the Ottoman empire and administered by the war office in Vienna, and it did not belong to central Europe in any of the ways usually meant.

24. Most influential in devising and propagating this argument was Mario Nobilo, who was appointed ambassador to the United Nations when Croatia gained membership on May 22, 1992.

25. Tomislav Marčinko, IDF managing editor, and Miroslav Lilić, Croatian Television (HTV) senior program editor, "Decree on Reporting from War Zones."

26. There is much debate over whether such a plan (RAM) existed, if this was its purpose, and who was behind it. It seemed to gather strength with the war in Bosnia-Herzegovina, in which the war gains of the Bosnian Serbs appeared to fulfill its military strategy. See discussion in chapter 5 on the Gow interpretation,

and the cautious elaboration in Dušan Janjić, "Gradjanski Rat i Mogućnost Mira u Bosni i Hercegovini (Civil war and the possibility of peace in Bosnia and Herzegovina)," in *Bosna i Hercegovina Izmedju Rata i Mira* (Bosnia and Herzegovina between war and peace) (Belgrade: Institut Društvenih Nauka, 1992), p. 119.

27. Written in either Latin or Cyrillic script, according to individual choice (and reflecting the religious element of ethnic identity in Bosnia-Herzegovina).

28. The critical principles of each of the constitutions, and the source of the greatest contention, were in their preambles. See Julie Mostov, "Democracy and the Politics of National Identity," paper prepared for the 1992 annual meeting of the American Political Science Association, Chicago, September 3–6, 1992, and her manuscript in progress using the Yugoslav case.

Karadžić was interviewed by Alan Little on BBC World Service, January 4, 1993. He expressed his unhappiness with the Vance-Owen Plan by saying "we must have our right to self-determination, that is, our right to secede, to create a state within a state of Bosnia." In documents presented by the Bosnian Serb delegation to the ICFY Geneva, January 22, 1993, Aleksa Buha, minister of foreign affairs of the "Republic of *Srpska*," insisted that the following passage, which he claimed was in the documents of the London conference but left out of the Vance-Owen Plan, be added to its preamble: "U.N. covenants on human rights according to which each nation has the right to self-government, to freely determine its political status, and to freely secure its economic, social, and political development."

29. Some prefer to call this the ethnic principle, but that introduces the confusion between nation—as a right to a state—and ethnicity—as a personal and cultural identity—mentioned above. As a claim to national rights in practice, however, the democratic principle of the expression of individual preference in a vote tends to be employed most by leaders who are looking to make ethnic identity national and claim control over territory thereby.

30. Aleksa Buha, minister of foreign affairs for the "Republic of *Srpska*," delegation to the ICFY Geneva, *Basic Information*, January 22, 1993, claimed territory "by historical right and by the right of ownership which can be verified in land registers."

31. The most famous was the great Serbian migration in 1690 in response to Emperor Leopold's invitation to the Serbian archbishop to bring his entire community to Vojvodina, but tensions during the 1991 war in Slavonia result from the postwar relocations of peasants in the 1920s and again in the 1940s from unarable, impoverished land in the interior of Croatia and Bosnia-Herzegovina to rich farmland abandoned by or expropriated from war collaborators.

Ivo Banac calls this the Jacobin principle to juxtapose it more clearly to the historicist principle and to portray Serbian state ideology as expansionist and integrationist. For his analysis of Serbian ideology, see Banac, *The National Question*, pp. 70–114.

32. Albanians claimed they were about 40 percent of the republic's population, whereas the Macedonian government insisted they were only 15 or 20 percent. The dispute was so politically threatening to Macedonian internal stability that the Council of Europe and the European Union funded an extraordinary census in June 1994 so as to establish the real numbers. Although radical Albanian leaders attempted again to effect a boycott, the European pressure became too great an embarrassment. After

much delay, they did participate, but found reasons in the procedures of the census to dispute the results showing their proportion (as citizens, not as residents) to be 23 percent (the notable lack of preparation and knowledge about Macedonia and its ethnic composition of the International Census Observer Mission did give them some causes for criticism). (Interview material and "Macedonian Census Results," *Radio Free Europe/ Radio Liberty Daily Report*, November 15, 1994, reporting results released by the Macedonian National Statistics Bureau.)

33. Vojin Dimitrijević, "The Yugoslav Precedent: Keep What You Have," in Anthony Borden and others, eds., *Breakdown: War & Reconstruction in Yugoslavia* (London: Institute for War and Peace Reporting, 1992), pp. 62–64.

34. In the second Yugoslavia, 26 percent of the Serbian population (according to the 1991 census) lived outside of the republic of Serbia.

35. Gligorov is a Belgrade-born, ethnically Macedonian political theorist. Vladimir Gligorov, "Is What Is Left Right?" in János Mátyas Kovács, ed., *Transition to Capitalism? The Communist Legacy in Eastern Europe* (New Brunswick, NJ: Transaction Publishers, 1994), pp. 147–72.

36. See Milan Andrejevich, "The Sandžak: The Next Balkan Theater of War?" *RFE/RL Research Report* (November 27, 1992), pp. 26–34, and *Memorandum on the Establishment of a Special Status for Sanjak* (Novi Pazar: Muslim National Council of Sanjak, 1993).

37. The SDA leadership of Bosnia-Herzegovina, in fact, began openly in 1993 to claim the Sandžak as "Bosnian territory" on historicist grounds; see chapter 10. Moreover, the important role in the SDA leadership of people from the Sandžak—the Sandžaklije—such as Ejup Ganić, was even greater than the analogous role of Herzegovinians in the HDZ leadership in Croatia. On the early organizing of the SDA in the Sandžak, see Lenard Cohen, *Broken Bonds: The Disintegration of Yugoslavia* (Westview Press, 1994), p. 144.

38. The Cvetković-Maček *Sporazum* to give Croatia autonomy in August 1939, signed between the Yugoslav prime minister (a Serb) and the leader of the dominant Croatian party, the Croatian Peasant party. President Tudjman declared this right and goal in public frequently, including in an interview with this author in Davos, Switzerland, on January 30, 1992. For the borders, see Greg Englefield, *Yugoslavia, Croatia, Slovenia: Re-emerging Boundaries*, Territory Briefing 3 (Durham, England: International Boundaries Research Unit, 1992), pp. 4, 6; and Mladen Klemenčić, *Territorial Proposals for the Settlement of the War in Bosnia-Hercegovina*, Boundary and Territory Briefing vol. 1, no. 3 (Durham, England: International Boundaries Research Unit, 1994), pp. 14–16, 28.

39. See Klemenčić, *Territorial Proposals for the Settlement of the War in Bosnia-Hercegovina*, pp. 30–33.

40. Confidential interviews with visiting U.S. Senators in August 1992 and a general survey of the press.

41. Commission on Security and Cooperation in Europe, *The Referendum on Independence in Bosnia-Hercegovina, February 29–March 1, 1992* (Washington, D.C., March 12, 1992), p. 11.

42. The irony was not lost on nonnationalist Serbs that it was originally a Croatian idea that a state should be based on their view that the south Slavs were

one, albeit triune, people, but that it had now become a primary weapon in the Serbian fight against Albanians in Kosovo.

43. Greek policy demonstrates that not only Yugoslavs seek to use national myths for governance. As Jonathan Eyal puts it, in "Managing the Balkan Conundrum," *Breakdown*, p. 75: "Athens claims to represent a homogeneous nation which, apart from Muslims in Western Thrace, does not contain any other ethnic minorities. Macedonia's independence, with its impact on the Slavs in Greece's north, will expose this claim."

44. "It Could Do the Most Harm to Vojvodina Hungarians," NÉPSZA-BAD-SÁG, July 9, 1991, in FBIS, *Daily Report: East Europe*, July 11, 1991, p. 40.

45. The Treaty of Trianon created large Hungarian minorities in Yugoslavia, Romania, Czechoslovakia (largely the Slovak republic), and Ukraine and in territories the MDF considered Hungarian as well, especially Vojvodina (an autonomous province of Serbia) and Transylvania (in Romania).

46. Accounts of the sale vary from 36,000 to 80,000 rifles. The scandal broke in January 1991. The late József Antall's favorite way to phrase his government's policy did open the way to consideration of innovative solutions to the national question in eastern Europe—that in the new world order "borders should take on a different meaning than they had in the past"—but it was not reassuring to those who had historically justified suspicions. By 1993, before Antall's death from cancer in December, public opinion in Hungary had seemed to distance itself from this sentiment, saying that "frontiers" were not an open question; such sentiments are, however, vulnerable to politicians' rhetoric and economic conditions.

47. Ralph Johnson, principal deputy assistant Secretary of State for European and Canadian Affairs in the U.S. Department of State, transparently revealed this confusion in relation to the Yugoslav situation in testimony on U.S. policy, June 11, 1992, before the subcommittee on European Affairs of the Senate Foreign Relations Committee: "to reiterate, we are prepared to accept any outcome in the region so long as it is based on:—Change achieved peacefully and democratically, consistent with CSCE principles;—Respect for all existing borders, and change to those borders only through peaceful and consensual means;—Support for democracy and the rule of law, emphasizing the key role of elections in the democratic process;—Safeguarding of human rights, based on full respect for the individual and including equal treatment of members of minority groups; and—Respect for international law and obligations, especially adherence to the Helsinki Final Act and the Charter of Paris."

## Chapter 8

1. This characterizes much of the commentary on the Yugoslav breakup. An example of a nonparticipant can be found in Paula Franklin Lytle, "U.S. Policy Toward the Demise of Yugoslavia: The 'Virus of Nationalism'," *East European Politics and Societies*, vol. 6 (Fall 1992), pp. 303–18.

2. The Croat writer Slavenka Drakulić captures this essence in "The Smothering Pull of Nationhood," *YugoFax*, October 31, 1991, p. 3.

3. As discussed in chapter 5, the origins of the National Socialist party (Nazis) of Germany are instructive, that the partisan loyalties of people—especially the unemployed—often depend most on who seeks them out and organizes them. See F. L. Carsten, *The Rise of Fascism* (University of California Press, 1982).

4. See discussion and data in Dušan Janjić, "Gradjanski Rat i Mogućnost Mira u Bosni i Hercegovini" [Civil war and the possibility of peace in Bosnia and Herzegovina], pp. 112–18, and in Vladimir Goati, "Politički Život Bosne i Hercegovine 1989–1992 [Political life of Bosnia and Herzegovina 1989–1992]," pp. 55, 57, and 61. Both in *Bosna i Hercegovina Izmedju Rata i Mira* (Belgrade: Institut Društvenih Nauka, 1992).

5. See Mark Thompson, *Forging War: The Media in Serbia, Croatia and Bosnia-Herzegovina* (Article 19, International Centre Against Censorship: May 1994).

6. Janjić, "Gradjanski Rat," p. 107, provides a summary for the case of Bosnia-Herzegovina, but the phenomenon was widespread. Mary E. McIntosh, Martha Abele Mac Iver, Daniel G. Abele, and David B. Nolle find, in their empirical study in 1991–92 of attitudes toward ethnic minorities, "Minority Rights and Majority Rule: Ethnic Tolerance in Romania and Bulgaria," *Social Forces* (forthcoming, March 1995), that the greatest predictor of ethnic intolerance among a wide range of determinants (education, age, gender, ethnic composition of community, rural/urban origin, political ideology, democratic values, economic outlook) was the "perception of threat from the target group . . . to one's state or personal security," specifically a possible impending attack from a neighboring country associated with the ethnic minority. They conclude that the "importance of actual and imagined irredentist challenges . . . suggests that assurances of secure borders could go a long way toward reducing ethnic tension in both countries."

7. Svetlana Slapšak, in "Bestial Words, Bestial War," *New York Times*, May 25, 1993, p. A23, describes this preparation in Serbia with unusual candor, but wonders therefore whether intellectuals who fought at the time for freedom of expression, for the rights of dissidents regardless of their message (as in the petition-writing campaign among intellectuals to support Vojislav Šešelj, before he became a right-wing radical extremist and stood accused by the international community as a war criminal for his activities in Croatia and eastern Bosnia), should instead have worried about protecting democracy. Which is more harmful to democracy, the expression of racist stereotypes or the measures taken to discourage such expression?

8. On the last part, see Janjić, "Gradjanski Rat," p. 107.

9. The charges and countercharges from both sides include numerous instances of actual or rumored rape, murder, and poisoning. Mark Thompson, *A Paper House* (Pantheon Books, 1992), pp. 129–30, provides needed perspective. The documentary and sensational literature together is huge; an attempt at neutrality can be found in Branko Horvat, *Kosovsko Pitanje* [The Kosovo question], 2d suppl. ed. (Zagreb: Globus, 1989). Documentation of human rights abuses can be found in the publications of Helsinki Watch (a division of Human Rights Watch, New York and Washington): *Increasing Turbulence: Human Rights in Yugoslavia* (October 1989); *Yugoslavia: Crisis in Kosovo*, with the International Helsinki Federation (March 1990); and *Yugoslavia: Human Rights Abuses in Kosovo 1990–1992* (October 1992); and in the Amnesty International Reports: *Yugo-*

*slavia: Torture and Deliberate and Arbitrary Killings in War Zones* (November 1991); *Europe: A Compilation Document: Concerns in Europe November 1990–April 1991, Human Rights and the Need for a Fair Asylum Policy* (November 1991); and *Yugoslavia: Further Reports of Torture and Deliberate and Arbitrary Killings in War Zones* (March 1992). See also Thompson, *A Paper House*, p. 128, and Brian Hall, *The Impossible Country: A Journey through the Last Days of Yugoslavia* (Boston: David R. Godine, Publisher, 1994), pp. 235–89.

10. Silva Mežnarić, "Gender as an Ethnic Marker: Violence, Women and Identity Politics in Albanian-Serbian Conflict," in V. Moghadam, ed., *Identity, Politics and Women* (Oxford University Press, 1992). On the role of Croatian symbols and the media in both Croatia and Serbia in generating emotions that were "increasingly hysterical," and the central role in the "Belgrade press's campaign of disinformation against the new regime in Zagreb [of] the idea that the latter was preparing genocide against the Serbs," see Ivo Goldstein, "Serbs in Croatia, Croatia in Yugoslavia," *East European Reporter*, Autumn/Winter 1990, pp. 65–66.

11. See Robert M. Hayden, "Recounting the Dead: The Rediscovery and Redefinition of Wartime Massacres in Late- and Post-Communist Yugoslavia," in Rubie S. Watson, ed., *Memory, History, and Opposition under State Socialism* (Santa Fe: School of American Research Press, forthcoming). For similar developments in Serbia, see Bette Denich, "Dismembering Yugoslavia: Nationalist Ideologies and the Symbolic Revival of Genocide," *American Ethnologist* (May 1994), pp. 367–90. For evidence that this is not only a Yugoslav phenomenon, see the fascinating analysis by Pamela Ballinger of Italian cave discoveries around Trieste, "The Politics of Submersion: History, collective memory and ethnic group boundaries in Trieste," Johns Hopkins University, Department of Anthropology, February 1993.

12. Misha Glenny provides numerous examples in *The Fall of Yugoslavia: The Third Balkan War* (Penguin, 1992), for example, pp. 66, 123. Another good source is *YugoFax/WarReport*, a periodical "critical briefing on the conflict in Yugoslavia" by journalists from all regions of the former country and others concerned to counteract the nationalized and censored flow of information, based in London. In a countrywide public opinion survey in May–June 1990 (a stratified, random sample of 4,232 persons over the age of 18), carried out by a consortium of the primary opinion survey institutions in each republic, television was found to be "the most popular source of information" about public affairs and government programs; between 45 percent (in Slovenia) and 64 percent (in Montenegro) used television as a regular source, while only 3 to 8 percent never watched television. "Public Opinion Survey on the Federal Executive Council's Social and Economic Reform," *Yugoslav Survey*, vol. 31, no. 3 (1990), pp. 3–5.

13. The newspaper *Oslobodjenje* challenged the constitutionality of the press law in March 1991 and won, but not without substantial and continuing harassment of its editorial board from members of the government.

14. For example, the column in the biweekly *Duga* by Brana Crnčević and the writings of Vojko Djogo and Vojislav Lubarda, who made fortunes on this theme, as did many others. The theme of *tamni vilajet* can be heard among Croats as well.

15. Its editor was given a lifetime achievement award by the Serbian government in 1991; letters of protest or defense from persons identified in its pages were rarely published.

16.  Mario Nobilo, in an interview in the presidential palace, Zagreb, July 16, 1991.

17.  Tomislav Marčinko, IDF managing editor, and Miroslav Lilić, Croatian Television (HTV) senior program editor, "Decree on reporting from war zones."

18.  A good summary for Croatia by Patrick Moore can be found in "The Media in Eastern Europe," *Radio Free Europe/Radio Liberty (RFE/RL) Research Report*, May 7, 1993, pp. 25–26. Milan Andrejevich discusses the situation in Slovenia, Serbia, and Montenegro, pp. 33–35, and Louis Zanga in Kosovo, p. 35. The HDZ also exerted its control over the printers to keep *Danas* from publishing until past debts were paid. Then *Danas* tried to publish in Slovenia or Austria, and the HDZ used its control over 80 percent of newsstands and the distribution system to put *Danas* out of business.

19.  Slapšak, "Bestial Words, Bestial War." On the campaign in Croatia against "five witches"—women journalists and writers suspected of not being sufficiently nationalist—see Vesna Kesić, "The High Price of Free Speech: Confessions of a Croatian Witch," *Women's Review of Books*, June 1993, pp. 16–17.

20.  This was not for lack of trying to terrorize opposition media, such as by sending thugs to vandalize the offices of the television station YUTEL and the weekly *Vreme*. Author's interviews with staff at YUTEL and *Vreme*.

21.  It would be interesting to speculate what the effect would have been if the normal (constitutional) rotation of the position of president to the HDZ (Croat) or SDS (Serb) had occurred. Was this initial advantage due to the SDA's tenure in that position and the international community's tendency to deal with single, rather than collective, leaders, or was it due to the ambiguity about Serb and Croat commitment to Bosnia and the obvious commitment of the Muslims in Bosnia-Herzegovina to its integrity and sovereignty within its republican borders?

22.  Government ministers focused their public speeches abroad on Bosnian history; for example, in a speech entitled "The Case for Bosnian Recognition," at The Woodrow Wilson Center, Washington D.C., on January 9, 1992, Haris Silajdžić (at the time minister of international cooperation of the Federal Republic of Bosnia-Herzegovina) gave a discourse instead on Bosnia in the Middle Ages. New histories were written and state symbols, such as a crest and a flag, were created. To what extent this represented a state's creating a nation, as the process in places such as Belarus might more properly be described, depends on one's ideological views toward Bosnia. And as historical and anthropological scholarship shows, this relation between state and nation is always dynamic, a relationship of interaction, and not one represented by unalterable givens. Foreign scholars have contributed to this process also. An example is Noel Malcolm, *Bosnia: A Short History* (New York University Press, 1994). See especially Robert Donia and John Fine, *Bosnia and Herzegovina: A Tradition Betrayed* (Columbia University Press, 1994).

23.  Some argue that extreme nationalist leaders in Bosnia-Herzegovina, such as the Serbs Radovan Karadžić and Nikola Koljević and the Croat Mate Boban, were more able to hold to their views that people could not live together because they originated in ethnically pure villages. *WarReport*, June 1993. A representative of the opposing view, architect Bogdan Bogdanović, who was mayor of Belgrade

from 1982 to 1986, is "Murder of the City," *New York Review of Books*, May 27, 1993, p. 20.

24. Silva Mežnarić, "Bosnia and Hercegovina: Selected Background Data and Analysis on Refugees, Migration, and Development," paper prepared for the workshop on Peace in Bosnia and Herzegovina, The Wilson Center, Washington, D.C., February 10–12, 1993 (Zagreb, January 1993), p. 12, and subsequent conversations.

25. Secret agreements between Bosnian Serbs and Croats also shaped the military outcome in Vareš, Kiseljak, Kupres, Jajce, and Bosanski/Slavonski Brod, and their mutual cease-fire largely held after the first offensive in 1992.

26. None of the fighting, particularly in Bosnia-Herzegovina, can be understood without placing the political goals of these wars at center stage, but this is a combination of the classical military tactic of cutting communication lines and of the political objective, including the reformation of loyalties and identities through propaganda. A. Ross Johnson reports an example from the Croatian wars in the summer of 1991, when the YPA cut local television links between Slavonia and Zagreb and replaced them with feeds solely from Belgrade. "The Self-Destruction of the Yugoslav People's Army" (November 1991), p. 3.

27. A. D. Smith, "States and Homelands: the Social and Geopolitical Implications of National Territory," *Millennium: Journal of International Studies*, vol. 10, no. 3, p. 187.

28. Marcel Fafchamps writes, "Even in developed economies, the occurrence of war or natural calamities revives solidarity and mutual assistance . . . whenever economic and social conditions are such that individual survival is extremely uncertain without some form of mutual insurance, informal solidarity mechanisms tend to emerge naturally." "Solidarity Networks in Preindustrial Societies: Rational Peasants with a Moral Economy," *Economic Development and Cultural Change*, vol. 41 (October 1992), pp. 148–49.

29. On the origins in patriarchal culture of patriotic loyalty, symbolized by this motto of the British crown, "Shame on him who thinks evil of it," see Julian Pitt-Rivers, "Honour and Social Status," in J. G. Peristiany, ed., *Honor and Shame: The Values of Mediterranean Society* (University of Chicago Press, 1966), pp. 19–78.

30. On rituals about death, see Denich, "Dismembering Yugoslavia."

31. The speech of common people caught in the war is not of the ethnic identities commonly asserted by outsiders but of the far stronger personal bonds of *komšije*—neighbors—and *kumstvo*—ritual kinship.

32. Although there is yet insufficient evidence of a deliberate policy, the widespread rape of women—particularly of Muslim women by Serbian soldiers—was a consequence of this explosive combination of mass media campaign, political rhetoric, rural culture, and war, helped along too well by pervasive drunkenness. It is true that fears of the demographic shift as a result of higher Muslim birthrates in Kosovo, Macedonia, and Bosnia-Herzegovina preoccupied nationalists in Slovenia, Croatia, and Serbia in the 1960s and 1980s, but whether this was a motivation for a campaign of rape by Serbian forces needs further analysis. Eyewitness accounts of massive rape in Bosnia-Herzegovina began to appear in Western media in October 1992: see Slavenka Drakulić, "Rape after Rape after Rape," *New York Times*, December 13, 1992, section 4, p. 17; and Amnesty International, *Bosnia-*

*Herzegovina: Rape and sexual abuse by armed forces* (London: January 1993). See also Alexandra Stiglmayer, ed., *Mass Rape: The War Against Women in Bosnia-Herzegovina* (University of Nebraska Press, 1994).

33. The president of the third Yugoslavia, from May 1992 to June 1993, Serbian writer Dobrica Ćosić, specialized in novels of World War I and II, for example, and President Tudjman of Croatia wrote a Ph.D. dissertation in history, subsequently published, to revise downward the numbers of dead in concentration camps under fascist Croatia during World War II. For a view on the storm over numbers this caused, see Ljubo Boban, "Jasenovac and the Manipulation of History," *East European Politics and Societies* vol. 4 (Fall 1990), pp. 580–92, and the comment by Robert M. Hayden, "Balancing Discussion of Jasenovac and the Manipulation of History," and Boban's reply, "Still More Balance on Jasenovac and the Manipulation of History" in vol. 6 (Spring 1992), pp. 207–17. "Like all nationalists of former Yugoslavia, the Serbians exaggerate their losses, sometimes claiming that more than 1 million Serbs were murdered in concentration camps of fascist Croatia alone. (Realistic estimates put the total of Serbian casualties between 500,000 and 600,000. Probably half were civilian victims of Croatian fascism.) Serbian nationalists are, however, right when they point out that Serbian casualties were both absolutely and relatively larger than those of any other Yugoslav group, and that only Serbs, Jews, and Gypsies were the victims of systematic and planned extermination. But Croatian and Muslim casualties were extremely high as well, and a considerable number of them were civilians who fell victim to Serbian extremists." Aleksa Djilas, "The Nation that Wasn't," *The New Republic*, September 20, 1992, p. 30. The most respectable numbers are those from the demographic study of Bogoljub Kočović, Žrtve drugog svetskog rata u Jugoslaviji [World War II victims in Yugoslavia] (Longon: Naše delo, 1985), calculating 487,000 Serb losses in the war.

34. The losses in World War II were greatest in Bosnia. "Of its 2.8 million people, 400,000 perished—every sixth Serb, eighth Croat, and twelfth Muslim." Djilas, "The Nation that Wasn't," p. 30.

35. This is not to engage in the ethical question, for this seems to become a vicious circle of accusation and redemption, such as the Croatian retort that the murder of 16,000 to 17,000 detainees returned by the British from Bleiburg in 1945 settled whatever question of Croatian guilt there might be and for which certainly Tudjman and contemporary Croats should not be held responsible. In this case also numbers were being inflated under nationalist attention in 1990–92. See, for example, Hall, *The Impossible Country*, pp, 26, 42.

36. "U šumi," "leave for the forests" was the common expression for joining the Partisan forces.

37. As discussed in chapter 2, the first question on acquaintance in Slavonia in the 1945–90 period was not "what do you do?" but "in whose house do you live?" In an interview with the author, February 5, 1992, in Belgrade, journalist and war correspondent Miloš Vasić argued that the pattern of warfare could be described less by geographic coordinates than by altitude. Paul Shoup concludes from an analysis of the ethnic composition of Serbian-inhabited regions of Croatia that districts most affected by the fighting were "not those where either Serbs or Croats

are in a clear majority but those where the two groups are more or less evenly balanced." "The Future of Croatia's Border Regions," *RFE/RL Report on Eastern Europe*, November 29, 1991, p. 32.

38.   1.3 million Greeks left Asia Minor, and about 400,000 Turks left Greece. The division of India and Pakistan involved about 12 million Hindu and Muslim refugees.

39.   According to James Gow in *Legitimacy and the Military: The Yugoslav Crisis*, (St. Martin's Press, 1992), p. 69, 25,661 Serbs and Montenegrins left Kosovo between 1981 and 1988.

40.   Robert M. Hayden refers to this as "constitutional nationalism" in "Constitutional Nationalism in the Formerly Yugoslav Republics," *Slavic Review*, vol. 51 (Winter 1992), pp. 654–73.

41.   Misha Glenny describes the pattern of intimidation and arbitrary violence against Serbs in Croatia in "The Massacre of Yugoslavia," *New York Review of Books*, January 30, 1992, pp. 30–35. On Serbian ethnic cleansing in Bosnia-Herzegovina, see *The Ethnic Cleansing of Bosnia-Hercegovina*, a staff report to the Committee on Foreign Relations, United States Senate (August 1992).

42.   *The Ethnic Cleansing of Bosnia-Hercegovina*, pp. 1–3.

43.   On population transfers taking place in Croatia, against Article 49 of the Fourth Geneva Convention, see Žarko Paunović, "Politics of Transfer," *YugoFax*, February 3, 1992, p. 3. On the practice of postwar population transfers in the entire region, see Charles Gati, "From Sarajevo to Sarajevo," *Foreign Affairs*, Fall 1992, pp. 64–78.

44.   For the conflict in Srebrenica, see David B. Ottaway, "Bosnian Muslims Bar Bid to Evacuate Town; Sarajevo Government Spurns 3-way Talks," *Washington Post*, April 7, 1993, p. A24. Under persistent criticism from the Bosnian government for assisting ethnic cleansing, the UN forces refused to assist an evacuation from Sarajevo organized by the Red Cross the previous November. See *Financial Times*, November 11, 1992, p. 3.

45.   Lt. Colonel Bob Stewart, in his memoir of his days commanding British UN soldiers in central Bosnia in 1993, *Broken Lives: A Personal View of the Bosnian Conflict* (HarperCollins, 1993), pp. 318–19, writes: "Bosnia is certainly complex beyond anyone's dreams. There are far more than three sides—Serb, Croat and Muslim—we hear about in the media. There are factions within groups and groups within factions. And without an established order, these different elements had created a situation as close to anarchy as I have yet witnessed. . . . Even the differentiation between military and civilian is impossible. . . . A civilian one minute is a soldier the next. . . . the war is mainly being fought by civilians. . . . A civilian soldier probably knows little about the established 'rules of war'. The use of detainees for digging trenches in the front line, where they are liable to be shot by their own side, might make sense to him. But both the ICRC and we were incensed by it. It is strictly against the Geneva Convention, we shout in exasperation. What's the Geneva Convention, comes the reply? How can someone like Commander Leko in Turbe be expected to know all the details of the 'civilized' conduct of war? Less than two years ago he was a teacher. He's had very little military training. What he is actually doing, of course, is defending his home, or what is left of it."

46. "Akashi Slams Serb Human Rights Violations," *RFE/RL Daily Report*, July 25, 1994. See also "Serbs Step Up Ethnic Cleansing," *RFE/RL Daily Report*, August 2, 1994.

47. Stephen Kinzer, "Croats Send Back Bosnian Refugees," *New York Times*, October 31, 1992, p. 3.

48. Aleksandra Mijalković, "The Vukovar Syndrome," *East European Reporter*, May/June 1992, p. 16.

49. Especially Zenica, Tuzla, Kakanj, and Vitez, towns that the Vance-Owen Plan for Bosnia-Herzegovina placed in majority "Muslim provinces" and that Mežnarić describes as "highly industrialized, ecologically destroyed, and densely populated." "Bosnia and Hercegovina: Selected Background Data," p. 8.

50. In the case of Bosnia-Herzegovina, Mežnarić looks for data to answer the question, Were the "three national groups, at the brink of the war, different to such an extent that the current clash would have been expected?" She finds no evidence in attitudinal data about social differences or tension but strong evidence in regional differences. According to economic and demographic data, there was an "ever wider developmental gap between specific regions in Bosnia," which can be linked to ethnic differences if pushed. "Bosnia and Hercegovina: Selected Background Data," pp. 4–5. Sociologists and economists in Zagreb warned in 1990 that tensions in Knin, Lika, and other areas subsequently part of the area in which Serbs claimed autonomy were a result of failed industrialization and increasing poverty and unemployed industrial workers that demanded immediate attention. Developmental programs were drawn up but rejected by the nationalist majority in the Croatian parliament.

51. Austro-Hungarian policy toward Bosnia-Herzegovina after it obtained trusteeship in 1878 was to insist on separate administration so as to prevent its union with either Serbia or Croatia and the creation of a strong south Slav state to its south. This, however, increased the confusion about where Bosnia-Herzegovina lay. Moreover, it left a bitter legacy. See Robert Lee Wolff, *The Balkans In Our Time* (W. W. Norton & Co., 1967), p. 96, on the striking parallel in method with the current period, such as the 1913 statement by the German Kaiser to the Serbs regarding the borders of a new Albanian state: "When His Majesty Emperor Franz Joseph demands something, the Serbian government must give way, and if it does not then Belgrade will be bombarded and occupied until the will of His Majesty is fulfilled." Wolff adds, "It was perhaps little wonder if this incendiary talk encouraged the Austrian Foreign Minister, Berchtold, to think highly of the policy of ultimatums to Serbia. The point is worth stressing, since the outbreak of World War I was then less than a year in the future," p. 94.

52. Mežnarić, "Bosnia and Hercegovina: Selected Background Data," p. 7. More than half of the Bosnian population (58 percent) had not moved, however, but remained in the rural or semirural settlements of less than 2,000 inhabitants in which they were born (p. 12).

53. Dr. Srdjan Bogosavljević, "Bosnia and Hercegovina in the Mirror of Statistics," p. 13. The fact that Serbs were a minority where they were once a majority (on the basis of which Bosnian Serb nationalists referred to Muslim-inhabited villages and towns in eastern Bosnia, for example, as "Serb land") was in part due to this economic emigration in 1971–91 and in part the result of the genocidal

murders of World War II. In the 67 of the total 108 communes in Bosnia-Herzegovina where population declined between 1963 and 1981, the majority had a Serbian majority and were in the *krajina* region and eastern Herzegovina; of those, only seven saw rising income, and of those, four were among the first targets of Serbian "cleansing." Mežnarić, "Bosnia and Hercegovina: Selected Background Data," p. 7.

54.  Vladimir Goati, "Politički Život Bosne i Hercegovine," p. 57. See also the story on Olovo, for example, "Ethnic Conflicts in Eastern Bosnia Described," *Borba*, December 8, 1991, p. 11, cited in Foreign Broadcast Information Service, *Daily Report: East Europe*, December 30, 1991, pp. 40–41 (hereafter FBIS, *East Europe*).

55.  John Burns's portrait of a 21-year-old Bosnian Serb soldier, Borislav Herak, who admitted and was convicted by a military court (on March 30, 1993) of war crimes, including "genocide, mass murder, rape and looting," along with the individual murder of twenty-nine people, provides almost a stereotype. "A Killer's Tale—a Special Report: A Serbian Fighter's Path of Brutality," *New York Times*, November 27, 1992, p. A1.

56.  On the same type of behavior and personality in Croatia in April 1991, see the description of anti-Serb, right-wing Croat gangs in Zadar in Thompson, *A Paper House*, pp. 261–64.

57.  James Gow, "The Role of the Military in the Yugoslav War of Dissolution," *Armed Conflicts in the Balkans and European Security*, an international conference April 20–22, 1993 (Ljubljana, Center for Strategic Studies, Ministry of Defence, June 1993), p. 74.

58.  Gow, "The Role of the Military"; Janjić, "Gradjanski Rat," p. 122; and Milan Vego, "Federal Army Deployments in Bosnia and Herzegovina," *Jane's Intelligence Review*, vol. 4 (October 1992), p. 445. Three army corps, totaling 45,000 men, were deployed in Bosnia-Herzegovina: the 17th corps at Tuzla, the 5th at Banja Luka, and the 4th at Sarajevo.

59.  Each brigade had several subordinate battalions, composed in turn of four or five eighty-two-man companies, 75 percent of which were ethnic Croats, drawn from the republic internal security police reservists, TDF members, and former YPA officers. It is equipped with light AFVs and ATGMs, and M-84 battle tanks produced in Croatia. MUP forces in Croatia were also in action with APCs and helicopters against Serbs in *krajina* even before the declaration of independence and included a special forces unit, "Blue Berets," for counterterrorism. David Isby, "Yugoslavia 1991—Armed Forces in Conflict," *Jane's Intelligence Review*, vol. 3 (September 1991), pp. 401, 403.

60.  Janjić discusses the "close relations between Croat army and proCroatian and proMuslim paramilitary and military formations in Bosnia-Herzegovina," from shared information and cooperation in propaganda, to the inclusion of actual units of the Croatian army in the war in "Croat areas" of Bosnia-Herzegovina, and the important role in heightening tensions and worsening relations with the YPA of returning Bosnian citizens, primarily ethnic Croats, who had been living or fighting in Croatia. "Gradjanski Rat," p. 120.

61.  According to a TANJUG (Yugoslav news agency) report of September 21, 1994, "Slovenia armed Bosnian Muslims in 1991, months before a civil war broke

out in Bosnia-Herzegovina in April 1992. This was evident from classified material of the Slovenian Defense Ministry, said a source which insisted on anonymity because of the secret nature of the documents. . . . In December 1991 and January–February 1992, at least 15 cargo planes carried different arms from Ljubljana to Bosnia . . . intended for Muslim paramilitary preparations to attack the then Yugoslav People's Army and the Bosnian Serbs" with the participation of a "Slovenian special army and police units." The arms trade from Slovenia and through Slovene ports had yielded weapons for Croatia as well. By 1994, however, the primary conduit for arms to Bosnia was from Iran through Croatian airports and seaports. According to Roger Cohen of the *New York Times*, Croatian defense minister Gojko Šušak said, "What I need, I get. . . . The arms market is saturated, so saturated you would pay three times the price if you got things legally." He added that Croatia was providing the Bosnian government army with antitank weapons, cannons, machine guns, and mortar ammunition. See "Arms Trafficking to Bosnia Goes on Despite Embargo," *New York Times*, November 5, 1994, p. A1.

62. An exception to joining one's local defense unit, whatever its party allegiance, followed a pattern seen in eastern Croatia: where there was a choice among units, volunteers would tend to choose the better-organized force in hopes of better personal security. Thus, in multiethnic Sarajevo, Bosnian Croats who identified as Sarajevans and Bosnians nonetheless chose to join the HVO rather than the Bosnian army because the HVO's earlier initiative had made it better organized (this was no longer an option after the fall of 1993 when the Bosnian government required HVO units in Sarajevo to integrate into the Bosnian army).

63. Serbia mobilized both police and TDF forces in early July, threatening to join TDF units of Serbs from Bosnia and move to protect Serbs in Croatia if the YPA did not. Isby, "Yugoslavia 1991—Armed Forces in Conflict," p. 403.

64. Ustasha comes from the verb to rebel; it was the name of the stormtroop units of the Croatian fascist state during World War II that were responsible for executing the terror and genocide against Jews, Romany (Gypsies), and Serbs. Four months before the Bosnian war began, 16,000 HOS troops were reported based in western Herzegovina. By mid-March, the HOS had mobilized 45,000. James Gow, "Military-Political Affiliations in the Yugoslav Conflict," *RFE/RL Research Report*, May 15, 1992, pp. 19, 25.

65. Janjić, "Gradjanski Rat," pp. 124–27.

66. Foreign mercenaries have fought on all sides of the war, the most colorful being the Serb-Australian Captain Dragan, who organized the "Martićevci" in Croatian *krajina*. West European fascists from Germany, France, and England joined Paraga's Black Legion, Islamic mujahedin from Iran, Saudi Arabia, Egypt, Algeria, Libya, Pakistan, and Morocco, some of whom had fought in the Afghan war, were recruited or volunteered for Bosnia, and 1,000 Russians were on the Serbian side in Bosnia by December 1992 (and Cossack units were forming to go in January 1993).

67. In villages in Bosnia-Herzegovina people report that arms appear out of nowhere, and unconfirmed but persuasive suspicions are that territorial defense forces distributed weapons to Serb villagers in the second half of 1991. Countless stories from villagers who left Bosnia-Herzegovina report this moment as decisive. They speak of neighbors appearing with arms and finding themselves without, except the random rifle in the barn that had not been fired for who-knows-how

long and which they must learn rapidly how to use. The record suggests, however, that all sides did so. For example, "Croatian 'Pro-Fascist' Party Members in Bosnia," TANJUG, April 6, 1992, in FBIS, *East Europe*, April 7, 1992, p. 38, reports on weapons being distributed to SDA members in Sarajevo, Bosanski Šamac, Bihać, Vlasenica, and Tuzla. The article adds that a report presented to the Bosnian presidency estimated that there were "about 600,000 armed people" in the republic.

68. See chapter 5. Prime Minister Marković continued his campaign against the army in mid-September 1991, when he demanded the resignations of Kadijević and Stane Brovet on the grounds that they had met secretly with General Yazov in Moscow on March 13 to arrange for the delivery of "a huge amount of weaponry." See "Marković Asks Army to Explain Moscow Arms 'Deal'," FBIS, *East Europe*, September 20, 1991, citing TANJUG of September 19, pp. 29–30, and the Defense Ministry's denial of any secret contacts or agreement about arms deliveries, in "Ministry Denies 'Secret Contacts' With Yazov," FBIS, *East Europe*, September 23, 1991, citing TANJUG of September 20, p. 29.

69. There is some dispute about this event. I accept the version of a reliable informant who was present and knows there was no attack (interview with the author).

70. "Bosnia, Macedonia Out of Monitoring Cease-Fire," TANJUG, September 5, 1991, in FBIS, *East Europe*, September 6, 1991, pp. 33–34. The same article reports that that same day, September 4, in Karlobag, the Croatian National Guard Corps (ZNG) "arrested and maltreated" the presidency's joint cease-fire monitoring group for Lika and northern Dalmatia. "Croatian Guards Mistreat Cease-Fire Group," TANJUG, September 5, 1991.

71. Janjić, "Gradjanski Rat," pp. 123–24.

72. Between the spring of 1992, when the Yugoslav Army was formed, and August 26, 1993, when the retirement of 42 generals, including the chief of staff, Colonel General Života Panić, was announced, 170 generals and admirals were officially retired, leaving only 7 on active duty.

73. Gow, "The Role of the Military," p. 71.

74. Citing Col. Jovan Čanak, "introduction" to a summary of findings on international involvement in the Yugoslav crisis and the Gulf war, in the military theoretical journal, *Vojno Delo*, July–October 1991, vols. 4–5, p. 15 (English translation). Gow, "The Role of the Military," pp. 72–75.

75. Miloš Vasić, "Yugoslav Army's Choice," *YugoFax*, December 28, 1991, p. 2. A third view comes from Bogdan Denitch, in *Ethnic Nationalism: The Tragic Death of Yugoslavia* (University of Minnesota Press, 1994), p. 164. He suggests that the floundering and change in strategy were linked to events in the former Soviet Union because the leaders of the army "were firmly convinced" that "they had a powerful ally, the Red Army, which faced similar foes in its own country. They and their political allies saw their last chance in the failed coup against Gorbachev in the summer of 1991." With its defeat, "both the Yugoslav army and the Milošević government faced total international isolation. In the place of a Yugoslavia that they had sworn to defend they left vast destruction."

76. In fact, the collapse of The Hague conference with the recognition of Croatia and its admission as a member state of the UN in May 1992 fundamentally altered the political assumptions on which the Vance Plan and UN mandate had

been based (not to prejudice the political outcome in negotiations) by granting Croatian sovereignty over this territory and beginning a long process of international pressure to get *krajina* Serbs to accept the consequences.

77. The Vance plan compensated Serbs in the UN protected areas (UNPAs) for their loss of protection from the army and their obligation to disarm by restoring their right to representation in local police forces in villages and districts where they were in the majority. One of the reasons for Babić's intransigence against the plan was Croatian president Tudjman's unwillingness to accept this provision, which he revealed in talks with UN negotiators in late January and early February 1992 over the terms of UN deployment when he demanded Zagreb's control over all local police units in the UNPAs (even if mixed, Serb and Croat), the authority of Croatian law in the UNPAs, and the exclusion of all Serb "rebel leaders" from local councils. Žarko Modrić, "Croatia denies raising new obstacles to UN peace plan," Croatian news agency (HINA), February 3, 1992. Another provision of the agreement for the withdrawal of the YPA from Croatia was that the rights of YPA personnel (for example, to their housing, consisting of 37,951 apartments) in Croatia be preserved, but this was violated by the Croatian government—by a law in 1992 that assigned empty, emptied, or abandoned YPA apartments to "war victims" (allocated by the Ministry of Defense); another law in 1992 that deprived anyone condemned of anti-Croatian activities (applied to all YPA officers who left for Belgrade, even if their families remained in Croatia) of citizenship rights; and a campaign beginning in mid-1991 that escalated to mass proportions in 1994 to evict families from those apartments without notice or right to appeal. (Interviews with the Center for Human Rights, UN headquarters, Zagreb, October 1994.)

78. United Nations Security Council Resolution 757, S/RES/757, May 30, 1992.

79. On the latter figure, Vego, "Federal Army Deployments in Bosnia and Herzegovina," *Jane's Intelligence Review*, p. 445.

80. Many argue that the army was the main defender of the conservative position on economic and political reform within the LCY, actively engaged against the liberal faction, and that this included support in bringing to power such persons as Slobodan Milošević. See, for example, Janjić, "Gradjanski Rat," p. 121. However, the policies of the general staff—especially by 1989–91—suggest that the army was as internally divided as the republics, at least along economic lines (with a faction favoring export production, technological modernization, and westernization) and that some were attempting to move the army toward civilian control and professionalization. Janjić himself notes that this "conservative" inclination was also manifest in an extreme nationalism among many officers (the local phrase is "chauvinism") that led them to desert to the national armies being formed in the republics at the same time that others shifted, with the collapse of the communist regime, to their *own* state-building project of a rump Yugoslavia (pp. 121–22).

81. The distinction for Serbs between Chetniks and Partisans still held in the wars of 1991–95. Many from the *krajina* of Croatia or in mixed villages and towns of Bosnia-Herzegovina were as likely to choose political loyalties, citizenship (where they had a choice), and paths of flight in opposition to Chetniks that was as great as that to Ustasha; rather than memories of ethnic conflict, it was the antifascist character of the World War II struggle that remained decisive.

82. Janjić cites one such example at the time of the incidents in Tuzla that included shots fired at the local mosque. The army response under Colonel Kadić was to deny reports that the Sarajevo Corps had armed only Serbs. Since no one had claimed this, Janjić and others saw it as a trick to test the readiness of Muslims for an armed uprising in support of a rump Yugoslavia. "Gradjanski Rat," p. 123.

83. The cause of these events, beginning May 2, 1992, is not clear. The confrontation began when President Izetbegović returned from negotiations in Lisbon and was kidnapped on arrival at Sarajevo airport. In the ensuing negotiations, mediated by UN envoys, the agreement was made to release Izetbegović and to require YPA withdrawal in exchange for unblocked barracks and a secured exodus. Yet Izetbegović did not arrive on the plane he announced to UN forces, which had gone to the airport to provide a safe escort, and instead stopped over in Rome without explanation (and thus arrived to no escort late in the evening). Moreover, despite the commitment to secure YPA exodus, an ambush was staged.

84. Aleksandar Ćirić and Miloš Vasić, "No Way Out: The JNA and the Yugoslav Wars," *WarReport*, no. 17 (January 1993), p. 4.

85. Vego, "Federal Army Deployments," pp. 445–48, attempts to estimate the number of troops and amount of equipment left when the YPA withdrew. He also cites a dispute over what proportion of troops were actually from Bosnia—"local Serbs"—between Belgrade, which claimed 80 percent of the 95,000 soldiers there in March 1992, and Sarajevo, which claimed no more than 20 percent, or 19,000. The YPA withdrew 14,000 troops by May 20.

86. Vego, "Federal Army Deployments," p. 446. A notable story about Mladić is that members of his immediate family were massacred in front of him by Croat Ustasha in World War II.

87. James Gow, "The Yugoslav Army—An Update," *Jane's Intelligence Review*, vol. 4 (November 1992), p. 501. This was not the last of the personnel changes, however, as Milošević proceeded over the next three years to weaken the army and coopt its best talent with higher salaries and benefits into the internal security police forces, which were, as for Tudjman in Croatia, his base of political power and loyalty.

88. See, for example, "Yugoslavia: Armament Industry Reportedly Booming," *Delo* (Ljubljana), September 21, 1993.

89. Tim van Beveren, "The Anglo-German Connection: Illegal Transfers Made Simple!" pp. 17–18; and Aleksandar Vasović, "Braced (and Armed) for Confrontation," *WarReport*, no. 17 (January 1993), p. 19; Zoran Kusovac, "Stalemate Ended by Crack Troops," *Jane's Defence Weekly*, November 7, 1992, p. 15; Milan Vego, "The Croatian Navy," *Jane's Intelligence Review*, vol. 5 (January 1993), pp. 11–16; Yves Debay and Paul Beaver, "Croatian Forces Open New Front," *Jane's Defence Weekly*, June 27, 1992, p. 1133. See also "Capability, Weapons Supply of Croatian Army," FBIS, *East Europe*, March 1, 1993, citing Belgrade *NIN* February 5, 1993, p. 15.

90. The Croatian navy was established September 11, 1991. Vego, "The Croatian Navy," pp. 11–16.

91. Serbia withheld food especially, a policy it attempted to defend in response to international criticism at the time of the May 1992 decision to impose economic sanctions on Serbia by arguing that Bosnians were making huge profits in selling

Serbian food and that food was needed in Serbia. Croatia interrupted transport links, for example by blowing up the bridge at Bosanski Šamac at the beginning of February 1992 and by putting barricades on the road and rail route connecting the Adriatic harbor at Ploče with Mostar and Sarajevo. In early February 1992, three weeks before the referendum on Bosnian independence, the price of cooking oil in Belgrade was 90 dinars a liter, in Sarajevo, 220 dinars; of milk, 30 dinars in Belgrade and 70 dinars in Sarajevo; of bread, 25 dinars in Belgrade and 50 dinars in Sarajevo. Average monthly salaries were in reverse proportion: 7,000 dinars in Sarajevo, and more than 15,000 in Belgrade. These figures are from the author's observations in both cities.

92.  Mihail Petkovski and others, "Stabilization Efforts in the Republic of Macedonia," *RFE/RL Research Report*, January 15, 1993, p. 34, and Hugh Poulton, "The Republic of Macedonia after UN Recognition," *RFE/RL Research Report*, June 4, 1993, pp. 23, 27.

93.  Gow, "Military-Political Affiliation," p. 17; see also Glenny, *The Fall of Yugoslavia*, pp. 108–09. In a confidential report to authorities in Zagreb (the president, prime minister, minister of defense, and minister of internal affairs) on August 18, 1991, a central representative in the government of Vukovar described the activities (and recall, through the intervention of Josip Manolić) of Merčep (who later became head of the influential organization of Croatian Volunteers for the Defense of the Fatherland) and appealed "for your intervention because the commune of Vukovar is a highly volatile crisis area in which armed conflicts on a large scale can break out any minute, and the city is almost under siege. The newly appointed persons continue the policy of Tomislav Merčep and the city is again victim of terror, armed strife and provocative shoot-outs with potentially unfathomable consequences. The policy pursued so far has created an atmosphere of terror among the Croatian and Serbian population. The Croatian part of the population unanimously denounces such behavior and feels disgraced and compromised and no longer wishes to bear responsibility for such a policy. As we do not feel in a position to sort things out with our local resources, we are asking you to urgently send here competent people who would help the legal institutions and authorities bring life back to normal."

94.  In a famous interview in the Belgrade weekly *Ilustrirana Politika* in March 1992, Stefanović admitted flying Šešelj all over the military front in July 1991, while General Aleksandar Vasiljević, former head of military intelligence services, admitted in an interview to *NIN* in 1992 that plans to stage a coup in Belgrade in September 1991 had failed because there were not sufficient military personnel present in the city.

95.  Despite the cease-fire negotiated by UN envoy Cyrus Vance in Croatia, Croatian forces retaliated for Vukovar with a counteroffensive on Papuk at the end of November.

96.  See Louise Branson, "Crossing the Line in Bosnia's War," *Christian Science Monitor*, October 19, 1992, p. 2.

97.  Prime Minister Janez Drnovšek admitted September 17, 1992, in a speech at the Center for Strategic and International Studies, Washington, D.C., that contracts signed with Iraq for tanks before Yugoslavia ended were being fulfilled as before by cooperating Slovene and Serbian firms. In April 1993, John Allcock,

a British expert on the former Yugoslavia, told a BBC interviewer that enforcement of the economic sanctions against Serbia was naive because it ignored one of the primary loopholes—Slovene firms.

98.   Tihomir Loza illustrates this problem with Kupres, in Herzegovina: the town had a slight Serb majority, followed by Croats and Muslims; it borders a district where Muslims form a small majority, followed by Croats and then Serbs. If division occurred along ethnic lines, "Kupres must be Serb while Bugojno must be Muslim. But the HDZ has already included Bugojno as part of Herzeg-Bosnia, and in order to join it with Tomislavgrad and Livno all they need is the Kupres plateau." Croat militias conquered the area in early 1992, the JNA and Serb paramilitaries took it from Croats, and because "the significance of the Kupres plateau is strategic rather than economic . . . further clashes can be expected." These occurred in late 1994, when a Bosnian government (Muslim) offensive led Bosnian Serbs to abandon the town to Bosnian Croats (in what appeared to be a secret agreement to prevent Bosnian Muslims from controlling the town). "Herzegovina: A Key Battleground," *YugoFax*, May 7, 1992, p. 9.

99.   Vukovar is a natural river port for the Sava-Danube basin, and the opening of eastern Europe led Danubian states to hope that links between Atlantic Ocean and Black Sea ports would provide a substantial stimulus for economic recovery. The widening of the Danube with the Gabčikovo/Nagymaros dam—disputed between Slovakia and Hungary in 1992—was critical, for example, to Slovakia's new development strategy based on Danube transport.

100.   This was illustrated powerfully on January 22, 1993, when the government in Zagreb chose to ignore the terms of its signed cease-fire arrangement in the UN protected zones and to retake militarily the area around the Maslenica bridge (the previous structure destroyed by fighting in 1991) which linked Zagreb to the Dalmatian coast at Zadar, and control over the Peruča dam that had been assigned to UN supervision.

101.   Jonathan S. Landay, "A Centuries-Old Serb Enclave Stands Firm," *Christian Science Monitor*, October 21, 1993, p. 6. One such case is the area of Mt. Ozren, a traditionally Serbian enclave of thirty-five villages surrounding a 500-year-old Serbian Orthodox monastery. Karadžić gave Ozren to the Muslim party at negotiations in August 1993 (the Owen-Stoltenberg plan). It is not economically viable and its communication and transportation lines are more oriented toward towns which the peace plans have put in Muslim-controlled areas. After the failure of this plan, however, the heavy loss of Serbian lives in fighting for Ozren and its religious-historical symbolism made this territorial concession nearly impossible politically for Karadžić in subsequent negotiations.

102.   For example, the airfield at Banja Luka and the fuel depot at Bosanski Brod were particularly important, early targets of Serbian forces; the Marshal Tito airforce school at Mostar, the Sokol aircraft factory, and Mostar's position on the Neretva River controlling supply routes from the coast, the hydroelectric plant at Jajce and along the Neretva valley, the coastal shipbuilding industry (with its large military component), and the gunpowder, rocket fuel, and explosives plant at Vitez were Croatian targets; and the industrial heartland of central Bosnia, where most defense plants were located, over which Croat and Muslim forces battled through most of winter-spring 1993.

103. Aleksa Buha, *Basic Information*, January 22, 1993. For example, the north-south rail line that was the "artery of economic life" in Bosnia-Herzegovina, and most of the hydroelectric plants, thermal energy potential, and coal basins remained outside Serb provinces.

104. On the first, see Hayden, "Constitutional Nationalism," pp. 654–73.

## Chapter 9

1. "The Community is like an adolescent facing the crisis of an adult," Delors is quoted saying. "It now only has the weapons of recognition and economic aid. If it were 10 years older, it might be able to impose a military peacekeeping force." In James E. Goodby, "Peacekeeping in the New Europe," *Washington Quarterly* (Spring 1992), p. 158.

2. At their fifth meeting on November 16, 1991, they adopted a peace treaty for all the republics and proposed the creation of an interparliamentary council, the specifics for which were drawn up by the Round Table's group of experts and presented at the sixth meeting, on January 11 and 18, 1992. The seventh meeting was scheduled in Sarajevo for February 15 (from the printed announcement).

3. "Exports to Be Controlled by Interior Ministry," *Borba*, December 10, 1991, p. 8, printed in Foreign Broadcast Information Service, *Daily Report: East Europe*, December 30, 1991, p. 39 (Hereafter, FBIS, *East Europe*.)

4. Kljuić subsequently formally submitted his resignation on February 2, 1992. "HDZ Official Explains Kljuić Resignation," Sarajevo Radio, February 3, 1992, in FBIS, *East Europe*, February 5, 1992, p. 51.

5. For example, in the first months of 1992, President Izetbegović made frequent public speeches to persuade children to continue to go to school, countering the fear campaign of Radovan Karadžić, leader of the Serbian Democratic party, urging them to stay home.

6. "EC Condemns Attacks," TANJUG, March 2, 1992, in FBIS, *East Europe*, March 3, 1992, pp. 20–21. One person was killed and five wounded in Sarajevo, and two killed in Doboj; bomb threats and barricades stopped rail traffic in many parts of the republic; and an SDS crisis committee in Sarajevo began negotiations with the Bosnian presidency.

7. There were alternatives. In negotiations in August 1991 between the SDS leadership and the leaders of the second, liberal, Muslim political party (the MBO), the two committed themselves to an integral Bosnia-Herzegovina; although President Izetbegović apparently supported the idea of these talks, he then denounced them and his rival, Adil Zulfikarpašić, when they were made public; see the interview by Emil Vlajki of Zulfikarpašić on June 4, 1993, reprinted in *South Slav Journal*, vol. 4 (Autumn–Winter 1994), pp. 78–84.

8. "Bosnian Croats Claim 'Genocide' in Herzegovina," TANJUG, October 22, 1991, in FBIS, *East Europe*, October 23, 1991, p. 53.

9. Author's interview with Karadžić in Sarajevo on February 6, 1992. In a radio interview in Belgrade on January 22, Karadžić proposed, in criticizing the "EC intentions to fragment the Serbian nation on this territory," the option of "Serbian regions in former Croatia, the Serbian regions in Bosnia-Herzegovina—which

would nevertheless be preserved somehow—and Serbia, form a sort of federation and perhaps form a confederation with others—be it Macedonians or Muslims—anyone who wishes to do it." "SDS Leader Calls for Serbian Federation," Radio Belgrade Network, January 22, 1992, in FBIS, *East Europe*, January 23, 1992, p. 56.

10. The dominance of the ethnic parties over political options had already gone quite far by early February. At the same time that citizens' groups were intently mobilizing a campaign in support of the referendum on Bosnian independence and politically aware citizens in Sarajevo were convinced that the war in Croatia would not erupt in their republic, they were already reacting defensively to this debate over maps. In interviews with this author on February 6–7, Sarajevo residents made a point of stating their outraged opposition to Karadžić's "green line" to cantonize the city. On the other hand, Ejup Ganić, member of the Bosnian presidency representing minorities (but in coalition in the parliament with the SDA and later an active leader of the SDA and the Muslim position), was already insisting on a "Bosnian" position *within* the ethnic principle: that cantonal administration could not extend to natural wealth—rivers, lakes, parks, mountains—which were the "common property" of all Bosnia and could not be divided.

11. One of Croatian president Tudjman's advisers, political scientist Zvonko Lerotić, argued in January 1992, three months before full-scale war in Bosnia, that "war is not necessary to finish off the republic, because that process is already complete," adding "war would only be necessary if one wanted Bosnia and Herzegovina to become a united and sovereign republic." Cited by Milan Andrejevich, "Bosnia and Herzegovina: A Precarious Peace," *Radio Free Europe/Radio Liberty (RFE/RL) Report on Eastern Europe*, February 28, 1992, p. 14.

12. It has since been accepted that the parties agreed to this plan. See David Binder, "U.S. Policymakers on Bosnia Admit Errors in Opposing Partition in 1992," *New York Times*, August 29, 1993 p. A10. While they may have given this appearance, and the language of rejection used the next week by President Izetbegović seems a clear reversal of the Lisbon position, the three parties had three very different maps in mind, as published at the time in the Belgrade newspaper *Politika*, suggesting in light of later disagreements that the three parties did not consider themselves in accord. I am grateful to Paul Shoup for this information. Robert Hayden provides a useful discussion of the talks and changing proposals in "The Partition of Bosnia and Herzegovina, 1990–1993," *RFE/RL Research Report*, May 28, 1993, pp. 6–8.

13. Many commentators assert, and the *New York Times* reports, that the U.S. ambassador to Yugoslavia, Warren Zimmermann, counseled President Izetbegović to reject the plan in favor of immediate recognition of an integral Bosnia-Herzegovina spearheaded by the United States. Ambassador Zimmermann denies this, although he acknowledges that the option was mentioned. Deputy Secretary of State Lawrence Eagleburger was known to be counseling Secretary Baker at the time that diplomatic recognition of the republic would prevent Serbian aggression, which could also have given this message. See Binder, "U.S. Policymakers on Bosnia Admit Errors."

14. Vasil Tupurkovski, the last representative of Macedonia to the federal presidency, who persisted longer than any other Yugoslav to try to find a diplomatic solution by Yugoslavs—he held fifty-seven meetings with Western heads of state

between June and December 1991—insisted to Genscher, Vance, and EC foreign ministers at the time that if the four remaining republics had been treated thus, as a package in the negotiations, there would have been a real chance for success without war and also for avoiding the disagreements that arose within the EC and between the EC and the United States. Author's discussions with Tupurkovski.

15. The timing of the German stand, after pressure for nearly six months, demonstrated the hand of Chancellor Kohl as well, since the December 15–16 meeting was held on the eve of the Christian Democratic Union and Christian Social Union (CDU-CSU) party convention. Italian cosponsorship of the recognition proposal and the agreement of even France and Britain were directly related to the meeting at Maastricht only days before (December 9–10, with the Treaty signing on December 11).

16. *Republika Srpska Bosne i Hercegovine.*

17. One of the many tragic ironies of this conflict is that this was the 500-year anniversary of the Jewish community in Sarajevo, given the name of "little Jerusalem" in 1492 for offering sanctuary, under Ottoman administration, to Jews fleeing the Inquisition.

18. In the judgment of a member of Vance's fact-finding team, the UN made the mistake from the beginning of seeing Bosnia as simply an extension of the Serb-Croat conflict. The same can be said for the United States and the EC. Interview, May 1992.

19. The cease-fire obtained by Cyrus Vance with President Tudjman of Croatia and the commander-in-chief of the Yugoslav army, General Kadijević, was signed at Sarajevo on January 2, 1992, and fifty military liaison officers were sent to help facilitate its implementation, arriving on January 14, the day before EC recognition changed the fundamental political terms of the Vance plan. The UN protection forces were established by SCR 743 on February 21, 1992, which requested the secretary-general to deploy persons immediately to develop an implementation plan. Peacekeeping troops first arrived in Belgrade March 8, making their way to Croatia on March 15. On the basis of the secretary-general's report on that implementation plan April 2, SCR 749, authorizing full deployment, was adopted on April 7.

20. Interviews at the United Nations May 8, 1992.

21. They returned again on July 7, focusing primarily on efforts to visit detention camps and prisoners of war which were continually obstructed, primarily by Bosnian Serbs, until mid-August and SCR 770 (August 13).

22. Vance was in Bosnia-Herzegovina April 14–18, two days after the EC talks had been reduced to discussion of a cease-fire by the SDA and HDZ rejection of the EC map on March 31, and Goulding spent the week of May 4–10.

23. The EC recalled its ambassador on May 11, the United States recalled Zimmermann the next day, and individual European countries followed as well during the month.

24. On May 4, the Bosnian government requested foreign military aid and the YPA announced it would complete withdrawal by May 19. The story of that withdrawal and the conflict between the YPA and the SDA leadership in the Bosnian government during May is replete with intrigue and treachery, including a brief kidnapping of President Izetbegović on May 2, the barricading of YPA

barracks, the reputed theft of the infamous "RAM" plan (see chapter 5), and a massacre of exiting conscripts that deserves a skilled investigative reporter.

25. Resolution 757 of May 30 imposed a universal, binding blockade on all trade and all scientific, cultural, and sports exchanges with Serbia and Montenegro; Resolution 760 of June 18 exempted humanitarian goods such as food and medicine and adopted a simplified and accelerated "no objection" procedure for processing requests for exemptions. Serbia and Montenegro were excluded from the CSCE for five months in May 1992 (after the Russian delegate objected to the Austrian and Hungarian proposals for permanent exclusion) and had not been readmitted as of the end of 1994, and from the United Nations in September 1992. Both organizations required the new Yugoslavia to apply for membership instead of granting them status as successor state to the former Yugoslavia. Resolution 777, September 19, 1992, was adopted by twelve members of the Security Council, with zero against and three abstentions (China, India, Zimbabwe), and the General Assembly concurred by adopting resolution 47/1 on September 22. This was in contrast to the contemporaneous treatment of Russia as successor to the Soviet Union.

26. There is perhaps no more symbolic a date in modern Yugoslav history. See chapter 6.

27. Mitterrand's gesture, to demonstrate it was "feasible to land," according to Dominique Moïsi speaking on BBC World Service that evening, was "what the French call 'panache.' " At the time, officials in the U.S. State and Defense departments were insisting repeatedly that they had "no reluctance" (as Secretary of State Baker said on May 23 in Lisbon) to provide naval and air support from their logistical base in Europe but, as Pentagon spokesman Pete Williams said on June 30, "I stress we have not yet been asked and until there's a request, we will do nothing."

28. The Security Council adopted a resolution (770) to that effect on August 13, 1992, under Chapter 7 of the Charter, committing member states to use "all measures necessary" to deliver humanitarian aid. But it was another month before a decision came, on September 10, to enlarge UNPROFOR troops for that purpose, bringing a rare public complaint on October 14 from Cyrus Vance that the UN was "extraordinarily slow" in delivering aid and protecting convoys.

29. Indeed, at the very moment when Milošević was expending substantial political capital to pressure the Bosnian Serb leadership in the spring of 1993, the United States was actively pushing its policy of "lift and strike," which included threats to bomb Belgrade and supply routes within Serbia.

30. Kerin Hope, "Serb Politician Charged in Belgrade Crackdown," *Financial Times*, June 5–6, 1993, p. 3.

31. Several months after the period covered in this book, during July and August 1994, President Milošević did finally threaten to cut off support to the Bosnian Serbs if they did not accept the most recent peace proposal of international negotiators, and then followed through on this threat in early August. He made it clear that this was in order to obtain a lifting of the economic sanctions that had become a serious threat to the Serbian economy and the macroeconomic stabilization program introduced the previous January. This led many to the conclusion that the "sanctions worked," without asking what the alternatives would have been

after May 1992 and whether sanctions might instead have prolonged the war, including its effective destruction of anything that could actually be called a "Bosnia and Herzegovina."

32. UN negotiators were inclined to add that the trouble with economic sanctions is that they are easy to put on, hard to remove, and work from the bottom up. As Western powers discovered in April–December 1993, when Bosnian Serbs appeared to defy Milošević's apparent efforts to end the sanctions by demanding they sign the Vance-Owen plan and moving to end supplies and the political support and privileges for Bosnian Serb leaders, sanctions are inflexible instruments—they can be tightened or lifted but not otherwise adjusted in response to behavior.

33. The Pulitzer Prize–winning report that broke the story of Serbian detention camps was by Roy Gutmann in *Newsday* on August 2 although governments and aid agencies were accused of knowledge more than two months earlier. See also his subsequent book, *A Witness to Genocide: The First Inside Account of the Horrors of Ethnic Cleansing in Bosnia* (Shaftesbury: Element Publishing Co., 1993). Television images from the camps at Omarska and Trnopolje began to arrive August 5, and a Senate Foreign Relations Committee Report, *The Ethnic Cleansing of Bosnia-Hercegovina*, written by staffers Peter Galbraith and Michelle Maynard, appeared August 15, 1992.

34. Security Council Resolution 795; on June 18, 1993, the United States added 325 troops to the 700-person Nordic battalion already deployed (SCR 842).

35. $152 million was pledged (author's interview with U.S. delegate to the conference). It was also about this time that Ogata began to be far more forceful in demanding that the international community create for refugees "the right to return" and "the right to stay." The situation also gave more visibility to the campaign of French president Mitterrand and his flamboyant Minister for Health and Humanitarian Affairs, Bernard Kouchner, who founded Médecins sans Frontières, for the right—and obligation—of the international community to interfere in internal affairs to defend human rights.

36. The main debate evolved in the U.S. Senate from August 3 to August 11, 1992, over a proposed Senate Resolution (S. Res. 330) but which expanded to a debate over U.S. involvement in former Yugoslavia in general and U.S. foreign policy in the post–cold war period, a debate that some senators called the best debate in foreign policy they had experienced. See *Congressional Record*, August 3–11, 1992 (August 3, pp. S11509–10; August 4, pp. S11405–07, S11437–40; August 5, pp. S11575–80; August 6, pp. S11638, S11643; August 7, pp. S11861–65, S11871–72; August 10, pp. S11991–S12060; August 11, pp. S12106–19, S12226–41, S12283–86, S12297).

37. The secretary-general expressed his frustration with Europe in particular when the permanent members of the Security Council pushed through a resolution requiring the UN to monitor the EC-negotiated cease-fire agreement of July 17 to put heavy weapons under international supervision, including an unusual public shouting match with British representative to the Security Council Sir David Hannay. On July 22, 1992, Boutros-Ghali said that the Security Council was in danger of paying "undue attention" to Yugoslavia rather than Somalia, where hundreds of thousands were dead and thousands were starving daily. He charged

the world with being concerned about "white Muslims" only and reminded the public (and later the citizens of Sarajevo in November 1992) that there were many other conflicts in the world of greater magnitude, such as Burma where there had been three civil wars in the preceding thirty years or the Sudan where more than a million lay dead in the most recent conflict.

38. The no-fly zone was discussed from July 1992 until Resolution 781 was voted on October 9, but it only allowed for monitoring flights. Pressure mounted for giving it military muscle until Resolution 816 of March 31. Air strikes were discussed seriously in the United States and Europe beginning July 1992, opposed by Britain and France, by the commanding officer of UNPROFOR troops in former Yugoslavia, General Satish Nambiar, and, after November, by Russia. NATO finally committed to the idea in August 1993 to "stop the strangulation of Sarajevo" and protect UN troops and repeated the threat at the NATO meeting in January 1994.

39. This was particularly influential on the question of sanctions. The United States began to pressure for toughening the May 30, 1992, sanctions (Security Council Resolution 757) during November. Although a naval blockade was imposed in the Adriatic to allow greater enforcement of the sanctions, the decision to tighten came only in April 1993 (Resolution 820 of April 17) after Russian efforts to delay the decision until after a referendum on presidential power was held April 25. U.S. acquiescence led to a rebellion among nonaligned countries on the Security Council and a compromise to delay its implementation until April 26. Russian behavior followed the same motives as those of Germany and the United States, defining national interests in terms of domestic politics and positioning among European powers, but this was invariably interpreted as "traditional" (historical, religious, ethnic) support for Serbia.

40. General Colin Powell elaborated what came to be called the Powell Doctrine in an interview with *New York Times* Pentagon correspondent Michael Gordon, "Powell Delivers a Resounding No On Using Limited Force in Bosnia," September 28, 1992, p. A1, and an editorial in that paper, "Why Generals Get Nervous," October 8, 1992, p. A35: that no U.S. military force should be committed until the political objectives were crystal clear and only then with sufficient ("overwhelming") force to ensure military victory; President Bush raised the question in the candidates' debates of the fall 1992 presidential campaign. Bush's secretary of defense, Richard Cheney, reiterated this view a year later, on the CNN program "Crossfire," October 22, 1993: "No one could ever define a clear-cut mission."

41. *The Islamic Declaration* was written by Izetbegović in 1970 and used by authorities as the basis of a political trial in 1983. It is a separate text from that written in 1980 and published in Belgrade in 1988 praising Islam, *Islam between East and West*.

42. Because the first ethnic party in Bosnia was created by Izetbegović, at a time when he was also a pan-Islamicist (to the extent that a secular liberal wing of the party eventually broke off to form a second Muslim party under Adil Zulfikarpašić), many observers find it difficult to absolve Izetbegović from all responsibility for the decline toward war, even though the Muslim population of Bosnia became its primary victims. See Paul Shoup's careful presentation in "Uloga Domaćih i Medjunarodnih Aktera Bosanskohercegovačke Drame" [The role of

domestic and international actors in the drama of Bosnia-Herzegovina], in *Bosna i Hercegovina Izmedju Rata i Mira*, pp. 81–82.

43.  Vladimir Goati outlines the different silences and vaguenesses in the three party platforms during the electoral campaigns of 1990 and the post-election constitutional confusions, in "Politički Život Bosne i Hercegovine, 1989–1992," pp. 53–61, and Dušan Janjić describes the vacillation of the parties and intellectuals on constitutional programs in 1991–92 and discusses the problem of "SDA and Alija Izetbegović [because] they had no clear conception for solving the problem of BH" (p. 116) in "Gradjanski Rat i Mogučnost Mira u Bosni i Hercegovini," pp. 116–18. Janjić also discusses the great exacerbation of relations with the Yugoslav army due to "frequent changes in the position of Alija Izetbegović and the SDA" (p. 124).

44.  From the transcript of the speech in "Policy Statement," August 26, 1992, British Information Services, New York, pp. 2–4.

45.  Prime Minister John Major at the London conference, August 27, 1993.

46.  The working group on Bosnia and Herzegovina was chaired by Martti Ahtisaari (a diplomat who became president of Finland in 1994), that on economic issues by Jean Durieux of Belgium, and that on ethnic and national communities by Geert Ahrens of Germany. The three other working groups were those on humanitarian issues (chaired by Sadako Ogata of Japan, as UN High Commissioner for Refugees), on succession issues (chaired by Jorgen Bojer of Denmark), and on confidence and security-building and verification measures (chaired by Vincente Berasategui of Argentina).

47.  The main work of consulting and drafting this proposal was done by Ahtisaari. Bosnian foreign minister Haris Silajdžić presented the plan at the London conference for a decentralized, secular state based on wide autonomy for the three national communities, ten provinces, and at least four regions with administrative centers in Sarajevo, Mostar, Banja Luka, and Tuzla.

48.  See *WarReport* and the newsletters of the Helsinki Citizens' Assembly for details of these proposals and efforts at influence. One example is the constitutional framework drawn up by professors of law at the University of Sarajevo, reprinted in Josep Palau and Radha Kumar, eds., *Ex-Yugoslavia: From War to Peace* (Madrid: Helsinki Citizens' Assembly; Movement for Peace, Disarmament and Freedom [MPDL], and Generalitat Valenciana, 1992), pp. 307–35. See also Payam Akhavan and Robert Howse, eds., *Yugoslavia, the Former and Future: Reflections by Scholars from the Region* (Brookings, 1995).

49.  President Bill Clinton reiterated the Bush warning after he assumed the presidency, and it was repeated by Secretary of State Christopher when he announced the new administration's policy toward the conflict on February 10, 1993.

50.  Bosnia was only one of seven or so foreign policy issues that Clinton selected to define the differences between him and his opponent, but when Bush's press secretary, Marlin Fitzwater, reacted on July 27 to a journalist's question about Clinton's proposal to bomb the Serbs by calling it "reckless," the issue moved to the top of the list, taking prominence from then on in the campaign.

51.  The United States was represented by Reginald Bartholomew, ambassador to NATO and a former under-secretary of state, who was replaced by Charles

Redman in September when Bartholomew took up an ambassadorship to Italy. Russia was represented by Vitaly Churkin.

52. Roger Cohen, "U.S. and Allies Differ on Arms for Bosnian Muslims," *New York Times*, April 22, 1993, p. A15.

53. Thomas L. Friedman, "Bosnia Reconsidered," *New York Times*, April 8, 1993, p. A1. "In effect," Friedman writes, "the Administration has gone from shaking its fist at the Serbs to throwing up its hands." See also Elaine Sciolino, "U.S. Offers Aid to Bosnia, But No Plan to End War," *New York Times*, December 1, 1993, p. A8.

54. "Decisions taken at the Council meeting on Monday, 2nd August 1993 at 3 p.m." (North Atlantic Council, NOTICE C-N (93) 42, August 3, 1993), which "noted that the Alliance had been ready since 22nd July to provide protective airpower in case of attack against UNPROFOR in the performance of its overall mandate, on the basis of UN Security Council Resolution 836" and "agreed that the Alliance will make immediate preparations for undertaking, in the event that the strangulation of Sarajevo and other areas continues, including wide scale interference with humanitarian assistance, stronger measures including air strikes against those responsible." See also "Decisions taken at the Council meeting on Monday, 9th August 1993 at 4 p.m." (North Atlantic Council, NOTICE C-N (93) 43, August 10, 1993), which approved the operational options for air strikes as decided on August 2. See Michael R. Gordon, "Conflict in the Balkans: Leading NATO on Bosnia," *New York Times*, August 3, 1993, p. A1.

55. Tensions between the United States and the UN (particularly the secretary-general) continued to rise during July and August as a result as well of troubles in the Somali operation. U.S. ambassador Madeleine Albright pronounced August 17, 1993, that it was "absolutely unconscionable" for UN officers—in this case Brigadier General Vere Hayes of Great Britain, who criticized the threat of air strikes—to question the president of the United States. Senator Robert Dole initiated the same day what appeared to be a Republican campaign against "multilateralism" (joined by Charles Krauthammer, George Will, and Henry Kissinger) with a criticism of U.S. acquiescence to UN action and of the secretary-general (Boutros-Ghali) as "obsessed about being in charge, rather than getting things done." William Claiborne, "Dole Decries U.S. Bosnia Policy, Acquiescence in U.N. Inaction Criticized in Address to Governors," *Washington Post*, August 18, 1993, p. A25. On September 27, 1993, President Clinton's maiden speech before the General Assembly called for greater scrutiny in initiating peacekeeping operations. Weekly Compilation of Presidential Documents, vol. 29, no. 39, p. 1909.

56. The first proposal from presidents Tudjman and Milošević came on June 16; see Paul Lewis, "Two Leaders Propose Dividing Bosnia into Three Areas," *New York Times*, June 17, 1993, p. A3. The detailed chronology of the ICFY efforts to negotiate a new peace plan after the failure of the Vance-Owen plan can be found in the periodic reports of the cochairmen to the secretary-general of the United Nations on their activities; see in particular, Report S/26260 of August 6, 1993; S/26922 of December 29, 1993; A/48/847 (to the General Assembly) of January 7, 1994; and S/1994/64 of January 21, 1994. While the cochairmen were in constant negotiating session, the peace talks themselves were only resumed on July 27,

among President Izetbegović, Mate Boban, and Radovan Karadžić; then on September 23, at which presidents Tudjman, Milošević, and Bulatović and ambassadors Churkin and Redman were also present; from November 29 to December 2 at Geneva, including in these meetings also foreign ministers of the EU; and with the parties in Brussels on December 22–23.

57. Referring to the Muslim forces in November 1993, a UN official in Bosnia-Herzegovina said, "They are in this for the long haul. We are no longer talking months now, but years." "The Frost Hardens in Bosnia," *Economist*, November 20–26, 1993, p. 51.

58. Abdić was also the other SDA representative on the Bosnian presidency, having received more votes in the elections held in November 1990 than Izetbegović himself. One reason for the campaign that now began against Abdić and led to his military defeat, temporarily, in August 1994, was revenge for the decision of Abdić and seven other members (of the nine-member) presidency to replace Izetbegović and Ganić as the Bosnian delegation at the Geneva talks on June 22. See Paul Lewis, "Bosnians Divide Over New Talks to Split Country," *New York Times*, June 23, 1993, p. A1. Another reason was to replace Abdić, who declared on September 28 an autonomous region of Western Bosnia, with someone loyal to the Sarajevo leadership.

59. French initiatives included a joint French-German proposal for revisions in the current peace proposal that would bring in terms for a settlement in Croatia, more territorial concessions by the Bosnian Serbs to the Bosnian government, and an easing of the sanctions on Serbia and Montenegro. "Europe Hopes New Proposal Will Revive Peace Talks in Balkans," *Chicago Tribune*, November 21, 1993, p. 9.

60. "Report of the Co-chairmen of the Steering Committee on the Activities of the International Conference on the Former Yugoslavia," presented to the Security Council, December 29, 1993, Report S/26922, p. 2.

61. There is immense dispute about who fired the mortar and whether it was yet another example of the Bosnian Serb siege of Sarajevo or part of a strategy by Bosnian government forces to invoke NATO's commitment to enforce the Sarajevo safe area and obtain air strikes against the Serbs. There were two separate UN investigations, the first considered technically faulty and the second demanded by Radovan Karadžić in exchange for agreeing to the Sarajevo cease-fire, in the belief that Serbs had not fired the mortar. The second UN investigation concluded that the shot could have come equally from either side, as it originated from an area on the confrontation line. This did not prevent continuing speculation and even unfounded declarations by high-level officials in Western capitals. David Binder, "Anatomy of a Massacre," *Foreign Policy*, Winter 1994–95, pp. 70–78.

62. "Decisions Taken at the Meeting of the North Atlantic Council on 9th February 1994 (1)" (NATO, DS/4). The phrase "peace from the bottom up" was commonly used by UNPROFOR officials to refer to what they were trying to accomplish on the ground to promote peace. It actually began the previous fall under UNPROFOR commander General Jean Cot, in Croatia, when in frustration with the lack of progress and continual collapse of negotiations over a general cease-fire between the Croatian government and Serbian authorities in Knin, he

decided to break the territory down and create "a hundred local cease-fires" with his own military negotiators.

63. Most influential was the "Sarajevo Initiative" of the *Sabor* (assembly) of the Croats of Bosnia-Herzegovina presented at a meeting in Sarajevo on February 6, 1994, and developed by representatives of political parties, cultural clubs, the Catholic church (particularly local Franciscan orders, as well as the Bosnian Archbishop), regional associations, and prominent local and émigré intellectuals such as Ivan Lovrenović and Ivo Komšić. The *Sabor* appointed an executive body, the Croatian National Council of Bosnia-Herzegovina (CNC), chaired by Komšić. See "Sarajevska Inicijativa" [The Sarajevo initiative], *Erasmus*, vol. 6 (1994), pp. 4–13; and also "New Presidency Member Komšić Sworn In," Sarajevo Radio Bosnia-Herzegovina, November 1, 1993, in FBIS, *East Europe*, November 2, 1993, p. 21.

64. The case of Tuzla airport demonstrates an even more complex confrontation of humanitarian and security interests. The second largest airport in Bosnia-Herzegovina, in a Muslim-majority city in largely Serbian-held territory declared a safe area, its opening for relief flights as a backup to the Sarajevo airport, which was frequently closed as a result of bad weather or hostilities, had a substantial appeal. To Bosnian Serbs, the opening would only make possible the covert supply of armaments to their enemies in the heart of territory they controlled. Together with the capacity to strike the capital of Serbia, Belgrade, from Tuzla airport, this made its opening an issue of immediate security concern to both the Bosnian Serbs and the government in Serbia. The most likely outcome of the demand for air strikes in January 1994 as a means to open Tuzla airport in place of bilateral negotiations was therefore the closing to UN forces of the land route from Belgrade through Serbia. Yet among other purposes, this was the only means (short of inefficient and costly air drops through the U.S.-initiated Operation Provide Promise) to get relief supplies to the three eastern enclaves—the safe areas of Žepa, Srebrenica, and Goražde; and because the only way to move sufficient quantities of supplies was over land, not by air, the result could be to reduce the amount of relief delivered.

65. A commission of experts was established to gather information on violations of international humanitarian law by UN Security Council Resolution 780 on October 6, 1992. During 1993, under chairman Cherif Bassiouni, it investigated mass graves in the UNPAs; allegations of sexual assault, torture, and detention camps in Bosnia-Herzegovina; alleged crimes against humanity in the Prijedor area of Bosnia; and the destruction of cultural property, particularly in Dubrovnik. It also coordinated with the special rapporteur for human rights for the former Yugoslavia, Tadeusz Mazowiecki, and with the judges of the international tribunal for the prosecution of war crimes committed in the territory of the former Yugoslavia since 1991. SC/5764, December 16, 1993, UN Information Service, Geneva. The tribunal was established by UN Security Council Resolution 808, adopted February 22, 1993. The idea was to make the UN the "conscience of the world."

66. It comprises eleven judges, sitting in The Hague. See Theodor Meron, "The Case for War Crimes Trials in Yugoslavia," *Foreign Affairs*, Summer 1993, pp. 122–35, and Sonja Biserko, ed., *Yugoslavia: Collapse, War, Crimes* (Belgrade:

Centre for Anti-war Action, Association of Independent Intellectuals "Belgrade Circle," 1993). See the speech at the U.S. Holocaust Museum on the subject by the guiding force behind this U.S. pressure, U.S. Permanent Representative to the UN, Madeleine K. Albright, "Bosnia in Light of the Holocaust: War Crimes Tribunals," *U.S. Department of State Dispatch*, vol. 5, no. 16, pp. 1–4.

67. Already at the time of the Lisbon negotiations, before diplomatic recognition, a commentator writing about that constitutional arrangement in the Zagreb daily *Vjesnik* worried, "Because a law-governed state no longer exists at all in B-H, and the republic Assembly and government are in the margin of events, it is an illusion to say that anyone will guarantee anyone rights and freedoms, especially those who will be left outside of their own respective ethnic regions." Mladen Mirosavljević, "Ethnic Groups Fear Mass Migrations," *Vjesnik*, March 21, 1992, in FBIS, *East Europe*, April 1, 1992, p. 46.

68. A group at Loyola University in Chicago worked voraciously from a variety of sources, largely newspaper accounts, to gather extensive documentation for legal proceedings. These were problematic sources, however; another problem, therefore, became the lack of interest among countries other than the United States (which has committed almost $15 million in 1994–95) in financing the investigative work necessary to press charges. Nonetheless, the appointment of the internationally esteemed Justice Richard J. Goldstone of the South African Constitutional Court as prosecutor of the tribunal, on July 8, 1994, reassured many legal scholars that the tribunal would apply the highest professional standards. Confidential interviews, September 1994.

69. Glenny, *The Fall of Yugoslavia: The Third Balkan War* (Penguin, 1992), p. 121.

70. See Mark Thompson, *Forging War: The Media in Serbia, Croatia and Bosnia-Hercegovina* (U.K.: Article 19, International Centre against Censorship, 1994).

71. The Cable News Network had won its vast audience with reporting from the Persian Gulf War in January–March 1991, just in time to be available for the Yugoslav conflict.

72. Quoted in Elaine Sciolino, "Christopher Spells Out New Priorities," *New York Times*, November 5, 1993, p. A8.

73. Some reliable estimates reached $1 billion. Confidential interviews.

74. Author's interview with UNHCR officials in July 1994. For more information, see *UNHCR Information Notes*, no. 10/94, pp. 2, 22–23, and *UNHCR Information Notes*, no. 7/94, p. 27.

75. The story of five-year-old Irma Hadžimuratović, who was airlifted out of Sarajevo and flown to London in August 1993, particularly highlighted the extent to which Western media influenced events in this conflict. Irma's doctor in Sarajevo went to reporters for help. The publicity they generated resulted in her being flown to London, at the order of British prime minister John Major, for treatment of shrapnel wounds of her spine. See John Pomfret, "39 Patients Flown Out of Sarajevo: Recipient Countries Quarrel with U.N. Over Motivations," *Washington Post*, August 16, 1993, p. A1, and William E. Schmidt, "Wounded and Sick Bosnians Land in London," *New York Times*, August 16, 1993, p. A6.

76. This is the CSCE approach to conflict management, and it is based on the critical assumption that parties to an agreement have made that agreement because

it is in their mutual interest. Thus once signed, they would and could enforce them, and the only task was to provide safeguards against cheating in a capacity to monitor, gather information, and create transparency to keep them honest to their own commitments. Called the liberal-institutionalist approach to cooperation in international relations, it assumes that parties represent the national interests of established, sovereign units—missing here—and that issues are subject to compromise and mutual interest, which did not appear to be the case between the Bosnian Muslim and Bosnian Serb leaderships over territory and state configurations or, despite the short-term example in the Washington Agreement, in the long run between the Bosnian Muslims and the Bosnian Croats.

77. General Philippe Morillon, speaking at the Woodrow Wilson Center, December 7, 1993.

78. Interview with Tomiko Ichikawa. The rough annual cost of UNPROFOR to the United Nations is $1.9 billion, met by assessed contributions from member states. *Information Notes: Update: May 1994*, United Nations Peace-keeping (PS/DPI/14/Rev.5-May 1994). The most recent statement of the budget, for the period July 1, 1993 to March 31, 1994, can be found in "Financing of the United Nations Protection Force," Report of the UN General Assembly, 48th Session: A/48/690/Add.4, August 16, 1994. The total size of UNPROFOR military and civilian personnel on September 6, 1994, was 42,999 persons; the next largest peacekeeping force was UNISOM II, in Somalia, which had 18,404 military personnel on April 30, 1994, when the total military personnel for UNPROFOR was 33,298 (United Nations Peace-keeping, *Information Notes: Update: May 1994*, United Nations Department of Public Information, DPI/1306/Rev.3-June 1994-7M).

79. Jonathan S. Landay, "A Centuries-Old Serbian Enclave Stands Firm," *Christian Science Monitor*, October 21, 1993, p. 6.

80. In October 1991, when residents of eleven Sandžak communes in Serbia and Montenegro were to vote for autonomy for the region, for example, the secretary of the SDA for the Sandžak, Rasim Ljajić, explained: "The Sandžak was discussed at the Berlin Congress in 1878 and in 1912 in London and then in 1945 in Novi Pazar, but the Muslim people were not consulted on any occasion. Therefore, if the right to self-determination applies to the Serbs in Croatia and to any other people in the country, why would this right be denied to the Muslim people in the Sandžak?" Dževad Kapetanović, "Sandžak Autonomy Referendum Examined," Sarajevo Radio, October 22, 1991, in FBIS, *East Europe*, October 23, 1991, p. 53.

81. Their position was summarized by Ivica Račan, leader of the Social Democratic party: "Unified Bosnia is in the strategic interest of the Croatian state and people." Quoted by Fabian Schmidt, *RFE/RL Daily Report*, September 9, 1993. Also, author's interview with Dražen Budiša, leader of the Croatian Social-Liberal party, in Washington, D.C., July 8, 1993. The opposition's statement of ten points was a direct response to the official proclamation on August 24 by Mate Boban of a state of Herzeg-Bosnia with its capital at Mostar in territory corresponding to the lines drawn on the Owen-Stoltenberg plan.

82. Accurate numbers of people considering themselves Macedonian are difficult to obtain because non-Bulgarian ethnic identification was politically discouraged under the Communist regime. Large numbers of people from areas now part

of Yugoslav Macedonia fled to Sofia at the end of the nineteenth century, and another exodus took place (particularly from the Ohrid area) after World War II. "To this day many Bulgarian cities are made up of people of almost wholly Macedonian origin." James Pettifer, "The New Macedonian Question," *International Affairs*, July 1992, p. 484.

83. Interview in Zagreb on September 16, 1994.

84. Foreign Minister of France, Alain Juppé, was quoted by the Yugoslav official news agency, TANJUG, from Paris, as saying "We should play Milošević as a trump card. If there is a chance for peace, we must not allow it to slip us." *Politika*, September 9, 1994.

85. "If confederal relations of Bosnian Serbs with Serbia are legalized, then we will also immediately demand such relations with Albania," Rugova said at a press conference in Priština, September 9, 1994, reported in *Borba* (*Bilten Vesti*, September 10, 1994, Savezna Republika Jugoslavija, Savezno Ministarstvo Inostranih Poslova, direkcija SIK, br. 1-697, 10.09.1994, p. 2). Rexhep Cosja, Kosovo intellectual and politician, went further. In an interview with the Belgrade *Monitor*, September 2, 1994, he said, "If the 1,200,000 Bosnian Serbs (one third of Bosnia's population) succeed in founding their own country (someone would say 'the fourth Serbian state which would unite with Serbia in the future') why should not 2,000,000 ethnic Albanians (90 percent of the Kosovo population) do the same in Kosovo?"

# Chapter 10

1. On December 11, 1992, the UN Security Council voted to redeploy 700 UNPROFOR troops from Bosnia-Herzegovina to Macedonia as monitors along the border with Serbia for the same purpose (to provide transparency against military movements on the assumption that war would begin by armed invasion from Serbia across the Macedonian border). They began to arrive January 6, 1993, in the first case of preventive diplomacy as proposed by UN Secretary-General Boutros Boutros-Ghali in his post–cold war proclamation in June 1992, an *Agenda for Peace*. They were joined in July by 325 U.S. troops. President Clinton, under pressure from European allies to show more commitment than air power if he wanted them to take more action, agreed to send the troops from Germany on June 18, 1993; they arrived the week of July 5–12. A year later the U.S. contingent in the UN command in Macedonia had risen to 535, almost half the total of 1,114. A military presence was an even stronger statement than CSCE monitors as a warning to President Milošević of UN and U.S. commitment to the sovereignty of Macedonia (even when the United States would not recognize the state because Greece continued to object to the name).

2. Two particularly informative works on the situation in Macedonia immediately after the breakup of Yugoslavia are James Pettifer, "The New Macedonian Question," *International Affairs*, vol. 68 (July 1992), pp. 475–86, and John Zametica, *The Yugoslav Conflict*, Adelphi Paper 270 (London: International Institute for Strategic Studies, 1992), pp. 34–36.

3.  On the flag of Serb nationalists, particularly those who claimed to be reviving the World War II right-wing Chetnik tradition, were four Ss (in Cyrillic, so that it would appear as four Cs), for: *Samo Sloga Spašava Srba,* "Only unity saves the Serbs."

4.  John Major, speaking at the London Conference, August 26, 1992, directed at Slobodan Milošević.

5.  Authorities of the federal republic of Yugoslavia (FRY) also complained that the Macedonian government had not yet in early 1995 recognized the existence and sovereignty of FRY either.

6.  For a similar argument, see Misha Glenny, "Hope for Bosnia?" *The New York Review of Books,* vol. 41, April 7, 1994, p. 8. Stefan Troebst outlines six scenarios in "Macedonia: Powder Keg Defused?" *RFE/RL Research Report,* vol. 3, January 28, 1994, pp. 33–41.

7.  Ten Macedonian Albanians, including Mithat Emini, formerly general secretary of the PDP, were found guilty of plotting to organize an Albanian irredentist army and sentenced to terms ranging from five to eight years (Emini received the heaviest sentence). Their defense was that the armament of Albanians in Macedonia, and the arms smuggling it involved, had taken place on grounds of self-defense and before a Macedonian army had been formed; they were tried under former Yugoslav law, the sentences were far heavier than those given to non-Albanians for similar crimes, and they have since incorporated into the army without complaint. The fact that members of the government had apparently reassured PDP leaders of light sentences (maximum 18 months) reinforced their perception that this represented anti-Albanian prejudice.

8.  Originally recruited by the Bosnian government, in mid-1994 they were estimated to number between 1,300 and 2,000.

9.  The most obvious example is that of the Croatian diaspora and the role of individuals such as Gojko Šušak, who became minister of defense in the independent Croatia and who spent decades organizing Croats in emigration in North America and raising funds to establish an independent Croatia (by supporting Franjo Tudjman and his political party).

10.  According to Mary McIntosh, Martha Abele MacIver, Daniel G. Abele, and David B. Nolle, "Minority Rights and Majority Rule: Ethnic Tolerance in Bulgaria and Romania," *Social Forces* (forthcoming, March 1995), this perception of threat by governments is widely shared by individual citizens, too.

11.  "Agreement on the Assurance of Special Rights of the Slovenian Minority Living in the Republic of Hungary and the Hungarian National Community Living in the Republic of Slovenia," November 6, 1992.

12.  According to Dr. Peter Vencelj, State Secretary in the Ministry for Foreign Affairs, in a communication with the author, they were not autochthonous or "indigenous" and therefore had no rights as national minorities.

13.  The Italian community in Istria and Dalmatia comprised about 35,000 people. In addition about 30,000 had left after World War II, and they began to press the Italian government in 1992–93 for recovery of their properties in Slovenia and Croatia. Although the Italian government had reassured Slovenia that its independence would not affect the border agreement in the 1975 Treaty of Osimo, that independence, popular pressure in Italy, the new right-wing government of

Prime Minister Berlusconi in 1994, and the activities of the Istrian Democratic Alliance in Croatia created great pressure by 1994 for bilateral revision of the treaty with Slovenia and Croatia to strengthen protections for the Italian minority and to regain property or receive compensation.

14.  Conditions were deteriorating so that on August 20, 1993, a subgroup on the protection of minorities of the UN Human Rights Commission submitted a draft resolution for discussion at the commission's annual meeting in Geneva that would demand that Belgrade revoke all discriminatory laws and facilitate the work of CSCE human rights observers; the UN Security Council condemned the Serbian government for expelling CSCE monitors in July 1993, in Resolution 855 of August 9, 1993. Also, Amnesty International has tracked the deteriorating situation, and especially Serbian police violence against ethnic Albanian civilians, in a number of reports throughout 1994. See *Yugoslavia: Ethnic Albanians—Trial by Truncheon* (AI index: EUR 70/01/94; February, 1994); *Yugoslavia: Police Violence Against Ethnic Albanians in Kosovo Province* (AI index: EUR 70/06/94; April 1994); and *Yugoslavia: Police Violence in Kosovo Province—the Victims* (AI index: EUR 70/16/94; September, 1994).

15.  Cited in Fabian Schmidt, "Amnesty International Blasts Rights Situation in Kosovo," *Radio Free Europe/Radio Liberty (RFE/RL) Daily Report*, November 24, 1993.

16.  The possibility that the separation of one part of the republic would provide the occasion for the remaining neighbors to divide the territory among them, erasing Macedonia altogether, was openly discussed during 1992–93 within ruling political circles in Greece, Serbia, Bulgaria, and Albanian communities.

17.  The exact numbers are unknown because the Albanians boycotted the 1991 census; any number cited reflects a political position, with the Macedonian government tending to undercount, at 15 percent, and the Albanian community tending to exaggerate, at 40 percent. Under sponsorship and funding of the Council of Europe, a new census was held in June 1994 to resolve this issue, but the official results announced tentatively in mid-November 1994 are also subject to differing interpretations (see chapter 7, note 32).

18.  This opened up what might have been an unnecessary struggle for the identities of other groups in Macedonia. The resulting developments gave the government reason to worry about the choice on identity to be made, in particular, by Romany, Turks, and Macedonian Muslims. Thus revised textbooks on Macedonian history and a curriculum reform begun in late 1992 aimed to develop Macedonian national consciousness and, with particular attention to the schooling of the Romany population in the Macedonian language, to regain their loyalties from their recent inclinations toward Albanian.

19.  A representative example, in conversations with the author in mid-1994, is Edward Mortimer of the *Financial Times*.

20.  Stan Markotich, "Istria Seeks Autonomy," *RFE/RL Research Report*, September 10, 1993, pp. 22–26.

21.  Information communicated to author by UN civil affairs personnel in Sector East, September 9, 1994.

22.  "Proceeding from the inalienable right to self-determination, following a policy of peace, tolerance and cooperation with other nations, and in order to

preserve national identity and safeguard the individual and collective rights of the Muslim nation of Sanjak, the Parliament of the Muslim National Council of Sanjak (MNCS), at its session of January 11, 1992, voted to establish *a special status for Sanjak* as the optimal solution for the Muslim nation, which is autochthonous on this territory. Consistent with this position, the Muslim National Council of Sanjak boycotted the elections in the remnants of Yugoslavia on May 31, 1992, and December 20, 1992, which action supported the Muslims [sic] nation of Sanjak by not participating in elections until there were a public resolution of the status of the Muslim nation of Sanjak." Dr. Sulejman Ugljanin [President, MNCS], "*Memorandum on the Establishment of a Special Status for Sanjak*" (Novi Pazar, Serbia: Muslim National Council of Sanjak, June 1993), p. i.

23.  "Tudjman Addresses UN General Assembly," Radio Croatia Network, September 27, 1994, in *Foreign Broadcast Information Service, Daily Report: East Europe* (hereafter FBIS, *East Europe*), September 28, 1994, pp. 46–48.

24.  Ethnic Hungarians living in Vojvodina numbered approximately 430,000 in 1992, or 22 percent of the total population in the province (somewhat fewer than the Serb population in Croatia and the Hungarian population in Slovakia). See Edith Oltay, "Hungarians Under Political Pressure in Vojvodina," *RFE/RL Research Report*, December 3, 1993, pp. 43–48.

25.  A project agreed on in 1977 by the Czechoslovak and Hungarian governments to dam the Danube River, making it more navigable for international vessels, assisting flood control, and feeding a hydroelectric power station. The postcommunist government in Hungary, responding to popular pressure organized by environmentalist groups, renounced and attempted to stop it in 1992. Because the river's diversion would change the border between the countries, an official from the Hungarian foreign ministry accused the Slovak government of violating their "territorial integrity." Cited in Ken Kasriel, "Danube Dam Spurs Hungary's Ire," *Christian Science Monitor*, October 30, 1992, p. 2.

26.  The independence-oriented Macedonian nationalists in Macedonia were pushing for independence by July 1990 along with Kosovo, Slovenia, and Croatia, but they did not win in the December 1990 elections and remained a minority party, operating as a radicalizing pressure from the Parliament.

27.  On its effects on the subsequent wars, see chapter 8.

28.  Calling itself the first "ecological state" in the world, it began an overall strategy for an environmentally clean, maritime area open to investment, tourism, and trade, which also had engaged lively interest at the World Bank. Any hope of financial support ended, however, when it "sided with Serbia," as its policies were described in Washington.

29.  Three reasons could be cited. A long and complicated historical debate over whether Montenegrins are Serbs (because they are south Slavs of the Eastern branch of Christianity) or Montenegrins appears to have been decided by foreign observers in favor of the former. See Ivo Banac, *The National Question in Yugoslavia: Origins, History and Politics* (Cornell University Press, 1984), pp. 23, 290–91. Montenegrin units of the Yugoslav army participated in the devastation of the area surrounding Dubrovnik in the war in Croatia; few asked whether they had a choice or if this reflected Montenegrin public opinion. As in the case of Serb recruits, stories of desertion and refusal to fight were given little publicity. See "BORBA

Reports Army Desertion, Replenishment Problems," TANJUG, October 18, 1991, FBIS, *East Europe*, October 22, 1991, p. 42. The political leadership of Montenegro chose to remain within Yugoslavia when the state broke up; it did not apply for recognition in December 1991 when the EC offered all six republics consideration, on the same grounds as Serbia—that its statehood had already been recognized by the Treaty of Berlin in 1878.

30. The first two-month blockade by Greece cost Macedonia $1.4 billion in needed supplies; trade losses from UN sanctions on Serbia were put at nearly $3 billion in mid-1993. Eric Bourne, "Brave in the Balkan Heartland," *Christian Science Monitor*, August 19, 1993, p. 20.

31. The tactics of President Islam Karimov of Uzbekistan in the first years after its precipitate independence (especially toward the opposition Erk) are a good example.

32. This applied even to those entities aiming at statehood, with two exceptions: the "Republic of Serbian Krajina" and "Herzeg-Bosnia." The choice of leadership in both, however, was not fully independent—in the first case strongly influenced by Serbian President Milošević and the second case fully under the control of Croatian President Tudjman.

33. Claus Offe, "Strong Causes, Weak Cures," *East European Constitutional Review*, vol. 1 (Spring 1992), pp. 21–23, suggests this problem is likely wherever "internal minorities . . . are at the same time external minorities of neighboring states, which are seen as foreign patron states of these minorities"—as is the case throughout eastern Europe, and the problem is reciprocal—"where each of two adjacent states has an external minority in the other (e.g., Slovakia and Hungary, Albania and Greece)."

34. See Chuck Sudetic, "A Shady Militia Chief Arouses Serbs," *New York Times*, December 20, 1992, p. A12, who quotes Ražnatović from a December 12 rally in Obilić, Serbia.

35. For example, secret negotiations taking place in November 1993 between Croatia and Serbia in Norway, encouraged by Geneva co-chairman, UN envoy, and former Norwegian foreign minister, Thorwald Stoltenberg, on the model of the successful PLO-Israeli talks, collapsed when President Tudjman leaked their existence to the press.

36. Pink zones are areas lying outside the boundaries of the UN protected areas but that were controlled by Serbs at the time of the Vance plan. They arose for two reasons: because the confrontation line between the Croatian government and Serb forces changed between the signing of the plan and the arrival of UN troops, and because the boundaries were drawn according to administrative borders of districts rather than actual military control. Adjacent to UNPAs, they came to fall within the ten-kilometer zone of separation established by the cease-fire agreement of March 29, 1994, and supervised by joint UN, Serbian, and Croatian patrols once mines had been removed.

37. The three villages were Divoselo, Čitluk, and Počitelj.

38. Milošević's electoral law had translated the Radicals' 10 percent of the electorate into one-third of the parliamentary seats.

39. Confidential communications to author.

40. See the most recent discussions on this old topic in Carol R. Ember, Melvin Ember, and Bruce Russett, "Peace Between Participatory Polities: A Cross-Cultural Test of the 'Democracies Rarely Fight Against Each Other' Hypothesis," *World Politics*, vol. 44 (July 1992), pp. 573–99. Good examples of this process *after* national independence can be found in the politics of Ukraine and Russia in 1992–93.

41. Fabian Schmidt, "Kosovo Update," *RFE/RL Daily Report*, September 8, 1993.

42. His foreign minister, Antonis Samaras, left the New Democracy party on this issue to form a separate party, the Political Spring party, bringing down the government. Although the campaign was fought largely on the domestic economy, the primary foreign policy issue was competition over how militant to be toward Macedonia.

43. His method was to create a governmental scandal over the discovery of arms-smuggling to the Bosnian government, allegedly by the Slovene president and associates of the prime minister, so as to bring the government down. See, for example, Jonathan S. Landay, "Slovenian Party Charged With Violating UN Ban On Yugoslav Arms," *Christian Science Monitor*, October 25, 1993, pp. 1, 20. According to Slovenes interviewed in June 1993, Janša's campaign aimed at the government of his rivals, President Milan Kučan and Prime Minister Janez Drnovšek, and included accusations that they were "re-integrationists" favoring renewed relations with republics of former Yugoslavia, even though he held a portfolio in this coalition government—with the ultimate aim of destabilizing the political system itself. As defense minister, Janša could not have been unaware of the transactions, and his complicity (as that of the Austrian government also) was later demonstrated in January 1994.

44. See the analysis of opinion poll results in "Udruže li se njegovi disidenti, HDZ bi u Saboru postao manjinska stranka i bez izbora pao s vlasti!" ("If its opponents were to ally, HDZ would become a minority party in the Sabor [Parliament] and without elections would fall from power!"), *Globus*, September 24, 1993, pp. 12–13; and "Katolička Crkva brani cjelovitu Bosnu i Hercegovinu" ("The Catholic Church defends an integral Bosnia and Herzegovina"), pp. 5–8, and "Popularnost HSLS-a ponovno raste!" ("The popularity of the HSLS is rising again!"), p. 11, in *Globus*, February 11, 1994.

45. Conflict within the Serbian Democratic Party in January 1992 was primarily over finances. The rebellion in Banja Luka against Karadžić's leadership came to a head over a financial scandal in which Karadžić was accused of imposing a surcharge on gas sold in Serbian-claimed areas for diversion to SDS party headquarters, in effect, secretly robbing local leaders of revenues they considered theirs.

46. See Srbobran Branković, "How Bolshevik is Serbia?" *East European Reporter*, vol. 5 (January–February 1992), pp. 8–11.

47. It is difficult to assess what portion of the vote for Milošević in the December 1992 elections was a direct result of the American campaign, although the opposition and independent analysts considered it extremely detrimental to their cause. It has been widely suggested in Europe, in fact, that the Bush administration did not want Milošević defeated, viewing him as a factor of stability in the region,

and that this was the real purpose of the Eagleburger accusation. Accusations of electoral fraud by the CSCE monitoring mission suggest that "seriously flawed" election procedures contributed substantially to Milošević's victory. According to final election results, Milošević received approximately 57 percent against Panić's 35 percent. Other candidates received a little more than 5 percent of the overall ballots cast. Milan Paroški of the People's party and Serbian opposition placed third with 3.4 percent of the vote. See "Results of the December 1992 Parliamentary and Presidential Elections," *Yugoslav Survey*, vol. 24, no. 1 (1993), pp. 3–50.

48. For example, the offensive of the first week of November 1993 (almost three months after the world community announced the "endgame" in Bosnia) was alone expected to create 150,000 refugees on the Croat side, according to Croatian foreign minister Mate Granić in a letter to the United Nations. Patrick Moore, "End Game for the Croats in Central Bosnia?" *RFE/RL Daily Report*, November 8, 1993.

49. The defeat of Fikret Abdić by the Fifth Corps of the Bosnian government army in August 1994 sent tens of thousands of refugees into the UN Protected Area Sector North and in the zone of separation of Croatia. Trapped there because Croatia would not permit them to enter Croatia or grant them transit to third countries, they became the fighting force for Abdić when he returned to the Bihać pocket in late November to fight to reclaim his "autonomous region of Western Bosnia" with the aid of Bosnian Serbs and Croatian Serbs. In the scenarios that predicted a resumption of war in Croatia in the spring of 1995, this example loomed large: that the Croatian government would take a cue from Abdić and incite hundreds of thousands of Croatian displaced persons to rush back to their homes in the UNPAs as the advance guard of the Croatian army.

50. The number was far less precise because the majority were placed with families, whereas they were easier to count in Croatia (672,000) and Slovenia (60,000) where they were largely confined to refugee camps.

51. "German cities struggle with Bosnian war refugees," Reuter wire service, February 28, 1994, and Reuter wire service briefs, March 8, 1994.

52. Illegal immigrants reportedly were flowing into the northwestern town of Tetovo—the seat of Albanian autonomist aspirations for a state of "Ilirida" and of radical political activity among Macedonian Albanians—at a rate of 100 persons a day. Confidential communication, July 1, 1994.

53. Milan Andrejevich, "Slovenia's Economic Woes," *RFE/RL Daily Report*, August 31, 1993, citing a study of the respected Economics Institute (renamed after its founder, Aleksandar Bajt, the Bajt Institute) in Ljubljana. Zmago Jelinčić won 10 percent of the vote in the elections of November 1992 for his position, among others, accusing 100,000 Bosnian refugees of fleeing economic deprivation rather than war. See "Slovenia's Voters Reject Balkans Diet of Nationalism," *Financial Times*, December 8, 1992, p. 2; and "Ultranationalists Campaigning Strongly in Slovenian Election," *Financial Times*, December 5–6, 1992, p. 2.

54. Rasko Močnik, "Slovenia: Domestic Strife Shakes the Peace," *YugoFax*, no. 6, October 31, 1991, p. 5, describes the continuation in Slovenia of the nationalist momentum: the one-sided, "chauvinistic" reporting of formerly independent and liberal newspapers, the public campaigns to "create differences," and so forth.

55. Interviews in Macedonia, 1994.

56. Paul Lewis, "UN Aides Cite Drawbacks to Bosnia Safe-Haven Plan," *New York Times*, May 30, 1993, p. A10.

57. Aleksandra Mijalković, "The Vukovar Syndrome," *East European Reporter*, vol. 5 (May–June 1992), p. 16.

58. A new business class (and potentially the new political elite) had emerged in Serbia by the fall of 1992 on the basis of sanction-busting. Some of the most spectacular successes were former émigrés, such as Jezdimir Vasiljević from Australia. See Chuck Sudetic, "A Belgrade Banker Makes Big Profits from Trade Sanctions," *New York Times*, February 16, 1993, p. A3, and John Kifner, "As Embargo Squeezes Yugoslavia, Trade Grows Brisk Over the Borders," *New York Times*, December 27, 1993, p. A6.

Émigrés were the critical conduit for illegal arms to Croatia as well. Criminal gangs in Sarajevo had become so powerful by the summer of 1993 that the first activities of the new government of Haris Silajdžić aimed at rounding them up. See John F. Burns, "Gangs in Sarajevo Spread Terror Unchecked by the Cowed Leaders," *New York Times*, October 22, 1993, p. A1; and John Pomfret, "Missed Hit Is Talk of Sarajevo: Many in City See Mobsters—not Politicians—Controlling Future," *Washington Post*, October 7, 1993, p. A35.

59. See discussion in chapter 8 and Tim van Beveren, "Uncontrolled Substances: The Export of Death," and "The Anglo-German Connection: Illegal Transfers Made Simple!" *WarReport*, no. 17 (January 1993), pp. 16–18.

60. John F. Burns, "Serbs and Croats Join in Devouring Bosnia's Land," *New York Times*, October 27, 1992, p. A1.

61. According to the U.S. Arms Control and Disarmament Agency (ACDA), Yugoslavia was one of six developing countries among the world's largest arms exporters. See U.S. Arms Control and Disarmament Agency, *World Military Expenditures and Transfers, 1990* (November 1991).

62. For example, the city of Mainz, Germany, had only 1,500 of the more than 40,000 refugees in Germany from the wars in Bosnia and Croatia, but the population of 175,000 received no aid from the federal government to help cover the cost (17 million marks [$9.9 million] in 1994) of basic necessities. Local officials feared the escalation of a resulting antiforeigner debate into the neo-Nazi and right-wing violence in other parts of Germany. Michael Christie, "German Cities Struggle With Bosnian War Refugees," Reuter wire service, February 28, 1994.

63. According to Heide Schmidt, the leader of the centrist party the Liberal Forum, "There is now a climate in this country that supports an increasing readiness to use violence." Stephen Kinzer, "More Letter Bombings in Austria Raise Fears of Neo-Nazi Terrorism," *New York Times*, December 7, 1993, p. A1.

64. It also changed rules on issuing visas in June 1993. See Jane Perlez, "Prague Fears Being Migrant Trails Last Stop," *New York Times*, June 30, 1993, p. A1.

65. Kosovo Albanians were prominent, especially in Switzerland, Germany, and Sweden, in heroin trafficking along the so-called Balkan route from Turkey and in organized crime; Dutch authorities complained in late 1993 that the Yugoslav gangs were particularly violent. See Graham H. Turbiville, Jr., "The Organized Crime Dimension of Regional Conflict and Operations Other Than War," in Robert

L. Pfaltzgraff, Jr., and Richard H. Shultz, Jr., eds., *Ethnic Conflict and Regional Instability: Implications for U.S. Policy and Army Roles and Missions* (Washington, D.C.: Strategic Studies Institute, U.S. Army War College, 1994), pp. 134–38.

66.   General Phillippe Morillon, former deputy force commander of UN forces, April 1992–October 1992, and commander of Bosnia-Herzegovina command, UNPROFOR, October 1992–July 10, 1993, speaking at the Woodrow Wilson Center in Washington, D.C., December 7, 1993.

67.   Many argue that Yeltsin's greatest frustration with this Parliament was its incessant pressure on the "Serbian question," criticizing Foreign Minister Kozyrev's policy and passing a series of resolutions to demand that Russia play a larger and more independent role in the Balkans as a matter of Russian national interest. Thus his exasperated surprise when the new Parliament elected in December showed no change on the issue—the agenda of its first session in January 1994 was deputies' salaries; the second day, the deputies returned to Balkan policy and the Serbian question. (Personal communication with Dr. Yelena Guskova, Balkan specialist, Russian Academy of Sciences, July 1994.) Yeltsin's warning that NATO expansion threatened to plunge Europe into "a cold peace" to the Budapest summit of the CSCE on December 5, 1994, and Moscow's use of armed force in Chechnya in December 1994 could be seen, in part, to follow.

68.   See the Russian military doctrine adopted November 2, 1993, in "The Basic Provisions of the Military Doctrine of the Russian Federation: Russia's Military Doctrine," *Rossiyskiye vesti*, November 18, 1993, in FBIS, *Daily Report: Central Eurasia*, November 19, 1993, pp. 1–11.

69.   The symbol for neo-Nazis in Austria in the 1990s was Count Rudiger von Starhemberg, the commander of forces that repelled the Ottoman assault on Vienna in 1683. Stephen Kinzer, "More Letter Bombings in Austria Raise Fears of Neo-Nazi Terrorism," *New York Times*, December 7, 1993, p. A1. The issue of Bosnia was the single most important political issue in Turkey in the fall of 1992, interrupted in public attention only briefly by the murder of one of Turkey's most popular journalists. Turkish doctors went to the aid of Muslim women raped in Bosnia-Herzegovina. As a result of forced expulsions and flight from the region at several points earlier in the century, there were a substantial number of Turkish citizens originally from Macedonia or Bosnia, many with immediate family ties still in former Yugoslavia.

70.   For more information on the estimated total cost to Bulgaria incurred from sanctions enforcement, see Embassy of the Republic of Bulgaria, "After Entry Into Force of the New Trade and Economic Sanctions Against the Federal Republic of Yugoslavia Imposed by the UNSC Resolution 820 From 17 April, 1993" (undated).

71.   The authority on mass killings and genocide in the twentieth century, Robert Jay Lifton, argues that any contact with such atrocities has reverberations that are all negative, leading to a general loss of moral compass, and that the problem of the extensive television coverage in the Yugoslav case is that it makes all viewers into knowing bystanders who then feel in some ways complicit for not having done more to stop it. See, for example, Robert Jay Lifton, "Introduction," to Zlatko Dizdarević, *Sarajevo: A War Journal* (New York: Fromm International, 1993), pp. xv–xxvi.

72. Samuel P. Huntington, "The Clash of Civilizations?" *Foreign Affairs*, vol. 72 (Summer 1993), pp. 22–49. U.S. Senator Bill Bradley (D-NJ) won substantial affirmation when he based his keynote address at the World Economic Forum annual meeting, in Davos, Switzerland, January–February 1993, on an early draft of Huntington's article.

## Chapter 11

1. *Yavashlik*, according to linguist and polymath Victor Friedman, is a Turkish word meaning "slowness," but it is used colloquially (particularly in the south) to mean, as he put it to me, "the kind of foot-dragging, promise-without-delivering, come-back-tomorrow avoidance of confrontation that is a classic Balkan method of conflict avoidance" (personal communication).

2. This group was now quite actively organized worldwide as the Friends of Bosnia and affiliated groups such as the Action Council for Peace in the Balkans in the United States. The Friends of Bosnia was organized by the U.S. government with seven other states—Albania, Austria, Bulgaria, Croatia, Hungary, Turkey, and Bosnia-Herzegovina—under the auspices of the CSCE in April 1992. Its membership enlarged de facto to seventeen by May; it gained particular impetus and support from countries of the Organization of the Islamic Conference, such as Malaysia, and centered its program on the lifting of the arms embargo on the government of Bosnia-Herzegovina and on sending arms.

3. The resulting mixed messages from these two impulses were on occasion particularly stark. For example, the day after a cessation-of-hostilities agreement obtained by UNPROFOR negotiators was signed by the Bosnian government and the Bosnian Serb leaders, on June 9, 1994, the U.S. House of Representatives voted 244 to 178 to amend the National Defense Authorization Act to require the president to terminate the arms embargo on the Bosnian government and to provide appropriate military assistance, upon receipt of a request for such assistance from the Bosnian government. See *Congressional Record*, daily ed., June 9, 1994, pp. H4232–H4252. The process to end the arms embargo, with amendments to the National Defense Authorization Act for fiscal year 1995 (S.2182), continued the next month, when the Senate responded with two amendments on August 11. One, sponsored by chairman of the armed services committee Sam Nunn, that passed by a vote of 56 to 44, would require the president to withdraw the United States from enforcement of the embargo on November 15 if the UN Security Council did not vote to do so by the end of October 1994. The other, sponsored by minority leader Robert J. Dole and Senator Joseph Lieberman, also passed, 58 to 42; it committed the United States to lifting the arms embargo unilaterally by November 15, regardless of UN action. See Daniel Williams, "Senate Seeks to Press Clinton on Bosnia Arms," *Washington Post*, August 12, 1994, p. A33. The Clinton administration introduced a resolution to exempt the Bosnian government from the arms embargo to the UN Security Council on October 28, 1994.

4. The threat to withdraw in the first week of December 1994—led by the French and accompanied by the first U.S. official commitment (announced De-

cember 8) to contribute ground troops to extraction—came the closest to the brink of all previous threats. Although the British defense minister, Malcolm Rifkind, announced as early as December 5 that his government would not withdraw unilaterally, the threat was reversed only at the European Union meeting in Essen, Germany, December 9. On the official U.S. offer, see Bruce Clark and Laura Silber, "UK Holds Back From Bosnia Withdrawal," *Financial Times*, December 9, 1994, p. 3; on the French threats of withdrawal, see, for instance, Emma Tucker, "Delors in Attack on Nato Plan to Expand," *Financial Times*, December 8, 1994, p. 1; on Rifkind's announcement, see Clark, "Major Says Bosnia War Could Spread," *Financial Times*, December 6, 1994, p. 3; on the joint UK–French decision to retain a peacekeeping presence, see Lionel Barber, "Britain and France Firm on Bosnia," *Financial Times*, December 10–11, 1994, p. 2. Ironically, moreover, Western governments and the UN Secretary-General found themselves in the opposite dilemma when Croatian president Tudjman formally demanded in January 1995 that the UN forces leave Croatia after the expiration of their current mandate on March 30, 1995, with withdrawal to be complete by June 30. They responded with a serious campaign of pressure to change Tudjman's mind.

5. Because international negotiations were committed to the republican borders and territorial integrity of Bosnia-Herzegovina, the ongoing talks between Croats and Serbs over partition had to remain secret. By the late summer and into the fall of 1994, the public language of Croatian officials in Zagreb suggested that these negotiations had settled on a new formula: a "smaller Greater Serbia." Croatia would accept the union of the Republic of the Serb People of Bosnia-Herzegovina with the Federal Republic of Yugoslavia in exchange for retaining Croatian sovereignty over the territory claimed by Croatian Serbs in the four UN protected areas (the "republic of Serbian *krajina*").

6. An interview with the new secretary-general of NATO, Willy Claes, in a Belgian newspaper (as reported on Voice of America on December 9, 1994, 12:19 GMT) summed up this approach: "Mr. Claes denies that NATO is paralyzed, and claims the alliance does have the military might to save the Bosnian enclave of Bihać. But, he admits NATO is losing part of its credibility because UN authorities refuse to authorize a military solution to the problem."

7. Bogdan Denitch argues that the "central problem for which the destruction of Yugoslavia provides useful insights is that of the relationship of the politics of identity, of nationalism, to democracy," in *Ethnic Nationalism: The Tragic Death of Yugoslavia* (University of Minnesota Press, 1994), p. 1, a book on the interaction between nationalism and democracy.

8. Vesna Pusić argues that elections have been used, in fact, to legitimize personal and emergency rule (what she calls "democratic dictatorships"), not to create the responsive governments and "civil freedoms [and] political competition" in periods between elections that characterize democracy. See Vesna Pusić, "Dictatorships with Democratic Legitimacy: Democracy versus Nation," *East European Politics and Societies*, vol. 8 (Fall 1994), pp. 396, 399.

9. In the fall of 1990 the Slovene government did commission a study of the economic effects of secession. However, radicals in the parliament rushed a referendum of sovereignty and secession before its results were available. When the study was ready in the spring of 1991, its analyses concluded that the economic

costs would be far greater than the benefits. Indeed, the government fell behind in the legally binding obligation from the December plebiscite to present a program for realizing independence before June because of the difficulty on an economic program and a parliamentary opposition that was increasingly vocal about the high economic price they would pay. "Slovenian Leadership Faces Problems on Secession," TANJUG, April 26, 1991, in Foreign Broadcast Information Service, *Daily Report: East Europe*, April 29, 1991, pp. 39–40 (hereafter FBIS, *East Europe*). Their action supports the argument that nationalism is "irrational," in the colloquial sense that its motivations are more powerful than economic gain. But such an interpretation requires an understanding of economic interest that ignores the essential political and state context of economic activity—who controls the resources and defines rights to property and to make economic policy. It also does not take into account the changing structure of opportunity in the international environment. For Slovenia (by 1994 accepted by European foreign offices and regional organizations as a member of central Europe rather than of southeast Europe), this changing structure predicted long-run economic advantage from secession, although this was not easy to measure at the time. Moreover, while the Yugoslav market had purchased 35 percent of Slovene goods in 1990 and its loss was one of the primary causes of economic difficulties in 1993 (according to an August 1993 study of the Bajt Economics Institute), the country's foreign currency reserves rose tenfold in 1993–94 as a result of earnings in the market for arms created by the wars in Croatia and especially in Bosnia.

10. The operative paragraph 12 of UN Security Council Resolution 820 ("The Security Council, acting under Chapter VII of the Charter of the United Nations, Decides that import to, export from and transshipment through the United Nations Protected Areas in the Republic of Croatia and those areas of the Republic of Bosnia and Herzegovina under the control of Bosnian Serb forces, with the exception of essential humanitarian supplies including medical supplies and foodstuffs distributed by international humanitarian agencies, shall be permitted only with the proper authorization from the Government of the Republic of Croatia or the Government of the Republic of Bosnia and Herzegovina respectively") was particularly criticized by *krajina* Serbs for this effect, which they considered discriminatory and pushed them further away from cooperation with the Zagreb government and closer to a sense of common destiny with Serbs in Bosnia-Herzegovina and in Serbia and Montenegro. The policy of isolating Bosnian Serbs in order to force their agreement to the Contact Group plan in the second half of 1994 and into 1995 included draconian restrictions on what Serbs in *krajina* could receive, as did the stricter prohibitions to prevent the flow of fuel oil, arms, and other materials to the Croatian and Bosnian Serbs that were added to the sanctions against Serbia and Montenegro January 12, 1995, when the UN Security Council extended for another 100 days the first step to lighten the sanctions by lifting restrictions on travel, sports, and scientific exchanges.

11. This is the phrase used uniformly by public officials, and the majority of Croats, to refer to the problem of Serbs in *krajina*. See, for example, "Introductory Address of the President of Croatia Dr. Franjo Tudjman to the UN Security Council," September 27, 1994, in FBIS, *East Europe*, September 28, 1994, pp. 46–48.

12. This blunt bargaining tactic by the stronger party to squeeze the weaker into concessions was also characteristic of Serbian policy toward ethnic Albanians in Kosovo, but the methods were more directly political than economic, by denying them rights and representation.

13. This was most apparent in the counterattack to reverse Bosnian government (5th Corps) gains in the Bihać pocket and help restore autonomist Fikret Abdić to his leadership of *Cazinska Krajina*, in November 1994. Such joint activity was particularly problematic for an international operation that was required to treat Croatia and Bosnia-Herzegovina separately according to their status as sovereign states, but this particular operation also led to the most severe crisis in NATO in its existence and marked a major reversal in U.S. policy when Secretary of Defense William Perry announced, on November 27, 1994, that air power could not defeat the Bosnian Serbs or reverse their gains around Bihać, even though it was declared a UN protected safe area. For an analysis of the change in U.S. policy, see Michael Gordon, "U.S. and Bosnia: How NATO's Changing Shape Altered Policy," *New York Times*, December 4, 1994, p. A1.

14. Named for its initial venture, as Pologne-Hongrie: Actions pour la Réconversion Économique, this had become the EU's primary source of economic aid to the postcommunist countries.

15. "Peace with Justice. Speech given by Prime Minister John Major at the opening of the London Conference on the Former Yugoslavia, August 26, 1992," *Policy Statement*, British Information Services.

16. See Walker Connor, *The Nationalist Question in Marxist-Leninist Theory and Strategy* (Princeton University Press, 1984), p. 155, on the subversive intention of national self-determination, not only for the Wilsonians but especially for the Bolsheviks.

17. This was one of the main characteristics that distinguished Milošević from ideological Serbian nationalists; the similarity with other former communists pursuing "national" interests such as Kučan of Slovenia and Gligorov of Macedonia may be one reason why they were able to negotiate common interests at certain moments.

18. This applied not only to leaders at war but also to the president of Macedonia. Macedonia was admitted to the United Nations under a tentative name but was not yet admitted to the CSCE (and therefore eligible for NATO Partnership for Peace, among other attractions) because of Greek objections.

19. Negotiation over the Helsinki Final Act had them in separate "baskets."

20. The campaign of *deložacija* (eviction) aimed to transfer ownership of apartments built by the Yugoslav state and leased primarily to Yugoslav army officers and their families to the Croatian state, but there was no due process and in the agreement on YPA withdrawal from Croatia, the government had explicitly agreed not to do this. Although occupants were of many national identities, the president of Croatia announced in a July 2, 1994, speech to the second annual assembly of the League of Croatian War Invalids of the Fatherland War that these evictions were justified because Serbs did not have a right to homes when they had expelled Croats from homes in the occupied territories. See "Budite tumači ispravne politike," and M. Prišćan, "Vratiti im sveti dug," *Večernji list*, June 3, 1994.

21. "The Washington Framework Agreement," March 1, 1994, and "The Constitution of the Federation of Bosnia and Herzegovina, draft copy, March 13, 1994."

22. Charles S. Maier, "Unsafe Haven: Why Minorities Treaties Fail," *The New Republic*, October 12, 1992, pp. 20–21. See the classic study of these treaties, Carlile Aylmer Macartney, *National States and National Minorities* (Oxford University Press, 1934); also Inis L. Claude, Jr., *National Minorities: An International Problem* (Harvard University Press, 1955). The one exception to international efforts to resolve these problems after World War I was the successful negotiation by the League of Nations for autonomy for the Åland islands within Finnish sovereignty. See James Barros, *The Åland Islands Question: Its Settlement by the League of Nations* (Yale University Press, 1968), and Horst Hannum, ed., *Documents on Autonomy and Minority Rights* (Dordrecht, the Netherlands: Martinus Nijhoff Publishers, 1993), pp. 115–43.

23. Important to the failure of these treaties was also their discriminatory character: the new states in Europe had to meet conditions that were not applied to the old states as if they would not protect minorities without international requirement and as if group rights were necessary in the East but not in the West. The same mistake was being repeated in 1992–94 when the Council of Europe (COE) was attempting to draw up a convention on minority rights that was stalled because countries that were already members, even if they also had substantial minorities (such as France, Spain, Greece, or Britain), did not accept the application of such a convention to them, and saw it as necessary to oblige only new members from central and eastern Europe. Nonetheless, the draft Framework Convention for the Protection of National Minorities was completed in the fall of 1994, adopted at the 95th session of the Committee of Ministers, Council of Europe, November 10, 1994, and obtained the requisite signatures from 12 member states in time for the next parliamentary session in January–February 1995. The convention would be included in the European Convention on Human Rights and, in contrast to the political commitments of CSCE signatories to its principles on minority protections, will entail legal obligations on signatory states. National legislatures will be obliged to transfer the convention granting rights to culture (including language and religion), freedom of expression, and use of minority language in surnames and public signs and inscriptions into national law within one year; to enforce it; and to agree to a monitoring mechanism of the COE Committee of Ministers.

24. Secretary of Defense William Perry, in remarks to the Fortune 500 Forum, November 3, 1994, identified "three basic categories in which our military forces are being used and will be used. The first is those where vital national interests are at stake; the second is where national interests are at stake but are not vital; and the third is where we have humanitarian interests." Bosnia (along with Haiti) "fall[s] in the second category . . . a national interest but not a vital interest."

25. Confidential interview with NSC staff.

26. Report of the Secretary-General on the work of the organization, "An Agenda for Peace: Preventive Diplomacy, Peacemaking, and Peacekeeping," June 17, 1992, A/47/277, S/24111.

27. But it also used the case of Bosnia to justify a new U.S. doctrine on peacekeeping, which urged even greater caution on the UN Security Council by listing conditions the United States would require. See *The Clinton Administration's Policy on Reforming Multilateral Peace Operations* (May 1994), known as Presidential Decision Directive 25. See Elaine Sciolino, "Christopher Explains Conditions for Use of U.S. Force in Bosnia: He Says Success and Quick Exit Must Be Likely,"

*New York Times*, April 28, 1993, p. A1, and "Press Briefing by National Security Advisor Tony Lake and Director for Strategic Plans and Policy General Wesley Clark," Office of the Press Secretary, The White House, May 5, 1994.

28.   My exposure to this European view has been largely through NATO specialists Jane Sharp of King's College, London, and Mario Zucconi, of Centro Studi di Politica Internazionale (CESPI) in Rome. French intellectual circles around Bernard-Henri Lévy, for example, are coming from a different place to the same view.

29.   In the communiqué of the EU ministerial meeting December 2, 1994, as discussed by former secretary-general of the WEU, Willem van Eeklen, in a speech at Spoleto, Italy, December 2, 1994.

30.   See Robert Lee Wolff, *The Balkans In Our Time* (W. W. Norton & Co., 1967); and The Carnegie Endowment for International Peace, *The Other Balkan Wars: A 1914 Carnegie Endowment Inquiry in Retrospect with New Introduction and Reflections on the Present Conflict by George F. Kennan* (Washington, D.C., 1993).

# Index